VORTH'S PRINCIPLES OF CRIMINAL LAW

ASHWORTH'S PRINCIPLES OF
CRIMINAL LAW

Eighth Edition

JEREMY HORDER

Professor of Criminal Law,
London School of Economics
and Political Science

OXFORD
UNIVERSITY PRESS

OXFORD

UNIVERSITY PRESS

Great Clarendon Street, Oxford, OX2 6DP,
United Kingdom

Oxford University Press is a department of the University of Oxford.
It furthers the University's objective of excellence in research, scholarship,
and education by publishing worldwide. Oxford is a registered trade mark of
Oxford University Press in the UK and in certain other countries

© Jeremy Horder 2016

The moral rights of the author have been asserted

Fifth edition 2006
Sixth edition 2009
Seventh edition 2013

Impression: 1

Public sector information reproduced under Open Government Licence v2.0
(http://www.nationalarchives.gov.uk/doc/open-government-licence/open-government-licence.htm)

Published in the United States of America by Oxford University Press
198 Madison Avenue, New York, NY 10016, United States of America

British Library Cataloguing in Publication Data
Data available

Library of Congress Control Number: 2015958678

ISBN 978–0–19–875307–0

Printed in Great Britain by Bell & Bain Ltd., Glasgow

PREFACE

This 8th edition is the first to be undertaken without the guiding hand of the original author, Andrew Ashworth, although he has continued be a constant source of encouragement, advice, and—where necessary—correction, for which I am very grateful. It follows that I alone take responsibility for text. Andrew generously gave me a free hand to re-write the book as I saw fit. Exercising that freedom has led me to re-think much of the approach taken in what were, until now, the justly famous first three introductory chapters of this work, dealing directly with principles of criminal law.

To begin with, there are now four introductory chapters, Chapter 1, 'criminal law process', deals principally with patterns of discretion exercised by criminal justice officials, such patterns being part—along with principles, rules, and standards—of what I call the 'fabric of criminal law' (Chapter 4). The influence of 'bureaucratic-administrative' structures for the exercise of discretion is analysed, along with the more familiar 'due process' and 'crime management' models.

There is a new Chapter 2, on 'criminal law history'. Including something in textbooks specifically on the criminal law's fascinating history inexplicably fell out of favour in the post-war period. That has been a shame, because there is so much to catch the imagination and so much to learn from it. Chapter 2 is intentionally provocative and selective in its focus, but (I hope) not too much the worse for that. Specifically, the influence of religious—and especially, biblical—thought is made central to the analysis of how the past has shaped the criminal law's values.

Chapter 3 is a new chapter dealing with, 'criminal law values'. I hope and expect that there will be a good deal that is unfamiliar but challenging to readers here. The focus is on the values the criminal law seeks to protect, through criminalization. In that regard, the analysis proceeds, first, by way of an analysis of key, 'intrinsic values', such as bodily integrity and sexual autonomy. Secondly, in an attempt to explain the very broad and diverse reach of the criminal law, the analysis proceeds by way of an examination of 'public goods,' in broadly the economists' sense, that the criminal law protects as part of its role in protecting our many different lives in common, as consumers, employees, users of roads and of public transport, and so on. Public goods are goods in which we have no individual right or share, but which benefit us in common with others. The security of the State, a tradition of racial and religious toleration, openness and integrity in corporate governance and public life, and the 'common pool resource' of a welfare system are all very different examples of public goods in this sense.

Amongst other things, this way of analysing criminal law values enables us to move the issue of corporate liability to the centre of the stage, rather than being kept, as it traditionally has been, as an appendage to a discussion of fault and of involuntary manslaughter. A very large proportion of offences are aimed mainly at businesses, even if there are few prosecutions of businesses in practice. An overview of the criminal law needs to address both of these facts, not just—as has traditionally been the case—the second one.

Chapter 4 discusses principles of criminal law, including one important new principle, the 'authoritarian' principle. Discussion of principles—given a revised definition—takes place alongside a discussion of rules, and of standards in criminal law. 'Rules' and 'standards' have to date been surprisingly under-analysed in many mainstream texts.

The tone of the discussion of principles—new and old—will be familiar to those who know earlier editions of this work, and the commitment to their moral importance is undiminished here. Even so, the earlier claims to the universality of the application of some of these principles across the criminal law does now come into question. Some principles are or should be of universal application, such as respect for human rights, and 'fair labelling' (the discovery of which was surely one of Andrew Ashworth's most significant contributions to criminal law jurisprudence).

However, other principles—like the principle of subjective fault—can be 'permissive' rather than mandatory in character, which is to say that whilst they clearly *may* be applied to the definition of an offence, there is no 'must' about it: other important moral considerations may outweigh a 'permissive' principle, in the case of some crimes.

These are major changes, but beyond that the 8th edition follows the pattern of previous editions closely. Chapters 5–12 have broadly the same headings as before, although naturally the analysis has in places changed to reflect the discussion in Chapters 1–4, and to accommodate new developments. Priority, in that regard, has been given to ensuring that text includes references to and discussion of recent legislation and case law. Whilst, of course, a number of new scholarly books and articles are also mentioned, scholarly commentary has now grown to such an extent that it is too difficult to provide a reasonably comprehensive account of it all in what is meant to be an introductory work.

I am very grateful to John Carroll at Oxford University Press for his patient and thorough guidance through the process, to Cheryl Prophett for her meticulous copy editing, and to Ailbhe O'Loughlin and Anna O'Mahony for their diligent research assistance. I am also very grateful to Niki Lacey, Stuart P Green, and Alice Moss for their invaluable critical comments on early drafts of key chapters.

St Vincent's Day, 2015.

NEW TO THIS EDITION

As indicated in the Preface, the original Chapters 1–3 of this book have been almost completely re-written. There are now four introductory chapters: a chapter on criminal law process, a chapter on criminal law history, a chapter on criminal law values, and a chapter on criminal law rules, standards, and principles.

The important work that has been done by the Law Commission in recent years is reflected principally by discussion of its proposals for insanity and automatism (2013), and for reform of non-fatal offences against the person (2014).

In terms of legislation, whilst there has been no change as significant as the Coroners and Justice Act 2009 was for the previous edition, mention is made of the Crime and the Courts Act 2013, which introduces deferred prosecution agreements, the Anti-Social Behaviour, Crime and Policing Act 2014, the Criminal Justice and Courts Act 2015, the Modern Slavery Act 2015, and the Serious Crime Act 2015.

Amongst recent cases worthy of mention are included:

- *R* v *Coley* [2013] EWCA Crim 223 (automatism)

- *R* v *Robson-Pierre* [2013] EWCA Crim 2396 (*actus reus*)

- *R* v *Grant* [2014] EWCA Crim 143 (transferred malice)

- *Natural England* v *Day* [2014] EWCA Crim 2683 (liability for the actions of a third party)

- As it affects the law of complicity, considerable attention is naturally devoted to the key decision of the Supreme Court in *R* v *Jogee* [2016] UKSC 8

- The courts have also continued to shed light, in a broadly common-sense way, on the homicide provisions of the Coroners and Justice Act 2009: *R* v *Dawes* [2013] EWCA Crim 322; *R* v *Bowyer* [2013] WLR(D) 130 (CA); *R* v *Ashmelash* [2013] EWCA Crim 157; *R* v *Jewel* [2014] EWCA Crim 414

CONTENTS

TABLE OF CASES

TABLE OF LEGISLATION

INTERNATIONAL INSTRUMENTS

1

CRIMINAL LAW PROCESS

1.1 THE SUBJECT-MATTER OF CRIMINAL LAW

If asked what kinds of wrongdoing their society regarded as criminal, most people are likely to mention offences against the person—murder, rape, or assault, for example—and offences against property, such as theft or fraud. In common with most other texts on criminal law, this book concentrates on such offences. As criminal law scholars, though, we should not be content to allow the focus of our work to be dictated solely by common sense thinking about what is most relevant. We need to take a critical look behind such thinking, to ask about the values on which it rests, and about the assumptions it makes. There are well over 9,000 offences in the criminal law of England and Wales (Scotland and Northern Ireland have separate criminal law jurisdictions within the UK). Why concentrate one's attention on such a select few crimes? Answering that question will occupy us over the first three chapters. Answering it requires us to reflect on the history of the criminal law, and on why textbook writers have thought it best for law students to study certain crimes, but also to reflect more broadly on the values that the criminal law seeks to protect and promote. We consider these issues in Chapters 2 to 4.

Before going any further, something needs to be said briefly about the relationship between what we are calling 'criminal law', and related disciplines such as the law of criminal procedure, the law of criminal evidence, and the law of sentencing. In common with other textbooks, this work is almost exclusively concerned with three things. First, very broadly speaking, there is analysis and discussion of the nature and content of a range of obligations (not to kill, not to steal, and so on), breach of which exposes someone to punishment by the state. Second, there is analysis and discussion of rules and standards governing special permissions to breach those obligations, permissions at issue when (say) self-defence is pleaded as a defence. Third, there is analysis of some of the exemptions and excuses for breaching those obligations, such as insanity, duress, or loss of self-control. Such obligations, permissions and excuses etc. are commonly known as the 'substantive' criminal law. The account of the substantive criminal law just given is not intended to be a definition of what is distinctive about a 'criminal' offence or defence,[1] but it serves in a rough and ready way as a basis for explaining the substantive criminal law's relationship with other closely related branches of law.

The close relationship between the substantive criminal law and these other branches of law (evidence, procedure, sentencing) can easily be illustrated. Punishments, the subject of the law governing sentencing, are not covered in any detail in this work. Details about the principles, rules, and standards governing punishment are to be found in works on sentencing, rather than in scholarly works on criminal law.[2] Yet, in one important way, it is impossible adequately to distinguish the substantive criminal law from (say) purely civil law obligations without reference to the role of sentencing or penalization more generally. The very fact that state *punishment*—sentencing, or other forms of penalization—may follow breach of a legal obligation, whether or not such a consequence is sought by the victim (if any), is a key factor leading us to describe that obligation as one imposed by the 'criminal' law.

A good example of the interrelationship between substantive criminal law and punishment—how the one influences the other—can be found in the law of murder. A conviction for murder must now be followed by the imposition of the mandatory sentence of imprisonment for life, but before 1965 the mandatory sentence in England and Wales was the sentence of death. There has always been a great deal of arbitrariness about mandatory penalties, in virtue of the fact that they are necessarily blind to the very different circumstances in which the crime to which the sentence is applied may be committed. That arbitrariness is thrown into particularly stark relief when the mandatory sentence in question is death. Consequently, over many centuries, the existence of the mandatory death penalty for murder led either the courts or Parliament to soften the hard edges of the penalty by developing, as a matter of *substantive* law, special defences to murder (unavailable for other crimes) to cover cases where there was substantial mitigation—such as loss of self-control, half-completed suicide pact, and diminished responsibility. If successfully pleaded, these defences reduce murder to manslaughter. The importance of this is that in manslaughter cases, the trial judge is free to pass such sentence as he or she thinks appropriate, taking into account the relevant sentencing guidelines. In all probability, these specialized defences would never have been introduced at all, if the sentence for murder had always been a matter for judicial discretion rather than a mandatory

---

[1] Duress and necessity, for example, have an application in the civil law.
[2] A. Ashworth, *Sentencing and Criminal Justice* (6th edn., 2015).

sentence.[3] The existence of those defences continues to this day to be a special feature distinguishing the substantive crime of murder from other crimes.[4]

The seriousness of crimes, and the punishments attached to them also heavily influences the rules of criminal procedure. For example, the procedural rule that a trial for murder must be on indictment in the Crown Court (murder may not be tried in the magistrates' court), is a rule designed to provide jury trial—and the highest level of protection from wrongful conviction—for those charged with such a serious offence. Turning to the substantive law and law of criminal evidence, these are in one way clearly separate matters. The law governing proof of an allegation that an obligation has been breached or that a defence exists (a matter for the law of evidence) presupposes the separate existence of that obligation or defence (the content of which is a matter for the substantive criminal law). Even so, as in the case of punishment and sentencing, there can be a close relationship between evidential and substantive law issues.[5]

For example, as a matter of substantive law, the nature and content of—say—a defence to a crime, may give rise to a legitimate concern about how that defence is to be proved or disproved, as a matter of evidence. It could be that once the defence has been raised by the defendant, it will then be unacceptably difficult for the prosecution to test and challenge the evidential basis for the defence as asserted by the defendant. That would not be in the public interest. So (rightly or wrongly), in some cases, the law may seek to resolve the problem by placing the evidential burden of proof, on the balance of probabilities, on the defendant. In such cases, the defendant will positively have to show that the conditions for the application of the defence are made out. He or she will not be able simply to assert that those conditions existed, leaving the prosecution to disprove that assertion beyond a reasonable doubt. An example involves the law's approach to defences based on mental disorder or abnormality of mental functioning. The defendant is not entitled simply to claim (a) that he or she was suffering from the relevant disorder or abnormality at the relevant time, (b) that it affected his or her conduct in such a way that liability for the offence should not arise, and (c) that it is now for the prosecution to disprove (a) and/or (b) beyond a reasonable doubt. Instead, a defendant making such a claim must, as a matter of law, produce medical evidence supporting the claim, evidence that may then be scrutinized by the prosecution's own expert witnesses.[6]

Putting these issues on one side for now, in this first chapter, we will take a step back from the substantive law, and from its relationship with other areas of law. Instead, we will consider the broader criminal justice landscape in which the traditional 'criminal' law itself is just one landmark.

---

[3] For fuller discussion see J. Horder, *Homicide and the Politics of Law Reform* (2012), ch 8. It is not uncommon for jurisdictions to have a narrower range of specialized defences to murder, if there is no absolute obligation to pass a mandatory life sentence in murder cases. New Zealand is an example.

[4] For discussion, see Chapter 8.

[5] P. Roberts and A. Zuckerman, *Criminal Evidence* (2nd edn., Oxford University Press, 2010).

[6] See, for example, s. 2(2) of the Homicide Act 1957. The defendant must prove on the balance of probabilities that the conditions for the applicability of the defence are met. Defendants never have to meet a 'beyond reasonable doubt' standard.

1.2. THE FABRIC OF THE CRIMINAL LAW: THE IMPORTANCE OF DISCRETION

We can think of the criminal law as comprised of a 'fabric', consisting of principles, rules, standards, and patterns influencing the exercise of discretion (discretion typically granted by a rule) by officials. Principles, rules, and standards of criminal law set down in cases and statutes—discussed throughout this book—are never applied automatically to those subject to them. At almost every point in the justice system, there must be discretion exercised by an official to progress a case, delay, or drop it. The exercise of this discretion is likely to be heavily influenced by the strength of the case against the accused, given the need to satisfy the applicable principles, rules, and standards if a conviction is to be obtained. For that reason, it is essential to have some grasp of the patterns shaping the exercise of discretion in the criminal process.

In that regard, in this chapter, we will set on one side the powers of the legislature and of the judiciary to create, interpret, and develop the law, important though they are. We will consider some of the ways in which the judges, in particular, perform these tasks in Chapter 4. Do they, for example, sometimes give too much weight to what we call the 'authoritarian' principle, and too little to the principle of respect for human rights? Most textbooks, like this one, are much taken up with discussion of the use of official power, judgment, and discretion at the highest level, the level at which the fabric of the law is given its authoritative legal shape. However, further down the system, every day there are thousands of officials asking questions and making decisions about the (non) application of the authoritative legal rules, principles, and standards of the criminal law. For example, they will ask themselves: 'Should this conduct be recorded as an offence by the police?'; 'Should someone be charged with this particular offence?'; 'Is this evidence of a crime compelling and reliable enough to be rightly subject to prosecution by the Crown Prosecution Service?' Study of the criminal law is not complete without at least an outline grasp of such issues. It is discretion exercised at this level that mainly concerns us in this chapter.

It would be unwise to assume that the criminal law as stated in the statutes and the textbooks reflects the way in which it is enforced in 'real life'. The key to answering the question of how the criminal law is likely to impinge on a person's activities lies in the discretion of the police and other law enforcement agents: they are not obliged to go out and look for offenders wherever they suspect that crimes are being committed; they are not obliged to prosecute every person against whom they have sufficient evidence. Having said that, they cannot prosecute unless the offence charged is actually laid down by statute or at common law. So we must consider the interaction between the law itself and the practical operation of the criminal process if we are to understand the social reality of the criminal law.

Even before the discretion of law enforcement officers comes into play, there is often a decision to be taken by a member of the public as to whether to report a suspected offence. The Crime Survey England and Wales (formerly the British Crime Survey) suggests that at least a half of all offences are not reported to the police,[7] often because they are thought to be too trivial, or because it is thought that the police would be unable to do anything constructive, or because it is thought that the police 'would not be interested'. Even where an assault results in hospital treatment, a significant proportion of victims fail to report the offence or at least to make a formal complaint.[8] If an offence is to have any chance of being recorded, either the victim or a witness must take the decision to report the offence to the authorities. About four-fifths of the offences which come to police attention are reported by the public. This means that people's (sometimes stereotyped) views on what forms of behaviour amount to criminal offences, and also on whether the police should be called, exert considerable influence on the cases entering the criminal justice system. For this and various other reasons, many offences committed at work or in the home remain concealed from official eyes. As for the one-fifth of offences that come to light in other ways, most of these are observed or discovered by the police themselves. There are some crimes, such as drug dealing and other so-called 'crimes without victims', which are unlikely to be reported and for which the police have to go looking. And there are other crimes, such as obstructing a police officer and some of the public order offences, which the police may use as a means of controlling situations—charging people who disobey police instructions about moving on, keeping quiet, etc.[9] In these contexts the police use the criminal law as a resource to reinforce their authority.

So, most police investigations of offences are 'reactive', that is, reacting to information from the public about possible offences. Only in a minority of cases do the police operate 'proactively'. Other law enforcement officials may have a larger proactive role. Her Majesty's Revenue and Customs (HMRC) investigate offences relating to taxation and smuggling. Various inspectorates are required to oversee the observance of legal standards in industry and commerce—the Health and Safety Executive (which includes seven inspectorates: Factory, Agriculture, Nuclear, Offshore, Mines, Railway, and Quarries), the Environment Agency, the Environmental Health Departments of local authorities, and so on. Although these agencies often react to specific complaints or accidents, much of their work involves visits to premises or building sites to check on compliance with the law. It is therefore proactive work: the number of offences coming to an inspectorate's attention is largely a reflection of the number of visits and inspections carried out, and the response depends on the general policies and specific working practices of that inspectorate.[10]

[7] C. Kershaw et al., *Crime in England and Wales* 2007–08 (Home Office Statistical Bulletin 07/08), 39, estimating that 42 per cent of crimes are reported to the police. The overall figure masks considerable variation: thefts of vehicles are the most likely to be reported (93 per cent), and theft from the person, vandalism, and assault with no injury least likely (32 per cent, 35 per cent, and 34 per cent in 2003–4). See now *Crime in England and Wales, year ending June 2012* (Office of National Statistics).

[8] See the research by C. Clarkson et al., 'Assaults: The Relationship between Seriousness, Criminalisation and Punishment' [1994] Crim LR 4.

[9] See the findings of D. Brown and T. Ellis, *Policing Low-Level Disorder: Police Use of Section 5 of the Public Order Act 1986* (Home Office Research Study No. 135, 1994).

[10] See K. Hawkins, *Law as Last Resort* (2002); B. Hutter, *Compliance: Regulation and Environment* (1997).

What happens when an offence has been reported to the police? The Crime Survey for England and Wales suggests that about one-half of all incidents reported to the police as crimes are not recorded as such: sometimes the evidence is thought unconvincing, or the offence too minor, or the incident redefined as lost property rather than theft of property. Of those that are recorded as crimes, the police trace around 28 per cent to an offender or suspected offender. The proportion of offences thus detected is much higher for offences of violence (around one half)—where the victim often sees and knows the offender—than for the offences where the perpetrator's identity will often be unknown (such as burglary, 13 per cent, and robbery, 20 per cent) and for offences that may be thought not to justify a great investment of police time and resources (e.g. criminal damage, 14 per cent).[11]

When the police find a suspect, they will invariably try to question this person. The Police and Criminal Evidence Act 1984 and its Codes of Practice require investigators to follow certain procedures before and during any interrogation, including notifying suspects of the right to a free and private consultation with a lawyer. The tape recording of suspects' statements is a routine feature at police stations, although statements (allegedly) made elsewhere remain admissible in evidence. Many of the miscarriages of justice uncovered in the late 1980s and early 1990s, after wrongly convicted people had spent many years in prison, stemmed from misconduct by the police at this stage of the investigation, including the falsification of notes of interviews. Following the quashing of convictions in the cases of the Guildford Four and the Birmingham Six, the Royal Commission on Criminal Justice was appointed in 1991 to examine the effectiveness of the criminal justice system. In its report the Royal Commission recognized that 'confessions which are later found to be false have led or contributed to serious miscarriages of justice',[12] but one of its key proposals, on preserving the right of silence, was rejected by the then government in favour of introducing a law that permits adverse inferences from failure to answer police questions.[13]

When the police have completed their questioning, they should release the suspect if they have insufficient evidence. If they believe they have sufficient evidence, or if the suspect has admitted guilt, there are choices to be made between a prosecution, giving the offender one of the forms of 'caution', and taking no further action. In recent years, young offenders have often received a caution, in the form of either a youth caution or a youth conditional caution under the Legal Aid, Punishment and Punishment of Offenders Act 2012.[14] For some years the policy had been to delay the entry of young people into the formal criminal justice system, in the belief that cautions were no less likely to be effective in preventing further offences, and that labelling a youth as a delinquent through formal court proceedings could reinforce that person's tendency to behave like a delinquent. The system of reprimands and warnings introduced by the Crime and Disorder Act 1998 was intended to be more rigorous and more demanding

---

[11] Kershaw et al., n 7, 169.   [12] Royal Commission on Criminal Justice, Report (Cm 2263 (1993)), 57.
[13] Sections 34–7 of the Criminal Justice and Public Order Act 1994, the impact of which is discussed in A. Ashworth and M. Redmayne, *The Criminal Process* (4th edn., 2010), ch 4.
[14] <www.yjlc.uk/youth-conditional-caution>, accessed 22 July 2015.

of young offenders: a warning also involves referring the young offender to a youth offending team, who may require the offender to participate in a scheme designed to prevent re-offending.[15] Thus, although the emphasis remains on the prevention of future offending, the rhetoric and the method have changed to confronting offenders with their behaviour and helping them to take more responsibility for their actions.[16] The emphasis of the Youth Justice Board remains on diverting most young offenders away from court, and making use of alternative approaches such as restorative conferences that may bring the offender face-to-face with the victim.[17] The proportion of young offenders receiving reprimands or warnings rather than prosecution is around two-thirds for boys and four-fifths for girls in the 12–14 age group, while in the 15–17 age group the proportions are about 45 per cent for boys and some two-thirds for girls.

For adults, the police may also decide to caution an offender, but again the use of cautions has declined somewhat from its peak in the early 1990s, so that around 20 per cent of adult male offenders and one-third of adult female offenders receive a caution. National Standards encourage the police to prefer a formal caution to prosecution where the offence is relatively minor, where the offender is old, infirm, or suffering from mental disturbance, and in other situations where there is little blame. Since 2003, the Crown Prosecution Service (CPS) has had the power to offer an offender a conditional caution, in cases where there is both an admission by the offender and objectively sufficient evidence. The conditions specified may include the making of reparation or participation in a restorative justice process. The offender is required to sign a document that spells out the conditions and records his admission of the offence.[18] There are also various out-of-court disposals, such as cannabis warnings, Penalty Notices for Disorder, and fixed penalties.[19]

Standing in contrast to the preferred use of prosecutions for suspected adult offenders (as distinct from juveniles) is the long-standing preference for alternatives to prosecution among the various inspectorates and other public authorities, such as HMRC, most of whom are dealing with businesses rather than with individuals. Many of these agencies regard their main aim as securing compliance rather than convictions. The Environment Agency, for example, states: 'We regard prevention as better than cure. Our general approach is to engage with business to educate and enable compliance.'[20] Such agencies therefore tend to rely on informal and formal warnings as a means of putting pressure on companies, employers, taxpayers, and the like to conform to the law. Most of these agencies regard prosecution as a last resort: the criminal law remains as a background source of the pressure towards compliance which the agencies are able

---

[15] For discussion, see C. Ball, 'Youth Justice? 'Half a Century of Responses to Youth Offending' [2004] Crim LR 167.

[16] Home Office, *No More Excuses: A New Approach to Tackling Youth Crime in England and Wales* (Cm 3809 (1997)), 1.   [17] See further <www.justice.gov.uk/youth-justice>.

[18] For fuller discussion, see Ashworth and Redmayne, n 13, ch 6.

[19] M. Maguire, R. Morgan, and R. Reiner (eds), *Oxford Handbook of Criminology* (5th edn., 2012), ch 32.

[20] Environment Agency, *Enforcement and Prosecution Policy* (issued 4 January 2011), 2, at <www.environment-agency.gov.uk>.

to exert. Thus, for example, the HMRC Prosecutions Office typically responds to tax evasion through civil procedures and rarely resorts to prosecution.[21] In these contexts, then, the criminal law is very much in the background, and the criminal process is experienced by relatively few of those caught breaking the law.[22]

Where the police are involved, however, prosecution remains the normal response for persons aged 18 and over. The initial decision whether or not to charge is taken under the 'statutory charging scheme' introduced by the Criminal Justice Act 2003. This means that police and prosecutors work together at this stage, but it is the CPS that takes the decision whether to charge and, if so, with what offence to charge the suspect. There are two factors on which the prosecution must base their decision. The first is evidential sufficiency: is there enough evidence on each of the elements required to prove the offence, so that it can be said that there is a realistic prospect of conviction? This requires the prosecutor to consider both the amount of evidence available and its admissibility in court (e.g. whether there has been a breach of the Police and Criminal Evidence Act 1984 and its Codes of Practice). The second, related, factor is whether a prosecution would be in the public interest. There is a Code for Crown Prosecutors (latest version, 2013) to provide general guidance on this and other decisions which prosecutors must take, and there is detailed guidance on prosecution policy for particular types of offence.[23]

It will be apparent from the preceding paragraphs that the defendants and offences brought to court form a highly selective sample of all detected crimes. Those convicted in court are certainly a small sample of the whole. The Home Office has estimated that if one takes account of those offences not reported, not recorded, not cleared up, and those that are cautioned rather than prosecuted, only some 2 or 3 per cent of crimes result in a conviction.[24] Although this rises to 10 per cent for crimes such as wounding, it would not be accurate to say that the cases brought to court involve the most serious offences and offenders, because:

(1) there are crimes for which a person under 18 would not be prosecuted, whereas a person of 18 or over would be;

(2) fairly serious crimes committed in the home or in certain workplaces may sometimes not be reported or prosecuted,[25] whereas prosecution is often the normal response to less serious offences in the street; and

(3) some of the crimes of petty theft which are prosecuted are, by almost any measure, less serious than many crimes which HMRC or other regulatory agencies deal with by warnings, civil penalties, or other alternative methods.

---

[21] See <www.hmrc.gov.uk/prosecutions/crim-inv-policy.htm>.
[22] See further Ashworth and Redmayne, n 13, 160–3.
[23] This may be found at <www.cps.gov.uk/publications/code_for_crown_prosecutors/>.
[24] *Home Office, Digest 4: Information on the Criminal Justice System in England and Wales* (1999), 29.
[25] See Ashworth and Redmayne, n 13, 187–90.

What emerges from this is that adults suspected of committing 'traditional' offences outside their own home are much more likely to appear in court than adults known to have committed more regulatory kinds of offence, such as tax evasion, pollution, having an unsafe workplace, and so on. Even leaving young people aside, then, court proceedings are a poor representation of the reality of crime in our society.

It will be evident, too, that it is not rules but discretionary decisions which characterize these early stages in the criminal process. Police decision-making is largely discretionary, structured only by the cautioning guidelines, local arrangements for dealing with young defendants, police force orders, and internal police supervision. As research into public order policing confirms, there are considerable variations in policy and practice, not just between police force areas but also among police divisions in the same force,[26] and this determines the nature and volume of cases placed before the CPS for consideration for prosecution. The same is largely true of the regulatory and other agencies which have the power to prosecute. Moreover, the elements of discretion do not stop with the decision whether or not to prosecute. A question of particular importance for our present purposes is that of deciding what offence to charge. In some cases there is little choice, but there are other cases where the prosecutor can choose between a more serious and a less serious offence. If there is a prosecution for the higher offence, it is usually possible for a court to convict of a lesser offence if it does not find the higher offence proved. But this does not mean that prosecutors routinely try for the higher offence. If, for example, the lower offence is triable only summarily (i.e. in the magistrates' court), whereas the higher offence is 'triable either way' (i.e. in the magistrates' court or at the Crown Court), the prosecutor may prefer the lesser charge so as to keep the case in the magistrates' court—for various reasons, one of which may be the belief that a conviction is more likely if the case is tried by magistrates rather than by a jury.[27] We will consider this issue further in sections 1.3 and 1.4.

Not only, then, are the cases prosecuted a selective sample of all crimes committed, but the offences for which convictions are recorded may sometimes underestimate the true seriousness of the crimes brought to court. The way in which offences are defined may facilitate or constrain many of the decisions that produce these results. So, the structure of the criminal law may have a greater direct influence at this point than at some earlier stages in the criminal process. However, the predominance of official discretion opens the way for other motivations, including bias and prejudice, to enter in. Although the ratio of male to female known offenders is around five to one, women are cautioned (rather than prosecuted) at a higher rate than men. The picture at the sentencing stage is rather complex, with some women receiving less severe sentences than comparable men, but some receiving disposals which may turn out to be more intrusive and therefore more severe.[28] There is also some evidence of racial discrimination

---

[26] T. Bucke and Z. James, *Trespass and Protest: Policing under the Criminal Justice and Public Order Act 1994* (Home Office Research Study No. 190, 1998).   [27] Ashworth and Redmayne, n 13, 298.

[28] The complexities are explored in C. Hedderman and L. Gelsthorpe (eds), *Understanding the Sentencing of Women* (Home Office Research Study No. 170, 1997).

in the pre-trial system,[29] although some of this is a form of structural bias stemming from the way in which the system imposes disincentives on those who elect Crown Court trial and who maintain a plea of not guilty.

This brief outline has demonstrated some of the ways in which the criminal law in action presents a different picture from that portrayed by the law as declared in the statutes and in court decisions. Little has been said about the ways in which defence lawyers may sometimes construct the defence around their own working priorities as well as around reconstructed versions of the defendant's narrative,[30] but that, too, is a factor in the presentation and the outcome of cases. So far as official agencies are concerned, each case brought to court is the product of a system which is heavily reliant on victims and other members of the public for the detection of offenders and the provision of evidence,[31] and which leaves considerable discretion in the hands of the police, other law enforcement agencies, and the CPS. We have seen that that discretion is exercised unevenly, in the sense that those who commit crimes on the streets and in other public places are likely to be prosecuted, even for relatively minor incidents, whereas offenders of certain kinds ('white-collar') are rarely brought to court. This not only emphasizes that the law in practice is different from the law in the books. It also raises questions about priorities and social justice: should we not have a ranking of crimes that makes it clear which are the most serious and which are the least serious, with the greatest efforts directed at enforcement against those who perpetrate the most serious offences, and the strongest measures taken against those offenders?[32]

1.3 CRIMINAL LAW AND THE CRIMINAL TRIAL PROCESS

For most people, the idea of a criminal offence conjures up a picture of a Crown Court or magistrates' court, where a suspect is tried before a judge or judges (or a judge and jury, in the case of the Crown Court). This simplistic picture can lead to a distorted perception of the way in which the criminal justice system works in practice. No less than 95 per cent of criminal cases are dealt with in the magistrates' court, and around 67 per cent of such cases will involve no contested trial because the defendant has pleaded guilty.[33] Statistically speaking, a contested Crown Court trial overseen by a bewigged judge, with similarly attired Counsel making their case to a jury that decides on guilt and innocence, is a rarity in England and Wales. Predominantly, prosecution

---

[29] C. Phillips and B. Bowling, 'Ethnicities, Racism, Crime and Criminal Justice', in M. Maguire, R. Morgan, and R. Reiner (eds), *Oxford Handbook of Criminology* (5th edn., 2012).

[30] See generally, M. McConville et al., *Standing Accused: The Organization and Practices of Criminal Defence Lawyers in Britain* (1994).

[31] See the fascinating study by P. Rock, *The Social World of an English Crown Court* (1993).

[32] See further A. Ashworth, 'Is the Criminal Law a Lost Cause?' (2000) 116 LQR 225.

[33] <www.cps.gov.uk/publications/reports/2009/ar_annex_c.html>. About 70 per cent of cases in the Crown Court also involve guilty pleas.

for a criminal offence leads not to a trial, but to a largely uncontested administrative processing of a guilty plea by officials, with some help from lawyers on each side.[34]

At best, then, we can say that criminal offences are cases in which alleged wrongdoing *may* lead to a contested trial, employing special procedural and evidentiary rules, before judges (or much more unusually, before a judge and jury). This legal possibility is, of course, meant to reflect what may be the potentially high seriousness of (or stigma attached to) an allegation against the defendant, and the severity of the sentence that he or she may face on conviction. Allegations concerning 'truly criminal' offences, many might say, must be open to rigorous testing of the evidence, must be subject to a beyond-reasonable-doubt standard of proof, and must be tried within a highly formal procedural setting designed to avoid miscarriages of justice. However, the heavy reliance of the criminal justice system on guilty pleas means that most criminal cases avoid anything like full compliance with these demands. A plea of guilty may simply be accepted more-or-less at face value, as proof beyond reasonable doubt of the allegation in question. As it was put in one case by Sachs LJ:

> [A] plea of guilty has two effects: first of all, it is a confession of fact; secondly, it is such a confession that without further evidence the court is entitled to and indeed in all proper circumstances will act upon it . . . result[ing] in a conviction.[35]

A guilty plea is not automatically subject to vigorous testing for its veracity, in the way that a plea of not guilty is tested. For example, whilst the Code for Crown Prosecutors (rightly) urges prosecutors to consider the interests of victims and their families before accepting a defendant's plea of guilty to a lesser charge, the code says nothing about the desirability of ensuring that such a plea can in fact be relied on as certain evidence of the truth about what happened.[36] What is more, judges and lawyers—even the defendant's own lawyer—are in many cases themselves involved in directing cases towards guilty pleas, and hence towards uncontested administrative processing of such cases.[37]

What has just been said presupposes that an individual person is subject to the pressure to plead guilty. In fact, similar pressures are more openly applied to companies—corporate 'persons'—accused of criminal wrongdoing. The most vivid contemporary example involves the company entering into a 'deferred prosecution agreement' respecting certain financial offences ('Sch 17 offences'), like bribery.[38] In exchange for a

[34] See D. Alge, 'Negotiated Plea Agreements in Cases of Serious and Complex Fraud in England and Wales: A New Conceptualisation of Plea Bargaining?' (2013) 19(1) Web JCLI, <www.webjcli.org/article/view/203/272#_Toc347515371>.

[35] *R v Rimmer* (1972) 56 Cr App R 196, 200, cited in J. Horne, 'Plea Bargains, Guilty Pleas and the Consequences for Appeal in England and Wales', in J. Hodgson (ed.), *Warwick School of Law Research Paper No. 2013/1* (Special Plea Bargaining). Horne adds: 'In contrast to the USA, there is no colloquy and the defendant will not give any account of the reasons for her [guilty] plea or the process that led to it.'

[36] <www.cps.gov.uk/publications/code_for_crown_prosecutors/guiltypleas.html>; <www.cps.gov.uk/victims_witnesses/resources/prosecution.html#a09>.

[37] See further, M. McConville and L. Marsh, 'Criminal Judges: Legitimacy, Courts and State-Induced Guilty Pleas in Britain' [2015] 42 *Journal of Law and Society* 319–24; McConville et al., n 30; Horne, n 35.

[38] Crime and Courts Act 2013, Sch 17.

prosecutor's agreement to defer a criminal prosecution, a company suspected of such offences may be asked to take a range of steps:

(a) to pay to the prosecutor a financial penalty;

(b) to compensate victims of the alleged offence;

(c) to donate money to a charity or other third party;

(d) to disgorge any profits made from the alleged offence;

(e) to implement a compliance programme or make changes to an existing compliance programme relating to P's policies or to the training of P's employees or both;

(f) to co-operate in any investigation related to the alleged offence;

(g) to pay any reasonable costs of the prosecutor in relation to the alleged offence or the deferred prosecution agreement.[39]

Should the company fail to take the steps, as agreed, the prosecution for the alleged crime may be revived. Yet, most if not all of the steps described in (a)–(g) above themselves already involve what most people would regard as penal sanctions appropriate for wrongdoing. This view is supported by the provision in para. 5 of Sch 17 to the 2013 Act indicating that in the statement of the facts of the case that must form part of the deferred prosecution agreement, *admissions* on the company's part may be included. Here, then, we have a sophisticated sanctioning system that is designed to operate alongside, but also largely instead of, the traditional sanctioning system, namely court trial. How should such developments be explained?

In relation to 'criminal' offences, both prosecution and defence have the right to insist on a court trial (other things being equal). That right does not benefit the parties alone but—to use an economist's term that we will look at closely in Chapter 3—has an element of 'public good' to it: the right is something of value as a resource open to and beneficial to all. However, even if there is a right to it, from the accused's point of view, not every case is best resolved through the trial process. Further, to use more economic terms, trials have both significant 'transaction costs' (best called 'participation costs', in this context),[40] and uncertainties about the outcome that are liable to encourage unduly risk-averse behaviour by both prosecution and defence.[41] A more or less formal strategy has long been in existence to reduce these costs and uncertainties, which we can call the 'crime-management' approach to criminal justice.[42] This approach is closely allied to, but not to be identified with, another approach, the 'bureaucratic-administrative' approach.

---

[39] Crime and Courts Act 2013, Sch 17, para. 5.

[40] F. H. Easterbrook, 'Criminal Procedure as a Market System' (1983) 12 *The Journal of Legal Studies* 289. In a public sector context like the prosecution of crime, prosecution 'transaction costs' are the costs of organizing and participating in the implementation of a policy or strategy (the prosecution of the defendant(s)). The defendant's transaction costs may include, for example, having to instruct Counsel on trial decisions, having to attend trial, and (possibly) give evidence.

[41] U. Segal and A. Stein, 'Ambiguity Aversion and the Criminal Process' [2006] 81 *Notre Dame Law Review* 1495.

[42] For an original discussion of different 'models' of how criminal law and justice operate, see H. Packer, 'Two Models of the Criminal Process' (1964) 113 *University of Pennsylvania Law Review* 1. See also M. Dubber, 'Preventive Justice: The Search for Principle', in A. Ashworth and L. Zedner (eds), *Prevention and the Limits of the Criminal Law* (2013), distinguishing 'law' and 'police' modes of governance.

1.4 THE CRIME-MANAGEMENT AND BUREAUCRATIC-ADMINISTRATIVE APPROACHES TO PROCESS

The crime-management approach involves bargaining in the shadow of the law, to reduce costs and resolve uncertainties for all concerned. It can be contrasted with the traditional but narrow focus on trials conducted on an adversarial basis, leading to the determination of guilt or innocence by a tribunal, which we can call the 'adversarial' approach to or understanding of criminal justice. The primary emphasis within the crime-management approach is on securing the agreement of the relevant parties (prosecution, defence, and sometimes also the judiciary) to an outcome that avoids a trial. The most common means by which this outcome is achieved is through a plea agreement or bargain.[43] Plea agreements or bargains are of different kinds. We will focus on 'charge' bargaining (to be explained shortly), and to a lesser extent on 'bargaining with the law'[44] (deciding to plead guilty to take the benefit of a discount for such a plea).

For example, suppose someone is charged with murder and pleads not guilty. The prosecution, on reflection, may decide that if the trial goes ahead, it will be difficult—if not impossible—for them to prove that the defendant had the necessary intent or that the defendant did not have a serious mental disorder. In other words, the prosecution faces either significant uncertainty or high participation costs in pursuing the murder charge. So, rather than press on with the risk of an acquittal on the murder charge, the prosecution may be willing to accept a plea of guilty to the lesser charge of manslaughter (charge bargaining), if the defendant offers such a plea. In that way, the costs and uncertainty of adversarial trial are avoided. There are also advantages in this process for defendants. The sentence for the crime admitted to should be lower, because of the guilty plea, as s. 144 of the Criminal Justice Act 2003 requires. Guidelines issued by the Sentencing Guidelines Council establish a sliding scale of sentence reductions, running from a one-third discount for indicating a guilty plea at the earliest opportunity down to a one-tenth reduction for a guilty plea 'at the door of the court' (bargaining with the law).[45] Average prison sentences for those pleading guilty are around a third below those convicted after a trial—a striking difference. Moreover, there are other procedural incentives to plead guilty, such as the right to ask the court for an indication of whether the sentence will be custodial or non-custodial (the court is not obliged to give the indication).[46]

As the murder case example just given illustrates, the state of the substantive law can have a significant impact on incentives to engage in bargaining over charge. The need to prove nothing short of an intention to kill or cause serious harm, in murder

---

[43] We have already come across the 'deferred prosecution agreement' above.

[44] For this phrase, see Ashworth and Redmayne, n 13, 301.

[45] Sentencing Guidelines Council, *Reduction in Sentence for a Guilty Plea: Revised Guideline* (2007).

[46] See Criminal Justice Act 2003, Sch 3, amending s. 20 of the Magistrates' Courts Act 1980; and *Goodyear* [2005] 3 All ER 117.

cases, may in some cases provide an incentive for the prosecution to avoid uncertainty in how the jury will decide that issue, by accepting a defendant's plea of guilty to manslaughter. That is because (in the relevant version of that crime), manslaughter requires proof only of a 'criminal and dangerous' act that caused death, a much easier thing to prove beyond reasonable doubt. Here is a slightly different example, involving the impact on charge bargaining that can be made by the existence of inchoate offences[47] underlying the completed offence. Suppose that it is alleged by the prosecution that a doctor committed murder by intentionally giving a terminally ill patient a lethal dose of painkiller, 'to end the patient's suffering'. The defence claims that it cannot be shown with any degree of certainty that the painkiller caused the patient's death, because the patient was so ill that death could have come about in a number of ways.[48] In such a case, the prosecution may have confidence in its case, but may be nonetheless concerned about the participation costs of a trial for murder, involving—as it will—an expensive and possibly inconclusive 'battle of the experts' between different doctors giving conflicting evidence on the cause of death. The prosecution must never pursue a charge (such as murder) simply in order to wring out of a defendant a willingness to plead guilty to a lesser charge.[49] However, bearing in mind that murder carries a mandatory life sentence, there is always the possibility that the doctor may offer to plead guilty to the inchoate offence of *attempted* murder, in exchange for the murder charge being dropped, on the basis of an admission that he or she intended to kill the patient, and did an act that was more than merely preparatory to that end (administering the high dose of pain killer).[50]

Efficient as it may sound, the crime-management approach has many risks attached to it. The most serious of these risks is the risk that some wholly innocent defendants may be drawn into pleading guilty to lesser crimes they did not commit, in order to avoid the possibility that they may be convicted at trial of an even more serious crime.[51] There are clearly some cases in which innocent persons feel driven to plead guilty.[52] Contrariwise, a defendant (perhaps especially, a corporate defendant) who has pleaded not guilty but is in fact guilty of a serious crime, may escape the penalty appropriate for that crime by pleading guilty to a lesser crime.[53] In spite of these risks, the European Court has accepted that, were crime management not to feature as part of the criminal process, seeking to further the interests of justice by having more criminal court trials might end up being a self-defeating strategy. When resources are necessarily limited (criminal justice is far from the only demand on public funds), the provision of court

---

[47] An offence, very roughly, in which D engages in the conduct element of the crime with the fault element, but where either or both of the circumstance or consequence elements do not occur, as when D shoots at V intending to kill (conduct and fault element), but misses V altogether (missing consequence element).

[48] For a well-known example of this kind, see <www.independent.co.uk/news/uk/doctors-dilemma-of-pain-or-death-dr-nigel-cox-will-be-sentenced-today-for-the-attempted-murder-of-1552676.html>.

[49] <www.cps.gov.uk/publications/code_for_crown_prosecutors/charges.html>.

[50] See further, Chapter 12 on attempts.

[51] See Horne, n 35; M. McConville, 'Plea Bargaining: Ethics and Politics' (1998) 25 *Journal of Law and Society* 562.   [52] For fuller discussion and references, see Ashworth and Redmayne, n 13, ch 10.

[53] See Alge, n 34.

time may involve costs that threaten a denial of justice, such as lengthy waiting times for trials.[54] Long waiting times are corrosive of justice, and not only because the threat of trial hangs over the defendant for a period that may be disproportionate to the allegation to be proved against him or her. Any delay affects the ability of witnesses to recall events accurately, and long delay may mean that they, or other key players, are no longer able to attend the trial at all (through death, or for other reasons).[55] The European Court has therefore agreed that the defendant can waive certain 'adversarial' rights that he or she may have, in the interests of speeding up the process of justice, without a breach of the defendant's human rights being involved:

> [The Court] has accepted that other considerations, including the right to trial within a reasonable time and the related need for expeditious handling of the courts' case-load, must be taken into account in determining the necessity of a public hearing at stages in the proceedings subsequent to the trial at first instance . . .[56]

In this case, the defendant waived his right to certain protections, having had the benefit of advice from two lawyers. The waiver was held to have been valid, in the circumstances.

Although prosecution and defence in a criminal case have a right to insist on a court trial, full-blooded court trials are in effect what economists call a 'scarce resource'.[57] That means that the public good constituted by the exercise of the right must be rationed, in order to maintain its integrity and value.[58] Clearly, in point of justice, it would be wholly wrong to apply a market solution to this scarcity, by allowing full criminal trials to be allocated to those willing to pay the most to have their case decided in this way. Crime-management techniques provide an alternative way of satisfying the demand for this scarce resource,[59] and also of doing justice in cases where there is no public interest in a full trial (e.g. where it would be extremely distressing for a key witness to have to give evidence[60]). Whether these benefits are worth running the risks involved in the use of such techniques, at least where individuals rather than companies are concerned, is another question.[61]

Alongside the crime-management approach, there is the closely allied 'bureaucratic-administrative' approach (the two approaches may overlap). The bureaucratic-administrative approach also departs from the traditional adversarial approach, by shifting the initial focus away from courts, trials, formal pleas of not guilty, and proof beyond

---

[54] See <www.cps.gov.uk/legal/a_to_c/abuse_of_process/>.

[55] The issues are aired in *R* v *Dunlop* [2006] EWCA Crim 1354, [2007] 1 Cr App R 8. This case makes clear that even a very long delay may not make a trial unfair. An example might be the discovery of evidence, linking someone to a crime, which is only discovered decades after the crime was committed.

[56] *Hermi* v *Italy* [GC], 18114/02, 18 October 2006, para. 80.

[57] E. Noam, 'Resource Allocation and Access to Criminal Courts: An Economic Model' (1982) 2 *Windsor Yearbook of Access to Justice* 208.

[58] See further, Chapter 3.   [59] See Noam, n 57.

[60] An example of this kind is the homicide case of *R* v *Hunes (Attorney General's Reference No 74, No 95 and No 118 of 2002)* [2002] EWCA Crim 2982.

[61] See McConville, n 30; Alge, n 34.

reasonable doubt. However, unlike the crime-management approach, the bureaucratic-administrative approach adopts more formal structures or systems (primary and secondary legislation; official guidelines) for penalizing wrongdoers at first instance. These systems or structures are sometimes run by justice officials, but are also very often run by non-court officials such as industry regulators. We have already come across an example of such a system or structure run by justice officials: the sentence discount system for guilty pleas.[62] An example involving officials outside the justice system is provided by the parking fine. Traffic wardens, who originally worked for the police but now work for local councils, decide the question of guilt or innocence, and impose the fixed penalty punishment, in the absence of the 'accused' driver.[63] In some cases, even if there are no protections against a finding of guilt and the imposition of a sanction in the first place, the procedure leading to penalization may nonetheless be considered fair and proportionate overall, if there is an adequate later opportunity to challenge the finding and sanction on appeal or on review.[64] What few people realize is how widespread across many domains of individual and business activity such civil penalties have become, not least because of the highly reduced level of participation costs involved.[65]

A complexity here is that civil penalties should not be confused with 'administrative' penalties. A civil penalty is a fixed punishment imposed where there is no legal possibility of court trial and punishment instead. By contrast, administrative penalties can be imposed where criminal trial is possible, but for some reason inappropriate in the circumstances. Administrative penalties are imposed when officials decide that it would be better to bring what would otherwise be a criminal process to a non-adversarial conclusion by the imposition of a penalty. We find an example under s. 16(3) of the Social Security Fraud Act 2001. If a benefit claimant knowingly fails to give notice to the authorities of a relevant change in his or her financial circumstances, he or she may be prosecuted in a criminal court, or may be subject to an administrative penalty, 'in less serious cases', whether or not there is an admission of guilt.[66] The presence of a system with formal structures and limits for imposing penalties without negotiation, and the ability to impose those penalties without an admission of guilt, are two important features of the bureaucratic-administrative approach that set it apart from the crime-management approach. The new system of deferred prosecution agreements (considered earlier), seems to be a blend of the crime-management and bureaucratic-administrative approaches. It relies on negotiation between prosecutors and the defendant to reach an

---

[62] See above, text at n 45.

[63] Although this decision can be challenged before the Traffic Penalty Tribunal: <www.trafficpenaltytribunal.gov.uk/>.

[64] Parking fines can be challenged, in a more adversarial spirit, before the Traffic Penalty Tribunal: <www.trafficpenaltytribunal.gov.uk/>. See also, <www.fca.org.uk/your-fca/documents/enforcement-information-guide>.   [65] See Law Commission, CP No 195 (2010).

[66] Department for Work and Pensions, *Penalties Policy: In Respect of Social Security Fraud and Error* (DWP, January 2015), para. 4.3.5. From 8 May 2012 the administrative penalty increased to 50 per cent of the amount overpaid subject to a minimum of £350 and a maximum of £2,000. The administrative penalty is payable in addition to any recoverable overpayment (para. 4.4.2). On 8 April 2014 the Government announced the intention to increase the maximum administrative penalty to £5,000, with the new limit being introduced in April 2015 subject to Parliamentary approval (para. 4.4.3).

agreed outcome (a crime-management aim); but it also sets out in legislation in quite a formal way the responsibilities of officials, and the nature and limits of the agreement that may be reached (a feature of the bureaucratic-administrative approach).

1.5 PROCESS, PROPORTIONALITY, AND 'CRIMINALITY'

What do we learn about the criminal law from these observations about the criminal process? It used to be said that one could identify 'criminal' offences by looking to see whether the wrongs in question were pursued in 'criminal' proceedings.[67] That definition, circular though it sounds, might have had some plausibility sixty years ago, when state penalization was associated almost exclusively with proceedings in the Crown Courts and in the magistrates' courts. However, as we now know, much has changed in that respect. Government departments, the police, local authorities, state prosecutors, and regulatory authorities of various kinds may all impose out-of-court penalties for wrongdoing. These penalties are likely to be fines but may include other sanctions, such as the removal of a licence.[68] In some instances, the penalties are far from trivial. For example, if the Home Office catches someone employing illegal immigrants, the employer may have a penalty imposed on him or her of up to £20,000 for *each person* illegally employed.[69] An even more dramatic example is the financial penalty of £5.25 million imposed by a regulatory body—the Financial Services Authority[70]—on the finance company, Aon. This penalty imposed was for the criminal-sounding wrong of, 'failing to take reasonable care to establish and maintain effective systems and controls to counter the risks of bribery and corruption associated with making payments to overseas firms and individuals'.[71] Compare that figure with the average fine imposed for breach of the criminal law under the Health and Safety at Work Act 1974, which stood at £16,730 in 2013.[72] The maximum fine available in the magistrates' court for the 'truly criminal' offences within its sentencing jurisdiction is just £5,000.

Now, here is a test. Which of the following is a criminal offence, which is an offence that may involve an administrative penalty, and which involves 'only' a civil penalty?

1. A person has been overpaid a social security benefit as a result of the fact that they negligently made an incorrect statement or representation, or negligently gave incorrect information or evidence, having failed to take reasonable steps to correct the error.[73]

---

[67] G. Williams, 'The Definition of a Crime' (1955) 8 CLP 107.

[68] *Didier* v *France (dec.)*, 58188/00, 27 August 2002.

[69] <www.gov.uk/penalties-for-employing-illegal-workers>.

[70] Now called the Financial Conduct Authority: <www.fca.org.uk/>.

[71] <www.fsa.gov.uk/library/communication/pr/2009/004.shtml>.

[72] <www.gov.uk/government/news/unscrupulous-employers-facing-tougher-health-and-safety-penalties>.

[73] The Social Security . . . Regulations 2012, made in exercise of the powers conferred by ss. 115C(2), 115D(1) and (2), 189(1), and 191 of the Social Security Administration Act 1992. See also s. 116(1) of the Welfare Reform Act 2012.

2. A company, and every company officer in default, fails to give notice to the Companies Registrar of the location of an overseas branch.[74]

3. A person who (subject to exceptions) between 14 May in any year and the following 4 August sells, exposes for sale, buys for sale, or consigns to any person for the purpose of sale, any description of oysters.[75]

The answer is that the first involves a civil penalty, the second is a criminal offence triable in the magistrates' court, and the third is an offence respecting which an administrative penalty may be paid in place of criminal prosecution. Can the answer be divined from an inspection of the elements of each offence, to see which involves genuinely reprehensible behaviour appropriate for criminalization? No, it cannot. Most importantly, as we have said, the imposition of the penalty in cases 1 and 3 is a matter for an official in the relevant government department, and is not a matter for trial in a court at first instance.

These facts about the criminal justice system bolster an argument for saying that one should not place heavy emphasis on what makes 'criminal' offences qualitatively different from other forms of penalization, namely that they are open to a full trial in accordance with specialized Crown Court or magistrates' court procedures. To insist on that emphasis is to focus too narrowly on the adversarial view of the way in which the criminal justice process plays out against the background of the substantive criminal law. Some eminent theorists have sought to argue that a distinctive feature of a true crime is that it involves a 'public wrong',[76] appropriate only for the adversarial procedures and protections available in the Crown Court and magistrates' court. However, the definition lacks a stable basis for generating genuine insights into the issue. For example, would it be possible, using this test, to determine which of the three 'test' examples given just now was or was not a 'criminal' wrong? It seems unlikely.

It would be more reflective of reality to view 'criminal' offences as just one basis from which the state seeks selectively to subject many different kinds of wrongdoing to (negotiated) penalization, through more or less formal procedures. In broad terms, the greater the stigma attached to an accusation of having committed that wrong, the stronger the case for procedures that protect the accused from wrongful conviction. Further, the more serious the wrong, the stronger the case not only for such protections, but also for sentencing powers that will reflect the degree of that seriousness, following a finding of guilt. This is an aspect of the 'proportionality' principle of criminalization.

The principle of proportionality is frequently encountered in the field of sentencing, as we will see in section 1.6. For example, Art. 49 of the EU Charter of Fundamental Rights stipulates that, 'the severity of the penalty must not be disproportionate to the

---

[74] Companies Act 2006, s. 130(2).

[75] Sea Fisheries (Shellfish) Act 1967, s. 16(1). See further: <www.gov.uk/government/uploads/system/uploads/attachment_data/file/314541/fap_guidance.pdf>, 15.

[76] Sir William Blackstone, *Commentaries*, Bk IV, ch 1; S. E. Marshall and R. A. Duff, 'Criminalization and Sharing Wrongs' (1998) 11 *Canadian Journal of Law and Jurisprudence* 7.

criminal offence'.[77] However, the proportionality principle also applies to the process of state penalization itself. An allegation of murder, engagement in terrorism or rape, clearly ought to be subjected to the most rigorous testing, with full protection of the accused from possible miscarriages of justice. That means, in practice, nothing short of Crown Court trial.[78] By contrast, parking illegally in the street may be appropriately dealt with by a low fixed civil penalty imposed by a low-level official, without any sort of hearing.[79] In between these two possibilities, there will be many variations in practice.[80] For example, the imposition of a Sexual Harm Prevention Order is a civil (non-criminal) procedure. However, there is obviously great stigma attached to being the subject of such an order. Consequently, although the proceedings are civil in character, the courts have insisted that the burden of proof that must be met in justifying the imposition of such an order is beyond reasonable doubt.[81]Put in pseudo-economic terms, in this new world of broad-ranging state penalization, the less serious and stigmatic an allegation, the greater the legitimate scope for adapting the process to reduce participation costs and uncertainty. We should note, though, that the proportionality principle can and should be made subject to certain 'red lines' that must not be crossed. For example, it would not be right to tolerate a penal procedure that might end in a sentence of imprisonment for the wrong done, unless the defendant enjoyed (amongst other things) the right to legal representation at a court hearing. More broadly, the Law Commission has said that where a penalty is unilaterally imposed by a state official, in the absence of any meaningful protections against miscarriages of justice, there should be appeal against the imposition of the penalty to an independent and impartial tribunal.[82] This follows the view taken by the European Court on the imposition of administrative penalties.[83]

1.6 SENTENCING IN CRIMINAL CASES

A person who has been found guilty of a criminal offence is liable to be sentenced by the court. A conviction may be bad enough in itself: it is a form of public censure, and many convictions (at least for non-motoring offences) make it difficult or impossible to

[77] This principle should also apply to administrative and civil penalties. See further, A. von Hirsch and A. Ashworth, *Proportionate Sentencing: Exploring the Principles* (2005). The Road Safety Act 2006, s. 3 makes it possible to vary a 'fixed' penalty according to the seriousness of the offence.

[78] Bearing in mind, though, the pressure placed on the accused to plead guilty at trial, that may threaten such protection.   [79] Although parking fines can be appealed: <www.gov.uk/appeal-parking-fine>.

[80] See, for example, the decision of the European Court in *Benham v the United Kingdom*, 19380/92, 10 June 1996, where it was held that certain rights, such as the right to free legal representation, depend on the severity of the penalty available on conviction.

[81] *B v Chief Constable of the Avon and Somerset Constabulary* (2001) 1 WLR 340.

[82] Law Com CP No 195. It follows that simply providing for an appeal may not be enough if the appeal body is effectively part of the same authority that imposed the penalty in the first place, and is thus insufficiently independent or impartial.

[83] *Čanády v Slovakia*, 53371/99, 16 November 2004. On a related point about proportionality, see *Falk v the Netherlands (dec.)* 66273/01, 19 October 2004.

obtain certain jobs or enter a profession. For most of the offences covered in this book, the sentence is likely to involve considerable deprivation, either of money or of liberty, or of both. The criminal law may therefore be said to open the way for coercive official sanctions against an offender. Indeed, we will see below that sentencing has considerable significance for the contours of criminal liability. When Parliament creates a crime, it authorizes not merely the affixing of a label of censure on the perpetrator, but also the imposition of certain deprivations by means of sentence.

The range of sentences available to English courts, and the actual exercise of judicial discretion in imposing sentences, can be outlined only briefly here.[84] The law of sentencing was consolidated in the Powers of Criminal Courts (Sentencing) Act 2000, but has since been altered in major ways by the Criminal Justice Act 2003 and other legislation. In brief, an absolute or conditional discharge may be thought sufficient for the least serious crimes or where the defendant has very strong mitigation. For many offences a fine will be the normal punishment. The size of the fine should reflect the seriousness of the offence, adjusted in accordance with the means of the offender.[85] If the offence is serious enough to warrant it, the court may consider imposing a community sentence. That sentence may contain one or more of twelve separate requirements, including a requirement to do unpaid work, a requirement to undergo drug treatment, and a curfew reinforced by electronic monitoring.

The most severe sentence is a custodial one, and a custodial sentence should be imposed only where the offence or offences are so serious that neither a fine alone nor a community sentence can be justified.[86] The length of any custodial sentence 'must be for the shortest term . . . that in the opinion of the court is commensurate with the seriousness of the offence'.[87] If the sentence is for up to two years, the court may suspend it and may require the offender to comply with certain requirements during the supervision period. Sentencing guidelines have been handed down in Court of Appeal judgments since the 1980s, but the main source of English guidelines is now the Sentencing Council (replacing the Sentencing Guidelines Council and Sentencing Advisory Panel), and guidelines have recently been issued on sexual offences,[88] and on fraud, bribery, and money laundering offences.[89] These are intended to guide the courts in setting the length of sentence for different types of offence. The high use of imprisonment continues to be a contentious issue. England and Wales have one of the highest rates of imprisonment in Europe, and on 26 June 2015 the prison population stood at just over 86,000 (compared with 42,000 in early 1993).[90]

How necessary is an understanding of sentencing law and practice to a study of the criminal law? Ideally the criminal law would be studied in conjunction with the

---

[84] For fuller discussion, see A. Ashworth, *Sentencing and Criminal Justice* (6th edn., Cambridge University Press, 2015).   [85] Powers of Criminal Courts (Sentencing) Act 2000, s. 128.

[86] Criminal Justice Act 2003, s. 152(2).   [87] Criminal Justice Act 2003, s. 153(2).

[88] <www.sentencingcouncil.org.uk/publications/item/sexual-offences-definitive-guideline/>.

[89] <www.sentencingcouncil.org.uk/wp-content/uploads/Fraud_bribery_and_money_laundering_offences_-_Definitive_guideline.pdf>.

[90] <www.gov.uk/government/statistics/prison-population-figures-2015>.

other elements of criminal justice, briefly discussed at the outset, with which it is so intimately linked in practice and in theory—prosecution policy and other aspects of pre-trial criminal process, the laws of evidence, and sentencing too.[91] At a minimum, the interactions between sentencing and criminal law must be kept in view. It is sentencing, largely, that gives the criminal law its bite, and so decisions on criminal liability should be viewed as decisions about the application of censure and coercion. An example of the impact of sentencing on the criminal law is that, as we shall see in Chapter 8, the shape of the law on murder and manslaughter has been influenced by the existence of the mandatory penalty for murder.

So, the aims of sentencing are not simply part of the background of the criminal law: they have implications for the shape of the criminal law itself. As argued earlier, proportionality should be a key element in the structure of the criminal law. It is a major function of the criminal law to grade offences and to label them proportionately. As Nils Jareborg expresses it, 'the threat of punishment is not only a conditional threat of a painful sanction. It is also an official expression of how negatively different kinds of action or omission are judged'.[92] At the level of judicial sentencing, the Criminal Justice Act 2003 requires courts to 'have regard to' some five different purposes of sentencing—punishment, deterrence, rehabilitation, public protection, and reparation.[93] Not only do these purposes conflict among themselves, but government-sponsored research demonstrates, for example, that the evidence for the effectiveness of deterrent sentences is unpromising.[94] The sentencing guidelines endeavour to save sentencing practice from the inconsistency that a 'pick-and-mix' approach to the purposes of sentencing might produce, by emphasizing that s. 143(1) of the Act insists upon proportionality of sentencing.[95] Proportionality thus has a central role, not only at the legislative stage of grading offences in the criminal law, but also at the judicial stage of passing sentence in individual cases. Although it may be a relatively abstract ideal, proportionality should be an important guiding principle, even for theorists who reject the idea that securing just deserts is the central aim of sentencing.[96] In that regard, we should note an important distinction between two kinds of proportionality.[97] One is cardinal proportionality, which requires that the severity of the punishment be in proportion to the seriousness of the offence. Exactly what the level of sentences should be remains a matter for debate, taking account of criminological research and, it is submitted, of the principle of restraint in the use of custody. The second kind of proportionality, more important for our present purposes, is ordinal proportionality. This requires an assessment of the seriousness of the crime in relation to other forms of offending, so as to establish acceptable relativities. The meaning of 'seriousness' is, of

---

[91] Cf. P. Alldridge, 'What's Wrong with the Traditional Criminal Law Course?' (1990) 10 *Legal Studies* 38.
[92] N. Jareborg, 'The Coherence of the Penal System', in his *Essays in Criminal Law* (1988).
[93] Criminal Justice Act 2003, s. 142(1).   [94] See references in n 52.
[95] Sentencing Guidelines Council, Overarching Principles (2004).
[96] N. Lacey and H. Pickard, 'The Chimera of Proportionality: Institutionalising Limits on Punishment in Contemporary Social and Political Systems' (2015) 78 *The Modern Law Review* 216.
[97] See further von Hirsch and Ashworth, n 77, ch 9.

course, highly contested, although at this stage it is enough to say that it will be much taken up with a combination of the gravity of the wrong or of the harm done or risked, together with the culpability of the offender in causing—or posing a risk of—the harm.

FURTHER READING

A. ASHWORTH, 'Is the Criminal Law a Lost Cause?' (2000) 116 LQR 225.

A. ASHWORTH, *Sentencing and Criminal Justice* (6th edn., Cambridge University Press, 2015).

A. ASHWORTH and M. REDMAYNE, *The Criminal Process* (Oxford University Press, 2010).

A. ASHWORTH and L. ZEDNER, 'Defending the Criminal Law: Reflections on the Changing Character of Crime, Procedure and Sanctions' (2008) 2 *Criminal Law and Philosophy* 21.

N. LACEY and H. PICKARD, 'The Chimera of Proportionality: Institutionalising Limits on Punishment in Contemporary Social and Political Systems' (2015) 78 *The Modern Law Review* 216.

N. LACEY and L. ZEDNER, 'Legal Constructions of Crime', in M. Maguire, R. Morgan, and R. Reiner (eds), *Oxford Handbook of Criminology* (5th edn., Oxford University Press, 2012), ch 6.

G. LAMOND, 'What is a Crime?' (2007) 27 *Oxford Journal of Legal Studies* 609.

M. MCCONVILLE and L. MARSH, 'Criminal Judges: Legitimacy, Courts and State-Induced Guilty Pleas in Britain' [2015] 42 *Journal of Law and Society* 319–24.

M. MCCONVILLE et al., *Standing Accused: The Organization and Practices of Criminal Defence Lawyers in Britain* (Oxford University Press, 1994).

2

CRIMINAL LAW HISTORY

2.1 INTRODUCTION

The eminent legal historian, S. F. C. Milsom once said of the criminal law that, '[t]he miserable history of crime in England can be shortly told. Nothing worthwhile was created. There is no achievement to trace.'[1] In this chapter, we will see why that claim is wrong. As we will see, whilst there is much to criticize in the way that the criminal law has developed over centuries, there is no doubting the fascination of its intellectual evolution. The brief history presented here seeks to develop the outline of an argument suggesting that Christian—and in particular Church of England—religious beliefs played an important historical role in England, in developing criminal law writers' understanding of what conduct ought to be criminal. That understanding became more secularized during the late-eighteenth and nineteenth centuries. This led to greater emphasis on a more rationalist approach on the part of later criminal law writers, concerned at least as much with organizing the form of the criminal law—through codification, in particular—as with its substance. This rationalism was, at least to some extent, buttressed by a new enlightenment 'humanism', that placed an emphasis on the need for punishments to be more 'proportionate' to the gravity of crimes, leading to abolition of the death penalty for many less serious crimes.

Prominent works on criminal law were for centuries primarily concerned with what were called the 'pleas of the Crown'.[2] The extensive jurisdictional reach of the criminal law, as a nationwide system, was based on royal authority. Pleas of the Crown were

---

[1] S. F. C. Milsom, *Historical Foundations of the Criminal Law* (1969), 353.

[2] See, e.g., Sir W. Staunford, *Les Plees del Coron* (Richard Tottell, 1557); Sir Matthew Hale, *The History of the Pleas of the Crown* (Gyles, Woodward and Davis, 1736); W. Hawkins, *A Treatise of the Pleas of the Crown* (J. Walthoe, 1716); E. East, *A Treatise of the Pleas of the Crown* (1803).

cases in which the Crown claimed jurisdiction over the alleged offence, taking precedence over the application of local law and custom, and over compensation arrangements between the offender and the victim (or between their families).[3] Moreover,
from the sixteenth century onwards, the legislature increasingly turned into pleas of
the Crown cases—many of which involved offences against religion or morality—that
had previously been within the jurisdiction of the Church courts. As we will see, this
development considerably broadened the remit of 'Crown law', with harsh and enduring consequences for offenders.

Pleas of the Crown were divided into treason, felonies—at one time, meaning the
betrayal of one's lord and master—and offences called misdemeanours.[4] Until the middle of the nineteenth century, many felonies were capital—death penalty—offences.
Felonies ranged from the most serious, such as murder, down to innumerable offences
involving the regulation and protection of trade, or state business, in the interests of
the common good. Historical examples of the latter were selling a horse to a 'Scotch-
man',[5] wilfully obstructing someone lawfully serving a writ in the Royal Mint,[6] or causing a nuisance on the highway or on a bridge.[7] Accordingly, the crimes included in
their treatises by early writers on criminal law were a broad-ranging collection, like
those included in major modern works directed at practitioners and the judiciary.[8]
Until the twentieth century, and the advent of the modern university law course, there
was no need for writers to concentrate only on a much narrower set of crimes, chosen
with an eye to enthralling student readers and impressing on them the potential gravity
of criminal law's concerns. We will say more about this in Chapter 3.

2.2 THE CHURCH OF ENGLAND AND THE FRAMEWORK OF ENGLISH CRIMINAL LAW

It is worth investigating briefly the values that guided the content of earlier works of
criminal law, to understand how much things have changed. In a way that too few
criminal law writers have appreciated, the importance of a citizen's loyalty to the monarch, and to the tenets of state religion, have played a fundamental role in shaping
English 'criminal' law.

Early works emphasized crimes touching on what were perceived as a citizen's fundamental obligations of loyalty, to the Crown and to the (protestant) church. This is

---

[3] See P. Crofts, *Wickedness and Crime: Laws of Homicide and Malice* (2013), 48–49; N. Hurnard, *The King's Pardon for Homicide to AD 1307* (1969).

[4] That distinction, which is still applied in some jurisdictions, was replaced in 1967 in England and Wales by the distinction between offences triable on indictment in the Crown Court, and offences triable only sum-marily, in the magistrates' court.

[5] 23 Henry VIII, chapter 16, perhaps unsurprising repealed by 4 James I, chapter 1.

[6] 9 George I, chapter 28.   [7] Hawkins, n 2, chs 76 and 77.

[8] The best known of which is J. Richardson (ed.), *Archbold's Criminal Proceeding, Evidence and Practice* (2015), first published in 1822.

an emphasis entirely absent from modern works on criminal law. Sir Matthew Hale (1609–76), whose *History of the Pleas of the Crown* was published posthumously in 1736, gave pride of place to the crime of treason. This was, and remains, a very broad offence. At one time, simply being a Catholic priest in England, without swearing an oath of loyalty to the monarch, amounted to treason.[9] To this day, treason includes killing the Lord Chancellor or a High Court judge[10] and having sexual intercourse with the King's wife, his eldest unmarried daughter, or the wife of the heir to the throne,[11] alongside 'compassing or imagining' the death of the King, the Queen, or the heir to the throne; although, thankfully, the rather remote possibility of being beheaded for treason was abolished in 1973.[12] In Hale's time, treason also included many forms of counterfeiting sealed documents, or coins.[13] Hale, who as an MP had helped ease the path to the restoration of Charles II as King in 1660,[14] did not explain the magnitude of the offence solely in terms of its threat to the, 'safety and preservation of the person, dignity and government of the king'. Hale also explained it in terms of the betrayal of loyalty owed by the citizen to the monarch:

> [A]s the subject has his protection from the king and the laws, so on the other side the subject is bound by his allegiance to be true and faithful to the king; and therefore all indictments of high treason run . . . as a breach of trust, that is owing to the king . . .[15]

William Hawkins, writing on pleas of the Crown in 1716, gave equal prominence to offences 'against God'. These encompassed not only specifically religious offences, but also some offences then regarded as immoral (particularly under the seventeenth-century influence of puritanism), such as sodomy[16] and 'open lewdness'. In Hawkins' view, such offences were at the heart of criminal law because religion and morality are together, 'the foundation of government'.[17] Falling under offences 'against God' were the

---

[9] Jesuits, etc, Act 1584 (a forerunner of this Act being the Act of Supremacy 1536, which made it high treason for a church office-holder to refuse to renounce papal authority). The execution of a priest under the 1584 Act became an issue in a case as late as 1995: *In re St Edmund's Churchyard, Gateshead* (1995) 3 WLR 253; see also, *In re St Mary the Virgin, Oxford* (2009) 2 WLR 1381.

[10] See G. McBain, 'Killing the Sovereign or Her Judges' [2009] 20 *King's Law Journal* 457.

[11] See G. McBain, 'High Treason—Violating the Sovereign's Wife' [2009] 29 *Legal Studies* 264.

[12] The death penalty for treason was abolished in 1998. Whilst the offence of treason lives on, it is now what lawyers call a 'dead letter' (an effectively unusable law). It has been overtaken in terms of coverage and importance by other crimes, including terrorist offences.

[13] Counterfeiting and forgery are now no longer treasonous, but have been turned into stand-alone offences contained in the Counterfeiting and Forgery Act 1981.

[14] At that time it was possible to serve as an MP and as a permanent judge at the same time, a position unchanged until the nineteenth century. It is still possible to serve as an MP and sit as a part-time recorder (a kind of judge) in criminal cases.   [15] Hale, n 2, 59.

[16] A broad sexual offence, but in practice mainly concerned with sexual intercourse between men. 'Buggery' became a capital crime under a statute in England in 1533 (25 Hen viii, c.6) aimed at, 'the punysshement of the vice of buggerie', as part of Henry VIII's efforts to reduce the criminal jurisdiction of the church courts. The suggestion that Catholic priests frequently engaged in buggery was part of the propaganda of reformation England. See P. Johnson and R. M. Vanderbeck, *Law, Religion and Homosexuality* (2014), 31–3.

[17] Hawkins, n 1, ch 6, section 5. See further, L. Moran, *The Homosexual(ity) of Law* (1996), 75.

capital (death penalty) common law offences of heresy, witchcraft, and sodomy, but also a host of non-capital offences. At common law, the latter included, 'scoffing at the scriptures',[18] blasphemies against God (including denying God's existence), and speaking or writing, 'seditious words in derogation of the established religion'. Under statute, Hawkins adds mention of, amongst other non-capital crimes, 'profane swearing and cursing', drunkenness, failing to go to church, and various examples of promoting or encouraging the 'Popish religion'.[19]

The importance accorded in law to treason, and to conduct contrary to God's will, reflected centuries of belief and practice. However, the idea that the two are intertwined in a special legal relationship is a product of the reformation period in England.[20] In 1528, leading protestant William Tyndale had written—in a work that may have been read and approved by Henry VIII himself—that

> He that judges the King judges God, and he that lays hands on the King lays hands on God, and he that resists the King resists God and damns God's law and ordinance. If the subjects sin, they must be brought to the *King's* judgment.[21]

One result of this change was that, during and after the reformation, it became the King's courts that were given the power to deal with most offences against God (as well as with other crimes). Offences against God had previously been tried and sentenced under a parallel jurisdiction enjoyed by church courts:[22] church courts had exercised jurisdiction over offences such as heresy, blasphemy, illegal sexual activity, fraud, and perjury.[23] The process of replacing the church's criminal jurisdiction with Royal jurisdiction began in earnest under Henry VIII, and involved harsh punishments for religious offences in particular.[24] For our purposes, an important landmark is a later statute: The Act for the Abolition of the Court of High Commission 1641.[25] By virtue of this Act, the Church courts lost much of their long-standing criminal jurisdiction.[26]

---

[18] A biblical notion: see 2 Peter, 3.   [19] Hawkins, n 2, chapter 15.

[20] Proponents of this view drew on scriptural passages, such as 1 Peter, 13: 'Submit yourselves for the Lord's sake to every authority instituted among men: whether to the king, as the supreme authority, or to governors who are sent by him to punish those who do wrong and to commend those who do right.'

[21] W. Tyndale, *The Obedience of a Christian Man* (Antwerp, 1528, reprint, 2000), (39–40 my emphasis). The Act of Supremacy 1534 decreed that Henry VIII had always been supreme head of the Church of England; and the Treason Act 1534 made opposition to the Act of Supremacy treason and punishable by death. Having been repealed under Mary, the Act was effectively revived by Elizabeth I in the Act of Supremacy 1559, which declared her 'Supreme Governor' of the Church of England. Tyndale himself was executed in Belgium, for daring to have translated the bible into English.

[22] For a fascinating account of the wide-ranging diet of cases tried in the Church courts, sometimes known as the 'bawdy' courts, because of their jurisdiction over sexual misconduct, see J. Briggs, C. Harrison, A. McInnes, and D. Vincent, *Crime and Punishment in England* (1996), ch 3.

[23] M. Jones and P. Johnstone, *History of Criminal Justice* (5th edn., 2015), 94.

[24] See, for example, The Act of the Six Articles (1539), that made punishable by death a number of actions deemed not to be in conformity with church doctrine.   [25] 1641, 17 Car I, cap 11.

[26] Other than when certain crimes were committed by those entitled to plead 'benefit of clergy': A.L. Cross, 'The English Criminal Law and Benefit of Clergy during the Eighteenth and Early Nineteenth Century' (1917) 22 *The American Historical Review* 544, at 551 onwards.

Offences against God hence became pleas of the Crown.[27] That led to extended discussion of such crimes in post-1641 works on criminal law in general.

The legacy of these developments, in conjunction with prevailing social attitudes, has been a shameful one. For centuries, in England and Wales, unashamed atheists or Catholics, and sexual adventurers outside religious and social norms, stood to be condemned by common law and statute on much the same basis as murderers and thieves. Indeed, A.D. Harvey has contended that, during the first thirty-five years of the nineteenth century, more than fifty men were hanged for sodomy in England.[28] This was roughly a seventh of the number of people executed for murder in the same period, although—seemingly incredibly—in 1806, there were more executions for sodomy than for murder.[29] This is an illustration of the fact that, for a long period of English criminal law, all such offenders were in one crucial respect condemned on the same basis: their alleged violation of God's law. So, for example, early-nineteenth century lawyer, Humphrey Woolrych (himself, an opponent of widespread use of the death penalty) understood the law's punishment of murder by the penalty of death to be justified by Genesis ix: 6.[30] He understood the Law's meting out of the same punishment for crimes against religion to be justified by Exodus xxii: 18[31] and Leviticus xix: 31,[32] and had this to say about sodomy:

> And there is no doubt that in the sight of God it is a most grievous and awful sin, and that his holy eyes must turn away from such a violation of his own image with disgust. There is not any question, also, but that He ordered the immediate execution of the sodomite, or unnatural person.[33]

Even after the death penalty for sodomy was removed, section 61 of the Offences Against the Person Act 1861 still saw fit to describe the crime (when involving anal intercourse) as, 'the Abominable Crime of Buggery'. The 1861 Act set out the sentence as

---

[27] W.M. Abbott, 'Anticlericalism and Episcopacy,' in B. Sharp and M. Fissel (eds), *Law and Authority in Early Modern England* (2007), 164. D. Eppley, *Defending Royal Supremacy and Discerning God's Will in Tudor England* (2007), 9. Part II of the 1641 Act read, '[No] . . . person or persons whatsoever exercising spiritual or ecclesiastical power, authority or jurisdiction by any grant, licence or commission of the King's Majesty [shall] . . . award, impose or inflict any pain, penalty, fine, amercement, imprisonment or other corporal punishment upon any of the King's subjects for any contempt, misdemeanour, crime, offence, matter or thing whatsoever belonging to spiritual or ecclesiastical cognizance or jurisdiction . . .'.

[28] A. D. Harvey, 'Prosecutions for Sodomy in England at the Beginning of the Nineteenth Century' (1978) 21 *The Historical Journal* 939.

[29] Harvey's figures (n 28) show a striking increase in prosecutions for sodomy in the early nineteenth century. Some contemporary writers gave lower figures for the number of those executed for sodomy immediately prior to this time. For example, speaking about the end of the eighteenth century, H. Woolrych, *The History and Results of the Present Capital Punishments in England* (Saunders and Benning, 1832), 144, claimed that, between 1757 and 1806, roughly one person was executed for sodomy every three years.

[30] 'Whoso sheddeth man's blood, by man shall his blood be shed.'

[31] 'Thou shalt not suffer a witch to live.'

[32] 'Do not turn to mediums or necromancers; do not seek them out, and so make yourselves unclean by them.'

[33] Woolrych, n 29, 143. See Leviticus 18:22: 'Thou shalt not lie with mankind as with womankind it is abomination.'

necessarily involving a minimum of ten years' imprisonment, up to life imprisonment. It was not until 1967 that sexual acts (with no other person present) between two males over twenty-one were decriminalized in England. It was not until the Sexual Offences (Amendment) Act 2000 that the 'no other person present' restriction was removed and the age of consent lowered to sixteen.[34] So far as blasphemy is concerned, whilst it was as long ago as 1697 that the last person was executed for blasphemy in England, there were a spate of prosecutions in the late-eighteenth century up until the middle of the nineteenth century, with a small number of prosecutions undertaken during the twentieth century.[35] Final abolition of this offence in England and Wales came as late as 2008.[36]

What is significant about these developments is the way in which changing values have altered perceptions of some of these early building blocks of criminal law. To use the criminal law to punish departures from loyalty to individual Crown commands, to an established religion, and to an associated fixed code of moral behaviour, is a breach of what we will call the principle of 'lifestyle autonomy'.[37] Such a use of the criminal law is wrong because it involves censuring people, and exposing them to state punishment, simply for speaking or behaving in a way that shows that their own loyalties, faith (if any), and beliefs do not lie with particular state officials, or with the state religion and its moral code. Lifestyle autonomy involves the freedom, amongst other things, to act on one's own beliefs and value judgements, to form personal relationships, including sexual relationships, and ties of loyalty of one's own choosing, to shape one's own life course, and so on, free from the threat of coercion (whether in the name of religion or otherwise).[38] We will have more to say about autonomy in Chapters 3 and 4. The importance of the principle in a more secular world meant that twentieth-century prosecutors increasingly made far less use of treason, or of religious offences (between 1922 and 1977, there were no prosecutions for blasphemy). Similarly, writers on criminal law found earnest discussions of treason and offences against God an embarrassment, and simply downplayed them or omitted discussion of them altogether. However, a conspicuous exception to these developments involved the continued criminalization of sexual activity between men. In late Victorian England, and well into the twentieth

[34] For a fascinating study of the way language was (ab)used in the course of the debates leading up to reform, see P. Baker, '"Unnatural Acts": Discourses of Homosexuality within the House of Lords Debates on Gay Male Law Reform' (2004) 8 *Journal of Sociolinguistics* 88.

[35] See D. Nash, *Blasphemy in Modern Britain: 1789 to the Present* (2000), chs 3 and 5. The best known twentieth-century trial is the case of *Whitehouse* v *Lemon* [1979] 2 WLR 281.

[36] Criminal Justice and Immigration Act 2008. The offence of profane swearing and cursing was abolished by s. 13 of the Criminal Law Act 1967. Sedition and seditious libel, as well as defamatory libel and obscene libel, were abolished by s. 73 of the Coroners and Justice Act 2009. 'Open lewdness' remains part of the common law offence of outraging public decency: see Law Commission, Simplification of the Criminal Law: *Public Nuisance and Outraging Public Decency*, Law Commission Consultation Paper no. 193 (2010).

[37] See Chapter 3.2 and 4.2. What we call 'lifestyle autonomy' is typically called 'personal autonomy'; but we avoid the latter term, because we wish to distinguish personal and inter-personal dimensions to 'lifestyle autonomy'.

[38] So long as one's choices do not themselves involve the use or threat of significant harm (not simply annoyance, affront, or disgust) to others. See Chapter 4.2. For a useful general discussion, see <www.plato. stanford.edu/entries/autonomy-moral/>; and more generally, J. Raz, *The Morality of Freedom* (1986).

century, difficulties with proving that sexual intercourse itself had taken place meant that gay men were being arrested and prosecuted in large numbers for the offence of 'gross indecency',[39] until the abolition of that offence in 2003.

2.3 THE RISE OF SECULAR VALUES, HUMANISM, AND CODIFICATION OF THE CRIMINAL LAW

As Randall McGowen remarks, 'for much of the eighteenth century . . . Divine justice was the normative model for human justice'.[40] Early criminal law texts, influenced by biblical writing,[41] gave homicide and theft or fraud offences a central role, in part because of their connection with the Ten Commandments ('thou shalt not kill'; 'thou shalt not steal'; thou shalt not bear false witness').[42] The Ten Commandments formed the theoretical benchmark against which criminal laws involving moral wrongs were to be judged.[43] The exercise of the King's jurisdiction over felonies in general—including murder and theft—was expressed and justified in theological terms. In explaining English law, Hale—brought up as a Puritan, and on graduating, originally intended for priesthood—sententiously pronounced, 'by the ancient divine law . . . the punishment of homicide was with death. Genesis ix 6'.[44] Clerics giving preliminary sermons, to the assize judges[45] and juries, saw it as their task to lend religious authority to the proceedings. As the Reverend John Lever graphically put it in his sermon at the Lancaster Assizes in 1771:

> When we see the poor affrighted wretch called up to the bar, to answer to the heavy charge brought against him; pale horror and the most dreadful anxiety painted in his countenance, perhaps his guilty conscience giving the lie to his words when he pleads not guilty; I say, when we view this affecting scene, let us remember that we must one day appear before the bar of a higher and more tremendous Tribunal.[46]

However, by the early-nineteenth century, reformist writing on pleas of the Crown was already becoming gradually more humanist, secularized, and rationalistic. For example,

---

[39]   Section 11 of the Criminal Law Amendment Act 1885. Between 1967 and 2003, 30,000 gay and bisexual men were convicted for behaviour that would not have been a crime had their partner been a woman: <www.theguardian.com/society/2007/jun/24/communities.gayrights>.

[40]   R. McGowen, '"He Beareth Not the Sword in Vain": Religion and the Criminal Law in Eighteenth-Century England' (1987–88) 21 *Eighteenth Century Studies* 192, 193.

[41]   See, e.g., Hale's discussion of capital punishment for murder: Hale, n 2, 2–3.

[42]   On the significance of the Ten Commandments to early understanding of crime, see Briggs, Harrison, McInnes, and Vincent, n 22. Hale devotes eighty-five pages of his treatise to homicide, and seventy-one pages to offences against property.

[43]   Briggs, Harrison, McInnes, and Vincent, n 22.

[44]   Hale, n 2, 2. The same biblical verse is later used in the same justificatory way by Woolrych: see text at n 30.

[45]   Judges trying cases on circuit around the country. Assizes were abolished as such in 1971, although judges still travel on circuit to try cases in local towns and cities.

[46]   J. Lever, *Prepare to Meet Thy God* (1771), 6, cited by McGowen, n 41.

in his work on the pleas of the Crown, Edward East sought to explain sodomy not as an offence against God but as an offence against the person;[47] and in his later history of English criminal law, Victorian judge, essayist, and jurist Sir James Stephen placed the offence under the heading of, 'Acts Injurious to the Public in General'.[48] More broadly, the secular and rational turn in analysis of criminal law was in part due to the influence of noted legal commentator and reformer Jeremy Bentham (1748–1832).[49] It was Bentham who coined the term 'codify',[50] and argued for the separation of church and state.

Taking Bentham's lead, in the early-nineteenth century work of the Criminal Law Commissioners[51] the focus turned to the systematization of offences, so that they could be embodied in an accessible and humane criminal code.[52] In their Fourth Report, the Commissioners dealt with the raggedly organized and often brutal law of theft.[53] In a famous passage, Bentham had sought to capture what he (as ever, exaggerating) believed was at the root of the harsh and unsystematized law of theft:

> The country squire who has his turnips stolen, goes to work and gets a bloody law against stealing turnips. It exceeds the utmost stretch of his comprehension to conceive that the next year the same catastrophe may happen to his potatoes. For two general rules . . . in modern British legislation are: never to move a finger until your passions are inflamed, not ever to look further than your nose.[54]

As Sir James Fitzjames Stephen put it, a detailed focus on such property crimes was justified in that they, 'contain[ed] material of the highest value for *systematic* legislation' (my emphasis).[55] A new influence also reinforced the preoccupation with such crimes. This was the influence of an Enlightenment value: the desire for proportionality between crime and punishment. As it was expressed, in relation to punishment, by one of its famous originators, Cesare Beccaria, in 1764:

> In order that punishment should not be an act of violence perpetrated by one or many upon a private citizen, it is essential that it should be public, speedy, necessary, the minimum possible in the given circumstances, proportionate to the crime, and determined by the law.[56]

---

[47] See Moran, n 17, 75.   [48] See Moran, n 17, 76.

[49] See, e.g., J. Bentham, *An Introduction to the Principles of Morals and Legislation* (1789).

[50] Although criminal codes have been around at least since the time of the sixth Babylonian King, Hammurabi, who issued his code in *c*.1754 bc: <www.commonlaw.com/Hammurabi.html>.

[51] There were eight reports completed by Her Majesties Commissioners on Criminal Law between 1834 and 1845. For an overview, see K. J. M. Smith, *Lawyers, Legislators and Theorists* (1998).

[52] See further, Wing-Cheong Chan, B. Wright, and S. Yeo (eds), *Codification, Macaulay and the Indian Penal Code: The Legacies and Modern Challenges of Criminal Law Reform* (2011).

[53] *The Jurist* (1840) vol. III, 778.

[54] Bentham MSS, in the library of University College London, cxl 92, cited in G. Postema, *Bentham and the Common Law Tradition* (1986), 264.

[55] Sir James Stephen, *A History of the Criminal Law of England*, vol. III (1883), x. We should note, though, that Stephen was himself, like his eighteenth-century predecessors, a defender of the view that the criminal law could legitimately be employed to deter and punish what he called, 'the grosser forms of vice', although he did not defend that view solely by pointing to the scriptures.

[56] R. Bellamy (ed), *Beccaria: On Crimes and Punishment and Other Writings* (1995), 113. On the proportionality principle, see Chapter 4.6.

In that regard, murder attracted increasingly critical attention amongst codifiers, precisely in virtue of the fact that, for many influential writers, politicians, and judges, it was fast becoming one of the few crimes for which the death penalty *was* commonly regarded as still uniquely appropriate.[57] By contrast, theft, forgery, and a variety of other property offences came in for criticism from some eighteenth- and nineteenth-century humanist writers, in virtue of what came to be regarded as the too-ready availability of the sledgehammer penalty of death in such cases.[58] Even Sir William Blackstone, for whom English Crown law in the eighteenth century was, 'with justice supposed to be more nearly advanced to perfection,'[59] could not reconcile this view with the existence of the death penalty for—amongst over 200 other offences—chopping down a cherry tree in an orchard.[60] From a modern perspective, of course, this state of affairs seems nothing short of barbaric, and agitators for reform from the late eighteenth well into the twentieth century never tired of pointing this out.

To understand historically rather than simply condemn, though, we must keep in mind the religious perspective from which this uniformity of harsh punishment for offences was justifiable.[61] Albeit focused on a wider range of conduct, the justice of the early criminal law was Old Testament-style justice, in which the penalty of death was to be used with little discrimination. In book 27, verse 24 of Deuteronomy, 'cursed is the man who kills his neighbour secretly'; but also cursed, in verse 23, 'is the man who sleeps with his mother-in law', and in verse 17, 'the man who moves his neighbour's boundary stone'. According to 22 Deuteronomy 25, if a man rapes a girl already pledged to be married, the man must die (but not the girl); but also, according to verse 22, if a man sleeps with another man's wife (with her consent), both are to be put to death. In a similar vein, Books 20 and 21 of Leviticus prescribe the death penalty—sometimes by fire—for many acts that would now seem relatively trivial: for example, cursing one's father or mother, or marrying both a woman and her daughter (in this case, all three were to be burned in the fire: 20 Leviticus 14). There is no evidence that the death penalty was in fact ruthlessly carried out in all such instances in the time of the early Hebrews (far from it), but that is also true of the use of the death penalty under early English criminal law. Nonetheless, what is clear is the scriptural authority for the wide availability of the death penalty for crimes both great and small.

---

[57] R. McGovern, 'History, Culture and the Death Penalty: The British Debates, 1840–70' (2003) 29 *Historical Reflections* 229–49.

[58] See the discussion in J. Horder, *Homicide and the Politics of Law Reform* (Oxford University Press, 2012), 7–15; 19–22, and in K. Smith, n 51, 141–5.

[59] Sir W. Blackstone, *Commentaries on the Laws of England* (1765–69), book 4, ch 1.

[60] 9 George 2, ch 22; 31 George 2, ch 42, discussed in Sir W. Blackstone, n 59, book 4, ch 1. These legislative developments Blackstone—influenced by Beccaria—attributed to, 'quackery in government'.

[61] See text at n 17. In relation to what is said next about Old Testament justice, we should recall that in the New Testament, Jesus is reported as saying, 'Do not think that I have come to abolish the Law (the Old Testament) or the Prophets; I have not come to abolish them but to fulfil them. I tell you the truth, until heaven and earth disappear, not the smallest letter, not the least stroke or a pen, will by any means disappear from the Law (the Old Testament) until everything is accomplished' (Matthew 5:17–18).

2.4 THE CODE THAT NEVER WAS: THE 1861 LEGISLATION AND ITS AFTERMATH

Contrary to the opinion commonly given in textbooks, as a result of these nineteenth-century initiatives English criminal law was to substantial degree systematized over 160 years ago. The almost universally held view that there has never been a criminal code in England and Wales[62] is in fact only a half-truth. A series of largely consolidating Acts passed in one year—1861—placed on a statutory footing: (a) the sentencing basis for murder and manslaughter, (b) abortion, (c) non-fatal offences of violence including major sexual offences, (d) criminal damage, (e) larceny, that is theft, (f) forgery, (g) complicity, and (h) what would now be regarded as 'terrorist' offences involving the use of explosives. From a twenty-first-century perspective, a good deal of the 1861 legislation is in many respects draconian, discriminatory, and oppressive. Small wonder, then, that most criminal law specialists have dismissed its significance as a whole, preferring to turn their fire on the parts of the 1861 legislation that are still valid and still form the basis for trials in England and Wales day in, day out. However, as with England's Victorian sewer system, we may think that the content of the 1861 legislation stinks, that it is out of date and that it is unable to cope with modern demands; but it is hard not to admit to a grudging admiration for the scale of the original achievement and for its longevity in some respects.

The 1861 legislation should be understood historically as a fledgling English criminal code. That it is not so regarded, leading to the partial myth of 'code-less England and Wales', stems from collective amnesia concerning events prior to the failure to enact what would have been a more complete code. This was Sir James Stephen's criminal code, that he drafted in the late-nineteenth century.[63] Stephen drafted a criminal code more comprehensive than the 1861 legislation, but itself also a work largely of consolidation and re-statement. This Bill was introduced into the House of Commons in 1873, and again in 1879. Stephen's efforts ended in failure in England,[64] although his code was adopted in Canada, New Zealand, and Australia.[65] It is true that Stephen's code, like the Crimes (New Zealand) Act 1908 that adopted it, would have been a single Act of Parliament, unlike the series of Acts that made up the 1861 legislation.

---

[62] See, e.g., Sir H. Brooke, 'The Law Commission and Criminal Law Reform' [1995] Crim LR 911; Lord Bingham, 'A Criminal Code: Must We Wait for Ever?' [1998] Crim LR 694; Mrs Justice Arden, 'Criminal Law at the Crossroads: the Impact of Human Rights from the Law Commission's Perspective and the Need for a Code' [1999] Crim LR 439. For an overview of the issues, see L. Farmer, 'Codification', in M. D. Dubber and T. Hörnle (eds), *The Oxford Handbook of Criminal Law* (2014), ch 17.

[63] See K. J. M. Smith, n 52, 146–9; L. Farmer, 'Reconstructing the English Codification Debate: The Criminal Law Commissioners, 1833–45' (2000) 18 *Law and History Review* 397.

[64] About which he memorably said: 'As to the code becoming law, Parliament is an ass made up of clever fellows who empty their talents merrily in ignoble squabbles, and pretty successful attempts to fall to the level of their constituencies which they properly despise': Letter to Lord Lytton, 29 August 1879, cited in J. Hostettler, *Politics and the Law in the Life of Sir James Fitzjames Stephen* (1995), 190–1.

[65] Another influential nineteenth-century criminal code, that of Lord Macaulay, was adopted in India in 1862, and is still the basis of the law in India and Pakistan. It was also adopted in Malaysia, Singapore, Burma, and Sri Lanka.

That being so, it might have been easier, constitutionally, for Parliament to accept that new criminal offences (howsoever understood) should be located by amendment or addition to that single Act. However, in that respect, rather than drafting a new code—which was always liable to create controversy—Stephen would have been better advised to urge Parliament to turn the existing 1861 legislation into a formal criminal code. New offences could then have been added to that code (as under the New Zealand Crimes Act 1908), as in fact happened on one occasion when the notorious Criminal Law Amendment Act 1885 repealed ss. 49 and 52 of the 1861 Act dealing with certain sexual offences.

That simple opportunity for codification having been lost, Parliament continued to enact important but still isolated criminal laws, even when these dealt with issues addressed by the 1861 legislation, such as the Larceny Act 1916.[66] This disjunctive strategy continues to the present day.[67] As a result of such efforts with individual pieces of legislation, the law may well have been modernized considerably. However, the nascent sense of a codified structure present in the 1861 legislation has been lost,[68] and along with it, the prospect of gaining some of the key objectives of codification. These are the largely formal virtues of clarity, certainty, and consistency. Over 150 years later, it is hard to see how these virtues could now ever be super-imposed on the existing law. Today, the sheer complexity and quantity of criminal law, the deep inter-connectedness of some of it with non-criminal legislation,[69] and increasing doubts over what offences should be called 'criminal' in any event, make the 1989 draft code proposed by the Law Commission read like a Beatrix Potter story.[70] The chance to codify the 'criminal' law completely will probably never come again.

Even if that is too gloomy a prognosis, there have always been, and continue to be, unresolved questions about what a code should include, and what it should leave out. By and large, the codifiers gave pride of place to a traditional focus on offences of violence, theft, and damage to property (although other crimes were included). This is what, in Chapter 3, we will call C. S. Kenny's 'gothic horror narrative' for criminal law,

---

[66] See, e.g., the Criminal Damage Act 1971 that replaced the Malicious Damage Act 1861.

[67] See, e.g., Law Com No. 218, *Legislating the Criminal Code: Offences against the Person and General Principles* (1993). Following subsequent governments' inaction, the Law Commission has now taken a fresh look at the issues in a Scoping Paper: *Reform of Offences Against the Person* (Law Com CP No 217). There has been sporadic legislation based on specific reports of the Law Commission on matters such as partial defences to homicide, corporate manslaughter, bribery, and contempt of court. Further preparatory work is also being undertaken on the insanity defence (<www.lawcommission.justice.gov.uk/areas/insanity.htm>), misconduct in a public office and firearms offences, amongst other things.

[68] In spite of the creation of a new draft code under the auspices of the Law Commission, following its foundation in 1965: Law Com No. 143 (1985); Law Com No. 177 (1989). See also A. T. H. Smith, 'The Case for a Code' [1986] Crim LR 285.

[69] The various Road Traffic Acts are an example of this.

[70] The Law Commission, after consultation, published its own Draft Criminal Code in 1989. Law Com No. 177 in two volumes: i. report and draft Bill, ii. commentary on the draft Bill. The Scottish Law Commission has published a Draft Criminal Code, prepared by a group of academic lawyers. Its relative brevity is to be commended, but it is open to similar social criticisms as its English counterpart: Scottish Law Commission, *A Draft Criminal Code for Scotland* (2003), discussed by P. W. Ferguson, 'Codifying Criminal Law (2): the Scots and English Draft Code Compared' [2004] Crim LR 105.

designed for university study.[71] Yet, there is an argument for trying to deal with all the most serious offences, rather than centring the codification effort on the traditional offences studied in universities.[72] For example, the Law Commission code did not deal with many serious offences carrying maximum penalties of seven, ten, or fourteen years (such as causing death by dangerous driving). Taking a step back, though, there is also a case for re-thinking the purpose of codification.

Suppose that the public interest test for codification is whether the code will in practical terms be of assistance to the widest range of members of the public. With that aim in mind, perhaps codifiers should start in a different place entirely, cutting across a serious/non-serious divide between offences. A 'people's code' might focus on offences concerning, for example: road traffic, health and safety at work, general issues applicable to the running of businesses, landlords and tenants, domestic violence, the care of children and the elderly, and tax and benefit obligations and entitlements. Most of these offences have never featured in old or modern proposals for a criminal code in England and Wales. That conspicuous absence gives rise to the suspicion that the traditional codifiers' menu in the twentieth century has had more to with the intellectual influence on liberal-minded reformers of problems raised by university study of criminal law. The traditional menu has, in consequence, little or nothing to say when it comes to giving practical assistance to the widest range of people who may encounter criminal law-based obligations at home and in the work place.

2.5 NEW DANGERS IN THE USE OF THE CRIMINAL LAW?

The analysis given in sections 2.2–2.4 might have left the impression that the development of the criminal law has been a slow but ultimately triumphal march towards a new era of rational improvement and protection for civil liberties. However, that kind of understanding of the criminal law's history should be resisted. The twentieth and twenty-first centuries are considered by many to have seen the emergence of a number of new threats to freedom from unwarranted state interference. No more than a sketch can be provided here.

First, there is the impact of the so-called 'war on terror', not least in the form of restrictions on freedom of speech. Such threats include the criminalization of 'glorifying' terrorism.[73] The aim of the legislation was to target those who, 'contribute to creating a climate in which impressionable people might believe that terrorism was acceptable'.[74] That is an unsatisfactory basis for the prohibition of free expression, not least because the justification for the prohibition is simply that 'impressionable' people *might* (not 'will', or even 'probably will') come to think that terrorism was acceptable. In theory, liberal and democratic states are committed to the view that, in the famous

---

[71] See Chapter 3.1.   [72] A. Ashworth, 'Is the Criminal Law a Lost Cause?' (2000) 116 LQR 225.
[73] Terrorism Act 2006, s. 1.   [74] 675 Parl Deb HL (5th Series) 2005, 1385.

words of Evelyn Hall: 'I disapprove of what you say, but I will defend to the death your right to say it.'[75] In practice, much of the freedom of speech enjoyed in Western countries is enjoyed on the fragile basis of *de facto* political restraint, rather than through legal rights and duties.

The legal framework one might expect to express Hall's view does nothing of the sort. Under Article 10 of the European Convention on Human Rights, freedom of expression can be curtailed on a number of authoritarian grounds. So long as a restriction on freedom of speech is (a) prescribed by law, (b) necessary and proportionate, and (c) pursues a legitimate aim, that restriction can be justified. In itself, that may seem unexceptionable. However, 'legitimate' aims include: the interests of national security, territorial integrity or public safety, the prevention of disorder or crime, the protection of health or morals, and maintaining the authority and impartiality of the judiciary. With such a wide-ranging menu of grounds on which the curtailment of freedom of expression can be justified, it is not hard to see how European governments have experienced little difficulty in setting that freedom to one side in the legislative 'war on terror'. Irresponsible and deluded though glorifiers of terrorism may be (and some may be worse than that), there is a respectable case for arguing that they are modern day 'folk devils':[76] the equivalent of unashamed Catholic priests and their supporters in earlier times.[77] What Blackstone said of active Catholics in the eighteenth century seems now to be applied by modern governments to glorifiers of terrorism:

> While they acknowledge a foreign power, superior to the sovereignty of the kingdom, they cannot complain if the laws of that kingdom will not treat them upon the footing of good subjects . . .[78]

Blackstone's argument begs the question. No one should have to be a 'good subject' in order to enjoy the benefits of civil liberty.

The curtailment of freely expressed political belief in the overthrow of the state is the hallmark of an authoritarian 'militant' democracy, rather than of a true liberal and democratic state. According to the writer who coined the term 'militant democracy', it is legitimate for the authorities to suppress by law any act or form of expression involving support for undermining a liberal and democratic state, if the alternative is thought to be the subversion of such a state from within:

> The liberal-democratic order deals with normal times . . . If democracy believes in the superiority of its absolute values . . . it must live up to the demands of the hour, and every effort must be made to rescue it, even at the risk and cost of violating fundamental principles.[79]

Regrettably, most European states that regard themselves as liberal and democratic in fact behave like militant democracies, when they believe themselves threatened as

---

[75] E. Hall, *The Friends of Voltaire* (1906), 199.
[76] See S. Cohen, *Folk Devils and Moral Panics* (3rd edn., 2002).   [77] See text at n 9.
[78] Sir W. Blackstone, n 59, book IV, 54. For reform, see the Roman Catholic Relief Acts 1791, and 1829.
[79] K. Loewenstein, 'Militant Democracy and Fundamental Rights' (1937), reprinted in A. Sajó (ed.), *Militant Democracy* (2004), at 245.

much by the exercise of freedom of expression as by the planning and execution of criminal acts.

A rather different threat to liberty is alleged to come from the seeming ubiquity of 'regulatory' criminal law, put in place to govern many areas of both business and individual activity.[80] Contrary to the impression often given by scholars, penal regulation in some form has been around as long as the legal system itself. It makes an appearance in Magna Carta,[81] and was a part of the sumptuary laws of medieval and early modern England.[82] Penal regulation played a role in the expanding Tudor state (especially during the ascendency of Thomas Cromwell),[83] and in the rise of the fiscal-military state in the period from 1693 to 1815 during which England was at war on different fronts for no less than fifty-six years.[84] Penal regulation was to be found in nineteenth-century legislation responding to the enthusiasm of a new breed of Benthamite reformers for raising or equalizing standards in schools, hospitals, places of work, and elsewhere (sometimes referred to by historians as 'inspection fever'[85]). It is also a feature of the legislation adopted by newly minted government departments in the early part of the twentieth century.[86] Even on the brink of world war, Parliament found time in 1939 to pass the following pieces of regulatory law (amongst others), which included penal provisions:

(a) Agricultural Produce (Grading and Marking) (Caerphilly Cheese) Regulations 1939;

(b) Prevention of Damage by Rabbits Act 1939;

(c) Hairdressers Act (Northern Ireland) 1939.

The merits of the dominance of regulation in the domain of the criminal and quasi-criminal law have been a hotly contested issue, both amongst scholars,[87] for politicians,[88] and in the press.[89] Criminal lawyers tend to treat penal regulation as if it were an alarming and unwelcome new infestation in the sanctuary of true criminal law, like

---

[80] See Law Commission CP No. 195; J. Chalmers, '"Frenzied Law-Making": Over-Criminalisation by Numbers' (2014) 67 CLP 483; J. Horder, 'Bureaucratic "Criminal" Law: Too Much of a Bad Thing?', in R. A. Duff et al. (eds), *Criminalisation: The Political Morality of the Criminal Law* (2014), ch 4.

[81] 'There shall be standard measures of wine, ale, and corn (the London quarter), throughout the kingdom. There shall also be a standard width of dyed cloth, russett, and haberject, namely two ells within the selvedges. Weights are to be standardised similarly.' This would have been enforced in local courts.

[82] For example, one of the Acts in the sumptuary legislation of 1336 declared, 'no knight under the estate of a lord, esquire or gentleman, nor any other person, shall wear any shoes or boots having spikes or points which exceed the length of two inches, under the forfeiture of forty pence.'

[83] See A. Ogus, 'Regulatory Law: Some Lessons from the Past' (1992) 12 *Legal Studies* 1.

[84] J. Brewer, *The Sinews of Power War: Money and the English State, 1688–1783* (1988).

[85] C. Steadman, *Policing the Victorian Community: The Formation of English Provincial Police Forces 1856–1880* (1984), at 54. See also O. Macdonagh, 'The Nineteenth-Century Revolution in Government: A Re-appraisal' (1958) 2 *The Historical Journal* 52, at 58.   [86] See Horder, n 80.

[87] See Chalmers, n 80; Horder, n 80; A. Ashworth, 'Is the Criminal Law a Lost Cause?' (2000) 116 LQR 225.

[88] D. Carswell and D. Hannan, *The Plan: Twelve Months to Renew Britain* (2008), ch 8.

[89] <www.theguardian.com/money/2015/jun/06/fine-more-penalties-modern-misdemeanours>.

Japanese knot weed in house foundations. In that regard, the Law Commission has remarked that

> [T]he criminal law should be employed to deal with wrongdoers who deserve the stigma associated with criminal conviction because they have engaged in seriously reprehensible conduct. It should not be used as the primary means of promoting regulatory objectives.[90]

There is much to commend in this claim, but notice that the use of the term 'primarily' rightly leaves open the possibility that—as is in fact the case—far from being an unwelcome intrusion, penal regulation in some form plays (as it always has) an important role in stiffening the spine of the interventionist administrative state. In that sense, penal regulation is a fundamental of such a state. Having said that, in the present context, what is most important about regulatory law is that the offences that underpin it are almost always 'prophylactic' in character: targeting conduct harmless-in-itself, so as to reduce the risks of harm occurring in the future, rather than targeting conduct that itself constitutes, causes, or threatens a harm.[91] For example, health and safety at work offences are aimed at conduct that poses unacceptable risks in the workplace; there are no offences concerned solely with causing harm in the workplace.[92] This is significant, in that it has been said in criticism of such crimes that they, 'are likely to generate over-criminalisation, since they frequently prohibit conduct that in itself creates no risk of harm'.[93]

That observation is all the more important, when one remembers that most regulatory crimes are not contained in primary legislation (drafted by parliamentary Counsel, for debate in Parliament). As we will see in Chapter 4, such crimes appear mostly in secondary legislation (drafted chiefly by civil servants in the relevant department, anticipating no debate in Parliament) made under the enabling primary legislation.[94] Crucially, legislation often makes the creation and content of criminal offences an entirely discretionary matter for an individual Minister's department. For example, under s. 11(1) of the Aviation Security Act 1982, the Secretary of State may serve a 'notice' on aircraft owners, aerodrome managers, those with access to aerodromes, and adjoining landholders, requiring them to provide information enabling the Secretary of State to perform his or her duties. Under s. 11(5) a failure to comply with a requirement of the notice, without reasonable excuse, is a criminal offence punishable by up to two years' imprisonment. So, in effect, the Secretary of State has the discretionary power when drafting the notice to write the individual terms of what will, if not complied with (and in the absence of reasonable excuse), be an imprisonable offence. Worries about ministers' discretionary

---

[90] Law Com CP No. 195, para. 1.29.

[91] See A. P. Simester, 'Prophylactic Crimes', in G. R. Sullivan and I. Dennis (eds), *Seeking Security: Pre-empting the Commission of Criminal Harms* (2012), 59–78.

[92] Health and Safety at Work Act 1974.   [93] Simester, n 91.

[94] It should be noted that objections to the use of powers delegated by legislation are not new. Great controversy about them has arisen from time to time for more than 250 years. A particularly well-known example, that led to a government Committee of Enquiry, was sparked in part by a diatribe against such powers written by the then Lord Chief Justice, Lord Hewart: Lord Hewart, *The New Despotism* (1929).

powers to create crimes as they go, led the Law Commission to recommend that imprisonable offences should be created only in primary legislation. That would make every proposal for such a law subject to democratic parliamentary scrutiny.[95]

A further threat to liberty is of more recent origin. There has been a great expansion in the use of preventative orders involving 'two-step' prohibitions.[96] These typically consist in a civil (non-criminal) order[97] obtained against a person that instructs that person not to engage in a certain kind of conduct—step 1—coupled with the threat of criminal prosecution and punishment should the order be breached—step 2. Almost all of the scholarly and critical attention has been focused on cases in which two-step prohibitions, such as the old anti-social behaviour orders, are imposed on individuals.[98] However, two-step prohibitions are also commonly used against businesses. One case is where a business is issued with a prohibition notice by the Health and Safety Executive, and subsequently breaches the terms of that notice.[99] A 'mixed' case (involving both an individual and a corporate dimension) is where someone who has been disqualified from acting as a company director, continues to direct a company as if entitled to do so.[100] Ian Dennis has noted that there are now at least seventeen different types of civil preventative order applicable to individuals, ranging in subject matter from football spectator banning orders to violent offender orders.[101]

Two-step prohibitions add an extra dimension to penalization in at least one important way. They seek to control an individual's behaviour by tailoring the threat of punishment to troubling features of that individual's own life course, rather than—as would be more usual—targeting the behaviour of an anonymous class of persons (like drivers) or of everyone.[102] So, to use a real but much-mocked example, suppose the problem is that someone is seemingly wasting the time of the emergency services by threatening to commit suicide too often by jumping, and then having to be rescued. In such a case, society's answer can be to impose an 'injunction to prevent nuisance or annoyance' banning that person from going near places where jumping to one's death is possible: rivers, railway lines, bridges, and multi-storey car parks.[103] A more typical case might involve the imposition of a Sexual Harm Prevention Order on someone

[95] Law Commission, CP No. 195.

[96] A. P. Simester and A. Von Hirsch, *Crimes, Harms, and Wrongs: On the Principles of Criminalisation* (2011), ch 12.

[97] Such as the injunction to prevent nuisance and annoyance: see Anti-social Behaviour, Crime and Policing Act 2014; or a Sexual Offence Prevention Order: see Sexual Offences Act 2003, s. 104.

[98] See, e.g., P. Ramsay, 'Substantively Uncivilized ASBOs' (2010) Crim LR 761; M. Tonry, 'The Costly Consequences of Populist Posturing: ASBOs, Victims, "Rebalancing" and Diminution in Support for Civil Liberties' (2010) 12 *Punishment & Society* 387.

[99] <www.hse.gov.uk/enforce/enforcementguide/court/sentencing-penalties.htm#P9_892>.

[100] Company Directors Disqualification Act 1986, s. 13; for an example, see <www.gov.uk/government/news/bankrupt-handed-prison-term-for-acting-as-a-company-director>.

[101] See I. Dennis, 'Security, Risk and Preventative Orders', in G. R. Sullivan and I. Dennis (eds), *Seeking Security: Pre-empting the Commission of Criminal Harms* (2012), 169 n 3.

[102] We note, though, that the addition of conditions to release from prison on parole which, if breached, lead to re-imprisonment, have long been a form of two-step prohibition.

[103] <www.theguardian.com/society/2005/feb/26/mentalhealth.uknews>.

convicted of certain offences, on the grounds that such an order is necessary to protect people from sexual harm from the individual in question.[104] The Order might, for example, prevent the individual from going within a certain distance of a school during certain hours, if his or her offending indicates that such a condition fulfils the necessity requirement just mentioned.

Such orders are a special kind of threat to liberty in that, like many regulatory offences of the sort discussed previously, (a) they concern possible harm anticipated rather than harm done, and (b) they involve writing specific terms of what will—if the Order is breached—effectively be an individualized criminal offence. The latter feature flirts with a departure from the long-standing view (reflected in the ban on Bills of Attainder in Article 1, section 9 of the US Constitution) that penalization should focus on a form of behaviour and not on an individual. A further feature that two-step prohibitions share with many regulatory offences is the frequent dependence of two-step prohibitions on expert evidence—such as psychiatric evidence—for their justification.[105] In the case of regulatory offences governing particular kinds of industry or business, such evidence commonly emerges during consultation with organizations that may be affected. However, when such evidence relates to an individual's propensity to cause further (serious) harm, the court will typically rely on actuarial assessments of the risk posed by offenders who share a similar background to the individual in question, coupled with some gloss placed on this by a psychiatrist or probation officer in the individual case. Sensible though that might seem, the reliability of such evidence in predicting outcomes with any certainty is hotly contested, and 'false positive' rates (mistaken judgements that someone is a risk) may run at the rate of 50 per cent or higher.[106]

Ian Dennis takes the view (probably rightly) that so long as two-step prohibitions are considered by criminal justice officials to meet rigorous tests of necessity and proportionality, they will continue to feature in modern criminal justice systems.[107] As Lord Bingham put it:

> Any prediction about the future behaviour of human beings . . . is necessarily problematical. Reasonable and informed minds may differ, and a judgment is not shown to be wrong or unreasonable because that which is thought likely to happen does not happen. It would . . . [be] irresponsible not to err, if at all on the side of safety.[108]

Perhaps so, but we should be alert to the danger of unjustified restrictions on liberty posed by two-step prohibitions.

---

[104] For fuller details, see the Anti-social Behaviour, Crime and Policing Act 2014, Sch 5. For a very clear discussion by a practitioner, see <www.1cor.com/1155/records/1103/Sexual%20offences%20-%20LT.pdf>.

[105] *Jones* v *The Greater Manchester Police Authority* [2001] EWHC Admin 189.

[106] See the discussion in L. Zedner, 'Erring on the Side of Safety: Risk Assessment, Expert Knowledge, and the Criminal Court', in G. R. Sullivan and I. Dennis (eds), *Seeking Security: Pre-empting the Commission of Criminal Harms* (2012); also, A. Ashworth and L. Zedner, *Preventative Justice* (2014).

[107] Dennis, n 101.

[108] *A and Others* v *Secretary of State for the Home Department* [2004] UKHL 56, at 29, cited by Zedner, n 106, 219.

FURTHER READING

M. Arden, 'Criminal Law at the Crossroads: the Impact of Human Rights from the Law Commission's Perspective and the Need for a Code' [1999] Crim LR 439.

A. Ashworth, 'Is the Criminal Law a Lost Cause?' (2000) 116 LQR 225.

A. Ashworth and L. Zedner, *Preventive Justice* (Oxford University Press, 2014).

J. H. Baker, *An Introduction to English Legal History* (4th edn., Butterworths, 2002).

J. Briggs, C. Harrison, A. McInnes, and D. Vincent, *Crime and Punishment in England* (UCL Press, 1996).

J. Chalmers, '"Frenzied Law-Making": Over-Criminalisation by Numbers' [2014] 67 CL 483.

G. de Burca and S. Gardner, 'The Codification of Criminal Law' (1990) 10 Oxford J Legal Studies 559–571.

Law Commission *A Criminal Code for England and Wales Volume 1: Report and Draft Criminal Code Bill* (Law Com No. 177, 1989).

L. Moran, *The Homosexual(ity) of Law* (Routledge, 1996).

P. Ramsay, *The Insecurity State: Vulnerable Autonomy and the Right to Security in the Criminal Law* (Oxford University Press, 2012).

J. A. Sharpe, *Judicial Punishment in England* (Faber, 1990).

K. J. M. Smith, *Lawyers, Legislators and Theorists* (Oxford University Press, 1998).

Sir James Stephen, *A History of the Criminal Law of England*, vol. III (Macmillan and Co, 1883).

G. R. Sullivan and I. Dennis (eds), *Seeking Security: Pre-empting the Commission of Criminal Harms* (Hart Publishing, 2012).

3

CRIMINAL LAW VALUES

We started Chapter 1 by asking why it is important to focus on certain types of crime—crimes against the person and against property—in a scholarly work on criminal law. In this chapter, we work towards an answer to that question, by looking at some of the values and practices that the criminal law protects.[1] Before doing that, in section 3.1, we will consider an old and rather implausible answer to the question, which nonetheless still resonates today and is important to discuss for that reason. In sections 3.3 to 3.5, we will move beyond a concern with such crimes, to explain why the criminal law also governs a wide range of human and corporate activity connected with what can be called our 'lives in common'. In that regard, it is important to note that in this chapter we will be largely concerned with some—but far from all—of the values and practices that drive the creation of criminal offences and penalties (values the criminal law protects). It will be in Chapter 4 that we turn our attention to values and practices that insist on or counsel restraint in the use of the criminal law (values and practices the criminal law must respect), although one such value—the value of autonomy, in its different forms—will feature in the discussion here, as its treatment in law transcends the 'protect/respect' distinction.

---

[1] We should add that the values discussed are not uniquely protected by the criminal law, but also feature in accounts of the civil (private) law as well.

3.1 A GLADIATORIAL ARENA? CRIMINAL LAW STUDY AS AN ENTERTAINMENT SPECTACLE

It would only be a slight exaggeration to say that criminal law scholarship, in the modern form that we know it in England and Wales, was properly developed at the University of Cambridge, in the first half of the twentieth century.[2] In his famed *Outlines of the Criminal Law*,[3] Cambridge academic C. S. Kenny wrote in 1902 of the study of criminal law that, not only did it have a direct bearing on 'the most urgent social difficulties of our time and on the deepest ethical problems of all times', but that

> [A]lmost all men, whether thoughtful or thoughtless, are fascinated by its dramatic character—the vivid and violent nature of the events which criminal courts notice and repress . . . Forcible interferences with property and liberty, with person and life, are the causes which bring criminal law into operation . . . Hence of all branches of legal study there is no other which stirs men's imaginations and sympathies so readily and deeply.[4]

In this passage, Kenny romanticizes the study of criminal law, which he sees as a kind of ongoing Gothic horror narrative, with the criminal court standing in as a setting for the traditional cursed castle or haunted house. The use of force is something by which men are 'fascinated', because it is 'dramatic . . . vivid and violent', thus exciting men's 'imaginations and sympathies': emotions it is one of the courts' functions to channel through the strict rules of procedure and evidence. In so conceiving of criminal law, the dated focus on 'men' is not insignificant. Perhaps, Kenny thought such XXX-rated material unsuitable for women students. Kenny's romanticizing about the benefits of studying criminal law would today be considered in poor taste. Moreover, it may have led to the relative neglect by textbook writers of less lurid but, constitutionally, equally significant crimes of long standing, such as false imprisonment or misconduct in a public office.

At Cambridge, Kenny's approach was reinforced by the work of Sir Leon Radzinowicz and J. W. C. Turner in criminology. They largely took it for granted that the primary concern of the criminal law was—in crude terms—murder, rape, and pillage. Influenced by Bentham,[5] they focused in what they called 'criminal science' on, 'intensive biological and social investigations' of individuals, and then on the basis of what the investigations revealed, they turned their attention to the question of, 'how best to fight against crime'.[6] Inevitably, such a focus limited the authors' ability to appreciate the importance of crimes committed by public or private companies and organizations, and to some extent also crimes committed by officials supposed to be leading the 'fight against crime' (itself, a morally loaded phrase).

---

[2] Through the work of scholars such as Courtney Kenny, Sir Leon Radzinowicz, J. W. C. Turner, and Glanville Williams.

[3] C. S. Kenny, *Outlines of Criminal Law* (1st edn., 1902).   [4] Kenny, n 3, 2.

[5] In particular, J. Bentham, *An Introduction to The Principles of Morals and Legislation* (Reprint of 1823 edition, 1907), first published in 1780.

[6] Sir L. Radzinowicz and J. W. C. Turner, 'Penal Reform in England' (1940) 1 *English Studies in Criminal Science* 1, 10.

However, Kenny was in a way right to draw out what is in effect a link between the concentration in criminal law courses on the use of immediate violence or force, and a kind unspoken and taboo voyeurism that motivates that concentration. It is much the same kind of voyeurism that once drew large crowds to attend public hangings, and that spawned demands for detailed accounts of the process of execution, once this process took place only behind closed doors.[7] Kenny was contrasting what he regarded as the allure of criminal law with the dry technicality (as he saw it) involved in studying the civil law; but Kenny might equally have asked rhetorically of the criminal law itself: why would one endure the tedium of studying the state's complex system for targeting benefit offenders who have over-claimed, when one could seek the thrill of making oneself an authority on murder or rape instead? The problem with this kind of argument is that the reasons Kenny gives us for concentrating on criminal law's Gothic horror narrative—murder, sexual offences, theft, and related offences—are to do with the satisfaction to be derived from sublimating (somewhat suspect) emotions, rather than with the significance of the values at stake. In what follows, we concentrate on such values.

3.2 INTRINSIC VALUES, AND HOW THEY MATTER TO US; PERSONAL AND INTER-PERSONAL GOODS

In the official criminal statistics, the police divide offences by category into 'victim-based' crime and 'other crimes against society'. Victim-based crime—that obviously includes crimes such as murder, sexual offences, theft, and so on—accounts for no less than 76 per cent of all police-recorded crime, whilst other crimes against society account for only 10 per cent of police-recorded crime (fraud offences make up the remaining 14 per cent[8]).[9] The recording by the police of an incident as a 'crime' is not a value-free activity, and so we may ask what value-priorities lead to victim-based crime looming so large in the statistics. One eighteenth-century argument that still resonates for some people is put by Blackstone. He said that even the slightest touching of someone, without consent or other justification, is unlawful, 'every man's person being sacred, and no other having a right to meddle with it in any the slightest manner.'[10] On this view, victim-based crimes against the person are unique in that they are violations of the *sacredness* of the body. In general terms,[11] it is not wrong to describe

---

[7] See, in this regard the discussion of the Ruth Ellis case by L. Seal, 'Ruth Ellis in the Condemned Cell: Voyeurism and Resistance' (2012) 199 *Prison Service Journal* 17.

[8] Most such cases are banking and credit industry offences, in relation to which an individual may be protected from loss by the bank. In such cases, the bank is in effect acting as the victim's insurer.

[9] <www.ons.gov.uk/ons/rel/crime-stats/crime-statistics/year-ending-june-2015/stb-crime--ye-june-2015. html#tab-Summary>.   [10] Blackstone, *Commentaries on the Laws of England* (1765–69), Book 1, 270.

[11] See Chapter 9 for further discussion.

victim-based crimes against the person as 'violations'.[12] However, there is something suspicious about the argument that an offence against the person is a violation only if our bodies are 'sacred'. How do we know that the body is sacred? If it really is sacred, perhaps I should think twice before cutting my hair or fingernails, for fear of violating the sacredness of my own body; but of course, other than exceptionally, I don't need to think twice about such things.

No one supposes that proprietary interests are sacred, but are invasions of such interests always 'violations'? Blackstone understood the right to property as closely analogous to the right to security of the body, in that crimes against them both involved personal violations.[13] That analysis may seem plausible in the case of burglary of someone's home, street robbery, or pick-pocketing. Even so, it does not accurately describe, say, minor shoplifting from a large supermarket, and shoplifting is more than twice as common as theft from the person.[14] Far from experiencing a sense of violation, large retailers (at whom shoplifting is most commonly targeted) are likely simply to write off such losses. They will treat them, insofar as they cannot be prevented, as business costs, like the need to compensate customers who have purchased faulty goods. That is emphatically not an argument for de-criminalizing 'shoplifting'; but it suggests the need for a different way of understanding the centrality, in our thinking about crime, of offences against property as well as offences against the person.

In the secular state, an individual's life has ultimate value, value not derived from any higher value. What gives real meaning and significance to individual life, over its course, is engagement in activities and relationships, and with other things—'goods'— that have 'intrinsic' value. That which is intrinsically valuable has value separate from or beyond being—like a bus ticket or a shoe lace—simply a means to an end. Things that have intrinsic value are activities, relationships, and other goods that are valued for their own sake, because they contribute constitutively to (they are an integral part of) a way of life. A parent's relationship with his or her child should have intrinsic value in this sense. By contrast, an online guide to good parenting has only instrumental value. The guide has value only as a means to set about improving and enriching that which has intrinsic value: the parental relationship. Bodily integrity (the freedom of the body from pain and injury) and bodily health, like the ability freely to express

---

[12] John Stanton-Ife explains the most serious offences as 'violations' as part of his thesis that murder and manslaughter are 'horrific' crimes: J. Stanton-Ife, 'Horrific Crime', in R. A. Duff et al. (eds.), *The Boundaries of the Criminal Law* (Oxford University Press, 2010).

[13] Blackstone, n 10, Book 1, 12, 'So great is the regard of the law for private property, that it will not authorise the least violation of it, no, not even for the general good of the whole community'.

[14] <www.ons.gov.uk/ons/dcp171778_371127.pdf>, 9. It would be right to point out that the overall cost of shoplifting to the retail sector is high; and systematic theft from retail stores can, of course, be experienced by the owner as a violation, especially when accompanied by criminal damage. See, more generally, <www.gov.uk/government/publications/crime-against-businesses-headline-findings-from-the-2013-commercial-victimisation-survey/crime-against-businesses-headline-findings-from-the-2013-commercial-victimisation-survey>.

[15] In the case of sexual choices, the intrinsic value of the choice will be context-dependent. So, e.g., for many people, a choice to engage in sexual relations will not have intrinsic value outside the bonds of marriage or a long-term relationship.

one's sexual identity and choices, normally have high intrinsic value to people.[15] That explains public concern about the level of violent and sexual offending, the priority given to its detection and prosecution, and its pre-eminent place as the focus of scholarly writing in articles and textbooks: what would it say about the police, the Crown Prosecution Service and legal scholars, if they thought it unimportant to pay attention to such offences?

Intrinsically valuable goods include 'personal' and 'inter-personal' goods. The intrinsic value of a good may be expressed in the way we are, in the way we think, in what we say, and in what we do. Further, it may be expressed either independently (personal good), or 'dependently', that is, jointly with other individuals (inter-personal good). Bodily integrity and health are personal goods,[16] as is our mature development as rational and emotional beings (our 'moral' autonomy),[17] and the expression our sexual identity (gay, straight, and so on). By contrast, the authentic expression of sexual or (more broadly) intimate partner *choice*, like engagement in genuine friendship, must of necessity be an inter-personal good. When the other person only participates unwillingly in such relationships, then the *inter-personal* good is not genuinely experienced by either person, even if there is still some perverse enjoyment, in seeking to carry on regardless, for the deluded or selfish first person.[18] Alongside bodily integrity and health, sexual identity and partnership choice, intrinsically valued goods of a personal or inter-personal nature may include a rewarding career, property-holding,[19] privacy, family life, and joint activities of different kinds like organized sport, political activity, or shared religious worship.[20] Many of these examples of intrinsically valued goods reflect an underlying good with great intrinsic value, the good of lifestyle autonomy: freedom from coercion or undue influence forming relationships, choosing a career, a family, and so on (to be discussed later, and again in Chapter 4). In many such cases, the law intervenes to protect the freely chosen (non-) participation in the personal or inter-personal good in question. The law may, for example, protect those participating or seeking (not) to participate in a good from discrimination, and from the use of force, coercion, domination, or exploitation.[21] Examples are the criminalization of forced marriages,[22] of 'stalking',[23] and of the harassment of a residential

---

[16] Although note that the goods of bodily integrity and health may sometimes be inter-personal in nature, as in the case of conjoined twins.   [17] See Chapter 4.3.

[18] Of course, that will be even more starkly true in a case where the participation of the other person is obtained through coercion or force etc., when the criminal law may become involved.

[19] Whether the property is real or personal in character.

[20] In relation to such joint activities, see the discussion of 'public goods' in section 3.3. We should note both that not all intrinsic values are of equal importance, but also that no one is obliged (in law or in morality) to rank-order intrinsic values in a particular way. So, for example, in spite of its importance generally as an intrinsic value, I can shun family life in order to live my chosen life as a monk; but in doing that, I do not have to deny that family life is of great intrinsic value.

[21] Sometimes, this is done through the use of the civil (private) law, as under the Equality Act 2010. We should note that the criminal law does not seek to protect us in equal measure from every instance of the use of force, coercion, exploitation, and domination, in every field of activity.

[22] Anti-Social Behaviour, Crime and Policing Act 2014, s. 121; and see <www.gov.uk/forced-marriage>.

[23] Protection from Harassment Act 1997, s. 2A.

occupier,[24] although—to give an example of a perhaps surprising omission—it is not an offence in English law to coerce someone into changing their religion.

The criminal law's protection of personal and inter-personal goods is central to the protection that it gives to autonomy. In this work, although we concentrate on the use of the criminal law to protect bodily integrity and health (personal good), sexual choice (inter-personal good), and proprietary interests (personal or inter-personal good[25]), the criminal law's protection goes beyond the creation of serious crimes against the body, against coerced sexual choices, or against invasions of property interests. The examples given in the previous paragraph illustrate this. To give some further examples, the importance of lifestyle autonomy (the freedom to be, whether or not in reliance or co-operation with others, an authentic author of one's own life) in part explains the passing of the historic Slavery Abolition Act 1833.[26] It is also the justification for the modern offence of holding another person in slavery or servitude, or requiring them to perform forced or compulsory labour.[27] To give a different kind of example of the law's concern for lifestyle autonomy, as a result of recent change, it is also a criminal offence knowingly to exercise controlling or coercive behaviour over or towards a close family member or intimate partner, when this has a 'serious effect' on the latter.[28]

In this context, the protection of children, the vulnerable, and those living under threat, is of special importance. Those responsible for the welfare of children may be held criminally liable for failures to support the physical and psychological needs and interests of the children, needs and interests the nurturing of which is central to the development of their moral autonomy.[29] The applicability of the offence of child neglect, but also of child abduction, to parents themselves is an illustration of this.[30] To give another example, a parental failure to ensure that a child is receiving appropriate full-time schooling may lead to the imposition of a school attendance order on the parent(s), a failure to comply with that order being a criminal offence punishable by a fine.[31] Mindful of these kinds of considerations, the police and the prosecution services may adopt policies specifically targeted at protecting the elderly,[32] the vulnerable,[33] or those living under threat of violence.[34]

---

[24] Protection from Eviction Act 1977, s. 1.

[25] Property can be an inter-personal good when it is for joint ownership or use.

[26] Repealed by the Statute Law (Repeals) Act 1998, following the enactment of the Human Rights Act 1998 that was considered to have made the 1833 Act redundant.

[27] Modern Slavery Act 2015, s. 1. One could add to this list, offences connected with false imprisonment: see Law Commission, *Simplification of the Criminal Law: Kidnapping and Related Offences* (Law Com 355, 2014).   [28] Serious Crime Act 2015, s. 76.

[29] Children and Young Persons Act 1933, s. 1, as amended by the Serious Crime Act 2015, s. 66. On 'moral' autonomy, see n 16, and Chapter 4.3.

[30] See Law Commission, *Simplification of the Criminal Law: Kidnapping and Related Offences* (Law Com 355, 2014).

[31] Education Act 1996, s. 443. <www.gov.uk/home-education>. We will deal with the case of a failure to ensure that a child attends regularly at school later in this chapter.

[32] <www.cps.gov.uk/publications/docs/caop_policy.pdf>.

[33] <www.met.police.uk/foi/pdfs/policies/safeguarding_adults_at_risk_policy.pdf>.

[34] <www.cps.gov.uk/Publications/Prosecution/domestic/index.html>.

3.3 LIFE IN COMMON: THE IMPORTANCE OF PUBLIC GOODS

Contrary to the oft-repeated claims of its critics, liberal and democratic thinking—of the sort that underpins the account of criminal law given in this work—is not exclusively 'individualist' thinking. That is in part demonstrated, not only by the attention paid to inter-personal as well as to personal goods, but also by the importance attached to our 'lives in common' in liberal and democratic thinking. The idea of 'life in common' is a loose but nonetheless coherent notion of people being identified or grouped according to some feature or characteristic they possess, some activity they engage in, a place where they live, a service they are using, and so on.[35] Whether they are aware of it or not, most people have a large number of lives in common, that may be more or less permanent, ephemeral, or constantly changing. One individual may participate in, say, the following lives in common with different groups of others: farmer, tenant, environmentalist, tax payer, tractor driver, animal owner, consumer, and internet user, amongst many other instances. In simply getting to work, one may experience different lives in common with different groups of others, as a train or road-traveller, then a station or car park user, and a finally a pavement walker.

Our lives in common are frequently rule-governed. One way that the law (but not only the law) subjects our lives in common to rules is through the protection of the 'public goods' through which our lives in common take place. Instances of public goods (to be defined shortly) and of their legal protection, relevant to the examples of the commuter's lives in common just given, are the co-ordination and safety gains achieved by (a) rules of the road, (b) rules covering the safety and security of passengers on trains and in station, or (c) rules regulating the use of pavements and car parks.[36] It would be a considerable task to assemble all the laws and official schemes of guidance—whether or not criminal laws—that address the lives in common of the commuter. Examples are the Road Traffic Acts 1988 and 1991, the Railways Act 1993 and 2005, the Highway Code,[37] and numerous by-laws creating minor offences.[38] What, though, is a 'public good', and what is the role of the criminal law in relation to such goods?

According to Joseph Raz, a public or common good is a good that

refers not to the sum of the good of individuals but to those goods which, in a certain community, serve the interests of people generally in a conflict-free, non-exclusive and non-excludable way.[39]

---

[35] The idea comes from T. Macklem, *Law and Life in Common* (2015), although he is not in any respect responsible for the way in which I have pursued the idea here.

[36] The last example being an example where a public good (the co-ordination of parking) may be upheld by the enforcement of rules created by a private individual or company, rather than by the state.

[37] On cycling, see, e.g., <www.gov.uk/rules-for-cyclists-59-to-82/overview-59-to-71>.

[38] <www.gov.uk/government/uploads/system/uploads/attachment_data/file/4202/railway-byelaws.pdf>.

[39] J. Raz, *Ethics in the Public Domain* (1994), 52.

Raz here restricts the meaning of public goods to those serving interests, 'in a certain community', but in a very pure form public goods are not so restricted. So, for example, pure public goods, goods which are open to all to enjoy or share without community or national limits, include sunshine, sea breezes, and beautiful skies. Having said that, humanly created public goods, that can be enjoyed in common and non-rivalrously, are often tied to particular communities. So, a nation's practice of religious tolerance, its cultural diversity, and its good humour, are public goods linked to that particular nation. For some economists, what makes a good a true public good is that it cannot be made subject to market exchange: I cannot, for example, create a market for beautiful cloud formations. Put another way, though, what matters about public goods is that—to benefit fully from them—no individual needs either a right to a specified share of the good, or (consequently) a right to exclude others on that ground from enjoying the good.[40] In order to enjoy the benefits of (say) a nation's tradition of altruism or of its practice of religious tolerance, neither do I have to seek 'my individual share' of such altruism or tolerance, nor do I need to seek to exclude others from the scope of the altruism or tolerance in order to sustain the value of 'my share'. The very nature of the tradition or practice of altruism or religious tolerance as public goods, something shared non-rivalrously and without fixed limit, means that one cannot meaningfully speak of individual 'shares' in it.

Public goods can be relatively stable or long-lasting; but public goods may equally be ephemeral, like the spontaneous formation of an orderly queue at a ticket office or cash dispenser. Some public goods provide institutional support for the pursuit of inter-personal goods, when the latter might be very difficult or impossible to pursue without the public goods in question. Examples of such public goods are nationally and locally supported facilities of various kinds: youth clubs, churches, voluntary networks, and so on. As these examples illustrate, public goods can sometimes be maintained by voluntary commitment, with or without state support. Further examples might be the practice of museums in keeping entry free of charge for those with a life in common as museum-goers, or the practice of newspaper editors in maintaining a letters page for the free exchange of opinion. As we have just said, in such instances no individual has either a right to a specified share of a public good, or (consequently) the right to exclude others on that ground from enjoying the public good. We should note that the provision of public goods through law may be inextricably linked with, and enhance, personal or inter-personal goods. For example, effective enforcement of sexual offence laws may create widespread confidence in the exercise of civil liberties, such as the freedom to go wherever we please at the time of day that suits us. Such confidence is a pubic good.

'Security' is a public good, other than when I am securing an essentially private space, such as a car, private house, or office. As a public good, security may be provided through private means (as by the employment of CCTV cameras or security guards in a shopping mall), or by the state (as through the maintenance of an army, police, intelligence services).[41] However, the provision of security as a public good cannot

---

[40] See, generally, I. Kaul, I. Grunberg, and M. A. Stern (eds.), *Global Public Goods* (1999).
[41] See Kaul, Grunberg, and Stern, n 40.

generate an individual right to security as such. The installation of CCTV in my local mall does not confer on me a 'right' to security that did not exist before, even though my security may have been marginally increased. The law outlaws violence and theft in the mall whether or not the mall benefits from any security measures. Likewise, the operation of (say) a state police force provides a measure of security that is to a greater or lesser extent enjoyed non-rivalrously by all—including those who commit crimes, or who have no right to be in the country—but no one has an individual 'share' of this benefit to which a right could attach.[42] Suppose that the police decide to save money by treating an area of a town prone to disturbances as a 'no go' area for law enforcement. In such circumstances, it is not the residents' supposed 'right' to security that is breached by the police (in)action, although the public good of security has wrongfully been allowed to diminish in value in that area. The residents' real complaint is a public law complaint against the police: there has been unfair or arbitrary treatment in the discharge of the management responsibilities that have been entrusted to the police respecting the public good of security. An attempt is being made by a public authority, on (*ex hypothesi*) improper grounds, to cut costs by reducing the value of the public good of security for some, whilst maintaining its quality at a higher level for others.[43]

It is important to keep in mind at this point a very significant constraint on the use of the criminal law to protect or promote security. Although security is a public good, that fact in itself does not give the state a licence to take *any* steps it sees fit to protect and promote that good. In protecting and promoting security, the state is bound to observe basic principles of respect (to be explored more fully in Chapter 4) bearing on criminalization. So, the invocation of 'security interests' is not, without more, a sufficient justification for failing to respect human rights, for ignoring the obligation to minimize the use of criminalization, for disregarding proportionality in response, and so on.[44]

Clearly, as well as public 'goods', there can be public 'bads' (a better word for the latter might be public 'negatives'). Suppose that you set up a chemical laboratory in your bedroom, and allow large clouds of evil-smelling gas to escape out of the window, affecting people for miles around. In effect, you create a public negative. This negative will be endured in common by your neighbours non-rivalrously, in the same way that the good of clear air would be enjoyed. In fact, it is possible to prosecute you for the (common law) crime of 'public nuisance' in such a case, or for an offence under the Environmental Protection Act 1990. The criminal law may be employed to tackle noise pollution in a similar way, although there are also civil powers, for example, to order the closure of premises giving rise to (a risk of) public negatives such as excessive noise

---

[42] Regrettably, too many theorists fail to understand that security is a public good, and so they concede that there is such a thing as a 'right' to security, and hence duties correlative to such a 'right' (even though duties can exist without correlative rights). This error can be found, even in the work of those unsympathetic to the notion of a right to security: see L. Lazarus, 'The Right to Security: Securing Rights or Securitising Rights', in R. Dickinson et al., *Examining Critical Perspectives on Human Rights* (2012).

[43] So, the resident has the standing—*locus standi*—to challenge the conduct of the police, but not on the basis that their action has breached an individual or collective 'right' to security.

[44] See generally, B. J. Goold and L. Lazarus (eds.), *Security and Human Rights* (Hart Publishing, 2007).

or public disorder.[45] Public negatives also include riots, violent disorder, and affray, which are made the subject of criminalization by the Public Order Act 1986.[46] In a way, these public negatives are just the obverse of a coin, the other side of which reflects a public good historically known as 'the Queen's peace'. Under an ancient power, someone can be 'bound over' to keep the peace, as a matter of civil law, and if they breach the conditions set by the Magistrate for 'keeping the peace', then they can be fined an amount that was agreed at the stage of bind-over.[47] Such powers, and indeed the broader way in which the law polices speech and behaviour in public spaces (whether or not under the Public Order Act 1986) are inevitably controversial.[48] For our purposes, though, what is important is that the concern is with obligations to sustain a public good (the Queen's peace) by punishing and deterring the perpetration of certain public negatives.

3.4 PROTECTING 'FRAGILE' PUBLIC GOODS

The law may become involved in the case of important public goods, supporting lives in common, when the goods are or may easily become fragile. Fragile public goods are goods whose value or existence may be threatened by over-use (commonly, in virtue of scarcity), or which are likely to be prone to injustice in point of access (perhaps, because of the way supply is used to satisfy demand). That being so, fragile public goods may have to be subject to one or more of formal co-ordination, regulation, rationing, and the deterrence and punishment of bad practice or of malevolent threats (when the criminal law typically comes in). Examples of fragile public goods include safe public places, security from external threats (like military invasion), unpolluted rivers, the maintenance of public health, adequate means to support the poor or out-of-work, and free-flowing but safe systems of transport. In these examples, one or more of co-ordination, regulation, or rationing may be necessary to maintain the value of these fragile public goods to lives in common connected to them, although the deterrence and punishment of bad practice and malevolence must play an important role.[49] For

---

[45] See, e.g., Anti-Social Behaviour, Crime and Policing Act 2014, s. 76. When a closure notice is in force, it then becomes an offence to be on the premises, or to obstruct a person lawfully executing the closure notice: s. 86.   [46] See <www.cps.gov.uk/legal/p_to_r/public_order_offences/>.

[47] <www.cps.gov.uk/legal/a_to_c/binding_over_orders/>. Although the proceedings are civil, the standard of proof to be satisfied is beyond reasonable doubt. So powers to bind over are an example of penalization beyond the scope of what is traditionally regarded as 'criminal' law: see Chapter 1.

[48] A. Ashworth, 'Preventive Orders and the Rule of Law', in D. Baker and J. Horder (eds.), *The Sanctity of Life and the Criminal Law* (2013), ch 3, 45–7; *Hashman and Harrup* v *UK* [2000] 30 EHRR 241; P. Ramsay, *The Insecurity State: Vulnerable Autonomy and the Right to Security in the Criminal Law* (2012), 198. As Ramsay points out, the power to bind over is now less significant, in the light of the power to impose injunctions to prevent nuisance annoyance under the Anti-Social Behaviour, Crime and Policing Act 2014.

[49] Where access to public goods must be restricted by rationing, or similar measures, economists refer to them as 'quasi-public' goods: see W. Blümel, R. Pethig, and O. von Dem Hagen, 'The Theory of Public Goods: A Survey of Recent Issues' (1986) 142 *Journal of Institutional and Theoretical Economics* 241. We do not find the term 'quasi-public' good to be very illuminating and so we have avoided use of it.

example, to maintain the value of the public good of access to public transport, and to avoid injustice at the point of access, rail operators are by law entitled to bring in and enforce systems of queuing for tickets.[50] With some other fragile public goods, there may be less of a need for co-ordination or rationing as such. Instead, the primary emphasis will be on promoting sound practice to maintain and enhance the goods in question, and deterring and punishing bad practice and malevolent threats. Examples of such public goods include the practice of racial and religious tolerance, a tradition of honesty in commercial activity or of incorruptibility in public service delivery, adherence to the rule of law, the stability of a system of property rights, and security from invasion or other threats.[51] However, one should not seek to harden these distinctions into categories. The emphasis will shift from one fragile public good to the next, as there are subtle differences between almost all of them.

An important case in point concerns property (both real and personal), and hence the justification for crimes against property. Property is a valuable but scarce resource; as Mark Twain is alleged to have advised, 'Buy land; they ain't making any more'. So, property may be subject to forms of rationing (as through restrictions on entitlement to social housing), or use-regulation (planning law), but these issues fall outside the scope of this work. More important are sound and unsound proprietary practices (generally dealt with by private law), and malevolent threats to proprietary interests (generally dealt with by the criminal law). It is tempting to think that the law protects property only because—like bodily integrity—it is a highly valued personal or inter-personal good,[52] as in the case of a home or an heirloom. However, by way of contrast with our common attitude to (say) bodily integrity, many items of our property are of merely instrumental value to us—they are valued purely as a means to an end—such as a car key. Further, some of our property frequently has no value to us at all: completed crosswords, perhaps, or the contents of our waste bins. The value people personally set on their own property does not, thus, provide a stable basis on which to protect their interests in property, because the nature of that value varies so greatly. In the eye of the law, the value related to property lies in the stability of a rational system of property-holding that protects our ownership or possession of *any* item of property. Such a system of property rights is a fragile public good, benefitting large numbers of people not only in England and Wales but internationally. However much (or little) property we have, and whatever its personal or inter-personal value to us, we benefit to some extent from the common good of a stable and rational regime for property-holding. To enhance the stability and predictability of the system as a public good, it is perfectly justified to give the same protection to the used cinema ticket left in my jacket pocket

---

[50] <www.gov.uk/government/uploads/system/uploads/attachment_data/file/4202/railway-byelaws.pdf>: '1.2. Any person directed by a notice to queue, or when asked to queue by an authorised person, shall join the rear of the queue and obey the reasonable instructions of any authorised person regulating the queue.'

[51] See, generally, Raz, n 38, Part I. In relation to threats, in emergency situations there may of course be a need for co-ordination of the public, and for the rationing of access to, for example, hospitals.

[52] The value of property may sometimes be inter-personal, as well as personal: think of a rowing team's joint ownership of a rowing boat designed for eight rowers.

as to the treasured heirloom that I also carry there.[53] The public good of a stable and rational system of property-holding may be undermined by the spread of unsound and unethical practice (dilapidations, nuisance, casual trespass, non-disclosure of liens at the point of sale, and so on), or by an increase in malevolent threats (theft, fraud). In either case, the law—be it the civil law[54] or the criminal law—will be needed to sustain the public good.

Many fragile public goods, such as a common pool of tax resources, the maintenance of public health, and the rule of law, as well as a stable structure of property rights, must in practice be supported (at least in part) by the state.[55] Such public goods can be created and upheld through democratic political and legislative action, or through the use of politically independent state bodies, such as the judiciary (or both). The need for state support will usually be for one or both of two reasons. It may simply be beyond the capacity of non-state institutions to support the fragile public good adequately, consistently, and universally. Alternatively, the good may be vulnerable to severe erosion by the actions of too many people—or too many powerful people—who are motivated by self-interest alone.[56] For example, in a state of any size and diversity, it is hard to imagine a worthwhile system of taxation being devised and supported only by the efforts of individuals and voluntary organizations.[57] Similarly, it is likely to prove impossible for individual employers and employers' organizations alone, however willing, to ensure that employees, and visitors to premises, are guaranteed a workplace that is safe.[58]

In all such instances, the threat of criminal sanctions may have an important role to play: for example, in countering the self-interest of those who care little for the public nature of a good.[59] So far as adherence to the rule of law is concerned, this fragile public good is served in part by the existence of offences such as contempt of court, failing to assist a constable, perverting the course of justice, perjury, and acting with intent to assist an offender after the offence.[60] To give a different example, the amount that the government raises in tax (the tax-take) is a fragile public good in the form of a 'common pool' resource.[61] Common pool resources are resources available in principle to be used by all, but they are in practice limited by the fixed amount there is to

[53] See the discussion of property rights in J. Gardner and S. Shute, 'The Wrongness of Rape', in J. Horder (ed.), *Oxford Essays in Jurisprudence: 4th Series* (2000).

[54] As through the maintenance of registers of title to, and interests in, property.

[55] See, e.g., M. Kleiman and S. Teles, 'Market and Non-Market Failures', in M. Moran, M. Rein, and R. Goodin (eds.), *The Oxford Handbook of Public Policy* (2006), ch 31.

[56] So, as Aristotle remarks in *The Politics*, Book VI, ch 5: 'If there are revenues, one should not allow popular leaders to distribute the surplus just to gain popularity among the people.'

[57] A point well understood by Aristotle. In *The Politics*, Book VI, ch 5, he says, 'it is necessary [for the legislator] to manage revenues soundly so that there will be a sustained surplus which can help the poor'.

[58] See, generally, <www.hse.gov.uk/>.

[59] E. Fehr and S. Gächter, 'Co-operation and Punishment in Public Goods Experiments' [2000] 90 *The American Economic Review* 980.

[60] For discussion of some of these offences, see D. Ormerod and K. Laird (eds.), *Smith and Hogan's Criminal Law* (14th edn., 2015), ch 9.

[61] See K. Yeung, 'Can We Employ Design-Based Regulation While Avoiding the Brave New World?' (2011) 3 *Law, Innovation and Technology* 1.

share around. In some cases—say, an oasis in a remote desert region—it may be impracticable to protect the common pool resource by law, and reliance must be placed largely on custom and practice. In the bureaucratic state, though, threats to common pool resources like the tax-take can be addressed in a sophisticated way, through the introduction of rules to govern the process of sharing. In that regard, the perennial political problem of whether governments should seek to minimize or to maximize the tax take—the amount of taxed income held as a common pool of resource—is accompanied by another key issue. There will always be some who fail to pay their tax when it is due, thus unjustifiably diminishing the common pool of tax revenue. What kinds of sanctions are fair and proportionate, in dealing with such people? Are fixed civil penalties enough, or is nothing less than a criminal offence acceptable?[62] Similarly, if tax officials persistently fail to do enough to bring in tax that is due, should these officials face only employment-based sanctions? Or, should they be prosecuted for a crime such as misconduct in public office instead? Currently, officials almost never face criminal sanctions for their part in the erosion of the common pool resource in question.

3.5 CRIMINAL LAW, VALUES, AND PUBLIC GOODS

What is the conclusion to be drawn from the analysis in sections 3.2 to 3.4? First, the criminal law has an important role in protecting people from the use of force, coercion, exploitation, or domination,[63] when these activities invade or threaten people's autonomy.[64] So, in the name of the lifestyle autonomy principle, along with prohibitions on causing bodily harm, the criminal law rightly outlaws forced, coerced, exploitative, or more generally un-freely chosen sex,[65] alongside, as we have seen, prohibitions on forced marriages, and harassment by (amongst others) obsessed stalkers persistently seeking unwanted personal relationships.[66] These crimes are a reflection of a general principle that a humane state is under a duty wider than simply *itself* avoiding the wrongful use of coercion, force, exploitation, or domination in relation to other people. The state must also strive to protect people from such conduct when threatened or engaged in by other (individual or corporate) people,[67] and to sustain the power to punish and deter such people.

That the criminal law may be permitted or required to keep at bay certain kinds of obstacle to the construction of an autonomous life shows us something else that is important. It is in the nature of the law's relationship with the lifestyle autonomy of

---

[62] <www.hmrc.gov.uk/prosecutions/crim-inv-policy.htm>; <www.gov.uk/guidance/customs-seizures-and-penalties>.   [63] But see n 21.

[64] See, J. Raz, 'Autonomy, Toleration and the Harm Principle', in R. Gavison (ed.), *Issues in Contemporary Legal Philosophy* (1987).   [65] Sexual Offences Act 2003: see Chapter 9.

[66] See text at n 23.

[67] See, e.g., *Osman* v *United Kingdom* [1998] EHRR 101. This case concerned the right to life protected by Art. 2 of the ECHR. Although no breach of that Article was found in *Osman*, the court nonetheless held that Art. 2(1) may, depending on the facts, impose a duty on a public authority to take all reasonable steps to protect a person from a real and immediate risk to his life posed by another person.

its citizens, that the law should not itself be used to try to coerce people into leading autonomous lives. Such a strategy would be self-defeating. A lifestyle choice will not be authentically autonomous, if it is followed through out of fear of the legal consequences should that choice be abandoned. So, no one should be coerced through threat of criminal sanctions into (say) making or retaining friendships or marriages, entering or staying in a particular profession or trade, playing sport, or maintaining religious faith. When such activities are engaged in out of fear of sanctions, then they lose any prospect of genuine meaning and intrinsic value for the participants and hence cannot meaningfully serve any greater good.

Political theorist J. S. Mill (1806–73), the originator of what is now called the 'harm principle' to be discussed in Chapter 4, sought to explain this point. He said that the threat of coercion should not be used solely to further someone's 'own good, either physical or moral'.[68] Mill thought that where determining one's own good was concerned, the mature individual was always 'sovereign' over body and mind.[69] However, that individualist way of making the point is not especially persuasive.[70] One does not need an account of the supposed 'sovereignty' of the individual over their choices in life to explain why the threat or use of coercion to determine those choices would be pointless, as well as harsh, insensitive, and in many instances a clear breach of someone's human rights. In broad terms, the criminal law has an important role to play in protecting people's ongoing prospects for an autonomous life, but in so doing it must itself respect people's autonomous choices, whether they are right or wrong for the individual(s) in question.[71] This dual 'protect and respect' approach is considered further in Chapter 4.

The 'respect' part of the law's approach to lifestyle autonomy is followed through, in liberal and democratic states, in relation to the law's support for public goods. A nation's sophisticated sense of humour, or its broad range of freely accessible cultural and sporting opportunities, are valuable public goods. Even so, their value would be damaged or entirely lost if, absurdly, a government sought to protect or promote these goods by making it a criminal offence not to participate in them. Laughter can be forced, but it should not be forced through state coercion. However, so long as this point is kept in mind, there is a crucial difference between the law's protection of lifestyle autonomy, and its protection of fragile public goods at the heart of our lives in common. However much I may rely on institutional support, the support of teachers, parents, friends, and so on,[72] to achieve true moral and lifestyle autonomy my achievement must—if it is to be authentic—be at least in part my *individual* achievement (or failure), whatever the contribution made by others.[73] However, the position is not the

---

[68] J. S. Mill, *On Liberty* (2nd edn., 1859), 22.   [69] See n 68.

[70] The language of sovereignty seems to overlook, for example, the dependence of people's prospects for an autonomous life on the past and present support of one or more of family, school, local community, friends, and others.

[71] See, e.g., the argument of J. Waldron, 'A Right to Do Wrong' (1981) 92 *Ethics* 21.   [72] See n 69.

[73] Perhaps there would be an exception to this, if there were a case in which twins become morally autonomous through genuinely joint thought and action, but even this example seems doubtful.

same where fragile public goods are concerned. As we have seen, these are an open resource, communally maintained. Their very existence commonly depends on our continued *joint* efforts, and so their maintenance is 'our' success, guided—where appropriate—by the law.

The significance of this 'collective endeavour' element to public goods is that we may all be placed under an obligation, not only to pose no threat to fragile public goods, but also—as actual or potential beneficiaries in common—to contribute positively to their maintenance. J. S. Mill himself recognized this point, when he observed that there are, 'many positive acts for the benefit of others, which [someone] may be rightly compelled to perform'.[74] He gave as examples the fact that people could be forced to give evidence in court (thus promoting the public good of justice), or made to 'bear their . . . fair share in the common defence, or in any other joint work necessary to the interest of the society of which [they] enjoy the protection' (thus promoting the public good of security[75]).[76] This statement of the position is broadly correct but not entirely satisfactory. It fails to acknowledge a point made earlier. As Mill was well aware, the exercise of the power to coerce people into making positive contributions to public goods, is subject to the need to respect autonomous choices in relation to personal and inter-personal goods. So, for example, when Mill speaks of people being made to do their 'fair share' towards common defence, he should expressly allow for the need for restrictions based not on 'fairness' considerations, but on considerations of (for example) the personal good of following one's conscience. If my religion forbids me to fight in any war, then I should not be coerced by the state into active service with the armed forces, even if an equal division of burdens—'fair shares'—would ordinarily demand this.[77] However, in general terms, Mill's concession that the state sometimes has the right to use coercion to make people contribute to the support of fragile public goods is rightly made.

For example, I—or my company—may be coerced into contributing to the maintenance of (say) a fragile environmental public good, such as high standards of waste management. Both waste management companies, and domestic householders, face sanctions if they fail to take all relevant measures as are reasonable in the circumstances to ensure that waste is transferred only to a person authorized to accept it.[78] I may also face sanctions if I fail to remove my dog's mess from a public area, if I abandon a vehicle on the highway, or (more controversially) if I put my waste bin out for collection at the wrong time.[79] In the first instance (the transfer of waste), breach of the provision is a criminal offence. In the latter three instances, the offences in question

---

[74] Mill, n 67, 24.

[75] For a critical examination of the protection of security by the criminal law, see V. Tadros 'Crimes and Security' [2008] 71 MLR 940; Ramsay, n 48.   [76] Mill, n 67, para. 1.11.

[77] M. Lippman, 'Recognition of Conscientious Objection to Military Service as an International Human Right' (1990–91) 21 California Western International LJ 31.

[78] Environmental Protection Act 1990, s. 34(1)(c) and (2)(A).

[79] These are often offences created by local authorities, under delegated powers. See, e.g., <www.wigan.gov.uk/Resident/Environmental-Problems/FPN.aspx>.

involved fixed penalties and are hence, as some would have it, not 'truly criminal', a point addressed in Chapter 1. As we may now see, other examples involve establishing a relationship between the need to protect a public good, and the wish to allow people space in which to pursue activities that may be of intrinsic value to them as personal or inter-personal goods.

For example, if I am licensed to own a weapon, I must—under pain of criminal sanction for failure—store the weapon in secure conditions.[80] I can pursue my hobby interest in collecting or shooting weapons, but I am made to take positive steps to ensure that the public good of security from potentially lethal attack or accident is not threatened by careless pursuit of that interest. For somewhat similar reasons—fragile public good reasons—if I wish to drive on public roads, I must pass a driving test, keep my car in adequate repair for that purpose, wear a seatbelt whilst driving, keep to the rules governing driving activity, ensure I have a minimum level of insurance, and so on.[81] For some people, there may be personal or inter-personal good, something of intrinsic value worth pursuing for its own sake, in being a gun or car owner.[82] This is what to some extent explains the law's willingness to permit such activities to be engaged in;[83] but in exchange for that permission the state (a) insists on a significant positive contribution to the public good of security threatened by the activity, (b) itself determines what that contribution is to be (not just requiring gun or car owners to do what appears to them reasonable in all the circumstances), and (c) backs these demands with significant sanctions in cases of breach. It would not, though, be right to leave these examples without mentioning that, in its enthusiasm to appear tough on crime, governments have sometimes created offences governing this area with scant regard for proportionality in response.[84] For example, causing death by careless or inconsiderate driving, contrary to s. 2B of the Road Traffic Act 1988, carries a maximum sentence of five years' imprisonment following trial on indictment, even though causing death by careless conduct in any other context is no offence *at all*.[85]

The examples just used involve laws affecting individuals. However, in terms of the sheer numbers of offences connected with the duty to promote (as well as not to threaten or detract from) public goods, it is likely that criminal and civil penalty law is mainly aimed at businesses rather than at individuals. Businesses large and small are always under general obligations—supported by the threat of penal sanctions for breach—to protect and promote public goods of one kind or another. An example already mentioned is the obligation to ensure the health and safety of employees or

[80] See <www.gov.uk/government/uploads/system/uploads/attachment_data/file/117794/security_leaflet.pdf>.
[81] See, e.g., the Road Traffic Act 1988; Road Traffic Act 1991.
[82] See further, J. Horder, 'Strict Liability, Statutory Construction and the Spirit of Liberty' (2002) 118 LQR 458. The inter-personal value may come, for example, from membership of a gun owners' or car owners' club.
[83] In the case of car driving it is, of course, also the high marginal utility of this activity for the many people dependent on it, as a form of transport, which means that people are willing to incur the participation costs involved in being able lawfully to take to the road.
[84] See Chapter 4.6 for discussion of the proportionality principle.
[85] Unless the carelessness amounted to gross negligence, in breach of a duty not to cause death, in which case it would be manslaughter: see Chapter 8.5(b).

visitors, so far as is reasonably practicable, which promotes the public good of safe places of work.[86] Businesses are also subject to a vast array of industry-specific duties respecting the protection and promotion of public goods, breach of which may attract a criminal or other penal sanction. Here is an example, mundane as it might seem. Under the Cosmetic Products (Safety) Regulations 2008, a cosmetics supplier is subject to the following obligation, breach of which is an imprisonable offence:

Labelling requirements:

12.—(1) No person shall supply a cosmetic product unless the container and packaging displays the following information in indelible, easily legible and visible lettering—

(a) the name or style and the address or registered office of the manufacturer or the person responsible for marketing the cosmetic product who is established within the EEA . . . Where the cosmetic product is manufactured outside the EEA, the country of origin must also be specified . . .

Once again, it would be right to point out that this offence appears to be in tension both with the proportionality principle (would imprisonment really ever be appropriate for breach of this obligation?), and with the principle of minimal use of the criminal law (could not a civil penalty adequately provide sufficient deterrence?).[87] Putting those issues on one side for now, this obligation is clearly not focused on the position of an individual consumer who may personally be at risk from, or have been harmed by, a cosmetic product. Instead, the legislation is better understood as a small part of a Europe-wide effort to promote the fragile public good of corporate accountability in respect of the supply of cosmetic goods.

This kind of legislation is, of course, a world away from the gothic horror narrative that Kenny constructed for criminal law studies.[88] Yet, as indicated earlier, criminal law scholars would do well to keep in mind that duties to protect and promote public goods imposed on businesses—supported by criminal offences in cases of breach— may well be the most common kinds of duties to be backed by criminal and civil sanctions in England and Wales. In that regard, before we turn in the next chapter to an examination of the values the criminal law is obliged to respect, we should take note of a common feature of offences connected with protecting and promoting public goods. This is that these offences are frequently 'anticipatory' in character. They are concerned primarily with deterring and punishing the creation of unacceptable risks of harm, rather than with deterring and punishing the causing of harm.

For example, it is an offence under s. 23 of the Financial Services and Markets Act 2000 to offer certain kinds of financial advice without authorization (or exemption) from the Financial Conduct Authority. The justification for seeking to regulate the market for financial advice in this way depends on an important assumption. This is the assumption that poor financial advice will be given with unacceptably greater

---

[86] Health and Safety at Work Act 1974, s. 2.
[87] For further discussion of these principles, see Chapter 4.   [88] See section 3.1 earlier.

frequency, leading to customers taking unwise financial risks far too often, unless a legal entitlement to give the advice is made dependent on prior screening and hence authorization. The assumption might seem eminently warranted (although similar assumptions underlying other anticipatory offences may not be so securely based). However, the plausibility of the assumption underpinning s. 23 depends on a number of factors. Two such factors are (i) the expertise and competence of those conducting the screening, and (ii) whether or not these expert screeners are adequately resourced to perform their prior screening and authorization tasks. All too easily, in a world of scarce resources for public servants, one or both of these factors can cease to obtain, pulling the rug from under the justification for the criminal offence. Customers may end up worse off, if financial advisers given authorization turn out to be no better or worse at advising, on average, than those who are (perhaps wrongly) denied authorization. As we saw at the end of Chapter 2, the question of whether or not an anticipatory (regulatory) offence, as opposed to a harm-based offence, has been committed frequently turns in part on the exercise of judgement by an expert official, to the effect that, say, a safety standard has not been met or cannot be met by a company.[89] So, if we have reason to doubt the ability of such officials systematically to deploy their expertise, in the way the legislation intended, then the foundation for the offence itself may be called into question. As John Gardner puts it, in relation to such offences:

> [T]he harm principle regulates achievement as well as endeavour. The law must actually prevent the harm it is intended to prevent, and must, moreover, do so in a way that is proportionate to the harm actually prevented. Herein lies the real power of the harm principle, as a constraint on legislators. It is easy to point to a harm that one's pet legislation is designed to eradicate; it is a lot harder to show that it eradicates it.[90]

FURTHER READING

E. Fehr and S. Gächter, 'Co-operation and Punishment in Public Goods Experiments' [2000] 90 *The American Economic Review* 980.

J. Gardner and S. Shute, 'The Wrongness of Rape', in J. Horder (ed.), *Oxford Essays in Jurisprudence: 4th Series* (Oxford University Press, 2000).

J. S. Mill, *On Liberty* (2nd edn., JW Parker & Son, 1859).

P. Ramsay, *The Insecurity State: Vulnerable Autonomy and the Right to Security in the Criminal Law* (Oxford University Press, 2012).

J. Raz, 'Autonomy, Toleration and the Harm Principle', in R. Gavison (ed.), *Issues in Contemporary Legal Philosophy* (Oxford University Press, 1987).

V. Tadros 'Crimes and Security' [2008] 71 MLR 940.

---

[89] The Health and Safety at Work Act 1974 provides an example.
[90] J. Gardner, 'Over-Criminalisation: The Limits of Criminal Law' (2008) *Notre Dame Philosophical Reviews* 03.

4

CRIMINAL LAW FABRIC

4.1 PRINCIPLES AND THE FABRIC OF THE CRIMINAL LAW

What is a criminal law 'principle', and why are principles important? Answering these questions provides an opportunity to explore in more detail part of what was called in Chapter 1 the 'fabric' of criminal law: the part of the fabric comprised of rules, standards, and principles. 'Rules', 'standards', and 'principles' are often—and not necessarily wrongly—terms that are used interchangeably, in constitutional law, private law, and criminal law. However, there are insights into the law to be gained from seeking to distinguish them.

> (1) Criminal law and civil penalty 'rules' are the primary means used to set out obligations to engage, or not to engage, in certain conduct, when breach of the obligation may be met with a finding of guilt and a sanction such as a fine, or imprisonment.

In law, these rules are established in different ways. Sometimes, the legislature will straightforwardly say that, 'It is an offence to . . .', and then set out the penalty for breaching the obligation in question in the statute (primary legislation) itself. So, for example, in s. 87(1) of the Environmental Protection Act 1990, Parliament says: 'A person is guilty of an offence if he throws down, drops or otherwise deposits any litter in any place to which this section applies and leaves it.'

According to an older 'common law' method, a second way of creating criminal law obligations is by implication in the relevant law, rather than through express statement. For example, surprising as it might seem, the Theft Act 1968 does not expressly say that it is an offence to commit theft. Instead, a declaratory rule in s. 1 of the 1968 Act provides a definition of theft as a matter of law, and later sections of the 1968 Act set out the meaning of terms in the definition, and lay down the maximum penalty upon conviction for theft (seven years' imprisonment).[1] The obligation not to commit theft is implied rather than expressly stated by these rules, but that is not a matter of great consequence. People are as bound to obey impliedly stated obligations as they are bound to obey expressly stated obligations. Like a number of other criminal laws, as the law of murder and manslaughter, the Theft Act 1968 appears primarily to be directed to officials (police, prosecutors, judges) who will be dealing with offenders, rather than being directed at all those under an obligation to obey the law.

An unwelcome (even if sometimes necessary) development, associated with the rise of secondary legislation as a mode of governance in the bureaucratic state,[2] has been the emergence of a third way in which criminal law obligations are created. Quite commonly, a statute will say something along these lines: 'It is an offence to breach regulations made under the powers granted by this statute.'[3] Under such a law, the obligation (breach of which is made a criminal offence under the statute) is largely empty of content. The law is an 'enabling' law. That is to say, it gives a legal basis for the future creation of offences by secondary legislation (in accordance with the first way of creating rules, described earlier) drafted by the relevant government department. Far and away the most important such law in England and Wales is to be found in s. 2(2) of the European Communities Act 1972, the Act that placed on a legal basis the UK's membership of the European Community (as it was then called). Section 2(2) says:

> (2) . . . Her Majesty may by Order in Council, and any designated Minister or department may by order, rules, regulations or scheme, make provision—

> (a) for the purpose of implementing any EU obligation of the United Kingdom, or enabling any such obligation to be implemented, or of enabling any rights enjoyed or to be enjoyed by the United Kingdom under or by virtue of the Treaties to be exercised; . . .[4]

Under this enabling power, regulations creating hundreds of criminal offences have subsequently been made since 1972, the vast majority aimed at businesses. Offences of this kind are regularly used not simply to require compliance with, say, safety obligations, but to assist officials by coercing businesses into co-operating with formal enquiries.[5] In this example, under the Eggs and Chicks (England) Regulations 2009 (SI No. 2163), 'O' is a public official:

---

[1] See Chapter 10.   [2] See Chapter 2.

[3] See, e.g., the Consumer Protection Act 1987, s. 12.

[4] Similar powers can be found in many other Acts, such as ss. 11 and 12 of the Consumer Protection Act 1987.

[5] See further, J. Horder, 'Excusing Information-Provision Crimes in the Bureaucratic State' (2015) 68 *Current Legal Problems* 1.

A person ('P') is guilty of an offence if they—

. . .

(b) fail to give to O any assistance or information that O may reasonably require of P for the performance of O's functions under these Regulations;

(c) furnish any false or misleading information to O; or

(d) fail to produce a record when required to do so to O.

It should be acknowledged that giving power to government departments to create laws simply and quickly in this way is probably necessary. We live in a governance environment in which all member states of the EU must ensure that they impose similar kinds of duties on a vast array of different kinds of business, businesses that are themselves constantly changing and developing their trading practices, giving rise to a need for new or further legislation.

However, there is an important question for the criminal lawyer. To find the substantive content of regulatory obligations made under an enabling Act, a search must be made of subsequent secondary legislation made (sometimes years later) under the relevant powers; and that may not be the end of it. Yet further secondary legislation, made under the same powers, may amend, restrict, or extend earlier secondary legislation, making the task of finding the law that is actually in force a formidable one, even—in some cases—for the Court of Appeal.[6] To give an eccentric but illustrative example, the Bovine Semen (England) Regulations 2007 (SI No. 1319), made under powers granted by an enabling provision—s. 10 of the Animal Health and Welfare Act 1984—implemented European Council Directive 88/407/EEC. The regulations laid down the animal health requirements applicable to intra-Community trade in and imports of semen of domestic animals of the bovine species. They replaced the Artificial Insemination of Cattle (Animal Health) (England and Wales) Regulations 1985 that had themselves been amended several times. By way of contrast with the 1985 Regulations, the 2007 Regulations fragmented the law by leaving Wales (along with Scotland and Northern Ireland), to make its own arrangements. The 2007 Regulations created numerous obligations binding those licensed to handle bovine semen.[7] To complicate matters further, the 2007 Regulations have now themselves been amended twice, in 2011 and again in 2013. The 2007 Regulations do not themselves create criminal offences for breach of those regulations. For such offences, one must turn to s. 10(6) of the Animal Health and Welfare Act 1984.[8] We hope that is clear so far.

Finding which substantive criminal laws are in force should not be this complex. The government needs (a) to provide a properly designed, complete, and regularly updated

---

[6] See *R v Chambers* [2008] EWCA Crim 2467; J. Chalmers, '"Frenzied" Law-Making: Overcriminalisation by Numbers' (2014) 67 CLP 483.

[7] See, e.g., s. 19, 'No person may collect semen from a bovine animal for use in artificial insemination unless the bovine animal—(a) is approved for that purpose by the Secretary of State . . . '; s. 21: 'No person may use a teaser animal to assist in the collection of semen unless it is approved for that purpose by the Secretary of State.'   [8] <www.legislation.gov.uk/uksi/2007/1319/memorandum/contents>.

online statement of all offences currently in force, and (b) to make local authorities (and other bodies—there are over fifty—entitled to create offences) do the same.

Another issue is this. Secondary legislation is not as closely scrutinized in Parliament as primary legislation, and—when it concerns technical matters—may not be taken seriously.[9] Yet, offences created by secondary legislation often carry maximum sentences involving substantial terms of imprisonment. For example, under ss. 4 and 5 of the General Food Regulations 2004 (SI No. 3279), made under powers granted by the Food Safety Act 1990, anyone who breaches or fails to comply with the food safety requirements of Regulation (EC) No. 178/2002 may be tried on indictment and if found guilty sentenced to a maximum of two years' imprisonment. We return to this issue when discussing the imprisonable offence principles in section 4.6.

One important function of rules is to act as potential guides to conduct. However, it is important to understand when the law must in practice act as a guide to be complied with directly, and when this direct guidance function is less significant. That is because what the law demands of me generally, if I am to be law-abiding, is that I 'conform' my conduct to the law (doing what the law says), not that I 'comply' with it by being guided by it directly. For example, before being allowed on the road, I have to learn enough about the law governing road-use. In other words, I have to know how the law intends to guide me, so that I know (say) that I have to stop in the right place when a traffic signal is showing red for the direction I am heading. However, in an important sense, for the purposes of road traffic law what matters is simply that I stop my car at the right point when the traffic light is showing red, putting my conduct in conformity with the law. From a road traffic law perspective, at that particular moment it does not matter that the only reason I stopped in the right place was, for example, that my car stalled. In other words, for the law's purposes, it does not matter whether my stopping at the light was or was not actually 'guided' by my understanding of what the law demands. This is true, even though—almost needless to say—a complex regulatory enterprise is highly unlikely to be sustained over a period of time unless most people governed by it are indeed guided by the law.

This point about the significance of conformity with the law is relevant to much more serious cases involving what lawyers call '*mala in se*'. *Mala in se* are actions wrongful in themselves, whether or not there is a law against them, such as rape or theft. The idea of *mala in se* is a controversial one, in so far as 'wrongfulness in itself' is a controversial concept. Moreover, sometimes something can come to be widely perceived as a *malum in se*—such as sex or race discrimination—only once a law has been passed to prohibit it. Nonetheless, in general, people conform to the rules governing, say, murder or criminal damage, without being guided by the substantive law itself. Indeed, something would have gone badly wrong if people had to consult lawyers and law books in order to know what their basic obligations are not to kill or to damage

---

[9] As demonstrated by this amusing clip from proceedings in the Swiss legislature concerning the implementation of regulations: <www.youtube.com/watch?v=Ps6e_toM26I>.

another's property.[10] In such cases, people are generally guided by or comply with, not the content of the substantive law, but either by morality, or (whatever the precise definition of the offence may be) by the justified fear that the punishment they will receive if caught might be severe. It is, though, still important that the laws governing such wrongs—*mala in se*—are as clear and precise as they can be, even though they are not meant primarily to guide individuals directly. That is because such laws must be readily understood by the police, prosecutors, judges, and juries who have to apply them to the acts that form the basis of the case against the defendant(s). Similarly, it is vital that defence lawyers can be clear about the exact nature of the prosecution argument on which they have to cast doubt.[11] We could call this requirement, for as much clarity and precision as possible at the investigative, prosecution, and trial stages, the 'adjudicative' (trial-focused) demand of the rule of law.

There are, though, many cases where the nature of the law is such that it is effectively impossible simply to conform one's conduct to it, and direct compliance is likely—barring an extraordinary coincidence—to be the only way to follow the law directly, with the benefit of legal or analogous forms of guidance (if need be). This is frequently the case where obligations imposed on companies are concerned, which is one reason why the costs to UK businesses of regulatory compliance are estimated at £500m each year.[12] Whilst it still may not matter, for legal purposes, whether I comply or simply conform, compliance is overwhelmingly likely to be the only way to conform. That is true, for example, of the corporate criminal offence of failing to keep a register of company members.[13] Similarly, owning firearms[14] and keeping wild animals,[15] are quite complex matters, legally speaking. The possibility of law-abidingness will effectively hinge on a knowledge of and reliance on the substantive demands of law itself, or at least on more or less official guides to the law's demands.[16] For small businesses (under ten employees), forming 96 per cent of UK businesses, this can be a particularly difficult challenge, involving significant risks of both over and under-compliance, as the government has itself frankly admitted.[17] The relevance of this is that, for the individuals affected, it will be important in such cases that the law be clear and precise in its terms. This is so that these individuals can avoid the kind of breach of their obligations that comes simply from mistaking what the law requires (such a mistake being no

---

[10] See generally, J. Waldron, 'The Rule of Law in Contemporary Liberal Theory' (1989) 2 *Ratio Juris* 79. There are some cases where people do need to be guided by a precise understanding of the law of murder. An example is physicians involved in caring for those who are dying. See, further the discussion of *Re A (conjoined twins)* [2004] 4 All ER 961, ch 5.

[11] For a general discussion, see J. Horder, 'Criminal Law and Legal Positivism' (2002) 8 *Legal Theory* 221.

[12] <www.bvdinfo.com/industrynews/compliance-and-due-diligence/uk-financial-compliance-costs-to-keep-rising/801554245>.   [13] Companies Act 1986, s. 133.

[14] See the Firearms Act 1968.   [15] See the Dangerous Wild Animals Act 1976.

[16] <www.gov.uk/licence-wild-animal>; <www.gov.uk/government/uploads/system/uploads/attachment_data/file/417199/Guidance_on_Firearms_Licensing_Law_v13.pdf>.

[17] <www.gov.uk/government/uploads/system/uploads/attachment_data/file/31614/10–1251-lightening-the-load-regulatory-impact-smallest-businesses.pdf>.

excuse in itself for committing a crime[18]). Ideally, such clarity can be provided without the need for professional legal advice. Such advice is mostly only affordable (and often only ever sought in advance) by the affluent, and it may be important not to deter people who cannot afford the advice from engaging in the activity in question. It ought, for example, to be relatively straightforward to negotiate one's way through the rules and regulations governing social security payments, or car ownership and the obtaining of a licence to drive, such that one does not have to resort to legal advice in order to avoid committing a criminal offence. We could, in contrast to the adjudicative demand of the rule of law, call this the 'activity-based' demand of the rule of law.

> (2) Criminal law 'standards' commonly have a double life. They provide a criterion or benchmark against which to judge people's conduct, for the purposes of deciding on criminal liability. Simultaneously, they provide rule-like guides to what is expected of us in our conduct, including what is expected of us both when are called on to exercise self-control or self-restraint, and when we form certain kinds of beliefs, or discharge duties of care.

For example, employers must ensure the health, safety, and welfare of their employees, so far as is 'reasonably practicable'.[19] Likewise, individuals may carry an offensive weapon in public only if they have lawful authority or a 'reasonable excuse' for doing so.[20] In such cases, employers, and would-be weapon carriers, can to some extent be guided by the law, and by law-related material. They can combine one or more of (say) industry-specific expertise, existing legal precedent and any official guidance on the meaning and limits of 'reasonably' and 'reasonable', to reach a well-informed view on what is required or permissible respecting their own activities.[21] At the same time, though, the terms, 'reasonably practicable' and 'reasonable excuse' provide a standard by which to judge the conduct of the employer or weapon-carrier, in an individual case. Suppose that the trial judge or jury finds that the safety measures the employer took, or the excuse given by the weapon-carrier for carrying the weapon in public, were insufficient—and outside the bounds of reasonableness. Then, the mere fact that the employer or weapon-carrier *thought* what they were doing was reasonable is not, as such, a defence to the charge.

A slightly different example of this type is to be found in the definition of rape under s. 1 of the Sexual Offences Act 2003. A man is guilty of rape if he has sexual intercourse with a person who is not consenting and, amongst other legal elements that must be satisfied by the prosecution, he lacks a 'reasonable belief', in all the circumstances, that the victim is consenting. Suppose that the defendant denies that he was at fault, by claiming that he thought the victim was consenting (even though the victim was not in fact consenting). In such a case, the task of the jury is to judge this belief against a standard: what might the reasonable man have been led to believe about the victim's attitude to consent, in all the circumstances? If the defendant's belief in the victim's consent was not reasonable, when judged against this standard, the defendant should be

---

[18] See A. Ashworth, 'Ignorance of the Law and Duties to Avoid it' (2011) 74 MLR 1. See section 4.5 later in the chapter.

[19] Health and Safety at Work Act 1974, s. 2(1).   [20] Prevention of Crime Act 1953, s. 1.

[21] See, e.g., <www.healthandsafetyatwork.com/hsw/risk-assessment/reasonably-practicable>.

convicted. However, s. 1 of the 2003 Act also provides an element of implicit conduct guidance. The broad message it conveys is that, if they are to avoid liability for rape, men must show adequate sensitivity to their sexual partner's desires and limits.[22]

(3) Principles are a kind of legal standard, giving guidance and providing criteria for judging conduct.[23] However, they differ from ordinary legal standards in that they have a 'supervisory' function. The role of principles is to provide a guide to making, and a critical standard for judging, the shape and character of rules and standards in the rest of the criminal law.

For example, one might criticize vague or unclear rules or standards for violating the rule of law demand for sufficient certainty of scope and definition.[24] Used in that way, the rule of law principle of certainty is operating as a higher or second-order legal standard. It is being employed to criticize other legal rules or standards, with respect to the specificity of the guidance they provide.

The role of principles in the criminal law is a complex one.[25] Some principles are *mandatory*, subject to any exceptions that limit them, and should always be respected. One example is the demand, embodied in Art. 3 of the ECHR, that no one be subjected to torture or to inhuman and degrading treatment.[26] Another example, embodied in Art. 7 of the ECHR, is the principle that criminal law and sanctions may not be made applicable retrospectively. In other words, criminal law and sanctions may not be made applicable to conduct engaged in *before* the law was brought into force that turned that conduct into a criminal offence.[27] At other times, principles are (or should be treated as) *permissive* in character. This means that, depending on the merits in context, it may or may not be right to drawn on them in the circumstances. To add to the complexity, principles may come into conflict with one another, as we may now see.

4.2 RESTRAINING PRINCIPLES, CONFLICTS BETWEEN PRINCIPLES, AND THE LIFESTYLE AUTONOMY PRINCIPLE

This book seeks to explain and judge the rules and standards of criminal law in the light of certain guiding principles of restraint in the construction and use of the criminal law. The element of restraint in these principles comes from a concern for values

[22] For more detailed discussion of these requirements, see Chapter 9.5.

[23] Jurisprudentially, we therefore prefer the understanding of principles given by F. Shauer, in *Playing by the Rules* (1993) to that given by R. Dworkin, *Taking Rights Seriously* (1977).

[24] The courts have the power to strike down regulations issued by government departments, if these are too vague: see, e.g., *Reilly and Wilson v The Secretary of State for Work and Pensions* [2013] EWCA Civ 66.

[25] For a thoughtful analysis, see J. Gardner, 'Ashworth on Principles', in L. Zedner and J. Roberts (eds.), *Principles and Values in Criminal Law and Criminal Justice: Essays in Honour of Andrew Ashworth* (2012), ch 1.

[26] <www.equalityhumanrights.com/sites/default/files/documents/humanrights/hrr_article_3.pdf>.

[27] Article 7 reads: 'No one shall be held guilty of any criminal offence on account of any act or omission which did not constitute a criminal offence under national or international law at the time when it was committed.' See C. Murphy, 'The Principle of Legality in Criminal Law under the European Convention on Human Rights' [2010] *Human Rights Law Review* 192.

that courts and legislatures ought to respect as limiting their powers, when creating, interpreting, or extending the criminal law.[28] Principles of restraint may include, for example, the principle of certainty, the principle of non-retroactivity,[29] the imprisonable offence principles, and the principle of strict construction of the scope of a criminal law statute in the accused's favour.

It is, though, not a defining feature of a criminal law 'principle' that it is a restraining principle. For example, we will contrast principles of restraint with another commonly encountered principle, the 'authoritarian' principle. The latter principle gives a relatively low priority to restraint in the way that it understands the legitimate scope of the criminal law. For example, the authoritarian principle stands for the view that a wide-reaching and flexible criminal law is justified, if it ensures that wrongdoing worthy of criminalization can more easily be brought within the scope of offences. In response to concerns about whether wide-reaching and flexible criminal laws might be abused by state officials, proponents of the authoritarian principle give the following answer. Wide-reaching or vague though the law may need to be to capture all possible forms of the relevant wrongdoing, placing trust in officials to use their discretion sensibly in administering it, is to be preferred to a clearer but narrower criminal law that may permit some wrongdoers to escape the law's net. We come back to this argument later.

A genuinely principled approach to criminal law does not entail a blanket rejection of extensions to criminalization. Indeed, sometimes an extension of the criminal law may be morally required. We have already encountered instances in which the protective reach of the criminal law has, on human rights grounds, been extended to outlaw (for example), forced marriages and the trafficking of people.[30] It is important to note, though, that people will legitimately differ over whether, on the one hand, extension or on the other hand, restraint, is dictated by considerations of principle. One well-known area in which this is obviously true concerns the law governing end-of-life decisions.[31] Let us put aside for now difficult cases in which an end-of-life decision is taken about someone who is incapable of giving consent.[32] Respect for the lifestyle autonomy principle made an important contribution to Parliament's decision in 1961 to de-criminalize suicide.[33] However, it remains a serious offence to assist or encourage the suicide of another person, even when the assistance or encouragement is voluntarily sought by person wishing to commit suicide.[34] For some, the lifestyle autonomy principle dictates that people of sound mind, deciding in a free and informed way, should be able to call on the assistance of others to help them end their own lives, at least when this happens in controlled circumstances:[35] a 'respect' approach.

---

[28] The principles are also to be observed in the application of the criminal law in practice, by police officers, the Crown Prosecution Service, and other officials.   [29] See text at n 27.

[30] See Chapter 3.2. See, more generally, on human rights-based obligations to create offences, A. Ashworth, *Positive Obligations in Criminal Law* (2013), ch 8.

[31] For discussion, see, e.g., E. Jackson and J. Keown, *Debating Euthanasia* (2011).

[32] See *Airdale NHS Trust v Bland* [1993] AC 789 (HL).   [33] Suicide Act 1961, s. 1.

[34] Suicide Act 1961, s. 2.

[35] See <www.dignityindying.org.uk/assisted-dying/lord-falconers-assisted-dying-bill/>.

Contrariwise, it is possible to concede that someone wishing to commit suicide has the right to do so, but yet maintain that it is wrong to assist that person. Such a protective approach could be justified in terms of the over-riding importance of reducing an important public negative:[36] bureaucratization, or—even worse—'abuse' in the making of end-of-life decisions.[37]

Similar conflicts over the right approach arise in other contexts. For example, is a free and informed lifestyle decision to enter the sex trade best respected by legalization of the sex trade,[38] or would such a step come at a price that it would be morally wrong to pay: an increase in a public negative, the amount of coerced or unwanted sex?[39] In England and Wales, Parliament has recently sought to tread a fine line: seeking to combine respect for the lifestyle autonomy of those for whom engagement in sex work reflects a free and informed decision, whilst at the same trying to reduce the risk that the price just mentioned must in consequence be paid.[40] In this regard, one of the most important social and ethical developments of the twentieth century has been the emergence, as a political priority, of the need to address public negatives affecting women, and/or black and ethnic minority people.[41] Here is an example where the criminal law has played a leading role. A woman can perform genital mutilation on herself (FGM), however horrifying others may find such an action: that shows the principle of lifestyle autonomy at work.[42] However, under the Female Genital Mutilation Act 2003, a much more restricted approach is taken to inter-personal conduct.[43] It is an offence for *another* person to excise, infibulate, or otherwise mutilate the whole or any part of a girl's labia majora, labia minora, or clitoris (other than for a very restricted range of reasons). Most importantly, for the purposes of this offence, 'girl' includes 'woman'.[44] So, even when an adult woman consents to FGM being performed on her by another person (assuming the narrow exceptions do not apply), the consent will be no defence to the other person's crime. In the knowledge that FGM is rarely sought by the

[36] For the term, 'public negative', see Chapter 3.2.   [37] J. Feinberg, *Harm to Self* (1986), 374.

[38] For a recent, controversial intervention in this debate, on the side of legalization, see <www.amnesty.org.uk/consultation-draft-policy#.VcJFKvlViko>.

[39] An important scholarly work on this issue is M. Madden Dempsey, 'Sex Trafficking and Criminalization: In Defense of Feminist Abolitionism' (2010) 158 *University of Pennsylvania Law Review* 172.

[40] There is now legislation criminalizing payment for sex where there is a risk that the sex to be paid for may be the product of exploitation: see the Sexual Offences Act 2003, s. 53A, and <www.cps.gov.uk/legal/p_to_r/prostitution_and_exploitation_of_prostitution/#a15>. For an earlier, influential discussion of the conflicting policies and principles, see the report of the Wolfenden Committee on Homosexual Offences and Prostitution in 1957.

[41] The criminal law has been closely involved in this process. For example, there are now not only crimes of inciting racial hatred and stirring up religious hatred (Public Order Act 1986, Part III; Racial and Religious Hatred Act 2006), but also specific crimes—such as assault—where, if there is proof that the offence was racially or religiously aggravated, a higher sentence than normal will be available to the judge: Crime and Disorder Act 1998, as amended. See <www.cps.gov.uk/legal/p_to_r/racist_and_religious_crime/>.

[42] Section 1 of the 2003 Act does not expressly exclude the possibility that someone performing FGM on herself could be guilty of the offence; however, this seems to be an implication. As in the case of suicide, anyone who assists a girl to perform FGM will be guilty of an offence: Female Genital Mutilation Act 2003, s. 2.

[43] For the distinction between personal and inter-personal goods, such as autonomy, see Chapter 3.2.

[44] Female Genital Mutilation Act 2003, s. 6(1).

victim herself,[45] the law seeks to deter the public negative of FGM through a prohibition on inter-personal performance of FGM, whilst protecting an individual's lifestyle autonomy by leaving it open to a woman to decide to perform the operation on herself.

This brings us to broader consideration of the principle of lifestyle autonomy, the principle that (broadly) we should be free from the use of undue influence or coercion in becoming authentic authors of our own lives, in expressing our choices in life, be they good, bad, or indifferent choices. What does the law (be it the criminal or the civil law) seek to respect, when it claims to respect the principle of lifestyle autonomy? Joel Feinberg provides a useful understanding of lifestyle autonomy (he does not himself use the term 'lifestyle'), as a value to be respected by the criminal law:

> [T]he most basic autonomy right is the right to decide how one is to live one's life, in particular how to make the critical life-decisions—what courses of study to take, what skills and virtues to cultivate, what career to enter, whom or whether to marry, which church if any to join, whether to have children, and so on.[46]

Feinberg is concerned here with what he considers to be the 'right' to lifestyle autonomy, but explaining autonomy in terms of rights may not always be helpful in this context.[47] Lifestyle autonomy is an intrinsic value, something valued for its own sake as constitutive of a life worth living.[48] The law's respect for lifestyle autonomy comes from the very high value set on it by most people, whether or not it is appropriate to speak of a 'right' to lifestyle autonomy. Further, speaking in terms of rights may unduly narrow the scope of moral inquiry. For example, I cannot make much of my 'right' to join a church if there are no churches in my country; I cannot meaningfully choose which courses of study to take if I have never received an education, or if there are no schools, or universities; and so on. In other words, the value and significance of the rights of which Feinberg speaks may be dependent on the (state, or non-state) provision and flourishing of public goods, like an education system, themselves in part supported by the criminal law (as we saw in Chapter 3).

How is lifestyle autonomy respected by the state? The important obligation to respect lifestyle autonomy is usually captured by J. S. Mill's theory that the state is bound by the 'harm principle'.[49] The state is guided by both 'permissive' and 'restrictive' aspects of the harm principle. We will deal first with the restrictive aspect. It will be recalled that, for Mill, consideration for someone's 'own good' is not in itself a sufficient justificatory basis for using coercion—including penal coercion—simply to make that person a better person.[50] In other words, someone should not be subject to criminal sanctions simply because they are (say) not a credit to their family, work-shy, or lazy, or the like. This issue has been the subject of vigorous debates about the proper ambit of the criminal law in the realms of sexual morality. In the notable exchanges between

---

[45] See <www.gov.uk/government/uploads/system/uploads/attachment_data/file/300167/FGM_leaflet_v4.pdf>, 4.   [46] J. Feinberg, *Harm to Self* (Oxford University Press, 1986), 54.

[47] As Feinberg recognized: see Feinberg, n 46, 37–47.   [48] Chapter 3.2.

[49] Chapter 3.5.   [50] Chapter 3.5.

Lord Devlin and Professor Hart,[51] Devlin's argument was that a society is entitled to use the criminal law against behaviour which may threaten its existence; that there is a common morality which ensures the cohesion of society; that any deviation from this common morality is capable of affecting society injuriously; and that therefore it may be justifiable and necessary to penalize immoral behaviour.[52] In response, Devlin's opponents have broadly followed the approach of John Stuart Mill,[53] in ruling out 'moral harm' as the sole or main basis for criminalization.

Lord Devlin's argument relies on an unacceptably loose concept of morality. Devlin proposed that the common morality could be discovered by assembling a group of ordinary citizens, in the form of a jury, and asking them to reach decisions on certain types of behaviour. However, not only would this method confuse prejudices with moral judgments, but it might also fail to elicit agreement on some subjects such as abortion. In effect, Lord Devlin assumes that immorality is to be defined and measured according to the strength of feelings of ordinary people. If certain behaviour evokes feelings of intolerance, indignation, and disgust among ordinary members of society, that is a sufficient indication that the behaviour threatens the common morality and is therefore a proper object of the criminal law. The difficulty is that these feelings of ordinary people may be more the expression of prejudice than of moral judgment. If a person's reaction to certain behaviour is to be termed 'moral', it ought to be grounded in reasons as well as in feelings, and those reasons ought to be consistent with other standards used by that individual to judge personal behaviour. A theory about morality and the criminal law must be based on a defensible definition of morality, not one which confuses it with mere feelings of distaste and disgust.[54]

Devlin's argument, if accepted, opens the way to justifying criminalization based on the fact that people find conduct highly offensive. In tackling this issue, the law draws a public–private distinction in respect of decency and shock to feelings. What 'offensive' conduct adults get up to in private is not regarded as the law's business, but what they do in the public domain *may* be the law's business if it is likely to give serious offence to the feelings of ordinary members of the public. However, a test based on whether conduct in public was found by members of the public to be 'seriously offensive' would be too simplistic. Many things may cause serious offence, and one person's sense of what is 'highly offensive' may differ entirely from another's. It is also not easy to establish a connection between offensiveness and wrongdoing. For example, if two gay people kiss in public, and sufficient numbers of people find this highly offensive, is that really enough to justify arresting the two engaged in kissing for a breach of the peace?[55]

Andreas von Hirsch and Andrew Simester argue for a different test of offensiveness. They suggest that the essence of the wrong involved in offensiveness lies in treating

---

[51] The principal essays written by the protagonists are collected in H. L. A. Hart, *Law, Liberty, and Morality* (1963), and P. Devlin, *The Enforcement of Morals* (1965).   [52] See Devlin, n 51, ch 1.
[53] J. S. Mill, *On Liberty* (1859), *passim*.   [54] Dworkin, n 23, ch 10.
[55] In *Masterson* v *Holden* [1986] 3 All ER 39 this was the situation. Shamefully, the court found that arrest was justified in these circumstances.

others with a gross lack of respect or consideration.[56] This subtly shifts the focus away from the effect D's conduct has on V (offensiveness), and towards the attitude displayed by D in his or her conduct (lack of respect for others). As with other principles, this one must be mediated by allowing other values to restrain criminalization. There should be a margin of social tolerance (being called a rude name should not be sufficient). Conduct that is readily avoided, by those who may be offended, should normally be excluded from criminalization. So, for example, there is scarcely a case for criminalization on the grounds of public indecency if a relatively secluded area for nude bathing is indicated or well-known, so that people can avoid it if they do not wish to be confronted by such behaviour. Finally, the conduct should be immediately offensive, and not simply create a risk of subsequent offence.[57]

How do these criteria apply? A test case is the criminalization of sexual acts in public places such as public lavatories.[58] The Crown Prosecution Service has explained the offence as follows:

> This offence has been introduced to give adults and children the freedom to use public lavatories for the purpose for which they are designed, without the fear of being an unwilling witness to overtly sexual behaviour of a kind that most people would not expect to be conducted in public.[59]

In broad terms, this justification fits with Simester and von Hirsch's explanation, because it suggests that it is the lack of consideration for others that matters, rather than whether or not the conduct causes 'offence'.[60] After all, if the offence is justified,[61] it still ought to apply if, say, a child might be frightened or worried by the conduct rather than offended. Another example of an offence in need of a justification along such lines may be found in the Indecent Displays (Control) Act 1981, which criminalizes the display of any indecent matter which is visible from a public place. Here, the questions concern the grossness of the lack of consideration, the margin of social tolerance, and of course the possibility that vulnerable people (particularly the young) will be exposed to the display.

4.3. THE PRINCIPLES OF AUTONOMY: RESPECTING 'MORAL' AUTONOMY

In order to be able meaningfully to exercise lifestyle autonomy, one must have 'moral' autonomy. Moral autonomy is a personal good,[62] which has different elements to it. To begin with, someone only becomes morally autonomous when they have the

---

[56] A. von Hirsch and A. P. Simester, 'Penalising Offensive Behaviour', in A. von Hirsch and A. P. Simester (eds.), *Incivilities: Regulating Offensive Behaviour* (2006), 120.

[57] Von Hirsch and Simester, n 56, 124–30.   [58] Sexual Offences Act 2003, s. 71.

[59] <www.cps.gov.uk/legal/s_to_u/sentencing_manual/s71__sexual_activity_in_a_public_lavatory/>

[60] For a possible example, see <www.theguardian.com/uk-news/2015/aug/12/couple-fined-for-revolting-sex-act-during-hyde-park-concert>.

[61] For the view that it is not justified, see <www.govyou.co.uk/repeal-s71-of-sexual-offences-act-2003-sexual-activity-in-a-public-lavatory/>.

[62] On personal goods, see the discussion in Chapter 3.2.

developmental maturity fully to understand, and evaluatively to distinguish, between choices they can or must make in life. If a five-year-old expresses a commitment to become a train driver, we should not treat that as a considered commitment, even if the child goes on to become a train driver in adult life. That is clearly because, at five years' old, someone does not have full moral autonomy in the sense just described. For such reasons, the law does not treat criminal liability as arising until a child is at least ten years' old, although that is a still low age for the criminal responsibility threshold, by European standards.[63] Until a child is developmentally mature enough adequately to understand the nature and significance of his or her actions when (say) hitting someone or damaging another's property, we should not treat those choices as morally autonomous choices fit for legal condemnation and state punishment. Beyond protecting young children themselves from criminal liability, given their lack of full moral autonomy, the law also takes steps to ensure that children have a proper chance to develop such autonomy. The criminal law may have a small but important role in this. Thus, alongside the criminalization of parental neglect or ill-treatment of children, the law insists that—if children cannot adequately be educated at home—parents must ensure that their children attend regularly to participate in the public good of schooling in common with other children.[64]

Linked with developmental maturity, moral autonomy involves the possession of adequate rational and emotional capacities. Famously, legal theorist H. L. A. Hart said that criminal liability should depend on whether someone had the 'capacity' and a 'fair opportunity' (in terms of the limits of their powers of self-control or self-restraint) to do other than they did.[65] To a greater or lesser extent, the law rightly seeks to shield those who lack such capacities or opportunities from full, or any, criminal responsibility, through the provision of defences such as insanity and (in a murder case) diminished responsibility.[66] Further, in *Cooke* v *DPP*,[67] the High Court said that it would be wrong to impose an anti-social behaviour order (now, an injunction to prevent nuisance or annoyance) on someone who was genuinely incapable of complying with it: in that case, the person against whom the order was being sought suffered from a personality disorder, post-traumatic stress disorder, and possibly also Asperger's syndrome.[68] Whether the law offers anything like enough protection to such individuals is another question.[69] The criminal justice system may all too easily end up as a dumping ground for people whose illnesses are difficult to treat, or who have multiple or complex problems.[70]

Even those with fully developed rational and emotional capacities may find those capacities put under intolerable strain in certain circumstances. Suppose that you

---

[63] See the discussion in Chapter 6.2.   [64] Education Act 1996, s. 444.

[65] H. L. A. Hart, *Punishment and Responsibility* (2nd edn., 2008), xxxiv–liii.

[66] See Chapter 6.2.   [67] [2008] EWHC 2703 (admin).

[68] See the discussion in Law Commission, *Insanity and Automatism: A Discussion Paper* (2013), 4.39.

[69] J. Peay, *Mental Health and Crime* (2010); Law Commission, *Insanity and Automatism: A Discussion Paper* (Law Commission, 2013).

[70] NACRO, *Liaison and diversion for mentally disordered offenders*, <www.nacro.org.uk/data/files/liaison-diversion-for-mdos-may06–936.pdf>.

are consumed by an intensely powerful emotion that dominates your thoughts and actions, reducing to a whisper the voice of reason that counsels restraint and self-control. In such circumstances, it may be said that—until you recover a sense of mental 'balance'—you temporarily lack an adequate capacity to act in a morally autonomous way: something that requires reason to have sufficient potential to influence conduct when emotion is running high. Perhaps you *could* have restrained yourself with exceptional difficulty, but in the circumstances the force of the emotion led you to vent it fully instead.[71] To a very limited extent, the law recognizes this effect on us that emotions can have, by providing defences such as duress (where death or serious harm is feared) to the commission of a crime,[72] and loss of self-control as a defence to murder.[73] These defences cater, on a restricted basis, for circumstances in which fear, or anger, understandably dominated the defendant's thoughts and led him or her to commit a crime whilst in the grip of one (or both) of these emotions.

At a more basic level, as a dimension of moral autonomy, rational capacity is an important feature of the general requirement that conduct—or possession, or some other relevant state of affairs—alleged to be criminal must have been 'voluntary'.[74] Rational capacity gives, within limits, control over the body and the mind. Many 'actions' are purely automatic and beyond our control—such as peristaltic movement. Even so, we have some capacity for directed, rational control even over actions that are normally automatic, such as breathing: you can deliberately speed up or slow down your breathing. In its interpretation of the voluntariness requirement, the law tends to focus on control of the body. If, for example, I slip on the road and accidentally barge into you, causing you to fall and injure yourself, I should be acquitted of any offence against you, however much harm you suffer. That is because my conduct in barging into you was not voluntary. Having slipped, I was then unable to bring to bear the force of reason to control my conduct so as to avoid injuring you, in the way the law demands. However, mere *difficulty* in controlling one's actions will not render them involuntary, for legal purposes.[75] So, drivers who have been charged with road traffic offences, and then claimed that (for example) the dangerous manner in which they drove was due to progressive hypoglycaemia associated with diabetes, have not been regarded as acting involuntarily. In the eye of the law, what is crucial is that they retained at least a measure of mental control over their conduct.[76] The law's apparently tough approach to difficulty with control over the body may be explained by the road traffic context in which many of these cases have arisen. If someone has a medical condition that is

---

[71] See J. Raz, *Engaging Reason* (1999), 43: 'My suggestion is that we can think of people who perform normally expressive actions as people who let themselves express their emotions . . . They permit themselves to do so . . . In the case of purely expressive actions we . . . allow the emotion to express itself, the will acting as the non-interfering gatekeeper.'

[72] See Chapter 7.3.   [73] See Chapter 8.4.

[74] *Bratty v AG for Northern Ireland* [1963] AC 386.

[75] *Attorney General's Reference (No 2 of 1992)* (1993) 97 Cr App R 89; *R v Coley* [2013] EWCA Crim 223.

[76] *Watmore v Jenkins* [1962] QBD.

likely to or has begun to affect their driving, they should simply stop driving rather than struggle on.

It can be argued that there is an inconsistency here between the law's refusal to recognize difficulty with retaining voluntary control of conduct, and its concession to difficulty in retaining self-control or self-restraint in loss of self-control or duress cases (considered briefly earlier). However, there are differences between the two kinds of case. Someone acting in response to fear or anger does not ordinarily lose voluntary control over their conduct: typically, they are capable of and do perform intentional actions. It is, in broad terms, the force of the emotion, and the justifiability of its cause, that is subject to scrutiny and judgement in such cases. Having said that, outside the driving context, there were some indications that the law was prepared to take seriously the idea that, albeit exceptionally, loss of rational control over the mind (as through, say, post-traumatic stress disorder, or involuntary drug-taking) can cast doubt on the voluntariness of actions, even when those actions are intentionally undertaken.[77] Respect for moral autonomy requires that the law remain open to such claims, when they are properly backed by medical evidence. However, more recently, where defendants have retained the capacity to engage in intentional behaviour, the law has become hostile to the view that such behaviour can nonetheless be regarded as non-voluntary in virtue of a disconnection between the behaviour and mental control over it (perhaps brought about by a stress-induced blackout).[78] Certainly, the law is entitled to be reluctant to accept such claims when the lack of mental control is self-induced,[79] and highly suspicious of them when they appear to be employed solely to camouflage the defendant's real motives.[80] We will come back to this issue in Chapter 5.2.[81]

4.4. THE PRINCIPLE OF MINIMALISM, AND THE PERMISSIVE ASPECT OF THE HARM PRINCIPLE

Chapter 3 was devoted to a discussion of what can now be recognized as the 'permissive' aspect of the harm principle, the aspect concerned with when it is legitimate—perhaps, even obligatory—to employ the criminal law to protect different kinds of value or good. Here, we consider further the nature and limits of the permissive aspect of the harm principle.

[77] *R v Charlson* [1955] 1 WLR 317; *R v Hardie* (1984) EWCA Crim 2; *R v T* [1990] Crim LR 256 (Snaresbrook Crown Court), discussed in J. Horder, 'Pleading Involuntary Lack of Capacity' (1993) 52 Cambridge LJ 298; B. McSherry, 'Criminal Responsibility, "Fleeting" States of Mental Impairment, and the Power of Self-Control' (2004) 27 *International Journal of Law and Psychiatry* 445.

[78] See *R v Coley* [2013] EWCA Crim 223, requiring 'complete destruction of voluntary control', discussed in Chapter 5.   [79] *R v Coley* [2013] EWCA Crim 223.

[80] See, e.g., the attitude of the CPS to claims that sexual offences have been committed whilst sleep walking: <www.cps.gov.uk/legal/d_to_g/defences_-_sleepwalking_as_a_defence_in_sexual_offence_cases/>.

[81] See further, the Law Commission, *Insanity and Automatism: A Discussion Paper* (2013), 4.33 and 4.60.

(a) JOEL FEINBERG'S ACCOUNT OF THE HARM PRINCIPLE

Joel Feinberg gives his account of the permissive aspect of the harm principle thus:

> It is always a good reason in support of penal legislation that it would probably be effective in preventing (eliminating, reducing) harm to persons other than the actor and there is probably no other means that is equally effective at no greater cost to other values.[82]

Notice that a permission (what Feinberg calls 'good reason') to use penal legislation, if the conditions he sets down are met, is not to be equated with an obligation to use it. Feinberg's conditions for the use of such legislation could be met, and yet the state could be right to stay its hand. For example, even if Feinberg's conditions are met, perhaps there is a high risk that the law would be, or be seen to be, operating in a manner that discriminated against a minority group: that might count decisively against criminalization of the activity in question.[83] Moreover, an issue of proportionality arises here. Penalization brings with it significant negative consequences for offenders. Perhaps, in some instances, the sum of human misery likely to be generated by the use of penalization to try to reduce or eliminate a harm is likely to be just too great, in comparison with the gain made in terms of harm reduction, to make the enterprise worthwhile: as some have argued powerfully in the case of drug use.[84]

If the criminalization of certain conduct, such as the possession of 'soft' drugs or various 'vice' offences, gives rise to social consequences that are hardly better than the mischief at which the laws aim, this militates strongly in favour of decriminalization. Thus drugs and vice laws may (i) produce active 'black markets', (ii) lead the police to adopt intrusive means of enforcement, (iii) allow the police to be selective in their enforcement, and (iv) lead to a degree of police corruption.[85] Prohibitions that have these consequences ought to be reconsidered. There is an ongoing debate about the propriety and wisdom of penalizing drug offences at all, and certainly so severely, when it appears that the law has little effect on the scale of drug use, importation, and supply.[86] There are other objections against criminalizing drug use, although some may still argue (notably in relation to 'hard' drugs) that the case for criminalization outweighs the other social consequences.[87] This leads on to a more general argument for restraint in criminalization: that, since the enforcement of the criminal law is selective and tends to bear down most heavily on the least advantaged (the enforcement of drug laws is one reason for the disproportionately high number of non-white offenders in prison in Britain and the USA), these injustices should be kept to a minimum.

---

[82] J. Feinberg, *Harm to Others* (1984), 26.

[83] See the discussion of restrictions on free speech, at the end of Chapter 2.

[84] See D. Husak, *Overcriminalization: The Limits of the Criminal Law* (2008); D. Husak, *Drugs and Rights* (1992).　　　　[85] See S. Kadish, *Blame and Punishment* (1987), 22–8, for elaboration of this argument.

[86] See, e.g., Husak, *Drugs and Rights*, n 84; UK Drug Policy Commission, *Final Report, A Fresh Approach to Drugs* (2012).

[87] Cf. the argument of Peter Alldridge, in ch 7 of his *Relocating Criminal Law* (2000), to the effect that dealers who supply drugs to addicts are committing the wrong of exploitation. His conclusion, however, is that there are powerful counter-arguments for continued criminalization.

A further important point is that Feinberg thought his statement of the permissive aspect of the harm principle to be, as it stands, over-inclusive in an important respect. As well as being (potentially) harmful, he thought that conduct must also be *wrongful*, if it is to permissibly penalized.[88] We touched on this justifying element of an offence in section 4.2, but it is worth reflecting on it further, in a slightly different context. To give a classic example, if I set up a business in competition with yours, that may lead you to suffer a setback to your interests—a harm—in the form of lost profits, or even bankruptcy. However, even if I intend my business to succeed and yours to fail, so long as I do not conduct my business in a wrongful way (through fraud, intimidation, and so on), the mere fact that I knowingly cause you harm does not bring my conduct within the scope of the harm principle, as set out by Feinberg. Even so, helpful though it is, the wrongfulness constraint may not prove to be a very significant bar to criminalization decisions. There are, quite simply, so many forms of wrongdoing whose relationship to a harm means that they—the wrongs—can easily be pressed into service in justification of a criminalization decision.

For example, consider a variation on the classic example just given. A group of ex-offenders sets up a car wash business in a local area. To help them in the medium term, the local authority bans (and subjects to a penalty) the setting up of rival car wash businesses within a mile of the ex-offenders' car wash. Then, if someone, in defiance of the ban, sets up a rival car wash business within the one-mile radius, they may be legitimately penalized for so doing. That is because, in establishing the penalty system, the local authority can rely for its justification on a form of wrongdoing. The reintegration of offenders as law-abiding members of the community is a valuable but fragile public good, and it can be wrong to undermine efforts to secure that good. However, it is important to bear in mind the point made right at the end of Chapter 3, which links with Feinberg's emphasis on 'effectiveness' in the passage cited earlier. Even when a wrong is, coupled with the threat of harm it involves, understandably used to justify a criminal offence or penalty, the principle of minimalism requires the use of the offence to be kept under active, periodic review. It is too often the case that we simply have no idea whether criminal offences or penalties remain proportionate and effective sanctions in dealing with the wrongful harm, or threat of such harm, that led to their creation. The need to secure proportionality and effectiveness ought to mean that, although wrongs are numerous, criminal offences or penalties dealing with wrongs should be very much smaller in number.

(b) THE NATURE OF MINIMALISM

That brings us a fundamental question. What is the case for being a minimalist about criminalization? There are at least two main bases on which minimalism can and should be promoted, when it is the criminal liability of individuals that is in issue. First, because sanctioning processes are a form of public censure—exposing someone to the possibility

---

[88] Feinberg, n 82, 36. The authoritative modern discussion is now A. P. Simester and A. von Hirsch, *Crimes, Harms and Wrongs* (2011), ch 2.

of hard treatment through punishment—it is especially important that legislatures and courts observe moral 'side-constraints' inhibiting the creation or extension of such processes. The most important of the side-constraints is the principle that human rights must be respected, and as a part of that, the principle that criminalization must not, in all the circumstances, be disproportionate (the proportionality principle). Secondly, at a deeper level, the principle of minimalism stems from a humane response to the recognition that—even when justified—criminalization does not involve only individual subjection in law to state authority (in what is meant to be a society of equally free people). Criminalization also entails subjection to an authority that has the right to censure and inflict punitive measures that, in serious cases, may cause great suffering, hardship, and impoverishment. The humane response to this recognition involves minimizing criminalization, because this response acknowledges that the censure and punishment of a fellow human being is a distasteful duty, and not a legitimate means by which full vent can be given to the righteous indignation of those affected by or informed of the crime. The humane response is the right one, because as legal philosopher John Finnis remarks, 'the criminal is an individual whose good is as good as any man's, notwithstanding that he ought in fairness to be deprived of some opportunities of realising that good'.[89]

Having said that, an often overlooked complicating factor means that a defence of minimalism must go further than this. As has been remarked a number of times in Chapters 1–3, a great deal of modern criminalization is aimed at business activity. Companies may be found to be at fault in criminal law,[90] but they are incapable of emotional suffering, they do not enjoy human rights to the same extent as natural individuals,[91] and most importantly, they are entirely subject to human direction. In both morality and law, they can legitimately be created or destroyed at will, and hence cannot enjoy the same status in law as human beings. Does that mean that minimalism, as a humanitarian principle, has no application to the legitimate scope of criminalization of companies? No, it does not. For millions of individuals, the prospects for the establishment of a secure basis for decent life depend on the flourishing of corporate activity: in 2013, only 19 per cent of working people were employed in the public sector in the UK.[92] Indirectly, thus, the application of minimalism, as a restraining principle applicable to corporate criminal liability, is of crucial importance for individuals, in so far as such liability threatens the commercial viability of the businesses they work in or otherwise depend on. This is to some extent reflected in the way that the criminal liability of businesses is made to depend in part on what a business can afford to do to avoid liability. For example, in deciding whether a company reduced safety risks below what was reasonably practicable, for the purposes of criminal liability under the Health and Safety at Work Act 1974, the Health and Safety Executive requires its staff to engage in, 'weighing a risk against the trouble, time and money needed to control

---

[89] J. Finnis, *Natural Law and Natural Rights* (1980), 264.   [90] See Chapter 6.3.
[91] Companies can benefit from, for example, the prohibition in Art. 7 of the ECHR on the imposition of retrospective criminal liability.
[92] <www.ons.gov.uk/ons/rel/pse/public-sector-employment/q3-2015/index.html>.

it'.[93] Similarly, under the Bribery Act 2010, it may be a defence to a corporate failure to prevent bribery that the firm had in place, 'adequate procedures' to prevent the offence occurring, where adequacy is linked in part to the size, nature, and resources of the organization.[94] Clearly, this argument spills over into the sentencing stage, where the punishments, in form of fines, should take account of the market consequences for employees, customers, and for fair competition, amongst other things.[95]

Beyond this, the most significant contribution of the minimalism principle to this issue is its insistence that criminalization must in most circumstances be a measure of last resort. This demand—often thought to have general application to all criminalization[96]—has great significance in the field of corporate criminal liability. That is because companies other than the very smallest have an organizational capacity (that individuals may lack) to engage with a range of alternatives to criminalization that can be used to deter or respond to corporate wrongdoing. Some of these, such as deferred prosecution agreements, were touched on in Chapter 1. Such agreements are one way that another important alternative to prosecution can come into play: community project work or otherwise 'restorative' measures, rather than retributive responses to wrongdoing.[97] Further, there has been an increasing trend to employ less stigmatizing civil penalties against businesses, especially small businesses, as an alternative form of sanction to court processes and conviction.[98] In point of process (participation cost[99]), such penalties are administratively cheaper for both parties, and more certain in terms of punitive outcome. These are factors whose importance was emphasized (although he was not speaking specifically of corporate liability) as long ago as 1789 by Jeremy Bentham, who claimed that there should not be punishment, 'where the mischief may be prevented . . . without it: that is, at a cheaper rate'.[100]

(c) A MORAL SIDE-CONSTRAINT: THE PRINCIPLE OF RESPECT FOR HUMAN RIGHTS

It is an important constitutional principle that the criminal law should respect fundamental rights and freedoms. Although human rights considerations can sometimes generate a positive case for criminalization,[101] respecting human rights usually

---

[93] <www.hse.gov.uk/risk/theory/alarpglance.htm>.

[94] See Law Commission, *Reforming Bribery* (Law Com no. 313, 2009), para. 6.109.

[95] See Sentencing Guidelines Council, *Corporate Manslaughter and Health and Safety Offences Causing Death* (2010), <www.sentencingcouncil.org.uk/wp-content/uploads/web__guideline_on_corporate_manslaughter_accessible.pdf>, 12–21. For a dramatic example of a multi-million pound fine being waived, in the light of a major's bank's perilous financial situation, see: <www.theguardian.com/business/2015/aug/12/co-op-bank-boss-niall-booker-praises-waive-120m-fine-pragmatic-solution>.

[96] For general discussion, see D. Husak, 'Criminal Law as Last Resort' (2004) 24 OJLS 207.

[97] See J. Braithwaite, *Restorative Justice and Responsive Regulation* (Oxford University Press, 2002).

[98] See the discussion in Law Commission, *Criminal Liability in Regulatory Contexts* (CP No. 195, 2010)

[99] For discussion of this concept, see Chapter 1.

[100] J. Bentham, *Introduction to the Principles of Morals and Legislation* (1789) (Oxford University Press, 1907), ch 13.

[101] For discussion, see A. Ashworth, *Positive Obligations in Criminal Law* (2013), ch 8.

involves observing constraints on criminalization. There are two sources of fundamental rights relevant to English criminal law—European Community law, and the European Convention on Human Rights. European Community law is potentially more powerful, since it takes priority over domestic law. However, its impact on English criminal law remains somewhat scattered, even if frequently underestimated.[102] The 'third pillar' of the European Union, as established by the Maastricht Treaty of 1992, relates to co-operation in the fields of justice and home affairs. The Amsterdam Treaty of 1999 defined the objective of the 'third pillar' as the creation of an 'area of freedom, security and justice'. The EU Constitutional Treaty anticipates its further development, and the provisions in Art. III-270 envisage harmonization of criminal laws as well as harmonized procedures, to go with mutual assistance and other co-operation (such as the European arrest warrant) already in place.[103]

More important in practice has been the change wrought by the Human Rights Act 1998, which may be loosely described as having incorporated into English law the European Convention on Human Rights. Reference has already been made to some Convention rights in Chapter 2.3 and 2.4. For present purposes, it is sufficient to make a broad sketch of the substantive rights guaranteed by the Convention, with some indication of their relevance to English criminal law:[104]

- Article 2 (right to life): self-defence and permissible force as exceptions; abortion; the surgical separation of conjoined twins; the right to self-determination, and assisting suicide.

- Article 3 (right not to be subjected to torture or inhuman or degrading treatment): protection through laws against sexual and physical violation; extent of defence of parental chastisement.

- Article 4 (right not to be held in slavery or servitude): protection through laws against forced labour and human trafficking.

- Article 5 (right to liberty and security of person): the defence of insanity; arrest for breach of the peace; and the 'quality of law' test.

- Article 6.2 (presumption of innocence): the burden of proof, and (possibly) offences of strict liability.

- Article 7 (prohibition on retroactive criminal laws): judicial lawmaking, and certainty in the definition of criminal offences.

- Article 8 (right to respect for private life): sexual offences; consent to physical harm; child abduction.

- Article 9 (freedom of religion): blasphemy (also Art. 10).

---

[102] See Chapter 1.3.

[103] See further S. Peers, *EU Justice and Home Affairs Law* (3rd edn., 2011), ch 8.

[104] For fuller discussion see B. Emmerson, A. Ashworth, and A. Macdonald (eds), *Human Rights and Criminal Justice* (3rd edn., 2012).

- Article 10 (freedom of expression): obscenity; racial hatred offences; contempt of court; incitement to disaffection; official secrets legislation; breach of the peace, and s. 5 of the Public Order Act 1986.

- Article 11 (freedom of assembly): breach of the peace, and various offences under the Public Order Act 1986 and the Criminal Justice and Public Order Act 1994 concerned with processions and demonstrations.

This list does not go into detail, but there will be references to the Convention and its jurisprudence at appropriate points in the later chapters. Nor is the list an exhaustive one. What is significant is that the Convention rights operate as a source of 'higher law' that can be used as a benchmark of the constitutionality of criminal legislation. Where a court finds that the definition of an offence interferes with one of the defendant's Convention rights and (if it is a right protected by Arts. 8–11) does so either without it being 'necessary in a democratic society' or proportionate to such a necessity, it may recognize this as the basis for a defence to liability.[105]

What has been the impact of the Human Rights Act on the criminal law? The reports and consultation papers issued by the Law Commission have taken considerable care to deal with possible Convention issues. The compatibility of legislation with the Convention should be assured by the procedure whereby the Minister sponsoring a Bill certifies that it is compatible with Convention rights,[106] but in fact certificates have been issued for some Bills whose compatibility has been much contested.[107] Section 6 of the Human Rights Act requires all public authorities (including the courts) to act in compliance with the Convention: this means that courts are bound to overrule judicial precedents which they find to be inconsistent with the Convention. Courts also have a duty under s. 2 of the Human Rights Act to 'take into account' decisions of the European Court of Human Rights. The wording of s. 2 makes it clear that the Strasbourg decisions are not binding: English courts have to interpret the Convention in the light of the Strasbourg jurisprudence, and may also consider other relevant decisions which may be drawn to their attention (e.g. decisions of the Privy Council, or constitutional cases from Canada, New Zealand, the USA, or South Africa). If the English courts were to decide not to follow a decision of the European Court of Human Rights, the right of an individual to petition to Strasbourg is available. In some spheres, where the Convention jurisprudence is weak (such as the burden of proof and Art. 6(2)), the English courts have gone further than the Strasbourg decisions and have followed the lead of other Commonwealth countries.[108] In other cases, the Supreme Court has refused to go as far, in protecting rights, as the European Court, most notably in relation to the dependence of conviction on hearsay evidence.[109]

---

[105] *Percy* v *DPP* [2002] Crim LR 835.   [106] Human Rights Act 1998, s. 19.

[107] E.g. the Bill that became the Sexual Offences Act 2003 (on which see Chapter 8.5 and 8.6); and the provision that became s. 76 of the Criminal Justice and Immigration Act 2008 (on which see Chapter 4.6(g)).

[108] *Lambert* [2002] 2 AC 545, and *Attorney General's Reference No. 4 of 2002* [2004] UKHL 43.

[109] See *R* v *Horncastle* [2009] UKSC 14.

Most powerful of all is s. 3 of the Act, which requires courts to construe legislation so as to comply with the Convention, 'so far as it is possible to do so'. This confers on courts a rather different interpretative role from that assumed at common law. Judicial discussions about 'the intention of Parliament' should be less frequent in cases where a Convention right is engaged, since the primary task is to reach an interpretation which protects the rights of individuals under the Convention—which may be the rights of defendants or of (potential) victims, for example. However, in some cases the courts have used this interpretative power extravagantly, so as to hold that a legislative provision bears a meaning that seems difficult to reconcile with its wording.[110] The courts do have an alternative approach in such situations: if a court is unable to read a statutory provision compatibly with the Convention, it will have to proceed as normal and the defendant will then appeal. An appellate court (Court of Appeal, Divisional Court, House of Lords) has the power under s. 4 to make a 'declaration of incompatibility' if it is satisfied that a statutory provision is incompatible with the Convention.[111] This may lead the government to take remedial action (s. 10), but the issue of a declaration of incompatibility itself has no effect on the continuing validity of the law or on the outcome of the proceedings in the case.

Since 2000, when the Human Rights Act came into force, twenty-nine declarations of incompatibility have been made in all areas of law.[112] They have included a 2003 declaration that Northern Irish legislation making it a crime for a man to have consensual anal intercourse with a woman[113] was incompatible with the right to a private life under Art. 8 of the ECHR.[114] The offending piece of legislation was repealed that same year by the Sexual Offences Act 2003, ss. 139, 140, Sch 6, para. 4 and Sch 7. In relation to human rights, what this shows is that their protection can involve a new constitutional idea: the idea that the development of the criminal law can be a matter of partnership between the courts and the judiciary.

In coming to grips with the Convention and its jurisprudence, it is important to note the difference in patterns of reasoning that it requires. The rights declared in the Convention have different strengths and, where they have exceptions, the structure of the exceptions may differ markedly. One pointer to this is Art. 15, which permits states to derogate from certain rights under the Convention 'in time of war or other emergency threatening the life of the nation', 'to the extent strictly required by the exigencies of the situation',[115] but specifically excludes from derogation the rights in Arts. 2, 3, 4(1), and 7. One might therefore construct the following hierarchy of rights:

- *Non-derogable rights*: the right to life (Art. 2), the right not to be subjected to torture, inhuman, or degrading treatment (Art. 3), the prohibition on slavery and forced labour (Art. 4(1)), and the right not to be convicted of a crime that was not

---

[110] Notably in *R* v *A* [2002] 1 AC 45.

[111] An example of its use was in *A* v *Home Secretary* [2004] UKHL 56.

[112] <www.publications.parliament.uk/pa/jt201415/jtselect/jtrights/130/13006.htm>.

[113] Offences Against the Person Act 1861 (NI), s. 62.

[114] *McR's Application for Judicial Review* [2003] NI 1.

[115] Article 15 was analysed by the House of Lords in *A* v *Home Secretary* [2004] UKHL 56.

in force at the time of the conduct (Art. 7). Article 2 does provide for certain exceptions, and the same exceptions should apply in some Art. 3 cases.[116] But those exceptions, discussed in Chapter 4.6, are narrowly circumscribed.

- *Strong rights*: the right to liberty and security of person (Art. 5), the right to a fair trial (Art. 6), and the right to enjoy Convention rights without discrimination on any ground (Art. 14). A State is permitted to derogate from these rights under the strict terms of Art. 15,[117] and the Strasbourg court has in some cases been content to afford States some margin of appreciation in respect of these rights.

- *Qualified rights*: the right to a private life (Art. 8), the right to freedom of thought and religion (Art. 9), the right to freedom of expression (Art. 10), the right to freedom of assembly (Art. 11). These are qualified or *prima facie* rights, their common feature being that the first paragraph of the Article declares the right, and the second paragraph sets out the circumstances in which the right may justifiably be interfered with. This affords considerable scope for argument, using the Strasbourg jurisprudence and other sources.[118] Thus freedom of expression may be curtailed by an offence of sending a grossly offensive message through a public communication system,[119] by offences of speech likely to stir up racial or religious hatred,[120] or by offences of inciting violence. There are bound to be difficult borderline decisions to be taken, as where an evangelical Christian was convicted under s. 5 of the Public Order Act 1986 for displaying a sign saying 'Stop Immorality, Stop Homosexuality, Stop Lesbianism', the court concluding that the interference with his rights to freedom of religion and freedom of expression was justified by the disorder and violence it provoked.[121]

The grounds for justifying exceptions to the qualified rights under the second paragraphs of Arts. 8 to 11 are fairly broad and wide-ranging, and turn on the two requirements of 'necessary in a democratic society' and 'proportionality'. Although the Strasbourg Court does not have an entirely consistent approach to the question of proportionality, its approach is more rigorous than that of the English courts to

---

[116] Now confirmed in Strasbourg by, e.g., *Rivas v France* [2005] Crim LR 305.

[117] In *A v Home Secretary* [2004] UKHL 56 the House of Lords found that the provisions for the detention without trial of suspected international terrorists were contrary to Art. 5 and were not saved by Art. 15, since, although their Lordships accepted the government's view that there was an emergency threatening the life of the nation, they held that the powers went further than strictly necessary and that they were discriminatory, by applying to non-nationals and not to British nationals. The government abandoned these powers and took different powers in the Prevention of Terrorism Act 2005.

[118] Sections 12 and 13 of the Human Rights Act require British courts to 'have particular regard to the importance of' the rights of freedom of expression and freedom of religion. The right to peaceful enjoyment of possessions, declared by Protocol 1, is also subject to a 'public interest' exception which places it within this broad category.

[119] *DPP v Collins* [2007] 1 Cr App R 5.

[120] But note s. 29J of the Public Order Act 1986 (inserted by the Racial and Religious Hatred Act 2006), re-stating freedom of expression as a value.

[121] *DPP v Hammond* [2004] Crim LR 851; cf. *DPP v Redmond-Bate* [1999] Crim LR 998, where the Divisional Court held that the interference with rights was not justified.

their preferred and looser concept of 'balancing'.[122] In summary, the rights declared in the Convention are not extensive and were never intended as a complete statement of the limits of the criminal sanction. As expected, the impact of the Human Rights Act on the substantive criminal law (as distinct from criminal procedure and evidence) has been rather small:[123] the issues surrounding the compatibility of the rules on self-defence and insanity have not yet come up for decision, and few of the reported cases have necessitated a re-writing of English criminal law.[124] However, there remains scope for critical discussion of the certainty of some aspects of English criminal law.

(d) RULE OF LAW PRINCIPLES: THE NON-RETROACTIVITY PRINCIPLE

According to the ideal of the rule of law, the law must be such that those subject to it can reliably be guided by it, either to avoid violating it or to build the legal consequences of having violated it into their thinking about what future actions may be open to them. People must be able to find out what the law is and to factor it into their practical deliberations. The law must avoid taking people by surprise, ambushing them, putting them into conflict with its requirements in such a way as to defeat their expectations and to frustrate their plans.[125] This is what was referred to earlier as the 'activity' dimension to the rule of law. It is a fundamental principle, binding in both civil and criminal law, with both procedural and substantive implications. It expresses an incontrovertible minimum of respect for the principle of lifestyle autonomy: citizens must be informed of the law before it can be fair to convict them of an offence (many of the *mens rea* and culpability doctrines discussed in Chapter 5 are connected to this), and both legislatures and courts must apply the rule of law by not criminalizing conduct that was lawful when done.

In many other jurisdictions, especially within Europe, it is usual to begin a discussion of general principles of the criminal law by stating the maxim *nullum crimen sine lege*, sometimes known as the principle of legality. However, the connotations of the principle of legality are so wide-ranging that it is preferable to divide it into three distinct principles—the principle of non-retroactivity, the principle of maximum certainty, and the principle of strict construction of penal statutes. The essence of the non-retroactivity principle is that a person should never be convicted or punished except in accordance with a previously declared offence governing the conduct

---

[122] B. Goold, L. Lazarus, and G. Swiney, 'Public Protection, Proportionality and the Search for Balance' (Ministry of Justice Research Series 10/07).

[123] See A. Ashworth, 'A Decade of Human Rights in Criminal Justice' [2014] Crim LR 325.

[124] The most significant appear to be *H.* [2002] 1 Cr App R 59 on parental chastisement (Chapter 4.8); *Percy* v *DPP* [2002] Crim LR 835 (s. 5 of the Public Order Act may interfere disproportionately with the defendant's Art. 10 right); and *Goldstein and Rimmington* [2005] UKHL 63 (public nuisance and Art. 7). Cf. *S.K.* [2011] EWCA 1691, where it was noted that the relevant legislation actually refers to Art. 4 on servitude and forced labour.

[125] J. Gardner, 'Introduction' to H. L. A. Hart, *Punishment and Responsibility* (2nd edn., 2008), xxxvi.

in question.[126] The principle is to be found in the European Convention on Human Rights, Art. 7: 'no one shall be held guilty of any offence on account of any act or omission which did not constitute a criminal offence under national or international law at the time when it was committed'. The rationale links back to the principle of lifestyle autonomy and to the concept of reliance inherent in the rule of law ideal: 'respect for autonomy involves respect for the ability to plan, which requires respect for the ability to rely on the law', which in turn generates the principle of non-retroactivity.[127] As we will see in section 4.5, on this point, the non-retroactivity principle conflicts with the 'authoritarian' principle.

Some years ago, the English courts did exercise the power, in effect, to create a new criminal offence. In *Shaw v DPP* (1962),[128] the prosecution had indicted Shaw with a 'conspiracy to corrupt public morals' at common law, in addition to two charges under the Sexual Offences Act 1956 and the Obscene Publications Act 1959. The House of Lords upheld the validity of the indictment, despite the absence of any clear precedents, on the broad ground that conduct intended and calculated to corrupt public morals is indictable at common law. The decision led to an outcry from lawyers and others. One objection to *Shaw* is that it fails to respect citizens as rational, autonomous individuals: a citizen cannot be sure of avoiding the criminal sanction by refraining from prohibited conduct if it is open to the courts to invent new crimes without warning. What happened in *Shaw* was that a majority of the House of Lords felt a strong pull towards criminalization because they were convinced of the immoral and antisocial nature of the conduct, and regarded their authority to criminalize that conduct as more important than the liberty of citizens to plan their lives according to the rule of law. However, it appears that the English courts no longer claim the power to create new criminal offences.[129] The question may occasionally arise whether a purportedly retrospective provision that is favourable to the defendant should be upheld. Both the Strasbourg Court and the Privy Council have held that a defendant should have the benefit of such a law.[130]

---

[126] The non-retroactivity principle does not affect the creation of defences to crimes, although the courts have sometimes deferred to the legislature on this matter. For theoretical discussion of this point, see P. H. Robinson, 'Rules of Conduct and Principles of Adjudication' (1990) 57 U Chic LR 729, and P. Alldridge, 'Rules for Courts and Rules for Citizens' (1990) 10 OJLS 487. Cf. Law Com No. 177, cl. 4(4). The non-retroactivity principle does not apply to retrospective changes that benefit an accused person: *Scoppola v Italy (no. 2)* [GC], no. 10249/03, 17 September 2009.

[127] B. Juratowitch, *Retroactivity and the Common Law* (Hart Publishing, 2008), 49.

[128] [1962] AC 220.

[129] *Knuller v DPP* [1973] AC 435, a case in which, paradoxically, the court appeared to create the offence of outraging public decency; *Rimmington and Goldstein* [2006] 1 AC 459, per Lord Bingham. The situation is different in Scotland, where the courts still retain the power to create new criminal offences: *Khaliq v HM Advocate*, 1983 SCCR 483. *Stallard v HM Advocate*, 1989 SCCR 248, discussed by T. H. Jones, 'Common Law and Criminal Law: the Scottish Experience' [1990] Crim LR 292.

[130] See, respectively, *Kokkinakis v Greece* (1993) 17 EHRR 397 and *Chan Chi-hung v R* [1996] AC 442. The question received a similar answer under European Community law in Cases C–358/93 and C–416/93 *Aldo Bordessa* [1995] ECR I–361: see E. Baker, 'Taking European Criminal Law Seriously' [1998] Crim LR 361, at 366–8, 376–7.

What about the extension of existing offences to new circumstances? As a counterpoint to the strictness of the non-retroactivity principle[131] as it applies to the creation of wholly new offences, the European Court has taken a perhaps surprisingly generous view of the scope that courts have to develop existing offences to cover new ground.[132] In 1992, the European Court was asked to consider the novel step taken by the House of Lords in abolishing the exception in the law of rape for a husband having sexual intercourse with his wife against her will. In abolishing the exception, the House of Lords upheld the conviction of the husband for rape, when he sought to take advantage of this long-recognized (if morally indefensible) legal exception.[133] Upholding the abolition of the exception and the justice of the conviction, the European Court said:

> Article 7(1) excludes that any acts not previously punishable should be held by the courts to entail criminal liability or that existing offences should be extended to cover facts which previously did not clearly constitute a criminal offence. It is, however, compatible with the requirements of Article 7(1) for the existing elements of an offence to be clarified or adapted to new circumstances or developments in society in so far as this can reasonably be brought under the original concept of the offence. The constituent elements of an offence may not however be essentially changed to the detriment of an accused and any progressive development by way of interpretation must be reasonably foreseeable to him with the assistance of appropriate legal advice if necessary.[134]

The majority of the Court went on to hold that the development of the law by the English courts did not go beyond the legitimate adaptation of the ingredients of a criminal offence to reflect the social conditions of the time. The decision creates a distinction between the 'constituent' elements of an offence (that may not be changed), and the—reasonably foreseeable—progressive development of those elements (that may involve legitimate change); but in some instances that will be a difficult distinction to maintain. Ironically, whilst there are certainly arguments to the contrary, it is perfectly arguable that the marital rape exception was a 'constituent element' of the crime of rape, because it in part defined the circumstance elements of the crime. The Court's decision was clearly affected by the subject-matter, since it purported to justify its narrow reading of Art. 7 by reference to the incompatibility between, 'the unacceptable idea of a husband being immune against prosecution for rape of his wife' and the, 'respect for human dignity' that is a fundamental objective of the Convention.[135] This decision implants a degree of flexibility into what ought to be a fundamental rule-of-law protection for individuals, making it more compatible with the authoritarian principle.[136]

---

[131] Which applies to the democratically elected legislature as much as to the bureaucratically selected courts.

[132] *S.W. and C.R.* v *UK* (1995) 21 EHRR 363; see Juratowitch, n 111, 127–38 for discussion.

[133] *R* v *R* [1992] AC 599, discussed by M. Giles, 'Judicial Law-making in the Criminal Courts: the Case of Marital Rape' [1992] Crim LR 407.

[134] (1995) 21 EHRR 363, at 390; cf. the even more doubtful decision in *C.* [2005] Crim LR 238.

[135] (1995) 21 EHRR 363, at 402.   [136] See section 4.5.

(e) RULE OF LAW PRINCIPLES: THE MAXIMUM CERTAINTY PRINCIPLE

The next principle—maximum certainty in defining offences—embodies what are termed the 'fair warning' and 'void for vagueness' principles in US law.[137] All these principles may be seen as constituents of the principle of legality, and there is a close relationship between the principle of maximum certainty and the non-retroactivity principle. A vague law may in practice operate retroactively, since no one is quite sure whether given conduct is within or outside the rule. Thus Art. 7 of the Convention is relevant here, since it is:

> not confined to prohibiting the retrospective application of the criminal law to an accused's disadvantage. It also embodies, more generally, the principle that only the law can define a crime and prescribe a penalty (*nullum crimen, nulla poena sine lege*) and the principle that the criminal law must not be extensively construed to an accused's detriment, for instance by analogy: it follows from this that an offence must be clearly defined in law. This condition is satisfied where the individual can know from the wording of the relevant provision and, if need be, with the assistance of the courts' interpretation of it, what acts and omissions will make him liable.[138]

However, the Strasbourg Court has also recognized that some vagueness is inevitable in order, 'to avoid excessive rigidity and to keep pace with changing circumstances', and that a reasonable settled body of case law may suffice to reduce the degree of vagueness to acceptable proportions.[139] It is for this reason that the court refers to access to legal advice in order to determine the precise ambit of a law.

The test applied under Art. 7 is the same as that applied as the 'quality of law' standard elsewhere in the Convention. Whenever a member state seeks to rely on a provision in the Convention in order to justify its actions—whether the arrest or detention of a citizen (Art. 5), or interference with one of the qualified rights in Arts. 8–11—it must establish that its officials acted 'in accordance with the law'. This means a valid law, and this requires the state to show that the relevant rule satisfies the 'quality of law' standard. As the Court stated in the *Sunday Times* case:

> Firstly, the law must be adequately accessible: the citizen must be able to have an indication that is adequate in the circumstances of the legal rules applicable to a given case. Secondly, a norm cannot be regarded as a 'law' unless it is formulated with sufficient precision to enable the citizen to regulate his conduct: he must be able—if need be with appropriate advice—to foresee, to a degree that is reasonable in the circumstances, the consequences which a given action may entail.[140]

The standard has been applied in a number of subsequent decisions. In *Hashman and Harrup* v *UK*[141] the applicants had been bound over to keep the peace and be of good

---

[137] See, e.g., *Kolender* v *Lawson* (1983) 103 S Ct 1855; the Supreme Court of Canada applied the principle in *Prostitution Reference* (1990) 77 CR (3d) 1.　　[138] *Kokkinakis* v *Greece* (1994) 17 EHRR 397, para. 52.

[139] *Kokkinakis* v *Greece* (1994) 17 EHRR 397, para. 40.

[140] *Sunday Times* v *UK* (1979) 2 EHRR 245, para. 49; see generally Emmerson, Ashworth, and Macdonald, n 104, ch 16.　　[141] (2000) 30 EHRR 241.

behaviour after disturbing a fox-hunt by blowing horns. The Strasbourg Court held that their Art. 10 right to freedom of expression had been breached by the binding over, since the interference with their right was not 'prescribed by law' inasmuch as the relevant law did not meet the 'quality of law' standard. The applicants had been bound over after a finding that they acted *contra bonos mores*, which was defined as behaviour that is 'wrong rather than right in the judgment of the majority of contemporary citizens'.[142] The Court held that this did not meet the standard because it failed to describe the impugned behaviour at all, whereas other provisions (such as conduct likely to provoke a breach of the peace) are acceptable because they describe behaviour 'by reference to its effects'.[143]

It remains unclear how far the 'quality of law' standard may be used to challenge various offences under English law. Many offences in the Theft Acts include a requirement that the defendant acted dishonestly, a concept that plainly does not, 'describe behaviour by reference to its effects'. The Court in *Hashman and Harrup* stated that the offences turning on dishonesty were different because dishonesty 'is but one element of a more comprehensive definition of the proscribed behaviour'.[144] Even if that is true, following leading House of Lords decisions,[145] it would hardly apply to a new general offence of dishonesty or of deception, as the Law Commission concluded.[146] There is considerable uncertainty of definition in common law offences such as cheating[147] and perverting the course of justice (although the conduct is defined by reference to its effects),[148] and they should be scrutinized in the light of Art. 7's requirements. When the House of Lords examined the offence of public nuisance in *Rimmington and Goldstein* (2006),[149] it narrowed the definition of the offence in order to avoid uncertainty, and Lord Bingham approved the statement (in a case of perverting the course of justice) that, if the ambit of a common law offence is to be enlarged, it 'must be done step by step on a case by case basis and not with one large leap'.[150] This is consistent with the Strasbourg position.

Why should such emphasis be placed on certainty, predictability, and 'fair warning'? As with the principle of non-retroactivity, a person's ability to know of the existence and extent of a rule is fundamental. Respect for the citizen as a rational, autonomous individual and as a person with social and political duties, requires fair warning of the criminal law's provisions and no undue difficulty in ascertaining them. The criminal law will also achieve this respect more fully if its provisions keep close to moral distinctions that are both theoretically defensible and widely understood by lay people.[151] A connected reason in favour of the principle of maximum certainty is that, if rules are

---

[142] *Hughes* v *Holley* (1988) 86 Cr App R 130.

[143] *Steel* v *UK* (1999) 28 EHRR 603 thus upheld the definition of 'breach of the peace', even though there remains some uncertainty in the definitions offered by the courts.

[144] (2000) 30 EHRR 241, para. 39.   [145] See the discussion of *Gomez* and *Hinks* in Chapter 9.2.

[146] Law Commission Consultation Paper (LCCP) No. 155, *Fraud and Deception* (1999), Parts V and VI; cf. the proposals in Law Com No. 276, *Fraud* (2002), which led to the Fraud Act 2006 (see Chapter 10.8), and which seek to avoid this problem by deploying an inchoate mode of drafting.

[147] *Pattni* et al. [2001] Crim LR 570.   [148] *Cotter* [2002] Crim LR 824.

[149] [2005] UKHL 63.

[150] [2005] UKHL 63, para. 33, quoting from *Clark* [2003] 2 Cr App R 363, para. 12.

[151] J. Gardner, 'Rationality and the Rule of Law in Offences Against the Person' [1994] Camb LJ 502.

vaguely drafted, they bestow considerable power on the agents of law enforcement:[152] the police or other agencies might use a widely framed offence to criminalize behaviour not envisaged by the legislature, creating the very kind of arbitrariness that rule-of-law values should guard against.

It will be noticed, however, that the principle is stated in a circumscribed form—the principle of *maximum* certainty, not *absolute* certainty—which indicates the compromise already inherent in the principle. In its pure form, the 'rule of law' would insist on complete certainty and predictability, but this is unattainable—'vagueness is ineliminable from a legal system, if a legal system must do such things as to regulate the use of violence . . .'.[153] Unless the criminal law occasionally resorts to such open-ended terms as 'reasonable' and 'dishonest', it would have to rely on immensely detailed and lengthy definitions which might be so complicated as to restrict the intelligibility of the law. As Timothy Endicott argues, neither vagueness nor discretion is necessarily a deficit in the rule of law, so long as the law can perform its function of guiding behaviour.[154] Even so, any government claim that a derogation from maximum certainty is necessary for the practical administration of the law must be scrutinized carefully. Thus those who adhere to the principle of maximum certainty would insist that the use of vague terms should be reinforced by other definitional elements, guidelines, or illustrative examples which inform the citizen and structure the court's discretion.[155]

(f) RULE OF LAW PRINCIPLES: THE PRINCIPLE OF STRICT 'CONSTRUCTION'

Two of the principles which are often brought under the umbrella of the principle of legality have already been discussed (non-retroactivity, maximum certainty); the principle of strict construction is the third. The difference here is that whereas the non-retroactivity principle applies to the lawmaking activities of Parliament and the courts, this principle relates to the courts' task in interpreting legislation. The formulation of the principle is a matter for debate. In its bald form, it appears to state that any doubt in the meaning of a statutory provision should, by strict construction, be resolved in favour of the defendant. One justification for this may be fair warning: where a person acts on the apparent meaning of a statute but the court gives it a wider meaning, it is unfair to convict that person because that would amount to retroactive lawmaking. Historically speaking, the principle seems to have originated either as a means of softening the effect of statutes requiring capital punishment, through the notion of construction *in favorem vitae*,[156] or as a response to statutory incursions into the common

---

[152] See the Home Office study of policing practice in Chapter 1, n 7.

[153] T. Endicott, 'The Impossibility of the Rule of Law' (1999) 19 OJLS 1, 6.

[154] Endicott, n 153, 17–18.

[155] E.g. the problem of defining the conduct element in attempts: see Chapter 11.3.

[156] L. Hall, 'Strict or Liberal Construction of Penal Statutes' (1935) 48 Harv LR 748. Similar reasoning (deriving more from the value of liberty than from capital punishment) may underlie the principle of giving the benefit to the accused when the Court of Appeal is faced with conflicting precedents: *Taylor* [1950] 2 KB 368.

law—which in turn led Parliament to enact more detailed, subdivided offences of the kind that still survive in the Offences Against the Person Act 1861.[157] Nonetheless, the early law was tolerably clear about the importance of the principle. In the words of Lord Esher MR:

> We must be very careful in construing this section, because it imposes a penalty. If there is a reasonable interpretation that will avoid the penalty, we must adopt that construction. If there are two reasonable constructions, we must give the more lenient one. That is the settled rule for the construction of penal sections.[158]

The status of the principle of strict construction is unclear. It has some connection with Art. 7 of the Convention in that, as we saw earlier, the Court has held that the non-retroactivity principle requires that the criminal law must not be extensively construed to an accused's detriment, for instance by analogy.[159] However, it is not clear how and when the Court would apply this principle. References to a principle of strict construction have been fitful both in England and the USA, leading to the claim that it is invoked more to justify decisions reached on other grounds than as a significant principle in its own right.[160] There is certainly no difficulty in assembling a list of cases in which it appears to have been ignored.[161] However, it may be that it was not properly understood in its more sophisticated form in England, since it is relatively recently that a sequence of principles to be applied when interpreting criminal statutes has been established. According to the House of Lords, the proper approach is not to be bound by any particular dictionary definition of a crucial word in a statute, but rather to construe a legislative provision in accordance with the perceived purpose of that statute.[162] In order to assist in ascertaining that purpose, a court may consult a Hansard report of proceedings in Parliament, a government White Paper, or the report of a law-reform committee so as to ascertain the gap in the law which the legislation was intended to remedy.[163] Having said that, if a Convention point arises, it is not a question of seeking the intention of Parliament but rather of applying s. 3 of the Human Rights Act 1998 and interpreting the statute, so far as possible, so as to comply with the Convention. Modern decisions appear to treat the principle of strict construction as a permissive principle,[164] albeit one of considerable weight, meaning that it can be outweighed by other principled considerations in construing statutes imposing criminal or civil penalty sanctions.[165]

---

[157] See Chapter 8.3.   [158] *Tuck v Priester* (1887) 19 QBD 629, 631.

[159] *Kokkinakis v Greece* (1994) 17 EHRR 397, para. 52, cited at n 138.

[160] J. C. Jeffries, 'Legality, Vagueness and the Construction of Penal Statutes' (1985) 71 Virginia LR 189.

[161] E.g. *Gomez* [1993] AC 442 and *Hinks* [2001] 2 AC 241 in the House of Lords, and many Court of Appeal decisions.

[162] *Attorney-General's Reference (No. 1 of 1988)* (1989) 89 Cr App R 60, affirming the Court of Appeal's decision at (1989) 88 Cr App R 191. *Attorney General v Associated Newspapers Ltd* [1994] 2 AC 238 (HL); *R v Z (Attorney General for Northern Ireland's Reference)* [2005] UKHL 35.

[163] Cf. *Black-Clawson International v Papierwerke Waldhof-Aschaffenber AG* [1975] AC 591 with *Pepper v Hart* [1993] AC 593.   [164] On permissive principles, see section 4.1.

[165] *Bogdanic v Home Office* [2014] EWHC 2872; *R v Z (Attorney General for Northern Ireland's Reference)* [2005] UKHL 35.

Those who disagree with the principle have sought to ridicule it by arguing that no system of criminal law can function adequately if absolutely every ambiguity has to be resolved in favour of the defendant.[166] But this line of attack misunderstands the true role of the principle, which has now been reasserted in the courts. Its proper place is in a sequence of points to be considered by a judge when construing a statutory offence. It will be an important advance in the development of English criminal law if other courts routinely follow the approach now established by the House of Lords, although the evidence suggests that neither courts nor counsel consider statutory interpretation to be a discrete subject with its own approach and its own precedents.[167] However, there are further important questions of interpretation to which no authoritative approach has been established. For example, uncertainty still prevails over the proper approach to interpreting statutory offences which do not include a fault requirement in their definition. The courts are still without a coherent approach to the question of strict liability, and no sooner is a high-sounding ('constitutional') principle declared than other courts ignore or circumvent it.

4.5 THE AUTHORITARIAN PRINCIPLE

As indicated earlier, the authoritarian principle holds that a wide-reaching and flexible criminal law is justified, if it ensures that wrongdoing worthy of criminalization can more easily be brought within the scope of offences. So, the authoritarian approach weakens the certainty demands of the activity-based dimension to the rule of law discussed earlier.[168] An example of such authoritarianism is the government's decision, against the recommendation of the Law Commission, to retain the very vague common law offence of 'conspiracy to defraud'.[169] The government believed that prosecutors needed the flexibility that this offence provides, even though in the fast-moving world of financial transactions that means it will be difficult for traders to know what amounts to a criminal form of financial misdealing. In theoretical terms, in this respect, authoritarian-minded judges have developed a counterpoint to the maximum certainty principle, the 'thin ice' principle. This follows Lord Morris's observation in *Knuller* v *DPP*[170] that, when it comes to definition of offences, 'those who skate on thin ice can hardly expect to find a sign which will denote the precise spot where he [sic] will fall in'.[171] The essence of this principle seems to be that citizens who know that their conduct is on the borderline of illegality take the risk that their behaviour will be held to be criminal. Another popular phrase for this would be 'sailing close to the wind'. On occasions the courts have applied this principle both to the creation of a new offence and to the extension of an existing offence.[172]

---

[166] Jeffries, n 160, and Law Com No. 177, para. 3.17.

[167] For fuller discussion see A. Ashworth, 'Interpreting Criminal Statutes: a Crisis of Legality?' (1991) 107 LQR 419, cited with approval in *Bogdanic* v *Home Office* [2014] EWHC 2872.

[168] See section 4.1.

[169] See Chapter 10.9.

[170] See n 129.

[171] [1973] AC 435.

[172] For the former see *Shaw* v *DPP* [1962] AC 220; for the latter see *Tan* [1983] QB 1053.

Putting legal flexibility into practice requires that officials—judges, police, prosecutors—be entrusted with additional kinds of discretion to the kinds discussed in Chapter 1, leading to the weakening of certainty and protection for rights in what might be called the 'investigative' dimension to the rule of law, as well as in the adjudicative dimension to the rule of law discussed earlier.[173] Under the authoritarian principle, police and prosecutors must be willing to use their discretion to test the limits of the law by bringing prosecutions in borderline cases where wrongdoing was perceived to be serious or harm done significant (or both).[174] A number of important laws are vague enough to leave room for the law enforcement agents to apply them to new forms of anti-social action: for example, the public order offences in the Acts of 1986 and 1994.[175]

Contrariwise, though, police and prosecutors should also seek to ensure that widely drafted laws are not used in an oppressive manner against those whose wrongdoing was slight or who did little harm (or both), not so much out of concern for human rights, but rather, lest the law be brought into disrepute and its authority questioned. An example where the government opted for the latter kind of authoritarian approach was in relation to the crime of engaging in sexual touching with someone under the age of sixteen, where both participants were themselves teenagers.[176] Rejecting clearer, rule-based solutions to this morally complex issue, the government decided to put its trust in the use of discretion by law enforcement agencies not to prosecute where the public interest in doing so was negligible.[177] To the objection that such crimes delegate far too much *de facto* power over citizens' lives to law enforcement agents, proponents of authoritarianism would reply that this should be tackled by means of internal guidelines and police disciplinary procedures rather than by depriving the police and courts of the means of invoking the criminal sanction against conduct which arouses social concern. The offences themselves appear to be worded objectively and neutrally (although they suffer from over-breadth) but their use may be selective, and not necessarily in a good way. So far as the judiciary are concerned, the classic statement of the authoritarian principle is to be found in the speech of Viscount Simonds in *DPP v Shaw*:[178]

> [T]here is in [the King's Bench] a residual power, where no statute has yet intervened to supersede the common law, to superintend those offences which are prejudicial to the public welfare. Such occasions will be rare, for Parliament has not been slow to legislate when attention has been sufficiently aroused. But gaps remain and will always remain since no one can foresee every way in which the wickedness of man may disrupt the order of society. I say, my Lords, that if the common law is powerless in such an event, then we should

---

[173] See section 4.1.   [174] As in *R v R* [1992] AC 599: see the discussion in the text at n 133.

[175] As confirmed by the Home Office research by D. Brown and T, Ellis, *Policing Low-Level Disorder: Police Use of Section 5 of the Public Order Act 1986* (1994), and by T. Bucke and Z. James, *Trespass and Protest: Policing under the Criminal Justice and Public Order Act 1994* (1998).

[176] Sexual Offences Act 2003, s. 9.

[177] For discussion, see J. Spencer QC, 'Child and Family Offences' [2004] Crim LR 930; N. Lacey, 'Beset by Boundaries: The Home Office Review of Sex Offences' [2001] Crim LR 3.

[178] [1962] AC 220.

no longer do her reverence. But I say that her hand is still powerful and that it is for Her Majesty's Judges to play the part which Lord Mansfield pointed out to them.[179]

In so saying, Viscount Simonds denied that this power involved a power to create new criminal offences. Instead, he was defending the power of the courts to invite a jury to apply a vaguely worded common law offence—conspiracy to corrupt public morals, in this case—to new circumstances. With such a vaguely worded offence, the difference between these positions is wafer thin; but it is true that the authoritarian principle does not entail permitting judges to create wholly new criminal offences, recognizing that this is the task of the democratic legislature.

One reason for the persistence and influence of the authoritarian principle is that it can to some extent be made consistent with the separation of powers and functions between the different branches of government. So, it is possible to be authoritarian about the role of the judiciary, and yet accept the following kinds of reasons for denying to the judiciary an extensive law-making role. In individual cases, judges cannot consult widely (indeed, hardly at all) with experts in the field, with interest groups, or with members of the public affected by the decision. Judges are also in practice limited in the range of relevant evidence that they can bring to bear on their decision, and in the time that they have to devote to the issues before their decision must be made. Additionally, judges have no power to insist that the rules they create, on the basis of predictions of what will happen with or without those rules in place, be systematically subjected to empirical testing or to regular, periodic reconsideration in the light of experience.[180] Judges do not have such a power, in part because this more holistic approach to law reform is meant to be a characteristic feature of legislative, not judicial, law reform. It is true that parliamentary intervention to correct or improve on judicial law-making is spasmodic, frequently unsatisfactory in that the cure turns out to be worse than the disease,[181] and is often itself unaccompanied by post-legislative scrutiny to determine the effects the intervention has brought about.[182] But in relation to a matter of such constitutional significance as the reach of the criminal law, it is with Parliament—warts and all—that the responsibility should lie for creating new criminal offences. As Lord Bingham put it in *Jones*:

> [I]it is for those representing the people of the country in Parliament, and not the executive and not the judges, to decide what conduct should be treated as lying so far outside the bounds of what is acceptable in our society as to attract criminal penalties.[183]

---

[179] [1962] AC 220, at 225.

[180] For example, the stringency of the rules governing the admissibility of evidence of voluntary intoxication in support of a defendant's exculpatory plea has been supported by judges on the policy basis that, without such stringency, 'public order [may] be threatened' (Lord Simon, in *DPP v Majewski* [1976] 2 WLR 640, at 641). Yet, evidence has subsequently suggested that the stringency of these rule has no proven connection with the level of alcohol-fuelled criminality: G. Dingwall, *Alcohol and Crime* (2013), 136.

[181] For an entertaining as well as helpfully critical evaluation, in this respect, see J. Spencer, 'The Drafting of Criminal Legislation: Need it be so Impenetrable?' (2008) 67 Cambridge LJ 585.

[182] See <www.parliament.uk/documents/commons/Scrutiny/csupostlegscrutiny.pdf>.

[183] [2007] 1 AC 136, at [29]; cf. also Lord Bingham in *Rimmington and Goldstein* [2006] 1 AC 549 (HL), at 33; *Norris v Government of USA* [2008] UKHL 16, at 55–6.

Nonetheless, that still leaves the important issue of whether, and to what extent, judges should use their interpretive powers to develop the existing law. A driving force behind the early-twentieth century intellectual development of criminal law studies at Cambridge[184] was resistance to two entrenched features of the legal landscape: the persistence of outcome-based criminal liability,[185] and the power of the judiciary to extend and develop existing offences. In relation to the latter—especially when common law crimes were in issue—the famous writer, critic, and law reformer Glanville Williams sought, in Benthamite fashion, to be the intellectual scourge of the judiciary.[186] Williams brushed aside those, like judge and jurist Sir James Stephen, who had sought to defend the way in which, by the end of the nineteenth century, the criminal law had developed, 'by very slow degrees and with absolutely no conscious adaptation of means to ends . . . [possessing] an internal organic unity . . . wanting in the [French] system'.[187] Instead, Glanville Williams argued, as Bentham had done, that

> [T]he expansion of the law [by judges is unavowed . . . the judges keeping up the pretence that they are mere mouthpieces of the law . . . [whereas] to the discerning eye [a judicial decision] is often no more than . . . rationalisation accompanied by misdirection and legerdemain.[188]

Such extreme views have always been overstated, and look dated to the modern eye, not only in virtue of the greatly increased professionalism of the judiciary, but also in virtue of the fact that Parliament itself relies—and must rely—on the exercise of judicial discretion in many important contexts, not least that of human rights.[189] The real problem is not so much the maintenance of a judicial 'pretence' that judges are no more than law-appliers. One very real problem is that, in an age when Parliament has long committed itself to the improvement of the law (if need be, through specialized agencies[190]), Parliament too often simply will not take the initiative to reform the law. Parliament too often rests content to leave judges to sort out important and intractable legal problems through the haphazard medium of case law development. Three important areas where this is so are the development of the law of complicity in murder cases,[191] the termination of life support,[192] and the law of murder and manslaughter.[193]

---

[184] See the discussion in Chapter 3.1.

[185] Liability based on the consequences caused, rather than on the fault of the offender in relation to what was done. For an important early Cambridge critique, see J. W. C. Turner, 'The Mental Element in Crimes at Common Law' (1936) 6 CLJ 31. See further Chapter 8.5.

[186] See G. Williams, *Textbook of Criminal Law* (2nd edn., 1983).

[187] Sir James Stephen, *A History of the Criminal Law of England*, vol. I (Macmillan and Co, 1883), 565.

[188] Williams, n 186, 16.

[189] See the discussion of the declaration of incompatibility in the text at n 111.

[190] See, e.g., the Law Commission Act 1965, s. 3: 'It shall be the duty of each of the Commissions to take and keep under review all the law with which they are respectively concerned with a view to its systematic development and reform, including in particular the codification of such law, the elimination of anomalies, the repeal of obsolete and unnecessary enactments, the reduction of the number of separate enactments and generally the simplification and modernisation of the law . . .'

[191] See Chapter 11.

[192] See Chapter 5.4.

[193] See Chapter 8.

Another more recent problem has been the ironic transformation of human rights law into an opportunity for authoritarian government. We have already seen that the European Court was quite content to say about non-retroactivity and the demands of Art. 7(1), that it is consistent with judicial creativity when:

> the existing elements of an offence [are] . . . clarified or adapted to new circumstances or developments in society in so far as this can reasonably be brought under the original concept of the offence . . . [so long as] progressive development by way of interpretation [is] reasonably foreseeable to [the defendant] with the assistance of appropriate legal advice if necessary.[194]

In so finding, the European Court gave scant attention to the problems besetting judicial creativity in this matter, set out earlier.[195] Moreover, what if someone has no access to legal advice in advance of acting, because they cannot afford it? The court's gloss on Art. 7 is perfectly consistent with adherence to the authoritarian 'thin ice' principle in the creation and interpretation of the criminal law.

At a more fundamental level, some of the 'protections' offered by basic human rights law are, in fact, also perfectly consistent with authoritarian government. An example is Art. 10 of the ECHR, which like Art. 8 (concerned with the protection of private and family life) makes freedom of expression subject to the following exceptions when it can be overridden:

> The exercise of these freedoms, since it carries with it duties and responsibilities, may be subject to such formalities, conditions, restrictions or penalties as are prescribed by law and are necessary in a democratic society, in the interests of national security, territorial integrity or public safety, for the prevention of disorder or crime, for the protection of health or morals, for the protection of the reputation or rights of others, for preventing the disclosure of information received in confidence, or for maintaining the authority and impartiality of the judiciary.

Were it not for the fig-leaf protection provided by the requirement that a restriction on expression be, 'necessary in a democratic society' (itself a highly contestable issue), there would be little here to trouble, and much to please, an out-and-out authoritarian. Even as it stands, Art. 10 clearly opens the path to the suppression of free speech under what was criticized at the end of Chapter 2 as 'militant democracy'. In virtue of being bound by the terms of Art. 10, judges must necessarily regard themselves as the agents of militant democracy, rather than as a bulwark against it.

The English judiciary has itself considered what maxims should govern their interpretive powers to develop the criminal law. In *C v DPP*,[196] Lord Lowry articulated five criteria for judicial lawmaking:

(1) if the solution is doubtful, the judges should beware of imposing their own remedy;

(2) caution should prevail if Parliament has rejected opportunities for clearing up a known difficulty, or has legislated leaving the difficulty untouched;

---

[194] *SW and CR v UK* (1995) 21 EHRR 363.   [195] See section 4.4(c) and (f).
[196] [1996] AC 1, at 28.

(3) disputed matters of social policy are less suitable areas for judicial intervention than purely legal problems;

(4) fundamental legal doctrines should not lightly be set aside;

(5) judges should not make a change unless they can achieve finality and certainty.

These are important principles, focusing on the constitutional aspects of judicial law-making, and they strike an important counter-authoritarian note, although strangely, Art. 7 was not mentioned as it should have been. Lord Lowry's criteria were cited when the Court of Appeal declined to change and to broaden the basis of corporate criminal liability.[197]

The authoritarian principle is not just a principle focused on placing trust in criminal justice officials to exercise wide discretionary powers in the public interest, although we should note, in this regard, that authoritarians tend to be resistant to the extension of this trust to juries acting in their capacity as official representatives of the public. It rests equally on an inherent *dis*trust of those who challenge prosecution or conviction by, for example, insisting that the prosecution prove its case without defence assistance, or by seeking to rely on an excuse or permission for breaches of the law. For example, the authoritarian principle supports the argument that ignorance of the criminal law should be no excuse. English law authorizes the conviction of persons who were unaware of the existence of a crime, even in circumstances where it would have been difficult for them to find out that they were committing it.[198] This derogation from the notions of maximum certainty and fair warning is supported by authoritarians who suggest that, if the defence were allowed, everyone would claim it and there would be large-scale acquittals. Such arguments should be regarded as unpersuasive but the basis for these arguments is of some theoretical interest.[199] The authoritarian principle is constructed on a foundation known as the 'bad man' theory of law (echoes of which are to be found in the speech of Viscount Simonds, in the passage cited earlier from *DPP* v *Shaw*). According to this theory, most famously propounded by American poet, physician, and jurist Oliver Wendell Holmes:[200]

> If you want to know the law and nothing else, you must look at it as a bad man, who cares only for the material consequences which such knowledge enables him to predict, not as a good one, who finds his reasons for conduct, whether inside the law or outside of it, in the vaguer sanctions of conscience.

Building on this 'bad man' theory of law, the authoritarian principle holds that one should devise rules on the assumption that the people to whom they apply will exploit them for their selfish ends. For authoritarians, the people targeted by the criminal justice system will always (a) be seeking to find gaps through which to escape conviction un-meritoriously, (b) making proof of guilt difficult for the prosecution even when

---

[197] In *Attorney-General's Reference (No. 2 of 1999)* [2000] 2 Cr App R 207, per Rose LJ, at 218.

[198] Discussed in Chapter 7.5.

[199] A. Ashworth, 'Ignorance of the Criminal Law, and Duties to Avoid It' (2011) 74 MLR 1, and Chapter 7.5.

[200] O. Wendell Holmes, 'The Path of the Law' (1897) 10 *Harvard Law Review* 457.

they are guilty, or (c) making bogus claims to a defence. So, the courts have resisted claims to excuse based on ignorance of the law on the (questionable) assumption that too many will try to exploit that excuse in doubtful cases. The courts have refused to recognize the excuse on the basis that someone who claims ignorance of the law as an excuse might in fact have been a 'good man', acting on a reasonable and honest understanding of his or her entitlement to act. As H. L. A. Hart said, responding to Holmes argument, 'why should not law be equally if not more concerned with the "puzzled man" or "ignorant man" who is willing to do what is required . . .?'.[201]

As an example, the authoritarian principle can also be seen at work in the neglect of the presumption of innocence by the legislature. Article 6(2) of the Convention declares that 'everyone charged with a criminal offence shall be presumed innocent until proved guilty according to law'. However, in English law, many offences are defined in such a way that the prosecution has to prove little, and then the defence bears the burden of exculpation. Section 101 of the Magistrates' Courts Act 1980 places on the defendant the burden of proving any excuse, exemption, proviso, or qualification in the definition of an offence tried summarily, a regime that is usually justified on grounds of expediency and economy. Neglect of the presumption is not confined to so-called regulatory offences: some 40 per cent of offences triable in the Crown Court—that is, the most serious offences in English law—place a burden of proof on the defendant.[202] It seems that the presumption has been so insignificant to policymakers and legislators that often they have not even regarded it as necessary to give a reason for placing a burden on the defence.[203]

Of course, there can be good reason to impose a burden of proof on the defendant. Certain matters are much easier for one party to prove than the other: it is generally far easier for a defendant to prove that he or she had a licence or permit than for the prosecution to prove the absence of one.[204] However, under the influence of the authoritarian principle, such a view can easily shade into the far less persuasive argument that D should prove any matter that 'lies within his own peculiar knowledge'.[205] That proposition might equally apply to intention, knowledge, and many other core elements of crimes. If taken at face value, it would thus undermine the presumption of innocence completely. This wider justification for reverse burdens embodies a viewpoint central to the authoritarian principle. This is that the law should be shaped to reflect the view that the 'bad' people targeted by the criminal justice system exploit difficulties that the prosecution will encounter proving matters within their (the bad people's) knowledge. So, the law must respond by adopting rules to counter such 'bad man' strategies.

What is wrong with the authoritarian principle? The principle is based on the idea that the state and its authorities were created to protect the law-abiding from wrongdoing by 'bad citizens'. Under the authoritarian principle, good citizens place their trust in

---

[201] H. L. A. Hart, *The Concept of Law* (1961), 39.

[202] A. Ashworth and M. Blake, 'The Presumption of Innocence in English Criminal Law' [1996] Crim LR 306.

[203] But see *R v Lambert* [2001] 3 WLR 206; *Attorney-General's Reference No. 4 of 2002* [2004] UKHL 43.

[204] See *Hunt* [1987] AC 352, discussed by J. C. Smith, 'The Presumption of Innocence' (1987) 38 NILQ 223, and by P. Roberts and A. A. S. Zuckerman, *Criminal Evidence* (2010), ch 6.

[205] Unfortunately even Lord Bingham in *Sheldrake v DPP* [2004] UKHL 43 relied on this flawed argument.

state authorities to act in the public interest when seeking to prevent such wrongdoing. This conception of society, and of how to protect the (largely mythical) law-abiding classes has a long history. For example, Magistrate and reformer Patrick Colquhoun wrote in 1800, in advocating the establishment of a police force for London, that London's crime 'problem' was due to:

> The enlarged state of Society, the vast extent of moving property, and the unexampled wealth of the Metropolis, joined to the depraved habits and loose conduct of a great proportion of the lower classes of the people; and above all, the want of an appropriate Police applicable to the object of prevention.[206]

In this respect, amongst many questionable assumptions made by the authoritarian theory, there is no coherent distinction that can be drawn between good and bad citizens. 'Good' citizens may also find themselves guilty of offences if, for example, they are convicted in spite of a perfectly reasonable ignorance of the law, if liability for the offence in question can be incurred without any fault (strict liability offences), of if they had no access to the legal advice that would have indicated that a proposed course of conduct might be ruled criminal by a court, using its inherent power to develop the law.[207] Moreover, the authoritarian principle operates in a 'top-down' way through its focus on the discretionary powers of authorities. It is thus in tension with a 'bottom-up' approach to criminalization, in which the focus is on clarifying the scope and nature of the freedom of the individual or company who may be subject to punitive state power, and hence on maximizing the certainty of the obligations that limit or define that freedom. As Philip Pettit memorably explains the point more generally, laws should be designed with certainty as a high priority so that people within the jurisdiction:

> Do not have to bow or scrape, toady or kowtow, fawn or flatter; they do not have to placate any others [such as the police or the CPS] with beguiling smiles or mincing steps. In short they do not have to live on their wits, whether out of fear or deference . . . [By contrast, they can] . . . walk tall among [their] fellows, conscious of sharing in the general recognition that no one can push [them] around with an expectation of impunity.[208]

4.6 IMPRISONMENT: AUTHORITARIANISM, THE RULE OF LAW, AND THE PROPORTIONALITY PRINCIPLE

In simple terms, the 'proportionality' principle requires that sentences—and in particular, the possibility of, and the length of, a sentence of imprisonment for a crime— be proportionate to the seriousness of the wrongful (threat of) harm. Naturally, in

---

[206] P. Colquhoun, *A Treatise on the Police of the Metropolis* (6th edn., 1800), 4.
[207] See section 4.4(d).
[208] P. Petit, 'Criminalisation in Republican Theory', in R. A. Duff et al. (eds.), *Criminalisation: The Political Morality of the Criminal Law* (Oxford University Press, 2014) 132, 138.

any individual case, the judge is under an obligation to weigh a large range of factors in coming to a decision about sentence that is, overall, within the bounds of proportionality; but we are concerned here with the broader issue of the framework within which such decisions are taken. For example, the fact that breach of an injunction to prevent nuisance and annoyance (contrary to the Anti-Social Behaviour Crime and Policing Act 2014) may end in a sentence of imprisonment of up to five years is disproportionate, not least because 'nuisance and annoyance' need involve no criminal offence in itself.[209] Alongside this well-known example, we should also note the less well-known predilection of government departments for using a 'standard' two-year maximum sentence for many offences under statute. A large array of provisions covering completely different issues—such as s. 389 of the Companies Act 2006, s. 15 of The Cattle Identification Regulations 2007, s. 13 of The Consumer Protection from Unfair Trading Regulations 2008, ss. 22 and 23 of The Energy Act 2008, and s. 34(4) of The Export Control Order 2008[210]—all have this two-year maximum sentence upon conviction in the Crown Court. The suspicion must be that the two-year maximum has become an off-the-peg solution to regulatory offences of middle-ranging seriousness, without a great deal of consideration having been given to the appropriateness of that maximum. For example, can it really be right that, whereas breach of an injunction to prevent nuisance and annoyance order carries a five-year maximum sentence, if someone knowingly transfers software goods that are destined for use outside the customs territory for the manufacture of weapons of mass destruction,[211] that offence carries only a two-year maximum sentence?[212]

Putting aside the issue of inconsistency in punishment as between offences of different types, the use of excessive maximum sentences of imprisonment is another manifestation of the authoritarian principle. Imprisonment is the harshest punitive measure that can be imposed on an individual committing an offence within the UK's criminal jurisdiction. One of the state's highest priorities when creating criminal offences should be the avoidance of greater-than-warranted discretion, granted to the judiciary, to impose such a punishment; but there is no evidence that avoiding this looms large on the mental map of UK legislators. In this, as in other criminal law matters influenced by the authoritarian principle, the state risks subjecting people to what has been called a kind of unacceptable 'domination' of those under its jurisdiction, domination in tension with the rule of law. According to Philip Pettit, the trouble with state (or any kind of) domination is that it increases, 'exposure to another's power of uncontrolled influence'.[213] The longer a maximum sentence, the greater such influence inevitably

---

[209] See A. Ashworth, 'Social Control and "Anti-Social Behaviour": the Subversion of Human Rights' (2004) 120 LQR 263.

[210] See also the General Food Regulations 2004, discussed in section 4.1.

[211] Export Control Order 2008.

[212] It is the task of the Sentencing Council in England and Wales to promote greater consistency in sentencing, but that usually means consistency as between different judges passing sentence for the same or similar offences countrywide; it does not normally mean reviewing the statute book to root out examples of excessive maxima: <www.sentencingcouncil.org.uk/>.

[213] P. Pettit, *On the People's Terms: A Republican Theory and Model of Democracy* (Cambridge University Press, 2012), 22 and 28.

becomes, even when the sentencing process is governed by sentencing guidelines, and subject to appeals against sentence.[214] On a moderate authoritarian view, the exercise of judicial discretion within a framework of long maximum sentences is acceptable, so long as there is a safety net against arbitrariness or abuse constituted by sentencing guidelines and an appeal process. Contrariwise, the proportionality principle dictates that it is wrong even to create the possibility of over-long maximum sentences, whether or not they will in practice ever be used.

In this respect, the requirements of the proportionality principle may seem vague, but they can easily be given concrete content. For example, one way to counter authoritarian tendencies is to prevent the possibility of imprisonment, or at least the possibility of sentencing in the Crown Court, being created through secondary legislation, rather than through primary legislation.[215] In that regard, s. 1054 of the Companies Act 2006 provides an excellent model of how to prevent 'discretion-creep' in relation to the ever-greater numbers of imprisonable offences created by regulations in England and Wales:

(2) Regulations under this Part may make provision for offence . . .

(3) The regulations must not provide—

(a) for imprisonment, or

(b) for the imposition on summary conviction of a fine exceeding level 5 on the standard scale and, for continued contravention, a daily default fine not exceeding one-tenth of level 5 on the standard scale.

Alongside this proposal, it is also strongly arguable that it should not be possible to imprison someone for a wholly strict liability offence, an offence that can be committed without any fault on the offender's part or without a sufficiently general defence, such as 'due diligence' shown.[216] For example, there is the offence committed by anyone who, 'has in his possession, or purchases or acquires, or manufactures, sells or transfers' any prohibited firearm.[217] The offence sounds serious, and carries a maximum sentence of ten years' imprisonment, and (for the most part) a minimum sentence of five years' imprisonment.[218] Yet, there is no requirement in the offence that the defendant was aware that the firearm he or she had in his or her possession, transferred, bought or sold was a prohibited firearm: even a reasonable belief that the firearm was not prohibited is no excuse.[219] Indeed, it is no excuse even if the defendant's belief was that the item in his or her possession was not a firearm at all.[220] The proportionality principle would

---

[214] <www.sentencingcouncil.org.uk/>. Only about 33 per cent of applications to appeal against sentence are successful before a single judge hearing the application, although if the application is renewed before the full Court of Appeal, the success rate rises to about 70 per cent. Ministry of Justice, *Judicial and Court Statistics, 2010 & 2011*, ch 7. See further, <www.icpr.org.uk/media/36503/transform-justice_appeals-report.pdf>.

[215] See Law Commission, *Criminal Liability in Regulatory Contexts* (CP 195, 2010), para. 3.158.

[216] A. Ashworth, 'Should Strict Liability be Removed from all Imprisonable Offences?' (2010) 45 *Irish Jurist* 1.

[217] Firearms Act 1968, s. 5.

[218] <www.cps.gov.uk/legal/s_to_u/sentencing_manual/section_5_firearms_act/>.

[219] *R v Howells* [1977] QB 614.

[220] *Deyemi and Edwards* (2008) 1 Cr App R 125.

dictate that either (a) this offence be modified to include a fault requirement or general defence, such as the absence of a reasonable excuse, or (b) the offence become one punishable by a fine or other non-custodial punishment, and a new, fault-based offence be created alongside it conviction for which, in virtue of having a fault requirement, can more legitimately be met with a sentence of imprisonment.

In the end, the difference between authoritarians and adherents of the proportionality principle may turn out for the most part to be one of degree, rather than one of kind, but in the field of criminal justice, differences of degree may be of great moral importance.

4.7 PROPORTIONALITY AND THE PRINCIPLES OF OFFENCE CONSTRUCTION

Respecting human dignity entails treating humans as persons capable of planning and plotting their future. Thus, respecting people's dignity includes respecting their autonomy, their right to control their future.[221]

The way that offences are designed—their ingredients—can have a negative impact on human dignity, and on people's prospects for lifestyle autonomy, as Joseph Raz describes them in this passage. For example, it might be argued that strict liability (considered at the end of the last section) disrespects autonomy because almost no plan, however well thought-out in advance, can guarantee that such liability will be avoided. This is especially problematic in cases where the very nature of an activity—driving; running a food manufacturing business—involves more or less constant exposure to the risks of such liability.[222] In the case of businesses, it may be argued that legal constructs such as companies (or public authorities) are not capable of attaining lifestyle autonomy, and do not have 'dignity' to be disrespected. So, it may not be wrong to use strict liability in such cases. Even so, in the case of many businesses involving just one person, or a family, that is a harsh argument, however much sense it may make in relation to big companies.[223] It can be argued that, in regulatory contexts, specialized investigators do not prosecute in strict liability cases unless, in fact, warnings have been given (or there is other evidence of prior fault).[224] Whilst not without merit, we should note that such an argument makes common cause with the authoritarian principle (see section 4.5), in placing reliance on the exercise of official discretion to mitigate the effect of broadly drafted criminal offences.

---

[221] J. Raz, 'The Rule of Law and its Virtue' (1977) 93 LQR 195, 204.

[222] See, e.g., *Smedleys* v *Breed* [1974] AC 839 (HL), where—following a line of argument favourable to the authoritarian principle—the House of Lords urged more use to be made of decisions not to prosecute in such cases.

[223] For discussion, see J. Horder, 'Strict Liability, Statutory Construction and the Spirit of Liberty' (2002) 118 LQR 458.

[224] See the discussion by G. Richardson, 'Strict Liability for Regulatory Crime: The Empirical Research' [1987] Crim LR 295. K. Hawkins, *Law as Last Resort* (Oxford University Press, 2003).

The greater the penalty for committing a strict liability offence, the greater will be the sense that it is disproportionate to impose that penalty when the accused was not at fault. Similarly, there may be proportionality objections to other features of offence construction. An example is 'constructive' liability, where criminal liability is imposed for consequences beyond those that were intended or foreseen, or could reasonably have been foreseen. For instance, someone may be found guilty of manslaughter if they intended to do or foresaw they might do some criminal wrong to the victim (such as a punch or rough push), but by bad luck the victim died as a result of the wrongdoing.[225] Is the imposition of liability for homicide in such as case (carrying with it, the possibility of a maximum life sentence) a fair and proportionate way to construct the crime of manslaughter? This issue will be discussed in Chapter 8.5, along with other moral issues bearing on offence construction, such as the need for fair labelling,[226] and for an adequate degree of correspondence between fault and the external elements of the offence.[227]

FURTHER READING

A. ASHWORTH, 'Interpreting Criminal Statutes: a Crisis of Legality?' (1991) 107 LQR 419.

A. ASHWORTH, 'Should Strict Liability be Removed from all Imprisonable Offences?' (2010) 45 *Irish Jurist* 1.

A. ASHWORTH, 'A Decade of Human Rights in Criminal Justice' [2014] Crim LR 325.

J. CHALMERS, '"Frenzied" Law-Making: Overcriminalisation by Numbers' (2014) 67 *Current Legal Problems* 483.

J. FEINBERG, *Harm to Others* (Oxford University Press, 1984).

J. GARDNER, 'Introduction' to H. L. A. Hart, *Punishment and Responsibility* (2nd edn., Oxford University Press, 2008).

N. LACEY, 'Criminalisation as Regulation: The Role of Criminal Law' in C. Parker et al., *Regulating Law* (Oxford University Press, 2004), ch 7.

C. MURPHY, 'The Principle of Legality in Criminal Law under the European Convention on Human Rights' [2010] *Human Rights Law Review* 192.

A. P. SIMESTER, 'A Disintegrated Theory of Culpability', in D. Baker and J. Horder (eds.), *The Sanctity of Life and the Criminal Law: The Legacy of Glanville Williams* (Cambridge University Press, 2013).

A. P. SIMESTER and A. VON HIRSCH, *Crimes, Harms and Wrongs* (Hart Publishing, 2011), ch 2.

A. VON HIRSCH and A. P. SIMESTER, 'Penalising Offensive Behaviour', in A. von Hirsch and A. P. Simester (eds.), *Incivilities: Regulating Offensive Behaviour* (Hart Publishing, 2006), 120.

L. ZEDNER and J. ROBERTS, *Principles and Values in Criminal Law and Criminal Justice* (Oxford University Press, 2012), chs. 1, 2, 3, and 5.

---

[225] See Chapter 8.5.   [226] See Chapter 6.7(a).
[227] See Chapter 6.4(a).

5

CRIMINAL CONDUCT: *ACTUS REUS*, CAUSATION, AND PERMISSIONS

5.1 THE GENERAL PART OF THE CRIMINAL LAW

This chapter and the following two chapters discuss what it is convenient to refer to as the 'general part' of the criminal law.[1] The general part is comprised in part of 'doctrines' (in the absence of a better word) which can be critically analysed without necessarily referring to the elements of a specific crime. Examples of such doctrines are (a) criminal 'conduct', (b) 'causation', (c) the 'unlawfulness' of conduct (impermissible conduct),[2] (d) varieties of 'fault', (e) 'capacity' to commit a crime, and (f) excuses for criminal wrongdoing. We will deal with (a) to (c) in this chapter, before turning to (d) and (e) in Chapter 6, and (f) in Chapter 7. Not all of these doctrines have the same status or nature, as aspects of the general part of the criminal law. For example, having sufficient physical and rational 'capacity', such that one may be found criminally liable, is what might be called a pre-condition of criminal liability. By contrast, when they are in issue, the conduct, causation, and fault doctrines are doctrines concerned with the defining elements of crimes (although not all crimes necessarily have causation or fault elements).

---

[1] J. Gardner, 'On the General Part of the Criminal Law', in R. A. Duff (ed.), *Philosophy and the Criminal Law* (1998).

[2] Some permissions are very context-specific. See, e.g., the defences to the crime of failing to ensure that a child attends regularly at school: Education Act 1996, s. 444.

In this chapter, we consider what is traditionally referred to by its Latin name as the *'actus reus'* element of crimes. Literally, this means, 'guilty act', but it is a potentially misleading term in that respect. It can be more helpfully broken down into different elements. To begin with, the criminal law sometimes makes it a criminal offence to 'omit' to do something, such as 'leaving' litter that has been dropped,[3] or a failure by a business employee in the regulated sector to report a suspicion that another person is engaged in money laundering.[4] Further, a criminal 'act' can include a 'state of affairs', such as being in possession of something (like an offensive weapon[5]). An act may also not be a 'guilty' act, in relevant sense, unless it has certain consequences (the consequence element), or takes place in certain circumstances (the circumstance element). So, consider the crime of causing, without reasonable excuse, a nuisance or disturbance to a staff member of the NHS working on the premises.[6] Here, the defendant's act (the conduct element) must cause a nuisance or disturbance to a staff member of the NHS (the consequence element), whilst the NHS staff member is working on the premises (circumstance element). In that regard, though, it is important to note that these distinctions—between conduct, consequence, and consequence elements—are drawn largely for the sake of explanatory convenience. In a criminal law case, so long as the prosecution proves that the relevant element was present, it does not matter much whether we call, say, the requirement that the victim be an 'NHS staff member' a consequence or a circumstance element.[7]

Finally, a 'guilty' act must be unlawful, in the sense of being something the defendant lacks permission to do. Some permissions are very context-specific, and we will not be concerned with those here.[8] However, some permissions—like some excuses— are sufficiently general in application to be treated as aspects of the general part of the criminal law. For example, under certain circumstances, even a shooting or stabbing may be permissible—and hence not unlawful—if it is intended to be in self-defence or prevention of crime.[9] Self-defence and prevention of crime are defences that give permission to do a number of what would otherwise be criminal acts (wounding, damaging property, and so on). In relevant cases, the applicability of these permissions is taken for granted: the existence of them is not usually mentioned in the definition of particular criminal offences. However, some offences do mention that the conduct in question will not be criminal if is permissible (or sometimes also, 'excusable', a matter considered in Chapter 7). An example is blackmail, where the wrongful conduct involves making an *unwarranted* demand with 'menaces'.[10]

---

[3] See Environmental Protection Act 1990, s. 87; ch 4.1.   [4] Proceeds of Crime Act 2002, s. 330.

[5] Prevention of Crime Act 1953, s. 1. The offence is committed only if the weapon is possessed in a public place, without reasonable excuse.

[6] Criminal Justice and Immigration Act 2008, s. 119. To commit the offence, the defendant must be on the premises at the time.

[7] Matters may be different when the charge is attempting to commit an offence: see Chapter 12.

[8] For an example, where 'reasonable excuse' must be understood in a context-specific way, see *R v Unah (Flora)* [2011] EWCA Crim 1837.

[9] See, e.g., the Criminal Justice and Immigration Act 2008, s. 76, discussed in section 5.6 later in the chapter.

[10] Theft Act 1968, s. 21(1).

It can be argued that permissions are of more fundamental importance than excuses. Conduct which is permissible gives a defendant a legal right to engage in it in appropriate circumstances, even if the conduct in question involves the intentional infliction of serious harm or even killing. This is quite different in theory from the operation of defences which are excuses, such as duress or mistake, discussed in Chapter 7. Someone seeking excuse concedes that they had no right to do as they did and that their act was wrongful. They nonetheless claim that they should be acquitted because they lacked culpability (in a broad sense) at the time. Where the defendant's act is regarded as permissible (say, in self-defence), the defendant claims the right to have done it.[11] Some of the importance of permissions comes from the fact that they mostly (if not in all cases) give some guidance to citizens on the circumstances in which they are permitted to (say) use force, cause damage, etc. It follows that the legal limits of such permissions ought, in so far as possible, to comply with standards of fair warning.[12]

5.2 INVOLUNTARY CONDUCT

(a) AUTOMATISM AND VOLUNTARINESS

Conduct may be found to have been involuntary on a number of bases.[13] In Chapter 4.3, we examined the theoretical basis for requiring that conduct be 'voluntary', if it is to attract criminal liability. A claim of 'automatism' is a denial of voluntariness, a claim that the ordinary link between mind and behaviour was absent, or that the link had become distorted in some fundamental way.[14] This can occur where what is prohibited by the law only occurred as a result of a set of involuntary movements of the body rather than as a result of voluntary acts. We should begin by noting that something that happens to one's body can be involuntary, without being 'automatic'. An example would be where someone (X) is forcibly seized by another (Y) and physically made to harm the victim or to damage their property. In such a case, Y is the real aggressor, whereas X is guilty of no crime because X's involvement was involuntary: controlled wholly by Y. Such cases are not further discussed here.

The more interesting cases involve behaviour that is involuntary because it is in some sense automatic (using that term fairly loosely). The law's understanding of involuntary—automatic—conduct extends to instinctive reactions, as where the defendant's driving is affected when he or she succumbs to a panic reaction when a swarm of bees enters his or her car. It also includes cases of what might be called 'mental disconnection', where the defendant appears to have control over his or her behaviour,

[11] Cf. J. Gardner, *Offences and Defences* (2007), ch 4.

[12] P. Robinson, 'The Modern General Part: Three Illusions', in S. Shute and A. P. Simester (eds), *Criminal Law Theory: Doctrines of the General Part* (2002); because the permissions guide conduct, M. Moore, *Placing Blame* (1997), ch 1, goes so far as to state that they belong to the 'special part'.

[13] See generally R. D. Mackay, *Mental Condition Defences in the Criminal Law* (Oxford University Press, 1995), ch 1; Law Commission Discussion Paper, *Insanity and Automatism* (2013).

[14] See, generally, H. L. A. Hart, *Punishment and Responsibility* (1968), 107.

but in fact does not. Examples may include committing offences whilst sleepwalking or when affected by serious concussion. Complex behaviour—such as driving—may occur in such cases, but it does not manifest itself in the form of voluntary conduct. Automatism is often regarded as a defence to crime rather than as a denial of an essential component of criminal conduct. Certainly, the discussion that follows has more in common with the treatment of various excuses in Chapter 7 than with the rest of this chapter. However, the common understanding is that automatism undermines the sense in which someone is engaging in 'conduct' at all, and thus amounts to a denial of the conduct element of the crime.[15]

As a matter of 'general part' thinking, the theory is that automatism prevents liability for all crimes. Since all crimes require a form of conduct, or of voluntary control over a state of affairs (as in possession cases), even if some of them do not require fault, it follows that automatism may lead to acquittal on any and every charge. Many of the early cases concerned motoring offences for which strict liability is imposed, and to which automatism is one of the few routes to acquittal. However, since a plea of automatism may apply to all, or almost all, crimes the courts have attempted to circumscribe its use, defining it fairly narrowly and developing major doctrines of limitation.

Where a defendant brings credible evidence to raise the possibility of involuntariness, the prosecution must establish beyond reasonable doubt that the accused was not in a state of automatism when the conduct occurred. In cases where the issue turns on mental malfunctioning ('I don't know what happened; I just suddenly blacked out'), that may involve the prosecution in an all-but impossible task if the defendant exercises his or her right not to undergo medical examination. Consequently, rare though automatism claims are, judges have said that, in cases such as that of the 'blacking out' example just given, the defence must rely on expert medical evidence bearing on the defendant's state of mind at the relevant time.[16] In particular, in such cases, D's own testimony as to his or her state of mind will be regarded an insufficient foundation for the judge to leave the issue to the jury, or for the magistrates to dismiss the charge.[17]

(b) THE ESSENCE OF AUTOMATISM

Examples of forms of involuntariness which might amount to automatism include convulsions, muscle spasms, or 'acts' following severe concussion. Criminal lawyers used to express the legal position in terms of a requirement of a voluntary act, going on to say that an act is voluntary if it is willed.[18] One criticism of this is that it does

---

[15] Thus in *Attorney General's Reference (No. 4 of 2000)* [2001] Crim LR 578 where a driver claimed that when he put his foot down to the brake pedal he pressed the accelerator instead and the bus shot forward out of his control, this was truly a claim of accident and not of involuntary conduct.

[16] See the helpful Crown Prosecution Service discussion of sleepwalking claims in the context of sexual offending: <www.cps.gov.uk/legal/d_to_g/defences_-_sleepwalking_as_a_defence_in_sexual_offence_cases/>.

[17] *Cook v Aitchison* [1968] Crim LR 266. See the discussion of *R v Coley* [2013] EWCA Crim 223 later in the chapter.

[18] The classic statement is that of J. Austin, *Lectures on Jurisprudence* (5th edn., 1885), 411–24. For an excellent application of the philosophy of action to criminal responsibility see R. A. Duff, *Criminal Attempts* (1996), chs 9–11.

not explain how the act of will itself occurs, and suggests an infinite causal regress;[19] another is that it misrepresents and exaggerates our awareness of the movements involved in our behaviour.[20] These criticisms led Hart to propose a 'negative' definition, describing involuntary actions as 'movements of the body which occurred though the agent had no reason for moving his body in that way'.[21] This switches attention to rare occasions of involuntariness, of which two types may be identified—behaviour which is uncontrollable, and behaviour which proceeds from severely impaired consciousness. Uncontrollable behaviour may be illustrated by epileptic fits, and reflex actions. Behaviour proceeding from a lack of consciousness can be illustrated by things done during a hypoglycaemic episode (which may be the result of taking insulin to correct diabetes). Both types of automatism should apply equally to offences of omission, excusing those who fail to fulfil a legal duty through physical incapacity arising from inability to control behaviour or through significantly reduced consciousness.[22]

Those final words bring us to an unresolved question. Must a court be satisfied beyond reasonable doubt that the defendant had a total lack of consciousness or of control over his or her behaviour, or will a lesser impairment suffice? In the first place, we should recall that the prosecution bears the burden of proof, ultimately, and all that the defence need do is to bring credible evidence of automatism. In *Broome* v *Perkins* (1987),[23] upholding a conviction for careless driving even though the defendant had been in a hypoglycaemic state, the Divisional Court held in effect that the defence must adduce credible evidence that the defendant was exercising no control over his bodily movements at the time. A similarly stringent test was applied in *Attorney General's Reference (No. 2 of 1992)*,[24] where there had been expert evidence about a condition known as 'driving without awareness', but the Court held that automatism requires a 'total destruction of voluntary control on the defendant's part', and that the alleged condition did not establish this. These decisions are inconsistent with earlier cases in which the defendant's consciousness was significantly reduced but not totally absent, and yet where this was held sufficient for an acquittal.[25] Both *Broome* and the *AG's Reference* case concerned road traffic offences, where a more stringent approach may be warranted because the defendant who is aware that he or she has a relevant medical condition can always refrain from driving.

However, *R* v *Coley*[26] has now affirmed that the stringent test has more general applicability. If the defendant was capable of engaging in, 'complex, organized behaviour,' then he or she is not to be regarded as acting in an involuntary way, even if he or she is acting under the influence of a 'deluded or disordered mind' (assuming that this

---

[19] A. I. Melden, 'Willing', in A. R. White (ed.), *The Philosophy of Action* (1968), 77.

[20] H. L. A. Hart, *Punishment and Responsibility* (2nd edn., 2008), 103.

[21] Hart, n 21, 255–6, reformulating (in response to criticism) the passage appearing at 105.

[22] See Model Penal Code, art. 2.01(1), draft Criminal Code (Law Com No. 177) cl. 33(2); A. Smart, 'Responsibility for Failing to Do the Impossible' (1987) 103 LQR 532.

[23] (1987) 85 Cr App R 321; see also *Isitt* (1978) 67 Cr App R 44.   [24] (1993) 97 Cr App R 429.

[25] E.g. *Charlson* [1955] 1 WLR 317; *Quick* [1973] QB 910. See the discussion of this point in Chapter 4.3.

[26] [2013] EWCA Crim 223. See T. Storey, 'The Borderline between Insanity and Intoxication' (2013) 77 J Crim Law 194.

state of mind does not, in law, amount to insanity, considered later).[27] In this case, under the influence of drugs voluntarily taken, D had got up in the night, dressed in dark clothing and a balaclava, broken into his neighbour's house, and stabbed the victim several times with a hunting knife that D had taken to the scene from his own knife collection. D said that his heavy cannabis consumption had previously led him to experience 'blackouts', which is what he said had happened on this occasion. His conviction for attempted murder was upheld, for the reasons just given, namely that D was obviously capable of engaging in, 'complex, organized behaviour'. The decision to uphold the conviction was bolstered by the probability that D's mental condition—his 'deluded or disordered mind'—was self-induced, as the Court noted.[28] However, as argued in Chapter 4.3, there should be greater flexibility and power to apply the automatism doctrine, where the influence on conduct of a deluded or disordered mind (falling short of insanity) is not self-induced. Nonetheless, the Law Commission has now followed the general trend, by provisionally proposing that automatism should be defined as, 'where at the time of the alleged offence the accused suffered a *total* loss of capacity to control his or her actions which was not caused by a recognised medical condition' (our emphasis).[29]

What, then, should be the extent of the involuntariness doctrine?[30] The cases focus on an absence of mental capacity.[31] There is, though, no concealing the questions of judgement this focus can leave open. The Law Commission's draft Code included within automatism any movement which '(i) is a reflex, spasm or convulsion; or (ii) occurs while he is in a condition (whether of sleep, unconsciousness, impaired consciousness or otherwise) depriving him of effective control of the act'.[32] This view is arguably wider, and more generous to the accused, than the Law Commission's new view, explained above. The key concept here is 'effective control', and this, combined with 'impaired consciousness', shows how difficult it is to eliminate questions of degree even from such a fundamental aspect of criminal liability. The *essence* of automatism lies in D's inability to control the movement (or non-movement) of his body at the relevant time, but it may be thought unduly harsh to restrict the doctrine to cases of apparently total deprivation. The phrase proposed by the Law Commission, 'depriving him of effective control', would expressly empower the courts to evaluate and judge D's worthiness for a complete acquittal, whereas if the decisions in *Broome v Perkins* and *Attorney General's Reference (No. 2 of 1992)* represent the law (at least within the sphere of road traffic offences) the doctrine of automatism is unavailable whenever the court believes that there was a residual element of control in the defendant's behaviour at the time. The advantage of the Law Commission's draft code formula would be to

---

[27] *R v Coley* [2013] EWCA Crim 223, para. 23 (Hughes LJ).

[28] *R v Coley* [2013] EWCA Crim 223, para. 24. For a sophisticated discussion of the case, see: J. Child and G. R. Sullivan, 'When Does the Insanity Defence Apply/some Recent Cases' [2014] Crim LR 788. However, that seems to beg the question whether, indeed, a hidden violent streak in Coley *was* brought out by the voluntary cannabis use, which seems a perfectly reasonable explanation of his behaviour, on the facts.

[29] Law Commission, *Insanity and Automatism: A Discussion Paper* (2013), para. 1.110.

[30] Hart, n 15, 106.   [31] G. Williams, *Textbook of Criminal Law* (2nd edn., 1983), ch 29.

[32] Law Com No. 177, cl. 33(1).

allow sensitivity to the special facts of unusual cases. Its disadvantage would lie in the freedom left to courts to incorporate extraneous considerations into their judgments.

At common law the courts have imposed at least three major limitations on the doctrine of automatism—by excluding cases involving insanity, intoxication, and prior fault—and it is to these developments that we must now turn.

(c) INSANE AUTOMATISM

Even if D's bodily movements are uncontrollable or proceed from unconsciousness, the doctrine of automatism will not be available if the cause of D's condition was a mental disorder classified as insanity.[33] The courts originally developed this policy for reasons of social defence, since it ensured that those who fell within the legal definition of insanity were subject to the special verdict and (at that time) to indefinite detention, rather than being allowed to argue that their condition rendered their acts uncontrollable, and that they should therefore have an unqualified acquittal on the grounds of automatism.

The policy behind this judicial approach is expressed most clearly in Lord Denning's speech in *Bratty* v *Attorney-General for Northern Ireland*.[34] D based his defence to a murder charge on psychomotor epilepsy, but the trial judge ruled that automatism was not available, holding that the true nature of the condition was a disease of the mind and that therefore insanity was the only defence. The House of Lords upheld the trial judge's approach, and Lord Denning affirmed that 'it is not every involuntary act which leads to a complete acquittal'. D's behaviour may have been involuntary, 'but it does not give rise to an unqualified acquittal, for that would mean that he would be left at large to do it again'. The proper verdict is one of insanity, 'which ensures that the person who suffers from the disease is kept secure in a hospital so as not to be a danger to himself or others'. Moreover, Lord Denning was inclined to give 'mental disease' a broad definition for this purpose, so as to include 'any mental disorder which has manifested itself in violence and is prone to recur'. In one sense, taken at face value, this view is too narrow: why not include mental disorders that lead people to commit theft, arson or burglary? In another sense, though, Lord Denning's view is too wide: not every mental condition that leads D to pose a persistent danger would be regarded by experts as a form of insanity.

In practice, the effect of this approach has not been greatly to swell the numbers of people pleading insanity. Typically, if a defence is based on automatism but the judge rules that, since the origin of D's condition was a 'disease of the mind', the defence should be treated as one of insanity, many defendants decide to plead guilty to the charge rather than to persist with an insanity defence. The Criminal Procedure (Insanity and Unfitness to Plead) Act 1991 grants courts a discretion to choose committal to

---

[33] Discussed in detail in Chapter 6.2. See now the Law Commission, *Insanity and Automatism: A Discussion Paper* (2013) para. 1.110.

[34] [1963] AC 386.

hospital, a supervision order, or an absolute discharge, if there is an insanity verdict.[35] This still places considerable emphasis on social defence, and may not be an attractive option if the defendant's condition bears little relation to the common understanding of insanity.

In recent years the courts have tended to transfer more varieties of involuntariness out of automatism and into insanity. The leading case is *Quick*,[36] where D's defence against a charge of causing actual bodily harm was that the attack occurred during a hypoglycaemic episode brought on by the use of insulin and his failure to eat an adequate lunch. The defence relied on automatism, whereas the prosecution sought and obtained a ruling that the condition amounted to insanity. The defendant then pleaded guilty and appealed. The Court of Appeal, quashing the conviction, held that a malfunctioning of the mind does not constitute a 'disease of the mind' within the insanity defence if it is 'caused by the application to the body of some external factor such as violence, drugs, including anaesthetics, alcohol, and hypnotic influences'. This 'external factor' doctrine was accepted by the House of Lords in *Sullivan* (1984),[37] where it was also restated that 'diseases of the mind' include both permanent and transitory conditions. Thus, where the malfunctioning of the mind is caused by an external factor, the legal classification is automatism rather than insanity, and the prosecution must disprove D's claim. Where it arises from an internal cause, the classification is insanity, and the burden of proof lies on D. This leads to the apparently strange result that a hypoglycaemic episode (resulting from the taking of insulin to correct diabetes) falls within automatism, whereas a hyperglycaemic episode (resulting from a high blood-sugar level which has not been corrected) falls within insanity, since it is an internal condition rather than a condition caused by an external factor.[38] Epilepsy falls within insanity for the same reason.

The courts have also applied the internal–external distinction to cases of somnambulism. In *Burgess*[39] the Court of Appeal held that, since there is no external cause of sleepwalking, this condition must be regarded as arising from internal causes and therefore classified as insanity, following *Quick* and *Sullivan*. The defendant in *Burgess* had not changed his plea to guilty but succeeded on a plea of insanity. Now, under the Criminal Procedure (Insanity and Unfitness to Plead) Act 1991, it would be open to a judge to grant an absolute discharge in these circumstances. However, the 'insanity' label might be unwelcome to many such defendants; yet English law has no other means of dealing with cases involving both danger and an absence of responsibility.[40] The case for an urgent review of the 'external factor' doctrine is strong.[41]

---

[35] For further discussion see Chapter 7.2(c).   [36] [1973] QB 910.   [37] [1984] AC 156.

[38] *Hennessy* (1989) 89 Cr App R 10; *Bingham* [1991] Crim LR 433.

[39] [1991] 2 QB 92; cf. *Bilton*, *The Daily Telegraph*, 20 July 2005, where a person who carried out serious sexual acts while sleepwalking was apparently acquitted entirely.

[40] For an illuminating discussion, see I. Embrahim et al., 'Violence, Sleepwalking and the Criminal Law: the Medical Aspects' [2005] Crim LR 614, and W. Wilson et al., 'Violence, Sleepwalking and the Criminal Law: the Legal Aspects' [2005] Crim LR 624.

[41] R. D. Mackay and B. Mitchell, 'Sleepwalking, Automatism and Insanity' [2006] Crim LR 901; Law Commission Discussion Paper, *Insanity and Automatism* (2013).

One type of condition that has not yet been classified authoritatively in England is 'dissociation', which is often marked by a short period of uncharacteristic behaviour accompanied by some degree of memory loss. In *Rabey*[42] the Supreme Court of Canada ruled, in the case of a defendant who attacked a woman who had rejected his admiration for her, that the dissociative state in which he acted could not be classified as automatism. Although D's rejection by the woman might be regarded as an external factor, 'the ordinary stresses and disappointments of life which are the common lot of mankind do not constitute an external cause constituting an explanation for a malfunctioning of the mind which takes it out of the category of a "disease of the mind"'. Thus the rejection was an external factor but not the primary cause of the dissociative state: the Supreme Court thought that this lay in the defendant's 'psychological or emotional make-up'. That approach left open the possibility that an utterly extraordinary event might suffice as an external cause, and a trial judge so ruled in *T*.[43] Here the defendant had been raped three days before she joined two others in a robbery, during which she said 'I'm ill, I'm ill' and then stabbed a bystander. Her defence was one of automatism arising from post-traumatic stress disorder caused by the rape. The judge ruled that the rape was a sufficient external cause to place the case within the doctrine of automatism rather than insanity.[44] However, the Law Commission has suggested that, in so far as post-traumatic stress disorder is a recognized medical condition, D should be acquitted for that reason—the influence of the recognized medical condition, as a defence—and not on the broader and more general basis that D was not engaged in voluntary conduct.[45]

(d) AUTOMATISM THROUGH INTOXICATION

The Court of Appeal in *Quick* held that automatism arising from intoxication does not fall within the definition of insanity. However, this does not mean that a person who causes harm whilst in such an intoxicated state as to have significantly reduced consciousness or to be unable to control movements of the body should be brought within the doctrine of automatism.[46] If the cause of the involuntariness is intoxication, then the courts treat the case as falling within the ambit of the intoxication doctrine. It is rare for the evidence to be strong enough to raise a reasonable doubt that D was sufficiently intoxicated as to be in a state of automatism, but this seems to have been accepted in *Lipman*,[47] where D had taken drugs and believed that he was fighting off snakes and descending to the centre of the earth, whereas he was actually suffocating his girlfriend. A defence of automatism was refused, and the case was treated as one of intoxication,[48]

---

[42] (1978) 79 DLR (3d) 414, on which see R. D. Mackay, 'Non-Organic Automatism—Some Recent Developments' [1980] Crim LR 350.

[43] [1990] Crim LR 256 (Snaresbrook Crown Court).

[44] The cases are discussed in Chapter 4.3, and in J. Horder, 'Pleading Involuntary Lack of Capacity' (1993) 52 Cambridge LJ 298.

[45] Law Commission, *Insanity and Automatism: A Discussion Paper* (2013), para. 4.60.

[46] See now *R v Coley* [2013] EWCA Crim 223.   [47] [1970] 1 QB 152.

[48] See now *R v Coley* [2013] EWCA Crim 223. See also Chapter 7.2.

drawing on the doctrine of prior fault discussed in (e) below. This would still be the result, under the Law Commission's recent provisional Proposals, because it would be a case in which the accused was 'culpably responsible' for the state of automatism.[49] However, suppose D's condition appears to have arisen through concussion resulting from a bump on the head, that itself was brought about by voluntary intoxication affecting D's ability to maintain balance. In such a case, the court may have to establish whether the concussion was a supervening influence on D's subsequent behaviour, an influence so significant that it made the initial voluntary intoxication merely part of the background. The distinction may seem a complication too far, but responsibility for one's condition can—exceptionally—be too remote to affect liability.[50]

(e) PRIOR FAULT

The aim of the doctrine of prior fault[51] is to prevent D taking advantage of a condition if it arose through D's own fault. In relation to automatism, the point was first made in *Quick*,[52] where Lawton LJ held that there could be no acquittal on this ground if the condition 'could have been reasonably foreseen as a result of either doing or omitting to do something, as, for example, taking alcohol against medical advice after using certain prescribed drugs, or failing to take regular meals whilst taking insulin'. According to this view, the question of prior fault is resolved by applying the test of reasonable foreseeability, the test of the reasonably prudent person in D's position. But in *Bailey*[53] the Court of Appeal held that a person should not be liable to conviction if the condition of automatism arose through a simple failure to appreciate the consequences of not taking sufficient food after a dose of insulin, even if the reasonably prudent person would have realized it. The defence of automatism should be available unless it can be shown that D knew that his acts or omissions were likely 'to make him aggressive, unpredictable and uncontrolled with the result that he may cause some injury to others'. On this view, prior fault requires awareness of risk, sometimes called subjective recklessness.[54] However, it has been long accepted that people can be taken to be aware of the disinhibiting effects of alcohol and many prohibited drugs. Where, as in *R v Coley*, self-induced intoxication leads directly to the commission of a crime, even when committed when D was suffering from some kind of mental 'blackout', automatism cannot be pleaded.[55]

(f) REFORM

The proposition that people should not be held liable for conduct that is involuntary is fundamental, and the common law on automatism has developed from it. However,

[49] Law Commission, *Insanity and Automatism: A Discussion Paper* (2013).
[50] *Stripp* (1979) 69 Cr App R 318.
[51] See J. Child, 'Prior fault: Blocking Defences or Constructing Crimes', in A. Reed et al. (eds) *General Defences in Criminal Law* (2014); Law Commission, *Insanity and Automatism: A Discussion Paper* (2013), para. 1.115.
[52] [1973] QB 910; for discussion of this development see A. Ashworth, 'Reason, Logic and Criminal Liability' (1975) 91 LQR 102.   [53] (1983) 77 Cr App R 76.   [54] On which see Chapter 6.5(c).
[55] *R v Coley* [2013] EWCA Crim 223, para. 17.

even accepting that cases of prior fault should continue to be excluded from automatism and that cases resulting from intoxication should be classified under the intoxication rules, one major unsatisfactory feature of the law on automatism is the line drawn between this doctrine and the defence of insanity. Since the courts have flexible powers of disposal under the 1991 Act, it may be argued that judicial persistence with the internal/external distinction does not have drastic implications for defendants. None the less, there can be no sense in classifying hypoglycaemic states as automatism and hyperglycaemic states as insanity, when both states are so closely associated with such a common condition as diabetes.[56] The difference in burdens of proof (prosecution must disprove automatism, defence must prove insanity) compounds the anomaly. The proper boundaries of the defence of insanity will be examined further in Chapter 6.2(c), but it is apparent from the discussion here that the present scope of the phrase 'disease of the mind' is too wide. On the one hand, there are many states in which the functioning of the mind is affected but which should not sensibly be included within the concept of insanity. On the other hand, it is difficult to arrive at a clear definition of automatism. The answer may lie in de-toxifying the label 'insanity', as the Law Commission provisionally proposes,[57] by replacing that term with a label such as 'recognized medical condition'. The argument is that, with such a change, there is less at stake, in terms of adverse labelling, in categorizing hypoglycaemic states, post-traumatic stress disorder or even epilepsy, as falling under a mental disorder-based defence, when such conditions lead someone to engage in criminal conduct.

5.3 ACTS, STATES OF AFFAIRS, AND POSSESSION

Accepting that a person should not be held liable for things which occur whilst he or she is not acting voluntarily, should there be a further narrowing requirement that liability should be based on 'acts'? Superficially, it might seem obvious that the answer should be, 'yes'. However, matters are not so simple.[58] There are three types of offence that appear to challenge the superficial view. First, there are offences relating to states of affairs. For example, under s. 128(1) of the Serious Organised Crime and Police Act 2005, it is an offence simply to be 'on' a designated site (such as Crown land[59]) as a trespasser, that is as someone with no right to be 'on' the site. Secondly, most criminal codes contain offences of possession, and it is questionable whether these require any act: if someone plants illegal drugs in my luggage, I am, in a basic sense, in possession of controlled drugs whether I am aware of what happened or not.[60] Thirdly, and most obviously, there are offences of omission. The essence of these offences is that they

---

[56] See the rather unsatisfactory discussion of this issue in *R v Coley* [2013] EWCA Crim 223, para. 20.

[57] Law Commission, *Insanity and Automatism: A Discussion Paper* (2013), para. 1.86 onwards.

[58] See A. P. Simester, 'On the So-Called Requirement for Voluntary Action' (1998) 1 Buffalo Crim LR 403.

[59] <www.gov.uk/government/publications/trespass-on-protected-sites-sections-128-131-of-the-serious-organised-crime-and-police-act-2005>.

[60] A valiant attempt was made to deny this basic point in *Warner v MPC* [1969] 2 AC 256, 282.

penalize a person for doing nothing when he or she should have done something. At the beginning of Chapter 4, we came across an the example of 'leaving' (omitting to pick up) litter that the person in question has dropped. We examine in the next section whether, and to what extent, offences of omission can be justified. In the remainder of this section, states of affairs and offences of possession are considered.

(a) SITUATIONAL LIABILITY

Are there good reasons for convicting a person simply because a state of affairs exists, without the person 'doing' anything to create or to continue that state of affairs? The leading case is *Larsonneur*,[61] where D left England because the duration of her permitted stay had come to an end. She went to Ireland, from where she was deported back to this country. On her return, she was convicted of 'being found in the United Kingdom' contrary to the Aliens Order 1920. Her appeal, based on the argument that her return to England was beyond her control, was dismissed by the Court of Criminal Appeal. The case is widely criticized: her return to this country was not her own act, and was contrary to her will and desire. The Court might have held that there was no voluntary act by the defendant, since it appears that various officials compelled her return to this country. It might then have given consideration to the degree of any prior fault on her part.[62] The judgment fails to discuss these points of principle, and the decision hardly shines as a beacon of common law reasoning. However, *Larsonneur* does not stand alone. In *Winzar* v *Chief Constable of Kent* (1983)[63] the Divisional Court confirmed a conviction for being found drunk on a highway, in a case where the defendant had been taken from a hospital on to the highway by the police. Another similarly worded offence is that of being drunk in charge of a motor vehicle, and there are many other offences that impose what Peter Glazebrook has termed 'situational liability'.[64]

However, the issue is one of statutory interpretation. In *R* v *Robinson-Pierre*,[65] two police officers lawfully broke into D's home, but were chased into the street and bitten by D's pit bull terrier. When asked by the officers to call the dog off, D replied that there was nothing that he could do. D was initially convicted of being the owner (a 'state of affairs') of a dog which had caused injury while dangerously out of control in a public place.[66] The Court of Appeal allowed D's appeal against conviction, on the grounds that Parliament must have intended that there be some act (or omission) attributable to D—a causal link—that connected D's ownership of the dog—the relevant 'state of affairs'—with the fact that whilst dangerously out of control, the dog injured someone. In other words, the mere fact that (a) D was the owner, and (b) the dog injured someone in a public place whilst dangerously out of control was not enough. In this case, perhaps

---

[61] (1933) 149 LT 542.

[62] Cf. the analysis by D. J. Lanham, '*Larsonneur* Revisited' [1976] Crim LR 276, suggesting that the decision may have been based on prior fault (see section 5.2(e)).

[63] *The Times*, 28 March 1983.

[64] P. Glazebrook, 'Situational Liability', in P. Glazebrook (ed.), *Reshaping the Criminal Law* (1978), 108.

[65] [2013] EWCA Crim 2396.   [66] Dangerous Dogs Act 1991, s. 3.

D's failure to call off the dog when reasonably asked might have been such an act/omission, but this possibility should have been put to the jury. In *R v Hughes*,[67] the Supreme Court had to consider whether the defendant should be convicted of causing death by driving whilst uninsured and without a full driving licence, when the victim was killed when he (V) veered across the road when tired and under the influence of illegal drugs, and was killed when his car collided with the defendant's car. The Supreme Court found that it was not enough for the prosecution simply to show that the defendant was 'driving' whilst unlicensed and uninsured (a state of affairs), when he was involved in a fatal accident involving both his car and the victim's car. It had to be shown that something (amiss) about the defendant's 'driving'—whilst uninsured and unlicensed—led to the fatal accident, otherwise it could not be said that the defendant caused the death 'by' driving. Arguably, that kind of analysis confuses a requirement of causation, that normally involves a fault-independent enquiry, with a requirement of fault.[68]

We will see in Chapter 6.3(b) how, in certain situations, the courts have imposed 'vicarious liability' on shop owners and employers by construing statutory words so as to achieve convictions. In effect, these individuals and companies are being held liable simply for states of affairs—for the fact that an employee sold American ham as Scottish ham, for example, even though the shop owner had specifically warned against this.[69] However, Andrew Simester has argued that in all these cases it is not the absence of a required act that is objectionable, but the absence of a fault element.[70] The proper approach, he submits, is evident from two New Zealand prosecutions of visitors for staying after the expiration of a visitor's permit. In *Finau v Department of Labour* (1984)[71] the conviction was quashed because D was pregnant and no airline would carry her. In *Tifaga v Department of Labour* (1980)[72] the conviction was upheld because D was at fault in running out of money, with the result that he could not afford a ticket. The offence did not require an act (or an omission), but rather a state of affairs for which D was responsible. Thus, it may be defensible to impose situational liability if the law is so phrased as to ensure that defendants are in control of their activities and know about their duty to avoid certain situations. This insists on a voluntariness requirement, but not an act requirement. So long as fair warning is given of the standards expected of those embarking on certain activities or enterprises, the principles of legality or 'rule of law' are satisfied and autonomy is respected. The English legislature, unfortunately, sees no objection to creating state-of-affairs offences such as 'being found' or 'being drunk in charge' without any voluntariness requirement. The courts have failed to develop the common law so as to provide a defence of compulsion or to insist on proof that D was responsible (i.e. voluntarily) for the conduct, result, or state of affairs proscribed, although in this respect perhaps *R v Robinson-Pierre*[73] and *R v Hughes*[74] may prove to be turning points in the courts' approach.

---

[67] [2013] UKSC 56.
[68] See further A. P. Simester and G. R. Sullivan, 'Causation as Fault' [2014] 73 CLJ 14
[69] As in *Coppen v Moore* [1898] 2 QB 306.   [70] Simester, n 59, 410–13.   [71] [1984] 2 NZLR 396.
[72] [1980] 2 NZLR 235.   [73] [2013] EWCA Crim 2396.   [74] [2013] UKSC 56.

It is interesting to contrast English law in this respect with the rules developed by the Supreme Court of the USA, taking us back to the 'prior fault' doctrine. In *Robinson v California*,[75] the Supreme Court held that it was unconstitutional, as a form of cruel and unusual punishment, to make someone criminally liable merely for being a drug addict. The *Robinson* decision has been used to strike down state laws criminalizing simple vagrancy or homelessness. However, in *Powell v Texas*,[76] this narrow concession was not built on further. The Court held that where D, a chronic alcoholic, was charged with being found in a state of intoxication in a public place, his inability (if such it was) to stop drinking to excess did not make it cruel and unusual to punish him when he appeared in that state in public. The *Powell* Court distinguished the *Robinson* case on the grounds that in the latter case, D had been punished with imprisonment merely for being in a certain state, namely alcoholism. By contrast, the defendant Powell could have avoided public places when intoxicated even if his intoxication was involuntary (which the Court doubted that it was). In *Powell*, thus, D's alcoholism was regarded as nothing more than an explanation of how he came—voluntarily—to commit the crime.

(b) OFFENCES OF POSSESSION

English law contains several offences of possession, relating to such items as offensive weapons,[77] any articles for use in a burglary, theft, or deception,[78] and controlled drugs.[79] Sometimes possession is the basic element of a crime in the inchoate mode, such as possessing drugs with intent to supply.[80] In ordinary language, one might agree that it is possible to possess an item without any act on one's part. Are offences of this kind therefore contrary to principle? Most of the difficulties with the concept of possession have arisen in drugs cases. The leading decision is that of the House of Lords in *Warner v Metropolitan Police Commissioner*,[81] but neither the speeches of their Lordships nor subsequent cases have rendered the law clear or principled.

The first proposition is that a person is not in possession of an item that has been slipped into his or her bag or pocket without his or her knowledge. The second proposition is that if a person knows that an article or container has come under his or her control, he or she is deemed to be in possession of it even if mistaken about its contents, unless the thing is of a wholly different nature from what was believed.[82] The exception is extremely narrow: Warner believed that certain bags contained scent when in fact they contained cannabis, but that was held not to be a sufficiently fundamental mistake, and his knowledge that he had the bag was sufficient. In *Warner* Lord Pearce stated that the mistake would not be sufficiently fundamental if D thought the containers held sweets or aspirins when in fact they held heroin.[83] The narrowness of this exception to the second proposition throws attention back to the first proposition, but

---

[75] 370 US 660 (1962).   [76] 392 US 514 (1968).   [77] Prevention of Crime Act 1953.
[78] Theft Act 1968, s. 25.   [79] Misuse of Drugs Act 1971, s. 5(2).
[80] Misuse of Drugs Act 1971, s. 5(3).   [81] [1969] 2 AC 256.
[82] These propositions were restated by the Court of Appeal in *McNamara* (1988) 87 Cr App R 246.
[83] [1969] 2 AC, 256, at 307.

that has also been confined tightly. In *Lewis*[84] it was held that D was rightly convicted of possessing controlled drugs when they were found in a house of which he was tenant but which he rarely visited. His defence was that he neither knew nor suspected that drugs were on the premises. The Court of Appeal appeared to hold that, since he had the opportunity to search the house, he should be held to possess items that he did not know about but could have found. In effect, this reduces the first proposition almost to vanishing point. Surely it could equally be said, of the person into whose bag drugs are slipped by some third party, that she could have searched her bag and found them? Probably this is another example of the so-called 'war against drugs' resulting in the distortion of proper legal standards.

The reason for enacting offences of possession is that they enable the police to intervene before a particular wrong or harm is done: in effect, these offences extend the scope of criminal liability beyond the law of attempts.[85] One ground for questioning possession offences is that they may criminalize people at a point too remote from the ultimate harm, not allowing for a change of mind. Another pertinent question is whether they depart from the voluntariness requirement. Although taking possession of an article will often (but not always) involve some act of the defendant, it is surely wrong to regard the conduct as *voluntary* if D was substantially mistaken as to its contents. Thus the first proposition in *Warner* is right in suggesting that possession is not purely a physical matter but does have a mental component, although wrong in restricting that fault element to the mere realization that some item or container has arrived in one's pocket, bag, or house. The Court of Appeal has been pressed to broaden the fault element, notably in *Deyemi and Edwards*,[86] chiefly by reference to those House of Lords decisions such as *B v DPP* and *K*,[87] which stated that the presumption of *mens rea* is a constitutional principle. The Court felt itself bound by previous decisions on possession of firearms, which follow the *Warner* approach, but certified a point of law of general public importance for the House of Lords. Until the decision in *Warner* is revisited, it remains objectionable that the English courts have failed to adhere to any basic voluntariness requirement, and have also ridden roughshod over normal principles of causation, which would operate so as to relieve D from liability when the voluntary act of a third party had brought about the possession.

5.4 OMISSIONS

Two questions arise, in relation to omissions.[88] What is the relation between an omission, as a piece of voluntary conduct or behaviour, and an act? Secondly, when, if ever, is it justified to make an omission a criminal offence? Turning to the first question,[89]

---

[84] (1988) 87 Cr App R 270, with commentary by J. C. Smith at [1988] Crim LR 517.
[85] See the discussion in Chapter 12.9(c).   [86] [2008] 1 Cr App R 25.
[87] [2000] 2 AC 428 and [2002] 1 AC 462 respectively, discussed in Chapter 6.5(a).
[88] See generally, A. Ashworth, *Positive Obligations in Criminal Law* (2013).
[89] See Duff, n 18, 317–20.

it is sometimes argued that certain verbs imply action and therefore exclude liability for omissions, and that the criminal law should respect the distinctions flowing from this. English courts have often used this linguistic or interpretive approach. It has led to a variety of decisions on different statutes,[90] without much discussion of the general principles underlying omissions liability. The Law Commission's draft Criminal Code may be said to signal the continuation of this approach, by redefining the homicide offences in terms of 'causing death' rather than 'killing', and redefining the damage offences in terms of 'causing damage', rather than 'damaging', so as 'to leave fully open to the courts the possibility of so construing the relevant (statutory) provisions as to impose liability for omissions'.[91] The draft code would therefore remove any linguistic awkwardness in saying, for example, that a parent killed a child by failing to feed it; but it does so in this specific instance, and without proclaiming a general principle that the act requirement may be fulfilled by an omission if a duty can be established. Attachment to the vagaries of the language is no proper basis for delineating the boundaries of criminal liability.

In some situations the courts, following the linguistic approach, have nevertheless found themselves able to impose omissions liability. In *Speck*[92] the defendant was charged with committing an act of gross indecency with or towards a child. The evidence was that an eight-year-old girl placed her hand on his trousers over his penis. He allowed the hand to remain there for some minutes, causing him to have an erection. The Court of Appeal held that the defendant's failure to remove the hand amounted to an invitation to the child to continue with the act, and that the offence would then be made out. In effect, the Court either held that his inactivity in those circumstances constituted an invitation which amounted to an act, or it created a duty in an adult to put an end to any innocent touching of this kind, with omissions liability for not fulfilling the duty.

The analysis is similar to that in *Miller*,[93] where D fell asleep whilst smoking, woke up to find the mattress smouldering, but simply left the room and went to sleep elsewhere. He was convicted of causing criminal damage by fire, on the basis that a person who initiates a sequence of events innocently and then fails to do anything to stop the sequence should be regarded as having caused the whole sequence. On this view the conduct constitutes a single, continuing act; Miller caused the damage because he took no steps to extinguish the fire he had innocently started. It must be doubted whether these efforts to find an act which then coincides in point of time with the defendant's knowledge or intention are convincing.[94] Surely the courts are imposing liability for an omission in these cases, by recognizing that a duty arises. *Speck* is a little different from *Miller* since the original act in *Speck* was that of the girl, and the duty must therefore amount to the recognition of an obligation on an adult to put an end to an indecent yet innocent touching by a child. In so far as these decisions appear to extend the statutory

---

[90] With different interpretations of words such as 'cause': see G. Williams, 'What should the Code do about Omissions?' (1987) 7 *Legal Studies* 92.

[91] Law Com No. 177, ii, para. 7.13; see generally paras. 7.7–7.13.   [92] (1977) 65 Cr App R 161.

[93] [1983] 2 AC 161.   [94] See the criticisms by J. C. Smith [1982] Crim LR 527 and 774.

wording, are they objectionable on grounds of retroactivity and lack of fair warning, or defensible as applications of existing common law doctrine to new situations?

In other situations it seems possible to offer plausible reasons for regarding the same event as either an act or an omission, and in some cases the courts have sought to exploit this ambiguity when dealing with problematic medical issues.[95] Yet it is one thing to say that a healthcare professional who decides not to replace an empty bag for a drip-feed has omitted to do something, whereas switching a ventilator off is an act. It is another thing to maintain that the act–omission distinction should be crucial to any determination of the criminal liability in the two situations. In *Airedale NHS Trust v Bland*[96] the House of Lords held that it would be lawful for a doctor to withdraw treatment from a patient in a persistent vegetative state, even though death would in-evitably be hastened by that conduct. The House held that the withdrawal of treatment would constitute an omission, and thus regarded the duties of the doctor as the central issue.[97] The decision was that a doctor has no duty to continue life-supporting treat-ment when it is no longer in the best interests of the patient, having regard to responsi-ble medical opinion.[98] However, the Court of Appeal declined to adopt this subterfuge in *Re A (Conjoined Twins: Surgical Separation)*,[99] holding that the surgical separation of the twins would undoubtedly be an act, and subsequently deciding that carrying out an operation which would result in the death of one twin in order to save the life of the other was permissible as a necessity. This required the Court, in effect, to recognize a new defence of 'balance of evils' in English law—which was what the House of Lords tried to avoid in *Bland*, by construing the withdrawal of treatment as an omission and then focusing attention on the existence of a duty.

The question thus arises again: is there any clear means of distinguishing acts from omissions? It has been argued that conduct should be classified as an omission if it merely returns the victim to his or her 'natural' condition, or the condition in which she would have been but for D's attempt to carry out treatment, or a rescue.[100] Discon-necting a life-support machine would therefore not be classified as an act because it merely returns the patient to the condition in which he or she would have been without any treatment. This view is open to several objections, notably that of deciding what the 'original condition' is in relation to each actor, and the implication that a person who has saved a non-swimmer from drowning could, on discovering that the non-swimmer is an enemy, leave him in the water. However, one advantage of categorizing the conduct as an omission is that it then makes liability depend on the recognition of a duty, which would be straightforward in the case of the rescued non-swimmer. This approach may therefore offer comfort to those who insist that the act–omission

[95] See I. Kennedy, *Treat Me Right* (1988), 169–74.   [96] [1993] AC 789.

[97] On this, see A. McGee, 'Ending the Life of the Act/Omission Dispute: Causation in Withholding Life-Sustaining Measures' (2011) 31 *Legal Studies* 467.

[98] Cf. now the Mental Capacity Act 2005, especially s. 4, and also M. Wilks, 'Medical Treatment at the End of Life—a British Doctor's Perspective', in C. Erin and S. Ost (eds.), *The Criminal Justice System and Health Care* (2007).   [99] [2000] 4 All ER 961.

[100] J. Rachels, 'Active and Passive Euthanasia' (1975) 292 *New England J of Medicine* 78.

distinction should not be used to avoid or foreclose moral arguments about the proper limits of criminal liability. But it is not a clear distinction, since it remains open to manipulation in different situations. The conclusion must therefore be that, although there are some clear cases of omission and some clear cases of act, there are many ambiguous cases in which the act–omission distinction should not be used as a cloak for avoiding the moral issues.

This demonstration of the fragility of the act–omission distinction and of the vagaries of the English language indicates that it may be simplistic to oppose omissions liability in principle. There are some clear cases of omission in which it is desirable to have criminal liability, such as the parent who neglects to feed her or his child or neglects to protect it from abuse.[101] Omissions can be involuntary or not, in the same way as acts; and, provided that the harm resulted because D failed to intervene, it can be argued that omissions are also causes.[102] Omissions liability may therefore satisfy the principle that no one should be held liable for bodily movements that he or she did not and could not direct. It may also satisfy the principle that no person should be held liable for conduct or consequences that he or she did not cause. But one point of the act requirement is to exclude liability for mere decisions and failures to think that do not result in some kind of behaviour, and omissions fall foul of that.[103] However, they are exceptions to the act requirement for a good reason—that certain positive duties to act are so important that they can rightly be made the subject of criminal liability. Of course, such a duty should also be defined with sufficient certainty, and should be adequately discoverable by those to whom it applies. So long as these formal requirements are fulfilled there can be no fairness objection to holding a person liable, provided that he or she is capable of taking some steps to carry out the duty.

5.5 CAUSATION

At the beginning of this chapter it was stated that causation can be one of the most basic requirements of criminal liability.[104] For those offences that merely require conduct the voluntariness requirement is crucial.[105] For the many crimes which specify proof of consequences, whether or not stemming from voluntary conduct, the requirement of causation assumes a central place. Of course, as we shall see in Chapter 6, the law often goes further and insists not only that the defendant voluntarily caused the offence but also that he did so knowingly, intentionally, and so on. Here, however, the concern is to explore the minimum conditions for criminal liability, of which causation can be one.

---

[101] E.g. *Emery* (1993) 14 Cr App R (S) 394, and the new duty imposed by the Domestic Violence, Crime and Victims Act 2004, discussed in Chapter 8.6.

[102] See R. A. Duff, *Answering for Crime* (2007), 111, and the discussion in section 5.5 on Causation.

[103] Duff, n 102, 112–13.

[104] See E. Witjens, 'Considering Causation in Criminal Law' (2014) 78 J Crim Law 164.

[105] For the view that voluntary conduct should not be analysed in terms of causing something to occur, see J. Gardner's review of M. Moore's *Act and Crime* (1994) 110 LQR 496.

Different kinds of consideration influence the law when deciding whether a person or persons 'caused' something to occur. First, there are rational expectations about how things will or may turn out, if something is done or not done. Suppose that you leave a dog locked in a car in extremely hot weather for the whole day, and fail to feed your baby for several days, and they both die. Unless some other exceptional and rationally plausible kind of explanation for the deaths is given, our expectation that the conduct you engaged in must inevitably—and therefore did—cause the deaths will prevail, especially if furbished (as would be normal at any trial) with scientific evidence showing the effects on the victims respectively of dehydration or lack of nutrition. Our expectations may be employed to establish causal links between events even when those event are not—by contrast with the examples just given—overwhelmingly likely to occur. Suppose D leaves a young baby in the middle of a wood, where the baby is later killed by a bird of prey or a fox. Such an outcome can be regarded as caused by D, if it is within the range of outcomes that might be expected to follow in the ordinary course of events from what D did. By contrast, then, if the baby left in the woods is killed by an earthquake, we are unlikely to say that the baby's death was 'caused' by D's conduct. Even though the baby would—we assume—not have been killed in the earthquake had he or she not been left in the woods, the death in the earthquake is outside the range of what might be expected to follow in the ordinary course of events from being left in the woods.

It is important to note that this 'expectations principle' can apply to human interventions, whether they are accidental or deliberate. Suppose, to vary the example, that an armed criminal strays into the woods. His gun then goes off unexpectedly and by a tragic accident the baby is shot dead by the bullet. In such a case, we are likely to say that the unexpectedness of such an outcome breaks the chain of causation leading from D's original act of abandoning the baby in the woods, to the baby's death. It is the armed criminal who caused the death, not D. However, that depends on the circumstances. In *R v Girdler*,[106] D, driving dangerously, accidentally pushed X's car into the path of oncoming traffic. Most of the traffic avoided X's car, but not V's car. Both X and V were killed in the collision between their cars. In relation to the deaths, the Court of Appeal held that, so long as D was found both to be driving dangerously, and to have been more than a slight or trifling cause of the deaths, then the jury should be instructed by the judge that

> The defendant will have caused the death(s) only if you [the jury] are sure that it could sensibly have been anticipated that a fatal collision might occur in the circumstances in which the second collision did occur.[107]

Finally, people's expectations must be described at the right level of specificity if they are to do the work they need to do to guide judgements in causation cases. For example, suppose D is chasing V with hostile intent through a dark forest, and in the dark V trips over a treasure chest, hits his head and dies. D may be found to have caused V's death, if tripping over *something*, falling and suffering a mortal wound in making reasonable efforts to escape D through a dark forest is the kind of accident we accept

---

[106] [2009] 2 EWCA Crim 2666.   [107] [2009] 2 EWCA Crim 2666.

as being within the range of things that could well happen to V in the circumstances. That tripping and falling over a *treasure chest* was wholly unexpected and unforeseeable is quite irrelevant.[108]

This brings us to the second kind of consideration of special relevance to the law's understanding of causation. This is dimension of moral autonomy, discussed in Chapter 4.3, concerned with recognizing the great causal significance of free, intentional, and informed actions.[109] This dimension to moral autonomy is sometimes employed by the courts to overlay or 'trump' the expectations-based set of causal considerations. Suppose D strikes V and leaves V unconscious in an area of town known for very frequent fatal shootings of vulnerable people so that the they can be robbed. Whilst unconscious, V is shot dead by a robber. In this case, the shooting may well be regarded as something coming within the range of what might be expected to occur as a consequence of D's actions. It will, nonetheless, not be regarded as a consequence brought about by D, if it was a free, deliberate, and informed act on the part of the robber.[110]

Before looking further into the common law approach, a further important factor must be mentioned. There can, of course, be more than one cause of an event. It would, therefore, be possible to find that two unconnected people had a hand in bringing about that event, for the purposes of establishing the separate liability of each in criminal or civil law.[111] Suppose D1 intentionally stabs V in order to cause a life-threatening injury. V is taken to hospital where, through negligence on the part of D2 (a doctor), inappropriate treatment is given to V, in circumstances where V's life might have been saved relatively easily. Let us assume that the treatment does not manifest negligence so appalling that it falls outside what might have been within the bounds of expectation, and thus does not in itself break the chain of causation from D's action to V's death (a point considered further later). In that case, both D1 and D2 may be found to have had a causal influence in killing V. It is thus perfectly possible for D1 to be found guilty of murder (causing V's death through an intention to kill or seriously injure), *and* for D2 to be found liable to pay damages in civil law for having caused V's death through a negligent breach of a duty of care to V.[112] Notice the implicit influence of certain assumptions that are made in reaching the latter conclusion. We now take it for granted that there are emergency services under a duty to take stab victims to hospital, and that when that happens, doctors and nurses owe duties of care—shaped

---

[108] See, more generally, M. Moore, in S. Shute, J. Gardner, and J. Horder (eds), *Action and Value in Criminal Law* (1993).

[109] It is important to note that an act may, in certain circumstances, be described as morally autonomous even if it lacks one or more of these characteristics, but that issue is not germane to the discussion here.

[110] For an application of the autonomy principle, in preference to the expectations principle (although these terms are not used) see *Kennedy (No. 2)* [2005] UKHL 38, discussed in the text at n 135.

[111] E.g. *Attorney-General's Reference No. 4 of 1980* (1981) 73 Cr App R 40.

[112] D2 cannot be found criminally liable for manslaughter unless D2's negligence in breaching the duty of case was 'gross' (see Chapter 8.5(b)); but if the negligence was indeed gross, then the treatment will normally be the kind of unexpected calamity befalling V likely to lead a jury to conclude that the chain of causation leading from D1's act to V's death was broken.

by exacting professional standards—to treat the victims as a high priority, and with all the skills at their disposal. These assumptions guide what falls within the scope of our expectations concerning what is likely to happen to injured victims of crime, and hence concerning who should be regarded as having had a hand in bringing about what happens to them. Analysis of who did what to who, whether in criminal or in civil law, cannot be undertaken in isolation from broader assumptions about the rights and duties created by social and political structures.

(a) THE GENERAL PRINCIPLE

The definitions of many crimes require that D caused a result (e.g. murder, grievous bodily harm, criminal damage) or that he caused a result by certain means (e.g. causing death by dangerous driving). In cases where it is clear that D either intended to cause the result or knowingly risked causing it, the causal enquiry is likely to be brief because no court will see much merit in the argument that the result was highly unlikely in the circumstances and probably a coincidence. Thus the dictum 'intended consequences are never too remote' is one expression of the strong effect which culpability has in hastening a finding of causation and overlooking restrictive policies which might otherwise be invoked.[113] Where the culpability element does not overshadow the issue—and particularly in crimes of strict liability, where no culpability may be required—the question arises what minimum connection must be established between D's conduct and the prohibited result. Although courts have occasionally succumbed to the temptation to say that causation is a question of fact for the jury or magistrates,[114] there ought to be guidance on the principles to be applied when assessing the significance of those facts. Some decisions have attempted to articulate principles, but how coherent they are is a matter of debate.

The general principle is that causation is established if the result would not have occurred *but for* D's conduct, although support for this principle in the courts is not unwavering. In *Cato*,[115] for example, the Court of Appeal expressly stopped short of the 'but for' test. D had been convicted of the manslaughter of V, whom he had injected with a heroin compound at V's request. On the issue of whether D's injection of the heroin could be said to have caused V's death, the Court stated that: 'as a matter of law, it was sufficient if the prosecution could establish that it was *a* cause [emphasis added], provided it was a cause outside the *de minimis* range, and effectively bearing upon the acceleration of the moment of the victim's death.'[116] The Court later stated that the

---

[113] Although, in some cases, it is in fact possible for intended consequences to be too remote to be attributed to the person trying to bring them about. Suppose D believes he can jump across the English Channel and land in France. As he jumps, a tornado sweeps him up and carries him across to France. Even assuming that, had he not initially jumped, the tornado would not have carried him all the way to France, the result's occurrence is too remote in causal terms from the way that D envisaged the result coming about to be described as intended. See, generally, R. A. Duff, *Intention, Agency and Criminal Liability* (1993).

[114] E.g. *Alphacell Ltd* v *Woodward* [1972] AC 824, but cf. the slightly more definite approach in *National Rivers Authority* v *Yorkshire Water Services* [1995] 1 AC 444. See generally N. Padfield, 'Clean Water and Muddy Causation' [1995] Crim LR 683.

[115] (1976) 62 Cr App R 41.   [116] (1976) 62 Cr App R 41, 45.

cause must be 'a cause of substance', although it held that the term 'substantial cause' would be putting the requirement too high.[117] Clearly, the Court was reluctant to accept 'but for' causation here, fearing that the link between D's conduct and V's death might be too tenuous. Whatever one makes of the Court's reasoning on the facts of the case, it was right not to endorse the but-for test wholeheartedly. The text is both under and over-inclusive. The Court in *Cato* was concerned about its under-inclusiveness: that the but-for text excludes some causes of events that are highly significant even if the events could or would have occurred without them. Suppose D1 makes V drink a poison that has a 60 per cent chance of killing V. Whilst V is incapacitated by the poison, D2 (unconnected with D1) later pours a weaker version of the poison down V's throat that raises the chance of V dying from the poison to 80 per cent. V dies from the effects of the poison. In this case, V might well have died from the effects of the poison even if D2 had done nothing but stand and watch. It cannot be proved that D2's contribution to events was a but-for cause of V's death. However, D2's contribution ought almost certainly to be regarded as *a* cause—along with D1's conduct—of V's death.

Without supplementation, the but-for test can also seem spectacularly over-inclusive, if it not understood in a sophisticated way. Suppose that D robs V. Someone might say, 'But-for the actions of D's grandparents in conceiving D's parents, D would never have existed to perpetrate the robbery. So, the grandparents were a but-for cause of the robbery'. That kind of reasoning takes too undiscriminating a view of causation.[118] The law's starting-point in its search for causes is the human conduct that led to the consequences complained of. The law's starting-point is not the human conduct—or other factors—that created or shaped the person themselves whose conduct then led to those consequences.[119] That principle leaves plenty of scope for the law to pay attention to, for example, the causal influence of other's people's conduct on the *conduct* of the person that caused the consequences. That is the normal approach when the question is whether X assisted or encouraged D in some way to commit a crime against V. The principle as it has just been expressed also leaves plenty of scope for considering the causes of D's conduct for the purposes of deciding if D should, say, be excused or exempted from liability on the grounds of, for example, duress or insanity. By contrast, whilst the actions of D's grandparents explain how D came to exist, they do not explain how D came to commit the crime.

To summarize, the *Cato* principle is that it is sufficient if D's conduct was a 'but for' cause which was more than minimal: it need not be a substantial cause,[120] but

---

[117] (1976) 62 Cr App R 41, 46; cf. *Cheshire* [1991] 1 WLR 844, referring to a 'significant contribution'.

[118] Although, of course, the grandparents' role may be relevant to other kinds of judgement that people may wish to make, such as whether 'criminality runs in the family'.

[119] See H. L. A. Hart and T. Honoré, *Causation in the Law* (2nd edn., 1985), ch 1, and H. Beynon, 'Causation, Omissions and Complicity' [1987] Crim LR 539.

[120] There are isolated exceptions: see Corporate Manslaughter and Corporate Homicide Act 2007, s. 1(3), stating that 'an organisation is guilty of an offence under this section only if the way in which its activities are managed or organised by its senior management is a *substantial element* in the breach' (my emphasis). See further Chapter 8.5(c).

it seems that a mere 'but for' cause will rarely be sufficient,[121] and it might be best to require D's conduct to be a 'significant cause'.[122] The principle has been illustrated here in relation to 'result-crimes' but the same approach should be adopted to crimes that penalize conduct or possession, although for those crimes the difficulties will usually concern the exceptions in (b) below.[123] The draft Criminal Code re-states the general principle in terms of 'an act which makes more than a negligible contribution to its occurrence',[124] and the Model Penal Code deals with the issue by excluding causes which are too remote to have a just bearing on responsibility.[125] The requirement of 'but for' causation is sometimes termed 'factual causation', which is then contrasted with 'legal causation'—not only to suggest that the law requires something more than 'but for' causation, but also to indicate that there are other aspects of the doctrine to be considered.

(b) INTERVENTIONS BETWEEN CONDUCT AND RESULT

A natural event occurring after D's conduct may be treated as terminating D's causal responsibility if it is a coincidence, but (as suggested earlier) not if it could reasonably be expected.[126] The contrast would be between D, whose assault victim catches scarlet fever in hospital and dies (which should be treated as a 'visitation of Providence' and as negativing any causal connection between D and the death), and E, who leaves his assault victim lying on a tidal beach, where he later drowns (this is within the risk which was reasonably foreseeable, and therefore not a sufficient coincidence to prevent causal responsibility for the death). What if D's act is followed by another human act, which intervenes before the result occurs? Because traditional causal theory does not review the entire situation but tends to focus on the last human act, one might expect an intervening human act to negative D's causal responsibility. But in at least three sets of situations—(i) the non-voluntary conduct of third parties; (ii) the conduct of doctors; and (iii) the conduct of the victim—this is not so, raising questions about what is the general rule and what is the exception.

'Non-Voluntary' Conduct of Third Parties: Since the general principle is said to be that the voluntary intervening act of a third party severs or supersedes the causal connection between D's act and the prohibited result, the courts have developed exceptions in cases where the third party's intervention would not be described as voluntary. If the third party is an infant or is mentally disordered, this lack of rational capacity may be sufficient to discount the third party's act in causal terms. The same applies if D sets out to use a responsible adult as an 'innocent agent', giving false information to that person in the hope that he or she will act upon it. The behaviour

---

[121] The old law on obtaining by deception (now replaced by the Fraud Act 2006, on which see Chapter 10.8) provided a possible example of 'but for' causation: see p. 125 of the fifth edition of this work.

[122] This was how Lord Bingham paraphrased *Cato* in *Kennedy (No. 2)* [2008] UKHL 1 AC 269, at 274.

[123] See the discussion of crimes of possession in section 5.3(b).   [124] Law Com No. 177, cl. 17(1)(a).

[125] American Law Institute, *Model Penal Code*, s. 2.03.

[126] Hart and Honoré, n 119, 342; the draft Criminal Code refers to an intervening act 'which could not in the circumstances have been reasonably foreseen', Law Com No. 177, cl. 17(2).

of the person who has been tricked is discounted as non-voluntary for these purposes. The case of *Michael* (1840)[127] illustrates the principle. D's child was in the care of a foster mother, and D, wishing her child dead, handed a bottle of poison to the foster mother, saying that it was medicine for the child. The foster mother saw no need for the medicine and placed it on the mantelpiece, from which her own five-year-old child later removed it and administered a fatal dose to D's child. The intended result was therefore achieved through the unexpected act of an infant rather than through the mistakenly 'innocent' act of an adult, but neither of these intervening acts was regarded as sufficient to relieve D of causal responsibility.[128]

A similar approach may be taken where the intervening act is one of compulsion, necessity, or duty. If the third party brings about the prohibited harm whilst under duress from D, then D may be regarded as the legal cause of the result.[129] The same analysis can be applied where D creates a situation of necessity, or where D's behaviour creates a duty to respond in the third party. Thus in *Pagett* (1983)[130] D was being pursued by the police and took his pregnant girlfriend hostage, holding her in front of him as a shield whilst he fired shots at the police. The police fired back at D, but killed the girlfriend. The Court of Appeal upheld D's conviction for the manslaughter of his girlfriend, even though the fatal shots were fired by the police and not by him. The Court offered two reasons in support of this conclusion: first, the police officer's conduct in shooting back at D was necessary for his self-preservation and therefore was not a voluntary act; and, secondly, that the police officer was acting from a duty to prevent crime and to arrest D. Both these reasons beg important questions. Did a necessity exist? Was there a duty? They contain no reference to a duty to avoid harm to the person being held hostage. Should not the liberty to act in self-preservation be subject to this qualification?[131] These points ought to have been explored at least. Perhaps a better rationale for this decision may be found in a doctrine of 'alternative danger', concerned with someone's freedom to choose. Where D places a person in the position of having to choose between two drastic courses of action, one threatening self-danger and the other threatening danger to another, that person lacks the range of options that would make their choice truly free. Accordingly, their choice—being unfree—should be attributed causally to the creator of the emergency, and not to the unfree person who has to choose. This leaves open the possibility of finding that a trained police officer ought to have acted with greater circumspection towards the hostage on the facts of *Pagett*, if that is a fair judgment on the facts of that case, since the law might justifiably expect more of a trained official than of a hapless citizen caught up in extreme events.[132]

Whatever one might say about the Court of Appeal's attempts to rationalize the causal responsibility of Pagett for his girlfriend's death, at least they kept some faith

---

[127] (1840) 9 C and P 356; cf. G. Williams, '*Finis* for *Novus Actus*' [1989] Camb LJ 391.

[128] Cf. *Cogan and Leak* [1976] 1 QB 217.   [129] *Bourne* (1952) 36 Cr App R 125.

[130] (1983) 76 Cr App R 279; see Hart and Honoré, n 119, 330–4.

[131] Art. 2 of the ECHR suggests so: see later in the chapter, section 5.6(b).

[132] See further Chapter 7.4; cf. the arguments of P. A. J. Waddington, ' "Overkill" or "Minimum Force"?' [1990] Crim LR 695, with the implications of Art. 2 of the ECHR.

with the fundamental principle that a voluntary intervening act breaks the causal chain. This cannot be said of one subsequent decision of high authority, *Environment Agency* v *Empress Car Co (Abertillery)*.[133] In this case the company had fixed an outlet from its diesel tank which would drain towards a river, governed by a tap that was not locked. An unknown person opened the tap and the river was polluted. The company denied that it caused the polluting matter to enter controlled waters, contrary to the Water Resources Act 1991. On normal principles, one would expect the deliberate act of a third party to negative its causal responsibility. However, the House of Lords held that if the company:

> did something which produced a situation in which the polluting matter could escape but a necessary condition of the actual escape which happened was also the act of a third party or a natural event, [the court] should consider whether that act or event should be regarded as a normal fact of life or something extraordinary.[134]

On the face of it, in articulating this view, the House of Lords appears to be discarding the general principle that a voluntary intervening act breaks the causal chain in favour of the distinction 'of fact and degree' between ordinary and extraordinary interventions. However, the conviction in this case stems from a clear policy decision to further the purpose of the Act that created the offence, aimed at imposing stringent duties on companies to take steps to prevent pollution, and convicting them for omissions to fulfil those duties. So, it may be that the decision was right in the particular statutory context. In *Natural England* v *Day*,[135] it was said that there might be strong reasons to follow the *Empress Car* case in certain cases. In this case, the defendant had been charged with causing someone in his employment to destroy woodland, contrary to s. 28E(1) and 28(P) of the Wildlife and Countryside Act 1981. It was held that the defendant could be found to have 'caused' this result even though (as is evident from the wording of the offence itself) the person who destroyed the woodland acted freely, knowingly, and intentionally. There is a difference between the cases in that, in *Natural England* v *Day*, the person who destroyed the woodland was under the broad authority of the defendant, unlike the person who opened the tap in the *Empress Car*. Even so, these cases demonstrate that sometimes general principles of criminal law may yield to the (perceived) need to further the aim of a statute.

The House of Lords returned to the subject, as a matter of general principle, in *Kennedy (No. 2)*. Lord Bingham held that the *Empress Car* decision was indeed to be confined to its facts (and hence its statutory context).[136] In *Kennedy (No. 2)*[137] D handed V a syringe of heroin with which V then injected himself and died. Overruling the

---

[133] [1999] 2 AC 22, overruling *Impress (Worcester) Ltd* v *Rees* [1971] 2 All ER 357.

[134] *Per* Lord Hoffmann at 36.

[135] [2014] EWCA Crim 2683.

[136] [2008] 1 AC 269, at 276, adding that the House 'would not wish to throw any doubt on the correctness of the *Empress Car* case'.

[137] [2005] 2 Cr App R 348; the Court's first decision in this case was also much criticized, see *Kennedy* [1999] Crim LR 65.

Court of Appeal's strained judgment in favour of a conviction for manslaughter, Lord Bingham recognized the criminal law's approach of treating individuals as autonomous beings, giving rise to the principle that 'D is not to be treated as causing V to act in a certain way if V makes a voluntary and informed decision to act in that way'. Thus the House of Lords unanimously held that there should be no conviction for manslaughter because D did not cause V to take the heroin: it was self-administered.

Conduct of Doctors: In cases where medical attention is given to a victim, there is rarely any doubt that it may properly be described as 'voluntary': doctors work under pressure, occasionally having to make rapid decisions, but they are trained and trusted to exercise clinical judgement in these circumstances. Doctors act under a duty to treat patients, but they surely do so voluntarily.

The courts have drawn a distinction between (a) cases where the injury inflicted by D remains a substantial and operating cause of death despite the subsequent medical treatment, in which case D remains causally responsible even if the medical treatment is negligent; and (b) those where the original wound becomes merely 'the setting in which another cause operates', in which case D's responsibility may be negatived by subsequent aberrant medical treatment.[138] The reference to an 'operating and substantial' cause may be regarded as more favourable to D than the general principle of causation, unless the term 'substantial' is read as meaning, simply, 'more than minimal'. This is confirmed by the statement in *Cheshire*[139] that a significant contribution is all that is required, and that the defendant's act does not need to be the sole or even the main cause:

> Even though negligence in the treatment of the victim was the immediate cause of his death, the jury should not regard it as excluding the responsibility of the accused unless the negligent treatment was so independent of his acts, and in itself so potent in causing death, that they regard the contribution made by his acts as insignificant.[140]

No clear reason is offered for discounting the voluntary intervening act of the doctor. If the doctor administers a drug to which the patient is known to be intolerant, or gives some other wrong treatment, the inappropriateness of the medical treatment should affect the causal enquiry. The courts' reluctance to discuss the causal significance of the medical treatment probably stems from a desire to ensure the conviction of a culpable offender, as in *Pagett*, and this suggests a strong attachment to a 'wrongful act' approach to causation, deciding the issue by reference to broader judgements of innocence and culpability. This appears to overlook the fact that D, who inflicted the original wound which gave rise to the need for medical attention, will still be liable for attempted murder or a serious wounding offence even if the medical treatment is held to negative his causal responsibility for the ensuing death. For adherents of the 'wrongful act' approach this would be insufficient: they want to see responsibility for the ultimate result pinned on the defendant. However, a court which declares that it

---

[138] *Smith* [1959] 2 QB 35, distinguishing *Jordan* (1956) 40 Cr App R 152; cf. the critical attack of A. Norrie, *Crime, Reason and History* (3rd edn., 2014), ch 7.

[139] [1991] 1 WLR 844.   [140] [1991] 1 WLR 844, 852.

is not the doctor who is on trial but the original wrongdoer[141] is merely offering an unconvincing rationalization of its failure to apply the ordinary causal principle that a voluntary intervening act which accelerates death should relieve the original wrong-doer of liability for the result. If that causal principle is thought unsuitable for medical cases, should we not be absolutely clear about the reasons, and then look closely at a doctrine of clinical medical necessity?[142]

Conduct or Condition of the Victim: The general principle that the law approaches causation by considering the effect of an autonomous individual's conduct upon a 'stage already set' is usually taken to extend to cases where the victim has some special condition which makes him or her especially vulnerable. This is sometimes known as the 'thin skull' principle, or the principle that defendants must take their victims as they find them. If D commits a minor assault on V, and V, who is a haemophiliac, dies from that assault, the principle applies to render D causally responsible for the death.[143] This principle of causation may have little practical effect on its own, since most of the serious criminal offences require proof of *mens rea* (proof that D intended or foresaw the risk of causing, say, serious injury), and it will usually be possible to show that the *mens rea* was lacking because D was unaware of V's special condition. However, where an offence imposes constructive liability (such as manslaughter in English and American law),[144] the 'thin skull' principle reinforces the constructive element by ensuring that there is no causal barrier to convicting D of an offence involving more serious harm than was intended or foreseen. The arguments for and against constructive manslaughter are set out in Chapter 8.5. An objection to the 'thin skull' principle is that such physical conditions are abnormal and that much of the standard analysis of causation turns on distinctions between normal and abnormal conditions.

What principles should apply to the causal effect of the victim's conduct after D's original act? Should V's conduct be subject to the normal rules of voluntary intervening acts? *Roberts*[145] was a case in which D, while driving his car, made sexual suggestions to his passenger, trying to remove her coat, at which point she opened the door and leapt from the moving car, suffering injury. The Court of Appeal upheld D's conviction for assault occasioning actual bodily harm, on the basis that a victim's 'reasonably foreseeable' reaction does not negative causation. Whether 'reasonable foreseeability' is an accurate way of expressing the point in question must be doubted. One might well say that the prospect of the woman jumping from the moving car was relatively unlikely. Surely it would be better to consider the principle of 'alternative danger': D's conduct had placed V in a situation of emergency in which she was left in an important way unfree to choose other than she did. That analysis might lead one to say that any victim reaction which cannot be regarded as wholly abnormal or 'daft'[146] should remain D's causal responsibility in such circumstances.

---

[141] *Per* Lord Lane CJ, in *Malcherek* (1981) 73 Cr App R 173.   [142] See section 5.7.
[143] A clear example, on these facts, is the American case of *State* v *Frazer* (1936) 98 SW (2d) 707.
[144] See, Chapter 8.5.   [145] (1972) 56 Cr App R 95; see also *Corbett* [1996] Crim LR 594.
[146] (1972) 56 Cr App R 95, at 97.

What if the victim refuses to accept medical treatment for the injury inflicted by D? The question presented itself starkly in *Blaue*.[147] D stabbed V four times, piercing her lung. V was advised that she would die from the wounds unless she had a blood transfusion, but, adhering to her faith as a Jehovah's Witness, she refused to undergo this treatment. She died. The Court of Appeal held D to be causally responsible for her death. Her intervening decision not to accept the 'normal' treatment did not negate D's causal responsibility, because, the Court argued, the situation was analogous to that covered by the 'thin skull' rule. Stating that 'those who use violence on other people must take their victims as they find them', the Court added that this 'means the whole man [*sic*], not just the physical man. It does not lie in the mouth of the assailant to say that his victim's religious beliefs which inhibited him [*sic*] from accepting certain kinds of treatment were unreasonable'.[148] Is this another example of a court stretching the principles of causation so as to ensure the conviction of a wrongdoer?

The 'thin skull' principle applies only to pre-existing physical conditions of the victim. The principle of individual autonomy suggests that, in general, any subsequent deliberate and informed act or omission by V should negative D's causal responsibility. Exceptions to this are where V's subsequent conduct falls within the 'reasonable foreseeability' notion in *Roberts*[149] or, more importantly, within the principle of 'alternative danger'. D's actions in *Blaue* can certainly be said to have caused a situation of alternative danger and emergency, and so then the question would be whether V's reaction should be classified as wholly abnormal in that context. In a statistical sense it surely was: it must be rare to refuse a blood transfusion knowing that death will follow that refusal. However, to follow this line of reasoning would be to make no distinction between one who refuses treatment for religious reasons and one who refuses out of spite.

A strong argument in favour of the court's decision is that the standard of normality should be informed by social values rather than enslaved to statistical frequency, that religious beliefs are a matter of conscience which should be respected, and therefore that acts or omissions based on religious conviction should not be set aside on the grounds of their 'abnormality'. Bolstering this argument is the point made about lack of true freedom, made earlier. Matters of conscience, taken seriously, leave someone to a significant degree *unfree* to do other than follow their conscience. That being so, it could be said that the victim was not acting freely when refusing to have a blood transfusion, preserving the link between the offender's wrongful act and her death. No doubt there was also much sympathy and respect for the victim, courageously adhering to her religious beliefs in the face of death, generating the argument that it would not be appropriate to hold her causally responsible for her own death.

There is also a long line of cases in which V has aggravated his or her condition by failure to attend to injuries or wounds, or even by deliberately re-opening them. The judicial approach is to hold that D can still be convicted if his conduct made an operative and substantial contribution to the result, even if V's own act or omission also

---

[147] (1975) 61 Cr App R 271.   [148] *Per* Lawton LJ, (1975) 61 Cr App R 271, 274.
[149] (1972) 56 Cr App R 95.

contributed.[150] Once again, the more rigorous approach of recognizing that V's own act broke the causal chain, and that D should therefore be convicted of an attempt or other offence, has been found unattractive by the courts.

(c) CAUSATION AND OMISSIONS

One of the difficulties sometimes raised about imposing criminal liability for omissions, in addition to those already discussed in section 5.4 earlier, is the problem of causation. How can an omission be said to cause harm? Or are these cases exceptions to the causal requirement?[151]

Starting with the most basic question, is it possible to say that, but for an omission, a harm would not have resulted? The existence of a duty justifies calling it an omission, and the non-performance of that duty in a situation where it arises can be said to cause the result. To take an extreme example, a parent who makes no attempt to save her or his child from drowning in shallow water can be said to cause the child's death. It is no answer to say that the child would have drowned anyway if the parent had not been there, because in that eventuality there would have been no one under a duty or rescue and hence no omission. On the facts as they were, the parent was present, and but for non-performance of the duty the child would not have died. When dealing with causation by acts, we have seen that the courts have used terms such as 'significant' and 'substantial' in some cases, chiefly to rule out remote or minimal causes, but this should create no special difficulty for omissions.

One counter-argument is that this approach may sometimes lead to the conclusion that many people caused a result: if, in a jurisdiction which imposes a duty of easy rescue, twenty or more people stand by without offering any help or raising the alarm, the conclusion must be that all these people caused the harm that occurred. This is true, but is hardly an argument against the causation approach since there can be multiple causes of events. Nor would it be a counter-argument to say that but for several omissions in the past many crimes would not have been committed: this is really no different from the argument against tracing causation to grandparents, mentioned earlier.

This is not to suggest that the application of causal arguments to cases of omission is without difficulty. For example, if A stabs V it is obvious that but for A's act V would not have suffered this wound; but if a parent makes no effort to save a child drowning in a pool, it is possible that the duty might have been fulfilled by summoning help (which might have caused delay, and the child's life might have been lost), or that the parent might not have been able to save the child's life anyway (if the child had already been in the pool some time before the parent arrived). The point of these examples is that the 'but for' clause may be less concrete in some omissions cases, and may occasionally

---

[150] See also *Dear* [1996] Crim LR 595.

[151] For discussions see A. Leavens, 'A Causation Approach to Omissions' (1988) 76 Cal LR 547; H. Beynon, 'Causation, Omissions and Complicity' [1987] Crim LR 539.

require a judgement to be made. However, at the very least there are many clear cases where ordinary causal analysis creates no more problems than it does in relation to acts.

(d) CAUSING OTHER PERSONS TO ACT

Can it ever be held that one person caused another to act in a certain way? The notion would seem to be inconsistent with the general, autonomy-based principle that a voluntary intervening act removes or displaces the previous actor's causal responsibility. Yet we have already noted one case in which a person can be said to cause another to act—the case of innocent agency, where the third party in the causal chain lacks rationality or has been tricked. Further cases arise in the law of complicity, that branch of the criminal law which holds people liable for helping or encouraging others to commit crimes, which will be discussed at length in Chapter 11.

One example of the type of case under discussion is where D goes to P and offers P money to injure or kill V.[152] The law will hold D liable for P's subsequent offence, in virtue of the fact that D assisted or encouraged P to commit the offence (in the old-fashioned words of the law, D 'counseled or procured' the offence). In this kind of case, one might say that D *causes* the offence, in some sense. However, D did not cause P to act as an innocent agent: P was not, we assume, lacking in rational capacity, and so on the general principle of individual autonomy P would be regarded as causally responsible for the result. D cannot, therefore, be held to have caused that result in the usual sense, but one might follow Hart and Honoré in suggesting that D may be said to have given P an effective reason for bringing it about.[153] This is a dilution of the general approach to causation, aimed specifically at rationalizing the criminal liability of certain accomplices. In that regard—assisting or encouraging ('counselling or procuring')—advice, information, and other acts of assistance and encouragement may be great or small, and may be readily obtainable from others if this would-be accomplice had declined. So, as an element of causal contribution to P's offence, D's 'aiding' may be insignificant indeed—certainly well below the 'but for' threshold, even in the extended sense adopted by the notion of 'occasioning'. Many writers now acknowledge that the element of causation is absent from some cases of 'aiding and abetting'.[154]

5.6 SELF-DEFENCE AND PERMISSIBLE FORCE

Many offences include a qualification such as 'without lawful excuse', 'without lawful authority or reasonable excuse', and so on.[155] We are not concerned here with the different shades of meaning attached to such phrases,[156] nor with the legislature's frequent

---

[152] *Calhaem* [1985] QB 808.

[153] H. L. A. Hart and T. Honoré, *Causation in the Law* (2nd edn., Clarendon Press, 1985), 51; cf. G. Williams, 'Finis for *Novus Actus*' [1989] Camb LJ 391, at 398.

[154] J. C. Smith, 'Aid, Abet, Counsel and Procure', in P. R. Glazebrook (ed.), *Reshaping the Criminal Law* (Sweet & Maxwell, 1978); cf. Part 2 of the Serious Crime Act 2007, discussed in Chapter 11.7.

[155] See, e.g., the Prevention of Crime Act 1953, s. 1.

[156] See R. Card, 'Authority and Excuse as Defences to Crime' [1969] Crim LR 359, 415.

use of the word 'excuse' to refer to permissions, but rather with some general doctrines which grant permissions to engage in conduct which would otherwise be criminal. Self-defence is the best known of these permissions, but there are others concerned with the prevention of crime, the arrest of suspected offenders, the protection of property, and so forth.

Lawyers frequently speak of these doctrines as defences, for example, 'the defence of self-defence', and procedurally that is how they function. If there is evidence, usually raised by the defendant, that the conduct may have been permissible, the prosecution bears the burden of proving beyond reasonable doubt that the conduct was *not* permissible or otherwise lawful. 'If the prosecution fail to do so, the accused is entitled to be acquitted because the prosecution will have failed to prove an essential element of the crime, namely that the violence used by the accused was unlawful.'[157] The consequences of presenting the permissions as the element of unlawfulness required in all crimes will not be taken further here.[158] Neither this, nor the procedural device of treating them as defences, should deflect attention from the fundamental significance of permissions. There are certain situations when individuals have a right or permission, to do things which would generally be prohibited because they cause harm or damage. The most extreme occasions are those on which the law permits one person to kill another. It is sometimes said that defences such as self-defence involve 'justifications' for conduct. An important point arising from this is that the rules governing permissions should ideally respect the various principles of legality and the rule-of-law for the same reason that offence-definitions should, that is, because they may be relied upon to guide behaviour.[159]

(a) SELF-DEFENCE AND AUTONOMY

The nature and limits of self-defence and prevention of crime have generated much critical discussion.[160] Historically, it is hardly surprising that decisions on self-defence formed an important and frequent element in the development of the English common law in days when there was no organized policing and when the carrying of deadly weapons was common. The issues here concern the basic right to life and physical safety. An individual who is either attacked or threatened with a serious physical attack must be accorded the legal liberty to repel that attack, thus preserving a basic right. A well-regulated society will provide a general protection, but it cannot guarantee protection at the very moment when an individual is subjected to sudden attack. The criminal law cannot respect the lifestyle autonomy of the individual if it does not make provision for this dire situation.

---

[157] *Per* Lord Griffiths in *Beckford* v *R* [1988] AC 130, at 144. See W. Wilson, 'How Defences Work', in A. Reed et al. (eds), *General Defences in Criminal Law* (2014).

[158] R. H. S. Tur, 'Subjectivism and Objectivism: Towards Synthesis', in S. Shute, J. Gardner, and J. Horder (eds), *Action and Value in Criminal Law* (1993).   [159] See section 5.1 earlier in the chapter.

[160] For detailed studies of the law on self-defence and the theory underlying it, see F. Leverick, *Killing in Self-Defence* (2006); S. Uniacke, *Permissible Killing: the Self-Defence Justification of Homicide* (1994).

(b) THE PROBLEM OF CONFLICTING RIGHTS

In terms of lifestyle autonomy,[161] one difficulty with this position is that these situations involve two individuals (at least). If the law gives the person attacked the liberty to wound or kill the aggressor, what happens to the aggressor's right to life and physical safety? The answer to this question must have as its starting point the European Convention on Human Rights, Art. 2 of which declares the right to life in these terms:

1. Everyone's right to life shall be protected by law. No one shall be deprived of his life intentionally save in the execution of a sentence of a court following his conviction of a crime for which this penalty is provided by law.[162]

2. Deprivation of life shall not be regarded as inflicted in contravention of this Article when it results from the use of force which is no more than absolutely necessary:

    a. in defence of any person from unlawful violence;

    b. in order to effect a lawful arrest or to prevent the escape of a person lawfully detained;

    c. in action lawfully taken for the purpose of quelling a riot or insurrection.

Articles 3 and 5 of the Convention protect a citizen's freedom from inhuman treatment and security of person, but, unlike Art. 2, they contain no explicit exceptions in favour of the permissible use of force, and the Court has had to imply such exceptions.[163]

As for the exceptions to Art. 2, two of them appear rather strange. To suggest that causing death may be absolutely necessary 'to effect an arrest' (Art. 2.2b) is somewhat absurd since, as Sir John Smith has pointed out, one cannot arrest a dead person.[164] A killing that is permissible to prevent a riot or insurrection (Art. 2.2c)—yet further evidence of deference to the authoritarian principle in the ECHR[165]—seems barely conceivable. However, Art. 2 has no expressly stated exception for killings in the prevention of any other non-violent crime. In theory, then, for example, a householder who kills a burglar ought to have no defence, if Art. 2 is applied, unless the circumstances can be said to have involved the defence of a person from unlawful violence; but the bizarre exceptions created for making arrests and quelling riots open the possibility for argument by analogy to such cases. We discuss this point later.

The approaches of other legal systems differ considerably. Some maintain that an innocent person's rights are absolute and thus recognize few limitations on those

---

[161] For a discussion of this concept, see Chapter 3.2 and Chapter 4.2.

[162] Note that Protocol 6 to the Convention requires the abolition of the death penalty. Several European states, including the UK, have agreed to this protocol, which is also brought into English law by the Human Rights Act 1998.

[163] *Rivas v France* [2005] Crim LR 305 and *RJ and M-J D v France* [2005] Crim LR 307.

[164] J. C. Smith, 'The Right to Life and the Right to Kill in Law Enforcement' (1994) NLJ 354.

[165] See the discussion of the authoritarian principle in Chapter 4.5.

rights, even when that person is repelling a minor assault or defending property.[166] This suggests that the aggressor forfeits the normal rights when he embarks on an attack, and that it is his misconduct in starting the conflict which justifies the law in giving preference to the liberty of his victim. The idea of forfeiture is not objectionable in itself.[167] However, it should be carefully circumscribed lest it allows the person attacked to stand fast and use whatever force is necessary to protect his rights of ownership and liberties of passage, however trivial the threat to them. The focus should be on the right to life, as the jurisprudence of the European Convention establishes.[168] Initial wrongfulness should only be taken to permit the proportionate use of force: the innocent subject of an attack should not be free to use whatever force is necessary to vindicate his threatened rights. Such an analysis would assign no value to the rights of the attacker. If the criminal law is committed to ensuring that everyone's life is protected and that force is inflicted as rarely as possible, it cannot accept a vindicatory approach which would allow the infliction of gratuitous, or at least disproportionate, harm. Forfeiture of life to protect a person from some minor hurt, loss, or damage would promote the value of honour or sheer self-assertion above respect for life and limb. The tendency of the English courts to reach for the concept of reasonableness, without setting out the relevant rights first, is an unfortunate aspect of legal culture.

(c) THE RULES AND THE PRINCIPLES

Self-defence is a long-standing defence in English law,[169] but it must be considered in the light of two statutory provisions. Section 3 of the Criminal Law Act 1967 states that 'a person may use such force as is reasonable in the circumstances in the prevention of crime'. The section was not intended to supplant the common law rules on self-defence,[170] and the courts have continued to develop those rules. It is true that in most situations of self-defence it could be said that the person was preventing crime (i.e. preventing an attack which constituted a crime), but that would still leave certain cases untouched—notably, attacks by a child under ten, by a mentally disordered person, or by a person labouring under a mistake of fact. Such aggressors would commit no offence, and so it is the law of self-defence, not the prevention of crime, which governs.[171]

Section 3 of the Criminal Law Act 1967 has now been buttressed by s. 76 of the Criminal Justice and Immigration Act 2008, which 'is intended to clarify the operation of the existing defences' (s. 76(9)), notably self-defence. It is rare for legislation

---

[166] See, most controversially, A. Dershowitz, *Preemption* (2006), 197–9. See also W. Wilson, 'How Defences Work', in A. Reed et al. (eds), *General Defences in Criminal Law* (2014).

[167] Uniacke argues that there is no conceptual difficulty with the notion of forfeiture so long as we accept that the right to life, like many other rights, is conditional on our conduct: n. 160, 201, and ch 6 generally.

[168] See text following n 181.   [169] A. Ashworth, 'Self-Defence and the Right to Life' [1975] CLJ 282.

[170] Ashworth, n 169, 285.

[171] See the judgment of Ward LJ in *Re A (Conjoined Twins: Surgical Separation)* [2000] 4 All ER 961.

to state on its face that it is for clarification: this curious notion must mean that the common law defence is not abolished,[172] but that the new provisions supersede the common law to the extent that they apply. However, as will appear from the following paragraphs, s. 76 deals with only a few of the many issues of principle arising in the law of self-defence.

Section 76(2) states that the section applies to the common law on self-defence and to s. 3 of the Criminal Law Act, which deals with force used in the prevention of crime or in effecting a lawful arrest. When the Law Commission considered the issue some years ago, it identified other possible bases for permitting the use of force, such as the prevention or termination of trespass on property that we will consider later in this chapter.[173] The principles should be the same as for the other permissions. However, where the force used is not physical but consists of damage to another's property, the legal principles are different. The permissible damaging of another's property requires only that D *believed* that 'the means of protection adopted ... would be reasonable having regard to all the circumstances'.[174] This hardly embodies a legal standard at all, since it turns on D's beliefs as to what is reasonable. One feature of the draft Criminal Code was that it would abolish the different rule for property damage.

(d) THE PROPORTIONALITY STANDARD

The law of self-defence has two elements: necessity and proportionality. The requirement that the use of force must be necessary (or, where the right to life is involved, 'absolutely necessary') is combined with a further requirement that the amount of force must be proportionate to the value being upheld. This shows respect for the rights of the attacker in self-defence cases, and for the rights of suspected offenders in relation to the other permissions. Even though the necessity part has subjective elements, as we shall see, the reasonableness of the force used depends not solely on D's beliefs but on an objective assessment.[175] Thus where D misjudges the amount of force which is reasonable, for example, to insist on passing along a path barred by another, to eject a trespasser, or to detain a poacher, this is a mistake of law rather than of fact. The Court of Appeal has confirmed that D's view of the amount of force that was reasonable is not determinative: the magistrates or jury should assess whether, in the circumstances existing at the time, the amount of force was reasonable.[176] The standard cannot be a precise one: s. 76 of the 2008 Act states that the force must not have been 'disproportionate', that is not out of proportion to the amount of harm likely to be suffered by the defendant, or likely to result if a forcible intervention is not made. What is crucial is that it should rule

---

[172] Cf. s. 59 of the Serious Crime Act 2007 ('the common law offence of inciting the commission of another offence is abolished'), discussed in Chapter 12.6.

[173] See section 5.6(e)(iii); Law Com No. 177, cl. 44, mostly re-stated in Law Com No. 218, *Legislating the Criminal Code: Offences Against the Person and General Principles* (1993), cl. 27.

[174] Criminal Damage Act 1971, s. 5(2).   [175] See e.g. *Jones, Milling* et al. [2007] 1 AC 136.

[176] *Owino* [1996] 2 Cr App R 128, not following *Scarlett* (1994) 98 Cr App R 290. See also *Tudor* [1999] 1 Cr App R (S) 197. Cf. the controversy surrounding the US case of *People v Goetz* (1986) 68 NY 2d 96, where D had shot and wounded four youths on the New York subway after they had demanded five dollars from him.

out the infliction or risk of considerable physical harm merely to apprehend a fleeing non-violent offender,[177] to stop minor property loss or damage, etc. As a nineteenth-century Royal Commission remarked, a law whose only requirement was necessity 'would justify every weak lad whose hair was about to be pulled by a stronger one, in shooting the bully if he could not otherwise prevent the assault'.[178] On this view, the proper approach is to compare the relative value of the rights involved, and not to give special weight to the rights of (say) a property owner simply because the other party is in the wrong (i.e. committing a crime).[179] Thus in *Rashford* (2006)[180] the Court of Appeal rightly held that self-defence should not be ruled out simply because D was the initial aggressor. If V's response to D's aggression was out of all proportion, D would be justified in using sufficient force to protect himself. If, however, D had intended to provoke V into attacking him, in order to then use fatal force on V, it is well established that self-defence would be unavailable.[181]

Although Art. 2 of the Convention does not specify a proportionality requirement, the Strasbourg Court has emphasized that the use of deadly force must be both absolutely necessary and strictly proportionate if it is to come within an exception to the right to life.[182] The American Model Penal Code provides that deadly force is not permitted, 'unless the actor believes that such force is necessary to protect himself against death, serious bodily harm, kidnapping or sexual intercourse compelled by force or threat'.[183] It is debatable whether this goes too far in allowing the lawful sacrifice of a life to prevent certain non-fatal assaults,[184] and it should be noted that Art. 2 of the Convention is vague on this question. Deadly force may be permitted, 'in defence of any person from unlawful violence', but how serious a violent attack? The Strasbourg jurisprudence is no more precise than English law on this point. The Model Penal Code formulation might be a worthwhile starting-point for analysis and argument, although it is arguable that the breadth and uncertainty of 'kidnapping' makes its inclusion in the list of threats that might warrant deadly force to resist them a controversial one.[185]

Should the judgment of proportionality be affected by the fact that the force was used against a law enforcement officer? Since English law renders an arrest lawful if the police officer has reasonable grounds for suspicion (even if the grounds turn out to be erroneous), this may be of importance. There are English decisions which draw a distinction between resisting a lawful—but mistaken—arrest (which is not permissible),

---

[177] As the European Court of Human Rights held in *Nachova v Bulgaria* (2006) 42 EHRR 933.

[178] Report of the Royal Commission on the Law Relating to Indictable Offences (1879, C. 2345), note B, at 44; see at 11 for an assertion of the principle that 'the mischief done by, or which might reasonably be anticipated from, the force used is not disproportioned to the injury or mischief which it is intended to prevent'.

[179] See Leverick, n 160, ch 6. For a different view see the judgment of the German Supreme Court, set out in P. H. Robinson, *Fundamentals of Criminal Law* (2nd edn., 1995), 488–90.   [180] [2006] Crim LR 546.

[181] For the eighteenth-century authorities, see Ashworth, n 169, 299–301.

[182] E.g. in *Andronicou and Constantinou v Cyprus* (1998) 25 EHRR 491, at para. 171; *Gül v Turkey* (2002) 34 EHRR 719, at para. 77; *Nachova v Bulgaria* (2006) 42 EHRR 933.   [183] Model Penal Code, s. 3.04.

[184] J. C. Smith, *Justification and Excuse in the Criminal Law* (1989), 109 and ch 4; Leverick, n 160, ch 7.

[185] Law Commission, *Simplification of the Criminal Law: Kidnapping* (Report No. 355, 2014), 3.85, does not go into this point.

and repelling the unlawful use of violence by police (which is permissible).[186] This principle is to be found both in the Model Penal Code and the draft Criminal Code.[187] It permits individuals to defend themselves against excessive force by the police, whilst requiring them not to use force against police who are effecting an arrest for which the officer may believe there are reasonable grounds (even if the arrestee believes otherwise).

(e) ASPECTS OF THE NECESSITY REQUIREMENT

The necessity requirement forms part of most legal regimes on permissible force. The first question to be asked is: necessary for what? We have seen that force may be permitted for any one of several lawful purposes. The necessity must be judged according to the lawful purpose which the defendant was trying to pursue: for self-defence, purely reactive defensive force will often be all that is necessary; in order to apprehend a suspected offender, on the other hand, a police officer or citizen will need to behave proactively. These differences may become particularly important in cases where there is a suspicion or allegation that the force was used by way of revenge or retaliation rather than in pursuit of a lawful purpose. What was the defendant's purpose? Could the conduct be said to be necessary for that purpose?

Does this reference to 'purpose' mean that there is a mental element in the permissions, such that a person cannot rely on a particular permission if he or she is ignorant of the basic facts needed to support that permission? In *Dadson* (1850)[188] a constable shot a fleeing thief. Such force was permissible only against 'felons', and a thief was a felon if he had two previous convictions. This thief had previous convictions and so was a felon, but the constable fired at him without knowing of these convictions. It was held that the constable could not rely on the permission to use force to apprehend a felon because he was unaware of the basic fact needed to constitute the permission. The Northern Irish case of *Thain* (1985)[189] takes this point further. D, a soldier on duty, stated from the outset that he did not fire the shot in order to apprehend V (who was running away at the time). He said that he shot in reaction to a sudden movement by V. It seems that D might have succeeded if he had maintained that his intention was to arrest, but he proffered another reason and was convicted of murder. This decision holds that D's beliefs or motives have a significant bearing on the permissibility of the use of force, and this is surely right. In many circumstances a greater use of force might be justifiable for law enforcement than merely for defence.[190]

---

[186] *Fennell* [1971] 1 QB 428; *Ball* [1989] Crim LR 579.
[187] Model Penal Code, s. 3.04(2)(a)(i); Law Com No. 177, cl. 44(4).
[188] (1850) 4 Cox CC 358.
[189] [1985] NI 457.
[190] Cf. *Nachova v Bulgaria*, earlier, n 177 and text thereat. For controversy over the *Dadson* principle, see R. Christopher, 'Unknowing Justification and the Logical Necessity of the *Dadson* Principle in Self-Defence' (1995) 15 Oxford JLS 229; J. Gardner, 'Justifications and Reasons', in A. P. Simester and A. T. H. Smith (eds), *Harm and Culpability* (Oxford University Press, 1996).

In most cases, where no problem of the mental element arises, the main issue is necessity. The English courts have continued to develop the common law, but without always relating the issues to any general themes and without explicit reference to the primacy of the right to life. An attempt is made here to organize the decisions around six aspects of necessity, referring to s. 76 of the 2008 Act where relevant.

Imminence: Although s. 76 is silent on the matter, there is authority that the use of force can be necessary only if the attack is imminent.[191] If there is time to warn the police, then that is the course which should be taken, in preference to the use of force by a private individual.[192] But this apparently does not mean that it is unlawful to prepare or keep armaments for an anticipated attack. In the *Attorney-General's Reference (No. 2 of 1983)*[193] D's shop had been looted during rioting which the police had struggled to control; D made some petrol bombs with which to repel any future attack, and the question was whether these were in his possession 'for a lawful object'. It was held that they were, if the jury accepted that D intended to use them only against an attack on his premises which the police could not control. This is an unusually indulgent approach for the criminal courts—a conviction followed by a discharge would be more normal, since it does not signal that such conduct is permissible—but it was a response to a particular type of situation. If the police are unable to offer protection and attack is imminent, the rationale for justifiable force is made out—although objects so lethal as fire-bombs should rarely be approved as lawful means of defending business premises, as opposed to defending a home or human beings.

This decision leaves a number of questions about the 'imminence' requirement unresolved. Where a woman who has been habitually subjected to physical abuse by her male partner has a reasonable fear that he may kill her next time, does this satisfy the 'imminence' requirement if she then kills him whilst he is asleep? True it may be that 'a "reasonable person" does not fear immediate death from a sleeping person',[194] but that reference to immediacy is surely too strict, and it may be argued that the real issue is whether the woman reasonably fears a danger to her life that she will be unable to avoid.[195] Another problem concerns the lawfulness of carrying a gun or an offensive weapon in order to repel an anticipated attack: the authorities would seem to suggest that, although the use of the weapon might be lawful if an attack takes place, its possession beforehand remains an offence.[196] A further unresolved question arises where a law enforcement officer shoots a fleeing suspect on the basis that the suspect

---

[191] E.g. *Attorney-General for Northern Ireland's Reference* [1977] AC 105; *Chisam* (1963) 47 Cr App R 130.

[192] See *Jones, Milling* et al. [2007] 1 AC 136; see also Lord Bingham's judgment on duress and the duty to avoid using force in *Hasan* [2005] 2 AC 467, discussed in Chapter 6.3.

[193] [1984] QB 456; see also *Cousins* [1982] QB 526.

[194] J. Dressler, 'Battered Women who Kill their Sleeping Tormentors' in S. Shute and A. P. Simester (eds), *Criminal Law Theory* (2002), 269.

[195] J. Horder, *Homicide and the Politics of Law Reform* (2012), at 252–5; Leverick, n 160, ch 5. Cf. also the loss of control defence, discussed in Chapter 8.4(b).

[196] See *Evans v Hughes* [1972] 3 All ER 412; Smith, n 184, 117–23; and D. J. Lanham, 'Offensive Weapons and Self-Defence' [2005] Crim LR 85.

is likely, if allowed to escape, to commit violent offences: must it be shown that those offences might or would be committed sooner rather than later?[197]

A Duty to Avoid Conflict?: One of the most technical but most significant elements in the common law of self-defence was the duty to retreat. Its technicality lay in its careful wording and its exceptions; its significance was that, from an early stage, the common law recognized limitations on the forfeiture principle and on the primacy of the non-aggressor's autonomy in these situations. However, the duty has now disappeared as such. In *Julien*[198] it was rephrased as a duty to demonstrate an unwillingness to fight, 'to temporize and disengage and perhaps to make some physical withdrawal'. In *Bird*[199] the Court of Appeal accepted that the imposition of a 'duty' is too strong. The key question is whether D was acting in self-defence or in revenge or retaliation. Evidence that D tried to retreat or to call off the fight might negative a suggestion of revenge, but it is not the only way of doing so. The modification of the law seems to derive from the suggestion in Smith and Hogan's textbook that the 'duty' as described in *Julien* is inconsistent with the liberty to make a pre-emptive strike.[200] It is not. The liberty to make a pre-emptive strike can easily be cast as an exception to the general duty to avoid conflict, and, as such, it is no more inconsistent with the rule than any other exception to a rule. The difficulty with regarding the duty to avoid conflict as merely one consideration to be borne in mind here is that it says nothing about the circumstances which might outweigh it. If the law is to protect everyone's right to life and to pursue the minimization of physical violence, the avoidance of conflict—or what Fiona Leverick refers to as the 'strong retreat rule'[201]— must be right in principle. Section 76 is silent on this.

Protection of the Home: One long-standing exception to the old duty to retreat was that a person attacked at home has no duty to withdraw.[202] This may be regarded as one remaining bastion of the view that the individual's home is sacrosanct. Undoubtedly many citizens feel that way about their homes today.[203] Before we turn to the law itself, though, here is an argument for a 'minimalist' approach to householders' rights in this situation. The first question is whether an exception to the duty to avoid conflict should be recognized here: *should* there be any obligation to 'temporize and disengage' if a person enters one's home unlawfully, manifesting an intent to steal property or to carry out an unlawful eviction? Much might be thought to depend on the situation and on D's purpose in acting. If D believes there is a threat only to personal property in the home and that there is no danger to D himself, it could be argued that reasonable force may be used only for the purpose of detaining the intruder.[204] If D believes

---

[197] A point left open by the European Commission in *Kelly* v *UK* (1993) 74 DR 139.

[198] [1969] 1 WLR 839.   [199] [1985] 1 WLR 816.

[200] J. C. Smith and B. Hogan, *Criminal Law* (5th edn., Butterworths, 1983), 327, quoted by the Court of Appeal in *Bird* [1985] 1 WLR 816; see now D. Ormerod and K. Laird, *Smith and Hogan's Criminal Law* (14th edn., Oxford University Press, 2015), 444.   [201] Leverick, n 160, 82, and ch 4 generally.

[202] *Hussey* (1924) 18 Cr App Rep 160.

[203] Paul Robinson and John Darley's subjects strongly maintained that there should be no duty to avoid conflict when attacked at home (and also declined to find full criminal liability when a person failed to retreat in a non-home setting): *Justice, Liability and Blame* (1996), 60.

[204] *Faraj* [2007] 2 Cr App R 25; J. Getzler, 'Use of Force in Protecting Property' [2006] 7 *Theoretical Inquiries in Law* 131.

that the threat is to evict him, it can be argued that D should have resort to the civil courts rather than using what may be considerable violence to defend his possession. Even if D believes there is a threat of violence from the intruder (as will often be the assumption[205]), and that he (D) is not capable of merely detaining the intruder, then it is arguable that life should be placed before property and D should retreat rather than (if this is possible) using violence against the intruder. Although popular sentiment appears to be otherwise, any other approach would value property interests more highly than life and limb.

However, English law now leans away from this minimalist approach, whilst not abandoning contact with it altogether, in the light of popular support for the 'rights' of the householder.[206] In several cases in which a firearm, sword, or knife has been used against a burglar with fatal results, the householder has been either acquitted or not prosecuted.[207] The law now supports such an approach, in virtue of s. 43 of the Crime and Courts Act 2013. The general provisions on self-defence in s. 76 of the Criminal Justice and Immigration Act 2008 have been amended by s. 43 to include the following provision:

> 76(5A) In a householder case, the degree of force used by D is not to be regarded as having been reasonable in the circumstances as D believed them to be if it was grossly disproportionate in the circumstances (our emphasis).[208]

The idea behind the provision is to give a householder greater scope to use force he or she thinks is reasonable, in the heat of the moment, even though—after the event—it is clear that far less force used would have been equally effective. Arguably, such is latitude is already present in s. 76 of the 2008 Act. Section 76(7) states that

> evidence of a person's having only done what the person honestly and instinctively thought was necessary for a legitimate purpose constitutes strong evidence that only reasonable action was taken by that person for that purpose.

It is possible that English law now violates the deceased's right to life, in so far as it allows the acquittal of a householder who uses fatal force against an offender who has not done or threatened 'unlawful violence'. Such a violation would occur, if the effect of s. 43 is to permit killings of trespassers in the home whose intention was believed by the householder to be only to steal or damage property. That is so, even allowing for the fact that an ordinary householder, acting in a situation of stress when confronting a burglar, may not be able to judge to a nicety whether the aim of the burglar is merely to take property, or also harm the householder if the householder seeks to prevent this happening. However, s. 43 applies only to the defence of 'self-defence'. Killing to

---

[205] See the Irish decision in *DPP* v *Barnes* [2006] IECCA 165 for an examination of the householder's rights and those of the burglar, concluding that the crime of burglary is itself an act of aggression, and that under the Irish Constitution there can be no duty to retreat from the home.

[206] See generally S. Skinner, 'Populist Politics and Shooting Burglars' [2005] Crim LR 275.

[207] D. J. Lanham, 'Defence of Property in the Criminal Law' [1966] Crim LR 368, 426; Smith, n 184, 109–12; and Leverick, n 160, 83–5.

[208] The provision applies only when the defendant was not a trespasser in a dwelling, but the victim was believed by the defendant to be a trespasser.

prevent theft is more properly regarded as action 'in prevention of crime' and not as self-defence. Having said that, a complication here is the ancient English Law dictum that an attack on the home has traditionally been regarded, in law, as tantamount to an attack on the person. In *Mead & Belt*,[209] Holroyd J said:

> the making an attack upon a dwelling, and especially at night, the law regards as equivalent to an assault on a man's person; for a man's house is his castle and therefore, in the eye of the law, it is equivalent to an assault.

This 'equivalence' is, of course, a fiction not to be taken seriously in a human rights context. Nonetheless, a difficult test case under s. 43 might be where a burglar seeks to snatch property from D's hand, and D intentionally kills the burglar to prevent this. Would that, if regarded in law as self-defence, be a violation of Art. 2?

Freedom of Movement: English law also recognizes an exception to the duty to avoid conflict (if such a duty exists) in those cases where D is acting lawfully in remaining at, or going to, a place, realizing that there is a risk that someone will force a violent confrontation there. The authority for this is *Field*,[210] where D was warned that some men were coming to attack him. D stayed where he was, the men came and made their attack, and in the ensuing struggle D stabbed one of them fatally. The Court of Appeal quashed his conviction, holding that he had no duty to avoid conflict until his attackers were present and had started to threaten him. The American case of *State* v *Bristol*[211] takes the point further, holding that D had no duty to avoid entering a bar where he knew his adversary (who had threatened him with attack) to be drinking. The American court declined to lay down a rule which might 'encourage bullies to stalk about the land and terrorize citizens by their mere threats'. These two decisions appear to promote the value of freedom of movement above any duty to avoid conflict in advance by, for example, informing the police of the threat.[212] However, in *Redmond-Bate* v *DPP*[213] the Divisional Court held that the defendant's right to preach should be protected, as an exercise of the right to freedom of expression under Art. 10 of the Convention, and it was only if the words spoken were likely to provoke violence in others that it would have been proper to arrest her: if her words were not provocative of violence, only those who used or threatened violence should have been arrested. This suggests a small qualification of a subject's right to freedom of expression, and there are surely strong arguments for this. Should not the minimization of physical violations (implicit in Art. 5) take precedence over freedom of expression (Art. 10) and movement? Is there not some analogy with omissions to assist in saving life, where a citizen's general liberty should also be outweighed by a specific social duty?[214] These remarks concern self-defence and the defence of property only; clearly, a person who acts with the purpose of preventing crime or arresting a suspected offender cannot

---

[209] (1823) 68 ER 1006.   [210] [1972] Crim LR 435.   [211] (1938) 53 Wyo 304.

[212] Cf. Lord Mance in *Jones, Milling* et al. [2007] 1 AC 136, with the arguments of F. McAuley and J. P. McCutcheon, *Criminal Liability: a Grammar* (2000), 760–1.

[213] [1999] Crim LR 998; cf. *Beatty* v *Gillbanks* (1882) 9 QBD 308 and *Nicol and Selvanayagam* v *DPP* [1996] Crim LR 318.   [214] See Chapter 4.4.

be expected to avoid conflict, and so the proportionality standard ought to assume primacy there.

Pre-Emptive Strike: The use of force in self-defence may be justifiable as a pre-emptive strike, when an unlawful attack is imminent.[215] This is a desirable rule, since the rationale for self-defence involves the protection of an innocent citizen's vital interests (life, physical security), and it would be a nonsense if the citizen were obliged to wait until the first blow was struck. The liberty to make a pre-emptive strike is not inconsistent with a duty to avoid conflict (if it were recognized), but it should be read as being subject to that duty. In other words, it would be possible and desirable to have a law which imposed a general obligation to avoid conflict but, where this was not practical, authorized a pre-emptive strike.[216] A law which allows pre-emptive strikes without any general duty to avoid conflict runs the risk, as Dicey put it, of encouraging self-assertion through violence.[217]

Necessity, Proportionality, and Law Enforcement: The point has already been made that a police officer or citizen whose purpose is to prevent a crime or to apprehend a suspected offender must behave proactively. The primary legal restriction on such conduct has been the standard of proportionality, in relation to the purpose that the actor was aiming to achieve.[218] How serious an offence was being or had been committed? Is there a danger of serious offences in the near future? Applying Art. 2 of the Convention, not only must the permission fall within paragraph 2(a), (b), or (c) of the Article, but the force must be shown to have been 'absolutely necessary' and 'strictly proportionate'—the adverbs emphasizing the sharper formulation of the tests under the Convention. This should be the benchmark for scrutinizing the so-called 'shoot-to-protect' policy adopted by the Association of Chief Police Officers in 2003, and defended after the London bombings. Although its details have not been made public, the Metropolitan Police Commissioner referred to shooting to kill 'a deadly and determined bomber who is intent on murdering many other people'.[219] Much then depends on whether reasonable grounds should be required for the belief that V is such a person.

Some of the leading European decisions are not uncontroversial. In *McCann and others* v *UK*[220] the European Court of Human Rights held (by a ten to nine majority) that the UK had violated the right to life of three suspected IRA terrorists who were shot dead by security forces in Gibraltar. The most important ruling was that Art. 2 requires law enforcement operations to be organized so as to 'minimize, to the greatest extent possible, recourse to lethal force'. The Court found that the planning of the operation failed to show the required level of respect for the suspects' right to life. It did not find that the soldiers who fired the shots violated Art. 2, although it did state that their reactions lacked 'the degree of caution in the use of firearms to be expected from law

---

[215] E.g. *Beckford* v *R* [1988] AC 130, at 144.   [216] See text at n. 200.

[217] A. V. Dicey, *Introduction to the Study of the Law of the Constitution* (8th edn., 1923), 489.

[218] See the discussion of *Thain* earlier, n 189 and text thereat.

[219] Sir Ian Blair in oral evidence to the House of Commons Home Affairs Committee, *Counter-Terrorism*, 13 September 2005, Qs 59–60.

[220] (1996) 21 EHRR 97; for analysis of the ECHR case law, see Leverick, n 160, ch 10, and B. Emmerson, A. Ashworth, and A. Macdonald (eds), *Human Rights and Criminal Justice* (2012), 748–57.

enforcement personnel in a democratic society, even when dealing with dangerous ter-rorist suspects'.[221] In *Andronicou and Constantinou* v *Cyprus*[222] the Court (by a five to four majority) held that Art. 2 was not violated when Cypriot security forces stormed a house where a hostage was being held, firing machine guns in all directions and kill-ing both the gunman and the hostage. This decision appeared to leave a considerable gap between the strict formulation of the tests and their application to the facts, but the Court distinguished it in *Gül* v *Turkey*.[223] The Court noted that in the *Cyprus* case the hostage-taker was known to be in possession of a gun, which he had fired twice already. In the *Turkey* case, there was insufficient reason to believe that Gül had a gun, and 'the firing of at least 50–55 shots at the door was not justified by any reasonable belief of the officers that their lives were at risk'.[224] It is fair to say that the Strasbourg judgments, particularly when applied to the facts of the cases, leave some scope for debate about what Art. 2 actually requires.[225] The English Courts have taken this to mean that, so long as a law enforcement official honestly believes in the need to use force, Art. 2 does not further require that the belief be based on reasonable grounds.[226]

(f) MISTAKEN BELIEF AS TO NECESSITY

In English law the rule has become established that a person who purports to use jus-tifiable force should be judged on the facts as he or she believed them to be.[227] Section 76(3) of the 2008 Act confirms that this subjective test represents English law, and s. 76(4) goes on to state that the reasonableness of the belief may be considered when assessing whether it was genuinely held.[228] However, in cases of killing under Art. 2, the Strasbourg Court has insisted on several occasions that the actions of those who take life should be judged on the basis of the facts that 'they honestly believed, *for good reason*, to exist'.[229] This is clearly an objective test which, in effect, places such a high value on the right to life as to require law enforcement officers to have adequate factual foundations for their beliefs before using lethal force in consequence. It is easy

---

[221] Cf. P. A. J. Waddington, '"Overkill" or "Minimum Force"?' [1990] Crim LR 695, for the argument that if officers do not shoot to kill they risk the possibility that an injured suspect might still be able to kill or wound someone—in which case, shooting to kill might be permissible in the first place.

[222] (1998) 25 EHRR 491.   [223] (2002) 34 EHRR 719.   [224] (2002) 34 EHRR 719, para. 82.

[225] However, it is widely recognized that the state has a positive duty to ensure that the right to life of all its citizens is protected, and to ensure that its police and military personnel conduct their operations with due respect for Art. 2. Passages in several judgments (e.g. *Isaveya* v *Russia* (2005) 41 EHRR 791, at para. 175) suggest that there may be grounds for charging senior police officers with negligent manslaughter if they fail in this duty. See also *Juozaitiene* v *Lithuania* (2008) 47 EHRR 1194.

[226] *R (Duggan)* v *HM Assistant Deputy Coroner* [2014] EWCA 3343 (Admin).

[227] By the Privy Council in *Shaw* v *R* [2002] 1 Cr App R 10; cf. *Martin* [2002] 1 Cr App R 27, where the Court of Appeal nevertheless held that psychiatric evidence to assist the jury to understand D's likely percep-tions was not admissible.

[228] Section 76(5) states that voluntary intoxication should be left out of account. General discussions of mistaken beliefs will be found in Chapter 7.4, and of intoxication in Chapter 7.2. See also *R v Oye* [2013] EWCA Crim 370 on the irrelevance of insane delusions about the need to act in self-defence.

[229] *McCann* et al. v *UK* (1996) 21 EHRR 97, at para. 200; *Andronicou and Constantinou* v *Cyprus* (1998) 25 EHRR 491, at para. 192; *Gül* v *Turkey* (2002) 34 EHRR 719, at paras. 78–82. See Leverick, n 160, ch 10.

to argue that this is unrealistic and may not always be possible, but such arguments often overlook the fact that what counts as a 'good' reason, or 'adequate' foundations for a belief, varies according to the circumstances. In confused and fast-moving situations, where it may be difficult—even for trained officers—to tell friend from foe, a 'good' or 'adequate reason to have shot with lethal intent may be found when it would not have been so regarded in a less pressured situation. Bearing that in mind, the objective test is best way to respect the right to life. For this reason, previous editions of this work have contended that it should be a principle of English law. The arrival of the Convention jurisprudence strengthens that case. The fact that the Strasbourg cases on Art. 2 deal only with law enforcement officers should not be crucial, since it is the state's duty to ensure that the law protects the lives of all victims, no matter who threatens them.[230]

In *Bubbins* v *UK* (2005)[231] the Strasbourg Court appeared to modify its position, reiterating the requirement of an 'honest belief, for good reason' but then softening it considerably by emphasizing the actual belief of the police officer at the time he shot V.[232] That recognizes the point made about officers acting in difficult situations, made earlier. Even so, it is true to say that the Strasbourg Court has had ample opportunity to point out any incompatibility between the English law of self-defence and the Convention, and has not done so,[233] a point picked up in the recent case of *R (Duggan) v HM Assistant Deputy Coroner* where the court concluded that a requirement that a belief in the need to use force be reasonable was not required by the Convention.[234] Yet, as the Joint Committee on Human Rights has pointed out, adopting the same argument as this book, the preponderance of Strasbourg jurisprudence favours the objective test of reasonable belief, and 'the very minimum required by human rights law' in order to protect the right to life of ordinary citizens is that the test of belief 'for good reason' should be introduced 'when force is used by state agents'.[235]

(g) PERMISSIBLE FORCE AND THE EMOTIONS

The foregoing paragraphs have examined principles which might produce outcomes that consistently uphold human rights in those varied situations in which a claim of permissible force might arise. Some might regard those principles as too mechanical for the sudden and confused circumstances of many such cases. It is well known that a sudden threat to one's physical safety may lead to strong emotions of fear and panic, producing physiological changes which take the individual out of his or her 'normal self'. According to this view, the most just law is the simplest: was the use of force an

---

[230] See, e.g., *Hertfordshire Police v Van Colle* [2008] UKSC 50.   [231] (2005) 41 EHRR 458.

[232] (2005) 41 EHRR 458, paras. 138–9.

[233] Per Collins J in *R (Bennett)* v *HM Coroner for Inner London* [2006] EWHC Admin 196; see also the government response to the Joint Committee, printed as Appendix 7 to the report at n. 235.

[234] [2014] EWHC 3343 (Admin).

[235] Joint Committee on Human Rights, *Legislative Scrutiny* (15th report, session 2007–08), para. 2.35.

innocent and instinctive reaction, or was it the product of revenge or some manifest fault?

This simple approach may have the great advantage of recognizing explicitly the role of the emotions in these cases. It is surely right to exclude revenge attacks from the ambit of justifiable force.[236] It is also consistent with the doctrine of prior fault for the law to construe the standards of reasonableness and necessity strictly against someone whose own fault originally caused the show of violence.[237] The question then is how much indulgence should be granted to the innocent victim of sudden attack who reacts instinctively with strong force. In the leading case of *Palmer* (1971),[238] Lord Morris stated that it is 'most potent evidence' of reasonableness that the defendant only did what he or she 'honestly and instinctively thought necessary'. The Strasbourg Court, despite its insistence on the requirement of 'good reason', deferred in *Bubbins* to the beliefs of 'an officer who was required to act in the heat of the moment to avert an honestly perceived danger to his life'.[239] Section 76(7) of the 2008 Act now gives legislative authority to this approach, by providing that a court should take account, when assessing reasonableness, of the considerations:

> that a person acting for a legitimate purpose may not be able to weigh to a nicety the exact measure of any necessary action; and

> that evidence of a person's having done only what the person honestly and instinctively thought was necessary for a legitimate purpose constitutes strong evidence that only reasonable action was taken by that person for that purpose.

The additional flexibility of this approach suggests that it is more accurate to state the law's requirement in terms of a 'not disproportionate' use of force rather than a proportionate response, but even then there must be limits. It cannot be right for absolutely any reaction 'in a moment of unexpected anguish' to be held to be justifiable,[240] particularly in the case of a trained firearms officer, even if it is right for the courts to consider 'how the circumstances in which the accused had time to make his decision whether or not to use force and the shortness of the time available to him for reflection, might affect the judgment of a reasonable man'.[241] To the extent that the law has moved away from objective standards towards indulgence to the emotions of innocent citizens, the rationale of permissions becomes diluted by elements of excuse.[242] This move may be inappropriate when the defendant is a trained firearms officer. We have

---

[236] These are explicitly excluded from the scope of defence of loss of self-control. See Chapter 8.5(b).

[237] See Leverick, n 160, ch 6.   [238] [1971] AC 814, at 832.

[239] *Bubbins v UK* (2005) 41 EHRR 458, at para. 139.

[240] A phrase from *Palmer*, above n 238. See also the insistence of the Joint Committee on Human Rights (earlier at n 235), para. 2.24, that allowing force which is not 'grossly disproportionate' would go too far and breach the state's obligations under Art. 2.

[241] *Per* Lord Diplock, in *Attorney-General for Northern Ireland's Reference* [1977] AC 105.

[242] On which see J. Horder, *Excusing Crime* (2004), 48–52. It is, though, clear that beliefs in the need to use force, or force of a certain degree, that are attributable to voluntary intoxication, or to delusions, will not be taken into account. See, on the former, Criminal Justice and Immigration Act 2008, s. 76(5); and on the latter, *R v Oye* [2013] EWCA Crim 1725.

seen that the confused and difficult circumstances in which officers may have to make decisions on 'shoot to kill' should be relevant to whether they had 'adequate' grounds for belief in the need to act; but that is not the same as arguing that—as in the case of ordinary civilians—a concession should also be made when officers' decisions are made on the basis of instinct or anguish.[243]

The fairness of this concession to what Blackstone termed 'the passions of the human mind'[244] is often supported by reference to the famous dictum of Holmes J, namely, that 'detached reflection cannot be demanded in the presence of an uplifted knife'.[245] This dictum is significant for its limited application: it concerns cases of an 'uplifted knife', that is typically, sudden and grave threats or attacks; it has no application to cases where the attack is known to be imminent and the defendant has time to consider his position. Nor should it necessarily be conclusive in relation to those who are trained to deal with extreme situations, such as the police and the army.[246] As the element of sudden and unrehearsed emergency recedes, the social interest in the minimal use of force becomes a firmer precept again. In this type of situation, the law ought to give consideration to the relative importance of the sanctity of life and the physical safety of all persons, including offenders, when compared with such other interests as the free movement of citizens. The aphorism about the 'uplifted knife' should not be used to prevent the principled resolution of cases to which it does not apply.

(h) CONCLUSIONS

The law relating to self-defence and permissible force depends on resolution of a clash between two aspects of the right to life—the individual's autonomy and right to protect life by using even fatal force if necessary, and the right to life of every citizen (including offenders). English lawyers have generally been reluctant to discuss the issues in these terms, and the government has rarely acknowledged its positive obligation under Art. 2 of the Convention to have in place laws that give maximum protection to the right of life of all citizens. The relevant law (whether on self-defence or the other forms of permission) is mostly common law, and the enactment of s. 76 of the Criminal Justice and Immigration Act 2008 to 'clarify' the common law is a disappointment, a missed opportunity to legislate at the detailed level rightly recommended by the Law Commission[247] and to engage with Art. 2 of the Convention and its requirements. An urgent re-assessment of the law on justifiable force is called for, taking full account of the issues discussed above.

---

[243] For further discussion of this point, see Chapter 8.4.

[244] *Commentaries on the Laws of England*, iii, 3–4.

[245] *Brown v United States* (1921) 256 US 335, at 343.

[246] Cf., however, the use of the concession in the *Andronicou* case, earlier at n 229, and in *Bubbins*, earlier at n 239.

[247] In the draft criminal code, Law Com No. 177, cl. 44.

5.7 CHASTISEMENT OF CHILDREN

For centuries it has been the common law that a parent is justified in using reasonable force to discipline her or his child.[248] Well into the twentieth century, it was permissible to use flogging as a form of state punishment for children. Reformers could do little in the eighteenth and nineteenth centuries to dim English enthusiasm for the punishment of flogging (whipping) for young offenders, although the practice was condemned by Bentham amongst others: 3,937 young offenders were sentenced between 1864 and 1871 to flogging for theft.[249] This particular form of inhuman and degrading punishment was ended in 1948. So far as parents are concerned, in *Smith*[250] a mother had asked the defendant (her partner) to smack her six-year-old child for disobedience, and he gave the child two strokes with his belt. Although it upheld the man's conviction for assault, the Court of Appeal recognized that the defence of reasonable chastisement exists and held that the prosecution must prove that D 'did more than inflict moderate and reasonable chastisement on the child'. However, in *A v United Kingdom* (1998)[251] the European Court of Human Rights held that the ill-defined nature of this defence failed to discharge the government's duty to ensure that the child's rights under Art. 3 of the Convention were protected. Article 3 declares that no person shall be subjected to 'inhuman and degrading treatment or punishment'.

In *A v UK*, the nine-year-old applicant had been beaten with a garden cane on several occasions by his stepfather, leaving marks that were visible several hours later. The judge had left the jury to decide on the reasonableness of the chastisement, and they had acquitted the man. The Strasbourg Court's finding of a violation of Art. 3 in this case did not require the criminalization of all smacking of children by parents, but rather a tightening of the law. The government accepted that it had a duty to ensure that the criminal law is so framed as to prevent degrading punishment, and that the then law failed to achieve this, and it conducted a public consultation on the matter.[252] Most of those working with children argued that the defence of reasonable chastisement should be abolished, as in Sweden and thirteen other European countries.[253] Some argue that the present law contributes to the cycle of violence and (as the United Nations Committee on the Rights of the Child has put it) fails to 'promote positive and non-violent discipline'.[254] The European Commissioner for Human Rights regards such consequentialist arguments as less powerful than the consideration that

---

[248] *Hopley* (1860) 2 F and F 202; see generally H. Keating, 'Protecting or Punishing Children: Physical Punishment, Human Rights and English Law Reform' (2006) 26 LS 394.

[249] R. L. Gard, *The End of the Rod: A History of the Abolition of Corporal Punishment in the Courts of England and Wales* (2009), 30.   [250] [1985] Crim LR 42.   [251] (1999) 27 EHRR 611.

[252] Department of Health, *Protecting Children, Supporting Parents* (2000); this paper and the responses are helpfully analysed by J. Rogers, 'A Criminal Lawyer's Response to Chastisement in the European Court of Human Rights' [2002] Crim LR 98.

[253] Commissioner for Human Rights, *Children and Corporal Punishment: 'the Right not to be Hit', also a 'Children's Right'* (2006) 43 EHRR SE17.

[254] UNHCHR, *Concluding Observations of the Committee on the Rights of the Child: United Kingdom* (2002), UN Doc CRC/C/15/Add.188, para. 35. See further Keating, *Protecting or Punishing Children*.

'the existence of special exceptions for violent ill-treatment of children in otherwise universally applicable laws against assault breaches the principle of equal protection under the law.'[255] However, the consultation suggested that a majority of members of the British public favoured retaining the defence (castigated by the European Commissioner as a 'disreputable legal concept') in order to allow parents to carry out their duty to bring up their children properly. These strong conceptions of parental duty prompt reflections on the rationale for this defence, which remains obscure and may reside (historically, at least) in some form of delegation by the State of its power to punish, or in an approach that permits parents to determine (within limits) what is in the 'best interests' of the child.

The law has now been changed by s. 58 of the Children Act 2004, which states that 'reasonable punishment' cannot be a defence to any offence under ss. 47, 20, or 18 of the Offences Against the Person Act 1861, or to the offence of child cruelty under s. 1 of the Children and Young Persons Act 1933. This leaves it open for D to raise the defence to a charge of battery. In order to ensure compliance with Art. 3, magistrates who try these cases[256] must ensure that they take account of all the relevant factors—such as whether an instrument was used, and the child's age—in deciding whether a particular battery amounted to reasonable chastisement.

5.8 PERMISSIONS, NECESSITY, AND THE CHOICE OF EVILS

The discussion so far has focused on self-defence and the permissions relating to law enforcement and the prevention of crime. Generally speaking, the permissions relating to self-defence may be linked directly to the principle of lifestyle autonomy, in the basic sense of self-preservation, whereas the permissions relating to law enforcement may be linked to the public good of security. In some situations, however, the principle of individual autonomy is compromised because it may not be possible to protect the autonomy of all persons involved. These are the 'choice of evils' cases, which must now be discussed.

(a) NECESSITY AS A PERMISSION

English law contains limited defences of duress and necessity, which apply when a person commits an otherwise criminal act under threat or fear of death or serious harm. The relevant law on duress is examined in Chapter 7.3, where it will become apparent that many statements about the ambit of the defences (especially in the courts) are ambivalent or even indiscriminate as to whether their basis lies in permissibility (D

---

[255] Earlier, n 253, at 228.
[256] By removing s. 47 offences from the ambit of the defence, the new law ensures that all such cases will now be tried in magistrates' courts.

had a right to use this force) or excuse (the use of force was impermissible, but D did not behave unreasonably in the dire circumstances). One apparently clear statement came when the House of Lords, in rejecting duress as a defence to murder, held in *Howe*[257] that, even if D's own life is threatened, it cannot be permissible to take another innocent life. What this means is that one innocent person who stands in danger of imminent death cannot be permitted to kill another innocent person. To kill an aggressor in self-defence is one thing, but to kill an uninvolved third party, even if this were the only means of preserving one's own life, could not be right even though it might be excusable, as we shall see elsewhere.[258]

What about the possibility of permitting the killing of an innocent non-aggressor when this will save two or more other lives? One example of this emerged from the inquest into the deaths caused by the sinking of the ferry *Herald of Free Enterprise* in 1987.[259] At one stage of the disaster several passengers were trying to gain access to the ship's deck by ascending a rope-ladder. On that ladder there was a young man, petrified, unable to move up or down, so that nobody else could pass. People were shouting at him, but he did not move. Eventually it was suggested that he should be pushed off the ladder, and this was done. He fell into the water and was never seen again, but several other passengers escaped up the ladder to safety. No English court has had to consider this kind of situation:[260] are there circumstances in which the strong social interest in preserving the greater number of lives might be held to override an individual's right to life?

Any residual permission of this kind must be carefully circumscribed. It involves the sanctity of life, and therefore the highest value with which the criminal law is concerned. Although there is a provision in the Model Penal Code allowing for a defence of 'lesser evil',[261] it fails to restrict the application of the defence to cases of imminent threat, opening up the danger of citizens trying to justify all manner of conduct by reference to overall good effects.[262] The moral issues are acute: 'not just anything is permissible on the ground that it would yield a net saving of lives'.[263] Yet there may be situations in which the sacrifice of a small number of lives may be the only way of saving a much greater number of lives, as where a dam is about to burst (flooding a whole town) unless a sluice-gate is opened (flooding a less densely populated area). Could a doctrine of necessity permit the intentional killing of people in the latter area in order

---

[257] [1987] AC 417.

[258] Cf. J. J. Thomson, 'Self-Defense' (1991) 20 *Philosophy and Public Affairs* 283, with R. Christopher, 'Self-Defense and Objectivity' (1998) 1 Buffalo CLR 537; on necessity as an 'excuse' see Chapter 7.3(a).

[259] Smith, n 184, 73–9.

[260] Cf. *Dudley and Stephens* (1884) 14 QBD 273, the case in which two men saved themselves by killing and eating the weakest member of a threesome who had been adrift in a boat for many days; but they were rescued the following day, and some have questioned the necessity of their act. See A. W. B. Simpson, *Cannibalism and the Common Law* (1984), and Chapter 7.4(a).

[261] Model Penal Code, s. 3.02; cf. G. P. Fletcher, *Rethinking Criminal Law* (1978), 788–98.

[262] Cf. the remarks of the House of Lords in *Jones, Milling* et al. [2007] 1 AC 136.

[263] Thomson, n 258, 309; see also J. Finnis, 'Intention and Side-Effects', in R. G. Frey and C. W. Morris (eds), *Liability and Responsibility* (1991), for the argument that it is never morally right to choose (intend) to take another's life.

to save the greater number, if there were no alternative? There are strong arguments in favour of recognizing some such extreme situations as involving a permission to kill, but there are those who would oppose this and would insist that there can never be a permission for intentionally taking life—although it may be acceptable to recognize a (partial) excuse in such cases.

Some situations give rise to the further moral problem of 'choosing one's victim', which arises when, for example, a lifeboat is in danger of sinking, necessitating the throwing overboard of some passengers,[264] or when two people have to kill and eat another if any of the three is to survive.[265] To countenance a permission in such cases would be to regard the victim's rights as less worthy than the rights of those protected by the action taken, which represents a clear violation of the principle of individual autonomy. Yet it is surely necessary to make some sacrifice if the autonomy of everyone simply cannot be protected. A dire choice has to be made, and it must be made in a way that fairly minimizes the overall harm. In an ideal world, a fair procedure for resolving the problem—perhaps the drawing of lots—would be employed. But here, as with self-defence and the 'uplifted knife' cases,[266] one should not obscure the clearer cases where there is no need to choose a victim: in the case of the young man on the rope-ladder, blocking the escape of several others, there was no doubt about the person who must be subjected to force, probably with fatal consequences.

(b) MEDICAL NECESSITY

Is it ever justifiable for a doctor to act contrary to the letter of the law for clinical reasons, on the grounds of necessity? Where doctors are considering a controversial or difficult treatment that will possibly kill, or have a serious impact on the autonomy of the patient, they will sometimes take the exceptional step of applying to the courts for a ruling on the lawfulness of what they propose. We will come to such cases in a moment. A basic question is whether doctors may take measures normally associated with palliative care, that end a patient's life. A simple case would be where painkillers are no longer having their intended effect, and so are used in a large dose to kill the patient (with, let us assume, that patient's full consent), or to help the patient end their own life. The Supreme Court has recently affirmed the long-standing rule that, just as when the death of the patient is directly intended, if the direct intention is to assist the patient to end his or her own life,[267] then there can be no defence that the patient's death was in his or her 'best interests', and thus in some sense 'necessary'.[268] However, matters are different if the patient's death is not directly intended but is only a foreseen side-effect of a genuine attempt to relieve pain (i.e. where pain relief is directly intended).

---

[264] *United States v Holmes* (1842) 26 Fed Cas 360.   [265] *Dudley and Stephens* (1884) 14 QBD 273.

[266] See *Brown v United States* (1921) 256 US 335.

[267] Contrary to the Suicide Act 1961, s. 2, which prohibits assisting or encouraging suicide.

[268] *R (on the application of Nicklinson) v Ministry of Justice* [2014] UKSC 38; J. Finnis, 'Case Comment: a British "Convention Right" to Assistance in Suicide?' (2015) 131 LQR 1; F. Stark, 'Case Comment: Necessity and *Nicklinson*' (2013) Crim LR 949.

At the celebrated trial of Dr Bodkin Adams, charged with murdering a patient by administering excessive doses of morphine, Devlin J stated the orthodox view that to shorten life by days and weeks is to cause death no less than shortening it by years. However, he added that a doctor 'is still entitled to do all that is proper and necessary to relieve pain and suffering even if the measures he takes may incidentally shorten life'.[269] Following this line of reasoning, in the case of Dr Cox, a doctor who administered a drug in order to stop the patient's suffering *by* causing her death—direct intent to kill—not simply to relieve pain, his act was considered (attempted) murder.[270] This distinction has now in effect been affirmed by the Supreme Court. As Lord Sumption put it, in the recent case of *Nicklinson*,[271] 'Medical treatment intended to palliate pain and discomfort is not unlawful, only because it has the incidental consequence, however foreseeable, of shortening the patient's life'.

The *Adams* approach was followed in *Dr Moor's case* in 1999,[272] where the trial judge again drew a distinction between administering drugs with intent to kill the patient and administering drugs as proper treatment to relieve pain and suffering. The courts are applying a version of the 'doctrine of double effect' to argue that the doctor does not cause death wrongfully, if the primary intention is to relieve pain, even though it is well known that this will shorten the patient's life.[273] In all these cases, doctors obtain the benefit of a distinction being drawn between acting on a 'direct' intention to kill (acting in order to kill), which will expose them to criminal liability, and acting on a so-called 'indirect' intention to kill: where death is not the aim, but is foreseen as virtually certain to occur in the course of an action aimed at a legitimate medical goal (in this case, the goal of pain relief). As we will see, ordinarily, the killer who kills when he or she foresees death as almost certain to occur is guilty of murder, just like the killer who directly intends to kill.[274] Why is it different for doctors? In law, there is not, as such, a 'special rule' for doctors in these kinds of situations (although doctors may obviously be governed by professional rules that do not apply to lay people), but in practice the law works as if there was a special set of rules. This is because (a) of the limitations the law places on the reach of the defence of necessity outside medical contexts, and (b) the fact that doctors' professional duties include the relief of pain through the use of medicaments that may in themselves shorten life.[275]

When dealing with patients nearing the end of their lives, doctors are likely to find that they can take advantage of a fine but important legal distinction. Directly intended killing is, other than wholly exceptionally in self-defence or prevention of crime, an action that is always unjustified (whatever the motive). However, when death is merely foreseen as a virtually certain consequence of an action—indirect intent—that opens up the possibility that the direct intention lying behind that action could justify the

---

[269] [1957] Crim LR 365.   [270] See (1992) BMLR 38.
[271] *R (on the application of Nicklinson)* v *Ministry of Justice* [2014] UKSC 38, para. 255.
[272] A. Arlidge, 'The Trial of Dr Moor' [2000] Crim LR 31.
[273] See, more broadly, E. C. Lyons, 'Slaughter of the Innocents: Justification, Excuse and the Principle of Double Effect' (2013) BJCL 232, 231.   [274] Chapter 6.4 and Chapter 8.3.
[275] See the discussion at section 5.8(a).

action in the circumstances; and cases in which patients are being treated provide a source of such justifications.[276]

Even though the law is clear that there is no necessity-based permission for killing, or assisting suicide, through a direct intention, it has been argued that there could be a (partial) *excusatory* defence to murder of 'compassionate killing'.[277] Strong though the argument is, it would, ironically, apply only where the killing was performed by a close relative or friend driven by strong emotion, and thus where professional safeguards and ethics, openness and accountability—the hallmark of medically permitted procedures—were absent.[278]

What about other kinds of medical necessity? The summing-up in *Bourne* (1939)[279] is sometimes cited as authority that a doctor may not be convicted (there, for carrying out an abortion) if it is necessary to save the life of the patient—a 'double effect' approach, although that particular area of the law is now subject to express statutory provisions.[280] More common in recent times has been the acceptance by the Courts of 'concealed defences' of medical necessity, by means of stretching established concepts. In the next chapter we will show how the House of Lords in *Gillick* v *West Norfolk and Wisbech Area Health Authority*[281] in effect extended the approach taken in cases such as Dr Moor's Case.[282] The House of Lords held that, so long as a prohibited result is not the directly intended product of a treatment decision by a medical practitioner, it can quite possibly be justified even if the prohibited result is foreseen as certain to occur. In this case, looking beyond cases concerned with pain relief, the treatment decision in question was a decision to prescribe contraceptives to a young girl, on the basis that this was in the best interests of her health.

One way of bringing such issues into the open would be to create a special defence, which might (following Paul Robinson's suggested draft) provide a permission for reasonable treatment for the promotion of the patient's health.[283] The definition would be quite elaborate, and much would turn on the criteria of reasonableness. Some would contend that 'reasonableness' should be determined by reference to practices 'accepted at the time by a responsible body of medical opinion',[284] whereas the ultimate determination ought surely to be that of the court.[285] Alternatively, the judges could be left to develop a defence at common law. One of the first English judges to confront some of the issues was Lord Goff in his speech in *Re F*,[286] where he distinguished three forms of

---

[276] See A. Ashworth, 'Criminal Liability in a Medical Context: The Treatment of Good Intentions', in A. P. Simester and A. T. H. Smith (eds), *Harm and Culpability* (1996).

[277] H. Keating and J. Bridgeman, 'Compassionate Killings: The Case for a Partial Defence' (2012) 75 MLR 697.

[278] For discussion of these points, see Law Commission Consultation Paper No. 177, *A New Homicide Act for England and Wales?* (2005), part 8.

[279] [1939] 1 KB 687.

[280] Abortion Act 1967.

[281] [1986] AC 112, discussed in Chapter 6.5(b). Smith, n 184, 64–70; Ashworth, n 276.

[282] See text at n 272.   [283] P. Robinson, *Criminal Law Defences* (Columbia University Press,1984), ii, 173.

[284] *Airedale NHS Trust* v *Bland* [1993] AC 789, *per* Lord Browne-Wilkinson at 883.

[285] As Lord Mustill argued in the *Bland* case.

[286] [1990] 2 AC 1; see S. Gardner, 'Necessity's Newest Inventions' (1991) 11 Oxford JLS 125.

necessity—public necessity, private necessity, and necessity in aid of another. The last category was not merely confined to medical cases (e.g. acting to preserve the life of a person who is in a condition that makes it impossible to give consent) but also extends to other cases of action to protect the safety or property of a person unable to give consent. The key element of the decision in *Re F* was that the necessity was determined by reference to the patient's best interests. It might be possible to reconcile the result of *Bourne*[287] with this approach, but the reasoning in that case was that the interests of the young mother should be allowed to override those of the foetus. That kind of balancing of interests was ruled out in *Dudley and Stephens*, but it underlies the reasoning of Brooke LJ in *Re A (Conjoined Twins: Surgical Separation)*,[288] where he distinguished *Dudley and Stephens* on the ground that in *Re A* there was no doubt about the person whose life should be sacrificed and why (that she was incapable of separate existence, and that a failure to operate would hasten the death of both twins). This frank approach to the problem is preferable to the distorting effect of some of the earlier decisions. However, the court was of the opinion that this case was unique—standing on the border of necessity and defensive action taken to save another's life—and cannot be treated as a peg on which to hang further extensions.

(c) NECESSITY AND JUDICIAL DEVELOPMENT OF PERMISSIONS

In the past almost all permissions were developed by the judges. If the criminal law is to be codified, should an exhaustive list of permissions be included? The Law Commission thinks not. Its draft Criminal Code includes provisions on duress and on permissible force, but clause 45(4) provides that a person does not commit an offence by doing an act that is permitted or excused by 'any rule of common law continuing to apply by virtue of section 4(4)'.[289] The intended effect is to preserve the power of the courts to develop defences, including permissions. There is an evident need for flexibility in responding to new sets of circumstances, but on the other hand the courts are not suited to the kind of wide-ranging review that ought to be carried out before a permission is recognized or even taken away.[290] A code should go as far as it can in formulating the permissions for what would otherwise be criminal conduct, even if it must rely on terms such as 'reasonable' at various points. This may mean the open discussion not merely of hitherto concealed defences such as medical necessity,[291] but also of broader concepts of necessity.

In general, conscious of their limited powers to weigh all the relevant factors, and enter into any kind of consultation process, the courts have been reluctant to permit the defence of necessity to develop beyond narrow boundaries. Thus in *Shayler*[292]

---

[287] [1939] 1 KB 687.
[288] [2000] 4 All ER 961, on which see J. Rogers, 'Necessity, Private Defence and the Killing of Mary' [2001] Crim LR 515.   [289] For discussion see Law Com No. 177, ii, para. 12.41.
[290] See Chapter 4.5, and S. Gardner 'Necessity's Newest Inventions' (1991) 11 Oxford JLS 125.
[291] See Chapter 7.3(c).
[292] [2001] 1 WLR 2206; the case went to the House of Lords on other grounds: [2003] 1 AC 247.

(disclosure of official secrets in order to expose alleged failures by the security services to protect citizens adequately) and again in *Jones, Milling* et al.[293] (damage to an airbase in order to impede aircraft leaving for the invasion of Iraq), the appellate courts took a highly restrictive approach to the prospect of a defence of necessity. One reason for this approach is that a plea of necessity may be employed to frustrate the purpose of a statutory scheme, as the court found in *S(C)*,[294] where D pleaded necessity as a basis for abducting her own child and taking the child outside the jurisdiction. However, whilst the conditions for the application of the defence ought to be tightly circumscribed, the mere fact that a plea of necessity may have a 'political' dimension to it, as in *Shayler* or *Jones*, is no reason to deny its existence.[295]

(d) STATUTORY RECOGNITION OF PURPOSE-BASED PERMISSIONS

There is an increasing tendency to insert into legislation some specific permissions, linked to D's purpose in acting. A long-standing example is s. 5(4) of the Misuse of Drugs Act 1971, allowing a defence to drugs charges if D's purpose in keeping the possession of the drugs was to prevent another from committing an offence or to hand them over to the authorities. Another example is s. 87 of the Road Traffic Regulation Act 1984,[296] creating exemptions from speed limits for emergency vehicles. Sections 1 and 4 of the Protection from Harassment Act 1997 both include defences for persons whose course of conduct (which might otherwise amount to 'stalking') was 'pursued for the purpose of preventing or detecting crime'.[297] Section 73 of the Sexual Offences Act 2003 states that a person cannot be convicted of aiding, abetting, or counselling a child sex offence if he acts 'for the purpose of (a) protecting the child from sexually transmitted infection, (b) protecting the physical safety of the child, (c) preventing the child from becoming pregnant, or (d) promoting the child's emotional well-being by the giving of advice'.[298] The presence of the permission depends here on the purpose or motive for which D acts, a point underlined by the further requirement that D does not act for the purpose of sexual gratification or in order to encourage sexual activity.

5.9 CONCLUSIONS

Many of the doctrines considered in this chapter hinge, at crucial junctures, on malleable terminology which leaves considerable discretion to those who apply the law. This is at its plainest with the ubiquitous term 'reasonable' in the permissions, although there is now some evidence of a more principled approach. Discretion is also conceded

---

[293] [2007] 1 AC 136.   [294] *S(C)* [2012] EWCA Crim 389.

[295] S. Gardner, 'Direct Action and the Defence of Necessity' [2005] Crim LR 371; cf. C. Clarkson, 'Necessary Action: a New Defence' [2004] Crim LR 81.   [296] As amended by s. 19 of the Road Safety Act 2006.

[297] See further A. Ashworth, 'Testing Fidelity to Legal Values: Official Involvement and Criminal Justice', in Shute and Simester (eds), *Criminal Law Theory*, at 322–30.

[298] See also the similar defence for principals in s. 14 of the Sexual Offences Act 2003 (facilitating the commission of a child sex offence).

by the proposition that the boundaries of omissions liability turn on the interpretation of particular words in statutes, by various concepts in the sphere of causation (e.g. *de minimis*, 'voluntary'), and by such notions as prior fault and 'external factor' in automatism. The presence of these open-ended terms does not empty the rules of their significance, but it raises doubts about the law's commitment to the values upheld by the principle of maximum certainty outlined in Chapter 4. It is one thing to leave the rules open-ended when persons are unlikely to rely on them as such (as with the excusatory defences discussed in Chapter 7), although even there the value of consistent judicial decisions should not be overlooked. It is another thing to leave the rules open-ended when citizens as well as courts may rely on them. In that respect, the enactment of s. 76 of the Criminal Justice and Immigration Act 2008 is almost an irrelevance, and certainly a sorely missed opportunity.

In this chapter we have also seen the first signs of the impact of the European Convention on English criminal law. More still needs to be done to bring the terms of the defence of reasonable chastisement of children into line with Art. 3, and there is a strong case for going further and abolishing the defence entirely. The effects of Art. 2 on the various rules governing the permission to use force are more difficult to gauge, partly because the leading Strasbourg decisions are not as clear as some would maintain. However, before Parliament accepted the amendment that became s. 76 of the 2008 Act there should have been a proper public assessment of the positive obligations stemming from Art. 2: the government's rather late and cursory treatment of the issue suggests less than full commitment to the Human Rights Act.

FURTHER READING

V. BERGELSON, 'Choice of Evils: In Search of a Viable Rationale' (2012) 6 *Criminal Law and Philosophy* 289.

I. DENNIS, 'On Necessity as a Defence to Crime: Possibilities, Problems and the Limits of Justification and Excuse' (2009) 3 *Criminal Law and Philosophy* 29.

R. A. DUFF, *Answering for Crime* (Hart Publishing , 2007), ch 5.

H. L. A. HART and T. Honoré, *Causation in the Law* (2nd edn., Clarendon Press , 1985), chs XII and XIII.

E. JACKSON, *Medical Law: Text, Cases and Materials*, (3rd edn., Oxford University Press , 2013), ch 5.4.

B. KOTECHA, 'Necessity as a Defence to Murder: An Anglo-Canadian Perspective' (2014) J Crim Law 341.

R. D. MACKAY, *Mental Condition Defences in the Criminal Law* (Oxford University Press , 1995), ch 1.

S. MILLER, ' "Grossly Disproportionate": Home Owners' Legal Licence to Kill' (2013) J Crim L 299.

A. NORRIE, *Crime Reason and History* (3rd edn., Cambridge University Press, 2014), chs 6–9.

B. SANGERO, *Self-Defence in Criminal Law* (Hart Publishing, 2006).

V. TADROS, *Criminal Responsibility* (Oxford University Press, 2005), ch 10.

6

CRIMINAL CAPACITY, *MENS REA*, AND FAULT

6.1 THE ISSUES

In Chapter 5 we examined some of the fundamental requirements of a crime that are usually embraced by the notion of *actus reus*—voluntary act, causation, and absence of justification. In this chapter we deal first with another fundamental requirement of a crime, criminal capacity. It is a precondition of criminal liability that the defendant is a person with sufficient capacity to be held responsible, and this leads to an examination of infancy and insanity as barriers to criminal responsibility (section 6.2). We then move to consider the capacity of companies or organizations to be found criminally liable (section 6.3). Having established that the defendant meets the preconditions for criminal responsibility, we then move to consider the fault requirements, or *mens rea* (as criminal lawyers often call them). An important fault element intention, proof of which is required in many crimes including major ones such as murder, rape, and robbery. The presence of a fault element may not mean that D was necessarily culpable, in an all-things considered sense. The latter depends on whether D's conduct was justified (Chapter 5) or was excused (Chapter 7). Those considerations apart, the fault element normally indicates culpability, and in section 6.4 we explore some of the reasons for and against the criminal law requiring proof of fault in any form. We then go on, in section 6.5, to give detailed consideration to the principal varieties of fault requirement in the criminal law.

We should note at this point that the majority of crimes in English law have no fault element and impose 'strict' liability. These are offences for which neither intention, nor recklessness, nor negligence needs to be proved. Most of these are summary offences, triable only in the magistrates' courts and carrying relatively low penalties.[1] Further, even when crimes do have a fault element, it may not relate to every part of the *actus reus*. Many such crimes are triable in the Crown Court. So, for example, the offence of, 'assault occasioning actual bodily harm' (contrary to s. 47 of the Offences Against the Person Act 1861), requires proof of fault only in relation to the element of 'assault'. There is no requirement to prove that the defendant was, or should have been, aware that the assault might, 'occasion actual bodily harm'. So, as far as the element of 'occasioning actual bodily harm is concerned, there is no need to prove any fault element; hence, this offence is of 'partial fault' only.[2]

It is therefore important, throughout this chapter, to distinguish between normative claims about the principles the law should observe and the realities of the law as it is. It may be argued that criminal conviction should always be founded on proof of fault, but it would require reform affecting thousands of offences to turn that aspiration into a reality. In order to underscore this point, section 6.5 of this chapter begins with a discussion of strict liability, before turning to intention, recklessness, and negligence.

Two further points must be made at this stage. One is that it is not unusual for an offence to have two or more different fault elements, relating to different aspects of the *actus reus*: the point may be illustrated by considering the several different elements in 'abuse of trust' offences in ss. 16–19 of the Sexual Offences Act 2003. These include the various requirements that D intentionally does the sexual activity, that D knows or could reasonably be expected to know of the circumstances by virtue of which he is in a position of trust in relation to the victim, and which requires no knowledge as to age if the victim is under 13 but requires reasonable belief that the victim is 18 if in fact he or she is aged 13–17. It is much clearer if crimes such as these are analysed in terms of their separate elements—for example, conduct, circumstances, result—so as to ascertain what form of fault is required in respect of each element. This leads to a second point: as we go through the specific offences in later chapters, we will see that it is not just the terminology of fault requirements that is diverse (many statutes contain words such as 'maliciously' and 'wilfully') but also their substance (e.g. requirements such as 'dishonestly' and 'fraudulently').

The discussion in this chapter does not purport to cover all fault terms and is confined to positive fault requirements, in other words, the mental element specified in (or implied within) the offence which the prosecution must establish. Selected for analysis are core fault terms such as intention, recklessness, knowledge, and negligence (the core fault elements under the US Model Penal Code), together with offences that use other terminology which has been held to impose a form of 'strict' or no-fault liability. One difficulty in focusing on a small range of fault terms is that the existing variety of approaches to fault is not captured, and that any generalization on the basis of

---

[1] A. Ashworth and M. Blake, 'The Presumption of Innocence in English Criminal Law' [1996] Crim LR 306.
[2] See further, Chapter 9(3)(d).

a few fault terms may lead to inaccurate conclusions.[3] We will return to that difficulty at the end of the chapter, after laying some foundations for wider discussion.

6.2 AGENCY, CAPACITY, AND MENTAL DISORDER

One of the fundamental presumptions of the criminal law and criminal liability is that the defendant is 'normal', that is, is able to function within the normal range of mental and physical capabilities. Many of the principles of respect discussed in Chapter 4 presuppose an individual who is rational and morally autonomous: otherwise he does not deserve to be liable to criminal punishment. A person who is mentally disordered may fall below these assumed standards of mental capacity and rationality, and this may make it unfair to hold him responsible for his behaviour. It is for this moral autonomy-based reason that most systems of criminal law contain tests of 'insanity' which result in the exemption of some mentally disordered persons from criminal liability. A similar rationale may be given for the voluntariness requirement, discussed in Chapter 5. There is also the prior question of whether the defendant is fit to be tried—whether the person can participate in the trial in a sufficiently meaningful sense. It is an essential precondition of a fair trial, as Antony Duff has argued,[4] that the defendant is a responsible citizen who is answerable before the court. The doctrine of 'unfitness to plead', embodies a procedural attempt to deal with this in relation to mentally disordered defendants.[5] Once it has been decided that a person is fit to plead, there is still the question whether at the time of the alleged act D was a sufficiently responsible moral agent: the defence of insanity, discussed in paragraphs (b) and (c) below, addresses this issue. Before, that, however, a few words must be said about young children, where legitimate concerns about answerability to the court and moral agency have received an unsatisfactory response from English lawmakers.

(a) THE MINIMUM AGE OF CRIMINAL RESPONSIBILITY

In England and Wales the minimum age of criminal responsibility is 10, substantially lower than the minimum age in many other European countries (although higher than in some US states), where teenage children are dealt with in civil tribunals up to the age of 13 (France), 14 (Germany), 15 (Scandinavia), or 16 (Spain and Portugal). At common law the presumption of *doli incapax* applied to children under 14, requiring the prosecution to establish that the child knew that the behaviour was seriously wrong

---

[3] For debate see J. Gardner and H. Jung, 'Making Sense of Mens Rea: Antony Duff's Account' (1991) 11 Oxford JLS 559; J. A. Laing, 'The Prospects of a Theory of Criminal Culpability: Mens Rea and Methodological Doubt' (1994) 14 Oxford JLS 57; J. Gardner, 'Criminal Law and the Uses of Theory: a Reply to Laing' (1994) 14 Oxford JLS 217.

[4] E.g. R. A. Duff, 'Law, Language and Community: Some Preconditions of Criminal Liability' (1998) 18 Oxford JLS 189.

[5] For further analysis, see Law Commission, *Unfitness to Plead* (CP No. 197, 2010): a final report is due in the Autumn of 2015; R. Mackay, *Mental Conditions Defences in Criminal Law* (1995), ch 6.

before the case could go ahead. The presumption was much criticized,[6] some arguing that children who failed to realize the wrongness of their behaviour were more in need of conviction and compulsory treatment,[7] and it was abolished by s. 34 of the Crime and Disorder Act 1998.[8] However, it remains important to think about fundamental issues in relation to the responsibility of young offenders. Are they fit to stand trial at the age of 10? Do they have sufficient understanding of the proceedings to participate meaningfully in them? In what sense are they responsible citizens at that age? Can it be said that, when they do criminal things with the required fault element, they are acting as moral agents, in a sufficiently full sense?[9] The first two points were discussed by the European Court of Human Rights in *V and T v United Kingdom* (1999),[10] drawing on the United Nations Convention on the Rights of the Child, which does not lay down a minimum age of criminal responsibility but does declare several other relevant standards.[11] The Court held that, although the trial process to which the two 11-year-old applicants were subjected did not amount to 'inhuman and degrading treatment' within Art. 3 of the Convention, the trial did violate Art. 6 in its failure to ensure that the boys understood the proceedings and had the opportunity to participate, and in the failure to reduce feelings of intimidation and inhibition. A subsequent Practice Direction sets out the steps that trial judges should take in these unusual cases in order to comply with Art. 6,[12] but the Strasbourg Court has held that this gives insufficient priority to the need to ensure that all young children have adequate opportunity to participate meaningfully in the criminal trial.[13]

The European Commissioner on Human Rights has specifically recommended that consideration be given to raising the age of criminal responsibility 'in line with norms prevailing across Europe', on the grounds that children of 10, 11, or 12 cannot have sufficient understanding of the nature and consequences of their actions.[14] The cognitive abilities of young children may not be sufficiently developed; their self-control may not yet have developed adequately; and they may be particularly susceptible to peer pressure at that age.[15] These are all aspects of moral development and, since childhood and adolescence are the time when moral reasoning and self-control should be learnt, it is not reasonable for the criminal law to demand as much from children as from adults.[16]

---

[6] Notably by the House of Lords in *C v DPP* [1996] AC 1.

[7] An argument expressed strongly by G. Williams, 'The Criminal Responsibility of Children' [1954] Crim LR 493, at 495–6.

[8] For discussion of whether a defence of *doli incapax* still exists, see *DPP v P* [2006] 4 All ER 628 and *T* [2008] 2 Cr App R 17.   [9] See the discussion in Chapter 4.3.   [10] (1999) 30 EHRR 121.

[11] G. van Bueren, *The International Law on the Rights of the Child* (1995), ch 7.

[12] *Practice Direction: Crown Court (Trial of Children and Young Persons)* [2000] 1 Cr App R 483.

[13] *SC v United Kingdom* (2005) 40 EHRR 226; L. Hoyano, 'The Coroners and Justice Act 2009: Special Measures Directions Take Two: Entrenching Unequal Access to Justice?' [2010] Crim LR 346.

[14] Office of the Commissioner of Human Rights, Report by Mr Alvaro Gil-Robles, *Commissioner for Human Rights, on his visit to the United Kingdom* (Comm DH (2005) 6), paras. 105–7.

[15] F. Zimring, 'Toward a Jurisprudence of Youth Violence', in M. Tonry and M. Moore (eds), *Youth Violence* (1998), 447.

[16] A. von Hirsch and A. Ashworth, *Proportionate Sentencing* (2005), ch 3.

A moral autonomy-based case for raising the minimum age of criminal responsibility in England and Wales is overwhelming.[17]

(b) THE SPECIAL VERDICT OF INSANITY

If the defendant is thought fit to stand trial, then the issue of mental disorder may be raised as a defence; namely, that at the time of the alleged offence D was too disordered to be held liable.[18] Medical evidence will be crucial in determining this,[19] but it is for the law to lay down the appropriate test. Mental disorder is a broad concept under the Mental Health Act 1983, as amended by the Mental Health Act 2007, and few would maintain that all those who fall within one of the four classes of disorder under that Act should be exempted from criminal liability. The criminal law has settled on a much narrower conception of 'insanity', proof of which should lead to a verdict of 'not guilty by reason of insanity'. In order to understand how this defence functions, however, it is important to bear in mind that until the Criminal Procedure (Insanity and Unfitness to Plead) Act 1991 came into force, the result of a successful defence of insanity was mandatory and indefinite commitment to a mental hospital. Whilst research revealed that about one-fifth of defendants thus committed were released within nine months,[20] there was no certainty of, or entitlement to, early release and the potentially severe effect of the insanity verdict was enough to lead many defendants to plead guilty and to hope for a more favourable disposal at the sentencing stage.[21] The 1991 Act gave the court the same discretion after an insanity verdict (except in murder cases, dealt with later) as it has after a finding of unfitness to plead: hospital order, supervision, absolute discharge.[22] This still leaves the possibility that the court will order deprivation of liberty, even though the defendant has 'succeeded' on a 'defence'. Insanity defences remain rare, with an average of fifteen per year from 1999–2001, but around half of the disposals are community-based, that is, supervision or absolute discharge.[23]

The possible legal consequences of the insanity verdict show the tension between considerations of individual autonomy and the public good of security in this sphere,

---

[17] See further H. Keating, 'Reckless Children' [2007] Crim LR 546.

[18] Law Commission, *Insanity and Automatism: A Discussion Paper* (2013); R. Mackay, *Mental Condition Defences in Criminal Law*, ch 2; V. Tadros, *Criminal Responsibility* (2008), ch 12.

[19] Section 1(2) of the Criminal Procedure (Insanity and Unfitness to Plead) Act 1991 requires the evidence of two doctors, at least one of them approved by the Home Secretary as an experienced psychiatrist.

[20] R. D. Mackay, 'Fact and Fiction about the Insanity Defence' [1990] Crim LR 247.

[21] The presence in prison, in consequence, of many offenders with mental disorders was criticized in Lord Bradley's Report, *People with Mental Health Problems or Learning Disabilities in the Criminal Justice System* (2009).

[22] Hospital orders, with a restriction indicating the minimum time to be spent in hospital to protect the public from serious harm, form roughly 38 per cent of disposals in insanity cases, with supervision orders being made in around 41 per cent of cases: R. D. Mackay, B. J. Mitchell, and L. Howe, 'Yet More Facts about the Insanity Defence' [2006] Crim LR 399.

[23] Mackay, Mitchell, and Howe, 'Yet More Facts about the Insanity Defence'.

and the same tension is manifest in the evidential and procedural provisions.[24] Insanity is the only general defence where the burden of proof is placed on the defendant,[25] a paradox when one reflects that the consequence of a successful defence may be a court order favouring social protection rather than the defendant's own interests. The prosecution may raise insanity if the defendant pleads diminished responsibility in response to a murder charge,[26] and, according to one view, can do so in all cases where D puts state of mind in issue.[27] The prosecution bears the burden of proving insanity here, which is much more appropriate given the consequences of the verdict of 'not guilty by reason of insanity'.

The requirements of the defence of insanity were laid down by the judges in *M'Naghten's Case* as long ago as 1843:[28]

> to establish a defence on the ground of insanity, it must be clearly proved that, at the time of committing the act, the party accused was labouring under such a defect of reason, from disease of the mind, as not to know the nature and quality of the act he was doing; or, if he did know it, that he did not know he was doing what was wrong.

A 'defect of reason' means the deprivation of reasoning power, and does not apply to temporary absent-mindedness or confusion.[29] It is, however, limited to cognitive defects, and therefore excludes from the insanity defence those forms of mental disorder that involve significant emotional or volitional deficiencies. Although in that respect the definition of insanity is very narrow,[30] in other respects it is so wide as to go well beyond even the general definition of mental disorder in the Mental Health Acts 1983–2007. Thus the phrase 'disease of the mind' has been construed so as to encompass any disease which affects the functioning of the mind—whether its cause be organic or functional, and whether its effect be permanent or intermittent—so long as it was operative at the time of the alleged offence.[31] This means, as we saw in Chapter 4.2(c), that any condition which affects the functioning of the mind and which results from an 'internal' rather than an 'external' cause will be deemed to be a 'disease of the mind', and if D relies on it in his defence he will be held to be raising the defence of insanity. The 'internal factor' doctrine has resulted in epilepsy,[32] sleepwalking,[33] and hyperglycaemia[34] being classified as insanity. This shows that the policy of

---

[24] See A. Loughnan, '"Manifest Madness": Towards a New Understanding of the Insanity Defence' (2007) 70 MLR 379, proposing a reinterpretation of the exceptional procedural and evidential provisions relating to insanity.

[25] T. H. Jones, 'Insanity, Automatism and the Burden of Proof on the Accused' (1995) 111 LQR 475; a challenge to this under Art. 6.2 of the Convention now seems unlikely to succeed, following the Court of Appeal's decision in *Lambert, Jordan and Ali* [2001] 1 Cr App R 205 to uphold the reverse onus in diminished responsibility.   [26] Criminal Procedure (Insanity) Act 1964, s. 6.

[27] Per Watkins LJ, in *Dickie* (1984) 79 Cr App R 213, at 219.   [28] (1843) 10 Cl and Fin 200.

[29] *Clarke* (1972) 56 Cr App R 226.   [30] See paragraph (d) later in this chapter.

[31] Per Lord Diplock, in *Sullivan* [1984] AC 156.   [32] *Sullivan* [1984] AC 156.

[33] *Burgess* [1991] 2 QB 92, overlooked in the rape case of *Bilton*, Daily Telegraph, 20 December 2006. See also the decision of the Canadian Supreme Court in *Parks* (1990) 95 DLR (4th) 27.

[34] *Hennessy* (1989) 89 Cr App R 10.

social protection has gained the upper hand, and that the judiciary has been prepared to overlook the gross unfairness of labelling these people as insane in order to ensure that the court has the power to take measures of social defence against them. Even then, the policy of protection has not been carried to its logical conclusion, since the law now perpetrates the absurdity of classifying *hyper*glycaemia as insanity (protective measures possible under the 1991 Act) whilst, because of the external/internal distinction, classifying *hypo*glycaemia as automatism (resulting in an outright acquittal unless prior fault can be shown).[35] More will be said about this later.

Where it is established that there was a defect of reason due to disease of the mind, it is then necessary to show that it had one of two effects.[36] First, the defence is fulfilled if D did not know the nature and quality of the act—in other words, did not realize what he was doing. In most cases this would show the absence of intention, knowledge, or recklessness; but since this mental state arises from insanity, considerations of protection are held to require the special verdict rather than an ordinary acquittal. Secondly, the defence is fulfilled if D did not know that he was doing wrong. English law appears ambivalent about the proper approach to this requirement: the Court of Appeal has confirmed that 'wrong' bears the narrow meaning of 'legally wrong',[37] although there is evidence that in practice courts sometimes act upon the Australian interpretation of 'failure to appreciate that the conduct was morally wrong' (usually, where D believes that he must, for some distorted reason, do the act).[38] The main difficulty with English law's insistence on confining this second limb to cases in which D knew that his or her act was legally wrong, is that it is using a test to judge those suffering from certain kinds of mental disorder that negate the moral relevance of the test. In terms of culpability, someone so deluded that he or she kills a boy because he or she thinks that the boy is the re-incarnation of Napoleon, is more or less on a par with someone so deluded that he or she kills a girl because he or she believes that the girl is at that moment trying to kill the Queen through the use of supernatural thought powers. Yet, formally, only the latter comes within the scope of the insanity defence. Only in the latter case does D's delusion mean that he or she does not appreciate that what he or she doing is 'legally' wrong because he or she believes that he or she is acting necessarily and proportionately in defence of another. By contrast, in the former case, D may think that what he or she did was not morally wrong (preventing a full-grown Napoleon re-appearing on the world stage), but may fully appreciate that it was legally wrong. This is unsatisfactory,

[35] See, more fully, Chapter 4.2.

[36] The fact that these limbs of *M'Naghten* are alternatives ought to mean that insanity may be a defence to strict liability crimes too, since the second test is applicable there, and a Divisional Court ruling to the contrary is difficult to support: *DPP* v *H* [1997] 1 WLR 1406, analysed critically by T. Ward, 'Magistrates, Insanity and the Common Law' [1997] Crim LR 796.

[37] *Johnson* [2008] Crim LR 132, applying *Windle* [1952] 2 QB 826, which had been followed by the majority of the Supreme Court of Canada in *Schwartz* (1979) 29 CCC (2d) 1.

[38] *Stapleton* v *R* (1952) 86 CLR 358; research evidence from R. Mackay and G. Kearns ('More Facts about the Insanity Defence [1999] Crim LR 714; and Mackay, Mitchell, and Howe, 'Yet More Facts about Insanity' at 406–7) shows that many psychiatrists interpret 'wrongness' in this wider sense, and that courts seem to accept this.

but it seems that legislative reform would be required to introduce the broader 'moral wrong' test.

(c) REFORM

Two major issues concerning defences of mental disorder emerge from the above discussion: the question of definition and the question of protective measures. In the past, the latter has often driven the former in that the definition has been expanded to include persons against whom compulsory measures are thought to be necessary, whether or not they would be regarded by experts as suffering from a serious mental disorder. The 1991 Act altered the balance somewhat, since committal to a mental hospital is now only a possible and not an inevitable consequence of a special verdict of not guilty by reason of insanity. But the label 'insane' remains, and it is manifestly unsuitable for those whose behaviour stemmed from epilepsy, somnambulism, or diabetes. In that regard in a welcome development, the Law Commission has proposed the replacement of the term, 'insanity', with the term, 'recognized medical condition'.[39]

Defence lawyers will rightly challenge aspects of the insanity doctrine under the Human Rights Act.[40] Article 6.1(e) of the European Convention allows that 'persons of unsound mind' may lawfully be deprived of their liberty, but the leading decision in *Winterwerp* v *Netherlands*[41] lays down three further requirements. First, there must be a close correspondence between expert medical opinion and the relevant definition of mental disorder: that can hardly be said of a test formulated in 1843 and subsequently held to encompass epilepsy, hyperglycaemia, and sleepwalking.[42] Secondly, the court's decision must be based on 'objective medical expertise', a requirement that could be used in conjunction with the 1991 Act to hold that psychiatric reports to the court should be accorded more weight than under the restrictive *M'Naghten* test.[43] Thirdly, the court must decide that the mental disorder is 'of a kind or degree warranting compulsory confinement', and until the law was changed in 2004 the court had no opportunity to make such a determination in murder cases.[44]

---

[39] Law Commission Discussion Paper, *Insanity and Automatism* (2013); R. D. Mackay and G. Reuber, 'Epilepsy and the Defence of Insanity—Time for Change?' [2007] Crim LR 782; R. D. Mackay and B. J. Mitchell, 'Sleepwalking, Automatism and Insanity' [2006] Crim LR 901; see also the discussion on automatism in Chapter 5.2(f).

[40] A Convention challenge to the *M'Naghten* Rules has already met with some success in Jersey: R. D. Mackay and C. A. Gearty, 'On Being Insane in Jersey' [2001] Crim LR 560.

[41] (1979) 2 EHRR 387.

[42] P. J. Sutherland and C. A. Gearty, 'Insanity and the European Court of Human Rights' [1992] Crim LR 418.

[43] E. Baker, 'Human Rights, M'Naghten and the 1991 Act' [1994] Crim LR 84.

[44] A new s. 5 of the 1991 Act, inserted by s. 24 of the Domestic Violence, Crime, and Victims Act 2004, gives courts a choice of orders following the special verdict in a murder case. If D is suffering from a mental disorder making detention in hospital appropriate under s. 37 of the Mental Health Act 1983, the judge has the power to make a hospital detention order. If the judge finds that D poses a threat of serious harm to the public, the judge can make an additional 'restriction' order, imposing a minimum time period before D can be considered for discharge from hospital: Criminal Procedure (Insanity) Act 1964, s. 5 (as amended).

Although arguments based on Art. 5 only have purchase at the stage where D is deprived of liberty, they are relevant in many cases and it would be best if the defence of insanity itself were reformed sensibly before piecemeal challenges are mounted under the Human Rights Act. The *M'Naghten* Rules are widely recognized to be outmoded. They refer only to mental disorders which affect the cognitive faculties, that is, knowledge of what one is doing, or of its wrongness, whereas some forms of mental disorder impair practical reasoning and the power of control over actions. This is now recognized in the 'diminished responsibility' doctrine in manslaughter,[45] which includes cases of 'irresistible impulse', and it should clearly be recognized as part of a reformed mental disorder defence. The Model Penal Code accomplishes this by referring to mental disorders which result in D lacking 'substantial capacity either to appreciate the wrongfulness of his conduct or to conform his conduct to the requirements of the law'.[46] The Butler Committee proposed to take this into account in a different way—by ensuring that one ground for a mental-disorder verdict is that, at the time of the alleged offence, D was suffering severe mental illness or handicap.[47] In other words, if the mental disorder was severe in degree, there should be no need to establish that it affected D's cognition: so long as the court is satisfied that the conduct was attributable to that disorder, the special verdict should be returned. It therefore includes both cognitive and volitional deficiencies, and places the insanity verdict more squarely on the ground of incapacity.[48] In doing so, however, it takes a somewhat static view of mental disorder, confining it more or less to the major psychoses.[49] It fails to recognize the variety of mental disorders, and the fact that some of them may substantially impair the patient's practical reasoning even though the diagnosis contains some contestable elements that not all experts agree on. Psychiatry has been attacked for offering diagnoses when these inevitably contestable elements are in issue, but the proper response is to recognize and discuss the contestable elements rather than to deny that they should influence criminal liability in any circumstances.[50]

Only to a small extent is this conservative approach to mental disorder mitigated by the second limb of the Butler proposals, also to be found in a revised form in the draft Criminal Code.[51] This provides for evidence of mental disorder to be adduced to show that D lacked the mental element for the crime. The Law Commission, unlike the Butler Committee, would limit the type of mental disorder that may be relied upon here to 'severe mental illness' and 'incomplete development of mind'. The Commission cited the danger of allowing too wide a definition, which would sweep in too many defendants.[52] However, the proposed definition is framed so as to include

---

[45] Homicide Act 1957, s. 2; see later in Chapter 7.4(e).   [46] Model Penal Code, s. 4.01.

[47] Butler Report, para. 18.30.

[48] Cf. Scottish Law Commission, *Report on Insanity and Diminished Responsibility* (2004), paras. 2.52–2.63, rejecting any volitional component in the insanity defence.

[49] Having said that, schizophrenia is in fact the most common basis for an insanity plea: Mackay, Mitchell, and Howe, 'Yet More Facts About the Insanity Defence'.

[50] K. W. M. Fulford, 'Value, Action, Mental Illness, and the Law', in S. Shute, J. Gardner, and J. Horder (eds), *Action and Value in Criminal Law* (1993).   [51] Law Com No. 177, cll. 34–40.

[52] Law Com No. 177, para. 11.27.

cases of 'pathological automatism that is liable to recur', and again classifies diabetes and epilepsy within mental disorder for reasons of social protection.[53] This is both contrary to the principle of fair labelling[54] and in violation of the European Convention, and should be abandoned. A separate form of defence should be devised for this group of conditions. Of course this leads to the problem of drawing a definitional line between 'insanity' and 'automatism', and it was the difficulty of doing so that led the Law Commission to bring these cases within the mental disorder defence, believing that this would be less 'offensive' and 'preposterous' than the insanity label.[55] Even if that answers the fair labelling argument, it leaves the European Convention challenge unaffected unless it is provided that no person with those conditions shall be deprived of liberty—and that, again, would require a separate definition.

In a valuable Discussion Paper, the Law Commission has proposed replacing the insanity defence with a defence of, 'not criminally responsible by reason of recognized medical condition' ('NCRRRMC').[56] The NCRRRMC defence has the great advantage of moving away from the formulaic, outdated, and partially ignored *M'Naghten* definition, and anchoring the replacement defence in contemporary medical practice. In that respect, such a change would tie in with the reforms in 2010 to the defence of diminished responsibility, which also now relies on proof that the defendant was suffering from a recognized medical condition.[57] In any event, the Law Commission takes the view that reform of the law governing unfitness to plead is more urgent, and if taken forward, would mean even fewer pleas of insanity or NCRRRMC.[58]

6.3 CORPORATE LIABILITY

(a) NATURAL AND CORPORATE PERSONALITY

Most discussion of criminal liability is concerned with individual defendants as authors of acts or omissions, raising questions of respect for the autonomy of individuals. However, many—perhaps most—criminal offences, certainly in regulatory spheres, are aimed at businesses large and small. This reflects the fact that corporate activities now play a major part in individual and commercial life. Companies are major employers, providers of goods and services (often in the public as well as in the private sector), providers of transport and of recreational facilities, and so forth. Since the nineteenth century, the criminal law has made increasing inroads into these spheres, spurred on in recent decades by the need to comply with European law. The courts have developed doctrines of vicarious and corporate liability, and the legislature had introduced new offences directed specifically as corporate activities in the financial and commercial

---

[53] Law Com No. 177, para. 11, 28.   [54] See above, section 6.7(a).
[55] Law Com No. 177, para. 11.28(c).
[56] Law Commission Discussion Paper, *Insanity and Automatism* (2013), para 1.22.
[57] See Chapter 8.4(C). Law Commission Discussion Paper, *Insanity and Automatism*, para. 4.141.
[58] Law Commission Discussion Paper, *Insanity and Automatism*, para. 1.14.

sphere (e.g. Financial Services and Markets Act 2000, and the Companies Acts 1985–9). Yet, historically, criminal law theorizing has developed around the notion of individual human beings as the bearers of rights and duties. It is still somewhat trapped in that framework, even though the idea of companies as separate legal entities from their shareholders and their management was established in the nineteenth century. A limited liability company has long been treated as a separate legal entity from the person or persons who control it.[59]

The present theory is that corporate personality attaches to companies just as natural personality attaches to individuals (with certain modifications). But does this theory, which has a secure grip in company law, mean that companies can be convicted of offences? The courts moved slowly in this direction in the mid-nineteenth century. Although still doubting whether companies could be said to *do* 'acts', the courts overcame any reluctance to hold companies liable for *failing* to act[60] and for committing a public nuisance.[61] The driving force behind these innovative decisions, both concerning railway companies in the early days of rail travel, was not legal theory but social protection: 'there can be no effective means of deterring from an oppressive exercise of power, for the purpose of gain, except the remedy by an indictment against those who truly commit it, that is, the corporation acting by its majority'.[62] And from there the law developed towards criminal liability for companies, acting through their controlling officers.[63]

(b) TOWARDS CORPORATE CRIMINAL LIABILITY

This subject was given a pressing social importance in the late 1980s by the series of disasters connected with corporate activities and involving considerable loss of life—for example, the Piper Alpha oil rig explosion, the Clapham rail disaster, the King's Cross fire, the sinking of the *Marchioness*, and in 1987 the capsize of the ferry *Herald of Free Enterprise*. It does not make sense to present each of these, and the string of subsequent transportation disasters, as the responsibility of a few individuals. Indeed, enquiries into the disasters have tended to emphasize the role of deficiencies in the systems of corporate management and accountability. Major disasters apart, a variety of organizations offer evidence of a constant stream of incidents of industrial pollution, unsafe working conditions, impure foods, and unfair business practices which impinge upon, or threaten to impinge upon, the lives of individual citizens.

Growing recognition of the significance of corporate harmdoing has not, however, been accompanied by substantial alteration of the framework of criminal liability. The trend, as we shall see, has been to attempt to fit corporate liability into the existing structure rather than to consider its implications afresh. More important in social

---

[59] *Salomon* v *Salomon* [1897] AC 22.   [60] *Birmingham and Gloucester Railway Co* (1842) 3 QB 223.
[61] *Great North of England Railway Co* (1846) 9 QB 316.   [62] *Per* Denham CJ at 320.
[63] Another landmark case was *Mousell Bros* v *London and North-Western Railway Co* [1917] 2 KB 836. For discussion of the history see L. H. Leigh, *The Criminal Liability of Corporations in English Law* (1969), ch 2, and Celia Wells, *Corporations and Criminal Responsibility* (2nd edn., 2001), ch 6.

terms, there has been little change of approach at the level of enforcement. It is one thing to have a set of laws which penalizes corporate wrongdoing as well as individual wrongdoing. It is quite another thing to have a balanced machinery of enforcement which strives to ensure the proportionate treatment of individuals and companies according to the relative seriousness of their offences. Present arrangements seem to draw a strong line between frequent police action against individuals and the relatively infrequent action of the various inspectorates, government departments, etc. against companies.[64] However, the social calculation cannot be presented simply as an imbalance in treatment between 'crime in the streets' and 'crime in the suites'. We must also take into account the finding of social surveys that it is street crimes that cause real harm and fear to people, not least to those who are already among the most disadvantaged in society.[65] It is therefore a question for discussion whether devoting large resources to the detection and prosecution of corporate harmdoers would be either defensible or socially acceptable. It is for reason of this kind that new approaches to corporate wrongdoing—fixed penalties and deferred prosecution agreements—have been introduced and become established.[66]

There are some straightforward applications of the doctrine that a company is a legal person, separate from the individuals involved in its operations. Thus, for example, two principal provisions of the Health and Safety at Work Act 1974 are as follows:

s. 2(1): 'It shall be the duty of every employer to ensure, so far as is reasonably practicable, the health, safety and welfare at work of all his employees.'

s. 3(1): 'It shall be the duty of every employer to conduct his undertaking in such a way as to ensure, so far as is reasonably practicable, that persons not in his employment who may be affected thereby are not thereby exposed to risks to their health and safety.'

These provisions, in conjunction with s. 33 of the Act (which creates an offence of failing to discharge either duty), are clearly directed at companies no less than at individual employers.[67] Thus in *British Steel plc*[68] the company was convicted of failing to discharge its duty under s. 3 of the Act. During an operation to re-locate a steel platform, under the supervision of a British Steel employee, an unsafe method of working led to the collapse of the platform and a sub-contracted worker was killed. The Court of Appeal upheld the conviction, on the basis that it was the employer on whom the duty was imposed, and the duty had clearly not been discharged. Similar reasoning can be used to hold companies liable for a whole range of offences of strict

[64] See A. Ashworth, 'Is the Criminal Law a Lost Cause?' (2000) 116 LQR 225, and the discussion by D. Nelken, 'White Collar Crime', in M. Maguire, R. Morgan, and R. Reiner (eds), *The Oxford Handbook of Criminology* (4th edn., 2007).

[65] T. Jones, D. Maclean, and J. Young, *The Islington Crime Survey* (1986); M. Gottfredson, *Fear of Crime* (Home Office Research Study No. 84, 1986).   [66] See the discussion in Chapter 1.

[67] *Associated Octel* [1996] 1 WLR 1543, a decision of the House of Lords. See also *Gateway Foodmarkets Ltd* [1997] Crim LR 512, imposing a duty under s. 2 of the Act on the employer in respect of the acts of all employees, not just those who were 'controlling minds' (see later).

[68] [1995] 1 WLR 1356; compare the much more restrictive approach in *Seaboard Offshore Ltd* v *Secretary of State for Transport* [1994] 1 WLR 541.

liability: just as much as any individual, company can cause pollution, sell goods, fail to submit annual returns, etc. An offence of strict liability is one which requires no fault for conviction: any person may be found guilty simply through doing or failing to do a certain act.[69] Thus, if a company owns the business or premises concerned, it may be convicted of failing to control emissions of pollutants, or for causing polluting matter to enter a stream, whether or not these events come about through fault on the companies part.[70]

(i) *The Possibility of Vicarious Liability:* Outside the criminal law there have been further developments, and the law of torts has established a doctrine of vicarious liability of employers for the conduct of their employees.[71] By contrast with federal law in the United States,[72] there is no such general doctrine in the criminal law, but various exceptions and quasi-exceptions are gaining a foothold. One is the 'delegation principle': where a statute imposes liability on the owner, licensee, or keeper of premises or other property, the courts will make that person vicariously liable for the conduct of anyone to whom management of the premises has been delegated.[73] This applies whether the defendant is an individual or a company. The underlying reason for this principle seems to lie in the assumption that such offences would otherwise be unenforceable, since delegation would remove responsibility from the person in effective control.[74]. The second exception revolves around the interpretation of such key words in statutes as 'sell', 'use', and 'possess'. The clearest example is where a statute prohibits the selling of goods in certain circumstances. *Coppen* v *Moore (No. 2)* (1898)[75] held the shop owner liable as the person who sold the goods in law, even though he was away from the shop at the time and an assistant carried out the transaction—in breach of the instructions left by the owner. So long as the assistant is acting as an agent rather than as a private individual, 'vicarious' liability is imposed.[76] In effect, a similar result flowed from the application of s. 3 of the Health and Safety at Work Act 1974 in the *British Steel* case, since the company was held liable for the inadequate supervision by

[69] See above, *Birmingham and Gloucester Railway Co*, n 60 and the discussion of strict liability in section 6.6(a).

[70] See the conviction under s. 85 of the Water Resources Act 1991 upheld in *Environment Agency* v *Empress Car Co (Abertillery)* [1999] 2 AC 22, criticized in Chapter 5.5(b).

[71] P. S. Atiyah, *Vicarious Liability in the Law of Torts* (1967).

[72] Where the sheer breadth of the vicarious liability doctrine has often been severely criticized. See, e.g., A. Weissmann, 'A New Approach to Corporate Criminal Liability' (2007) 44 *American Criminal Law Review* 1319.

[73] Cf. *Allen* v *Whitehead* [1930] 1 KB 211 with *Vane* v *Yiannopoullos* [1965] AC 486; see P. J. Pace, 'Delegation: A Doctrine in Search of a Definition' [1982] Crim LR 627.

[74] The doctrine was criticized by the Law Commission in, Consultation Paper No. 195 (2010), *Criminal Liability in Regulatory Contexts*, paras 7.35–7.57. in *St Regis Paper Company Ltd* [2011] EWCA Crim 2527, the delegation principle was confined to licensing cases. Modern legislation sometimes employs a different structure to deal with such situations, by (very broadly speaking) making it an offence for the owner or licensee etc. to allow unauthorized activity to go on: see, e.g., the Licensing Act 2003, s. 136.

[75] [1898] 2 QB 306.

[76] A. P. Simester and G. R. Sullivan, *Criminal Law: Theory and Doctrine* (3rd edn., 2007), 252, argue that this is not an example of vicarious liability because the owner does the *actus reus* himself since he is the seller. However, the physical act is that of his employee, so at least it is a form of quasi-vicarious liability.

its own employee.[77] A third exception or quasi-exception arises where a statutory offence penalizes conduct that appears to require a personal act, such as 'using' a motor
vehicle with defective brakes: in *James & Son* v *Smee*[78] the Divisional Court held the
company liable, on the basis that the use of the vehicle by an employee in the course of
employment constituted use by the employer.

The doctrine of vicarious liability is in tension with rule-of-law values, in that it is
unclear that it provides adequately for fair warning of the standards expected. Further,
fair warning is not assured if decisions are made by way of statutory interpretation in
the courts, rather than clearly by the legislature. Why the legislature continues to leave
such crucial matters to the courts, in criminal cases, remains one of the legal systems
enduring mysteries.

(ii) *The Identification Principle:* We now return to corporate liability as such. Most
of the instances discussed so far concern offences of strict liability, where it is often
easier to construe a statute so as to impose direct liability on a company. In 1944 the
courts began to develop a new doctrine which imposes liability on companies for offences requiring a mental element. In *DPP* v *Kent and Sussex Contractors Ltd*[79] the
defendant company was charged with two offences—making a statement which was
known to be false, and using a false document with intent to deceive. The Divisional
Court held that the company could be convicted of both offences, on the basis that its
officers possessed the required 'knowledge' and 'intent to deceive', and that those states
of mind could therefore be imputed to the company itself. As Viscount Caldecote CJ
held, 'a company is incapable of acting or speaking or even thinking except in so far as
its officers have acted, spoken or thought'. Thus the company is identified with those
officers who are its 'directing mind and will' for these purposes.[80]

This identification principle was applied in the leading case of *Tesco Supermarkets*
v *Nattrass* (1971),[81] where the company had been convicted of offering to sell goods
at a higher price than indicated, contrary to the Trade Descriptions Act 1968. A shop
assistant at a local Tesco store had failed to follow the manager's instructions, with
the result that the goods were offered at a higher price than advertised. The House of
Lords quashed the conviction, holding that the manager of one of the company's supermarkets was not sufficiently high up in the organization to 'represent the directing
mind and will of the company'. The identification principle is therefore fairly narrow
in its scope. It allows large companies to disassociate themselves from the conduct
of their local managers, and thus to avoid criminal liability. Moreover, where a large
national or multi-national company is prosecuted, the identification principle requires
the prosecution to establish that one of the directors or top managers had the required
knowledge or culpability. Managers at such a high level tend to focus on broader policy
issues, not working practices. Thus it may be considerably easier to achieve convictions

---

[77] See n 68 and accompanying text.
[78] [1955] 1 QB 78, discussed by Simester and Sullivan, *Criminal Law*, see n 76, 253.
[79] [1944] KB 146.
[80] Two other cases decided in the same year confirmed this approach: *ICR Haulage Ltd* [1944] KB 551,
and *Moore* v *I Bresler Ltd* [1944] 2 All ER 516.   [81] [1972] AC 153.

in respect of the activities of small companies than of large corporations, because there will tend to be more 'hands-on' management in smaller companies.[82]

The seeds for an expansion of the *Tesco v Nattrass* test have been sown by Lord Hoffmann, speaking for the Privy Council in *Meridian Global Funds Management Asia Ltd v Securities Commission* (1996).[83] Courts should be prepared to go beyond the people who represent the 'directing mind and will' of a company, and to enquire, in the context of the particular offence, 'whose act (or knowledge, or state of mind) was *for this purpose* intended to count as the act, etc., of the company?' The reach of this extension is unclear, since much turns on the statutory context. In this case it enabled the conviction of the company on the basis of the knowledge of two investment managers that they were making unlawful investments. When the Court of Appeal was invited to extend the identification principle along these lines in *Attorney-General's Reference (No. 2 of 1999)*,[84] a case arising from the Southall train crash, it declined to do so. Rose LJ held that

> The identification theory, attributing to the company the mind and will of senior directors and managers, was developed in order to avoid injustice: it would bring the law into disrepute if every act and state of mind of an individual employee was attributed to a company which was entirely blameless.[85]

The terms of this statement beg a number of questions, but it was clear from the judgment that the Court of Appeal thought that any significant extension of the judge-made identification principle should be left to Parliament.[86]

(c) INDIVIDUALISM AND CORPORATISM

The history of legal developments in this sphere suggests a somewhat slow progress towards integrating corporations into a legal framework constructed for individuals, with few gestures towards the differences between corporations and individual human beings.[87] There are those who argue that social phenomena can only be interpreted through the actions and motivations of individuals, and abstractions like corporations constitute barriers to proper understanding. Only individuals can *do* things, and so the law is right to concentrate its attentions upon them. Indeed, any other view might threaten the principle of individual autonomy by holding people liable when they did no voluntary act.

The weakness of this argument is that individual actions can often be explained fully only by reference to the context in which they were carried out. When the

---

[82] Cf. *JF Alford (Transport) Ltd* [1997] 2 Cr App R 326 (see Chapter 10.3(b)), and the conviction of manslaughter of a small outdoor pursuit company and its managing director in respect of the deaths of young canoeists sent out in poor weather with inadequate training and supervision (*OLL Ltd and Kite, The Times*, 9 December 1994), with the difficulty of identification in *Redfern* [1993] Crim LR 43.

[83] [1995] 2 AC 500.   [84] [2000] 2 Cr App R 207.   [85] [2000] 2 Cr App R 207, at 211.

[86] See also *St Regis Paper Co Ltd* [2011] EWCA Crim 2527, for a decision to apply the identification doctrine, in the particular statutory context.

[87] See C. Wells, *Corporations and Criminal Responsibility* (2nd edn., 2001), ch 3; G. R. Sullivan, 'The Attribution of Culpability to Limited Companies' (1996) 55 Camb LJ 516.

managing director of a company is announcing a commercial strategy, he or she is acting not merely as an individual but also as an officer of the company. Without reference to the structure and policies of the company and to that person's role within it, there can be no proper explanation of what was said and done. The argument, therefore, is that the behaviour of individuals is often shaped by their relationship to groups and collectivities—'shaped' in a meaningful sense, not 'determined' in the sense that individual autonomy is lost in the process (since individuals normally have some liberty to disengage themselves from the corporation). The thrust is that companies often have a policy structure and a dynamic of their own which to some extent transcend the actions of their individual officers.[88] Perhaps the clearest application of this can be found in offences of omission, particularly those involving strict liability. In a case like *Alphacell Ltd v Woodward*,[89] where polluting matter escaped from the company's premises into a river, it seems both fairer and more accurate to convict the company rather than to label one individual as the offender: where the law imposes a duty, the company should be organized so as to ensure that the duty is fulfilled.

None of this is meant to suggest that individuals within a corporation should not bear personal responsibility for their conduct. In appropriate cases they should do so, provided that they had fair warning of any special duties attached to the activities of the company.[90] The most common way that the law achieves this is to make it possible for directors to be guilty of the offence committed by the company if they 'consented or connived' at the commission of the offence by the company;[91] but of course if, say, a company director gives someone a bribe to enter into a contract with the company, the director can be individually liable for this criminal act, as well as opening up the path to liability of his or her company itself. The important point is that companies should be open to both criminal and civil liability, since it is they who create the structural context for the individual's conduct *qua* company officer. The corporation appoints the individual and sustains him in this position—the individual is in that place, doing that thing, because of the corporation—and so it is right that the corporation should bear primary liability, or at least concurrent liability with its officer. This does not mean that legality and 'rule of law' principles should be neglected: companies are run by individuals, who ought to receive fair warning of their duties. All these arguments may need adjusting for small, even one-person, companies and also for non-profit organizations. Moreover, they leave open the question whether the criminal law in its traditional form is the most appropriate means of dealing with corporate harmdoing.

---

[88] For further development of this idea, see L. Price, 'Finding Fault in Organisations—Reconceptualising the Role of Senior Managers in Corporate Manslaughter' (2015) 35 *Legal Studies* 385.

[89] [1972] AC 824; cf. the early decision in *Birmingham and Gloucester Railway Co* (1842) 3 QB 223.

[90] Wells, *Corporations and Criminal Responsibility*, 160–3; cf. J. Gobert and M. Punch, *Rethinking Corporate Crime* (2003), ch 8, with their discussion of companies as accomplices in ch 2.

[91] See, e.g., the Health and Safety at Work Act 1974, s. 37; <www.hse.gov.uk/enforce/enforcementguide/investigation/identifying-directors.htm>.

(d) CHANGING THE BASIS OF CORPORATE LIABILITY

The theoretical arguments in favour of corporate criminal liability seem strong, but developments at common law have been slow. The 'identification principle' in *Tesco Supermarkets* v *Nattrass*[92] has a relatively narrow sphere of operation, and there has been little judicial enthusiasm for the greater flexibility proposed in the *Meridian* case.[93] A small number of statutes impose direct or vicarious liability on companies, the Health and Safety at Work Act 1974 being an example, but there is no such general approach. An alternative strategy of placing the emphasis on individual liability would be unlikely to work with larger companies: any particular individual might be dispensable within a corporation (e.g. the 'Company Vice-President responsible for going to gaol'), allowing the company to continue on its course with minimal disruption. It might also be difficult to identify the individual responsible, not least because the lines of accountability within companies are sometimes unclear, although with smaller companies, which are far more numerous, this might be workable.

A number of different approaches have been canvassed in recent years. One approach would be to use company policies, or their absence, as the basis for liability. This follows the approach of Brent Fisse and John Braithwaite and, in particular, their concept of 'reactive fault'.[94] In their view, rather than expending prosecutorial energy and court time trying to disentangle the often convoluted internal structures and policies of corporations, the law should require a company which has caused or threatened a proscribed harm to take its own disciplinary and rectificatory measures. A court would then assess the adequacy of the measures taken. The concept of fault would thus be a *post hoc* phenomenon. Rather than struggling to establish some antecedent fault within the corporation, the prosecution would invite the court to infer fault from the nature and effectiveness of the company's remedial measures after it has been established that it was the author of a harm-causing or harm-threatening act or omission. The court would not find fault if it was persuaded that the company had taken realistic measures to prevent a recurrence, had ensured compensation to any victims, and had taken the event seriously in other respects. The whole orientation of the system would be different: every death caused, whether purely accidental or not, would be treated as potentially a serious offence until the company established otherwise.[95] A legal version of this approach was adopted in the Bribery Act 2010. Section 7 of the 2010 Act created a strict liability corporate offence of 'failing to prevent bribery' by a person associated with the company, but s. 7(2) provides a defence involving proof by the company that it had 'adequate procedures' in place to prevent such actions. There has been some suggestion that this model could be used more widely, in tackling corporate failures in relation to tax

---

[92] [1972] AC 153.   [93] See, e.g., *St Regis Paper Co Ltd* [2011] EWCA Crim 2527.
[94] B. Fisse and J. Braithwaite, *Corporations, Crime and Accountability* (1993).
[95] See the analysis by G. R. Sullivan, 'Expressing Corporate Guilt' (1995) 15 Oxford JLS 281.

and fraud offences committed by individual and businesses seeking to obtain business for the company.[96]

Following a lengthy process of discussion and negotiation, a new form of corporate liability was introduced in the limited (but high profile) area of homicide.[97] The Corporate Manslaughter and Corporate Homicide Act 2007 introduces a new offence of corporate manslaughter, which can be committed only by 'organizations' and not by individuals. The legislative framework of the new offence is highly technical, but for present purposes we can focus on the mechanism by which liability is imposed. Section 1 of the 2007 Act provides:

> An organisation . . . is guilty of an offence if the way in which its activities are managed or organised—
> * causes a person's death, and
> * amounts to a gross breach of a relevant duty of care owed by the organisation to the deceased.

Three features of the new Act's approach stand out. First, it applies to 'organizations', which include companies, partnerships, and various associations and government departments. This is controversial, but is not pursued here. Secondly, the offence is only committed if 'the way in which its activities are managed and organized by its senior management is a substantial element in the breach' of duty. This focus on 'senior management' is developed by s. 1(4), which provides that senior managers must be persons who 'play significant roles' in either decision-making or managing the whole or a substantial part of the organization's activities. This shows that the model of corporate liability adopted in the 2007 Act has not strayed far from the 'identification principle' that has developed at common law.[98] It is, to be blunt, doubtful if the manager of a large Tesco superstore plays a significant role in managing a substantial part of Tesco's activities. If the company is to be prosecuted under the 2007 Act, it must be shown that people at a higher level in a large organization organized the relevant activities in such a way as to amount to a substantial element in the breach. Thirdly, however, s. 8 of the Act directs the jury to consider any alleged breach of health and safety legislation, and permits the jury to take account of evidence of 'attitudes, policies, systems or accepted practices within the organization that were likely to have encouraged' any failure to meet safety standards. This suggests that evidence of what is sometimes called 'corporate culture' may be determinative in some cases.

Whether this new approach will be thought to achieve justice in homicide cases remains to be tested.[99] Certainly it seems to be a rather narrow approach to serve as

---

[96] See HM Revenue and Customs, 'Tacking Offshore Tax Evasion: A New Corporate Criminal Offence of Failure to Prevent the Facilitation of Evasion (Consultation Document, July 2015), <www.gov.uk/government/consultations/tackling-offshore-evasion; <www.kingsleynapley.co.uk/news-and-events/blogs/criminal-law-blog/preventing-economic-crime-will-we-see-a-further-extension-of-corporate-criminal-liability-in-the-uk>.   [97] See the detailed discussion in Chapter 8.5(c).

[98] See L. Price, 'Finding Fault in Organisations—Reconceptualising the Role of Senior Managers in Corporate Manslaughter' (2015) 35 *Legal Studies* 385.

[99] See now S. Field and L. Jones, 'Five Years On: the Impact of the Corporate Manslaughter and Corporate Homicide Act 2007: Plus ça Change?' (2013) 24 ICCLR 239.

a model for corporate criminal liability generally, and so the quest for a fairer set of principles must go on.[100] The new approach also serves to raise the wider question of whether it is the conviction of organizations that is the most important aspect, or whether the sentencing of organizations should be regarded as important too. A company can hardly be imprisoned, moderate fines can be swallowed up as business overheads, and swingeing fines may have such drastic side-effects on the employment and livelihoods of innocent employees as to render them inappropriate.[101] Fisse and Braithwaite have proposed a range of special penalties, some of which are rehabilitative (putting corporations on probation to supervise their compliance with the law), some of which are deterrent (punitive injunctions to require resources to be devoted to the development of new preventive measures), and others of which have mixed aims (e.g. community service by companies).[102] In their view, the primary search should be for a regime which ensures maximum prevention. The 2007 Act provides for three types of sentence—publicity orders (requiring the organization to make it known that it has been convicted of this offence); remedial orders (requiring the offender to remedy the causes of the homicide); and fines (which may prove problematic for the reasons given above, and which are questionable in so far as they may have deleterious effects on the level of public service provided by organizations such as hospital trusts and the police).[103]

6.4 FAULT AND *MENS REA*: GENERAL PRINCIPLES

(a) *MENS REA* AND FAULT

It has already been argued that there should be no criminal liability without fault for imprisonable offence.[104] Indeed, there is a respectable argument for saying that there should *never* be criminal liability without fault;[105] but whilst that view seems persuasive in relation to the liability of individuals, it is perhaps less persuasive where the liability of businesses is concerned, particularly in cases where there is a defence to the crime in question of 'due diligence shown' (or the like).

The claim that criminal offences should include *mens rea*—guilty mind—requirements reflects the view that criminal liability should be imposed only on persons who can be said 'subjectively' to have associated *themselves* through their behaviour with the wrongful conduct in question (including the circumstance or consequence

---

[100] See D. Ormerod and R. Taylor, 'The Corporate Manslaughter and Corporate Homicide Act 2007' [2008] Crim LR 589.

[101] See generally, M. Woodley, 'Bargaining Over Corporate Manslaughter—What Price a Life?' (2013) J Crim L 33.

[102] Fisse and Braithwaite, *Corporations, Crime and Accountability*; cf. Gobert and Punch, *Rethinking Corporate Crime*, ch 7.

[103] <www.sentencingcouncil.org.uk/wp-content/uploads/web__guideline_on_corporate_manslaughter_accessible.pdf>.   [104] Chapter 4.6.

[105] For a sophisticated defence of this view, see A. P. Simester, 'A Disintegrated Theory of Culpability', in D. Baker and J. Horder (eds), *The Sanctity of Life and the Criminal Law: The Legacy of Glanville Williams* (2013).

elements of the offence, if any). In broad terms, this occurs when people engage in wrongful conduct intentionally, knowingly, recklessly, whilst possessing similar mental states such as indifference, awareness, or suspicion, or when they are complicit in the wrongdoing of others. The subjective *mens rea* approach encompasses the belief principle, which holds that criminal liability should be based on what defendants believed they were doing or risking, not on facts which were unknown to them at the time.[106] For example, according to the belief principle, if D is found in possession of class A drugs, but claims he believed he was in possession of class B drugs, if the prosecution cannot prove otherwise, he should be acquitted of 'possessing class A drugs'. It should not be sufficient to show that he knew he was in possession of prohibited drugs unless, of course, as under the present law, there is a specific offence of possessing 'a prohibited drug'.[107]

By contrast, liability is sometimes based on a broader set of fault elements that are said to go beyond a finding of 'guilty' mind. These are fault elements traditionally thought to involve judging people after the fact, as 'grossly negligent' or as having shown a 'lack of due care and attention'. Such evaluative ('objective') judgments are the means by which a fault-focused association between the defendant's behaviour and the wrongful conduct is brought about later *by the judgment of others* (judge or jury), rather than by the defendant him or herself in virtue of what he or she intended, knew, or realized, *etc.* In relation to the belief principle as it applies to possession offences, for example, the objective, judgmental approach would ask the question, 'Should D have realized at the relevant time exactly what was in his or her possession'? If D had no reason to suppose he or she was in possession of something it is prohibited to possess, then the objective judgmental approach would advocate acquittal.

In many cases, the more subjective *mens rea* approach is supported, in broad terms, by the principle of fairness and proportionality of offence construction, set out briefly in Chapter 4.7.[108] This approach may also be claimed to enhance the constitutional values of legality and rule of law, by reassuring citizens that they will be liable to conviction, and to the exercise of state coercion against them, only if they intentionally, knowingly, or recklessly, etc. cause or risk causing a prohibited harm. If this were achieved, the criminal law would ensure that, 'each person is guaranteed a greatest liberty, capacity and opportunity of controlling and predicting the consequences of his or her actions compatible with a like liberty, capacity and opportunity for all.'[109]

However, English law does not adopt the subjective *mens rea* approach to the definition of many crimes, even quite serious ones. For example, manslaughter may be

---

[106] A. Ashworth, 'Belief, Intent, and Criminal Liability', in J. Eekelaar and J. Bell (eds), *Oxford Essays in Jurisprudence, 3rd Series* (1989).

[107] Misuse of Drugs Act 1972, s. 5(2). The law, more generally, flouts the belief principle by taking the approach that if D knew or believed he or she was in possession of something, then it will be assumed he or she knew what that 'something' was: see *Warner* [1969] 2 AC 256 (HL).

[108] Cf. A. Brudner, 'Agency and Welfare in Criminal Law', in S. Shute, J. Gardner, and J. Horder (eds), *Action and Value in Criminal Law* (1993), and R. Lippke, *Rethinking Imprisonment* (2007), 84–98.

[109] D. A. J. Richards, 'Rights, Utility and Crime', in M. Tonry and N. Morris (eds), *Crime and Justice: An Annual Review* (1981), iii, 274.

based on a demonstration of a defendant's 'gross negligence' (an objective judgment about the fault in someone else's association with a death caused). Similarly, rape can also be found, in law, where a defendant has non-consensual intercourse with another in the absence of a reasonable belief that the other is consenting to the intercourse:[110] the question whether a defendant's belief in consent was 'reasonable' is a matter for evaluative judgment after the fact by the jury at trial. So, the subjective *mens rea* approach involves what was referred to at the end of Chapter 4.1 as a 'permissive' principle of criminal law. This is a principle that may be permissibly applied in many circumstances, but will not necessarily be appropriately applied in many circumstances: rape is a good example of a crime where the subjective *mens rea* approach is not appropriate.[111]

Moreover, there is less of a difference than is sometimes supposed between the subjective *mens rea* approach to fault, and the approach to fault based on objective judgment. When someone is negligent, there is something to blame about their state of mind at the time of the offence, not just something to blame with the benefit of hindsight at trial. Where someone truly has been negligent, there will have been an absence of thought about the circumstances or the consequences where such thought could and should have been given at the time, or there will be a belief reached without proper regard for its basis.[112] In that respect, it can be argued that the objective, judgmental approach *is*, in fact, a *mens rea* or guilty mind-based approach to criminal culpability.

Associated with the subjective *mens rea* principle—but in fact having a more general basis—is what is commonly termed the principle of 'correspondence'.[113] This principle—also a permissive principle in English law—insists that the fault element for a crime should correspond to the conduct, circumstance, or consequence element specified for the crime. Thus, if the conduct element is 'causing serious injury', then the fault element ought to be 'intention or recklessness as to causing serious injury'; a lesser fault element, such as 'intention or recklessness as to a mere assault', would breach the principle of correspondence.[114] However, it is important to note that the correspondence principle can—and should—be applied to instances in which fault can be found on the basis of objective judgment. For example, in cases of gross negligence manslaughter, it should not be enough to show that, in causing death, the defendant was grossly negligent as to causing only some harm. The correspondence principle insists that the prosecution must prove that, in causing death, the defendant was grossly negligent as to causing *death*, because that is the consequence the defendant is to be held liable for bringing about.[115]

---

[110] Sexual Offences Act 2003, s. 1. See Chapter 9.6(D).   [111] See Chapter 9.6(D).

[112] The outstanding modern discussion is that of A. P. Simester, 'Can Negligence be Culpable?', in J. Horder (ed.), *Oxford Essays in Jurisprudence, 4th Series* (2000).

[113] A. Ashworth, 'A Change of Normative Position: Determining the Contours of Culpability in Criminal Law' (2008) 11 New Crim. L. R. 232.   [114] See the discussion of this issue in Chapter 9.3(c).

[115] See *Adomako* [1995] 1 AC 171 (HL); Chapter 8.6(b).

(b) CONSTRUCTIVE LIABILITY AND 'MORAL LUCK'

So-called 'constructive' liability attracted a great deal of critical attention from the influential Cambridge criminal law theorists of the early twentieth century.[116] A 'constructive' liability approach is an approach that gives primacy of place to outcomes in determining liability. In itself, that might not be too contentious, but what makes constructive liability 'constructive', is what makes criminal liability turn on outcomes, at the expense of the correspondence principle as it relates to fault in bringing about those outcomes. In other words, on a constructive liability approach, one may be found liable for outcomes one brought about by engaging in certain acts, even if one did not know at the time that one's act might have these outcomes. The argument in favour of constructive liability runs something like this. If D (say) did in fact kill V, or was in fact in possession of (say) an illegal firearm, and so on, then such outcomes should form the basis for finding D criminally liable, even if—for fairness reasons, and to draw distinctions between offences according to their gravity—*some* fault element may also be required before conviction is appropriate. A classic case, mentioned right at the start of this chapter, is the offence of assault occasioning actual bodily harm (s. 47 of the Offences Against the Person Act 1861). D is liable for occasioning the actual bodily harm—the outcome—even if he or she only had the fault element for the assault, and did not appreciate that actual bodily harm might result from that assault. All actions bring about unintended as well as intended outcomes, the argument continues, and we cannot claim credit for bringing about the good (unintended) outcomes whilst denying any blame for bringing about the bad (unintended) outcomes. In an outcome-generating world of action, we have to shoulder responsibility for 'moral luck' in bringing about those bad outcomes, just as we rejoice and take credit for bringing about the good outcomes.

On the other side of the argument, some theorists reject the view that someone should be found criminally liable respecting any outcome they produce, whether or not it was intended.[117] On this uncompromisingly non-consequentialist view, if I stab you intending to kill you and you die of your wounds, then I should be found criminally liable only in respect of the action I controlled—the risk posed to your life—but not for the outcome which I do not exercise control over: your death. So, on this view, there could be no crime of 'murder'; only a crime of 'intentionally risking death'. Why? As German philosopher G. W. F. Hegel memorably put it (in 1820), citing an old proverb, 'the stone belongs to the devil when it leaves the hand that threw it'.[118] However, adherents of the correspondence principle do not necessarily need to go nearly so far as this.[119] All they insist on is that, when criminal liability depends on consequences brought about, or on the presence of certain circumstances, defendants must be proved to have been at fault respecting—known about, intended, realized (or, possible also, been negligent regarding)—the bringing about of the consequences, or the presence of the circumstances.

---

[116] See Chapter 3.1. and J. W. C. Turner, 'The Mental Element in Crimes at Common Law' (1936) 6 CLJ 31.

[117] L. Alexander and K. Ferzan, *Crime and Culpability: A Theory of Criminal Law* (2009).

[118] H. B. Nisbet (trans.), G. W. F. Hegel, *Elements of The Philosophy of Right* (1991), 148, para. 119A.

[119] For further argument, compare A. Ashworth, 'Taking the Consequences', in S. Shute, J. Gardner, and J. Horder (eds), *Action and Value in Criminal Law* (1993) and V. Tadros, *Criminal Responsibility* (2005), 90–8, with R. A. Duff, *Criminal Attempts* (1996), ch 12.

A test case is the justification for the offence of manslaughter by a criminal and dangerous act.[120] Suppose I punch you during an argument, you fall, hit your head and die. This is commonly known as 'one punch manslaughter'.[121] The law fixes me with liability for the death of the victim, even though I only intended to hurt the victim by punching. This is constructive liability in operation. Liability is based on the outcome—death—caused, and only some fault element (an intentional or recklessly committed criminal act) is required to justify the case as one of manslaughter, so long as the criminal act in question posed an obvious risk of causing some harm to the person. By contrast, on the strictly non-consequentialist view just outlined, criminal liability should go no further than the punch, or the creation of a risk of harm by punching. In between these views, there are different positions.[122] One such position reflects the correspondence principle: there should be no liability for the death—and hence, for manslaughter—unless the death was foreseen as a possible outcome of the punch, or (on the objective judgment view) unless there was negligence with regard to causing death by punching.[123] However, the extended basis for liability provided by the objective judgment view involves accepting a less secure basis for the criminal law's adherence to a key principle of the rule of law.[124] It is much harder to avoid criminal wrongdoing in advance if liability can be extended beyond the wrongdoing you intentionally did, or realized might occur, to encompass the risks of wrongdoing you failed to see in advance (even if you ought to have seen them).

(c) THE PRINCIPLE OF PROPER COINCIDENCE BETWEEN FAULT AND ACTION

In very broad terms, the principle of proper coincidence holds that the fault element must coincide 'in the proper way' with the conduct element, in order to amount to an offence.[125] Suppose I am tracking you down armed with a gun in order to kill you. I turn a corner, accidentally bump into you and my gun just goes off, killing you. In this example, I cannot be found guilty of murder, even though I intended to kill you and did kill you. My fault element coincided in point of time with my causing of your death, but did not coincide in the proper or right way, so to make this an 'intentional killing'. An intentional killing in this case would have involved—very roughly—my pointing my gun at some vital area of your body, pulling the trigger, and thereby killing

---

[120] See Chapter 8.5.

[121] <www.cps.gov.uk/legal/s_to_u/sentencing_manual/involuntary_manslaughter/>, where it is made clear that a much more severe sentence will be given to the single punch killer than would ever be given to the person who simply punches another causing (say) a bruise.

[122] See, e.g., J. Gardner, 'Rationality and the Rule of Law in Offences against the Person' (1994) 53 Camb LJ 502, at 509.

[123] In French law, homicide can be committed by simple negligence, whereas 'manslaughter' by negligence in English law requires proof that the negligence was gross. See, for a general discussion, J. Spencer, 'Approaches to Strict and Constructive Liability in Continental Criminal Law', in A. P. Simester (ed.), *Appraising Strict Liability* (2005), 237.

[124] See text at n 106.

[125] An early general statement was that of Lord Kenyon CJ in *Fowler* v *Padget* (1798) 7 Term Rep 509.

you. Clearly, I can maintain an intention (to kill, to see Alaska, to visit a relative) over a long period of time. I can also maintain an action over a period of time (cycling, running, driving). An intention is exhausted or extinguished by its fulfillment in action, in the right or proper way, by the person who has that intention. So, in the case just given where I am tracking you down, my intention was not exhausted or extinguished by my killing you, because I did not kill you intentionally; but for obvious reasons, I would soon enough abandon my intention on discovering that I had killed you accidentally.

An action may continue until it stops, is stopped, or transforms into a different action, whether or not that is someone's intention, or it may become intended as it continues. An example of the latter might be this: when I first learn to cycle, I may start cycling without realizing that is what exactly what I am doing, but then carry on (joyfully!) cycling intentionally. Contrariwise, I may start to pour milk into my coffee intentionally, and then become distracted, so that I carry on pouring (unintentionally) long past the point at which I meant to stop. Homely as these examples may seem, they provide an important background to the understanding of the law's approach to 'continuing acts'. Here is an example where someone, as in the cycling case, finds that they are doing something, and then intentionally continues. In the famous case of *Fagan* v *Metropolitan Police Commissioner* (1969)[126] D accidentally drove his car on to a policeman's foot, and then deliberately left it there for a minute or so. The defence to a charge of assault was that the conduct element (applying force) had finished before the fault element began; the act and the intent never coincided. The Divisional Court held that D's conduct in driving the car on to the foot and leaving it there should be viewed as a continuing act, so that the crime was committed when the fault element (D's realization of what had happened and decision to leave the car there) came together with the continuing conduct.

This is not the only occasion on which the courts have invoked the notion of a 'continuing act' to justify liability on the basis that there has been a proper coincidence between conduct and fault.[127] However, a different approach was taken by the House of Lords in *Miller*.[128] This was the case in which a squatter was smoking in bed, accidentally set the mattress on fire, but simply moved to another room without attempting to remedy the problem, with the result that the house caught fire. Lord Diplock did not reject the view that the fire was a continuing act that began accidentally but could then be connected with D's fault when he realized that the mattress was on fire. However, his Lordship expressed a preference for the 'duty' analysis, whereby the accidental creation of danger gave rise to a duty (a continuing duty to avert the danger caused) which in this case D knowingly failed to discharge.

The continuing act approach seems to exert an influence in another area. In *Thabo Meli* v *R* (1954)[129] the plan was to kill V in a hut and then throw his body over a cliff:

---

[126] [1969] 1 QB 439.
[127] E.g. in rape, *Kaitamaki* v *R* [1985] 1 AC 147, now confirmed by the Sexual Offences Act 2003, s. 79(2), and in theft (on appropriation), *Hale* (1978) 68 Cr App R 415).
[128] [1983] 2 AC 161. See the discussion in Chapter 4.4.   [129] [1954] 1 WLR 228.

this was what D believed he was doing, but in fact V died from the fall down the cliff and not from the beating in the hut. The argument for the appellant was based on the lack of proper coincidence between conduct and fault (this time it was intent first, death later), but the Privy Council rejected this, holding that the beating and the disposal over the cliff formed part of a planned series of acts which should be regarded as a single course of conduct.[130] On this analysis, the presence of the fault element at any stage during the planned sequence would suffice. The analysis creaks a bit, as the victim was supposed to have been killed by beating and the disposal over the cliff was not in itself intended to kill. So, there was no proper coincidence between conduct and fault at either stage. However, murder is a 'result' crime, involving the causing of death. So, the case is perhaps defensible on the basis (a) that there was proper coincidence between the fault element and the conduct intended to cause death (the beating), and (b) V's eventual death could be traced back causally to the beating.[131] A better view is perhaps that D was guilty of attempted murder at the first stage, and manslaughter at the second stage.

It is convenient to deal here with one more awkward situation relating to the link between conduct and fault. In *Attorney-General's Reference (No. 4 of 1980)* (1981),[132] it appeared that D was arguing with his female partner at the top of a flight of stairs, that he pushed her away and she fell backwards down the stairs, that he concluded she was dead, and then dragged her back to their flat with a rope around her neck and cut up her body. The Court of Appeal held that there could be a conviction on these facts, even though it was not clear which of D's acts caused death. So long as the jury was satisfied that D had sufficient fault for manslaughter when he pushed her backwards, and sufficient fault for manslaughter when he cut up her body,[133] it was immaterial which act caused death. The facts of this case are somewhat stronger than the facts of *Thabo Meli*, *Church*, and *Le Brun*, since in all of those cases it was clear that it was not D's initial act that caused death. In the *AG's Reference* case, it should have been possible to convict D if the court was satisfied that there was a sequence of events and that D had the required fault element at some stage; the actual facts, however, were taken not to raise this point.

6.5 VARIETIES OF FAULT

We now move to the core fault elements. First to be considered is strict liability, when criminal liability may be incurred without fault. It has already been argued that strict liability is wrong, if individuals face prison sentences when convicted.[134] One reason

---

[130] This kind of analysis has been used in other result crime cases, such as manslaughter: *R v Church* [1966] 1 QB 59; *R v LeBrun* [1992] QB 61.

[131] For further discussion, see K. J. Arenson, 'Thabo Meli Revisited: The Pernicious Effects of Results-Driven Decisions' (2013) 77 J Crim Law 41.   [132] [1981] 1 WLR 706.

[133] An intention merely to assault would suffice: see the discussion in section 6.4(b) earlier in the chapter.

[134] Chapter 4.6 and 4.7.

for considering strict liability offences first is that they are the most numerous, a fact that belies the prominence often given to intention and recklessness in the rhetoric of English criminal law. We then turn to the *mens rea* terms of intention, recklessness, and knowledge, before exploring the concept of negligence.

(a) STRICT LIABILITY

There is no clear convention about when criminal liability should be classified as 'strict'.[135] We will use the term here to indicate those offences of which a person may be convicted without proof of intention, knowledge, recklessness, or negligence. Some offences prescribe liability without fault, but allow the defendant to avoid liability on proof of 'due diligence' shown in seeking to avoid the commission of the offence. There is dispute about whether offences with such provisos are properly termed 'strict liability' offences, although classification is perhaps less important as an issue than whether the existence of a 'due diligence' defence (or the like) will do enough to mitigate the moral objection to strict liability in relation to any particular crime. For present purposes, such offences will be included within the concept of strict liability. This corresponds with the Canadian approach, which separates strict liability (where a defendant can avoid liability by establishing that there was no negligence) from absolute liability (where the only defences available relate to fundamental elements of capacity or necessity).[136]

The term 'absolute liability' has its own difficulties, however, since one can argue that liability should only be described as absolute where there is no defence available at all to someone who is proved to have caused the prohibited event. What this shows, above all, is that there is no settled terminology to give simple expression to the numerous permutations of conditions for liability. If one takes account of the device of shifting the burden of proof on to the defendant, then the permutations range from requiring *mens rea*—with the burden of proof on the prosecution—to defining special defences or provisos with an evidential burden on D, defining special defences or provisos with a legal burden of proof on D, requiring proof of negligence by the prosecution, creating a no-negligence defence to be proved by D, imposing liability with no due diligence defence at all, and even to a dispensation from proving an element of the offence.[137]

(i) *Some Arguments For and Against Strict Liability*: Let us leave aside the complexities introduced by changes in the burden of proof, and formulate a central question: what are the arguments for imposing criminal liability with no due diligence defence available? The main argument is based on the undoubted importance of protecting and promoting security from harm as a public good. The argument is that strict liability for causing or threatening harm does something significant to promote this good, by

---

[135] See the searching exploration of this topic in A. P. Simester (ed.), *Appraising Strict Liability* (2005).

[136] There is ample authority that automatism is a defence to strict liability offences, but some disagreement on whether insanity may afford a defence: cf. *Hennessy* (1989) 89 Cr App R 10 with *DPP v H* [1997] 1 WLR 1406, discussed in section 6.2(c).

[137] A. Ashworth, 'Towards a Theory of Criminal Legislation' (1989) 1 *Criminal Law Forum* 41.

making the circumstances in which we breach our obligations to others uncompromising and crystal clear ('no excuses!'), thereby enhancing the deterrent effect of the law.[138] If that argument sounds plausible, recall that behind it lurks the influence of the authoritarian principle, criticized in Chapter 4.5. According to the authoritarian principle, as we have seen, it is preferable to place our trust in the proper exercise of discretion by officials—in this case, concerning when to prosecute—rather than give legal scope to defendants to deny fault or plead excuses in a way that might mean their case did not fall within the scope of the offence. Further, the argument (a) does nothing to show that strict liability would be a *proportionate* response, in accordance with the principle of fairness in offence construction outlines in Chapter 4.7, and (b) makes the assumption that strict liability contributes meaningfully to increased security, but without hard evidence to back it up.

The fairness issue, in relation to offence construction, is one which runs through this chapter. Bearing in mind that the criminal law is society's most condemnatory instrument, in so far as the criminal trial has a communicative function, strict liability impairs this. It does this by severely limiting D's ability to explain, excuse, or justify the conduct, and by requiring a conviction in all but exceptional circumstances. Moreover, so far as individuals are concerned, respect for lifestyle autonomy requires that criminal liability be imposed only where there has been genuine fault, meaning that the commission of the offence could have been avoided. This is a fundamental requirement.

What about the position where the liability of businesses is in issue? Whilst they can be found responsible for committing crimes, businesses are artificial legal constructs and so, unlike their owners or workers, they cannot enjoy lifestyle autonomy. What is more, they can sometimes escape what are meant to be the longer-lasting effects of criminal condemnation by re-creating themselves as a new company (so called 'phoenix' companies), or by merging with another company. So, as Braithwaite has argued, is there not something incongruous, in a world in which avoidable deaths and injuries are much too frequent and cause much grief and insecurity, for the State meticulously to observe the 'intent' and 'belief' principles, the presumption of innocence, and other fairness principles so as to facilitate the acquittal of clumsy, ignorant, but nevertheless dangerous corporate people?[139] One answer to that question comes from looking at the way businesses are dealt with by prosecution authorities in practice.

Many of the regulatory agencies with the authoritarian power to invoke strict liability offences adopt what may be termed a 'compliance strategy' towards law enforcement—that is, aiming to secure conformity to the law without the need to process and penalize violators.[140] Regulatory activities focus on obtaining compliance, and

---

[138] In effect, this was the argument of the Department for Education in making the case for the effectiveness of strict liability in relation to the offence of failing to ensure a child regularly attended school, in the well-known case of *Barnfather* v *London Borough of Islington Education Authority* [2003] EWHC 418 (Admin).

[139] J. Braithwaite, *Corporate Crime in the Pharmaceutical Industry* (1984), ch 9.

[140] A. Reiss, 'Selecting Strategies of Social Control over Organizational Life', in K. Hawkins and J. M. Thomas (eds), *Enforcing Regulation* (1984).

prosecution is reserved for the few cases where either the violator is recalcitrant or the violation is so large that public concern can only be assuaged by a prosecution. This may also mean that prosecutions tend to be brought only in cases where there is fault: indeed, there are regulatory agencies which pursue such a policy, even though they have no-fault offences at their disposal.[141] There is little evidence among the regulatory agencies of a 'deterrence strategy', using criminal prosecution as a primary means of preventing breaches of the law.[142] So, one conclusion that could be drawn is that the right way to structure a regulatory scheme, aimed at corporate activity, is to confine the use of the criminal law to instances in which harm has been done or grave risk posed through fault, and pursue less serious incidents through the use of civil penalties.[143] Indeed, if regulation in such spheres as industrial safety had been harnessed to relatively serious offences requiring proof of fault, then those offences might now be taken much more seriously, integrated into people's thinking about offences against the person rather than being regarded as 'merely regulatory' and 'not real crime'.[144]

A fault-based approach to offence construction reflects the value of individual autonomy, but many of the harms which afflict, or threaten to afflict, citizens today are the result of the acts or omissions of corporations. Pollution, defective products, food and drugs, safety at work, transport systems—all these sources of danger are dominated by corporate undertakings. We saw in section 6.3 that the traditional doctrines of the criminal law have various shortcomings when applied to corporate decision-making and responsibility. Once a secure basis for corporate liability is found, the next question would concern the appropriate conditions of liability for companies. In the modern world, corporate activity is highly rule-governed. Everyone running a business is at some level aware of the need for regulatory compliance, and directors should always be aware that they may need to take legal advice, or consult advisory bodies or government departments and agencies, before conducting their business in a particular way. That explains the emphasis given, in the crimes created to target corporate activity, to 'due diligence' defences, and the like. It can therefore be argued that the principle of fairness in offence construction does not necessarily forbid the use of strict liability in the corporate sphere, so long as there are defences that themselves encourage efforts to secure regulatory compliance. This final qualification is particularly important when one bears in mind that the majority of UK businesses have a sole proprietor, or are small-scale family concerns.[145]

---

[141] The leading study is K. Hawkins, *Law as Last Resort* (2003). For shorter reviews, see G. Richardson, 'Strict Liability for Regulatory Crime: The Empirical Research' [1987] Crim LR 295, and R. Baldwin, 'The New Punitive Regulation' (2004) 67 MLR 351.

[142] That approach to law enforcement is more typical of the police, who rarely occupy themselves with the so-called regulatory offences aimed at commercial and industrial safety etc.

[143] For fuller discussion see the Law Commission, *Criminal Liability in Regulatory Contexts* (CP No 195, 2010).

[144] Cf. decisions such as *Seaboard Offshore Ltd* v *Secretary of State for Transport* [1994] 1 WLR 541, *British Steel* [1995] 1 WLR 1356, *Associated Octel* [1996] 1 WLR 1543, and *Gateway Foodmarkets Ltd* [1997] Crim LR 512.

[145] See J. Horder, 'Strict Liability, Statutory Construction and the Spirit of Liberty' (2002) 118 LQR 458, at 472–4.

Is it an argument in favour of, or against, strict liability that the offence is a minor one or a grave one? The English courts have used both triviality and gravity as arguments in favour of strict liability. Many offences with low penalties are, or have been held to be, offences requiring no proof of fault.[146] This reasoning derives some justification from an economic argument based on ease of prosecution: such trivial offences are not worth the public expenditure of prosecution and court time in proving fault. There is hardly any stigma in being convicted of such offences, and so it is thought to be in the public interest to dispose of them quickly (although the result may be to dilute the moral legitimacy of the criminal law). But none of this can apply to serious offences. Principles of individual fairness, even if overridden by economic considerations in respect of minor offences, should surely be central to the question of conviction for serious offences. One clear benchmark here is the availability of imprisonment as a punishment. The American Model Penal Code proposes that imprisonability should be a conclusive reason against strict liability (as was argued in Chapter 4.5 and 4.6).[147] In Canada, the Supreme Court has held that an offence of strict liability which carries the possibility of a custodial sentence is contrary to the Charter of Rights, unless there is a no-negligence defence.[148] However, the jurisprudence of the European Court of Human Rights is equivocal on the matter.[149]

(ii) *The Development of Strict Liability:* No presumption against the imposition of no-fault liability for imprisonable offences has been enunciated in this country; indeed, English law contains several examples of courts using the seriousness of the offence as an argument in favour of strict liability—a course of reasoning which inevitably results in no-fault liability for some imprisonable crimes. The nadir of such judicial reasoning was probably reached in *Howells*,[150] where D was charged with possessing a firearm without a certificate, an offence contrary to s. 1 of the Firearms Act 1968, with a maximum penalty of three years' imprisonment. D sought to rely on s. 58 of the Act, which exempted 'an antique firearm which is ... possessed as a curiosity or ornament'. When evidence was given that the gun was not an antique but a reproduction, D then put the point that he believed it to be an antique, since it had been sold to him as such. This would be a defence only if some requirement of knowledge or belief could be read into the statute. The Court of Appeal ruled this out and upheld strict liability:

> First, the wording would, on the face of it, so indicate. Secondly, the danger to the community resulting from the possession of lethal firearms is so obviously great that an absolute prohibition against their possession without proper authority must have been the intention of Parliament when considered in conjunction with the words of the section. Thirdly, to

---

[146] *Alphacell Ltd v Woodward* [1972] AC 824, following the notion of 'quasi-crimes' outlined by Lord Reid in *Sweet v Parsley* [1970] AC 132.

[147] Model Penal Code, s. 6.02(4). For discussion in the context of the US Constitution see A. Michaels, 'Constitutional Innocence' (1999) 122 Harv LR 829.

[148] *References re Section 94(2) of the Motor Vehicles Act* (1986) 48 CR (3d) 289; see D. R. Stuart, *Canadian Criminal Law* (4th edn., 2001).

[149] Whether the presumption of innocence ought to have any implications for strict criminal liability is a matter that has been debated extensively. See, e.g., the contribution by Sullivan in Simester (ed.), *Appraising Strict Liability* (2005); V. Tadros and S. Tierney, 'The Presumption of Innocence and the Human Rights Act' (2004) 67 MLR 402; and A. Ashworth, 'Four Threats to the Presumption of Innocence' (2006) 123 SALJ 62.

[150] [1977] QB 614. See also *Bradish* [1990] 1 QB 981.

allow a defence of honest and reasonable belief that the firearm was an antique and therefore excluded would be likely to defeat the clear intentions of the Act.[151]

This is poor reasoning. The powerful expression of the second point, the danger to the
community, gives no weight at all to the argument against rendering a person liable
to imprisonment without proof of fault; indeed, the argument seems not to have been
mentioned. The 'danger to the community' argument is surely questionable in itself. Is
it really being contended that the more serious the (potential) harm, the stronger the
argument for strict liability? Would this support strict criminal liability for all killings?
Moreover, the assertion about the original intention of Parliament is unsupported:
there is no reference in the judgment to the history of this part of the Firearms Act.
The third point in the quotation merely restates the assertion. Everything depends on
whether Parliament, by failing to include any fault terms in the relevant section of the
Act, did intend to exclude fault, or whether it was merely leaving the issue to be determined by the courts.[152] This brings us back to the first point, that the wording 'on the
face of it' favours strict liability. This is a monumentally unhelpful statement, which
calls for some discussion of the respective functions of the legislature and the courts
in these matters.

Part of Parliament's function in defining offences should be to state any fault requirement for liability. It discharges this function in many statutory provisions, but in
many others it remains silent, merely enacting a provision that penalizes an act or an
omission without any reference to fault. Over the years the courts have had to interpret
these provisions on many occasions, deciding whether or not to insert a fault requirement. Not only do strict liability crimes account for over half of some 10,000 offences
in English criminal law, but half of the offences serious enough to be tried in the Crown
Court have a strict liability element too.[153] The courts' approach to interpretation has
not been a model of consistency. In some cases they avoid the substantive issue by
proceeding as if it were merely a linguistic matter. In others they make high statements
of principle, which may raise hopes that a consistent framework is to be established.
This is the present position, the House of Lords having recently handed down two decisions that extol the presumption of *mens rea* as a 'constitutional principle'.[154] In the
past, any hopes of a more consistent judicial approach have usually been dashed, as the
supposed principle is progressively whittled away or, more damningly, simply ignored.
Consistency does not, of course, rule out the possibility of reasoned exceptions. But, as
the following small selection from the enormous variety of offences (including many
in the field of road traffic) shows, there is little evidence of consistency on any level.

One of the earliest statements of principle was that of Wright J in *Sherras v de
Rutzen*,[155] who stated that: 'there is a presumption that *mens rea* ... is an essential

---

[151] *Per* Browne LJ, at 626.   [152] P. Devlin, Samples of *Lawmaking* (1970), esp. 71–3.
[153] Ashworth and Blake, 'The Presumption of Innocence'.
[154] *B v DPP* [2000] 2 AC 428 and *K* [2002] 1 AC 462, discussed later at section 6.5(a)(iii). The decisions
were applied by the Court of Appeal in *Kumar* [2005] Crim LR 470.
[155] [1895] 1 QB 918.

ingredient in every offence; but that presumption is liable to be displaced either by the words of the statute creating the offence or by the subject-matter with which it deals, and both must be considered'. What 'subject-matter' displaces the presumption? One example given by Wright J was 'acts which are not criminal in any real sense', where the criminal penalty is attached to acts which are not regarded as morally wrong. This was a reference to offences involved in regulating the sale of tobacco, food, alcohol, and so forth. There were a number of judicial decisions in the 1960s which held persons liable for quite serious drug offences without proof of any fault, in the belief that public policy demanded this, but this trend was arrested in what is probably the leading case, *Sweet* v *Parsley*.[156] The case involved a schoolteacher who was prosecuted for being concerned in the management of premises used for the purpose of smoking cannabis; she had rented her farmhouse to a group of students who, unbeknown to her, smoked cannabis there. The case went up to the House of Lords on the question whether any fault had to be proved. If one takes the language 'on its face', to refer back to the quotation from *Howells*,[157] it suggests liability without fault. The premises were used for smoking cannabis, and D was concerned in their management. But their Lordships were unanimous in holding that the statute should be construed in the light of the presumption that *mens rea* is required. They took the view that the courts had no power to impose negligence liability in such cases: the choice lay between *mens rea* and strict liability, and the presumption should be in favour of the former.

This presumption did not fare well during the next decade. It was soon held to be displaced in another House of Lords case, *Alphacell Ltd* v *Woodward*,[158] where a company was convicted of causing polluted matter to enter a stream. Three reasons played a part—the linguistic one, that the word 'cause' was thought to favour strict liability; that the low maximum penalty favoured dispensing with fault; and the assumption that pollution offences were not criminal in a real sense. The decision in *Howells*[159] is hard to reconcile with *Sweet* v *Parsley*, as is *Pharmaceutical Society of Great Britain* v *Storkwain Ltd*,[160] where the House of Lords held that a person may be liable to conviction for selling drugs without a valid prescription, contrary to the Medicines Act 1968, without proof of fault. The decision was reached by analysing the statute, with scant reference to any presumption of *mens rea* and without giving weight to the fact that the offence carried a maximum sentence of two years' imprisonment.

(iii) *A New Constitutional Principle?*: The new millennium brought an apparent change of direction. In *B* v *DPP*[161] the House of Lords had to decide whether, in the offence of indecency with a child under 14 contrary to the Indecency with Children Act 1960, there was strict liability as to the age of the child or the prosecution had to establish knowledge of the child's age. The House unanimously held that 'the common law presumes that, unless Parliament has indicated otherwise, the appropriate mental

---

[156] [1970] AC 132.   [157] See previously, n 150.
[158] [1972] AC 824; see also *Environment Agency* v *Empress Car Co* [1999] 2 AC 22, discussed in Chapter 4.6(b).   [159] See n 150 and accompanying text.   [160] (1986) 83 Cr App R 359.
[161] [2000] 2 AC 428.

element is an unexpressed ingredient of every offence'.[162] Not only does this decision apply the presumption stated in *Sweet* v *Parsley* in preference to the older view that, in sexual offences, it is morally justifiable to impose strict liability as to age,[163] but Lord Steyn accepted the description of the presumption of *mens rea* as a 'constitutional principle' that is not easily displaced by a statutory text.[164] The same approach was taken by the House of Lords in *K* (2002),[165] where the charge was indecent assault on a girl under 16. The defence was that the girl had told D that she was 16. The question was whether this section of the Sexual Offences Act should continue to be regarded as imposing strict liability as to age, or whether the presumption of *mens rea* applied. Again, not only did the House of Lords find unanimously in favour of the presumption of *mens rea*, but both Lord Bingham and Lord Steyn described the presumption as a 'constitutional principle'.[166]

(iv) *Exceptions to the Constitutional Principle?:* What does the term 'constitutional principle' mean? It is clearly intended as a principle of judicial interpretation. Whether it is a principle of which Parliament ought to take account is another matter: in the Sexual Offences Act 2003 it certainly did not, overruling the effect of both the House of Lords decisions.[167] Even for the judges, it is a principle and not a rule. Thus, for example, Lord Nicholls held in *B* v *DPP* that courts may rebut the presumption of *mens rea* by reference to 'the nature of the offence, the mischief sought to be prevented, and any other circumstances which may assist in determining what intent is properly to be attributed to Parliament when creating the offence'.[168] One might comment that if the presumption can be rebutted so easily it may prove to be worth little. It may be justifiable to rebut the presumption for minor offences which may be described as 'not criminal in any real sense', but the failure to regard the possibility of imprisonment as a crucial distinction is a major weakness.[169] A powerful example of this is *Gammon* v *Attorney-General for Hong Kong* (1985).[170] Following the collapse of a building, the defendants were charged with offences against the construction regulations which carried high fines and a maximum prison sentence of three years. Lord Scarman, giving the opinion of the Privy Council, reaffirmed the presumption of *mens rea* laid down in *Sweet* v *Parsley*, and added that 'the presumption is particularly strong where the offence is 'truly criminal' in character'. He went on:

> the only situation in which the presumption can be displaced is where the statute is concerned with an issue of social concern; public safety is such an issue . . . Even where a stat-

---

[162] *Per* Lord Nicholls at 460.

[163] *Prince* (1875) LR 2 CCR 154; cf. R. Cross, 'Centenary Reflections on Prince's Case' (1975) 91 LQR 520 and J. Horder, 'How Culpability Can, and Cannot, Be Denied in Under-age Sex Crimes' [2001] Crim LR 16.

[164] *Per* Lord Steyn at 470, borrowing the expression from Sir Rupert Cross, *Statutory Interpretation* (3rd edn., 1995, by Bell and Engle), at 166.   [165] [2002] 1 AC 462.

[166] Lord Bingham at [17], Lord Steyn at [32]. Lord Bingham made similar remarks in the recklessness case of *G* [2004] 1 AC 1034, discussed later in section 6.6(c).

[167] See the discussion of sexual offences in Chapter 9.5.   [168] [2000] 2 AC at 463–4.

[169] In addition to *Howells* and *Muhamad*, see also decisions such as *Storkwain* (earlier in chapter, at n 160), *Gammon* v *Attorney-General for Hong Kong* [1985] AC 1 and *R* v *Wells Street Magistrates' Court and Martin, ex p Westminster City Council* [1986] Crim LR 696.   [170] [1985] AC 1 at 14.

ute is concerned with such an issue, the presumption of mens rea stands unless it can also be shown that the creation of strict liability will be effective to promote the objects of the statute by encouraging greater vigilance to prevent the commission of the prohibited act.

The last few words support the principle that strict liability should not be imposed where there is nothing more a defendant could reasonably be expected to do in order to avoid the harm.[171] This means that liability is tethered, however loosely, to the defendant's control; liability is not completely strict in these cases. However, the earlier part of the quotation demonstrates how muddy the waters still are. In some cases the courts say that strict liability is appropriate for minor offences which are not truly criminal.[172] Yet they also seem to hold, as in *Gammon*, that it is appropriate where offences relate to public safety or social concern—a description which (as pointed out earlier) could extend to large areas of the criminal law. That the *Gammon* decision was cited by the House of Lords in *B v DPP* without any attempt to confront this problem indicates a pessimistic outlook for the 'constitutional principle'.

In a search for principled exceptions, let us examine two areas of the law—firearms and sexual offences—where the courts have taken a different view. The decision of the Court of Appeal in *Deyemi and Edwards*[173] is of particular importance, since the defence placed strong reliance on the 'constitutional principle' of *mens rea*. The defendants were found in possession of an article that they believed to be a large torch but which was in fact a stun-gun. They were convicted of possessing a prohibited weapon, contrary to s. 5 of the Firearms Act 1968 and the judge, having examined the facts, gave them a conditional discharge. The Court of Appeal recognized the significance of the House of Lords decisions establishing the 'constitutional principle', but held that it was bound by a long line of authority (including *Howells*, see earlier) to hold that this is a strict liability offence. The House of Lords decisions were each 'concerned with the proper meaning of the statutory provisions in question', held Latham LJ, a dismissal that confines their sphere of influence to statutory provisions that have not yet been the subject of an authoritative interpretation. On the substantive issue, presumably the argument is that strong reasons of public policy require the courts to impose strict liability in firearms cases, otherwise measures of control would be weakened. But the outcome here—conditional discharges for the two defendants—suggests that an acquittal in this kind of case would not weaken the law. The convictions were unfair, as the sentences indicate. The line of firearms cases which the Court applied ought to be overruled.

Turning to sexual offences, the decision of the House of Lords in *G*[174] confirms that the offence of rape of a child under 13 in s. 5 of the Sexual Offences Act 2003 imposes strict liability as to age. The House was unwilling to accept human rights arguments to the effect that this breaches the presumption of innocence in Art. 6(2) and breaches the Art. 8 rights of the accused (who was aged 15 only).[175] The majority view, expressed by

---

[171] See *Lim Chin Aik* v R [1963] AC 160.

[172] For an example, see *Harrow LBC* v *Shah* [2000] 1 WLR 83 (selling lottery tickets to a person under 16: strict liability as to age approved so as to help enforcement). [173] [2008] 1 Cr App R 26.

[174] [2008] UKHL 37. [175] For fuller discussion of the decision, see Chapter 9.6(a).

Baroness Hale, was that strict liability is necessary here in order to ensure the protection of children from the sexual attentions of others. The implication is that allowing a defence of reasonable mistake (a negligence standard) would reduce that protection unacceptably; on this view, the unfairness and stigma of convicting a mistaken defendant of this serious offence is less important, even when that defendant is also below the age of consent (and could have been charged with a lesser offence). Both the empirical and the normative strands in that attempted justification call for close examination.

(v) *Conclusion:* Despite pronouncements of high authority on the existence of a 'constitutional principle' requiring fault, English law remains in an unsatisfactory state. The judgments in *B* v *DPP* and in *K* refer to the possibility of rebutting the principle or presumption; there are decisions since 2000 that show how easy it is for a court to find a reason for rebutting the presumption;[176] and it seems that courts will follow precedents on the precise statute rather than resorting to the broader authorities on the 'constitutional principle'.[177] So long as different statutes are promoted by different government departments without an overall grammar or standard, progress towards a consistent approach will be hampered. The first move should be for Parliament, probably prompted by the Law Commission, to establish a principled way of proceeding.[178] If there are persuasive economic and social arguments in favour of strict liability for minor offences—and those arguments must be rigorously evaluated—then this may be permitted so long as imprisonment is not available. There should be recognition of the principle that no person should be liable to imprisonment without proof of sufficient fault.[179] This principle should inform the distinction between minor and non-minor offences. The classification of an offence as 'regulatory', whatever that may mean, should be irrelevant to the imposition of strict liability: if imprisonment is available as a sanction, then fault should be required whether it is called 'regulatory' or not. Similarly, the 'public safety' test stated in the *Gammon* case should be discarded, not least because it points in exactly the wrong direction by arguing in favour of strict liability for more serious offences.

(b) INTENTION

The term '*mens rea*' has conventionally been used to connote the following fault requirements: intention or recklessness as to a specified consequence, and knowledge of, or recklessness as to, a specified circumstance.[180] In discussing offences of strict

---

[176] E.g. *Muhamad* [2003] QB 1031 (offence of materially contributing to insolvency by gambling); *Matudi* [2003] EWCA Crim 697 (offence of importing products of animal origin, not citing either *B* v *DPP* or *K*).

[177] As in *Deyemi and Edwards* (see n 173 earlier). See also the speculation of Colin Manchester on how the Licensing Act 2003 will be interpreted, in 'Knowledge, Due Diligence and Strict Liability in Regulatory Offences' [2006] Crim LR 213.

[178] See now, Law Commission, *Criminal Liability in Regulatory Contexts* (CP No. 195, 2010), Pt 6.

[179] See further R. A. Duff, *Punishment, Communication and Community* (2001), 149–51.

[180] In that respect, as we discussed at the beginning of this chapter, '*mens rea*' is a term narrower in scope that the term 'fault element', because the latter clearly includes negligence.

liability, we have considered the main arguments in favour of requiring fault as a condition of criminal liability. Now we move to the more detailed and specific question of drawing distinctions between the four main forms of fault which generally fall under the umbrella of *mens rea*. The task is important, because of the key role of intention in serious crimes. Sometimes the intent is the essence of an offence, as in doing an act with intent to impede the apprehension of an offender, all crimes of attempt, and offences defined in terms of 'doing x with intent to do y' (such as burglary: entering as a trespasser with intent to steal).[181] Sometimes the law uses intention as the main method of grading offences: both the murder–manslaughter distinction and the dividing line between wounding under s. 18 of the Offences against the Person Act 1861 (maximum penalty of life imprisonment) and wounding under s. 20 (maximum penalty of five years' imprisonment) turn on the presence or absence of intention.

(i) *Intention in Principle:* It is quite possible—indeed, quite normal—to do things with more than one intention in mind. I can demolish a fence with the simultaneous intentions of making way for a new fence, providing wood for the fire, and so on. The approach of the criminal law, however, is generally not to ask with what intentions D committed the act, but to ask whether one particular intention was present when the act was committed. The law, generally speaking, is interested in the presence or absence of one particular intention—that specified in the definition of the offence charged—and not in conducting a general review of D's reasons for the behaviour in question. Did D intend to kill the crew of the aircraft on which he placed a bomb, as well as intending (as he admits) to claim the insurance money on the cargo? Did D intend to assist the enemy by his actions, as well as intending (as he admits) to save his family from a concentration camp?[182]

The law's approach in selecting one intention, and then abstracting it from D's other reasons and beliefs at the time, calls for careful consideration. It is essential to keep in mind the particular intent required by the definition of the offence. It is quite possible to say 'D pulled the trigger of the gun intentionally', without implying that D intended to kill V when he pulled the trigger. The offence of murder turns (broadly)[183] on the presence or absence of an intention to kill; whether the trigger was pulled intentionally or accidentally may be an important part of the case, but the legally required intention is that D *intended to kill* V. Loose references to whether D 'acted intentionally' can blur this distinction: it is unhelpful to refer to intention without relating it to a particular object or consequence, which in a legal context means the intent specified in the indictment or information.[184]

---

[181] Burglary is discussed later in Chapter 10.6. On intent-based crimes see generally A. Ashworth, 'Defining Criminal Offences without Harm', in P. F. Smith (ed.), *Criminal Law: Essays in Honour of J. C. Smith* (1987), and J. Horder, 'Crimes of Ulterior Intent', in A. P. Simester and A. T. H. Smith (eds), *Harm and Culpability* (1996).   [182] See the discussion of *Steane* later, n 204 and accompanying text.

[183] See Chapter 8.3(c).

[184] For further study see R. A. Duff, *Intention, Agency and Criminal Liability* (1990), chs 3, 4, and 6, critically discussed on this point by A. P. Simester, 'Paradigm Intention' (1992) 11 *Law and Philosophy* 236.

This approach to intention may avoid some errors, but the proper definition of intention remains the subject of theoretical debate and judicial disagreement. The core of 'intention' is surely aim, objective, or purpose; whatever else 'intention' may mean, a person surely acts with intention to kill if killing is the aim, objective, or purpose of the conduct that causes death. When drafting, however, it may be best to avoid the term 'purpose' (which may give rise to confusion with D's ultimate purpose in doing the act), and instead to define intention in terms of 'acting in order to bring about' the result.[185] Similarly in *Mohan*[186] James LJ defined intention as 'a decision to bring about [the proscribed result], in so far as it lies within the accused's power, no matter whether the accused desired that consequence of his act or not'. This definition has the advantage of stating that desire is not essential to intention (one may act out of feelings of duty, for example, rather than desire); it has the disadvantage of referring to a 'decision', whereas in many offences of violence and other crimes the events happen so suddenly and rapidly that an action can be engaged in intentionally without there have been deliberation about the alternatives beforehand. In law, a spontaneously formed intention is as much an intention as an intention that is the product of lengthy deliberation.[187]

The *Mohan* case involved an attempted crime, and intention is thought to be crucial to attempts, because one cannot be said to *attempt* to produce a result unless one *intends* to produce it (see Chapter 12.3(a)).[188] The decision in *Mohan* goes some way towards stating the core of the concept of intention, that is, acting in order to bring about a result.[189] It is important to note that, in intending to bring about an end, one must also intend the means adopted to achieve it, because otherwise D could always avoid liability by pointing to some ulterior motive for the action: 'it was not my purpose to kill V, because my real purpose in shooting at V was to inherit V's money after V's death'. Such a purported detachment of the means from the end is quite unconvincing. Both are part of the intention with which D fired the shot, and the criminal law is interested only in whether the killing was intentional.

Should the concept of intention be more extensive than that, in the context of criminal liability? Lawyers have long worked with a concept of intention includes not only acting in order to bring about *x* but also acting with foresight of certainty that *x* will result—that D can be said to have intended a result if he or she realized that the result was certain to follow from the behaviour in question. An early example of this may be found in Bentham's writings, and his distinction between direct and oblique intention

---

[185] LCCP 177, *A New Homicide Act?*, paras. 4.36–37, adopting the argument of A. Khan, 'Intention in Criminal Law: Time to Change?' (2002) 23 Statute LR 236.   [186] [1976] QB 1.

[187] R. Cross, 'The Mental Element in Crime' (1967) 83 LQR 216.

[188] An exception involves cases in which someone tries to do something in order to show that it is impossible to achieve, such as seeking to jump over the roof of a very high building. Here, there may be an attempt without an intention to succeed, but such cases are rare. If such a case arose in a criminal context, it would not count as a criminal attempt, because there was no 'intent to commit the offence', as required by the Criminal Attempts Act 1981, s. 1(1).

[189] Compare J. Finnis, 'Intention and Side-Effects', in R. G. Frey and C. W. Morris, *Liability and Responsibility* (1991), 32, with A. P. Simester, 'Why Distinguish Intention from Foresight?', in Simester and Smith (eds), *Harm and Culpability* (1996).

is one way of expressing the point.[190] One might say that a consequence is *directly* intended if D acts in order to produce it, and that it is *obliquely* intended if it is not D's aim but is known to be certain.[191] To regard both these mental attitudes as forms of intention is to make a moral point. It is not necessarily being claimed that ordinary people in their everyday language use the term 'intention' in this way.[192] The claim is that the person who foresees a consequence as certain should be classified as having intended that result rather than as having been merely reckless towards it—and the claim is being made in the knowledge that some killings would thus be classified as murder rather than manslaughter, some woundings described as 'with intent' rather than merely as unlawful, and so on. As soon as the argument moves from the moral to the legal, such questions of classification arise. What has to be established is not that all cases of foresight of certainty are socially or morally as bad as all cases of purpose, but that it is more appropriate to classify them with 'intention' than with 'recklessness'.

If we pursue the moral part of the argument further, we find that the shorthand phrase 'foresight of certainty' is perhaps too brief in this context. Few future events in life are absolutely certain, and a reference to consequences as 'certain to follow' would generally mean 'practically certain to follow' or 'certain, barring some unforeseen intervention'.[193] A familiar example is D, who places a bomb on an aircraft with the aim of blowing it up in mid-flight in order to claim the insurance money on the cargo. D knows that it is practically certain that the crew of the aircraft will be killed as a result of the explosion. One might say that D's *purpose* is to claim the insurance money, but if the charge is murder, that is irrelevant. The key question is whether D intended *to kill*. Let us assume that D did not act in order to kill, that is, that he had not intended the death of the air-crew as the means to his end. Should the law extend the definition beyond such a direct intent to cover D's awareness of the practical certainty that the crew would be killed? The argument in favour of this is that D's behaviour shows no respect for the value of human life at all: D knows that the crew will die, and yet he still pursues the aim of blowing up the aircraft. There is little social or moral difference between that and planning the explosion in order to kill the crew. It is sometimes thought that the 'test of failure' argues against this:[194] since D would not regard the explosion as a failure if the cargo were destroyed but the crew were not killed, this serves to differentiate him from someone whose purpose is to kill. But to establish that a philosophical distinction exists between D and the purposeful killer is not to conclude the matter: to transfer the argument from morality to law, it has to be decided whether the person who foresees death as virtually certain should be bracketed with the directly intentional killer (murder) or treated as merely reckless (manslaughter).[195] Recklessness, as we shall see

---

[190] Bentham, *Introduction to the Principles of Morals and Legislation*, ch VIII, on direct and oblique intent. Bentham's definition of oblique intent was wider than that described here, a point discussed by G. Williams, 'Oblique Intent' (1987) 46 Camb LJ 417.　　　　　　　　　　　　　　　　　　　　　　　　[191] Ibid.

[192] See the discussion of 'ordinary language' later.

[193] The phrase of Lord Lane CJ, in *Nedrick* (1986) 83 Cr App R 267.

[194] Duff, *Intention, Agency and Criminal Liability*, ch 3.

[195] For extensive discussion, see I. Kugler, *Direct and Oblique Intention in the Criminal Law* (Ashgate, 2002).

later, includes the taking of relatively small risks. There is a strong argument that some-one who takes a risk of death that amounts to a virtual certainty comes very close, in point of culpability, to the person who chooses someone's death as the means to an end. They both show no respect at all for human life. The Law Commission accepts this, preferring a definition that includes not only the person who acts in order to bring about the prohibited consequence but also the person who 'thought that the result was a virtually certain consequence of his or her action'.[196]

(ii) *Intention in the Courts:* At present there is no legislative definition of inten-tion. How have the courts approached the question? The leading decisions concern the crime of murder, to be discussed in a later chapter,[197] but their effect can be sum-marized here. The first of the leading cases is *Moloney*,[198] in which the House of Lords held that judges should generally avoid defining the term 'intention', beyond explain-ing that it differs from 'desire' and 'motive'. Only in exceptional cases should the judge depart from this golden rule, notably, where the essence of the defence is that D's pur-pose was only to frighten, not to harm, the victim. Here the jury should be instructed to decide whether D foresaw the prohibited consequence as 'a natural consequence' of the behaviour: if the answer was yes, they could infer intention from that. In the course of his speech Lord Bridge gave hints of the sort of cases he meant to include—cases where the consequence was a 'little short of overwhelming', or 'virtually certain'—but unfortunately the centrepiece of his speech was the term 'natural consequence'. When this was used by the judge to direct the jury in *Hancock and Shankland* (1986),[199] it was held to be unsatisfactory. The House of Lords overruled its own test of 'natural consequence', and Lord Scarman stated that juries should be told that 'the greater the probability of a consequence the more likely it is that the consequence was foreseen, and that if that consequence was foreseen the greater the probability is that that conse-quence was also intended'.

These decisions left unclear the precise legal meaning of intention and the proper approach to directing a jury, and Lord Lane CJ attempted to synthesize the House of Lords decisions when presiding in the Court of Appeal in *Nedrick*:[200]

> Where the charge is murder and in the rare cases where the simple direction is not enough, the jury should be directed that they are not entitled to infer the necessary intention, un-less they feel sure that death or serious bodily harm was a virtual certainty (barring some unforeseen intervention) as a result of the defendant's actions and that the defendant real-ized that such was the case.

This direction now has the authority of the House of Lords. In *Woollin*[201] the House disapproved a direction in terms of whether D had realized that there was a 'substantial risk' of serious injury, and held that the *Nedrick* formulation should

---

[196] Law Com No 304, *Murder, Manslaughter and Infanticide* (2007), para 3.27.   [197] Chapter 8.3(c).
[198] [1985] AC 906.   [199] [1986] AC 456.   [200] (1986) 83 Cr App R 267.   [201] [1999] AC 82.

be followed—with one modification. Where *Nedrick* states that if D foresaw the relevant consequence as virtually certain the court is 'entitled to infer' intention, *Woollin* states that the court is 'entitled to find' intention.[202] This change has little practical significance, and it leaves open the possibility that, if courts are 'entitled' but not required to find intention in these cases, then there may occasionally be cases where they may lawfully decide not to find intention despite foresight of virtual certainty.[203]

In English law, therefore, intention is not defined in terms of (a) acting in order to bring about a result or (b) acting in the knowledge that the result is virtually certain to follow. The indirect or oblique element, (b), is said to be something on the basis of which intention can be found, and not a species of intention. The reluctance of the judiciary to commit themselves to a particular definition of intention confirms that they see the need to preserve an element of flexibility so that they can continue to allow occasional divergences from the 'standard' (a) or (b) definition. Appellate decisions over the years reveal a variety of departures from what might be termed the 'standard definition' of intention. Thus in *Steane*[204] the Court of Criminal Appeal quashed D's conviction under wartime regulations for the offence of doing acts likely to assist the enemy, with intent to assist the enemy. The Court held that if D's acts were as consistent with an innocent intent (such as saving his family from a concentration camp) as with a criminal intent, the jury should be left to decide the matter. This diverges from the standard definition, since it was never discussed whether D knew that it was virtually certain his acts would assist the enemy. The Court could probably have used the defence of duress to quash the conviction, but it evidently thought that adopting a narrow definition of intention provided a simpler route to the desired result. Similarly, in the civil case of *Gillick* v *West Norfolk and Wisbech Area Health Authority*[205] the House of Lords held that a doctor who gives contraceptive advice to a girl under 16 for clinical reasons, whilst realizing that this would facilitate sexual activity, is not guilty of aiding and abetting the offence of sexual activity with a child. The decision might well have been placed on some such ground as 'clinical necessity',[206] but instead Lord Scarman explained that 'the bona fide exercise by a doctor of his clinical judgement must be a complete negation of the guilty mind'. With this sweeping statement it was held that the doctor did not have the intention required for aiding and abetting, even though it may be assumed that prescribing the contraceptives was foreseen as virtually certain to assist the commission of an offence.

---

[202] Applied by the Court of Appeal in *Matthews and Alleyne* [2003] 2 Cr App R 30, although Rix LJ commented that 'there is very little to choose between a rule of evidence and one of substantive law'.

[203] Commonly discussed examples involve situations of emergency, where a defence of necessity is unavailable because the defence has no application, as in murder cases. Consider an example in which D and her baby are trapped by an advancing fire at the top of a high building, and D throws the baby off the edge in the vain hope that someone below may by a miracle catch the baby. In such a case, even if D foresaw the baby's death as certain to occur as a result of her action, a court might not infer from that D intended to kill the baby by that action.   [204] [1947] KB 997.   [205] [1986] AC 112.

[206] See the discussion in Chapter 4.5(a).

To set alongside these two decisions which favour a narrow definition of intention it is not difficult to find decisions pointing in a different direction. In *Smith*[207] D had offered a bribe to an official, solely in order to demonstrate that the official was corrupt. The Court of Criminal Appeal upheld his conviction for corruptly offering an inducement to an official, holding that D had an intention to corrupt so long as he intended the offer to operate on the mind of the offeree. In this case D's law-abiding motivation was held to count for nothing. Similarly in *Chandler v DPP*,[208] the defendants' convictions of acting 'for a purpose prejudicial to the safety or interests of the State' were upheld by the House of Lords. They had infiltrated a military airfield, and this was regarded as prejudicial to the State's interests. The defendants' argument that their own purpose was to promote the safety and interests of the State (by promoting peace), rather than to prejudice them, was discounted.

What these decisions demonstrate is that the courts do not adhere to a single definition of intention. Various observations may be made about this. One common reaction is to treat it as evidence for a 'realist' interpretation of how courts behave: they decide on the desired result, and then define the law in whatever way happens to achieve it. But the evidence is limited to a small number of appeal court decisions, and may not reflect the everyday operation of the criminal courts. Even if it were true to some degree (and few suggest that the courts have an absolute freedom in these matters), what is it that leads courts to adopt these reasons for reaching these particular results? Judges in the appellate courts are fond of referring to 'ordinary language' as a justification for their decisions, but this often appears to be a camouflage for moral judgments. Critical writers have made much of the tensions revealed by the varied judicial approach. Thus Nicola Lacey scrutinizes the shifting language of the appellate judges and argues that this reflects their attempt to keep the law fairly close to popular conceptions (and thereby to enhance its legitimacy) whilst trying to ensure that the interests of the powerful are not significantly challenged.[209] Thus a model direction stating that, where a court is satisfied that D foresaw a result as virtually certain, it is 'entitled to find' that D intended the result, may operate so as to allow the courts to expand and contract the definition so as to reflect other factors, including moral judgments of a defendant's background and situation.

(iii) *Intention Concluded:* In delivering the unanimous judgment of the House of Lords in *Woollin*, Lord Steyn observed that the appeal concerned the crime of murder and that 'it does not follow that "intent" necessarily has the same meaning in every context in the criminal law'.[210] However, the variable approaches to intention described in the previous paragraphs have not been explained by judges on an offence-specific basis, and there would surely need to be particular arguments in favour of adopting a

---

[207] [1960] 2 QB 423; see also *Yip Chiu-Cheung* [1995] 1 AC 111, discussed in Chapter 12.5.

[208] [1964] AC 763.

[209] N. Lacey, 'A Clear Concept of Intention: Elusive or Illusory?' (1993) 56 MLR 621. See also A. Norrie, *Crime Reason and History* (3rd edn., 2014), ch 3.

[210] [1999] AC 82, at 90; see the observations of V. Tadros, 'The System of the Criminal Law' (2002) 22 LS 448, at 451–6.

different definition for a certain crime or class of crimes. The *Woollin* definition may therefore be treated as established, and yet we have seen that the House of Lords left the door ajar: the phrase 'entitled to find' preserves an element of 'moral elbow-room' which many judges believe to be essential to doing justice. The Law Commission accepts this view: in recommending that 'an intention to bring about a result may be found if it is shown that the defendant thought that the result was a virtually certain consequence of his or her actions',[211] the Commission argues that this element of flexibility is 'the price of avoiding the complexity' needed if a comprehensive definition were attempted, and that broad terms such as 'extreme indifference' would create greater uncertainty. The reason judges adopted variable meanings of intention in the decisions discussed above is largely that the standard definition, in combination with the range of available defences to liability, sometimes fails to capture moral distinctions which are thought important. The term 'intent'—sometimes the determinant of liability, sometimes a primary way of grading offences—is not one that necessarily incorporates elements of moral evaluation, unlike the other *mens rea* term 'reckless' (discussed below).[212] Thus when faced with a strong moral pull towards exculpation the courts have sometimes, as in *Steane* and in *Gillick*, manipulated the concept of intention rather than developing a defence to criminal liability. However, it would surely be better to adopt a tighter definition of intention, excluding the permissive words 'may be found' in the Law Commission's recommended definition, and to place greater emphasis on appropriate defences. Under the criminal code the courts would have a power to develop new defences,[213] so as to ensure that what they regard as important moral distinctions are marked appropriately.

(c) RECKLESSNESS

Much of the preceding discussion about the proper limits of the concept of intention in the criminal law has inevitably concerned the dividing line between recklessness and intention. The argument was that there are some cases in which D knows the risk of the prohibited consequence to be so very high (i.e. practically certain) that it is more appropriate to classify his mental attitude within the highest category of culpability (intention) rather than in the lesser category of recklessness. We may note that some would draw the dividing line lower, arguing that if D foresaw the prohibited consequence as a *probable* result, this should be classified as intention, leaving only the lesser degrees of risk within the category of recklessness.[214] Another avenue, not explored in English law, would involve employing the US Mode Penal Code term 'knowledge'

---

[211] Law Com No. 304, para 3.27; see generally paras 3.18–3.26.   [212] See section 6.5(c).

[213] Expressly preserved by cll. 4(4) and 46(4) of the draft Criminal Code. See now *Re A (Conjoined Twins: Surgical Separation)* [2000] 4 All ER 961, discussed later in Chapter 8.2; and more generally, A. Ashworth, 'Criminal Liability in a Medical Context: the Treatment of Good Intentions', in Simester and Smith (eds), *Harm and Culpability* (1996).

[214] This was one of the views expressed in *Hyam* v *DPP* [1975] AC 55, by Lord Diplock (not dissenting on this point); see J. Buzzard, 'Intent' [1978] Crim LR 5, with reply by J. C. Smith at [1978] Crim LR 14.

that something will occur: to cover states of mind where D foresees a high certainty of the occurrence. We will now move away from these arguments, but they do remind us that debates about the boundaries of intention relate to the grading of culpability and so of offences. The same is true of the lower boundary between recklessness and negligence: when criminal lawyers refer to offences as requiring '*mens rea*', they usually mean that either intention or recklessness will suffice for liability but that negligence will not. Thus, once again, the debate concerns not so much language as the limits of criminal liability.

An abiding difficulty in discussing the legal meaning of recklessness is that the term has been given several different shades of meaning by the courts over the years. In the law of manslaughter, 'reckless' has often been regarded as the most appropriate adjective to express the degree of negligence ('gross') needed for a conviction:[215] in this sense, it means a high degree of carelessness. In the late 1950s the courts adopted a different meaning of recklessness in the context of *mens rea*, referring to D's actual awareness of the risk of the prohibited consequence occurring:[216] we shall call this 'advertent recklessness'. Controversy was introduced into this area in the early 1980s, when the House of Lords purported to broaden the meaning of recklessness so as to include those who failed to give thought to an obvious risk that the consequence would occur:[217] as we shall see in paragraph (ii) later, the House of Lords has now reversed itself on this point.[218] The law of manslaughter will be left for discussion later:[219] here we will focus on the other meanings of recklessness.[220]

(i) *Advertent Recklessness:* It was in *Cunningham* that the Court of Criminal Appeal held that, in a statute, the term 'malicious' denotes intention or recklessness, and that recklessness means that 'the accused has foreseen that the particular kind of harm might be done and yet has gone on to take the risk of it'.[221] There are essentially three elements in this definition, and they are the same ones found in the Model Penal Code's definition of recklessness as 'the conscious taking of an unjustified risk'. First, it requires D's actual awareness of the risk;[222] this is why it is referred to as 'advertent recklessness', and it is regarded as the key element in bringing recklessness within the concept of *mens rea*. A person should be held to have been reckless about a particular result only if the court is satisfied that he or she was aware of the risk at the time. The second element is that a person may be held to have been reckless if he or she was aware of *any degree* of risk: we have seen that when the risk is so high as to be a practical certainty, D may be classed as intending the consequence, but any risk, however slight, may be sufficient as a minimum for recklessness, so long as D is aware of it and it materializes. In its recommendations for reform of the law of homicide, the Law

---

[215] See *Andrews* v *DPP* [1937] AC 576 and *Adomako* [1995] 1 AC 171, discussed later in Chapter 7.6.
[216] *Cunningham* [1957] 2 QB 396, adopting the definition offered by C. S. Kenny, *Outlines of Criminal Law* (1st edn., 1902; 16th edn., 1952).   [217] *Caldwell* [1982] AC 341, and *Lawrence* [1982] AC 510.
[218] In *G* [2004] 1 AC 1034.   [219] Chapter 8.6(b).
[220] A further meaning of recklessness was adopted in sex cases (see *Kimber* [1983] 1 WLR 1118, *Satnam S and Kewal S* (1984) 78 Cr App R 149), but the enactment of the Sexual Offences Act 2003 relegates this to a matter of historical interest only.   [221] [1957] 2 QB 396.   [222] Model Penal Code, s. 2.02(s)(c).

Commission proposes a narrower definition of recklessness—that D must be aware of a 'serious risk', that is, one that is 'more than insignificant or remote'.[223] It is not clear whether this would alter the outcome of many cases, but it is right that an offence such as murder should be more tightly defined. The third element is that the risk which D believes to be present must be an unjustified or unreasonable one to take in the circumstances. This is an objective element: courts have rarely discussed it, but it exerts a significant background influence.

A typical example of the objective element is the surgeon who carries out an operation knowing that death will probably result.[224] In this example, assuming that there is a clinical justification for the operation, even exposing the patient to a high degree of risk from the operation itself may well be fully justified. In general, thus, 'the responsibility line is drawn according to an evaluation of the nature of the activity and the degree of the risk'.[225] However, the circumstances in which an activity is undertaken may be as important as the nature of the activity itself, Suppose, in the example just given, that (for a bet) the surgeon tried to conduct the same operation wearing a blindfold. Even if the surgeon was so skilled that most experts would say he or she posed no extra risk to the patient when blindfolded, the surgeon's gratuitous introduction of an extra potential source of risk would be regarded as acting recklessly. The evaluative task of determining objective risk has rarely been performed by the courts but, as Alan Norrie rightly points out, this is because prosecutors have often made their own evaluations at an early stage and no prosecution (or at least no prosecution for a serious offence such as manslaughter) has been brought in most such cases.[226] Thus we have scant judicial authority relating to the objective element in recklessness.

The justifications for the advertent definition of recklessness are grounded in the principle of individual autonomy and the importance of respecting choice, outlined earlier.[227] The distinction between recklessness and negligence turns on D's awareness or unawareness of the risk. In both cases there is an unreasonable risk taken, but D should only be held to have been reckless if he or she was aware of the risk. A person who is aware of the risk usually chooses to create it or to run it, and therefore chooses to place his or her interests above the well-being of those who may suffer if the risk materializes.[228] Choosing to create a risk of harmful consequences is generally much worse than creating the same risk without realizing it. Moreover, holding a person reckless despite unawareness of the risk would result in a conviction in a case like *Stephenson* (1979).[229] D, a schizophrenic, made a hollow in a haystack in order to sleep there; he felt cold, and so lit a small fire, causing the whole haystack to go up in flames,

---

[223] Law Com No. 304, paras. 3.36–3.40, relating to first degree murder and to reckless murder (second degree); for further discussion, see Chapter 8.3(c).

[224] Criminal Law Revision Committee, 14th Report, *Offences against the Person* (1980), 8.

[225] D. J. Galligan, 'Responsibility for Recklessness' (1978) 31 CLP 55, at 70.

[226] Norrie, *Crime, Reason and History*, ch 4. For example, prosecutions for offences of recklessness have been unusual in respect of large-scale transportation disasters.   [227] See earlier, section 6.4(a).

[228] For an analysis of fault in such terms, see, e.g., A. Brudner, 'Agency and Welfare in the Penal Law', in S. Shute, J. Gardner, and J. Horder (eds), *Action and Value in Criminal Law* (1993).   [229] [1979] QB 696.

and resulting in damage of some £3,500. The defence relied on medical evidence that D may not have had the same ability to foresee the risk as a mentally normal person. The Court of Appeal, quashing D's conviction, held that the definition of recklessness clearly turned on what this defendant actually foresaw, and the medical evidence should have been taken into account on this point. This decision, then, strongly affirms the element of individual fairness in the advertent or subjective definition. An entirely objective test would exclude this.

Does concentration on the element of awareness always produce decisions in accord with fairness? There are at least two types of awkward case for a test of liability which requires the court to be satisfied that the defendant actually saw the risk, however briefly. One is where a person acts impulsively in the heat of the moment. This is often expressed in ordinary speech by saying 'I acted without thinking', or 'I just didn't think'. D denies that he or she was aware of the risk at the time of acting. In *Parker* (1977)[230] D tried unsuccessfully to make a telephone call from a payphone; in his frustration he slammed down the receiver and broke it. The Court of Appeal upheld his conviction for causing criminal damage recklessly, despite his defence that it did not occur to him that he might damage the telephone. The Court held that he must have known that he was dealing with breakable material, even if that fact was not at the forefront of his mind when he slammed the receiver down. He had 'closed his mind to the obvious', or suppressed this knowledge at the time of the act.[231] It is quite evident that this decision involves some stretching of the awareness element which is thought to be central to advertent recklessness. In effect, it broadens the time frame from the moment of the act itself to an earlier and calmer time, when D would almost certainly have answered the question: 'What might happen if you slammed down a telephone receiver?', by saying: 'It might break'. The reason for thus broadening the time frame is presumably to prevent bad temper resulting in an acquittal, since this would be socially undesirable: people should control their tempers. But it does sully the subjective purity of this definition of recklessness. In that regard, an important difference between *Parker* and *Stephenson* concerns the reasons why each did not foresee the possible damage that might be done by their conduct. In Stephenson's case, the explanation was a mental disorder the effects of which he could not control. By contrast, in Parker's case, the explanation was his loss of temper, something he simply failed to control. However, as we will see, the House of Lords has rejected any attempt to finesse the definition of recklessness by reference to such factors.

The second problem is the 'couldn't care less' attitude: D might not have thought about a particular consequence, because it was irrelevant to his interests. If this version of events is accepted, D must be acquitted on the advertent definition of recklessness. Antony Duff has argued that these cases can and should be included within the meaning of recklessness, by invoking the concept of 'practical indifference'. This is 'a matter, not of feeling as distinct from action, but of the practical attitude which the action itself

---

[230] [1977] 1 WLR 600.   [231] See the discussion by Geoffrey Lane LJ in *Stephenson* [1979] QB 695, and M. Wasik and M. P. Thompson, 'Turning a Blind Eye as Constituting Mens Rea' (1981) 32 NILQ 328, at 339. In *Booth v CPS* (2006) 170 JP 305 the Divisional Court upheld a finding of recklessness on the basis that D had 'closed his mind' to the obvious.

displays'. Moreover, it may include cases in which D fails to advert to certain aspects of the situation: 'what I notice or attend to reflects what I care about; and my very failure to notice something can display my utter indifference to it'.[232] The argument is that people who are practically indifferent to certain key features of a situation may be just as much to blame as those who do advert to them. This argument was put strongly in relation to the pre-2003 law of rape, contending that judgments of practical indifference should be made on the basis that men *ought* to consider the victim's interests in such cases. Defensible as that approach is in that context,[233] the question is whether it is subjective, since it brings within the concept of recklessness some defendants who do not actually advert to these matters. Duff's response is that requiring practical indifference is just as subjective, and just as respectful of individual autonomy, as requiring awareness of risk. The practical indifference test looks to D's attitude at the time, on the basis of his acts and words. In practice, it is likely that juries applying the test of advertent recklessness would convict such defendants on the basis that they must have realized the risk; but that merely suggests that it may be unnecessary to confront Duff's point, not that it is wrong.

Thus there are at least two types of situation in which the 'awareness' requirement, the centrepiece of advertent recklessness, is problematic (on some views) and may fail to yield an acceptable grading of blameworthiness. One is the person who acts impulsively or in a temper, 'without thinking'. The other is the person who fails to think about the consequences out of indifference to them. A third possibility would be where D states that he was so preoccupied with other aspects of what he was doing as to give no thought to a particular consequence (although the courts might be reluctant to accept such a defence).[234]

(ii) *Caldwell Recklessness:* In *Caldwell* (1982)[235] the House of Lords introduced a new objective definition of recklessness that, incidentally, would encompass the three types of situation with which the traditional definition does not deal convincingly. It was heavily criticized, and for all practical purposes the subsequent decision in *G* (2004)[236] overrules it. Nonetheless, a brief discussion is appropriate here, in order to identify some of the issues of principle raised by the *Caldwell* decision and twenty-eight years of applying it (mostly in criminal damage cases, since it was never accepted throughout the criminal law).[237] In *Caldwell*, Lord Diplock formulated the following model direction: a person is guilty of causing damage recklessly if:

> (i) he does an act which in fact creates an obvious risk that property would be destroyed or damaged and (ii) when he does the act he either has not given any thought to the possibility of there being any such risk or has recognized that there was some risk involved and has nonetheless gone on to do it.

---

[232] Duff, *Intention, Agency and Criminal Liability*, 162–3.

[233] The Sexual Offences Act 2003 alters the definition of rape in this direction: by introducing a reasonableness test of belief in consent, it ensures that practically indifferent defendants should be convicted. See Chapter 9.5.

[234] See G. Williams, 'The Unresolved Problem of Recklessness' (1988) 8 *Legal Studies* 74, at 82.

[235] [1982] AC 341. The case of *Lawrence* [1982] AC 510 was decided on the same day.

[236] [2004] 1 AC 1034.   [237] For a fuller discussion, see the 4th edition of this work, at 183–7.

It will be noticed that this definition includes the advertent element (by referring to the person who recognizes the risk and takes it), but then goes further, extending to all those who fail to give any thought to the possibility of a risk which may be described as obvious. The formulation in the reckless driving case of *Lawrence* goes a little further by requiring proof that the risk was 'obvious and serious', the latter term implying that the ordinary prudent person would not have considered the risk negligible.[238] Lord Diplock's primary justification for thus expanding the definition of recklessness was that it may be no less blameworthy for a person to fail to foresee an obvious risk than it is to see the risk and knowingly to take it. In other words, Lord Diplock challenged the common law distinction between recklessness and negligence on the ground that it fails to draw the line in the right place. It will be observed that Lord Diplock did not appear to be altering the balance between individual responsibility and social protection. He did not argue that the definition of recklessness should be widened because a person who fails to give thought to an obvious risk is just as *dangerous* as the person who realized the risk. Rather, he attacked fundamental conceptions of responsibility by arguing that the idea of *mens rea*, as encompassing intention and subjective recklessness, is unsatisfactory because it omits some equally culpable cases.[239] As we have seen, some of the supporters of advertent recklessness accept that it is under-inclusive, in that they have attempted to stretch it to include actions during fits of temper and actions out of indifference.

A major problem with Lord Diplock's test of what would have been obvious to the reasonable person was that it admitted of no exceptions. The effect was to convict young children and mentally impaired defendants by applying to them an objective standard of foreseeability that they could not meet.[240] Thus, even if the *Caldwell* test were to be regarded as an improvement because it extended to thoughtless and inconsiderate wrongdoers, the absence of a capacity exception produced unfair convictions in some cases. The case of G[241] involved two children aged 11 and 12 who set fire to some newspapers beneath a rubbish bin and then left, after which the fire spread and caused major damage to nearby shops. The House of Lords considered whether to preserve the *Caldwell* test and engraft a capacity exception on it so as to exempt those (such as children and the mentally disordered) who might be incapable of attaining the objective standard; but this solution was rejected on the ground that the *Caldwell* test was already complicated and that this would over-complicate it to the extent of risking confusion among juries and magistrates.[242] The leading speech by Lord Bingham

---

[238] [1982] AC 510 at 527, reiterated in the reckless driving case of *Reid* (1992) 95 Cr App R 391.

[239] Lord Goff in *Reid* (1992) 95 Cr App R at 405–6 took the same view, arguing that unawareness of risk stemming from drink, rage, an attitude of indifference, or wilful blindness ought to be regarded as culpable and as reckless.

[240] See, e.g., *Elliott v C* (1983) 77 Cr App R 103 (mentally handicapped girl of 14), *Stephenson* [1979] QB 695 (man with schizophrenia).   [241] [2004] 1 AC 1034.

[242] *Per* Lord Bingham at para. 38. For substantive argument, see V. Tadros, 'Recklessness and the Duty to Take Care', in S. Shute and A. P. Simester (eds), *Criminal Law Theory: Doctrines for the General Part* (2002), at 255–7.

accepts the substance of the criticisms of *Caldwell*—the lack of legal foundation for the decision, the unfairness of its effects in some cases—and marks a reversion to the traditional, more subjective definition of recklessness based on the defendant's awareness of the risk. This closes one of the common law's less distinguished chapters,[243] and more or less returns the criminal law to a single definition of recklessness. But it does not advance the debate about the types of case that strictly fall outside that traditional definition of recklessness: the indifferent D who, precisely in virtue of his or her indifference, appears not to have thought of the risk at all,[244] and D who acts in sudden rage or temper and claims not to have realized the risk of harm.[245]

(d) KNOWLEDGE AND BELIEF

In general terms, the requirement of knowledge is regarded as having the same high status as a fault requirement as intention, except that knowledge relates to circumstances forming part of the definition of the crime, and intention relates to the consequences specified in the definition of the crime. This is probably acceptable as a dividing line, even though the distinction between circumstances and consequences is not without difficulty when applied to the definitions of some offences.[246] Requirements of knowledge, belief, and variations on these terms are widespread in the criminal law:[247] for example, the Licensing Act 2003 created several offences of 'knowingly' allowing a licensable activity to be carried on without authorization (s. 136), knowingly selling alcohol to a person who is drunk (s. 141), and so forth.[248]

It is instructive to approach the question by means of the basic definition of the offence of criminal damage—damaging property belonging to another with intent to damage property belonging to another: Criminal Damage Act 1971, s. 1(1).[249] One can argue that the only fault element required here is intention—does D intend to damage property belonging to another? But it is also possible to divide the fault element into two: Does D intend to damage property? Does D know that the property belongs to another? The knowledge relates to a fact or circumstance: although it will

---

[243] For the detailed history of the rise and fall of *Caldwell* recklessness, and suggestions for further development, see A. Halpin, *Definition in the Criminal Law* (2004), ch 3.

[244] For a discussion of different kinds of indifference, in this context, see J. Horder, 'Gross Negligence and Criminal Culpability' (1997) 47 *University of Toronto Law Journal* 495.

[245] On this point one may compare German criminal law, which also adopts this broader form of recklessness with a capacity exception—the question being whether D would or should have foreseen the risk, given his intellectual capacities and knowledge at the time. See J. R. Spencer and A. Pedain, 'Strict Liability in Continental Criminal Law', in A. P. Simester (ed.), *Appraising Strict Liability* (2005), 241.

[246] See the instructive study by S. Shute, 'Knowledge and Belief in the Criminal Law', in S. Shute and A. P. Simester (eds), *Criminal Law Theory*, (2002), esp. at 172–8.

[247] For discussion of the potential problems see G. Williams, 'The Problem of Reckless Attempts' [1983] Crim LR 365, R. J. Buxton, 'Circumstances, Consequences and Attempted Rape' [1984] Crim LR 25, and R. A. Duff, 'The Circumstances of an Attempt' (1991) 50 Camb LJ 100. The issue is discussed in Chapter 12.3.

[248] See C. Manchester, 'Knowledge, Due Diligence and Strict Liability in Licensing Offences' [2006] Crim LR 213.

[249] The offence may also be committed recklessly, but that is not relevant here. See more fully D. W. Elliott, 'Criminal Damage' [1988] Crim LR 403.

usually be relevant to D's reasons for acting, one can separate it analytically from the result which D intends. Such an analysis is essential for those crimes which require no result or conduct, such as possessing a controlled drug, where knowledge becomes the key element in the crime.[250] The matter is absolutely clear in the many offences which include the term 'knowingly' in their definition, such as being knowingly concerned in the importation of prohibited goods into the country.[251] There are also some offences in which the requirement is extended slightly, such as handling stolen goods knowing or believing them to be stolen, where the reference to 'believing' is taken to include people who may not *know* that the goods are stolen but may have no substantial doubt that they are.[252]

It is at this point, however, that a significant difference opens up between intention and knowledge as fault requirements. One can intend a result, whether or not it actually occurs: D can intend to kill by, say, shooting at V; if D's shot missed, then D still intended to kill and may be convicted of attempted murder. If the intention fails to come to fruition, it is none the less an intention. But this does not apply to knowledge. If we return to the basic offence of criminal damage as described earlier, we can consider the facts of *Smith (D R)*:[253] D was renting a flat, and during the course of his tenancy he fixed some panelling to the walls to conceal the wires of his stereo equipment. When his tenancy ceased, he took down and destroyed the panelling—which he had put up for his own convenience. He was charged with criminal damage, on the basis that, in law, the panelling became the property of the landlord once it was fixed to the walls. The Court of Appeal quashed his conviction for criminal damage, pointing out that although he did intend to damage property, he believed that the property was his own, and therefore he lacked the fault element for the crime. If D had been asked whether the panelling was his own, he would surely have replied: 'Yes'. Yet it would be inaccurate to say that he *knew* this, since it was not in fact true. It is more accurate to say that he *believed* the panelling to be his own; this belief should not be described as knowledge, because it does not accord with the true position. Although one can intend something which does not come to fruition, one cannot know something which is not in fact (or in law) true.

It is relatively unusual for the element of 'knowledge of circumstances' to be contested in serious crimes. Neither murder nor manslaughter is committed if D does not know that the object against which he uses force is a human being, but it is rare for a defendant to argue that the target was believed to be a dummy.[254] In rape, before the Sexual Offences Act 2003, it was necessary for the prosecution to prove that D knew V was not consenting or knowingly risked the possibility that V was not consenting, and the landmark decision in *DPP v Morgan*[255] held that D should be acquitted where the jury was left in reasonable doubt whether D mistakenly believed that V was consenting.

---

[250] See the discussion of possession offences at Chapter 5.3(b).
[251] Customs and Excise Management Act 1979, s. 170; see, e.g., *Taaffe* [1984] AC 539.
[252] See *Hall* (1985) 81 Cr App R 260, and the discussion later in Chapter 9.6.   [253] [1974] QB 354.
[254] See G. Williams, 'Homicide and the Supernatural' (1949) 65 LQR 491.   [255] [1976] AC 182.

Lord Hailsham stated that as a matter of 'inexorable logic' the absence of the necessary knowledge (because of a mistaken belief) must lead to an acquittal, since the prosecution has not proved its case. This decision has effectively been reversed by the 2003 Act,[256] but the 'inexorable logic' has been pursued by the courts in other cases.

Thus offences of assault and wounding are defined not just in terms of the use of force against another, but the *unlawful* use of force. As we saw in Chapter 5.6, force may be lawful if it is used in self-defence or the prevention of crime, for example. The 'logical' argument is that, if D used force in the belief that he was preventing a crime, when in reality this was not so, D would lack the knowledge that the use of force was unlawful and should therefore be acquitted of the offence.[257] However, as argued in Chapter 7.4 later, the 'inexorable logic' does not stand unchallenged, and there are powerful arguments for creating exceptions and for introducing requirements of 'reasonable belief' into certain offences and defences. This may be seen as running counter to the subjective thrust of some recent decisions of high authority, particularly those proclaiming a 'constitutional principle' that, unless Parliament indicates otherwise, 'the appropriate mental element is an unexpressed ingredient of every offence'.[258] The justifications for departing from that principle are examined in Chapter 7.4. The important point here is that, where the term 'knowingly' appears in an offence or where knowledge is otherwise required, it requires subjective awareness by D of each of the facts or circumstances in the definition of the crime to which it applies.

(e) RECKLESS KNOWLEDGE

Just as recklessness as to consequences is often an alternative form of *mens rea* to intention, so recklessness as to circumstances is sometimes an alternative form of fault to knowledge. What may, for convenience, be called 'reckless knowledge' exists where D believes that there is a risk that the prohibited circumstance exists, and goes on to take that risk. It is therefore a subjective requirement, on the same level as advertent recklessness as to consequences. However, in some cases it has been held to include 'wilful blindness', that is where D knows that there is a risk that a prohibited circumstance exists, but refrains from checking it.

An example is *Westminster City Council* v *Croyalgrange Ltd* (1986),[259] where D was charged with knowingly permitting the use of premises as a sex establishment without a licence. The House of Lords held that

> it is always open to the tribunal of fact, when knowledge on the part of a defendant is required to be proved, to base a finding of knowledge on evidence that the defendant had deliberately shut his eyes to the obvious or refrained from enquiry because he suspected the truth but did not want to have his suspicion confirmed.[260]

---

[256] See later in Chapter 9.6(i).   [257] *Williams (Gladstone)* (1984) 78 Cr App R 276.
[258] *B* v *DPP* [2000] 2 AC 428 and *K.* [2002] 1 AC 426, discussed earlier in the chapter.
[259] (1986) 83 Cr App R 155; see also the draft Criminal Code, Law Com No. 177, cl. 18(a).
[260] *Westminster City Council* v *Croyalgrange Ltd* (1986) 83 Cr App R 156.

It will be seen that Lord Bridge used the language of inference here, suggesting that a court might infer knowledge from wilful blindness in the same way as he suggested that intention might be inferred from foresight of virtual certainty.[261] There is well-known authority to the effect that wilful blindness should be treated as actual knowledge.[262] However, D does not *know* the relevant circumstance in such cases, since he has refrained from finding out, and it may not be easy to establish that he had an overwhelmingly strong belief (that it is virtually certain) that the prohibited circumstance exists. Wilful blindness should therefore be treated as a form of reckless knowledge, and relevant only when reckless knowledge is sufficient, unless it can be shown that D refrained from making inquiries because he was virtually certain that his suspicion would be confirmed.[263]

(f) NEGLIGENCE

Traditionally, books dealing with English criminal law afford an extremely brief discussion to negligence as a standard of liability. Among the common law crimes, only manslaughter rests on liability for (gross) negligence,[264] and careless driving and dangerous driving are among the few common offences based on negligence. Yet there are many offences of negligence among the statutory offences regulating various commercial and other activities, often taking the form of an indictable offence of doing an act 'with intent' to contravene the regulations, supported by a summary offence of negligence in committing an act in such a way as to 'have reason to believe' that the regulations will be contravened.[265] Moreover, other systems of law tend to have a larger group of offences of negligence, and may look askance at a set of laws which penalizes negligence where death is caused but does not penalize it where serious injury or suffering is caused or risked.

One reason for the opposition of many English text-writers to criminal liability for negligence is that it derogates from the subjective principles stated at the beginning of this chapter.[266] These elements are missing where mere negligence is sufficient: there is no need to prove that D adverted to the consequences at all, so long as the court is satisfied that a reasonable person in that situation would have done so. To have negligence as a standard of liability would therefore move away from advertence as the foundation of criminal responsibility, and in doing so might show insufficient respect for the principle of autonomy. The counter-argument to this might challenge the relevance to culpability (and to the public censure of criminal conviction) of 'the distinction between foreseen effects and effects that were unforeseen only because the agent was

---

[261] See *Moloney* [1985] AC 905; cf. *Woollin* [1999] 1 AC 82, earlier at n 201.

[262] The classic statement is that of Devlin J, in *Roper v Taylor's Garages Ltd* [1951] 2 TLR 284, at 288.

[263] See G. R. Sullivan, 'Knowledge, Belief and Culpability' and V. Tadros, 'Recklessness and the Duty to Take Care', in Shute and Simester (eds), *Criminal Law Theory*, at respectively 213–14 and 252–4.

[264] See later in Chapter 8.6(c).   [265] Some examples are collected at [1980] Crim LR 1.

[266] See earlier, at section 6.4(a).

not paying as much attention as he could and should have paid'.[267] It might be argued that a person who negligently causes harm could have done otherwise: he or she could have taken the care necessary to avoid the harm. So long as the individual had the capacity to behave otherwise at the time, it is fair to impose liability in those situations where there are sufficient signals to alert the reasonable citizen to the need to take care. Autonomy is a fundamental principle, but this does not mean that advertence should always be required so long as there is fair warning and a fair opportunity to conform to the required standard.

Three features of this counter-argument should be noted. First, its focus on capacity should not be dismissed as 'objective', for that would be an undiscriminating use of the term. As Hart has shown, it is perfectly possible to allow exceptions for those who cannot be expected to attain the standard of foresight and control of the reasonable citizen. One only has to supplement the question, 'did D fail to attain a reasonable standard of care in the circumstances?', with the further question; 'could D, given his mental and physical capacities, have taken the necessary precautions?'.[268] Negligence liability need be 'objective' only in so far as it holds liable those who fail to take precautions when they could reasonably have been expected to do so. Liability can be termed subjective in so far as it takes account of the limited capacities of the particular person. Taking objective and subjective aspects together, the blameworthiness may be expressed as 'the culpability of unexercised capacity'.[269] As AP Simester puts it:

> Without external standards, judgement is impossible. Without reference to the defendant, judgement cannot lead to blame. The device of the reasonable man is, in a sense, one means by which the law seeks to reconcile the impersonal with the humane.[270]

In addition, empirical research suggests public support for some such individualization of negligence liability.[271] Secondly, negligence liability may also derogate from any principle of contemporaneity, in the sense that the culpable failure to take precautions often pre-dates the causing of the harm: the rail worker failed to check the signals or the track, so that a crash occurred later; D misunderstood the mechanism of the gun, so that when he later pulled the trigger it killed someone. The enquiry into capacity and opportunity necessitated by negligence liability widens the time frame of the criminal law, giving precedence to the doctrine of prior fault over the principle of contemporaneity.[272] Thirdly, the argument is in favour of negligence liability, not strict liability. Existing law imposes obligations on people who engage in various activities: the obligations of those operating systems of public transport; or the obligations of driving a motor vehicle; or the obligations of owning or managing a factory; or the obligations

---

[267] J. Gardner, 'Introduction', at xxxv, summarizing the views of H. L. A. Hart, *Punishment and Responsibility* (2nd edn., 2008).

[268] This is the argument of Hart, *Punishment and Responsibility* (1968) chs 2 and 6. The absence of an incapacity exception was a major argument against the *Caldwell* test.

[269] See the detailed discussion by M. S. Moore, *Placing Blame* (1997), ch 9 and 588–92.

[270] A. P. Simester, 'Can Negligence be Culpable?', in J. Horder (ed.), *Oxford Essays in Jurisprudence, 4th Series* (2000), 106.   [271] P. H. Robinson and J. M. Darley, *Justice, Liability and Blame* (1995) 123.

[272] See section 6.4(f).

of engaging in a particular trade or business. Strict liability was criticized in paragraph (a) earlier. Negligence liability, on the other hand, is not open to the same objections.

The discussion thus far should have established that people who cause harm negligently may be culpable, in so far as they fail to take reasonable precautions when they have a duty and the capacity to do so. What it does not establish is that negligence is an appropriate standard for criminal liability, for it must be borne in mind that criminal liability is the law's most condemnatory form, and in principle it should be reserved for serious wrongs.[273] How might it be argued that the English doctrinal tradition of drawing the line of criminal liability below intention and recklessness, and above negligence (at least for 'conventional' crimes, such as those in the draft Criminal Code) is ill-founded? One approach would be to establish that some cases of negligence manifest greater culpability than some cases of subjective recklessness—the principal justification for the *Caldwell* decision. Thus it could be claimed that a person who knowingly takes a slight risk of harm is less culpable than another person who fails to think about or recognize a high risk of the same harm: D, a shooting champion, fires at a target, knowing that there is a slight risk that the bullet will ricochet and injure a spectator, which it does; E, who rarely handles guns, is invited to participate in a shooting party and fires wildly into bushes, failing to consider the possibility of others being there, and one is injured. Is D manifestly more culpable than E? A different comparison would be between someone who knowingly takes the risk of a small harm occurring and someone who fails to recognize the risk of a serious harm occurring: a criminal law which convicts the former and not the latter could be said to be transfixed by the notion of a 'consistent' general part. Why maintain that negligence is never an appropriate standard of criminal liability, even where the harm is great and the risk obvious?

The argument is therefore moving towards the conclusion that negligence may be an appropriate standard for criminal liability where: (i) the (potential) harm is great; (ii) the risk of it occurring is obvious; (iii) D has a duty to try to avoid the risk; and (iv) D has the capacity to take the required precautions. This opens up further debates on various points. The thesis is that negligence may be an appropriate standard where there are well-known risks of serious harm. This argues in favour of negligence as a standard of liability for certain serious offences against the person, including some serious sexual offences,[274] and also for some serious offences against the environment and property. But it must be debated whether liability for serious crime should be confined to *gross* negligence, not simple negligence. And it would be vital to protect 'rule of law' expectations, and thus to ensure that people receive fair warning of any duties that may form the basis of criminal negligence liability.[275] The spread of negligence liability would not have to result in the broadening of the traditional category of *mens rea*: negligence could be admitted as a form of fault, whereas intention and recklessness would

---

[273] A. Ashworth, 'Is the Criminal Law a Lost Cause?' (2000) 116 LQR 226.

[274] As now adopted in the Sexual Offences Act 2003, discussed in Chapter 9.5.

[275] On this and other points, see J. Horder, 'Gross Negligence and Criminal Culpability' (1997) 47 U Toronto LJ 496.

remain the two forms of *mens rea*. It would be perfectly possible for a criminal code to provide separate crimes of negligence, with lower maximum sentences, at appropriate points in the hierarchy of offences. A further issue is whether the offences of negligence should be in the inchoate mode—'failing to take reasonable precautions'—or should be tied to the occurrence of the particular harm. Careless driving is of the former type, manslaughter of the latter.[276]

Even granted this argument in favour of criminalizing certain instances of negligence, what would be the point of doing so? This takes us back to the aims of the criminal law. It might be tempting to maintain that the general preventive aim of the criminal law cannot be served by offences of negligence: the notion of deterrence presupposes rational reflection by D at the time of offending, whereas the distinguishing feature of negligence is that D failed to think (when a reasonable person would have done). However, it can be argued that crimes of negligence may exert a general deterrent effect, by alerting people to their duties and to the need to take special care in certain situations. The practical prospects of deterrence here seem no less propitious than in relation to offences requiring intention or recklessness. The principal justification, however, would be that negligent harmdoers deserve criminal conviction because and in so far as they are sufficiently culpable. This is a question of degree and of judgment, on which views may differ.[277]

(g) OBJECTIVE VERSUS SUBJECTIVE

Much of the discussion of the law in this section of the chapter has concerned the interplay of subjective and objective factors in the definition of the core fault terms. It has been suggested that in crimes where strict liability is imposed on individual defendants, the courts have generally placed insufficient emphasis on respect for individual autonomy and the importance of requiring fault. When dealing with recklessness and mistake, however, the tendency of some text-writers and judges has been to regard the advertent or subjective approach as axiomatic, thus excluding from conviction certain people who may be no less culpable than those who are convicted. The *Caldwell* test could be seen as a way of supplementing the narrow conception of moral fault embodied in advertent recklessness, but it was flawed in other respects (notably, the absence of an incapacity exception) and it perished.[278] An alternative is Duff's test of practical indifference, which relies considerably on objective judgments as evidence of a person's attitude when behaving in a particular way. A further alternative would be to introduce more offences of negligence and, in respect of mistaken belief, more objective limitations on defences to criminal liability—a task on which the legislature embarked in the Sexual Offences Act 2003. It is evident that, in many cases examined in this chapter, an approach that focuses solely on advertence fails to capture some

---

[276] See Chapter 8.6 and 8.7.

[277] Some 'subjectivists' might accept a case for some criminal negligence liability, while insisting that it is categorically different from liability based on choice: see Moore, earlier at n 269.

[278] See the discussion in section 6.6(c).

moral distinctions and to satisfy all social expectations.[279] Subjective tests heighten the protection of individual autonomy, but they typically make no concession to the notion of duties to take care and to avoid harming the interests of others. However, if we are to move towards greater reliance on objective standards, at least two points must be confronted. First, objective tests must be applied subject to capacity-based exceptions. This respects the principle of moral autonomy, by ensuring that no person is convicted who lacked the capacity to conform his or her behaviour to the standard required. Secondly, any improved moral 'fit' obtained by moving more towards objective standards must be weighed against the greater detraction from the principle of maximum certainty that is likely to result. Objective standards inevitably rely on terms such as reasonable, ordinary, and prudent. They appear much more malleable and unpredictable than subjective tests that ask whether or not a defendant was aware of a given risk, and they explicitly leave room for courts and even prosecutors to make social judgments about the limits of the criminal sanction: the hallmark of the authoritarian principle.

6.6 THE VARIETY OF FAULT TERMS

Although the focus so far has been upon intention, recklessness, and knowledge, an examination of criminal legislation in force—some modern, some from the nineteenth century—reveals a diversity of fault terms. Even if the draft Criminal Code were to be enacted, its provisions would not be restricted to the core fault terms discussed so far. Moreover, the Code would cover only some 200 out of perhaps 10,000 criminal offences, so the diversity will inevitably remain for some years. A full survey of the different fault terms cannot be offered here, but some general remarks may be worthwhile.

Nineteenth-century legislation such as the Offences against the Person Act 1861 makes considerable use of the term 'maliciously'.[280] It is now settled that this term should be interpreted to mean intention or recklessness, which simplifies the criminal lawyer's task.[281] Unfortunately, certain other terms have not been interpreted consistently in line with the core terminology. Many offences are defined in terms of 'permitting', a word that has usually been interpreted as requiring full knowledge, but which has sometimes been held to impose strict liability, even on individuals.[282] Some statutory offences, both ancient and modern, rely on the term 'wilfully'. Although in *Sheppard*[283] the House of Lords held that the term meant 'intentionally or recklessly' in the context of the crime of wilful neglect of a child, there are other offences in which 'wilfully' has

---

[279] Cf. Gardner's view that 'once we go beyond the paradigm of intention ... the mentalities of crime quickly fragment and lack any intelligible ordering': J. Gardner, 'On the General Part of the Criminal Law', in R. A. Duff, *Philosophy and the Criminal Law* (1998), 231.

[280] See the discussion of specific offences in Chapter 9.3.

[281] *Cunningham* [1957] 2 QB 396; *Savage, Parmenter* [1992] AC 699. See now Law Commission, *Reform of Offences Against the Person: A Scoping Consultation Paper* (2014).

[282] Compare, e.g., *James and Son v Smee* [1955] 1 QB 78 with *Baugh v Crago* [1976] Crim LR 72.

[283] [1981] AC 394.

been held to include 'indifference', in the sense of not caring whether or not something (harmful) occurs.[284] It seems that this extended meaning of 'wilful' has now been carried forward into the healthcare context, where 'ill-treatment' or 'wilful' neglect of a patient by a member of staff has now been made a serious criminal offence.[285]

More to the point, however, is the fact that many major criminal offences rely on fault terms that bear little relation to any of those discussed so far. Theft and several other Theft Act offences rely on the term 'dishonestly', which, as we shall see,[286] encompasses a mixture of elements of subjective awareness and motivation with elements of objective moral judgment. Some fraud offences turn on whether the act or omission was done 'fraudulently'. And a number of public order and racial hatred offences impose liability where a certain consequence is 'likely' to result from D's conduct, without reference to whether D is aware of this likelihood. Thus, for example, a person commits the offence of creating 'fear or provocation of violence' by the use of threatening, abusive, or insulting words or behaviour *either* with intent to cause another person to believe that immediate unlawful violence will be used, *or* 'whereby that person is likely to believe that such violence will be used or it is likely that such violence will be provoked'.[287] Similarly, the offence of publishing or distributing racially inflammatory material is committed if *either* D intends thereby to stir up racial hatred *or* 'having regard to all the circumstances racial hatred is likely to be stirred up thereby'.[288] Offences that rely on the court's assessment of the probable effect of certain conduct may be said to impose a form of strict liability, or at least liability for negligence, if it is assumed that the defendant ought to have known what effect was likely. However, suffice it to say that criminal offences in English law vary in their use of fault terms. The arguments for and against the core terms, examined in this chapter, should provide a framework for considering the justifications for most other fault terms that may be encountered.

6.7 THE REFERENTIAL POINT OF FAULT

To say that a certain crime should require intention or recklessness is not enough. One must enquire: intention (or recklessness) as to what? It might be said loosely that 'the crime of manslaughter requires proof of intention or recklessness': the reason this is a loose statement is that the intent or recklessness required may be the same as that for assault or some other criminal act, whereas the liability imposed is that for homicide. Close analysis of the elements of the crime will show that the required fault and the result specified in the definition are not on the same level. This is what the principle of correspondence, outlined earlier, aims to eliminate.[289] Whenever one is discussing intent or recklessness, its referential point should always be established.

---

[284] See J. A. Andrews, 'Wilfulness: A Lesson in Ambiguity' (1981) 1 *Legal Studies* 303.
[285] Criminal Justice and Courts Act 2015, ss. 20 and 21.   [286] In Chapter 10.2.
[287] Public Order Act 1986, s. 4(1); see Chapter 8.3.   [288] Public Order Act 1986, s. 19(1).
[289] See section 6.4(a).

(a) FAULT, CONDUCT, AND RESULT

The argument may be carried further by considering the width or narrowness of the definitions of offences. This raises an issue central to fairness in offence construction, and that is the principle of 'fair labelling'. This is the principle that, broadly speaking, what a defendant has done (in terms of fault, conduct, and—if relevant—consequences and circumstance elements) should adequately represent the wrong at which the offence in question strikes.[290] For example, if D kills V through negligence, 'murder' would not be a fair label to attach to what D did, even if the correspondence principle is respected by requiring that the negligence be as to the causing of death. Similarly, if D has sexual intercourse with an under-age V in circumstances where D could not have known or guessed that V was under 16 years of age, it would not be fair to label D as—in effect—a child sex offender.[291] The fair labelling principle has important implications for the reform and restructuring of offences.

For example, it would be far easier to establish intent for a broad offence—such as intentionally causing physical harm to another—than to establish intent in a system with a hierarchy of graded offences—such as attempted murder, causing serious injury intentionally, causing injury intentionally, and common assault—which would require proof of more specific mental states. Similarly, a law which includes a general offence of intentionally causing damage to property belonging to another makes it far easier to establish the intent, than a law with a series of offences differentiated according to the type of property damaged. Do these different legislative techniques have significant implications for the doctrines of fault?

Surely they do. One could argue that a single broad offence of 'intentionally causing physical harm to another' would obliterate the distinction between intending a minor assault and intending a major injury, and that a single broad offence of 'intentionally damaging property belonging to another' obliterates the distinction between intending damage to a cheap item and intending damage to an expensive item.[292] Broadening offences in this way waters down the prospects for fair labelling, by rendering the offence label unable to reflect what the defendant has done.

How should this problem be solved? It is hardly practical to allow each person to nominate those factors which he or she regarded as significant in any particular event: who is to say whether fidelity to individual choice and control requires two or twenty grades of criminal damage, or two or four grades of offences of violence? Nonetheless, the implications for fault principles of these labelling decisions[293] should be kept firmly in mind. We will consider the issues in more depth when we consider the Law Commission's Consultation Paper on reform of the non-fatal offences against the person.[294]

[290] See A. Ashworth, 'The Elasticity of *Mens Rea*' in C. Tapper (ed.), *Crime, Proof and Punishment* (1981).
[291] In this example, the fair labelling principle is in accord with the correspondence principle.
[292] Cf. the facts of G [2004] 1 AC 1034, where the two children set fire to paper beneath a dustbin, and the ultimate result was damage to buildings costing around £1 million.
[293] See the discussion of the principle of fair labelling in Chapter 3.6(s).
[294] Law Commission, *Reform of Offences Against the Person: A Scoping Consultation Paper* (2014).

The argument may be taken still further, for there are cases where it is plain that D intended to cause a different result from the one which actually occurred. How ought the law to deal with such cases? Should it respect D's choice, and provide for a conviction of attempting to do X (which was what D intended to do)? Or should it regard the result as the dominant factor, ignore the difference in D's intention, and convict on the basis of 'sufficient similarity' between the intention and the result? English law adopts the latter, more pragmatic approach. The Law Commission, in introducing a provision into the draft Criminal Code which follows the traditional approach, confirms the emphasis on results by stating that a conviction for attempt would be 'inappropriate as not describing the *harm done* adequately for labelling or sentencing purposes'.[295] The traditional English approach rests on three doctrines—unforeseen mode, mistaken object, and transferred fault.

(b) UNFORESEEN MODE

When D sets out to commit an offence by one method but actually causes the prohibited consequence in a different way, the offence may be said to have been committed by an unforeseen mode. Since most crimes penalizing a result (with fault) do not specify any particular mode of commission,[296] it is easy to regard the difference of mode as legally irrelevant. D intended to kill V; he chose to shoot him, but the shot missed; it hit a nearby heavy object, which fell on V's head and caused his death. Any moral distinction between the two modes is surely too slender to justify legal recognition. To charge D with *attempting* to kill V when he *did* kill him seems excessively fastidious. Pragmatism is surely the best approach here, and English law is generally right to ignore the unforeseen mode.

(c) MISTAKEN OBJECT

When D sets out to commit an offence in relation to a particular victim but makes a mistake of identity and directs his conduct at the wrong victim, the offence may be said to have been committed despite the mistaken object. The same applies if D intends to steal one item of property but mistakenly takes another. So long as the two objects fall within the same legal category, it may be said that any moral distinction between them is too slender to justify legal recognition. However, much depends on the breadth of definition of the relevant offence: there is surely some moral significance in the plea: 'I thought the picture I damaged was just a cheap copy; I had no idea that a valuable painting would be kept in that place'. English law favours the pragmatic answer of reflecting shades of moral culpability at the sentencing stage, but one might argue on principle that to convict this person of intentionally or recklessly damaging a valuable painting is a gross mislabelling of the wrong. In one sphere, English law's

---

[295] Law Com No. 177, ii, para. 8.57 (my emphasis).
[296] The offences of fraud form an exception: see later in Chapter 10.7.

general approach of ignoring mistake of object within the same offence is not followed. This is the law of complicity: where A gives assistance to D who plans to kill X, and then D decides to kill Y, there is long-standing authority to the effect that A cannot be convicted for aiding and abetting D's murder of Y.[297] The complexities of the moral distinctions drawn here are discussed in Chapter 11.5, but if it is accepted that the identity of the victim is so important in this type of case, one may enquire more widely whether there really is inadequate moral significance in the plea: 'I intended to kill my enemy, X, and never meant any harm to the poor innocent, Y'. The pragmatic approach adopted elsewhere in the criminal law (apart from complicity) may fail to mark significant moral distinctions in some cases, and many might be dissatisfied if the only conviction were for attempting to murder X.

(d) TRANSFERRED FAULT

When D sets out to commit an offence in relation to a particular person or a particular property but his conduct miscarries and the harm falls upon a different person or a different property, English law regards D's intent as transferred and the offence as committed against the actual victim or property. When the fault is transferred, any defence which D may have is transferred with it.[298] As with unforeseen mode and mistaken object, the fault may only be transferred within the same class of offence.[299] Thus, if D throws a brick at some people, intending to hurt them, and the brick misses them and breaks a window, the intent to injure cannot be transferred to the offence of damaging property.[300] In this situation, the possible offences are an attempt to cause injury, and recklessly damaging property. As with the doctrine of mistaken object, the breadth of definition of the offence has some importance here. It is one thing to accept that D, who swung his belt at W and struck V, should be convicted of injuring V;[301] it is quite another thing, in moral terms, to accept that E, who threw a stone at a window, should be convicted of intentionally damaging a valuable painting which, unbeknown to him, was hanging inside. Yet English law would convict E, applying the broad wording of the Criminal Damage Act 1971 (any 'property belonging to another'), without any need to rely on the doctrine of transferred fault.[302] Thus the ambit of all three doctrines is much affected by the breadth of each offence definition.

The doctrine of transferred fault and its relationship with conceptions of subjective guilt remain sources of considerable controversy.[303] Rather surprisingly, in view of its long pedigree in English law, the doctrine was denounced by Lord Mustill in the

---

[297] See Law Com No. 177, ii, para. 8.31, and later in Chapter 10.6(a).

[298] *Gross* (1913) 23 Cox CC 455 (partial defence of provocation transferred).

[299] See A. Ashworth, 'Transferred Malice and Punishment for Unforeseen Consequences', in P. Glazebrook (ed.), *Reshaping the Criminal Law* (1978).   [300] *Pembliton* (1874) 12 Cox CC 607.

[301] As in the leading case of *Latimer* (1886) 17 QBD 359.   [302] See Ashworth, n 299, 89–93.

[303] Cf., e.g., D. Husak, 'Transferred Intent' (1996) 10 Notre Dame J Law, Ethics and Public Policy 65, with A. M. Dillof, 'Transferred Intent: An Inquiry into the Nature of Criminal Culpability' (1998) 1 Buffalo Crim LR 501. See also, P. Westen, 'The Significance of Transferred Intent' (2013) 7 *Criminal Law and Philosophy* 321.

House of Lords for 'its lack of any sound intellectual basis'. In *Attorney-General's Reference (No. 3 of 1994)*[304] D stabbed his girlfriend in the stomach, knowing that she was pregnant. Two weeks later the child was born prematurely, and because of its grossly premature birth it failed to thrive and died after four months. The House of Lords held that on these facts D could not be convicted of murder, holding that transferred malice could have no application because the foetus had no separate existence at the time the mother was attacked. The facts of this case are unusual, thankfully, but the House of Lords failed to deal convincingly with the relevance of the doctrine of unforeseen mode (should it matter that the child's death resulted from the premature birth, not from any direct wound?) and with the relevance of the extended principle of contemporaneity (if the death was part of an unbroken sequence of events following the stabbing, should not D's original intent be connected with the ultimate death?).[305] It could be argued that it would go too far if three artificial doctrines (transferred fault, unforeseen mode, and extended contemporaneity) were combined to find someone guilty of the highest crime in the land. Indeed, it has been argued that the law should recognize a further restrictive principle, the remoteness doctrine, so as to ensure that there is no conviction of an offence (e.g. murder) if the way in which the death of the unanticipated victim occurred was so remote from what D intended or anticipated that to convict D of murdering the actual victim would be an unrepresentative label.[306] Be that as it may, the courts have continued to find novel ways to apply the doctrine. In *R v Grant*,[307] D shot at V1 with intent to kill. He missed, but his shots caused serious injury to V2 and to V3. The Court of Appeal upheld D's convictions for (a) the attempted murder of V1, and (b) causing grievous bodily harm to V2 and V3 with intent, contrary to s. 18 of the Offences Against the Person Act 1861.[308] D's intent to kill encompassed an intent to do grievous bodily harm, and the latter intent could thus be transferred to the injuries inflicted on V2 and V3.

(e) ESTABLISHING THE REFERENTIAL POINT

A system of criminal law which succeeded in reflecting the varying degrees of importance which people attribute to aspects of their intention (the mode of execution, the identity of the victim, the value of the property) might be a 'law professor's dream', but it is clearly not practical. Such an individuated or fine-grained approach to fault has to give way, at least in some respects, to claims of administrative efficiency. But that does not establish that the traditional English approach is the most appropriate. The draft Criminal Code provides for the continuation of the pragmatic approach, arguing that this is simpler for prosecutors and that a conviction for attempt in the above situations

---

[304] [1998] 1 Cr App R 91.

[305] See the discussion of this principle in section 6.4(c) earlier.

[306] J. Horder, 'Transferred Malice and the Remoteness of Unexpected Outcomes from Intentions' [2006] Crim LR 383; but see, S. Eldar, 'The Limits of Transferred Malice' (2012) 32 OJLS 633.

[307] [2014] EWCA Crim 143.   [308] See Chapter 9.3(b).

would ignore the harm actually done.[309] Does its pragmatism stretch too far? Would it not be better to analyse some of these cases in terms of an unfulfilled intention, combined with an accidental (or perhaps reckless) causing of harm? Some would argue that the present law of inchoate offences would not ensure a conviction in all these cases of miscarried intent and miscarried recklessness:[310] according to this view, the three doctrines are not merely effective in returning convictions and symbolically right in their emphasis on results,[311] but also necessary if justice is to be done in all cases. There is, it may be argued, no serious distortion of 'desert' or proportionality involved in the three doctrines, since the doctrines do not misrepresent the class of harm that D set out to commit. Yet there remains the law's ambivalence about the importance of a victim's identity: if this really is significant to offenders and people's judgments of them, as the law of complicity implies, should not prosecutors make more use of the law of attempts, where it is clearly applicable?[312]

FURTHER READING

A. ASHWORTH, 'A Change of Normative Position: Determining the Contours of Culpability in Criminal Law' (2008) 11 New Crim LR 232.

R. A. DUFF, *Answering for Crime* (Hart Publishing, 2007), ch 3.

R. A. DUFF 'Whose Luck is it Anyway?', in C. Clarkson and S. Cunningham (eds), *Criminal Liability for Non-Aggressive Death* (Ashgate, 2008).

J. GARDNER, 'Introduction', to Hart (2008).

H. L. A. HART, *Punishment and Responsibility* (2nd edn., Oxford University Press, 2008), chs 2 and 6.

A. NORRIE, *Crime, Reason and History* (4th edn., Cambridge University Press, 2014).

A. P. SIMESTER (ed.), *Appraising Strict Liability* (Oxford University Press, 2005).

V. TADROS, *Criminal Responsibility* (Oxford University Press, 2005), ch 8.

---

[309] In effect, cl. 24 of the draft Criminal Code is a 'deeming' provision: see Law Com No. 177, ii, paras. 8.57–59.

[310] G. Williams, 'Convictions and Fair Labelling' [1983] CLJ 86.

[311] Cf. the discussion of luck and results in section 6.4(b).

[312] Cf. J. Horder, 'Transferred Malice and Remoteness', with A. P. Simester and G. R. Sullivan, *Criminal Law: Theory and Doctrine* (3rd edn., 2007), 156–8.

7

EXCUSATORY DEFENCES

7.1 EXCUSES AND OTHER DEFENCES

Criminal lawyers sometimes speak and write as if criminal guilt turns on the presence or absence of *mens rea*, but observations in previous chapters have already hinted that matters are not so simple. The notions of fault and culpability go further and deeper than *mens rea* and require a discussion of other doctrines broadly termed 'defences'. It is technically incorrect to use the term 'defence' when referring to the 'defence of mistake' or the 'defence of accident', since these (along with intoxication) are simply 'failure of proof' arguments; 'mistake' or 'accident' is merely a way of explaining why the prosecution has failed to prove the required knowledge, intention, or recklessness in respect of a particular ingredient of an offence.[1] Defences of various kinds have been discussed in earlier chapters. The absence of a voluntary act (Chapter 5.2) is often referred to as the defence of automatism. The various justificatory defences, such as self-defence, were analysed in Chapter 5. Defences of lack of capacity, particularly insanity, were discussed in Chapter 6.

In the present chapter, the focus is on excuses and potential excuses for wrongful acts. Excuses may take the form of a 'confession and avoidance'. Here, D admits committing the conduct element with the fault element if any (the 'confession'), but seeks nonetheless to avoid liability. The 'avoidance' claim may involve proof of a mental disorder linked with the commission of the crime (discussed in Chapter 6); but it may also

---

[1] See P. H. Robinson, 'Criminal Law Defenses: A Systematic Analysis' (1982) 82 Columbia LR 199, *Structure and Function in Criminal Law* (1997), ch 5, and *Criminal Law Defences* (1984), for a five-fold classification of defences: (i) failure of proof defences; (ii) offence modifications (e.g. withdrawal in complicity); (iii) justifications; (iv) excuses; and (v) non-exculpatory public-policy defences (e.g. time limitations). This chapter is concerned with (iv) and with some forms of (i).

involve a claim that the commission of the crime was, in the circumstances, something falling within the range of actions that could reasonably have been expected of someone with ordinary capacities for reasoning and emotional restraint. So, sometimes, it is the influence of an emotion, under extreme circumstances, that forms the basis for such a confession-and-avoidance excuse: duress is a central case in point (section 7.3), although loss of self-control—addressed in Chapter 8—is another, more controversial example. On other occasions, people can be regarded as having done something falling within the bounds of normative expectations, even when they engaged in the crime, in virtue of some cognitive or knowledge-based defect that explains their conduct. Were ignorance of the law to be an excuse (Chapter 6.5), this would fit such a model,[2] but more pertinently, reasonable mistake of fact falls under such a heading (Chapter 6.4). We will return, at the end of the chapter, to take stock of the various rationales.

It would be possible for much complexity to be avoided if the law provided simply that a defendant should be acquitted of any crime if he or she had a 'reasonable excuse' for committing it, in the eyes of the jury or magistrate. However, that simplistic solution is ruled out by the need to ensure that key principles applicable to the law generally do not gain a foothold in individual criminal trials. For example, there should be no general defence of reasonable excuse for kidnapping, because it should not be possible to plead, as a 'reasonable excuse' for kidnapping a child, that the parents of the child had other children whereas the kidnapper had none and so took the child to rid herself of continuing envious thoughts. For these and other reasons, the law generally confines excuses closely, focusing mainly on (in a broad sense) cognitive defects, defects of the will, and cases in which an extreme threat cannot reasonably be avoided other than by committing a crime. The law excludes cases in which the defendant, in the pursuit of his or her own agenda, simply treats the victim's interests as expendable.

First, we will deal with the difficult case of intoxication. In a way, intoxication should really be dealt with in a discussion of the fault element in crime, rather than under an excuse heading. That is because the main relevance of intoxication is that it can sometimes provide evidence that the defendant did *not* have the fault element at the relevant time. It is, in other words, commonly used not as a 'confession and avoidance' defence, but as a basis for denying that an element of the crime—the fault element—was missing. However, its close connection with 'confession and avoidance' excuses means that it is not too misleading to deal with it here.

7.2 INTOXICATION

Research confirms that many of those who commit crimes of violence and burglary (at least) have taken some kind of intoxicant beforehand.[3] Alcohol is probably the most widely used of intoxicants, but narcotic or hallucinogenic drugs are involved in some

---

[2] See the discussion in Chapter 4.5.

[3] G. Dingwall, *Alcohol and Crime* (2006); the British Crime Survey reports that 45 per cent of victims of violent incidents believed the offender(s) to be influenced by alcohol and 19 per cent believed their offender(s) to be influenced by drugs: C. Kershaw et al., *Crime in England and Wales 2007/08* (2008), 76–10.

cases, too, and our discussion will relate to those who have taken alcohol, drugs, or a combination of the two. The usual effects are a loosening of inhibitions and, perhaps, a feeling of well-being and confidence.[4] It is well known that people who have taken intoxicants tend to say or do things which they would not say or do when sober, and, in that sense, intoxicants may be regarded as the cause of such behaviour. But, as we saw in Chapter 6, the criminal law's conception of fault has tended to concentrate on cognition rather than on volition. Thus the approach to intoxication has not been to examine whether D's power to choose to cause the prohibited harm was substantially reduced, but has been to focus on its relation to *mens rea*. However, the law has been reluctant to allow intoxication simply to negate *mens rea*: instead, rather like its approach to automatism (see Chapter 5.2), it has drawn on arguments of prior fault and public security in order to prevent the simple acquittal of those who cause harm when they lack awareness because of intoxication. This, as we shall see, has caused various doctrinal difficulties for English criminal law.

(a) THE ENGLISH INTOXICATION RULES

It is not surprising to find that a person who deliberately drinks himself into an intoxicated state in order to carry out a crime will have no defence. As Lord Denning declared in *Attorney-General for Northern Ireland v Gallagher*:[5]

> If a man, whilst sane and sober, forms an intention to kill and makes preparation for it . . . and then gets himself drunk so as to give himself Dutch courage to do the killing, and whilst drunk carries out his intention, he cannot rely on this self-induced drunkenness as a defence to a charge of murder.

Cases such as this are rare. More frequent are cases in which D has become intoxicated 'voluntarily', that is where there is no reason to regard it as 'involuntary',[6] and has then done something whose nature, he argues, he would have appreciated and avoided but for the influence of alcohol or drugs.

It could be said that there is an 'inexorable logic'[7] that if *mens rea* is not present, whether through intoxication or otherwise, D should not be convicted. However, considerations of social protection have led the courts to introduce an unusual distinction to avoid this consequence in many cases. The decision in *DPP v Majewski*[8] divides crimes into 'offences of specific intent' and 'offences of basic intent', and allows intoxication as a 'defence' (in the form of a denial of fault) to the former but not to the latter. For reasons that will become clear, it would be more helpful if the distinction was expressed as one between crimes of specific 'fault', and basic 'fault' (rather than specific or basic 'intent'), but for now this must remain a background consideration.

---

[4] See, for a recent study, A. Newbury and G. Dingwall, '"It Lets Out All My Demons": Female Young Offenders" Perceptions About the Impact of Alcohol on Their Offending Behaviour' (2013) 41 *International Journal of Law, Crime and Justice*, 277.

[5] [1963] AC 349, at 382.   [6] See the discussion in section 7.2(d) later in the chapter.

[7] The phrase of Lord Hailsham in *DPP v Morgan* [1976] AC 182, at 214.   [8] [1977] AC 443.

Murder (involving intent to kill or cause serious harm), and wounding with intent to do grievous bodily harm, are crimes of specific intent. In law, the misleading term 'specific' here indicates that proof of nothing less than the intent in question will suffice for conviction. If the 'specific' intent cannot be proved, the prosecution fails in relation to that crime, and it matters not what the reason is for the lack of intent (including the influence of voluntary intoxication). However, in such cases, there will sometimes be a lesser crime of 'basic' intent underlying the specific intent crime—in the examples just given, manslaughter, and wounding—of which the defendant can be convicted even if the prosecution for the more serious specific intent crime fails.

Various theories have been advanced in an attempt to explain why murder and wounding with intent (together with other specific intent crimes such as theft, handling, conspiracy, and all crimes of attempt) are crimes of 'specific intent' whereas others are not, but none is satisfactory.[9] In *Heard*[10] Hughes LJ tried to simplify matters by offering the opinion that crimes of specific intent require proof of purpose; but the theory fails to convince because it takes the 'intent' element in the notion of 'specific intent' too literally. For example, the crime of handling stolen goods is a specific intent crime, after *Durante*,[11] even though the key fault element for that crime is not intent but knowledge or belief that goods are stolen at the time of the handling. To go back to the point made earlier, handling stolen goods is a crime of specific *fault* (involving the need to prove the relevant knowledge or belief) even though it does not involve proof of intent in relation to the 'stolen' quality of the goods handled. Moreover, many crimes—rape is an example—contain some elements for which only intent will suffice and others for which recklessness or negligence is sufficient; and so they cannot be neatly categorized as 'purposive' or non-purposive.[12] However, as so often in law, what does not work in theory works perfectly well in practice. The courts have restricted the operation of the 'inexorable logic' of *mens rea* to the few offences of specific intent or fault. As most such crimes are underpinned by a lesser offence of basic intent or fault, there have not been a raft of unjustified complete acquittals.

What of 'basic' intent or fault? The policy expressed in *Majewski*, through the idea of 'offences of basic intent', was expressed slightly differently in *Caldwell* (1982)[13] in terms of 'recklessness'. Thus, where recklessness is a sufficient fault element for the crime, the crime is one of basic intent or fault, and evidence of voluntary intoxication is irrelevant: anyone who was voluntarily intoxicated is deemed to have been reckless. This is a simpler rule to apply, although it appears not to have displaced the *Majewski* test.[14] It is subject to an exception, as we shall see in section 7.2(d) later, in cases where the

---

[9] Their inadequacy is demonstrated by G. Williams, *Textbook of Criminal Law* (2nd edn., 1983), 428–30, and A. Ward, 'Making Some Sense of Self-induced Intoxication' [1986] CLJ 2410. Perhaps the best modern analysis of that is R. Williams, 'Voluntary Intoxication—a Lost Cause?' (2013) 129 LQR 264.

[10] [2008] QB 43, on which see D. Ormerod, [2007] Crim LR 6510.   [11] [1972] 3 All ER 962.

[12] S. White, 'Offences of Basic and Specific Intent' [1989] Crim LR 271.   [13] [1982] AC 341.

[14] The discussion of 'drunken accidents' in *Heard* (n 10) pays little regard to the possibility of recklessness in certain situations.

intoxication can be regarded as to some degree 'involuntary'. Section 6(5) of the Public Order Act 1986, which applies only to offences in that Act, reads as follows:

> a person whose awareness is impaired by intoxication shall be taken to be aware of that of which he would be aware if not intoxicated, unless he shows either that his intoxication was not self-induced or that it was caused solely by the taking or administration of a substance in the course of medical treatment.

This provision, though couched in the terminology of awareness instead of advertent recklessness, may be thought to express the law's general approach.[15]

The effect of all these rules is that voluntary intoxication rarely functions as a ground of exculpation. Here, as with automatism and some mistakes, the 'logic' of the standard doctrines of *actus reus* and *mens rea* has been subordinated to considerations of public security. Thus, where it is alleged that intoxication induced a state of automatism, the case is treated as one of intoxication (the cause) rather than automatism (the effect).[16] The same approach has been quite vigorously pursued in cases of intoxicated mistake, bringing them under the rules of intoxication (the cause) rather than mistake (the effect). At common law, in *O'Grady*,[17] where the defence took the form of a drunken mistaken belief in the need for self-defence, the Court of Appeal held that D could not rely on his mistake if it stemmed from intoxication. This means, in effect, that where the normal subjective rule for mistake clashes with the objective rule for intoxication, the latter takes priority. The Court of Appeal confirmed this in *Hatton*,[18] declining an invitation to depart from *O'Grady* and confirming a conviction for murder of someone who made an intoxicated mistake in self-defence.[19] The common law approach has now been enshrined in statute, by s. 76 of the Criminal Justice and Immigration Act 2010. In relation to a mistaken belief in the need to use force in self-defence or prevention of crime, ss. 76(4) and (5) say:

(4) If D claims to have held a particular belief as regards the existence of any circumstances—

    (a) the reasonableness or otherwise of that belief is relevant to the question whether D genuinely held it; but

    (b) if it is determined that D did genuinely hold it, D is entitled to rely on it for the purposes of subsection (3), whether or not—

        (i) it was mistaken, or

        (ii) (if it was mistaken) the mistake was a reasonable one to have made.

(5) But subsection (4)(b) does not enable D to rely on any mistaken belief attributable to intoxication that was voluntarily induced.

The current law may have some logic behind it. It may be appropriate to take a different approach to the relevance of intoxication depending on whether D is denying fault, or

---

[15] *Aitken* (1992) 95 Cr App R 304, *Richardson and Irwin* [1999] 1 Cr App R 392.

[16] *Lipman* [1970] 1 QB 152; see Chapter 10.2.

[17] (1987) 85 Cr App R 315; there is debate about whether this ruling was merely *obiter dictum*, but it has now been applied in *O'Connor* [1991] Crim LR 135 and in *Hatton*, n 18.   [18] [2006] 1 Cr App R 110.

[19] See also *Fotheringham* (1989) 88 Cr App R 206, dealing with the pre-2003 law on rape.

claiming a (putative) defence to a crime respecting which he or she admits have possessed the fault element. However, the approach also involves a need for fine distinc-
tion-making of a kind that becomes more troublesome the more serious the crime in
issue. For example, consider D's potential for liability for murder, with its mandatory
sentence of life imprisonment, in the following examples:

1. D, a very strong individual, was so voluntarily intoxicated that he believed at the
   time that the heavy wooden pole with which he repeatedly struck V until V died
   was made of a lightweight wood that would not cause serious harm even when
   repeated blows were struck.
2. D was so voluntarily intoxicated that he mistakenly thought that V, who was
   walking towards D, intended to attack D there and then with lethal force, and so
   he struck V repeatedly with a heavy wooden pole, causing V's death.

In example 1, D is denying that he or she had the fault element (intention to kill or
to do serious harm). As murder is a crime of specific intent, D's state of voluntary
intoxication—and hence D's explanation of his or her actions—may be considered by
the jury in determining whether D had the fault element when striking V. So, D has a
route to conviction for manslaughter only, on the basis of denial of the fault element
for murder. By contrast, in example 2, D admits (we may assume) having the fault element for murder, but claims that—due to voluntary intoxication—he believed that he
was acting in self-defence. Applying s. 76 of the 2008 Act, D will not be able to rely on
his honest but mistaken belief that V was about to attack him with lethal force, and will
accordingly have no route to manslaughter because (we are assuming) he admits having killed whilst having the fault element for murder. However, stepping back from the
strict application of the law, one may ask whether there is enough, morally speaking, in
the distinction between examples 1 and 2 to justify providing a route to manslaughter
in the first, but not in the second. Assuming that they are both telling the truth, does D
clearly deserve the mandatory life sentence in example 2, in a way that D in example 1
does not? There is a case for saying that both examples should be treated as instances of
reckless killing, and therefore as a highly culpable form of manslaughter.

(b) THE ATTACK ON THE ENGLISH APPROACH

The approach of the English courts has been attacked on several grounds. The distinction between 'specific intent' and 'basic intent' is ill-defined, even if it does have a
greater degree of coherence when understood as a distinction between specific fault
and basic fault. The approach of deeming intoxicated persons to be reckless rests on a
fiction, and the attempts of Lord Elwyn-Jones in *DPP* v *Majewski* to argue that intoxicated persons really are reckless because 'getting drunk is a reckless course of conduct'[20]
involve a manifest confusion between a general, non-legal use of the term 'reckless' and
the technical, legal term, which denotes (for almost all offences) that D was aware of

---

[20] [1977] AC 443, at 4710.

the risk of the result which actually occurred. In most cases it is far-fetched to argue that a person in the process of getting drunk is aware of the type of conduct he or she may later indulge in.

These criticisms of the courts' attempts to stretch the established meaning of 'intent' and of 'recklessness' in order to deal with the problems of intoxication have been joined by other arguments. Some have held that the intoxication rules are inconsistent with s. 8 of the Criminal Justice Act 1967, which requires courts to take account of all the evidence when deciding whether D intended or foresaw a result.[21] However, the effect of *DPP* v *Majewski* is to deny that evidence of intoxication is 'relevant' unless the crime is one of specific intent, and s. 8 extends only to legally relevant evidence.[22] Another argument is that the intoxication rules are inconsistent with the principle of proper coincidence between fault and action,[23] in that they base D's conviction (of an offence of basic intent) on the antecedent fault of voluntarily taking intoxicants:[24] but of course the 'proper coincidence' principle is only a permissive principle,[25] a principle that may, but not must, be applied. Perhaps it is right not to insist on it simply because to do so would keep the law simpler. Whatever the merit of these criticisms, it is undeniable that the intoxication rules in English law rest on fictions and apparently illogical legal devices. Is it the policy of restricting the defence of intoxication which is wrong, or merely the legal devices used to give effect to the policy?

(c) INTOXICATION, CULPABILITY, AND SOCIAL POLICY

One may concede that, in fact, a person may be so drunk as not to know what he or she is doing when causing harm to others or damage to property, and yet maintain that there are good reasons for criminal liability. What might these reasons be? At the root of the public security arguments is the proposition that one of the main functions of the criminal law is to exert a general deterrent effect, so as to protect major social and individual interests. In that regard, so the argument runs, any legal system which allows intoxication to negative fault would present citizens with an easy route to impunity. Indeed, the more intoxicated they became, the less likely they would be to be held criminally liable for any harm caused. As a matter of human experience, it is far from clear that this argument is soundly based. There are several common law jurisdictions which have declined to follow the English approach and which simply regard intoxication as one way of negativing fault.[26] Two comments may be made here. First, these jurisdictions can be taken to be reinforcing the important and often neglected point

[21] See J. C. Smith, 'Intoxication and the Mental Element in Crime', in P. Wallington and R. Merkin (eds), *Essays in Honour of F. H. Lawson* (1987).

[22] [1977] AC 443, at 475; *Woods* (1981) 74 Cr App Rep 312. See C. Wells, 'Swatting the Subjectivist Bug' [1982] Crim LR 2010.   [23] Chapter 6.4(c).

[24] Voiced by majority judges in the High Court of Australia, in *O'Connor* (1980) 146 CLR 610.

[25] See the discussion at the end of Chapter 4.1.

[26] See *Keogh* [1964] VR 400, and *O'Connor* (1980) 146 CLR 64 in Australia, and *Kamipeli* [1975] 2 NZLR 610 in New Zealand: compare G. Orchard, 'Surviving without *Majewski*—a View from Down Under' [1993] Crim LR 426 with S. Gough, 'Surviving without *Majewski*?' [2000] Crim LR 7110.

that it is extremely rare for a defendant to be able to raise even a reasonable doubt that he was unaware of what he was doing. All that is required for proof of intent or recklessness is a momentary realization that property is being damaged or that a person is being assaulted, etc. Thus, even if evidence of intoxication were relevant, D's condition would not usually be acute enough to prevent conviction. Secondly, and alternatively, the rarity of acquittals based on intoxication in these jurisdictions may simply be because juries and magistrates are applying a normative test rather than a purely factual test. Thus the confidence of the majority judges in the High Court of Australia that juries and magistrates will not be too readily persuaded to acquit in these cases[27] may derive less from the rarity of acutely intoxicated harmdoers, than from a belief that the courts will simply decline to return verdicts of acquittal where D is regarded as unworthy or culpable in some general way. This would suggest that both the English and the Australian approaches are unsatisfactory in their method—the English because it deems intoxicated harmdoers to be 'reckless' when they are not, the Australian because it relies on juries to make covert moral assessments and not simply the factual assessment that the law requires—even if they usually produce socially acceptable outcomes.

There remains the question of individual culpability. What distinguishes evidence of intoxication from many of the other explanations for D's failure to realize what most ordinary people would have foreseen is the element of prior fault. It was D's fault for taking drink or drugs to such an extent as to lose control over his behaviour. Does this mean that, in order to support a finding of culpability, it must be established that D knew of the likely effects of the intoxicants upon behaviour? Probably not, for it would be regarded as perfectly fair to assume that all people realize the possible effects of taking alcohol or drugs (apart from the exceptional situations to be discussed in paragraph (d) below). 'It is common knowledge that those who take alcohol to excess or certain sorts of drugs may become aggressive or do dangerous or unpredictable things.'[28] This is plainly an objective standard, but it is so elementary that it should not be regarded as unfair on anyone to assume such knowledge. Thus there is an element of culpability in intoxication cases which serves to distinguish them not only from insanity cases (which arise without fault) but also from many cases of simple absence of fault.

But in what does the culpability consist? Specifically, is D to blame for becoming intoxicated or for causing the proscribed harm? It is fairly simple to establish culpability for becoming intoxicated if there is no evidence that it was 'involuntary'. It is fairly difficult to establish culpability for causing the proscribed harm if we follow normal principles: we must assume acute intoxication at the time of the act, and if we look back to the period when D was becoming intoxicated, it is unlikely that one could establish actual foresight of the kind of harm eventually caused. Perhaps some people who regularly assault others when drunk may realize that there is a risk of this occurring, but in order to encompass the majority of cases, it would be necessary to rewrite the

---

[27] Cf. S. Gough, 'Intoxication and Criminal Liability: the Law Commission's Proposed Reforms' (1996) 112 LQR 335, at 337.

[28] *Bailey* (1983) 77 Cr App R 76, *per* Griffiths LJ at 80.

proposition about 'common knowledge' so as to maintain that people should realize that, when intoxicated, they are likely to cause damage or to assault others. The culpability, in other words, is somewhat unspecific—as in many instances where prior fault operates to bar a defence.[29] Sentencing decisions suggest that intoxication may mitigate on the first occasion it is raised, if the offence can be portrayed as 'out of character', but it will not mitigate any subsequent offences committed in an intoxicated state.[30]

(d) VOLUNTARY AND NON-VOLUNTARY INTOXICATION

We have already noted that non-voluntary intoxication may constitute an exception to the general intoxication rules, and we saw that s. 6(5) of the Public Order Act 1986 recognizes an exception where the intoxication was not 'self-induced'. There is, however, no sharp distinction between the voluntary and the non-voluntary: rather, there is a continuum of states in which D has more or less knowledge about the properties of what he is consuming. The English courts, consistently with their generally restrictive approach, have been reluctant to exempt defendants from the intoxication rules. Thus in *Allen* (1988),[31] D's argument was that he had become intoxicated because he had not realized that the wine being given to him had a high alcohol content. The Court of Appeal held that, so long as a person realizes that he is drinking alcohol, any subsequent intoxication is not rendered non-voluntary simply because he may not know the precise strength of the alcohol he is consuming. In some circumstances this might be quite a harsh ruling, but in broad terms it is compatible with judicial statements about the unpredictability of alcohol.

A different problem arose in *Hardie*,[32] where D took a quantity of Valium tablets 'for his nerves' and later set fire to an apartment. The Court of Appeal quashed his conviction. The main distinguishing factor here was that Valium is widely regarded as a sedative or soporific drug, and is not thought likely 'to render a person aggressive or incapable of appreciating risks to others'. This suggests that one basis for the distinction between voluntary and non-voluntary intoxication is a division of intoxicants into those that are sedative and others that may have aggressive effects. The Court in *Hardie* added that D would nonetheless be treated as reckless if he had known, contrary to general beliefs, that Valium might have disinhibiting rather than sedative effects.[33] It should be noted that s. 6(5) of the Public Order Act 1986, set out earlier, allows D a defence where the intoxication 'was caused solely by the taking or administration of a substance in the course of medical treatment'. In line with the general approach, this should be confined to cases where D was not warned of the possible effects, or where those effects were not widely known.

---

[29] See P. H. Robinson, 'Causing the Conditions of One's Own Defence' (1985) 71 Virginia LR 1, at 50–1.

[30] For the uncompromising judicial response to repeated offences of drunken violence, see *Sheehan and O'Mahoney* [2007] 1 Cr App R (S) 149 and *McDermott* [2007] 1 Cr App R (S) 1410.

[31] [1988] Crim LR 6910.   [32] (1985) 80 Cr App R 1510.

[33] This follows the reasoning in *Bailey* (1983) 77 Cr App R 76 on diabetes and automatism.

The question of non-voluntary intoxication is raised most directly by *Kingston*.[34] The evidence suggested that certain sedative drugs had been introduced into D's coffee, and that he had then carried out indecent sexual acts on a sleeping boy. The Court of Appeal quashed D's conviction, holding that if D had been placed in an altered mental state by the stratagem of another, and this led him to form an intent that he would not otherwise have formed, he should have a defence. This approach accepts that D may have had the mental element required for the crime, but looks to the *cause* of that condition: in effect, a doctrine of prior lack of fault. The House of Lords restored the conviction. If the non-voluntary intoxication is so acute as to negative *mens rea*, then it may lead to an acquittal of any offence requiring *mens rea*, whether of specific or basic intent. Where non-voluntary intoxication is not so acute as to negative fault, Lord Mustill held that there is no basis for an acquittal unless the courts were to create a new defence (a doubtful claim, as we will see shortly).[35] This the House was unwilling to do, because their Lordships could see no significant moral difference between this case and *Allen*, and because the opportunity for false defences was considerable. The matter was one for the Law Commission and Parliament.

What, then, is the position? If the intoxicant is in the soporific category, it seems from *Hardie* that D may have a defence if he can show that he lacked the mental element required for the crime. The general rule would prevent evidence of intoxication being adduced to show that he was not reckless but, if the intoxication was non-voluntary, evidence of the intoxication should be admitted. However, where the intoxicant is not so powerful as to remove D's awareness of what he is doing, it seems immaterial whether it is in the soporific or the 'aggressive' category. *Kingston* holds that there is no defence available and D is therefore convicted on the basis of his intention or recklessness. Even if D can establish that the intoxicant was administered without his awareness—the 'laced' or 'spiked' drink[36]—this appears insufficient to alter the analysis. The House of Lords in *Kingston* dismissed as irrelevant D's absence of fault in bringing about the condition; but arguably that was to overlook the potential application of automatism as it affects the mind rather than the body. This was a point raised in Chapter 4.3, namely whether a lack of moral autonomy—where D acts intentionally with cognitive awareness, but lacks moral control due to some temporary mental defect not amounting to insanity or voluntary intoxication—should count as a kind of automatism. We saw in Chapter 4.3 that the courts have equivocated over the extension of automatism in this direction, but the defendant in *Kingston* should at least have been given a better opportunity to argue the point.[37]

---

[34] [1995] 2 AC 355.

[35] His Lordship concluded that the few distant authorities in favour of the defence were unpersuasive, and so the House of Lords (rightly) considered the issue afresh.

[36] For an example see *Blakely and Sutton* [1991] Crim LR 763.

[37] For further discussion of this case, see G. R. Sullivan, 'Making Excuses', in A. P. Simester and A. T. H. Smith (eds), *Harm and Culpability* (1996).

(e) FINDING A LEGAL SOLUTION

A simple solution compatible with the ordinary logic of the liability rules is to regard evidence of intoxication as relevant on issues of *mens rea*, following various decisions in New Zealand and in the non-Code states of Australia. There will only rarely be acquittals, and these may be regarded as part of a small price for respecting the principle of individual autonomy—like occasional acquittals of clumsy and thoughtless individuals. In practice the behaviour of most defendants who allege intoxication will show some elements of intention, knowledge, or awareness.[38] However, an objection to the Antipodean approach is that it seems to yield the anti-social maxim 'more intoxication, less liability', and public outcries at certain acquittals have led some Australian states to abandon the simple 'logical' approach.[39] It gives no weight to the elements of choice and risk involved in getting drunk. Usually the choice is to loosen one's self-restraint rather than to commit a crime, let alone a particular kind of crime; but the retention of control over one's behaviour might fairly be regarded as a social duty, and its abandonment as a form of wrongdoing. This argument may be weakened where D is addicted to alcohol or drugs, since the element of choice may have been exhausted long ago.[40]

In this country the various proposals for reform seem to fall into one of two different camps. On the one hand there are those who argue that the essence of the wrongdoing in most cases lies in becoming intoxicated, and that it is unfair to label a defendant as a certain kind of offender (wounding, indecent assault, etc.) if he really was so intoxicated as not to realize what he was doing. Along these lines was a Consultation Paper issued by the Law Commission in 1993, proposing that courts be allowed to take account of evidence of intoxication on any issue of fault (following the Antipodean approach), but also introducing a new offence of causing harm whilst intoxicated—a 'state of affairs' offence designed to achieve a measure of social defence without unfair labelling of the offender (in line with German law).[41] However, the prevailing approach to reform is an adaptation of the common law. A government version is to be found in a draft Bill of 1998:[42]

> For the purposes of this Act a person who was voluntarily intoxicated at any material time must be treated—

---

[38] C. N. Mitchell, 'The Intoxicated Offender—Refuting the Legal and Medical Myths' (1988) 11 Int J Law and Psychiatry 710.

[39] S. Gough, '"Surviving without *Majewski*?": the Law Commission's Proposed Reforms' (1996) 112 LQR 335, also discussing the Canadian decision in *Daviault* (1995) 118 DLR (4th) 469 and its consequences.

[40] Cf. H. Fingarette, 'Addiction and Criminal Responsibility' (1975) 84 Yale LJ 413 with J. Tolmie, 'Alcoholism and Criminal Liability' (2001) 64 MLR 688.

[41] Law Commission Consultation Paper No. 127, *Intoxication and Criminal Liability* (1993). German law adopts this approach, allowing intoxication to negative intention (applying the 'inexorable logic') but then applying an offence of 'dangerous intoxication' that consists of committing the conduct element of another offence while culpably intoxicated: see J. Spencer and A. Pedain, 'Strict Liability in Continental Criminal Law' in A. P. Simester (ed.), *Appraising Strict Liability* (2005), 244–5. On fair labelling, see Chapter 6.7(a).

[42] Home Office, *Violence: Reforming the Offences Against the Person Act 1861* (1998), draft Bill, cl. 19, based on the criminal code proposals in Law Com No. 177, draft Bill, cl. 22. An intervening report from the Law Commission, Law Com No. 229, *Legislating the Criminal Code: Intoxication and Criminal Liability* (1995), was not adopted in its central recommendations.

as having been aware of any risk of which he would have been aware had he not been intoxicated; and

as having known or believed in any circumstances which he would have known or believed in had he not been intoxicated.

The first part of this means that in most cases an intoxicated actor will be deemed reckless, which is not far from the present law and its distinction between specific and basic intent.[43] The 1998 Bill also deals with intoxicants taken on medical advice, and includes a definition of voluntary intoxication. It does not provide a separate defence of involuntary intoxication, and indeed creates a presumption that intoxication was voluntary.

More recently, the Law Commission has proposed a way of rationalizing the current law without using the confusing terms 'specific' and 'basic' intent.[44] In its place, the Law Commission draws a distinction between crimes in which the fault element is an 'integral' element, and crimes in which the fault element is not an 'integral' element. Only in the former may voluntary intoxication be used as a way of denying the fault element. The Commission lists those species of fault the inclusion of which in the definition of the offence will make them 'integral' to the offence, meaning that the prosecution will have to prove that D had the fault element even if D denies having it on the grounds that he or she was voluntarily intoxicated:

Recommendation 3

   (1) Intention as to a consequence;

   (2) Knowledge as to something;

   (3) Belief as to something (where the belief is tantamount to knowledge);

   (4) Fraud;

   (5) Dishonesty.

This proposal is to be welcomed in so far as it requires judges, when considering if a crime is one to which voluntary intoxication may be evidence of lack of fault, only to decide whether the fault element falls within one of the categories just mentioned. They would no longer have to wrestle with the application of the more abstract and indeterminate notions of 'specific' and 'basic' intent, and hence the risk of mis-categorizations—such as that in *Heard*[45]—might be avoided more often. In making this advance, though, the Law Commission relies on another distinction that is not without difficulty, namely the distinction between crimes where the fault element is 'integral' to the offence, and crimes where it is not. Clearly, the notion of fault being 'integral' to the offence cannot mean simply that a fault element is expressly included in the offence; otherwise, the distinction would be doing no work. In its understanding of what is 'integral' to the offence, the Law Commission

---

[43] Sir John Smith rightly questioned (b), which might have unexpected consequences in attributing to people beliefs they did not hold: 'Offences Against the Person: the Home Office Consultation Paper' [1998] Crim LR 317, at 321.

[44] Law Commission, *Intoxication and Criminal Liability* (No. 314, 2009).   [45] [2008] QB 43 (CA).

is alluding instead to the wrongdoing that underlies the offence. The idea is that, in some crimes—murder, theft, fraud, for example—the fault element is integral to the wrongdoing itself: morally speaking, there can simply be no 'murder' without intention, no 'theft' without dishonesty, and so on. So, the argument runs, it would be unfair to deny D the possibility of denying the fault element in such crimes (whatever the reason for the absence of the fault element), given how central the fault element is to the moral wrong underlying the crime in question. By contrast, it is said, in some crimes—criminal damage is an example—the fault element may be added to the definition, as a matter of fairness to the accused, but is not integral to the underlying wrong. One may question how helpful this distinction really is. For example, is handling stolen goods 'knowing or believing' them to be stolen a crime in which the fault element is integral to the wrong, or not? Happily, under the Law Commission's scheme, such troublesome theoretical questions would not have to be tackled in the courts, who would look for guidance directly to Recommendation 3 (see earlier).[46]

All of this might be described as 'workable', although it ignores the moral arguments made by those who favour the modified German–Antipodean approach to which the Law Commission was temporarily attached in 1993. The case for a purely subjective approach to intoxication seems unconvincing, but the arguments about how the intoxicated wrongdoer should be labelled and sentenced remain keenly contested.[47]

7.3 DURESS AND NECESSITY

This part of the chapter deals with cases in which D's behaviour fulfils the conduct element and the positive fault requirements of an offence, but in which D acted in response to threats from another person (duress by threats),[48] or in order to avert dire consequences (called 'duress of circumstances'). At the outset, these were called, 'confession and avoidance' defences. We have already seen, in Chapter 5.8, that some cases of necessity might give rise to a claim that what would otherwise be a criminal action was permissible, but those are likely to be rare cases where there is a net saving of lives. Having said that, in focusing here on the *excusatory* defences of duress, we will find that the development of the common law has been characterized by confusions over whether, when D responds to pressure by committing an offence, D acts permissibly or only excusably.

---

[46] For detailed analysis see Williams, 'Voluntary Intoxication—A Lost Cause?'.

[47] Cf. A. Ashworth, 'Intoxication and the General Defences' [1980] Crim LR 556 with Gough, 'Intoxication and Criminal Liability'.

[48] Within this category, there used to be an unusual defence of 'marital coercion', which was abolished by the Anti-Social Behaviour, Crime and Policing Act 2014, s. 177.

(a) REQUIREMENTS OF THE DEFENCES

The courts have generally held that the requirements of duress by threats and of duress of circumstances are in parallel.[49] Although both defences require some danger external to D,[50] they arise in different factual circumstances, and it might be best to illustrate this by contrasting two cases. In *Hudson and Taylor*[51] two teenagers were prosecution witnesses at a trial for wounding. They testified that they did not know the man charged and could not identify him as the culprit. The man was acquitted but the young women were charged with perjury. They admitted that they gave false evidence, but said that they were under duress, having been threatened with violence by various men, one of whom was in the public gallery at the original trial. The Court of Appeal quashed their convictions because the defence of duress had been wrongly withdrawn from the jury. In *Conway*[52] two men approached D's car, whereupon D, urged on by his passenger, drove off at great speed and in a reckless manner. D's explanation was that he knew that his passenger had recently been threatened by two men who had fired a shotgun. D feared that these two men intended harm, and his driving was in response to that emergency. The Court of Appeal quashed the conviction for reckless driving because the trial judge had failed to leave the defence of duress of circumstances to the jury. A difference between these two cases is that for the defence of duress there should typically be a threat intended by the threatener to coerce D into committing a particular offence, whereas for duress of circumstances there will typically be a situation of emergency (involving perceived danger) that leads D to do something that would otherwise be an offence. However, there are additional subtle differences between the defences (although these may not have legal consequences):

1. In duress by threats cases, the crime D is to commit to avoid the threat will be specified by the threatener; in duress of circumstances cases, it is D who decides that the commission of a particular crime is the only reasonable course of conduct to take if the threat is to be avoided.

2. In duress by threats cases, one issue for D is a character assessment of the threatener in the shape of an assessment of his or her credibility: how likely is it that the threatener can or will implement the threat if D refuses to comply with the demand? In duress of circumstances, the equivalent issue for D is a risk assessment: how likely is it that the threat will have an impact on D in a way that makes commission of the crime the only reasonable course of action?

3. Unlike duress by threats, duress of circumstances overlaps with self-defence (if that defence is given a broad understanding). For example, *Conway*[53] could be seen as a case in which D acted in self-defence rather than under duress, if

---

[49] See *Willer* (1986) 83 Cr App R 225, *Conway* (1988) 88 Cr App R 159, *Martin* (1989) 88 Cr App R 343, discussed by D. W. Elliott, 'Necessity, Duress and Self-Defence' [1989] Crim LR 611.

[50] *Rodger and Rose* [1998] 1 Cr App R 143 (D's own suicidal tendencies are not a 'threat' that can found either defence).   [51] [1971] 2 QB 202, doubted in *Hasan*, see n 70.

[52] [1989] 3 All ER 10210.   [53] [1989] 3 All ER 1025, discussed earlier.

self-defence is deemed to include avoiding action that takes a form other than the use of force. If ducking to avoid something thrown at one's head is conduct that is self-defensive in nature, D's conduct in *Conway* should be analysed in a similar way.

What, then, are the general requirements of the two defences? First, they appear to be restricted to cases where D acted as he did out of fear of death or serious injury,[54] including cases in which D wrongly but reasonably believed that he or she faced such a threat.[55] In *R v GAC*,[56] D sought to avoid a conviction for importing a class A drug. D applied to the Court of Appeal to review her conviction, in the light of new evidence that she was suffering at the time from 'learned helplessness' (battered women's syndrome) brought about by abusive conduct by a co-defendant with whom she was romantically involved. The Court of Appeal upheld her conviction, on the basis that, although she may have been subjected to violence and suffered the condition, there was no evidence that it amounted to an immediate threat of serious violence.[57] Threats to property or to reputation have been held to be insufficient,[58] as has a threat of unwanted sexual contact.[59] Further, a threat of false imprisonment is unlikely to be sufficient.[60] In a sense it seems strange that the degree of threat or danger should be fixed in this way, since the seriousness of the crimes in respect of which duress is raised may vary considerably. A threat of death or serious harm should be necessary to excuse a person who caused a grave harm, but does it follow that some lesser threat should not be sufficient to excuse a lesser offence? One problem might be the fear of duress claims becoming too common a currency in less serious cases. Suppose, at school, that Nelson threatens to punch Milhouse unless Milhouse steals Bart's lunch money for Nelson. Does such a case require a defence of duress, or is it sufficient that the duress—if accepted as having taken place—can be taken into account in sentencing along with any other mitigating factors?[61] There is arguably a need to deal with more minor threats made by, for example, criminal gangs known to be willing and able to escalate the threat in order, say, to secure the involvement of children living in the area or at school in the area where the gang operates to assist in drugs and other gang-related offences.[62] In such cases, as we will see, the law currently takes a hard line by requiring someone threatened to report the matter to the police rather than give in to the threat.

Additionally, the threats must be such that 'a sober person of reasonable firmness' would not have resisted them.[63] This objective condition has been tested in cases in

---

[54] *DPP for Northern Ireland* v *Lynch* [1975] AC 653; *Bowen* [1996] 2 Cr App R 157.

[55] *Safi and others* [2003] EWCA Crim 1809.   [56] [2013] EWCA Crim 1472.

[57] [2013] EWCA Crim 1472. 'Learned helplessness' may have more relevance to the 'immediacy' condition: see later.

[58] In, respectively, *DPP* v *Lynch* [1975] AC 653 at 687, and *Valderrama-Vega* [1985] Crim LR 220.

[59] *Hammond* [2013] EWCA Crim 2709.   [60] See *R v Van Dao* [2012] EWCA Crim 1717.

[61] For an analysis of the policy reasons for keeping the defence confined to threats of death or serious injury, see *R v Van Dao* [2012] EWCA Crim 1717.

[62] See <www.theguardian.com/society/2014/jan/05/drug-gangs-using-children-as-mules>; T. Bennett and K. Holloway, 'Gang Membership, Drugs and Crime in the UK' (2004) 44 BJ Crim 305.

[63] *Graham* (1982) 74 Cr App R 235, confirmed by the House of Lords in *Howe* [1987] AC 4110.

which there have been attempts to introduce evidence to the effect that D's personality rendered him or her particularly susceptible to threats. In *Bowen*[64] the Court of Appeal held that the question is whether D responded 'as a sober person of reasonable firmness sharing the characteristics of the defendant would have done'. In applying this test a court should not admit evidence that D was more pliable, vulnerable, timid, or susceptible to threats than a normal person, and characteristics due to self-abuse (alcohol, drugs) should also be left out of account. But the Court did suggest that it would be proper to take account of age, sex, pregnancy, serious physical disability, or a 'recognized psychiatric condition'.[65] In view of the re-affirmation of the objective standard of self-control in loss of self-control cases,[66] this broadening of the ambit of duress may appear anomalous. However, the comparison with the operation of a partial defence to murder (i.e. loss of control) is not an apt one. The objective standard in loss of control can be maintained, in the expectation that mentally disordered defendants will have resort to the separate partial defence of diminished responsibility that also reduces murder to manslaughter. Duress is a complete defence to crimes other than murder or attempted murder. Unless the matter is to be left to sentencing following conviction, the only way to take account of mental disorder in duress cases, where insanity is not in issue, is by relaxing the objective standards.[67]

The threats need not be addressed to D personally:[68] the defence is available if the threats are against D's family or friends. In the unusual case of *Shayler*,[69] the defence was that D revealed official secrets because he believed that (unidentified) people were placed in danger by MI5's activities. The Court of Appeal held that, for the defence to be available, the threat or danger must be to D himself or 'towards somebody for whom he reasonably regarded himself as being responsible'.[70] This arguably introduces an unnecessary complication to the defence. Suppose that a bank robber threatens to shoot a bank customer or employee, unless an employee or customer volunteers to help with the robbery; D, a customer, agrees to help the robber. In this example, D is not in any way responsible for the welfare of any other customer saved by his or her decision to help the robber; yet, it would seem harsh to deny the defence to D. Would it really be held by the courts that D, being a customer, could not invoke the defence whereas, had a bank employee volunteered instead of a customer, the defence would have been available, because bank employees have a degree of responsibility for their customers? Such a distinction seems arbitrary.

The threat must be 'present' and not a remote threat of future harm, but how long an interval may elapse? In *Hudson and Taylor*,[71] the facts of which were outlined earlier,

---

[64] [1996] 2 Cr App R 157.

[65] For the suggestion that this phrase has wider implications than the Court realized, see A. Buchanan and G. Virgo, 'Duress and Mental Abnormality' [1999] Crim LR 517.

[66] Coroners and Justice Act 2009, discussed in Chapter 8.4(b).

[67] See further J. Horder, *Excusing Crime* (2004), 183–10.

[68] *Gill* (1963) 47 Cr App R 166; and Law Com No. 83, *Defences of General Application* (1977), 2–3.

[69] [2001] 1 WLR 2206.

[70] Lord Bingham in *Hasan* [2005] 2 AC 467 approved this formulation as 'consistent with the rationale' of duress (para. 21(3)).   [71] See n 50, and accompanying text.

the Court of Appeal held that it is not necessary that the threat would be carried out immediately, so long as its implementation was imminent. The same approach was taken in *Abdul-Hussain* et al.,[72] where a group of Shiite Muslims from Iraq had hijacked an aircraft to Stansted airport. When they surrendered, they claimed that they had acted out of fear of persecution and death at the hands of the Iraqi authorities. The trial judge withdrew the defence from the jury on the ground that the threat was not sufficiently close and immediate, but the Court of Appeal held that imminence is sufficient and that the execution of the threat need not be immediately in prospect. However, in *Hasan*[73] Lord Bingham opposed the drift towards the looser concept of 'imminence' and held that older authorities in favour of a requirement of immediacy should be restored: there is a duty to take evasive action where possible, particularly where the threat 'is not such as [D] reasonably expects to follow immediately or almost immediately on his failure to comply with the threat'.[74] Lord Bingham regarded *Hudson and Taylor* as wrongly decided, commenting that he could not accept 'that a witness testifying in the Crown Court at Manchester has no opportunity to avoid complying with a threat incapable of execution there and then'. This strong line may, though, leave intact the concession to the defendants' youth in *Hudson and Taylor*— 'having regard to his age and circumstances, and to any risks to him which may be involved in the course of action relied upon'.[75] Having said that, more broadly, Lord Bingham's conception of duress evidently finds no place for those who cannot measure up to reasonable expectations.

Another objective element is that the defendant is not entitled to be judged on the facts as he believed them to be. Contrary to the generally subjective approach to mistaken beliefs,[76] the Court of Appeal in *Graham*[77] held that the test for duress is whether, as a result of what D *reasonably* believed that the duressor had said or done, he had *good cause* to fear death or serious injury. Lord Lane offered no convincing reasons for departing from the subjective orthodoxy of the time, and in *Safi*[78] the Court of Appeal appeared to favour a subjective approach, although the point was not argued to a clear conclusion.[79] The decision in *Hasan* has probably concluded the argument in favour of the *Graham* approach.

Both duress by threats and duress of circumstances are subject to the considerations of prior fault. In *Sharp*[80] D joined a gang of robbers participating in crimes where guns were carried, but when he tried to withdraw he was himself threatened with violence. The Court of Appeal held that the defence of duress is unavailable to anyone who

---

[72] [1999] Crim LR 570.   [73] [2005] 2 AC 4610. The decision is also known as Z.

[74] [2005] 2 AC 4610, para. 210.   [75] [1971] 2 QB 202, at 2010.

[76] See section 7.4; the Divisional Court erroneously applied this general approach to duress in *DPP* v *Rogers* [1998] Crim LR 202.

[77] (1982) 74 Cr App R 235; much of Lord Lane's judgment proceeds on an analogy with provocation, even though the preponderance of authority favours a subjective test for belief in provocation cases—see Chapter 10.4, and W. Wilson, 'The Structure of Criminal Defences' [2005] Crim LR 1010.

[78] [2003] Crim LR 721.

[79] It is tolerably clear from the strong objectivism of Lord Bingham's speech in *Hasan* [2005] 2 AC 467, notably at para. 38, that he would support the *Graham* test.   [80] [1987] QB 853.

voluntarily joins a gang 'which he knows might bring pressure on him to commit an offence and was an active member when he was put under such pressure'. In *Shepherd*[81] the Court added that: 'there are certain kinds of criminal enterprises the joining of which, in the absence of any knowledge of propensity to violence on the part of one member, would not lead another to suspect that a decision to think better of the whole affair might lead him into serious trouble'. The doctrine of prior fault does not only operate in the context of joining criminal enterprises: it also applies where drug users become indebted to drug dealers who have a reputation for violence. The leading decision now is *Hasan*,[82] where D associated with a man who was known to use violence, and who allegedly forced D (by threats) to carry out two burglaries. Lord Bingham held that there should be an objective test, based on the foreseeability of violence being threatened by the people with whom D was associating, and not requiring foresight of coercion to commit crimes of a particular kind:[83]

> The policy of the law must be to discourage association with known criminals, and it should be slow to excuse the criminal conduct of those who do so. If a person voluntarily becomes or remains associated with others engaged in criminal activity in a situation where he knows or ought reasonably to know that he may be the subject of compulsion by them or their associates, he cannot rely on the defence of duress to excuse any act which he is thereafter compelled to do by them.[84]

Thus the subjective element in *Sharp*, 'which he knows . . .', is superseded by the strongly objective approach running through Lord Bingham's speech in *Hasan*. However, Baroness Hale's speech favours the subjective approach in *Sharp*, and also argues that the foreseen threat must have been a threat to commit crimes rather than a general threat of violence.[85] The latter point is surely right: the likelihood of being subjected to violence or threats thereof is different from the foreseeability of threats being used to force D to commit crimes, and the latter should be required.

(b) THEORETICAL FOUNDATIONS FOR THE DEFENCES

Why should defences of duress be allowed? One argument is that acts under duress are permissible in the sense that they constitute a lesser evil than the carrying-out of the threat: the credentials of this rather narrow argument were discussed in Chapter 5.8. In general the courts have tended to mix arguments about permissions with those of excuse, without noticing the distinction. How strong are the arguments for excusing D rather than saying that the act is permissible? It is fairly clear that duress does not negative intent, knowledge, or recklessness: D will know only too well the nature and consequences of the conduct. It also seems unlikely that duress negatives the voluntary nature of D's conduct: the elements of unconsciousness and uncontrollability of bodily

---

[81] (1988) 86 Cr App R 410.   [82] [2005] UKSC 22.
[83] Overruling *Baker and Ward* [1999] 2 Cr App R 335 on this point.
[84] [2005] UKS 22, at para. 38; see also *Ali* [2008] EWCA 7110.   [85] [2005] UKSC 22, at para. 77.

movements which are regarded as the hallmark of involuntary behaviour[86] are not typically to be found in duress cases. Two separate rationales, with somewhat different implications, warrant further discussion—the first seeing duress as characterized by moral involuntariness, the second regarding it more as a reasonable response to extreme pressure.

Although conduct in response to duress or necessity is not *in*voluntary, it may be described as *non*-voluntary. The argument is that there is a much lower degree of choice and free will in these cases than in the normal run of actions. George Fletcher has termed this 'moral or normative involuntariness', arguing that the degree of compulsion in these cases is not significantly less than in cases of physical involuntariness.[87] The phrases used by the Court of Appeal in *Hudson and Taylor*—'effective to neutralize the will of the accused', and 'driven to act by immediate and unavoidable pressure'— have been repeated in many subsequent decisions. Even though 'neutralizing the will'[88] puts it rather too strongly, the idea of moral 'involuntariness' seems to encapsulate the approach of English judges, who also draw on a supposed analogy with loss of self-control. Full acceptance of the 'moral involuntariness' rationale might lead to an entirely subjective version of duress, in which the degree of pressure experienced by D would be the main issue: a denial of moral autonomy.[89] In fact, English law imposes a standard of reasonable steadfastness, but of course that could be explained as a means of avoiding false defences (as courts and reform committees often state) rather than a rejection of the basic rationale. The weakness of the moral involuntariness account of duress is that it mis-describes most actions taken under duress, which are coerced but are neither involuntary nor non-voluntary. It is possible to imagine circumstances in which a threat could break D's will to resist. An example might be where D is subjected to prolonged and agonizing torture, and then threatened with a continuation of the torture unless he or she complies with a threatener's demand. Conceivably, a severe case of 'learned helplessness' ('battered women's syndrome') might also be analysed in such a way.[90] In such a case, D may genuinely lack the will to resist, but such cases will be rare.

An alternative rationale is to regard the successful duress defence as recognition that D responded in a reasonable way to his or her fear, when faced with extreme danger. It is important not to read too much into the element of reasonableness here. It is not being claimed that D had a right to respond as he did, save perhaps in the small group of cases where a net saving of lives is in prospect.[91] Duress usually operates as an excuse, recognizing the dire situation with which D was faced and limiting the defence to cases where D responded in a way that did not fall below the standard to be expected

---

[86] See Chapter 5.2.

[87] G. P. Fletcher, *Rethinking Criminal Law* (1978), 803, adopted by Dickson J in the Supreme Court of Canada in *Perka* v *R* (1984) 13 DLR (4th) 1. For discussion see C. Wells, 'Necessity and the Common Law' (1985) 5 Oxford JLS 471.

[88] See also *R* v *GAC* [2013] EWCA Crim 1474 for use of this kind of language.

[89] See Chapters 4.3 and 5.3   [90] See *R* v *GAC* [2013] EWCA Crim 1474.

[91] Discussed in Chapter 5.8.

of the reasonable citizen in such circumstances. On this rationale, the person of reasonable firmness assumes a central role, not so much in announcing a standard that should be followed, or reducing the risk of false defences, but rather in recognizing that D was not lacking in responsibility for what was done. D is excused for giving way to the threat or danger when resistance could not reasonably be expected in the circumstances—which means that self-sacrifice is required in certain (lesser) situations.

That leaves the issue of citizens who, for one reason or another, cannot attain the standard of reasonable firmness in these situations. We saw that in *Bowen*[92] the Court of Appeal recognized a small group of conditions which might be allowed to modify the standard of reasonable firmness, whilst maintaining that the standard should be upheld for those falling outside that short list. The 'moral involuntariness' rationale argues in favour of including these people in the defence of duress, on the basis of the severe reduction of their free will. But they fall outside the 'reasonable response' rationale, to which the standard of reasonable steadfastness is central. English law knows no general defence, falling short of insanity, of diminished capacity or extreme mental or emotional disturbance.

A more radical approach would be to argue that, since there are so many questions of degree in duress cases (degree of threat, degree of immediacy, seriousness of crime), they are much more appropriate for the sentencing stage than the liability stage.[93] On that view, the duress defences should be abolished altogether. At present English law takes the view (except in murder cases) that there is a point at which threats or an emergency may place so much pressure on an individual that it is unfair to register a conviction at all, so long as the individual does not fall below the standard of reasonable firmness, but that in lesser situations claims of duress sound only at the sentencing stage. Mitigation may be right if 'desert' is the basis for sentence, but supporters of deterrent sentencing have a particular problem. Their general approach is to maintain that the stronger the temptation or pressure to commit a crime, the stronger the law's threat should be in order to counterbalance it.[94] The law and its penalties should be used to strengthen the resolve of those under pressure. Yet, Bentham also accepted that criminal liability and punishment are inefficacious where a person is subject to such acute threats (e.g. death, serious injury) that the law's own threat cannot be expected to counterbalance it: in these cases, he said, there should be a complete defence.[95] The difficulty with this analysis is that it suggests heavy deterrent sentences for all cases except the most egregious, where it prescribes no penalty at all—a distinction with momentous effects but no clear reference point. There is surely a sliding scale of intensity of duress and necessity. If, in the dire circumstances that confront D, he or she responds in such a way that one could not reasonably expect more of a citizen, then surely neither conviction nor punishment is deserved. Mitigation of sentence should

---

[92] [1996] 2 Cr App R 157.
[93] See section 7.8(a), and M. Wasik, 'Duress and Criminal Responsibility' [1977] Crim LR 453.
[94] J. Bentham, *Introduction to the Principles of Morals and Legislation* (1789), ch XIV, para. 10.
[95] Bentham, *Introduction to the Principles of Morals and Legislation*, para. 11.

be available for less extreme cases, to reflect strong elements of pressure that did not amount to the full defence.

(c) DURESS AND THE TAKING OF LIFE

Although most of the elements of these defences seem to be based on a rationale of excusing a person's understandable submission to the threat, the troubled issue of whether the defences should be available to murder has led the courts to draw on permission-based rationales. The tone was set in the late-nineteenth century with *Dudley and Stephens*,[96] where two shipwrecked mariners killed and ate a cabin-boy after seventeen days adrift at sea. Lord Coleridge CJ held that no defence of necessity (now called duress of circumstances) was available in a case of taking another person's life. In the first place, he argued, there is no *necessity* for preserving one's own life, and there are circumstances in which it may be one's duty to sacrifice it. Then, secondly, if there were ever to be a similar case, who would judge which person is to die? (This point might be overcome by drawing lots.) So he concluded that, terrible as the temptation might be in this kind of case, the law should 'keep the judgment straight and the conduct pure'. The sentence of death was later commuted to six months' imprisonment, thus emphasizing the obvious conflict between the desire to reaffirm the sanctity of life and the widely felt compassion for people placed in an extreme situation.[97]

In *DPP* v *Lynch*[98] the House of Lords accepted, by a majority of three to two, that duress by threats should be available as a defence to an accomplice to murder, reflecting the law's compassion towards a person placed under such extreme pressure. But then the Privy Council in *Abbott* v *R*[99] held that duress was unavailable as a defence to the principal in murder, and in *Howe*[100] the House of Lords had to decide whether to perpetuate this distinction between principals and accomplices. Their Lordships decided not to do so, unanimously favouring a rule which renders duress and necessity unavailable as defences in all prosecutions for murder.[101] The primary reason for their decision was that the law should not recognize that any individual has the liberty to choose that one innocent citizen should die rather than another. All duress cases involve a choice between innocents, D and the intended victim, and the law should not remove its protection from the victim. Thus D is required to make a heroic sacrifice. A secondary argument, similar to that employed a century earlier in *Dudley and Stephens*, was that executive discretion could take care of deserving cases—either by releasing D on parole at an early stage or even by refraining from prosecution.[102]

---

[96] (1884) 14 QBD 273.

[97] For detailed consideration of the case in its social context, see B. Simpson, *Cannibalism and the Common Law* (1984). [98] [1977] AC 653.

[99] [1977] AC 755; I. Dennis, 'Duress, Murder and Criminal Responsibility' (1980) 96 LQR 2010.

[100] [1987] AC 417.

[101] The House of Lords held in *Gotts* [1992] 2 AC 412 that, by logical extension, duress should not be available as a defence to attempted murder. [102] *Per* Lords Griffiths and Mackay, at 446 and 457.

Both these arguments are open to criticism. The argument based on protection for the innocent victim seems to assume that duress is being advanced as a permission for killing: this enables the judges to assume that, because the killing of an innocent person is impermissible, duress should not be a defence. It was argued earlier that a killing under duress might be permissible if there were a net saving of lives,[103] but that is not the issue here. Where it is a question of liability for taking one innocent life to save another, the rationale must be one of excuse, not justification. It can therefore be put alongside other situations in which a killing may be excused in whole or in part (e.g. mistaken self-defence, intoxication, loss of self-control), without being permissible.[104] Utilitarians might argue that a rule denying duress as a defence to murder is preferable because over the years it might achieve a net saving of lives. This kind of argument not only fails to take the defendant's interests into account, but also assumes that persons under duress will know of the law's approach and will be influenced by it, an assumption which will rarely be true. The second argument, in favour of convicting the person under duress and then invoking executive clemency to reduce the punishment, lack real conviction. For one thing, there can be no certainty that the Parole Board will view these cases more favourably than others. For another, if we are satisfied that D was placed under extreme pressure, we ought to declare that publicly either by allowing a defence or, if not, by allowing a partial defence to murder on an analogy with loss of self-control. The argument in favour of merely a partial defence should not be understated: it is possible both to recognize the sanctity of life as a fundamental value, and to demonstrate compassion to the person who takes a life.[105]

The case for a partial defence in duress cases has arguably been strengthened by the extension of the partial defence to murder of loss of self-control to cover cases in which D lost self-control and killed V when in fear of serious violence from V.[106] The requirement in duress cases that the threateners have insisted on immediate or almost immediate compliance[107] is strongly analogous to a requirement for loss of self-control. Further, whilst it is true that in loss of self-control cases it must be the person threatening the violence who is killed, rather than an innocent third party (as in duress cases), this is arguably no more than a factor to take into account when deciding whether the person of reasonable steadfastness might have done as D did. In its 2005 Consultation Paper, the Law Commission proposed that duress should be available as a partial defence to first degree murder, reducing it to second degree murder, and that the *Bowen* test of relevant characteristics should be tightened so as to run in parallel to the partial defence of loss of self-control.[108] There were other, complicated proposals about how this approach should be adapted to defences of duress to second degree murder and to manslaughter, but the consultation process persuaded the Commission to abandon this whole approach. Although recognizing that consultees were 'more divided on duress' than on any other aspect, the Commission has now reverted to its earlier

---

[103] See Chapter 5.8.   [104] P. Alldridge, 'The Coherence of Defences' [1983] Crim LR 665.
[105] See, further, K. J. Arenson, 'The Paradox of Disallowing Duress as a Defence to Murder' (2014) 78 J Crim Law 65.   [106] Coroners and Justice Act 2009, s. 55(3). See further, later in Chapter 7.
[107] *Hasan* [2005] 2 AC 467 (HL), para. 210.
[108] LCCP 177, *A New Homicide Act for England and Wales?* (2005), Part 10.

view that in principle it would be morally wrong to convict of any crime a defendant who satisfies the stringent requirements of the defence of duress, having reacted as a person of reasonable fortitude might have done.[109] The Commission recognizes that recommending duress as a partial defence might have been a compromise acceptable to many, but it states that the argument against a complete defence based on the sanctity of life is not conclusive because of cases of 'ten year olds and peripheral secondary parties becoming involved in killing under duress'.[110]

The reference to age is sharpened by the subsequent decision in *Wilson*,[111] where a boy of thirteen was pressed by his father into helping with the killing of a neighbour and no defence of duress was available on the charge of murder, despite considerable evidence that he was so frightened that he could not disobey his father. The Law Commission's principal argument is that as a matter of moral principle a person who is found by a jury to have reacted to extreme circumstances as a reasonable person might have done 'should be completely exonerated despite having intentionally killed', adding that youth is a relevant factor in determining reasonableness.[112] Thus the Commission insists that the threat must be believed to be life-threatening, and that D's belief that the threat has been made is based on reasonable grounds. The argument for adopting the *Graham* approach is that, compared with loss of control and self-defence (which have no such requirement of reasonable belief), there is a less immediate temporal or physical nexus between the threat and the killing in duress cases.[113] This also becomes the primary argument in favour of the Commission's recommendation that the burden of proof be reversed where duress is raised as a defence to homicide[114]—that the separation of the threat from the killing creates extra difficulties for the prosecution. However, the Commission supports the tightening of the law by the House of Lords in *Hasan*, one aspect of which was the replacement of the former 'imminence' requirement with one of immediacy; so the temporal separation cannot be great, and reference to 'time to reflect' takes insufficient account of the great emotional turmoil brought about by threats of this kind.[115]

7.4 REASONABLE MISTAKE AND PUTATIVE DEFENCES

For the first three-quarters of the twentieth century, the approach of the common law to mistake was that if the defendant wished to rely on this defence it must be shown that he had reasonable grounds for his mistaken belief. The leading case was *Tolson*,[116]

---

[109] Law Com No. 304, *Murder, Manslaughter and Infanticide* (2006), Part 6; the earlier report adopting the same approach was Law Com No. 218, *Legislating the Criminal Code: Offences against the Person and General Principles* (1993). [110] Law Com No. 304, *Murder, Manslaughter and Infanticide* (2006), para 6.46.

[111] [2007] QB 960. [112] Law Com No. 304, paras. 6.53 and 6.142–3.

[113] Law Com No. 304, para. 6.79.

[114] For criticism of this recommendation, see A. Ashworth, 'Principles, Pragmatism, and the Law Commission's Recommendations on Homicide Law Reform' [2007] Crim LR 333, at 340–2.

[115] The Ministry of Justice's Consultation Paper 19 on *Murder, Manslaughter and Infanticide: Proposals for Reform of the Law* (2008), much discussed in Chapter 8, does not cover the duress recommendations.

[116] (1889) 23 QBD 168.

where the Court for Crown Cases Reserved held that a mistake of fact on reasonable grounds would be a defence to any criminal charge. Despite being cited as the leading case, the ambit and status of *Tolson* were never clear, since Stephen J devoted much of his judgment to the proposition that if the mental element of the crime is proved to have been absent, the crime so defined is not committed.[117] Certainly it is authority for the proposition that reasonable mistake is a defence to crimes of strict liability.[118] It is also authority on the crime of bigamy, and was expressly preserved by the House of Lords in *DPP* v *Morgan*[119] when it introduced (or, in the light of Stephen J's judgment, reintroduced) the proposition that if the mental element is missing in respect of one of the conduct elements specified in the definition of the crime, then as a matter of inexorable logic D should be acquitted even if the mistake was wholly unreasonable.

The 'inexorable logic' argument may be accepted as a starting point, but the question is whether considerations of moral fault indicate that in certain types of case it should be abandoned. We have already seen that the 'inexorable logic' has not been followed in respect of intoxication (where special restrictive rules have been created). When the House of Lords in *Morgan* opted for the 'inexorable logic' approach, treating the claim of mistake as a mere denial of the required mental element, it expressly left un-disturbed two different rules—the *Tolson* principle (above), as applied to bigamy, and the requirement that mistakes relating to a defence should be reasonable. This second requirement relates to 'defences' resting on permission: if there is a mistake about the circumstances giving rise to the permission, this makes it a putative defence (i.e. an *excuse* rather than a *permission*, because the circumstances for permission were absent and D merely believed they were present). The persistence of the objective approach to mistake in these cases owed more to assumption and repetition than to principled argument. Its chief application was in self-defence, where courts had tended to require that any mistake about the circumstances should be based on reasonable grounds.[120] But this reasonable mistake doctrine, left intact in *Morgan* itself, was swept away by decisions of the Court of Appeal and Privy Council in the 1980s.[121] Thus a putative defence will succeed wherever the prosecution fails to prove that D knew the relevant facts (i.e. that D did not hold the mistaken belief claimed), no matter how outlandish that belief may have been. Thus in *Williams* (1984)[122] V saw a man, X, snatch a bag from a woman in the street; V ran after X and forcibly detained him; D then came upon the scene and asked V why he was punching X; V said, untruthfully, that he was a police officer; D asked V for his warrant card, and when V failed to produce the card,

---

[117] See A. P. Simester, 'Mistakes in Defence' (1992) 12 Oxford JLS 295, and R. H. S. Tur, 'Subjectivism and Objectivism: Towards Synthesis', in S. Shute, J. Gardner, and J. Horder (eds), *Action and Value in Criminal Law* (1993).   [118] Confirmed by the House of Lords in *Sweet* v *Parsley* [1970] AC 132.

[119] [1976] AC 182.

[120] The leading cases were probably *Rose* (1884) 15 Cox CC 540 and *Chisam* (1963) 47 Cr App R 130. The only careful analysis was that of Hodgson J in the Divisional Court in *Albert* v *Lavin* (1981) 72 Cr App R 1710. See, though, the subjective approach to mistake in provocation cases: *Letenock* (1917) 12 Cr App R 221, *Wardrope* [1960] Crim LR 770.

[121] *Kimber* (1983) 77 Cr App R 225, followed by *Gladstone Williams* (1984) 78 Cr App R 276 and by *Beckford* [1988] 1 AC 130.   [122] (1984) 78 Cr App R 276.

D struck V. D was charged with assaulting V, and his defence was that he mistakenly believed that his actions were permissible in the prevention of crime. It is plain that his actions were not in fact permissible, since V was acting lawfully in trying to detain X.[123] The law requires the prosecution to satisfy the court that D was aware of the facts which made his action unlawful, and he was not. He was mistaken. The Court of Appeal held that his conviction should be quashed: 'The mental element necessary to constitute guilt is the intent to apply unlawful force to the victim. We do not believe that the mental element can be substantiated by simply showing an intent to apply force and no more.'

The courts in *Williams* and *Beckford* presented this as an application of the 'inexorable logic' approach in *Morgan* (overlooking the fact that *Morgan* left this aspect of the law unchanged), reasoning as follows:

(i) unlawfulness is an element in all crimes of violence;

(ii) intention, knowledge, or recklessness must be proved as to that element; and therefore;

(iii) a person who mistakenly believes in the existence of circumstances which would make the conduct lawful should not be criminally liable.

The crucial step is the first: how do we know that unlawfulness is a definitional element in all crimes? Not all crimes are defined explicitly in this way. So it is, rather, a doctrinal question. Andrew Simester has argued that unlawfulness cannot be an ingredient of the *actus reus*, since only when there is *actus reus* with *mens rea* can we conclude that conduct was unlawful.[124] Might this not be a question of terminology? Some would argue, as we saw in Chapter 5.6, that there is no *actus reus* where the conduct is permissible. If 'absence of permissible' is substituted for 'unlawfulness' in the above reasoning, does not the difficulty claimed by Simester disappear? A stronger argument is that, irrespective of the definitional boundaries of the *actus reus*, there is a need to confront the moral issue whether there should be some grounds for doing so before using force against another. Using force is *prima facie* wrongful and so citizens should not use force without grounds for doing so, bearing in mind that the circumstances in which D has to act will affect what is regarded as adequate grounds. This distinguishes cases of putative defence from other cases of mistake in which D does not think what he is doing is wrongful or dangerous.[125]

Rather than relying on the logic of steps (i), (ii), and (iii) above, the law should adopt this more context-sensitive approach, taking some account of the circumstances of the act, of D's responsibilities, and of what may reasonably be expected in such situations. The consequence may be not to require knowledge of a certain circumstance in the definition of the offence, but to require reasonable grounds for a belief. In rape

---

[123] S. Uniacke, *Permissible Killing* (1994), discussed in Chapter 5.6, would say that D's conduct was agent-perspectivally permitted to act but not objectively permitted.
[124] Simester, 'Mistakes in Defence' n 117.
[125] *McCann v UK*, discussed in Chapter 5.6(g); see also Simester, 'Mistakes in Defence', n 117.

cases, these considerations militate in favour of a requirement of reasonable grounds for any mistake, as the Sexual Offences Act 2003 now provides.[126] Reasonable grounds should also be required in respect of age requirements for consensual sexual conduct, although in this respect the 2003 Act goes further and imposes strict liability in some circumstances.[127]

In principle, it is also right to require reasonable grounds before allowing the acquittal of a police officer with firearms training, as in *Beckford* v *R*.[128] Of course, any such infusion of objective principles must recognize the exigencies of the moment, and must not demand more of D than society ought to expect in that particular situation. In that regard, one may question the appropriateness, in evaluating the conduct of armed professionals, of the provision in s 76(7) of the Criminal Justice and Immigration Act 2008, that in determining whether force was reasonable in self-defence a court must take account of 'what the person honestly and instinctively thought necessary'.[129] Perhaps, when an armed officer is taken completely by surprise, this provision may have some relevance; but surely, in general, we would expect more of professionals trained to use firearms than they instinctively shoot from the hip when the need to use (perhaps lethal) force arises?[130] These arguments may be no less strong in many cases of putative defences of duress, where a reasonableness requirement has been imposed.[131] A question arising from this analysis is whether cases of mistaken belief in permission are necessarily cases of excuse, or whether they may be treated as forms of permission. Any confusion here stems from a failure to distinguish reasons to act from reasons to believe. Although an action itself may be unjustified, the belief in the need to act in that way might have been justified.[132]

English law currently takes variable approaches to these questions. In recent years the judges have often seemed to be firmly in the embrace of the 'inexorable logic' approach to mistake,[133] but there have been some deviations which perhaps suggest recognition of the complexity of the issues. As noted in the discussion of duress in section 7.3(a) earlier, the poorly reasoned decision in *Graham*,[134] holding that a mistake about the nature of the threat must be a reasonable one if the defence of duress is to be available, has now been championed on strong protectionist grounds by Lord Bingham in *Hasan* and adopted by the Law Commission.[135] The objectivist approach in the Sexual Offences Act 2003 suggests a more context-sensitive treatment of mistake about consent. There is a strong case for saying that this approach is the right one: the law should

---

[126] See Chapter 9.5(d).   [127] See Chapter 9.6(a), discussing *G* [2008] UKHL 310.

[128] Compare *Beckford* [1988] AC 130 with *McCann* v *UK* (1995) 21 ECHR 97, 5.7(f)(vi). The High Court of Australia has required 'reasonable grounds' in all cases of mistaken self-defence: *Zecevic* v *R* (1987) 162 CLR 645.   [129] Discussed in Chapter 5.6(g).

[130] For an outstanding analysis of this issue, see J. Gardner, *Offences and Defences* (2007), ch 6.

[131] See section 7.3(c) earlier, and the Law Commission Consultation Paper No. 139, *Consent in the Criminal Law* (1995), ch 10.

[132] Gardner, *Offences and Defences*, ch 4; R. A. Duff, *Answering for Crime* (2007), 270–6.

[133] For recent affirmations see *B* v *DPP* [2000] 2 AC 428 and *K* [2002] 2 AC 462 discussed in Chapter 6.5(a)iii.   [134] (1982) 74 Cr App R 2310.

[135] [2005] 2 AC 467, discussed in section 7.3(a) of this chapter.

in general require beliefs to be reasonable, but ensure that the jury understands how to assess the reasonableness of a belief in its context.

7.5 REVIEWING THE ROLE OF DEFENCES

It would not necessarily be wrong to deal with all 'confession and avoidance' excuses (see section 7.1), such as duress, by excluding them from the criminal trial, and dealing with them at the sentencing stage, on the grounds that—by way of contrast with mistake—in such cases D admits engaging in the prohibited conduct with the fault element. The objection to this approach is that a criminal conviction is rightly regarded as condemnatory: it is unfair to apply such official censure when the accused was doing only as a reasonable person might have done (in the absence of any reasonable alternative), or under the influence of severe mental disorder; but that objection is perhaps not conclusive. It creates the risk of arbitrariness between those factors deemed acceptable as formal 'confession and avoidance' excuses, and factors excluded from having this kind of legal impact. Unless the penalty is mandatory (as, in English law, for murder), courts are able to reflect the strength of the excuse in the sentence they pass. Even so, care must be taken with this solution. To begin with, there has been insufficient recognition of the importance of ensuring that defendants have the same evidential safeguards, in relation to sentencing considerations, as they would have had if the same factors arose in a criminal trial.[136] Secondly, there is no clear recognition that there is a right to have mitigating evidence taken into account. The matter is often presented as discretionary, suggesting that courts may withhold a reduction in sentence if they wish to do so: a reflection of the authoritarian principle discussed in Chapter 4.5. This is unsatisfactory, and reflects the general lack of structure of English sentencing law in respect of mitigating factors.

There are also procedural remedies to deal with cases where there are strong mitigating factors, although such remedies will carry authoritarian baggage because of their reliance on official discretion. The most powerful procedural approach is not to prosecute at all. Prosecutors may decide that a prosecution would not be 'in the public interest', if mitigating factors are strong enough, as for example in cases where the defendant is very young or elderly, or is, or was at the time of the offence, suffering from significant mental or physical ill health. Both of these factors are to be weighed against the seriousness of the offence. In practice, non-prosecution and discontinuance of prosecution are responses to many cases involving mentally disordered persons, who may then be admitted to hospital or a treatment programme informally. However, a deeper issue is whether a prosecution should be stayed once it has been commenced. This powerful remedy has been held appropriate in cases of entrapment, and in one case of officially induced mistake of law.[137] The reason it is particularly appropriate in these types of case is that the involvement of officials in 'creating' the offence makes it

---

[136] See A. Ashworth, *Sentencing and Criminal Justice* (4th edn., 2005), 342–6.
[137] *Postermobile plc v Brent LBC, The Times*, 8 December 1997.

wrong for the prosecution to be heard by the courts at all. Providing a defence to liability would not be enough: it is so fundamentally wrong for the state to prosecute that D should not be put to the trouble of defending himself.

In this connection it is worth mentioning that some have put the case for a defence of 'social deprivation' or 'rotten social background' on the basis of diminished capacity. Thus it has been argued that social deprivation should excuse because it causes criminal behaviour; that socially deprived people may find themselves under pressure to commit crime, or in a situation where crime is the 'lesser evil'; or that socially deprived people who have been abused and maltreated by others have already suffered and therefore should not be punished further, or at least fully, for their own crimes.[138] It could be argued that some of these people are trapped in a criminal lifestyle, with scarcely more capacity for free choice than the person under duress, and that therefore society has no warrant for expecting them to achieve the normative expectations appropriate to others. Critics suggest that this confuses explanation with excuse: research may demonstrate a causal link between social deprivation and offending behaviour, but this does not deny the capacity or a fair opportunity to behave otherwise.[139] Judge Bazelon, a strong proponent of the 'social deprivation' defence, subscribed to the diminished capacity argument but put greater weight on the state's responsibility for the defendants' predicament: 'It is simply unjust to place people in dehumanizing social conditions, to do nothing about those conditions, and then to command those who suffer, "Behave— or else!"'[140] Whilst that might be true, the question is whether a doctrinal approach to the issue—providing a formal excuse—is the right response. A more flexibly humane response might be to make social deprivation a factor to be considered in the decision on the public interest in prosecuting a particular case, or in allowing a private prosecution to continue, as in (say) some cases of small-scale shoplifting or minor burglary.

FURTHER READING

R. A. Duff, *Answering for Crime* (Hart Publishing, 2007), ch 11.

J. Gardner, *Offences and Defences* (Oxford University Press, 2007), chs 4, 6 and 10.

H. L. A. Hart, *Punishment and Responsibility* (2nd edn., Oxford University Press, 2008), chs 2 and 7, and Introduction by John Gardner.

J. Horder, *Excusing Crime* (Oxford University Press, 2004), ch 3.

S. Kadish, *Blame and Punishment* (Macmillan, 1987), ch 10.

A. Norrie, *Crime, Reason and History* (3rd edn., Cambridge University Press, 2014), part IV.

A. Reed and others, *General Defences in Criminal Law: Domestic and Comparative Perspectives* (Ashgate, 2014).

V. Tadros, *Criminal Responsibility* (Oxford University Press, 2005), chs 10 and 11.

P. Westen, 'An Attitudinal Theory of Excuse' (2006) 25 *Law and Philosophy* 2810.

---

[138] See the judicious but critical assessment of these arguments by S. Morse, 'Deprivation and Desert', in W. C. Heffernan and J. Kleinig (eds), *From Social Justice to Criminal Justice* (2000).

[139] M. Moore, 'Causation and the Excuses' (1985) 73 Cal LR 1091.

[140] D. Bazelon, 'The Morality of the Criminal Law' (1976) 49 S Cal LR 3810.

8

HOMICIDE

There are a surprising number and variety of homicide and homicide-related offences in English law.[1] This chapter deals with the most important instances in which the criminal law prohibits and punishes behaviour that causes death or risks causing death. Murder, manslaughter, and several other homicide offences are discussed, and one recurrent issue here is fair labelling: does English law respond proportionately to the different degrees of culpability manifested in cases where death is caused?

8.1 DEATH AND FINALITY

Homicide may fairly be regarded as the most serious offence in the criminal calendar. It is sometimes argued that treason or terrorism are more serious offences, since they may strike at the very foundations of the State and its social organizations, but this line of thinking has little substance for two reasons. First, both treason and terrorism-related offences cover a large range of conduct, much of which is very remote from any harm done.[2] Treason-related offences, for example, include the common law offence of 'compounding treason'. This involves agreeing, in exchange for some benefit, not to prosecute someone who has committed treason. This is wrongdoing that in all probability would now be treated rather less dramatically either as bribery or as perverting the course of justice. Secondly, in speaking of an offence as 'more' or 'less'

---

[1] For a non-exhaustive list, see J. Horder, 'The Changing Face of the Law of Homicide', in J. Horder (ed.), *Homicide Law in Comparative Perspective* (2007).   [2] See, e.g., Terrorism Act 2000, s. 57.

serious one presupposes that offences are commensurable, that they can be effectively weighed against one another in a set of moral scales. That is not true of a comparison between homicide and treason (when this offence does not involve causing or threatening death). The two kinds of offence are qualitatively different, even if they are both very serious. It was said in Chapter 3.2 that life has ultimate value (value not derived from any higher value), and that in itself marks out homicide not just as serious but as a special kind of wrongdoing. Even in crimes of violence which leave some permanent physical disfigurement or psychological effects impinging on the intrinsic value in V's life, the victim retains that which is of ultimate value—his or her life.

Although many deaths arise from natural causes, and many others from illnesses and diseases, each year sees a large number of deaths caused by 'accidents', and also a number caused by acts or omissions which amount to some form of homicide in English law. In 2000, for example, the statistics showed that there were some 13,000 accidental deaths, of which some 3,200 occurred on the roads and the remainder either at work or in the home.[3] By comparison, the number of deaths recorded as criminal homicide is much smaller: it rose from around 600 per year at the start of the 1990s to around 700 per year in the early years of this century, since when it has fallen back to 638 in 2010–11 and to 550 in 2011–12.[4] This includes all the murders and manslaughters, but it leaves further questions to be confronted. For example, are we satisfied that the 700 deaths recorded as homicide are in fact more culpable than all, or even most, of the deaths recorded in other categories? In other words, does English criminal law pick out the most heinous forms of killing as murders and manslaughters, or are the boundaries frozen by tradition? For example, the number of offences of causing death by dangerous driving, causing death by careless driving whilst intoxicated, and causing death by careless driving now stands at around 400 per year:[5] some of these offences result in sentences more severe than those handed down for some forms of manslaughter,[6] which prompts the question whether these offences should be brought into manslaughter or other offences should be removed from that category.

We will see in sections 8.5 to 8.7 that Parliament has created four new homicide offences in the last few years. For one of them (corporate manslaughter) it has used the term manslaughter. For the others it has either used the terminology of 'causing death by' (the two offences introduced by the Road Safety Act 2006)[7] or provided no label at all (the offence under s. 5 of the Domestic Violence, Crime and Victims Act 2004).[8] Various questions may be raised: are these labelling decisions acceptable? Are these extensions of homicide law defensible, or is the distance between the defendant's fault and the consequent death too remote? What implications, if any, should the different labels have for sentence levels? These and other problems in the

---

[3] *Social Trends 2000* (2001).

[4] P. Taylor and S. Bond, *Crimes detected in England and Wales 2011/12* (2012), Table 1.

[5] Taylor and Bond, *Crimes detected in England and Wales 2011/12*, 409 in 2010–11 and 400 in 2011–12.

[6] Sentencing Guidelines Council, *Causing Death by Driving* (2008); M. Hirst, 'Causing Death by Driving and Other Offences: A Question of Balance' [2008] Crim LR 339.

[7] See section 8.7.   [8] See section 8.6.

reform of homicide law will be examined, after the contours of the present law have been discussed.

8.2 THE CONDUCT ELEMENT: CAUSING DEATH

English law distinguishes between the offences of murder and manslaughter, as we shall see, but the two crimes do have a common conduct element. It must be proved that the defendant's act or omission caused the death of a human being. The requirements of causation in the criminal law were discussed in Chapter 4.5, and already some problems came to light. Thus, the standard doctrine is that to shorten life by days is to cause death no less than shortening it by years, and this raises questions about the liability of doctors who administer drugs which they know will have the effect of shortening life, even though their primary purpose is to relieve pain. We noted that, in the rare trials of doctors for murder, the approach has been to direct the jury (in effect) to determine whether the doctor's primary motive was to relieve pain or to accelerate the patient's death[9]—an approach that conflicts with the orthodox approach to intention. It would be more consistent with prevailing doctrine for the courts to accept that a doctor may be clinically justified in administering a form of treatment he or she foresees as almost certain to hasten death (so long as death is not directly intended), but may have a suitably refined defence of clinical necessity in this situation, in spite of fulfilling both the conduct and fault elements for murder.[10]

At what points does an organism start and cease to be a person within the protection of the law of homicide? The current view, both in English law and in that of many other European countries,[11] is that a foetus is not yet a person and therefore cannot be the victim of homicide. Thus, in the difficult case of *Attorney-General's Reference (No. 3 of 1994)*,[12] where D had stabbed his pregnant girlfriend, also injuring the foetus, and the child was born prematurely and died some four months later from the wound, the House of Lords held that the doctrine of transferred intention could not be applied because it could only operate to transfer intention from one person to another, and not from a person to (what was at the relevant time) a foetus. Only when the child is born alive and has an existence independent of its mother does it come within the protection of the law of homicide, although there are other serious offences capable of commission before birth, notably child destruction (which carries a maximum of life imprisonment).[13] The

---

[9] Cf. the cases of Dr Bodkin Adams, Dr Moor, and Dr Cox, discussed in Chapter 4.5.

[10] See n 14 and accompanying text, where the Court of Appeal adopted this approach in the somewhat analogous 'conjoined twins' case.

[11] See the discussion by the European Court of Human Rights in *Vo v France* (2005) 40 EHRR 259, holding that a foetus does not come within the protection of Art. 2 of the Convention, which guarantees the right to life. Cf. E. Wicks, 'Terminating Life and Human Rights: The Fetus and the Neonate', in C. Erin and S. Ost (eds), *The Criminal Justice System and Health Care* (2007).

[12] [1998] AC 245; the doctrine of transferred intention, and the impact of this decision on it, was discussed in Chapter 5.5(d).

[13] Essentially, the killing of a foetus capable of being born alive: Infant Life Preservation Act 1929, s. 1.

point at which the protection of the law of homicide begins was a crucial factor in the case of *Re A (Conjoined Twins: Surgical Separation).*[14] The twins were conjoined and both would have died within months if left conjoined, but the stronger twin had good prospects of survival if surgical separation was performed. The Court of Appeal held that the weaker twin was sufficiently capable of independent breathing to be classed as a human being: she was independent of her mother, even though she was dependent on the vital organs of her twin for survival. Once it was decided that she was a person within the protection of the law of homicide, it followed that the operation to separate the twins would constitute the conduct element of murder in relation to the weaker twin (who would inevitably die shortly afterwards) unless there was some legal justification for the homicide, which the Court, invoking a version of necessity, held that there was.

It seems that a person will be treated as dead if he or she has become irreversibly 'brain dead', the definition of brain death being largely left to medical practice.[15] Thus switching off the life support machine of someone who already fulfils the criteria of brain death would not amount to the conduct element of murder. What if the patient does not fulfil those criteria, but is in a persistent vegetative state? This was the situation in the case of Tony Bland, who was being kept alive by food from a naso-gastric tube and by occasional administrations of antibiotics.[16] The House of Lords held that it would be lawful to discontinue treatment, thus allowing the patient to die. The elements of criminal homicide would not be present, they held, because discontinuing treatment was not causing death: it was allowing the patient to die of his pre-existing condition. Discontinuing treatment was properly regarded as an omission, not as an act. Further, it was not a criminal omission because there was no duty to treat the patient, given that there was no hope of recovery and it was no longer in his best interests to be kept alive. The controversial aspects of this decision cannot be pursued here.[17]

At common law there was also a rule that a person could only be convicted of a homicide offence if the death occurred within a year and a day of the accused's act or omission. Advances in medical science now make it possible for some victims to be kept alive for years after being injured or wounded, and the argument that the passage of years should not prevent a homicide prosecution was accepted by Parliament in the Law Reform (Year and a Day Rule) Act 1996, which abolished the old rule. The Act relies on prosecutorial discretion to prevent oppressive or unfair prosecutions: s. 2 provides that, where more than three years have elapsed since the injury and the defendant has already been convicted of a non-fatal offence, a prosecution for homicide may only be instituted with the Attorney General's consent. It would be helpful to see the publication of some principles or guidelines on which this discretion should be exercised.

---

[14] [2000] 4 All ER 961.   [15] *Malcherek and Steel* (1981) 73 Cr App R 173.

[16] *Airedale NHS Trust* v *Bland* [1993] AC 789.

[17] Cf. Chapter 4.4; J. Coggon, 'Ignoring the Moral and Intellectual Shape of the Law after *Bland*' (2007) 27 LS 110; A. McGee, 'Finding a Way Through the Ethical and Legal Maze: Withdrawal of Medical Treatment and Euthanasia' [2005] 13 Med LR 357.

8.3 DEFINING MURDER: THE INCLUSIONARY QUESTION

(a) THE PROCEDURAL CONTEXT

If causing death is to be regarded as the most serious harm, it would seem to follow that the most blameworthy form of homicide (the greatest wrong) should result in the most severe sentences imposed by the courts. Indeed, many systems of criminal law impose a mandatory sentence for murder (or whatever the highest form of homicide is called in that system). In some jurisdictions this is a mandatory sentence of death.[18] In the United Kingdom the penalty for murder is the mandatory sentence of life imprisonment.[19] The existence of the mandatory sentence has a significant impact on the shape and content of the remainder of the law of homicide: as we shall see, the dividing line between murder and manslaughter may be affected by the inability of courts to give different sentences for murder, and there are those who believe that the strongest reason for retaining provocation or 'loss of control' as a partial defence to murder is that otherwise a judge could not reflect degrees of culpability in the sentence (for murder).

The mandatory sentence of life imprisonment is divided into three portions: the first is now known as the minimum term (formerly, the tariff period), and is intended to reflect the relative gravity of the particular offence. It is a term that is served in full, and the early release provisions applicable to all determinate custodial sentences do not apply here. Once the minimum term expires, the second part consists of imprisonment based on considerations of public protection, and a murderer who is thought still to present a danger may be detained until the Parole Board decides that it is safe to order release. The third portion is after release from prison: the offender remains on licence for the rest of his life. Although until 2003 the Home Secretary had the final say on the minimum term and ultimate release, those decisions have now passed to the courts and the Parole Board respectively.[20] However, the government wished to fetter the judges so as to ensure that minimum terms were not set too low. Thus s. 269 of the Criminal Justice Act 2003 requires a court, when setting the minimum term to be served by a person convicted of murder, to have regard to the principles set out in Sch 21 of the Act. The structure of that Schedule is to indicate four starting points:

- (for those over 21 at the time of the offence) a whole life minimum term for exceptionally serious cases, such as premeditated killings of two people, sexual

---

[18] There are also some jurisdictions in which capital punishment is discretionary. See generally R. Hood and C. Hoyle, *The Death Penalty: a World-wide Perspective* (4th edn., 2008).

[19] The process of abolishing the death penalty was completed by s. 36 of the Crime and Disorder Act 1998 (dealing with treason and piracy), thus ensuring compliance with Protocol 6 to the European Convention.

[20] The change resulted from the decision of the European Court of Human Rights in *Stafford* v *United Kingdom* (2002) 35 EHRR 1121 and subsequently of the House of Lords in *R (on the application of Anderson)* v *Secretary of State for the Home Department* [2003] 1 AC 837, fundamentally because the Home Secretary cannot be regarded as an 'independent and impartial tribunal' as required by Art. 6 of the Convention.

or sadistic child murders, or politically, religiously, or ideologically motivated murders;

- (for those over 18 at the time of the offence) thirty years for particularly serious cases such as murders of police or prison officers on duty, murders involving fire-arms or explosives, sexual or sadistic killings, or murders aggravated by racial or sexual orientation, or cases that would have attracted a 'whole life' term starting point, had the offender been 21 at the time of the offence;

- (for those over 18 at the time of the offence) twenty-five years for murder com-mitted with a knife or other weapon intentionally taken to the scene in order to commit the crime, or to have the weapon available for use, and it was used;

- (for those over 18 at the time of the offence) fifteen years for other murders not falling within either of the higher categories.

It should be borne in mind that to compare the minimum term with a determinate sentence one should double it: in other words, a minimum term of fifteen years is the equivalent of a determinate sentence of about thirty years.[21] However, the language of Sch 21 leaves considerable latitude to the sentencing judge. Although criteria are enu-merated for the whole life and thirty-year starting points, they are expressed as factors that would 'normally' indicate such a sentence. There is then provision for the court to take account of any further relevant factors, and an explicit statement that 'detailed consideration of aggravating and mitigating factors may result in a minimum term of any length (whatever the starting point)'. The Lord Chief Justice amended the previous guidance to reflect the 2003 provisions when he issued a Practice Direction in May 2004.[22] He has subsequently emphasized that s. 269(3) merely states that the judge must specify the minimum term that 'the court considers appropriate', and indeed went on to say that so long as the judge bore in mind the principles set out in Sch 21, 'he is not bound to follow them'—although an explanation for departing from them should be given.[23] Nonetheless, anomalies can arise. Suppose that a farmer's wife chooses to accede to her terminally ill husband's request by shooting him with a shotgun. On the face of it, in such a case, thirty years is the indicated minimum and premeditation may take the minimum term even higher, although the sentencing judge might have to bal-ance these factors against the mitigating factors mentioned in para. 11(d) and 11(f) of Sch 21, namely provocation brought about by prolonged stress, and the fact that the killing was intended as an act of mercy.[24]

The system introduced by the 2003 Act means that judges can vary the minimum term to reflect degrees of culpability in murder, but the overall framework of the

---

[21] As noted by Lord Woolf CJ in *Sullivan* (n 23). This is because a determinate sentence of thirty years means fifteen years in prison (followed by fifteen years on supervised licence), whereas a minimum term for murder is not subject to the general provisions on early release and is served in full.

[22] *Practice Direction (Crime: Mandatory Life Sentences) (No. 2)* [2004] 1 WLR 2551.

[23] *Sullivan* [2005] 1 Cr App R (S) 308.

[24] See the examples discussed by the Law Commission in LCCP 177, *A New Homicide Act for England and Wales? A Consultation Paper* (2005), paras. 1.112–18.

mandatory sentence means that judges cannot set the maximum term to be served, as they do for other serious offences. On expiry of the minimum term, release is determined on public protection grounds by the Parole Board. This constraining effect of the mandatory life sentence means that the justifications for retaining it must be scrutinized afresh. One argument in favour of the mandatory life sentence is that it amounts to a symbolic indication of the unique heinousness of murder. It places the offender under the State's control, as it were, for the remainder of his or her life. This is often linked with a supposed denunciatory effect—the idea that the mandatory life sentence denounces murder as emphatically as possible—and with the supposed general deterrent effect of declaring that there is no way of avoiding the life-long effect of this sentence. It might also be argued that the mandatory life sentence makes a substantial contribution to public safety.

None of these arguments is notably strong, let alone conclusive. The mandatory penalty does indeed serve to mark out murder from other crimes, but whether the definition of murder is sufficiently refined to capture the worst killings, and only the worst killings, remains to be discussed. As we shall see in section 8.3(c), it is sufficient for murder if D killed without intent to kill but with intent to cause serious harm, and the lesser intent is merely a mitigating factor from the various starting points in Sch 21 of the 2003 Act. Whether the life sentence is regarded as a sufficient denunciation depends on the public's perception of what life imprisonment means: if it is widely believed that it results in an average of about ten years' imprisonment, the effect will be somewhat blunted, even if the belief is untrue. The same applies to the general deterrent argument: its effectiveness depends on whether the penalty for murder affects the calculations of potential killers at all, and, if it does, whether the prospect of life imprisonment influences them more than the alternative of a long, fixed-term sentence.

As for public protection, this depends on executive decisions with regard to release; it raises the question whether it is necessary for public protection to keep most 'lifers' in for so long.[25] It is sometimes claimed that murderers should be treated differently because they are particularly dangerous: anyone who chooses to kill once can choose to kill again. But this is an over-generalization that takes little account of the situational variations of murder cases. Moreover, the argument will seem less persuasive when we have discussed cases of manslaughter by reason of diminished responsibility: where a murder is reduced to manslaughter, the judge has a wide sentencing discretion and may, according to the facts of the case, select a determinate prison sentence, a hospital order, or life imprisonment. There is no evidence that those who kill and are convicted of manslaughter by reason of diminished responsibility are less dangerous than those convicted of murder, and yet the judge has sentencing discretion in one case and not in the other.

[25] On this, see the cautious words of S. Brody and R. Tarling, *Taking Offenders out of Circulation* (Home Office Research Study No. 64, 1980), 33.

[26] HL Select Committee on Murder and Life Imprisonment (1988–9), HL Paper 78, paras. 101–22, adopting the reasoning of D. A. Thomas, 'Form and Function in Criminal Law', in P. R. Glazebrook (ed.), *Reshaping the Criminal Law* (1978); cf. also M. D. Farrier, 'The Distinction between Murder and Manslaughter in its Procedural Context' (1976) 39 MLR 414.

Considerations of this kind led the House of Lords Committee on Murder and Life Imprisonment to recommend the abolition of the mandatory sentence for murder.[26] A committee chaired by the former Lord Chief Justice, Lord Lane, reached the same conclusion in 1993.[27] Both committees favoured judicial sentencing discretion to mark the relative heinousness of the murder, subject to review on appeal.[28] A discretionary sentence of life imprisonment would still be available for those cases in which it was thought appropriate. Such a reform could bring improvements in natural justice without loss of public protection, but successive governments have been reluctant to contemplate the abrogation of the mandatory sentence for murder, and the latest reform proposals are premised on the retention of the mandatory penalty.[29]

(b) THE STRUCTURE OF HOMICIDE LAW

The structure of the law of homicide varies across jurisdictions,[30] and recent proposals for reforming English law will be discussed later. It must be said that the current structure of the English law of homicide is rather strange. Although formally there are two offences—murder and manslaughter—the latter includes two distinct varieties: 'voluntary' manslaughter (killings which would be murder but for the existence of defined extenuating circumstances); and 'involuntary' manslaughter (killings that are in fact the product of voluntary conduct, but for which there is no need to prove any awareness of the risk of death being caused, but for which there is nonetheless thought to be sufficient fault to justify liability for a killing). The arguments therefore tend to focus on three borderline questions: What is the minimum fault required for conviction of murder? In what circumstances should murder be reduced to manslaughter? What is the minimum fault required for a conviction of manslaughter?

(c) REQUIREMENTS FOR MURDER

In English criminal law, satisfying the fault requirement for murder involves the prosecution in proof that D possessed one of two states of mind: either an intent to kill, or an intent to cause grievous bodily harm. What do these requirements mean? Do they extend the definition of murder too far, or are they too narrow?

An intent to kill may be regarded as the most obvious and least controversial form of fault element for murder. In part, though, that judgment hinges on the meaning given to 'intent' in the criminal law. The meaning of intent has been the subject of a number

---

[27] *Committee on the Penalty for Homicide* (1993).

[28] See further M. Wasik, 'Sentencing for Homicide', in A. Ashworth and B. Mitchell (eds), *Rethinking English Homicide Law* (2000).

[29] Law Com No. 304, *Murder, Manslaughter and Infanticide* (2006), and Ministry of Justice, Consultation Paper 19, *Murder, Manslaughter and Infanticide: proposals for reform of the law* (2008).

[30] See J. Horder (ed.), *Homicide Law in Comparative Perspective* (2007).

[31] See the discussion of *Moloney* [1985] AC 905, *Hancock and Shankland* [1986] AC 455, and *Woollin* [1999] 1 AC 82 in Chapter 6.5(b).

of House of Lords decisions,[31] and yet the definition is still not absolutely clear. A broad definition would be that a person *intends* to kill if it is his or her aim to kill by the act or omission charged, in the sense that he or she would regard it as a failure if V was not killed by the act or omission (although the courts do not themselves use this so-called 'test of failure', which is merely a helpful explanatory tool). In practice, the 'golden rule' is the first to be applied—that intention should be left without description or definition in most cases, and the full definition should be reserved for cases where D claims that his purpose was something other than to cause serious injury. This is because the full definition includes a further possibility, in addition to proof of aim or purpose of killing on D's part. This is proof that D foresaw that V's death was virtually certain to follow from his or her act or omission, whether or not V's death was aimed at (i.e. whether or not D would have regarded V's survival of the incidence as a 'failure' on D's part to achieve his or her goal). If the jury is sure that D acted with this state of mind, they are entitled to infer that D intended to kill (we will look further at this issue).

To this extension of the meaning of intent must also be added that, as was mentioned above, it is sufficient for the prosecution to show that, in killing V, D intended to cause grievous (serious) harm to V, and hence it will be enough for the prosecution to show that D foresaw grievous bodily harm as virtually certain to occur. So, in a case where D has killed V, in the absence of any justification or excuse:

1. if D intended to kill: *murder*;

2. if D intended to cause grievous (serious) bodily harm: *murder*;

3. if D foresaw death or grievous bodily harm as virtually certain to occur: *murder*, if the jury infers that D intended to kill or cause grievous bodily harm.

A fairly typical set of facts is provided by *Nedrick*,[32] where D had a grudge against a woman and had threatened to 'burn her out'. One night he went to her house, poured paraffin through the letter-box and onto the front door, and set it alight. One of the woman's children died in the ensuing fire. When asked why he did it, D replied: 'Just to wake her up and frighten her'. A defence of this kind, a claim that the purpose was only to frighten and not to cause harm, requires the full definition of intention (i.e. including the reference to foresight of death or grievous bodily harm as a virtual certainty) to be put to the jury. The question is: granted that D's aim was to frighten, did he nonetheless realize that it was virtually certain that his act would cause death or grievous bodily harm to someone? The jury should answer this, as in all criminal cases, by drawing inferences from the evidence in the case and from the surrounding circumstances.

As was pointed out in Chapter 6.5(b), the decision of the House of Lords in *Woollin*[33] leaves some leeway in the application of the test by holding that, where the jury concludes that D foresaw that death or grievous bodily harm was virtually certain to ensue, it is 'entitled to find' that D had the intention necessary for murder. The test

---

[32] (1986) 83 Cr App R 267.   [33] [1999] 1 AC 82.

remains a permissive principle of evidence rather than a rule of substantive law, although the Court of Appeal has accepted that, once there is an appreciation of virtual certainty of death, 'there is very little to choose between a rule of evidence and one of substantive law'.[34] However, the test is so formulated in order to leave a degree of indeterminacy,[35] and this could allow juries to make broader moral or social judgments when deciding whether the fault element for murder is fulfilled in a case where death (or grievous bodily harm) was known to be virtually certain.[36]

What about the alternative element in the definition, an intent to cause grievous bodily harm? This has considerable practical importance, since this is all that the prosecution has to prove in order to obtain a verdict of guilty of murder. It must be shown that the defendant intended (which, again, includes both acting in order to cause the result and knowledge of practical certainty) to cause 'really serious injury' to someone, although the use of the word 'really' is not required in all cases.[37] The House of Lords confirmed this rule in Cunningham:[38] D struck his victim on the head a number of times with a chair, causing injuries from which the victim died a week later. D maintained throughout that he had not intended to kill, but there was evidence from which the jury could infer—and did infer—that he intended to cause grievous bodily harm. The House of Lords upheld D's conviction for murder: an intent to cause really serious injury is sufficient for murder, without any proof that the defendant even contemplated the possibility that death would result.

Does the 'grievous bodily harm' rule extend the definition of murder too far? If the point of distinguishing murder from manslaughter is to mark out the most heinous group of killings for the extra stigma of a murder conviction, it can be argued that the 'grievous bodily harm' rule draws the line too low. The rule departs from the principle of correspondence (see Chapter 6.4(a)), namely that the fault element in a crime should relate to the consequences prohibited by that crime. By allowing an intent to cause grievous bodily harm to suffice for a murder conviction, the law is turning its most serious offence into a constructive crime. Is there any justification for 'constructing' a murder conviction out of this lesser intent?

One argument is that there is no significant moral difference between someone who chooses to cause really serious injury and someone who sets out to kill. No one can predict whether a serious injury will result in death—that may depend on the victim's physique, on the speed of an ambulance, on the distance from the hospital, and on a range of other medical and individual matters unrelated to D's culpability. If one person chooses to cause serious injury to another, he or she has already crossed

[34] Per Rix LJ in Matthews and Alleyne [2003] 2 Cr App R 30, at 45.
[35] As the Law Commission has accepted: LCCP 177, A New Homicide Act for England and Wales? (2005), para. 3.8.
[36] See the discussion of the views of N. Lacey and A. Norrie, Chapter 6.5(b)(ii). The Law Commission recommends that the common law approach in Woollin should form the basis of a new law: Law Com No. 304, 57–8.
[37] Cf. Janjua [1999] 1 Cr App R 91, where there had been a stabbing with a five-inch knife, with Bollom [2004] 2 Cr App R 6, where the Court of Appeal approved a definition in terms of 'seriously and grievously to interfere with the health or comfort of the victim'.   [38] [1982] AC 566.

one of the ultimate moral thresholds and has shown a sufficiently wanton disregard for life as to warrant the label 'murder' if death results. The counter-arguments, which would uphold the principle of correspondence, are that breach of that principle is unnecessary when the amplitude of the crime of manslaughter lies beneath murder, and also that the definition of grievous bodily harm includes a number of injuries which are most unlikely to put the victim's life at risk. In the leading case of *Cunningham* Lord Edmund-Davies (dissenting) gave the example of breaking someone's arm: that is a really serious injury, but one which is unlikely to endanger the victim's life.[39] So in practice the 'grievous bodily harm' rule goes beyond the point at which the arguments of its supporters still carry weight. In its charging standards, the Crown Prosecution Service gives the following account of when it is appropriate to charge D with the offence of wounding with intent to do grievous (serious) bodily harm, an account that will also serve as a guide to cases in which, if V dies, it will be appropriate to charge murder:

- injury resulting in permanent disability, loss of sensory function or visible disfigurement;
- broken or displaced limbs or bones, including fractured skull, compound fractures, broken cheek bone, jaw, ribs, etc.; injuries which cause substantial loss of blood, usually necessitating a transfusion or result in lengthy treatment or incapacity;
- serious psychiatric injury. As with assault occasioning actual bodily harm, appropriate expert evidence is essential to prove the injury.[40]

It must be recognized that many other legal systems also have a definition of murder that goes beyond an intent to kill.[41] What other approaches might be taken? The fault element for many serious offences is intent or recklessness: why should this not suffice for murder? One question is whether all killings in which the defendant is aware of a risk of death are sufficiently serious to warrant the term 'murder'. An answer sometimes given is that they are not, because a driver who overtakes on a bend, knowingly taking the risk that there is no vehicle travelling in the opposite direction, should not be labelled a murderer if a collision and death happen to ensue.[42] This example assumes that sympathy for motorists will overwhelm any tendency to logical analysis: the question is whether motorists are ever justified in knowingly taking risks with other people's lives. Yet if the example is modified a little, so that the overtaking is on a country road at night and the risk is known to be slight, it becomes questionable whether the causing of death in these circumstances should be labelled in the same

---

[39] [1982] AC 582; see also the criticism by Lord Mustill in *Attorney-General's Reference (No. 3 of 1994)* [1998] AC 245 at 258–9, and by Lord Steyn in *Powell and Daniels* [1999] AC 1, 15.

[40] <www.cps.gov.uk/legal/l_to_o/offences_against_the_person/>

[41] Both Federal and state law in the US extends murder beyond an intention to kill; that is also true of, for example, the Indian Penal Code, and of most states in Australia.

[42] An example given by Lord Goff, 'The Mental Element in the Crime of Murder' (1988) 104 LQR 30, at 48.

way as, say, an intentional killing by a hired assassin. This is not to suggest that motorists, in particular, should be treated differently. The point is rather that, even though knowingly taking risks with other people's lives is usually unjustifiable, taking a slight risk is less serious than intentionally causing death. In discussing the boundaries of murder, we are concerned with classification, not exculpation.

To classify all reckless killings as murder might be too broad, but the point remains that some reckless killings may be thought no less heinous than intentional killings. Can a satisfactory line be drawn here? One approach would be to draw the line by reference to the degree of probability. Murder would be committed in those situations where D caused death by an act or omission which he knew had death as the probable or highly probable result. A version of this test of foresight of high probability is used in several other European countries;[43] it was introduced into English law by the decision in *Hyam* v *DPP*,[44] but abandoned in *Moloney*[45] on grounds of uncertainty. A related approach, applicable to certain terrorist situations, would be to maintain that someone who intends to create a risk of death or serious injury endorses those consequences to the extent that, if they occur, they can fairly be said to be intended.[46]

A second approach is to frame the law in such a way as to make it clear that the court should make a moral judgment of the gravity of the defendant's conduct. Section 210.2 of the Model Penal Code includes within murder those reckless killings which manifest 'extreme indifference to the value of human life'.[47] Scots law treats as murder killings with 'wicked recklessness', a phrase which directs courts to evaluate the circumstances of the killing.[48] Both the Model Penal Code test and the Scots test may be reduced to circularity, however, for when one asks how extreme or how wicked the recklessness should be, the only possible answer is: 'wicked or extreme enough to justify the stigma of a murder conviction'. Admittedly, the Model Penal Code does contain a list of circumstances which may amount to extreme indifference, which assists the courts and increases the predictability of verdicts in a way that Scots law does not. Having said that, under both approaches there is no precise way of describing those non-intentional killings which are as heinous as intentional killings. The advocates of this approach argue that the law of murder has such significance that the principle of maximum certainty should yield to the ability of courts to apply the label in ways more sensitive to moral/social evaluations of conduct. Opponents argue that the principle of maximum certainty is needed here specifically to reduce the risk of verdicts based on discriminatory or irrelevant factors, such as distaste for

[43] See, e.g., A. du Bois-Pedain, 'Intentional Killings: The German Law', in J. Horder, *Homicide Law in Comparative Perspective* (2007).

[44] [1975] AC 55.   [45] [1985] AC 905.

[46] A. Pedain, 'Intention and the Terrorist Example' [2003] Crim LR 579.

[47] This was recommended as one ground for a murder conviction by the Law Reform Commission of Ireland, *Homicide: Murder and Involuntary Manslaughter* (2008), also requiring that D took a 'substantial and unjustifiable risk' with another's life.

[48] See P. R. Ferguson and C. McDiarmid, *Scots Criminal Law: A Critical Analysis* (2nd edn., 2014), 9.12–9.13.

the defendant's background, allegiance, or other activities, especially if the mandatory life sentence is at issue.[49]

A third, more precise formulation now favoured by the Law Commission is that a killing should be classified as murder in those situations where there is an intention to cause serious injury coupled with awareness of the risk of death.[50] Neither an intention to cause serious injury nor recklessness as to death should be sufficient on its own, but together they could operate so as to restrict one another and perhaps to produce a test which both satisfies the criterion of certainty and marks out some heinous but non-intended killings.

A fourth approach, adopted by English law until 1957 and still in force in many American jurisdictions, is some form of felony-murder rule: anyone who kills during the course of an inherently dangerous felony should be convicted of murder.[51] Thus stated, there is no reference to the defendant's intention or awareness of the risks: the fact that D has chosen to commit rape, robbery, or another serious offence, and has caused death thereby, is held to constitute sufficient moral grounds for placing the killing in the highest category. Plainly, this is a form of constructive criminal liability: the murder conviction is constructed out of the ingredients of a lesser offence. Presumably the justification is that D has already crossed a high moral/social threshold in choosing to commit such a serious offence, and should therefore be held liable for whatever consequences ensue, however accidental they may be.[52] The objections would be reduced if awareness of the risk of death was also required: in other words, if the test were the commission of a serious offence of violence plus recklessness as to death. The effect of that test would be to pick out those reckless killings which occurred when D had already manifested substantial moral and legal culpability, and to classify them as murder.

Four alternative approaches have been described, and others could be added. The point is that the traditional concept of intention does not, of itself, appear to be sufficiently well focused to mark out those killings which are the most heinous. The law must resort to some kind of moral and social evaluation of conduct if it is to identify and separate out the gravest killings. Some would defend the GBH rule on this basis as a form of 'rough justice', and that argument could be extended to some of the cases in the fourth category above, as William Wilson has proposed.[53]

[49] This is particularly relevant to killings resulting from the activities of (allegedly) terrorist groups. The HL Select Committee on Murder etc., para. 76, concluded that: 'It is neither satisfactory nor desirable to distort [general principles] in order to deal with the reckless terrorist and other "wickedly" reckless killers, who will, in any event, be liable to imprisonment for life [i.e. for manslaughter].'

[50] Law Com No. 304, Part 3, following the CLRC 14th Report (1980), para. 31, adopted in the Draft Criminal Code cl. 54(1) and supported by the HL Select Committee on Murder etc., para. 71.

[51] See C. Finkelstein, 'Two Models of Murder: Patterns of Criminalisation in the United States', in J. Horder, *Homicide Law in Comparative Perspective* (2007).

[52] In their empirical research, P. Robinson and J. Darley found that most of their sample agreed that an accidental killing during a robbery should be punished more severely than other negligent killings, but they did not agree with classifying it as murder: *Justice, Liability and Blame* (1995), 169–81. As the authors express it, the majority view was in favour of a felony-manslaughter rule, not a felony-murder rule.

[53] W. Wilson, 'Murder and the Structure of Homicide', in A. Ashworth and B. Mitchell (eds), *Rethinking English Homicide Law* (2000).

At the other end of the spectrum were the Law Commission's provisional proposals, which proposed to deal with the issue by means of a distinction between first degree murder and second degree murder. The mandatory life sentence would remain for first degree murder, the definition of which would be refined by confining it to cases where there is an intent to kill.[54] Second degree murder would then include cases where D is proved to have killed while intending to do serious harm, defined more tightly than in existing law,[55] and also cases where D is proved to have killed with reckless indifference as to causing death. Second degree murder would carry a maximum sentence of life imprisonment, together with the label 'murder', and is an attempt to allow some 'moral elbow-room' in the definition of murder outside the mandatory penalty.[56] However, in its final report the Law Commission sought a compromise that enlarges first degree murder beyond intention to kill and yet does not encounter the objections made against the GBH rule. In effect, the Commission adopts the third approach above, arguing that first degree murder should extend beyond an intent to kill to those cases where there is an intent to cause serious injury coupled with an awareness of a serious risk of causing death.[57] The Law Commission's view is that cases involving both these elements are morally equivalent to cases of intent to kill, or at least are closer to those cases than to cases placed in the other offence of murder in the second degree.

What cases would fall within murder in the second degree? The Law Commission identified two types of case—where D kills with an intention to do serious injury (those not accompanied by an awareness of the risk of death and therefore not within murder in the first degree), and where D 'intended to cause injury or fear or risk of injury aware that his or her conduct involved a serious risk of causing death'. The latter category is designed to capture bad cases of reckless killing and to sweep them into an offence with the label murder (in the second degree). One issue with this provision is whether the breadth of the concepts of 'injury' and 'serious risk' enables the proposal to distinguish fairly between these cases and others that fall into manslaughter. Another issue is whether the introduction of the provision would place too many choices between closely related mental states that the jury must juggle, in deciding whether D is guilty of first degree, second degree murder, or manslaughter. There is a considerable

---

[54] Research shows moderate public support for the mandatory life sentence, but some disagreement about the types of homicide for which the measure is appropriate: see LCCP 177, *A New Homicide Act?*, App A, 'Report on Public Survey of Murder and Mandatory Sentencing in Criminal Homicides', by B. Mitchell. See now B. Mitchell and J. V. Roberts, 'Public Attitudes to the Mandatory life Sentence for Murder: Putting Received Wisdom to the Empirical Test' [2011] Crim LR 456.

[55] For the broad definition now adopted, see n 42; the new definition would relate serious harm to either endangering life or causing permanent or long-term damage to physical or mental functioning—LCCP 177, *A New Homicide Act?*, para. 3.144.

[56] For discussion, see W. Wilson, 'The Structure of Criminal Homicide' [2006] Crim LR 471, and A. Norrie, 'Between Orthodox Subjectivism and Moral Contextualism: Intention and the Consultation Paper' [2006] Crim LR 486.

[57] Law Com No. 304, Part 3, discussed by A. Ashworth, 'Principles, Pragmatism and the Law Commission's Recommendations on Homicide Law Reform' [2007] Crim LR 333. Cf. Law Reform Commission of Ireland, *Homicide: Murder and Involuntary Manslaughter* (2008), recommending retention of an intent to cause serious injury as sufficient for murder.

likelihood that, were the provision introduced, there would be more disagreements between individual jurors as to which offence category (if any) it fell into, and hence more cases in which the jury failed to agree on a verdict. This would mean that a fresh trial would have to be ordered, with all the witnesses having to given their evidence again, with no guarantee that a fresh jury would be more likely to agree on a verdict.[58] In any event, the government indicated that it was not minded to pursue the first degree/second degree distinction, and would be focusing on reform of the partial defences to murder.[59]

8.4 DEFINING MURDER: THE EXCLUSIONARY QUESTION

Even in a legal system which had the narrowest of definitions of murder—say, premeditated intention to kill—there would still be an argument that some cases which fulfil that criterion should have their labels reduced from murder to manslaughter because of extenuating circumstances. Just as the discussion of the *inclusionary* aspect of the definition of murder travelled beyond the concepts of intent and recklessness, so the discussion of the *exclusionary* aspect (i.e. which killings fulfilling the definition should be classified as manslaughter rather than murder) must consider the circumstances in which the killing took place and other matters bearing on the culpability of the killer.

(a) THE MANDATORY PENALTY

The existence of the mandatory penalty has significant effects on the shape of the substantive law of homicide. One argument is that the main reason for allowing such matters as loss of self-control to reduce murder to manslaughter is to avoid the mandatory penalty for murder: if the mandatory penalty were abolished, it would be sufficient to take account of loss of self-control when sentencing for murder. However, this argument neglects the symbolic function of the labels applied by the law and by courts to criminal conduct. Surely it is possible that a jury might decline to convict of murder a person who intentionally killed following a loss of self-control, even though they knew that the judge could give a lenient sentence, because they wished to signify the reduction in the defendant's culpability by using the less stigmatic label of manslaughter. Since there are two offences—and particularly in jurisdictions where there are three or more grades of homicide—surely it is right and proper to use the lesser offence to mark significant differences in culpability. This may be seen as an application of the principle of fair labelling. When a jury takes the decision between the two grades of homicide, this may also assist the judge in sentencing, and help the public to understand the

---

[58] For criticism along these lines, see R. Taylor, 'The Nature of Partial Defences and the Coherence of (Second Degree) Murder' [2007] Crim LR 345.

[59] Ministry of Justice, *Murder, manslaughter and infanticide: proposals for reform of the law* (2008), para. 9.

sentence imposed.[60] A second major effect of the mandatory penalty for murder derives from the long minimum terms (plus the detention for public protection and then
the licence for life) imposed for murder, as compared with the considerably shorter
sentences for manslaughter upon loss of self-control or by reason of diminished responsibility. Thus the sentencing guidelines for manslaughter upon loss of self-control
indicate a starting point of twelve years' imprisonment where minimal provocation led
to a loss of self-control is low, and starting points of eight and three years for more serious provocation leading to a loss of self-control.[61] The difference between the highest
starting point for manslaughter following a loss of self-control—twelve years (release
on licence after six years)—and the lowest starting point for murder—fifteen years
(which means fifteen years at least before release on licence)—is so considerable that,
in practice, 'there is the greatest of pressure to distort the concepts of provocation and
diminished responsibility to accommodate deserving or hard cases. This pressure will
continue as long as each case of murder carries the mandatory life sentence.'[62]

(b) MANSLAUGHTER FOLLOWING A LOSS OF SELF-CONTROL

Killings are generally thought to be less heinous when they are the result of grave provocation, or of a fear of violence stemming from words or conduct on V's part. Before
important legislation in 2009, only provocation (not a fear of violence) had historically
been accepted as a ground for reducing to manslaughter a killing which would otherwise be murder.[63] From time to time, there continue to be cases where the provocation
is so gross and so strong that a court imposes a very short prison sentence or even a
suspended sentence for the manslaughter—typically, cases where a wife, son, or daughter kills a persistently bullying husband or father. In cases of this type (amongst others), though, the motivation may not be provocation so much as a fear of continuing
violence, but where—for one reason or another—the complete defence of self-defence
or action in prevention of crime cannot succeed. The Coroners and Justice Act 2009
sought to address this gap in the law. The 2009 Act put a fear of serious violence on a
par with provocation, as a basis for reducing the offence from murder to manslaughter,
so long as—putting on one side a number of restrictions and qualifications—in either
case (or where both are pleaded together) D acted during a loss of self-control. The issues here are whether either or both of these 'partial' defences (defences to murder that
reduce the crime to manslaughter) have any place in the modern law, or contrariwise,
whether there is a case for extending them.[64]

[60] This was the view of the HL Select Committee on Murder etc., paras. 80–3, agreeing with the CLRC,
14th Report (1980), para. 76.

[61] Sentencing Guidelines Council, *Manslaughter upon Provocation* (2005).

[62] Law Com No. 290, *Partial Defences to Murder* (2004), para. 2.68.

[63] A fear of violence featured sporadically in explanations for the existence of the provocation defence
from the seventeenth century onwards, but was not clearly and authoritatively accepted as such.

[64] See now, J. Horder, *Homicide and the Politics of Law Reform* (2012), ch 8; A. Reed and M. Bohlander
(eds), *Loss of Self-control and Diminished Responsibility: Domestic, Comparative and International Perspectives*
(2011).

The 2009 Act made highly significant changes to the law governing the partial de-fences. However, it is helpful to start with a brief explanation of the old structure, built from a mixture of common law and legislation, that was replaced by the 2009 Act: to a considerable extent, the 2009 Act still relies on that old structure. Before the coming into force of the 2009 Act, the doctrine of provocation (as it was commonly known) had two main elements. These emerge in s. 3 of the Homicide Act 1957, which the new law replaces:

> Where on a charge of murder there is evidence on which the jury can find that the person charged was provoked (whether by things done or by things said or by both together) to lose his self-control, the question whether the provocation was enough to make a reason-able man do as he did shall be left to be determined by the jury; and in determining that question the jury shall take into account everything both done and said according to the effect which, in their opinion, it would have on a reasonable man.

This was not intended to be a complete statement of the law on provocation, but it settled the form of the main requirements. First, there had to be evidence that D was provoked to lose self-control and kill. Then the jury had to decide whether the provo-cation in question was enough to make a 'reasonable man' who had lost self-control do as D did. Importantly, D did not bear the burden of proving any of this him or herself. In a murder trial, when evidence of provocation was given or emerged in the course of the trial, the burden of showing beyond reasonable doubt that the requirements of s. 3 were *not* satisfied lay upon the prosecution.[65] If the prosecution failed to discharge that burden to that standard, D was entitled to an acquittal on the murder charge on the grounds of provocation, and would be convicted of manslaughter instead. In prac-tice, then, in any case where evidence of provocation became relevant, the prosecu-tion would focus on one, or both, of two things. First, the prosecution could seek to convince the jury that D never lost control, however grave the provocation might have been. Secondly, the prosecution could seek to convince the jury that, even if D did lose self-control, the provocation was not of such a grave kind that it might have moved even a reasonable person to lose self-control and kill with the fault element for murder.

(i) *The Subjective Requirement and its Replacement:* The first requirement of the pre-2009 qualified defence of provocation was predominantly subjective—evidence that D was provoked to lose self-control and kill. Without this, there would be no way of excluding planned revenge killings as a response to provocation, and the argument is that they should be excluded from the defence. A person who coolly plans a murder as a response to an affront or a wrong is defying the law in so doing, and (barring the applicability of some other defence) there can be no excuse for that. By contrast, the killer provoked to lose self-control is, for the duration of the loss of self-control, not fully master of his or her mind, and so—in theory—is not deliberately defying the law in the same way. As Richard Holton and Stephen Shute argue, the paradigm case is

---

[65] See *Acott* [1997] 2 Cr App R 94.

where D normally had sufficient self-control to suppress violent inclinations, but the provocation aroused those inclinations and undermined D's controls.[66] In the old case of *Duffy*,[67] Devlin J (before he became Lord Devlin) expressed this idea in the following famous passage:

> [C]ircumstances which induce a desire for revenge are inconsistent with provocation, since the conscious formulation of a desire for revenge means that a person has had time to think, to reflect, and that would negative a sudden temporary loss of self-control, which is of the essence of provocation.

In what ways has this requirement for a loss of self-control been altered by the reforms effected by the 2009 Act?

The wording of s. 3 of the Homicide Act 1957 (the residual elements of the common law having been abolished) has now been replaced by ss. 54 and 55 of the 2009 Act. These sections introduce a partial defence renamed 'loss of control'. The defence includes a new version of the old 'provocation' defence (the second limb of the defence), but also includes a new defence focused on a loss of self-control stemming from a fear of serious violence at V's hands (the first limb of the defence). In relation to the subjective requirement, the new law retains the requirement that D's acts or omissions in doing or being party to a killing resulted from D's loss of self-control (s. 54(1) of 2009 Act).[68] The 2009 Act also re-states in a new form two ancient common law doctrines that served to restrict the defence in important ways. The first, just mentioned, is that the defence of loss of self-control will not apply where D acts on, 'a considered desire for revenge' (s. 54(4)). The second is that the defence will not apply if D's loss of self-control stemmed from something that D him or herself incited to be done or said *in order to* provide an excuse to use violence (s. 55(6)(a) and (b)). An example would be where D dares V to hit him, saying that V will prove himself to be nothing but a coward if V fails to do it; so, V hits D, upon which D loses self-control and stabs V to death.[69]

More significantly, the 2009 Act makes the following changes to the old law:

1. Section 54(6) says that the defence must only be left for the jury to consider where, 'sufficient evidence is adduced to raise an issue with respect to the defence . . . [namely where] . . . evidence is adduced on which, in the opinion of the trial judge, a jury, properly directed, could reasonably conclude that the defence might apply'.

2. Section 54(2) says that the loss of self-control need no longer be 'sudden'.

---

[66] R. Holton and S. Shute, 'Self-Control in the Modern Provocation Defence' (2007) 27 OJLS 49.

[67] [1949] 1 All ER 932n.

[68] So long as that loss of self-control resulted from a 'qualifying trigger', namely a justifiable sense of being seriously wronged (provocation), or a fear of serious violence at V's hands.

[69] This sensible provision in fact imposes greater restrictions than were in place at common law. At common law, the 'self-induced' character of provocation was merely a factor that the jury was to take into account in deciding whether the reasonable person might have done as D did: see *Johnson* [1989] Crim LR 738, disapproved on this point in *Dawes* [2013] EWCA Crim 322, para. 58, which correctly indicates that the statutory scheme is narrower: focused on words or conduct *intended to* provide an excuse for violence.

Let us turn first to consideration of this second change. In the passage cited earlier, Devlin J referred to the need at common law for a 'sudden temporary' loss of self-control. This supposed requirement at common law was ever-afterwards controversial. To begin with, it is unclear what is added by stipulating that a loss of control must be 'temporary'. A loss of self-control cannot indefinitely sustain itself or be sustained for very long, even if, having subsided, it then periodically overtakes D as he or she reflects from time to time on some provocation or on some threat of violence from V. Secondly, it was never clearly the case at common law in any event that a loss of self-control had to be 'sudden' (i.e. immediately following a provocation, rather than happening at a slightly later point as D reflected on something said or done earlier).[70] In many cases prior to 2009, this supposed requirement was ignored by both judges and juries.[71] Critics of the suddenness requirement also claimed that it slanted the defence in favour of male defendants and prejudiced it against female defendants, in so far as the latter, unlike the former, tend not to lose self-control instantly but to react in a more 'slow burning' way.[72] Whatever one's view about this, though, there was always a certain amount of tension at common law, and now in the legislation, between the removal of the supposed requirement of suddenness, and the exclusion by s. 54(4) from the scope of the defence of killings prompted by a 'considered desire for revenge'.

To begin with, although this is not acknowledged by the legislation, a provoked killing, even following a loss of self-control, normally has a vengeful motivation: the 'desire for retaliatory suffering' as ancient Greek philosopher Aristotle called it. So, on the one hand, it is perfectly consistent with pleading the defence that D did not react instantaneously and brooded on what was said or done, perhaps even forearming him or herself in readiness to confront V.[73] That is the effect of s. 54(2) even though, ironically, evidence of delay (such as the detour to the garage to fill up the car in *Baillie*[74])—and even more so, evidence of pre-planning—can be powerful evidence that D's supposed loss of self-control at the time of the killing was *not* genuine or never occurred. On the other hand, by virtue of s. 54(4), in cases in which D acted from a 'considered' desire for revenge the defence is simply inapplicable. The combined effect of these provisions seems to be that, even if D does take time to brood on vengeful thoughts and even if D to some extent has prepared for a retaliatory attack on V, so long as D (a) had lost self-control at the time of the killing and (b) was not at that time motivated by any preconceived decision to exact vengeance that he or she may have come to previously, the defence may apply. That position is intelligible, legally and morally, but is based on fine distinctions that it may be very difficult to draw, not least in circumstances where

[70] In *Ahluwalia* [1992] 4 All ER 889 (CA), the Court of Appeal rejected the view that there was such a requirement at common law.

[71] See, e.g., *Baillie* [1995] Crim LR 739, where the provocation defence was left to the jury even though D had fetched a gun from his attic, and then filled his car with petrol from the garage before heading to V's house.

[72] For an example, see *Thornton* [1992] 1 All ER 306, where D took the time to sharpen a kitchen knife before returning to the living room and stabbing her abusive husband to death. The provocation defence was left to the jury. See also *Ahluwalia* [1992] 4 All ER 899.

[73] See the cases discussed at nn 71 and 72.   [74] *Baillie* [1995] Crim LR 739.

it is likely that D's account of his or her own thoughts, feelings, and actions will be the only or main source of evidence for those thoughts, feelings, and actions.

The Law Commission had originally argued strongly against the retention of any loss of self-control requirement.[75] In the Commission's view, there should instead simply be a negative test of whether D acted on a considered desire for revenge; if he or she did not, then the defence would be available in principle. However, it is not entirely clear that this approach would have resolved the difficulties in distinguishing deserving from undeserving cases in this area.[76] It is one thing to exclude cases like *Ibrams*[77] from the defence: not merely was there a gap of some five days between provocation and killing, but there was evidence of planning and premeditation. It is another thing to exclude defendants with slow-burning temperaments, who do not react straight away to an insult or wrong, but go away and then react after minutes or even hours of festering anger. However, the problem then is that allowing lapse of time between the provocation and the retaliation—as suggested in *Ahluwalia*[78]—not only helps women defendants but also broadens the time frame for men, and may thus weaken the excusatory force that derives from acting in uncontrolled anger. In *Dawes*,[79] the Court of Appeal made the important point, in this context, that delay between a stimulus and the loss of self-control may be a product of the 'cumulative impact' of events, an especially important explanation for losses of self-control when the defendant and the victim were living together for a long period of time.[80]

(ii) *The Subjective Requirement and the Role of the Judge:* We now turn to the first change effected by s. 54(6). The opening words of the old s. 3 of the Homicide Act 1957 ('Where on a charge of murder there is *evidence* on which the jury can find that the person charged was provoked') were construed by the courts in such a way that almost any evidence of a provoked loss of self-control would make provocation an issue in the trial, and the prosecution would come under an obligation to show that the elements of the defence were not made out, as described above. What was required, stated Lord Steyn in *Acott* (1997),[81] is 'some evidence of a specific act or words of provocation resulting in a loss of self-control', whereas 'a loss of self-control caused by fear, panic, sheer bad temper or circumstances (e.g. a slow down of traffic due to snow) would not be enough'. However, what may properly be defined as 'provocation' in this context proved controversial. In *Doughty*[82] the crying of a 17-day-old child was held to be sufficient to satisfy the requirement for a 'provoked' loss of self-control, even though a child's crying is scarcely even voluntary conduct, let alone conduct that is intended to or known to be likely to provoke. *Doughty* did not, of course, decide that a baby's crying was to be regarded as such that a reasonable person might have done as D did in

---

[75] Law Com No. 290, paras. 3.28–30; 3.315–17.

[76] For further discussion, see J. Horder, *Homicide and the Politics of Law Reform* (2012), 213–22.

[77] (1981) 74 Cr App R 154.   [78] 1992] 4 All ER 889 (CA).   [79] [2013] EWCA Crim 332.

[80] See further, T. Storey, 'Loss of Self-Control: The Qualifying Triggers, Self-induced Loss of Self-Control and "Cumulative Impact"' (2013) 77 J Crim Law 189.   [81] [1997] 2 Cr App R 94, at 102.

[82] (1986) 83 Cr App R 319, on which see J. Horder, 'The Problem of Provocative Children' [1987] Crim LR 654.

that case. The point the Court of Appeal made was that even a baby's persistent crying was 'evidence . . . that the person charged was provoked' such that the defence became an issue at trial and the prosecution had to convince the jury that its elements were not satisfied. It was a waste of the court's time, and of counsels' time, to have to address defences when, as in *Doughty*, they had such little chance of success. What is more, albeit exceptionally, some juries were acquitting D of murder, following a direction from the judge on the provocation issue, in cases where the provocation was so trivial that, as a matter of justice, it ought never to have been put before the jury. An example is *Naylor*.[83] D picked up a prostitute (V) in his car, and then refused to pay as agreed for the services he had received. When V remonstrated with him he strangled her with such force that he broke bones in her neck. As there was 'evidence . . . that the person charged was provoked', the defence of provocation was put to the jury, which (surprisingly) acquitted him of murder and convicted of manslaughter only.

So far as the second limb of the defence is concerned,[84] it may be argued that s. 54(6) seeks to snuff out the possibility that cases such as *Doughty* and *Naylor* might end in manslaughter verdicts on the grounds of loss of self-control. It does this by providing that the loss of self-control defence is not to be put to the jury unless the judge is of the opinion that a jury, having been given proper directions, might reasonably conclude that the defence applied. This gives the trial judge an important and broad responsibility and discretion to exercise, in the role of 'gatekeeper', to the loss of self-control defence. Were cases with facts similar to those in *Naylor* and *Doughty* to recur, on any view it is hard to see how they would pass the judicial 'gatekeeper', given the height of the new hurdle (to be considered shortly) that D must surmount if he or she is to make loss of self-control an issue in the case in relation to the second limb of the defence; but how broad is the 'gatekeeper' function provided by s. 54(6)? In *Dawes*,[85] the Court of Appeal emphasized that, when s. 54(6) speaks of the judge reaching an 'opinion' on whether a properly instructed jury could reasonably conclude that the defence might apply, that does not mean that—since opinions differ—a judge could never be wrong when reaching such a decision. Nonetheless, if the evidence passes muster under s. 54(6), taking a view on this that is most favourable to the defendant, the defence must be left to the jury.[86]

So far as the first limb of the defence (addressed later) is concerned—a fear of serious violence from V—s. 54(6) is less dramatic in its effect in this respect. It is still meant to deny the defence to Ds who raise wholly implausible claims to have lost self-control due to a fear of serious violence at V's hands, but as we will now see, s. 54(6) is a less powerful tool in that regard in relation to the first limb of the defence than in relation to the second limb.

---

[83] (1987) 84 Crim App R 302.   [84] See text preceding n 65.

[85] [2013] EWCA Crim 322; see also *Workman* [2014] EWCA Crim 575.

[86] On this, see *Clinton* [2012] EWCA Crim 2, para 46; *Jewel* [2014] EWCA Crim 414. That the defence may be rightly withdrawn from the jury where the provocation is trivial is illustrated by *R v Bowyer* [2013] WLR (D) 130 (CA); *R v Hatter* [2013] WLR(D) 130 (CA).

In relation to the first limb of the defence, s. 55(4)(b) is at the heart of the 2009 Act's replacement for the subjective requirement in what were formerly provocation cases. It requires that a loss of self-control as a result of something said or done (or both together) cause D 'to have a justifiable sense of being seriously wronged'. These are the words designed to replace the old notion of a 'provoked' loss of self-control under the 1957 Act, and are referred to in the legislation as being part of a 'qualifying trigger' bringing the defence into play (s. 55(2)).[87] It seems immediately apparent how the wording of s. 55(4)(b) will be likely to exclude cases such as *Doughty* from the scope of the loss of control defence, at the point when the judge has to decide whether a properly directed jury might reasonably conclude that the defence may apply. This is because s. 55(4)(b) avoids the language of 'provocation', by employing instead the notion that D must have had a justifiable sense of being seriously wronged. In this way, the law introduces the idea that, for the purposes of the second limb of the defence, D must have had good cause to feel that he or she was the victim of some kind of serious injustice, insult, or other glaring instance of denigration or derogatory conduct at the hands of another: nothing short of that will, assuming it sparks a loss of self-control, be sufficient to bring the defence into play (other things being equal). A crying baby is, quite simply, not capable of behaving in such a way towards another person, however frustrated or enraged that person may be by the crying. The way that the law achieves this, though, is by introducing an objective (judgmental) element into what was formerly an almost purely factual, subjective question concerning whether D was provoked to lose self-control. The objective, judgmental element is represented by the requirement that D's sense of being seriously wronged by some piece of conduct must be a 'justifiable' sense of being seriously wronged.[88] It is worth noting the contrast, in this respect, with the subjective requirement for the first limb of the defence (the other 'qualifying trigger' bringing the defence into play), which does not involve this heavily judgmental element. Section 55(3) requires no more than evidence of a 'fear of serious violence from V against D or another identified person'. Such evidence will bring the loss of self-control defence into play, when this limb of the defence is relied on, whether or not the fear of serious violence was 'justifiable'.[89] This is likely significantly to complicate the judge's task in discharging the gatekeeper function, and in directing the jury, when D pleads (as he or she is entitled to do) both limbs of the defence together.

[87] The other part of the qualifying trigger in the second limb, the requirement for provocation 'of an extremely grave character' is considered below, as part of the objective requirements of the defence.

[88] The justifiability element appears to have two separate effects. First, in cases where D believes that he or she has been seriously wronged, but this view is based on a mistake on D's part about what has been said or done, that mistake must be justifiable. Secondly, in so far as D believes that he or she has been *seriously*—not just trivially—wronged, that belief must also be justifiable.

[89] The difference in approach is doubtless explained by the fact that when D is pleading self-defence or prevention of crime as a (complete) defence to murder, a subjective belief—whether or not justifiable—in the existence of deadly threat will be sufficient to bring the defence into play: Criminal Justice and Immigration Act 2008, s. 76(4). By contrast, s. 55(4)(b) effectively overrules the old decision in *Letenock* (1917) 12 Cr App R 221, a decision that had appeared to make the question whether or not D understood V's conduct as embodying a grave provocation a purely subjective one: see n 81.

(iii) *The Objective Requirement; The New Elements:* It is helpful to begin by focusing on what the 2009 Act puts in place of the old provocation defence (the second limb of the defence, under s. 55(4)), and in that regard starting with a brief discussion of the pre-2009 law. Under s. 3 of the Homicide Act 1957, the jury had to decide not only whether D had lost self-control at the time of the killing, but whether the provocation was such as might have made a reasonable man do as D did. The latter question is the objective requirement, and it is still part of the post-2009 law (in a more sophisticated form, as we will see). Its function is to ensure that not every homicidal loss of self-control reduces the offence from murder to manslaughter. It would, for example, be unacceptable if the defence served to reduce from murder to manslaughter an intentional killing involving the act of a possessive spouse angered by no more than his or her partner's decision to go out alone for an evening, or the act of someone who flies into rage when lawfully arrested for a crime he or she has committed. Only those provocative acts serious enough to unbalance the reactions of a person with reasonable self-control should suffice.[90] However, the 1957 Act did not elaborate on the kinds of provocation that might form the basis of a successful plea.[91] The authors of the 1957 legislation were content to leave that question to be decided by each jury on a case–by-case basis.[92]

Regrettably, though, the Appeal Courts could not resist the temptation to introduce legal complexity to the relatively simple provisions of the 1957 Act. They sought to spell out, case by case, the characteristics of the 'reasonable person' as a matter of law, and hence dictate to the jury what should, and should not, be taken into account in deciding whether the reasonable person might have done as D did in the circumstances. In so far as it affected his or her reaction, could the reasonable person still be reasonable when jealous, depressed, temperamental, or touchy on the subject of a disability or a previous criminal record? Could the 'reasonable' person possibly be someone who had a mental disorder that affected their capacity to maintain self-control? Judges needlessly set themselves the task of answering all these questions—and more of a similar kind. Naturally, when considering these questions, judges disagreed amongst themselves over the right answers, over the kinds of characteristics that could, and could not, be regarded as features of the reasonable person. This served only to push the law even further into obscurity.[93] We will return to this issue shortly.

---

[90] For a contrary view, though, see B. Mitchell, R. Mackay, and W. Brookbanks, 'Pleading for Provoked Killers: In Defence of Morgan Smith' (2008) 124 LQR 675.

[91] The common law was, historically, much more forthcoming in this respect. See, e.g., *Mawgridge* (1707) 1 Kel 119.

[92] On the history of the legislation, in that regard, see J. Horder, *Homicide and the Politics of Law Reform* (2012), ch 8.

[93] The highest court even used its Privy Council status, hearing appeals from other jurisdictions where the law was in substance the same as in England and Wales, to disagree with decisions by the House of Lords on the law governing England and Wales, an unacceptable practice when driven simply by disagreement on the substantive issues rather than by some special feature of the law in the overseas jurisdiction: see *Attorney-General for Jersey* v *Holley* [2005] 2 AC 580. It took a further decision of the Court of Appeal to decide that the *Holley* case represented English law: *James* [2006] QB 588.

A very significant effect of the 2009 Act is to bring to the fore, and make explicit, an objective requirement that was only implicit in the pre-2009 law: the requirement for the conduct that sparked D's loss of self-control to be an instance of very grave provocation. Section 55(4) says that, in addition to being something that gave D a justifiable sense of being seriously wronged (a requirement that we have already considered), the conduct that sparked D's loss of self-control will not amount to a qualifying trigger unless (s. 55(4)(a)) it, 'constitutes circumstances of an extremely grave character'. It will still be, as it was under the law prior to the 2009 Act, a matter for the jury whether what was done or said that led D to lose self-control and kill constituted circumstances of an extremely grave character. However, it is clear that s. 55(4)(a) was intended to raise the bar that D must surmount in order to bring the defence into play: the provocation must not merely be serious, but 'extremely grave'.

In the parliamentary debate on the issue in 2008–9, Baroness Scotland, speaking for the government, gave as an example a hypothetical case in which a refugee living in the UK encountered a man responsible for rounding up members of his old village, locking them in a church, and then setting the church alight. The man laughs at the incident and describes in some detail what happened to the refugee's family killed in the fire. The refugee thereupon lost self-control and killed the man. Baroness Scotland went on the say:

> We consider that the words and conduct limb of the partial defence needs to be included in this kind of extremely grave example, where the defendant would have a justifiable cause to feel seriously wronged. We remain of the view that the partial defence should succeed only in the gravest of circumstances.[94]

Baroness Scotland's example, coupled with this explanation, suggests two things.

First, what is to count as an 'exceptionally grave' provocation must be judged in context. There can never be a list of exceptionally grave provocations detached from consideration of circumstantial and contextual issues such as who the provoker and the provoked person were, the relationship between them, and the manner in which the provocation was given.[95] For example, if the hypothetical war criminal in the example given by Baroness Scotland had given his account of the events at the church to a young British person who was born long after the incident took place, and knew nothing of it, the gravity of the provocation would be reduced. It might still be a grave provocation, but arguably no longer an exceptionally grave provocation. So, as the Law Commission put it (considering its own version of the test): 'The jury should be trusted to evaluate the relative grossness of provocation, in whatever form it comes, according to their own sense of justice in an individual case.'[96] Under the 1957 Act, this was also the position, following the overruling in *DPP* v *Camplin*[97] of the old case of *Bedder* v *DPP*.[98]

---

[94] HL debates, 7 July 2009, col 582–3.
[95] For confirmation that this is the right approach, see *Dawes* [2013] EWCA Crim 322, para. 65.
[96] Law Com No. 304, at 85.　　　[97] [1978] AC 705 (HL).　　　[98] [1954] 2 All ER 201.

In *Bedder* v *DPP*, D, who was sexually impotent, was taunted about his impotence and kicked in the groin by a prostitute with whom he had been attempting to have sexual intercourse, whereupon he lost self-control and killed her. The House of Lords held that the jury should consider the effect of these acts on a 'reasonable' man, without regard to the sexual impotence. That was a difficult rule to apply, because it is hard to see how the gravity of the provocation constituted by a taunt about impotence can be properly understood without reference to whether the person taunted is indeed impotent. The House of Lords in *Bedder* v *DPP* failed to consider whether it was possible to take into account D's impotence, in assessing the gravity of the provocation, whilst at the same time insisting that the provocation must be so grave that it might lead even a person with reasonable powers of self-control to lose control and kill.[99] The effect of the decision in *DPP* v *Camplin* was to adopt the latter approach. Lord Diplock held that a court should consider the effect of the provocation on 'a person having the power of self-control to be expected of an ordinary person of the sex and age of the accused, but in other respects sharing such of the accused's characteristics as they think would affect the gravity of the provocation to him'. We will consider the first part of this ruling in due course. So far as the second part of the ruling is concerned—characteristics affecting the gravity of the provocation—following the decision in *Camplin*, increasingly few, if any, limits were set to the kinds of characteristics that may affect the gravity of the provocation. In *Morhall*,[100] D was a glue-sniffing addict who had been taunted about his glue-sniffing by the victim, whom D subsequently stabbed. The Court of Appeal held that in applying the objective test the jury should be directed not to take account of discreditable characteristics such as glue-sniffing (or paedophilia). The House of Lords disagreed, and held that a jury should be directed to take account of any matter relevant to an assessment of the strength of the provocation. As we will see, in broad terms, this is now the approach under the new law.

Does this mean that there are no boundaries at all to what personal attributes may be taken into account in assessing the gravity of the provocation? What about the case of a racist who believes that it is gravely insulting for a non-white person to speak to a white man unless spoken to first?[101] Lord Taylor in *Morhall* put the case of 'a paedophile upbraided for molesting children',[102] which raises similar issues. The implication of the House of Lords decision in *Morhall* is that the judgment of such matters must be left to the jury without much guidance. It could be argued strongly that is unsatisfactory: there ought to be a normative element that excludes attitudes and reactions inconsistent with the law or inconsistent with the notion of a tolerant, pluralist society that upholds the right to respect for private life without discrimination (Arts. 8 and 14 of the Convention). However, the significance of that argument has sharply diminished in the light of the reforms effected by s. 55(4)(a) of the 2009 Act, and its

---

[99] See A. Ashworth, 'The Doctrine of Provocation' [1976] 35 Camb LJ 292.
[100] [1996] 1 AC 90.
[101] These issues were perhaps first raised in relation to English law by A. Ashworth, 'The Doctrine of Provocation' (1976) 35 CLJ 292.   [102] (1994) 98 Cr App R 108, at 113 (CA).

requirement that provocation be of an 'extremely grave' character. Further, Baroness Scotland's second point in the passage cited earlier from her speech indicates that s. 55(4)(a) is meant to be a restatement of what was originally envisaged by the legislature when debating the 1957 Act, namely that commonly encountered provocations— even very annoying or wounding ones, such as persistently inconsiderate behaviour by a neighbour or the discovery that a spouse is in another relationship—should not be capable of forming the basis of a successful plea.[103] In the years following the reform of the defence in 1957, it would be fair to say that courts had—whilst making the law ever more complex—also allowed juries to consider a provocation plea in a far wider range of cases, involving commonly encountered provocations, than the legislature had envisaged in 1957. To that extent, s. 55(4)(a) is a welcome development.

It is against that background that we should consider s. 55(6)(c), which provides that, 'In determining whether a loss of self-control had a qualifying trigger . . . the fact that a thing done or said constituted sexual infidelity is to be disregarded'.[104] As these words indicate, s. 55(6)(c) concerns a (dis)qualifying trigger, but it is illuminating to discuss it more generally as part of the post-2009 modification of the objective requirements of the loss of self-control defence. In policy terms, the provision was intended to stop possessive men, in particular, pleading a partner's infidelity as a basis for reducing murder to manslaughter: something that it was open to them to do (with no guarantee of success, of course) under the old law.[105] The provision is, though, so clearly and obviously incapable of doing that (except in rare cases), that it is probably better to regard its importance as lying not so much in the extent to which it narrows the scope of the law, as in its symbolism as a commitment to taking domestic violence more seriously. The case for regarding it as more important symbolically than normatively is expressed in Baroness Scotland's explanation of the section, worth citing at length:

> Even accepting that a great deal has been done in recent years to address this problem, and that pleas of provocation on the basis of sexual infidelity generally do not succeed, it is still true that, under the current law, the defence can be raised and could technically succeed. We want to make it clear in the Bill that this can no longer be the case, and that it is unacceptable for a defendant who has killed an unfaithful partner to seek to blame the victim for what occurred. It is important to correct a misconception here. By doing this, we are not saying that people are not entitled to feel upset and angry at a partner's unfaithfulness: we are concerned here with a partial defence to murder and the circumstances in which it is appropriate to reduce liability for murder to that of the less serious offence of manslaughter. We are saying that killing in response to sexual infidelity is not a circumstance in which such a reduction can be justified.[106]

---

[103] For example, the war criminal hypothetical was also used as an illustration of the need for the defence in the debates preceding the 1957 Act, although it was given greater significance at that time because of the continuing application of the death penalty.

[104] For critical evaluation, see D. Baker and L. X. Zhao, 'Contributory Qualifying and Non-qualifying Triggers in the Loss of Self-Control Defence: A Wrong Turn on Sexual Infidelity' (2012) 76 J Crim Law 254.

[105] HC Public Bills Committee, 3 March 2009, col 439.   [106] HL debates, 7 July 2009, col 589.

The case for saying that s. 55(6)(c) is of little normative significance was to an extent conceded by the government itself, when it stated that it is only sexual infidelity in itself that must be disregarded in a provocation case.[107] If there is other evidence that constitutes a qualifying trigger, then the case may be considered by the jury notwithstanding the part played in D's reaction by sexual infidelity. This point was hammered home by the Lord Chief Justice in the Court of Appeal's decision in *Clinton*.[108] Indeed the Court of Appeal went on to say that even evidence of sexual infidelity itself could be given, 'where sexual infidelity is integral to and forms an essential part of the context in which to make a just evaluation whether a qualifying trigger properly falls within the ambit of subsections 55(3) and (4)'.[109]

The case for saying that s. 55(6)(c) will have only a negligible impact in cases where possessive men have used violence against women (and against their sexual partners in particular) has been much commented on, not least in *Clinton* itself.[110] To adapt an earlier example, if D loses control and kills V simply because V wishes to have a night out without D present, that evidence will not be ruled out as a basis for a plea of loss of self-control by s. 55(6)(c). Similarly, a plea of loss of self-control will not be ruled out by that section in any of the following examples:

(a) D 'stalks' a celebrity with whom he is obsessed (although they have never met), losing control and killing her when he sees her having dinner with a man;

(b) D loses control and kills V, his 16-year-old daughter, when V says that she intends to start dating;

(c) D loses self-control and kills V, his partner, when V says that she will never have sexual intercourse with him again.

In these examples, it is highly unlikely that the defence of loss of self-control would be put to the jury, or if put to the jury it is highly unlikely that the defence would succeed; but that is not because of the existence of s. 55(6)(c). It is because of the combined effect of s. 54(6)—that requires the judge to withdraw a case from the jury if a properly directed jury could not reasonably conclude that the defence might apply—and s. 55(4)(a), that requires the evidence to constitute circumstances

---

[107] HC debates, 9 November 2009, col 83 (Claire Ward), cited by D. Ormerod, *Smith and Hogan's Criminal Law* (13th edn., 2011), 521.

[108] *Clinton, Parker and Evans* [2012] EWCA Crim 2, paras. 40–4.

[109] *Clinton, Parker and Evans* [2012] EWCA Crim 2, para. 39. Confusingly, though, having said that it would approach the interpretation of s. 55(6)(c) as an ordinary language question (para. 4), the Court of Appeal went on to suggest that s. 55(6)(c) should be understood so as to extend its reach beyond an ordinary language construction. So, the Court said that the section should be understood to cover untrue 'confessions' of sexual infidelity, and also reports to D by others of sexual infidelity (para. 28), even though by no stretch of the imagination could these 'constitute' sexual infidelity. Perhaps this line of argument was adopted as part of the courts' well-known duty to avoid statutory constructions that lead to absurdity; but in the case of s. 56(6)(c), it is hard to know in what directions such a duty would take the law.

[110] *Clinton, Parker and Evans* [2012] EWCA Crim 2, paras. 17–25. See also *Dawes* [2013] EWCA Crim 3222.

of an extremely grave character. Were it not for the perceived great importance of the symbolic function of s. 55(6)(c), it is strongly arguable that sexual infidelity cases should have been left to be weeded out by the same combination of ss. 54(6) and 55(4)(a).

(iv) *The New Limb of Loss of Self-Control: A Fear of Serious Violence:* Section 55(3) creates a new basis for reducing murder to manslaughter, under the heading of loss of self-control. As we have seen, a qualifying trigger for the loss of self-control defence is that D's loss of self-control 'was attributable to D's fear of serious violence from V against D or against another identified person'. This short statement of the first limb of the defence captures both the subjective element, '*fear* of violence' (already considered), and an objective requirement that the violence feared must have been 'serious'; s. 55(3) does not say as much, but it would be wholly inconsistent with the tenor of the provisions as a whole were it to be a matter solely for D whether the violence he feared was serious. It should not, for example, be possible for a gang member to say that he responded with lethal violence to a punch from a member of a rival gang, because he regarded violence offered by rival gang members to be much more serious than other kinds of violence. 'Serious' should probably be understood to mean, 'constituting at least serious bodily harm'. However, the application of the first limb may not be all that straightforward in some circumstances.

Consider the facts of the case of *Uddin*, that arose under the old pre-1957 common law.[111] D was a Moslem who killed another Moslem (V) when V threw a pigskin shoe at him. At the trial, expert evidence of the religious significance of shoe throwing (and in particular, no doubt, of *pigskin* shoe throwing) was given to assist the jury in understanding the gravity of the provocation. That would almost certainly also happen were D in a similar case now to plead loss of self-control under the second limb, on the basis that this was exceptionally grave provocation that gave him a justifiable sense of having been seriously wronged. However, were D to claim that he intentionally killed V solely on the grounds that he faced 'serious' violence from V, how should that claim be treated? It is submitted that the claim should fail. The incident was serious only as a form of provocation, not as a form of violence (a far more objective question). However, as has already been pointed out, D would be entitled to plead the two limbs of the loss of self-control defence together, entailing a tricky task for the judge in directing the jury. That direction would be further complicated if, as indicated earlier, D was mistaken about what V threw at him, thinking it was a pigskin shoe when in fact it was a plastic container of some kind.

The underlying explanation for s. 55(3) is principally the difficulty that may arise, highlighted in the Law Commission's analysis of the provocation defence,[112] when a woman kills an abusive husband or partner (V) without reacting suddenly in the face of a final provocation or threat from V. In such cases, it will often make more sense, in terms of the moral narrative, to describe her ultimate reaction in killing the husband as

---

[111] *The Times*, 14 September 1929, discussed in Ashworth, n 99.
[112] Law Commission, *Partial Defences to Murder* (Consultation Paper No. 173, 2003).

attributable to fear for her own or her children's safety rather than to anger (although motives may be understandably mixed).[113] It will also make sense, in those terms, to explain her reaction as delayed because of (amongst other things) an inequality between her size and strength and his—that necessitates waiting until he is off guard to defend herself—rather than because of sheer malevolence or a purely vengeful motivation. Neither of these points was capable of accommodation under a defence of provocation tied, as it was under the old law, to the notion of a sudden and angry loss of self-control.

Moreover, although solid evidence to prove this one way or another has been hard to come by, juries have been considered reluctant to apply the complete defence of self-defence in such circumstances, even though that defence is sensitive to considerations such as a disparity in size between those involved, such that the weaker person may (more justifiably) use a weapon or wait until the stronger person is off his guard.[114] As we have seen, so far as the loss of self-control defence is concerned, the new law has dispensed with the suddenness requirement (s. 54(2)), but crucially, it retained the requirement for a loss of self-control (s. 54(1)). The government departed from the Law Commission's view: that the latter should be abolished, as it was doing as much as the former to make things difficult for a battered woman who had killed her abusive partner, having waited until he was off his guard. Although there is certainly truth in this, that does not mean that the government's retention of the loss of self-control requirement was necessarily wrong. This first limb of the loss of self-control defence has an application in a number of contexts when what would otherwise be murder is the result of a fear of serious violence: such as when someone lashes out with lethal intent when attacked in a public house brawl, or when an armed police officer shoots a man dead without warning because the officer believes that the man may be threatening him. In both such cases, a jury may be reluctant to acquit completely on the grounds of self-defence, but has the option of reducing murder to manslaughter under the first limb of the defence. In such cases, it is much more understandable that the law would be reluctant even to see murder reduced to manslaughter, unless the killer could say, as part of the excusatory explanation for his or her reaction, that he or she had lost self-control.[115]

(v) *The Old Objective Requirement Modified:* Should D by some miracle surmount the hurdles to pleading loss of self-control just discussed, there is still one hurdle left to jump. That is the test set out in s. 54(1)(c), reflecting a requirement of the old common law, alluded to in the previous version of s. 3 of the 1957 Act. The test—formally, part of the qualifying trigger for the defence—is whether someone of D's sex and age, with a normal degree of tolerance and self-restraint, and in D's circumstances, might have

[113] See S. Edwards, 'Loss of Self-Control: When His Anger is Worth More Than Her Fear', in A. Reed and M. Bohlander (eds), *Loss of Self-Control and Diminished Responsibility* (2011), ch 6.

[114] For an outstanding analysis, see A. McColgan, 'In Defence of Battered Women who Kill' (1993) 13 OJLS 508.

[115] For deeper analysis see J. Horder, *Homicide and the Politics of Law Reform* (2012), 239–55.

reacted in the same or in a similar way. Added to this, in s. 54(3), is an elaboration of the meaning of D's 'circumstances':

> [T]he reference to 'the circumstances of D' is a reference to all of D's circumstances other than those whose only relevance to D's conduct is that they bear on D's general capacity for tolerance or self-restraint.

It is unclear how much is really added by these two provisions, given that the loss of self-control defence cannot come into play, in any event, unless one of the limbs of the defence is satisfied, and the disqualifying triggers (a 'considered revenge' motive; self-induced loss of self-control; reliance solely on sexual infidelity, and so forth) do not apply. If, for example, under the second limb of the defence, someone is found to have intentionally killed having lost control in the face of an exceptionally grave provocation that gave them a justifiable sense of being seriously wronged, is that not just another way of saying precisely that, in the circumstances, a normal person in D's position might indeed have acted in the same or in a similar way?[116] In fact there may be some room for these provisions to have an impact. An example is where, at the time of the killing, D occupied a role that demanded of him or her greater self-restraint than an ordinary member of the public might be expected to show. A case in point might be where D, a police officer from an ethnic minority seeking to control a violent crowd, is subjected to continued pushing and shoving, coupled with continuous racist abuse. After an hour of this treatment, the officer loses self-control, knocks over a demonstrator and stamps on his head, killing him. In such a case, the first limb of the defence might be satisfied (exceptionally grave provocation giving D a justifiable sense of having been seriously wronged). However, a jury might nonetheless find that a person with a normal degree of tolerance and self-restraint *who was a police officer on crowd-control duty* (these being 'the circumstances of D') would not have reacted in the same or in a similar way.[117]

As indicated above, under the pre-2009 law, the higher courts took upon themselves the task of explaining to the jury the characteristics of the 'reasonable man' (as it was then termed), but continually disagreed amongst themselves over which characteristics were and which were not attributable to the 'reasonable man'. Indeed, following the enactment of the Homicide Act 1957 the House of Lords or Privy Council considered some aspect of the provocation defence (and this is not a complete list) in 1968, 1973, 1978, 1996 (twice), 1997, 2001, and 2005, with the Court of Appeal considering it in many more cases. In few areas (with the exception of complicity, dealt with in Chapter 11) can Dickens' characterization of Chancery lawyers have been more appropriate in the criminal law: 'some score of members of the High Court . . . mistily engaged

---

[116] For an analogous argument in relation to the defence of duress, see K. J. M. Smith, 'Duress and Steadfastness: In Pursuit of the Unintelligible' [1999] Crim LR 363.

[117] For a powerful analysis of provocation and loss of self-control when D is on duty as a member of the police or army, see J. Gardner, 'The Gist of Excuses' (1998) 1 *Buffalo Criminal Law Review* 575. See also, under the old law, *R v Clegg* [1996] 1 AC 482 (HL), where a soldier in Northern Ireland was convicted of murder when he shot at a car both before and after it had passed a checkpoint.

in one of the ten thousand stages of an endless cause, tripping one another up on slippery precedents, groping knee-deep in technicalities, running their goat-hair and horse-hair warded heads against walls of words …'.[118] It would not be appropriate to go through those 'slippery precedents' now that s. 54(1)(c) replaces them, as (in broad terms) that provision aimed to set the law as described in *Attorney-General for Jersey* v *Holley*[119] on a statutory footing.

What s. 54(1)(c) seeks to ensure is that the jury does not take into account, in D's favour, some feature of his or her psychological make-up that makes him or her prone to explode into violent rage in circumstances where ordinary people would have kept their tempers in check, or would have responded in a less violent (or non-violent) way. For example, D may be someone for whom jealousy leads to extreme anger,[120] who may suffer from Intermittent Explosive Disorder, or who may be suffering from a tumour affecting the brain such that his or her reactions to stress have become unpredictable or uncontrollable (or both).[121] Whether or not any of these factors are D's 'fault', they are not to be taken into account by the jury. This is because they affect the level of restraint that can be expected of D in general; they do *not* necessarily relate to the gravity of the provocation or to the seriousness of the violence feared on the occasion in question. Where D simply struggles to or cannot control him or herself in the way that a person of ordinary tolerance and self-restraint should do, and it is that— rather than the gravity of the provocation or a fear of serious violence—which explains his or her loss of self-control and lethal use of violence, the right plea is diminished responsibility, and not loss of self-control.

Although the relevant provisions of the 2009 Act do not mention the issue of intoxication specifically, this robust approach has been applied (as in other areas of the law) to evidence of voluntary intoxication.[122] Such evidence will not be relevant if tendered as evidence of a reduced capacity for self-control. Arguably the position must be that even involuntary intoxication or chronic alcoholism should be treated in the same way, because such evidence is evidence of a reduced capacity for self-control, but it is possible the courts may take a different view in order to avoid an element of arbitrariness: whilst a plea of diminished responsibility may be available to someone suffering from chronic alcoholism, it would not be available to someone under the temporary influence of involuntary intoxication.[123]

More broadly, this explanation of s. 54(1)(c) is something of an over-simplification. For example, even the person of ordinary tolerance and self-restraint may be affected by irritability or tiredness in such a way that they are more likely to 'fly off the handle'. In such a case, D's irritability or tiredness may well form part of the 'circumstances of D' that are relevant to judging the possible reaction of a person of ordinary tolerance and self-restraint, for the purposes of s. 54(3). However, it is hard to see how that will

---

[118] Charles Dickens, *Bleak House*, 14.   [119] [2005] 2 AC 580.

[120] *Weller* [2003] Crim LR 724 (CA), now no longer good law.

[121] *Luc Thiet-Thuan* v R [1997] AC 131.   [122] *R* v *Asmelash* [2013] EWCA Crim 157.

[123] It should not, of course, be forgotten that evidence of intoxication, whether or not voluntary, can be tendered as evidence that the intent for murder was lacking: see Chapter 7.2.

help D much, if his or her violent reaction was not in response to an exceptionally grave provocation or a fear of serious violence (although it might help to explain, in an appropriate case, why D made a mistake about the provocation or threat offered). Section 54(1)(c) also creates its own exception to the general rule, by stipulating that D's 'sex and age' can affect the level of self-restraint and tolerance to be expected of D in the circumstances. Quite why, for example, D's sex is thought especially likely to affect D's level of tolerance (or, for that matter, her capacity for self-restraint) is something of a mystery. Even if men are, say, generally less racially or religiously tolerant than women,[124] should a jury really be making allowances for this? Again, the issue is unlikely to arise, because the need to satisfy the requirements of the first and second limbs (a fear of—objectively—serious violence, or an extremely grave provocation giving D a justifiable sense of being seriously wronged) will tend to mean that reactions attributable to racial stereotyping or religious intolerance will fall at the first hurdle.

(c) MANSLAUGHTER BY REASON OF DIMINISHED RESPONSIBILITY

General considerations:[125] Diminished responsibility was formerly one of the most frequently used qualified defences to murder, but in recent years the numbers have fallen from eighty per year in the early 1990s to around twenty per year (twenty-two in 2004, for example). Diminished responsibility was introduced into English law only in 1957, in response to long-standing dissatisfaction with the insanity defence. Insanity was, and still is, a complete defence to crime, as we saw in Chapter 5.2, but its confines are narrow, and on a murder charge a verdict of not guilty by reason of insanity requires the court to make a hospital order with restrictions.[126] Diminished responsibility has a wider ambit, but its effect is merely to reduce murder to manslaughter. Moreover, by way of contrast with the defence of loss of self-control, the burden is on the accused to show (on the balance of probabilities) that he or she is suffering from diminished responsibility.[127] The judge then has a discretion in

---

[124] There is, e.g., some evidence of greater racial tolerance amongst women than men, although the evidence shows that it is a minor influence on racial attitude formation generally: M. Hughes and S. Tuch, 'Gender Differences in Whites' Racial Attitudes: Are Women's Attitudes Really More Favourable?' (2003) 66 *Social Psychology Quarterly* 384.

[125] For detailed discussion, see R. Mackay, 'Diminished Responsibility and Mentally Disordered Killers', in Ashworth and Mitchell (eds), *Rethinking English Homicide Law* (2000); R. Mackay, 'The New Diminished Responsibility Plea' [2010] Crim LR 290; R. Fortson QC, 'The Modern Partial Defence of Diminished Responsibility', in A. Reed and M. Bohlander (eds), *Loss of Control and Diminished Responsibility* (2011), chs 1 and 2; L. Kennefick, 'Introducing a New Diminished Responsibility Defence for England and Wales' (2011) 74 MLR 750.

[126] If the conditions for such an order are fulfilled: see s. 24 of the Domestic Violence, Crime, and Victims Act 2004, and Chapter 5.2.

[127] This is to avoid a situation in which D claims that his or her responsibility was diminished, but produces no medical evidence to back this claim, and refuses to be examined by the medical experts advising the prosecution. It would be wrong to sentence D on the basis of unproven claims about his or her mental disorder. However, in theory at least, it would be possible to insist that a claim of diminished responsibility is backed by medical evidence without going as far as to place the burden of proof on the accused on the balance of probabilities.

sentencing, and in recent years about half of the cases have resulted in hospital orders without limit of time.[128] The existence of the diminished responsibility defence is one of the reasons for insisting that the loss of self-control defence is insensitive to mental disorders affecting D's levels of tolerance and powers of self-restraint: D must be 'normal' in this respect (s. 54(1)(c)). For, if D is clinically abnormal in this respect (and it is that which explains D's reaction), he or she is free to plead diminished responsibility which, if successful, has the same effect as a plea of loss of self-control in reducing murder to manslaughter.

The Post-2009 Law: The wording with which s. 2 of the Homicide Act 1957 introduced diminished responsibility was generally regarded as unsatisfactory and has now been replaced (by s. 52 of the 2009 Act) with the following provisions:

(1) A person (D) who kills or is a party to the killing of another is not to be convicted of murder if D was suffering from an abnormality of mental functioning which—

    (a) Arose from a recognized medical condition,

    (b) Substantially impaired D's ability to do one or more of the things mentioned in subsection (1A), and

    (c) Provides an explanation for D's acts or omissions in doing or being a party to the killing.

(1A) Those things are—

    (a) To understand the nature of D's conduct;

    (b) To form a rational judgment;

    (c) To exercise self-control.

(1B) For the purposes of subsection (1C), an abnormality of mental functioning provides an explanation for D's conduct if it causes, or is a significant contributory factor in causing, D to carry out that conduct.

The aim of the reforms was to bring greater clarity of definition to the terms employed to describe diminished responsibility, and to ensure that those terms were capable of adaptation to developing clinical diagnostic practices. Hence, the abnormality of mental functioning from which D suffers must arise from a 'recognized medical condition', where it is understood that, over time, what count as recognized medical conditions may change as knowledge about mental functioning advances.[129] In practice, under the old law, where a diminished responsibility plea was backed by medical evidence, it was simply accepted by the prosecution—meaning that D would be convicted of manslaughter only, without the need for a full trial to go ahead—in 77 per cent of cases. Whether or not there is reason to think that this

---

[128] See the research by R. D. Mackay in Law Com No. 290, *Partial Defences to Murder*, App B.

[129] Under the old law, there was a fixed list of conditions from which the abnormality of mind (as it was then called) had to arise, although few lawyers or psychiatrists paid much attention to it.

statistic will alter, in the light of the change of definition of diminished responsibility, and in the light of the new relationship it forms with the loss of self-control defence, is something to be considered when the ingredients of the defence have been analysed.

The Nature of the Conditions: The notion of an 'abnormality of mental functioning' arising from a 'recognized medical condition' suggests that whether or not D suffers from such a condition is essentially an expert question.[130] It would be inconsistent with the tenor of the legislation, and unfair to D, to leave members of the jury to decide whether or not D's condition meets the criteria if that matter is not in dispute between the experts. The emphasis in the new law is different to the path adopted by the old law, under which an abnormality of mind was said to be 'a state or mind so different from that of ordinary human beings that the reasonable man would term it abnormal'.[131] This was unsatisfactory, not least because it suggests that the state of mind in question must be something not experienced in any form by mentally normal people (schizophrenia, for example); whereas, many abnormalities of mental functioning are states of mind very familiar—at least in a moderate form—to 'ordinary human beings', such as pathological jealousy or intermittent explosive disorder.[132] However, in cases where experts disagree over whether or not there is an abnormality of medical functioning, or over whether the abnormality stems from a recognized medical condition, the matter will have to go to the jury. Even if this issue is not in dispute, the jury should be told that they are free to decide whether or not D's condition, established on the basis of expert opinion, 'substantially impaired D's ability to do one or more of the things mentioned in subsection (1A)'. It will also be for the jury to decide whether the abnormality of mental functioning was the cause, or a significant contributory factor in causing, D's condition, although they may be assisted on this issue by expert evidence.[133] Again, these are matters on which D bears the burden of proof on the balance of probabilities.[134]

What kinds of conditions will meet the criteria? In *Byrne*,[135] D strangled and then mutilated a woman after her death. Evidence was given that from an early age Byrne had suffered from extremely strong perverse desires that he found it all-but impossible to control, and it was such a desire that had overwhelmed him when he killed the woman. Such a case would fall within the scope of the defence, because it involves an abnormality of mental functioning substantially impairing D's ability to exercise control over violent impulses, an abnormality recognized as a medical condition. The well-respected Diagnostic and Statistical Manual of

[130] On the meaning of 'recognized medical condition', see now the Law Commission Discussion Paper, *Insanity and Automatism* (2013).

[131] *Byrne* [1960] 2 QB 396, per Lord Parker CJ.

[132] In practice, under the old law, a broad range of abnormalities of mind was accepted as meeting the criteria.

[133] For a case where a causal link was not established, although D suffered from ADHD, see *Osborne* [2010] EWCA 547.

[134] As usual, if the prosecution wishes to refute the defence evidence, it must do so to the beyond-reasonable-doubt standard.   [135] [1960] 2 QB 396.

Mental Disorders (DSM-4) lists some sixteen different kinds of recognized mental disorder, including:

- Disorders Usually First Diagnosed in Infancy, Childhood, or Adolescence
- Delirium, Dementia, and Amnestic and Other Cognitive Disorders
- Mental Disorders Due to a General Medical Condition
- Substance-Related Disorders
- Schizophrenia and Other Psychotic Disorders
- Mood Disorders
- Anxiety Disorders
- Somatoform Disorders
- Dissociative Disorders
- Sexual and Gender Identity Disorders
- Eating Disorders
- Sleep Disorders
- Impulse-Control Disorders Not Elsewhere Classified
- Adjustment Disorders
- Personality Disorders
- Other Conditions That May Be a Focus of Clinical Attention

This is not a list of disorders drawn up for legal purposes, and so not all of these disorders, even if they affected D's conduct, would be capable of substantially impairing D's ability to (s. 52(1)(a)) understand the nature of his or her conduct, to form rational judgment, or to exercise self-control. Even so, the DSM gives an indication of the breadth of expert opinion concerning abnormalities of mental functioning. Certain to be included are the effects of alcohol dependency,[136] of depressive illnesses resulting from, for example, long-term abuse at the hands of a violent partner,[137] or from the stress of long-term care for a terminally ill relative.[138]

Picking up on the final example, some critics of the new law complained that the 2009 reforms would end the practice of 'benign conspiracy' (allegedly sometimes entered into by the prosecution and the defence, in agreeing not to contest the case) to allow those who had taken a premeditated and rational decision to kill a terminally ill relative (at the latter's request) to plead guilty to manslaughter only.[139] That is a curious objection, since the very fact that the practice could only be sustained by a benign

---

[136] Under the old law, see *Tandy* [1989] 1 All ER 267. [137] *Hobson* [1998] 1 Cr App R 31.

[138] See the discussion in Law Commission Consultation Paper No. 177 (2005), *A New Homicide Act for England and Wales?*, part 8.

[139] See Kennefick (n 125). See also the evidence of 'Dignity in Dying' to the Joint Committee on Human Rights, 8th Report, 2008–9, para 1.150, cited by D. Ormerod, *Smith and Hogan's Criminal Law* (13th edn., 2015), 531 n 160; *Cocker* [1989] Crim LR 740 (CA).

conspiracy shows that the practice was, in fact, inconsistent with the legal requirement for any abnormality of mental functioning arising from the stress of long-term care for the terminally ill person to have a medically recognized origin (to use the modern language of the 2009 law). Excuses for rationally perpetrated euthanasia, whether or not they are partial excuses, should be introduced after open democratic debate on their merits, and not introduced through a back door route created by lawyers manipulating defences that were intended as a humane way of treating only those with medically recognized abnormalities of mental functioning. The irony is that, as the Law Commission was at pains to point out in an almost wholly neglected part of its Consultation Paper on the subject,[140] many of those who kill terminally ill relatives following years of stressful long-term care are indeed suffering from such an abnormality of mental functioning that both substantially impairs their judgment and control, and makes a significant contribution to their conduct in killing V; and that can be true whether or not V consented to be killed. We consider this issue further below.

Where a mental disorder has been aggravated by the effects of voluntary intoxication, the pre-2009 law was that the judge should instruct the jury to answer the question, 'Has the defendant satisfied you that, despite the drink, his mental abnormality substantially impaired his mental responsibility for his fatal acts?'[141] This focuses on the 'substantial impairment' element of the partial defence, and the Court of Appeal took the same approach in *Wood*,[142] where the underlying clinical condition was alcohol dependency syndrome and D had also drunk much alcohol. The jury should decide whether the clinical condition 'substantially impaired' D's responsibility, discounting any effects of alcohol consumed voluntarily. In effect, the jury are left to determine how much of D's drinking derived from his alcohol dependency and how much was 'voluntary'. This inevitably involves a good deal of speculation by the jury on which the assistance that expert evidence can provide may be limited. In such cases, it is arguable that evidence of voluntary intoxication should not simply rule out a plea of diminished responsibility, even if the voluntary intoxication made some causal contribution to D's conduct in killing V. This approach is warranted, because the issue of voluntary intoxication is more complicated than when alcohol affects a mentally normal person. Research shows both that alcohol dependency or heavy drinking may generate psychiatric disorders and that, vice versa, those with psychiatric disorders often become alcohol dependent or heavy drinkers: in an effort, for example, to offset the unwanted and unpleasant effects of a disorder.[143]

The focus should be on whether or not the abnormality of mental functioning (which may include the lasting effects of excessive drinking over a long period) substantially impaired D's understanding, judgment, or control, and whether that made a significant contribution to D's conduct in killing V. In that regard (and indeed generally, in

---

[140] See the discussion in Law Commission Consultation Paper No. 177 (2005), *A New Homicide Act for England and Wales?*, Part 8.

[141] *Dietschmann* [2003] 1 AC 1209, *per* Lord Hutton at 41.   [142] [2008] 2 Cr App R 34.

[143] V. Modesto-Lowe and H. R. Kransler, 'Diagnosis and Treatment of Alcohol-Dependent Patients with Comorbid Psychiatric Disorders' (1999) 23 *Alcohol Research and Health* 144.

relation to this defence), it will be important to establish the meaning of 'substantial impairment'. Clearly, 'substantial' does not mean 'complete', for otherwise there would be too much overlap with the defence of insanity, and scant justification for a conviction of manslaughter. At the other end of the scale, 'substantial' impairment may mean simply, 'more than trivial or insignificant', and that was the view taken under the old law in *Simcox*.[144] This approach has now been endorsed as the right one under the new law in *Golds*,[145] although unhelpfully, the court suggested that a judge could rightly refuse to comment on the meaning of the term at all, in a direction to the jury. That is unhelpful, because it is quite likely that a jury will apply a more stringent test of 'substantial impairment' if the jury is revolted by what the defendant has done. They should at least be told that this is not an appropriate way to approach the issue, even if—behind closed doors—they end up adopting it.

That brings us to an important case of new law, the decision in *Dowds*.[146] In that case, D had, whilst heavily intoxicated, killed his partner V with a knife, inflicting some sixty stab wounds in the process. The evidence suggested that D periodically drank very heavily, but retained control over when he started drinking. In support of his plea of diminished responsibility, D nonetheless claimed that his acute intoxication at the time of the offence was a 'recognized medical condition' for the purposes of the new law, even though the intoxication was voluntary. D relied on a World Health Organization classification of acute intoxication as a medical condition (WHO ICD-10). D was convicted and his appeal was dismissed by the Court of Appeal. Hughes LJ said (para. 40) that, even when D is suffering from a recognized medical condition, that is only a necessary element to be satisfied if D is to raise diminished responsibility. The presence of a medically recognized condition will not in and of itself always be sufficient for that purpose. In support of that conclusion. Hughes LJ pointed to the fact that the Dictionary of Scientific Medicine (DSM) itself warns that there is what it refers to as an 'imperfect fit' between clinical diagnosis and legal concepts.[147] By way of example, Hughes LJ highlights the fact that the DSM includes as possible basis for a clinical diagnosis 'unhappiness', 'irritability and anger', and 'paedophilia', none of which could ever come to be regarded as 'recognized medical conditions' for the purposes of the defence of diminished responsibility (a point made earlier). In Hughes LJ's view, voluntary intoxication, however acute, should be placed in the same category. That is to say, even if it is a recognized medical condition, it is not a medical condition appropriate for recognition in law as capable of giving rise to an abnormality of mental functioning substantially impairing D's ability in the relevant respects.

The Court of Appeal's approach, then, is to admit that acute voluntary intoxication can be a recognized medical condition, but to carve out some space for judicial discretion to rule that not all recognized medical conditions will suffice to bring the diminished responsibility defence into play. As we have just indicated, that approach is consistent with what the DSM itself says about the 'imperfect fit' between clinical

---

[144] [1964] Crim LR 402. [145] [2014] EWCA Crim 748.
[146] [2012] EWCA Crim 281. [147] DSM-IV, introduction.

and legal analysis. However, even if one puts aside the case of voluntary intoxication as a special case, the approach has the broader potential both to give rise to significant difficulties for trial judges in deciding whether or not to put the defence to the jury in contested cases, and to give rise to tensions between legal and clinical analysis that it was one purpose of the s. 52 reform to reduce. A more radical view of the reform would be that (a) any recognized medical condition is in principle capable of founding a defence of diminished responsibility, (b) that it is D's task to prove (on the balance of probabilities) that the condition gave rise to an abnormality of mental functioning that had the effects s. 52 requires it to have, and (c) that it is the prosecution's task to show the contrary beyond a reasonable doubt. On this radical view, if such an approach means more contested cases in which the prosecution seeks to rebut defence evidence that a recognized medical condition met the conditions of s. 52, then so be it. However, not the least of the problems with the radical view is that it places in jeopardy the prospect of establishing a satisfactory relationship between the defences of diminished responsibility and of loss of self-control.[148] As we have seen, the Court of Appeal has—rightly—made it clear that there is a need for some consistency of approach to the defences of loss of self-control and diminished responsibility when it comes to evidence of the effect of voluntary intoxication.[149]

Pleading Loss of Self-Control and Diminished Responsibility Together: There is nothing to stop D pleading both loss of self-control and diminished responsibility together. One cynical reason for D to take this course is the hope that if, say, the loss of self-control that led to the killing was not triggered by very grave provocation, and D was suffering only from a mild form of mental disorder, the jury will nonetheless put these two pieces of evidence together and bring in a manslaughter verdict even though, strictly speaking, that would be a case of adding 2 and 2 together in order to reach the required '5'. This is because if neither the evidence relating to the loss of self-control defence itself, nor the evidence for the diminished responsibility defence itself, is independently sufficient to satisfy the criteria respectively for each of those defences, the verdict should be murder. There should be no mixing and matching of half-fulfilled criteria on each side to make a 'whole' defence to murder. To that end, a judge should instruct a jury considering both defences to ignore evidence relevant only to one of them, when considering the other.[150] So, suppose that D claims that he reacted with murderous rage to a mildly offensive remark made by V not only because he (D) lost self-control, but also due to the influence on him of a medically recognized abnormality of mental functioning. D calls evidence from a psychiatrist who has examined him to say that D suffers from a mental abnormality that means that he sometimes finds it impossible to control his temper. The judge should tell the jury that this evidence is not relevant to the plea of loss of self-control (other than to show, if need be, that D had

---

[148] It is noteworthy, in this regard, that Dowds himself unsuccessfully pleaded both loss of self-control (on the basis of a fear of serious violence) and diminished responsibility.

[149] See the discussion of *Asmelash* [2013] EWCA Crim 157, at section 8.4(b)(iii).

[150] See the seminal article by R. D. Mackay, 'Pleading Provocation and Diminished Responsibility Together' [1988] Crim LR 411.

in fact lost self-control at the time of the killing). In particular, the psychiatrist's evidence cannot affect (a) whether D 'justifiably' has a sense of being seriously wronged, (b) whether the loss of self-control was attributable to circumstances of an extremely grave character, or (c) whether a person of D's sex and age with a normal degree of tolerance and self-restraint might have reacted as D did. Consequently, we may expect to see a shift in popularity towards diminished responsibility and away from old-style provocation in its newly restricted form as the loss of self-control defence. This is because—financial resources permitting—it is likely to prove easier to find a medical practitioner somewhere in the UK (or, if need be, in the world) willing to give evidence that D suffers from an abnormality of mind stemming from a 'medically recognized condition' that influenced his or her conduct, than it is to fulfil the requirements of the narrow loss of self-control defence.[151] To that end, a 'recognized' medical condition is not necessarily one that a substantial body of medical practitioners would accept as such: it can include, for example, a condition discovered by an individual practitioner who has published the results of his or her own medical research in a peer-reviewed journal.[152] All this suggests that, in the future, we may see more contested trials than we have been used to on the issue of diminished responsibility.

At a superficial level, the two defences of loss of self-control and diminished responsibility can seem as if they are two sides of a single coin, the former excusing normal people, and the latter abnormal people, who—for the reasons specified in each defence—could not be expected to contain an urge to kill. Moreover, they are often raised in similar circumstances: where, for example, a man has killed his partner following an argument or alleged infidelity.[153] However, the appearance is something of an illusion. In each case, the reasons for excusing differ so greatly that, ethically speaking, these defences have little or nothing in common. In cases of loss of self-control, the basis for excuse is that no more could reasonably have been expected of D—any ordinary person might have reacted in that way—although, given the nature of the motive for which D acted (retaliation; revenge-taking), there is not enough in this to warrant a full excuse and hence an acquittal. By contrast, 'reasonableness' plays no part at all in the assessment of D's homicidal conduct in diminished responsibility cases. In effect, D is saying, 'I was only to an extent morally responsible for my actions, and to the extent that I was *not* morally responsible, I should not be judged by the standards of ordinary people at all'. Those acting under the influence of provocation or a fear of violence are 'morally active' (in evaluative control), and hence morally accountable—if not fully to blame—for their conduct, whereas those acting under diminished responsibility are morally more 'passive' (less capable of evaluative control), and less justly held fully to account for their conduct.[154] Accordingly, the defence of diminished responsibility may have just as clear an application to cases of, for example, premeditated, sexually motivated, or mass killing as it does to killing in the heat of the moment. Even a

[151] See Horder, *Homicide and the Politics of Law Reform*, at 233.
[152] See Public Bill Committee Debates, 3 March 2009, col 414.
[153] For critical discussion of this common feature, see J. Horder, *Excusing Crime* (2004), 165–9.
[154] See Horder, *Excusing Crime*, ch 1.

homicidal war crime could be reduced to manslaughter if there was evidence that the perpetrator's responsibility was diminished, whereas no amount of provocation could ever excuse—let alone justify—such an act.

The absence of theoretical connection between the two partial defences to murder is an illustration of a broader problem in the law of homicide. Currently, there is little more than a jumble of instances in which murder can be reduced to manslaughter, if one also adds in the curious case of a part-completed suicide pact (s. 4 of the Homicide Act 1957), all with their own rationales for existence, none of which is wholly convincing in its own terms.[155] Were the mandatory sentence for murder to be abolished, it would be possible—with the assistance of statutory guidelines if need be—to rid the law of these anomalous excuses and regard the issues (provocation, fear, mental disorder, etc.) as matters of sentence mitigation. Not the least of the benefits of such a scheme would be that it would cease to matter which precise defence pigeonhole D's actions fitted into, with all the current implications that has for the admissibility of evidence (ir)relevant to the defence in question. It would be possible to take account of both diminished responsibility and fear of violence or provocation, depending on the degree to which they had a just bearing on the appropriate sentence. Ironically, under current sentencing guidelines, when D is convicted of murder because the specific defences based on these factors have been rejected by the jury, it is precisely this approach that influences what sentence D receives.[156]

(d) KILLING IN PURSUANCE OF A SUICIDE PACT

Section 4 of the Homicide Act 1957 provides that a person who kills another in pursuance of a suicide pact is guilty of manslaughter, not murder. A suicide pact exists where two or more people, each having a settled intention of dying, reach an agreement which has as its object the death of both or all.[157] Some suicide pacts may be regarded as the highest expression of individual autonomy, by means of a mutual exercise of the individuals' rights of self-determination, but the Law Commission reported concern that the majority of cases involve men taking decisions to end the lives of the spouses or partners for whom they are caring.[158] The Criminal Law Revision Committee recommended that killings in pursuance of a suicide pact should be a separate offence, on the ground that the stigma and maximum penalty for manslaughter are inappropriate in these cases.[159] This is a more contentious stance than might at first glance be supposed. In principle, for example, s. 4 would cover the following cases:

(A) a cult leader secures the agreement of all his 300 followers that they will die together with him in a barn that he will set alight. He sets the fire with that intention in mind but, finding it hot, changes his mind and makes his escape while the 300 followers die.

---

[155] See Horder, *Homicide and the Politics of Law Reform*, ch 8.
[156] Criminal Justice Act 2003, Sch 21 to s. 269.
[157] The burden of proof will be on the survivor to prove this, on the balance of probabilities.
[158] LCCP 177, *A New Homicide Act?*, paras. 8.68–83.   [159] 14th Report (1980), para. 132.

(B) Two terrorists are on the run from the police. They return to their apartment and agree that one will shoot the other dead before shooting himself dead, to avoid the capture and questioning of either. One shoots the other dead, but then changes his mind about killing himself and decides to fight to the death with the pursuing police instead. When the police arrive later he gives up on that intention as well, and allows himself to be arrested without resistance.

An offence dealing with suicide pacts must be up to the task of fair labelling in such cases, and it is strongly arguable that the right label is (at least) manslaughter.[160] Consequently, the Law Commission recommended no change to the law until there is a wider review of 'consensual' and 'mercy' killings. However, it abandoned its earlier proposal that s. 4 should be abolished and all cases dealt with under the partial defence of diminished responsibility if they were to fall outside the scope of murder. This was because there might be cases in which a suicide pact was the product of a rational decision by mentally normal people, and such cases required consideration alongside similar 'ending of life' decisions, rather than being dealt with in isolation:[161]

> Y has terminal cancer and is determined to bring about her own death one way or another. X, Y's husband, does not wish to live on if Y is dead. So, X and Y decide to end both their lives by jumping off a high cliff on to the rocks below. They hold hands at the top of the cliff, count to three in unison, shout, 'Go!', and then jump off. X survives the fall but Y dies.

Were it not for s. 4, X would in theory be guilty of the murder of Y because, with the intention that they should both die, his acts of assistance and encouragement play a causal role in bringing about Y's death, although the law almost always treats such a role in another's death as the specific offence of doing an act capable of encouraging or assisting suicide rather than as murder.[162] Had Y survived instead of X, it would be Y who was guilty of murder or of encouraging/assisting suicide, for identical reasons. Yet, it is perhaps not all that easy to see why X's decision to end both their lives *with Y's agreement* should make such a fundamental difference to the legal outcome. Suppose Y had asked X to push her off the cliff, and X had agreed; but secretly, X always harboured the intention to jump off the cliff immediately afterwards, a decision he did not communicate to Y for fear of causing her even greater distress. In such circumstances, if X jumps off the cliff immediately afterwards and survives, he is nonetheless guilty of the murder of Y and has no defence. Indeed, given that he pushed her off the cliff, there is no case for treating what X did as merely encouraging or assisting suicide. This kind of example illustrates that it would make more sense for the law to consider all forms of 'ending of life' decisions together, when considering how far to extend

---

[160] The Royal Commission on Capital Punishment (1949–53) had recommended that suicide pacts in which one person agreed to kill another person before killing himself ('you, then me' pacts) should remain murder, and only 'die together' pacts should be manslaughter. The government of the day decided to draw no distinction between the two and both are covered by s. 4. In examples (A) and (B), the first is a 'die together' pact and the second a 'you, then me' pact. On fair labelling, see Chapter 6.7(a).

[161] Law Com No. 304, paras. 7.42–45.

[162] Assisting or encouraging suicide is an offence, punishable with up to 14 years' imprisonment, contrary to s. 2(1) of the Suicide Act 1961.

the scope of defences to murder, rather than permitting only an exception for suicide pact cases that is morally so arbitrary in its range and application. For similar reasons, the relationship between murder and s. 4 manslaughter needs to be considered in the light of the specific offence of encouraging or assisting suicide. For example, why is the latter not manslaughter, if V dies having been influenced by D's encouragement or assistance, with killing in the course of a suicide pact being treated as a separate specific offence instead?

(e) DOING AN ACT CAPABLE OF ASSISTING OR ENCOURAGING SUICIDE OR ATTEMPTED SUICIDE

Suicide and attempted suicide ceased to be criminal when the Suicide Act 1961 became law, in recognition of the right to self-determination. However, as indicated at the end of the last section, it is an offence contrary to s. 2(1) of the Suicide Act 1961 if:

(a)   Does an act capable of encouraging or assisting the suicide or attempted suicide of another person, and

(b)   D's act was intended to encourage or assist suicide or an attempt at suicide.

(1A)   The person referred to in subsection (1)(a) need not be a specific person (or class of persons) known to, or identified by, D.

(1B)   D may commit an offence under this section whether or not a suicide, or an attempt at suicide, occurs.

(1C)   An offence under this section is triable on indictment and a person convicted of such an offence is liable to imprisonment for a term not exceeding 14 years.[163]

This version of the offence is a version modified by s. 59 of the Coroners and Justice Act 2009, although the changes were intended simply to modernize the language of s. 2(1),[164] and clarify the law.[165] It may appear paradoxical to legalize an activity (suicide), but at the same time make it a serious offence to encourage or assist that lawful act. Further, many of the cases governed by s. 2 involve compassionate assistance, where many may think there is little case for prosecuting. However, the rationale for the offence is illustrated by *McShane*,[166] where a woman was convicted of an attempt to counsel her mother's suicide by encouraging her repeatedly to take an overdose, and it was shown that the mother's death would greatly alleviate the defendant's financial problems. There remains a need to protect the vulnerable from persuasion on such a crucial matter as the ending of life. Just because suicide is not a criminal offence does not mean that it has ceased to involve an unjustified harm through the elimination of

---

[163] Under French law, the equivalent offence carries a maximum sentence of only three years. Imprisonment: Art. 221–13.

[164] To reflect the language of the offences of encouraging and assisting crime under the Serious Crime Act 2007.

[165] Further provisions to clarify the law in s. 2A will not be addressed here.

[166] (1978) 66 Cr App R 97.

a human life. That being so, there can be a legitimate case for criminalizing the encouragement or assistance of suicide, and *McShane* is an illustration of the kind of case where it seems justified to employ the deterrent and retributive powers of the criminal law.[167]

The consent of the Director of Public Prosecutions (DPP) is required before a prosecution under s. 2 is commenced, and that has brought under scrutiny the prosecution policy adopted by the DPP in relation to such prosecutions. A number of difficulties have arisen in relation to scope of the offence. For example, suppose someone (V) attempts to kill themselves through an overdose. The emergency services arrive whilst V is still conscious and in need of urgent treatment, but V refuses treatment under any circumstances. It might seem as if to attempt forcibly to treat V would be to assault V, and the courts have confirmed that this is indeed so.[168] However, doctors and the emergency services are under a duty to take positive action to help those in their care, and those needing immediate treatment for whom they have assumed responsibility, meaning that an omission can count as an 'act' for legal purposes. So, do doctors and the emergency services do 'an act capable of . . . assisting' V to commit suicide by allowing V to die unaided? It would seem that they do not.[169] So, in seeking to provide an escape route from the dilemma in which care workers may find themselves, in such situations, the law errs on the side of the right to self-determination and avoids paternalism (seeking to improve someone's prospects even when they are themselves fully capable of deciding where their own best interests lie). It is probably right to do so, in so far as to permit the forcible administering of treatment on a sane and mature adult against their will is likely to be an inhuman and degrading process for that person, and will hence involve a breach of Art. 3 of the European Convention on Human Rights. In some countries, the law has gone further, and does not look unfavourably even on doctors who take positive steps to assist suicide.[170]

That still leaves unclear what policy should be adopted towards the ordinary citizen who seeks to assist,[171] in a variety of circumstances, someone who wishes to die. All prosecutions must pass tests not only of evidential sufficiency, but also of public interest, and it is in relation to the public interest factor in prosecuting s. 2(1) cases that devising prosecution policy is most difficult and controversial. On the one hand, taking it for granted that the criminalization of assisting suicide is the right legal policy in general,[172] there would be a strong public interest in prosecuting someone who set up a commercial operation in the UK to help people end their lives.[173] On the other

---

[167] See also *Cumming* [2007] 2 Cr App R(S) 20.   [168] *Re B (Refusal of treatment)* [2002] 2 All ER 449.

[169] *B (Refusal of treatment)* [2002] 2 All ER 449.

[170] See, e.g., J. Griffiths, 'Assisted Suicide in the Netherlands' (1995) 58 MLR 232, and M. Blake, 'Physician-Assisted Suicide: A Criminal Offence or a Patient's Right?' (1997) 5 Medical LR 294.

[171] Unless there is a radical change in ethical and legal thinking, it seems clear that the law should make little or no allowance for the person who *encourages* (as opposed to assists) another to commit suicide.

[172] A matter on which, of course, people differ strongly, but consideration of which is beyond the scope of this work.

[173] Although perhaps not such a strong public interest as to make it desirable to criminalize UK citizens if and when they engage in this conduct in countries where doing so is tolerated.

hand, if a wife simply agrees with her terminally ill husband's request not to give him any more of the medicine he needs to stay alive for the few more days that the medicine can realistically give him, or buys tickets for them both to visit a country where he can be assisted to die, there may—depending on the precise facts—be little or no public interest in a prosecution.

In *R (on the Application of Purdy)* v *DPP*,[174] the applicant sought to compel the DPP to reveal or devise a published policy for prosecuting under s. 2, so that she could make a properly informed decision on whether to ask her husband to assist her to travel abroad to die. The House of Lords agreed with the argument that Art. 8—the right to respect for private and family life—was engaged by the prohibition on s. 2. Even so, Art. 8(2) provides that public authorities may legitimately interfere with respect for private and family life, but only—amongst other things—if the interference is 'in accordance with the law'.[175] The prohibition in s. 2 itself is, of course, in accordance with the law. However, the DPP is himself also a 'public authority' seeking to interfere or impinge on a matter of private and family life. In that regard, the House of Lords said that the absence of a published prosecution policy in relation to s. 2, meant that there was a risk that prosecutions would not be 'in accordance with the law', if it was not possible for individuals like Purdy to make highly important personal decisions against a sufficiently clear legal policy background. So, the DPP was obliged to publish a code setting out the factors to be considered in any prosecution decision in relation to s. 2.[176]

This argument involves a sleight of hand, because there was never any suggestion that a prosecution would be undertaken other than 'in accordance with the law'.[177] It is true that forcing the DPP to draw up a comprehensive prosecution policy in relation to s. 2 would assist citizens the better to assess the risk that they might be prosecuted if they took certain steps. However, that argument might equally apply to cases in which someone is contemplating committing, assisting or encouraging, or conspiring to commit euthanasia (murder, in English law).[178] Moreover, the issuing of official guidelines in relation to the prosecution of a particular offence (s. 2, in this instance) opens up the prospect of secondary litigation testing whether, in any allegedly borderline case, the guidance had been correctly followed. That could lead to prosecutions being stayed for lengthy periods whilst the secondary litigation is conducted to answer the point, or to convictions being quashed long after the event, on procedural fairness grounds that would have no application to crimes closely analogous to assisting suicide (where there was no official guidance), such as euthanasia. Perhaps the answer

---

[174] [2009] UKHL 45.

[175] The interference must also be, 'necessary in a democratic society . . . for the prevention of crime, for the protection of health or morals, or for the protection of the rights and freedoms of others'.

[176] See <www.cps.gov.uk/publications/prosecution/assisted_suicide_policy.pdf>, discussed in P. Lewis, 'Informal Legal Change and Assisted Suicide: the Policy for Prosecutors' (2011) 31 LS 119.

[177] See further, J. M. Finnis, 'Invoking the Principle of Legality against the Rule of Law' (2010) *New Zealand Law Review*, 601–16.

[178] In cases of inchoate assisting and encouraging crime contrary to the Serious Crime Act 2007, any offence is subject to defence of 'reasonableness'. *A fortiori*, it ought to follow that guidance on the use of the inchoate offence must also be issue, where the inchoate offence relates to s. 2, and perhaps also euthanasia.

is that all serious crimes should come with comprehensive official guidance on prosecution policy, whose implementation in any individual case can be challenged by the
individual prosecuted or convicted (or perhaps also by a third party, such as Dignity
in Dying). That would take the law into a new era in which public law principles of
judicial review were potentially as important as criminal law principles to the outcome of cases, something that English law has witnessed in private litigation against
the State.[179] That might not be such a bad thing, although it would draw the courts into
making authoritative decisions not only on the scope of the substantive law (as they
have always done), but now also on the boundaries within which a decision based on
a pre-announced policy will be regarded as reasonable, and as having taken into account relevant—and disregarded irrelevant—considerations. Inevitably, there would
be tensions between judicial interventions of this kind, and the broader position so far
as the accountability of the DPP on policy matters is concerned: the DPP is answerable
politically, on policy questions, to the Attorney General (a member of Parliament).

Amongst the factors listed as being relevant to a prosecution decision are:

In favour of prosecution:

1. the would-be suicide is under 18 years of age;

2. the suspect not being wholly motivated by compassion;

3. the suspect being unknown personally to the would-be suicide, and encouraging
   or assisting through, for example, the provision of specific information through
   website material;

4. the suspect being paid by the would-be suicide, or providing assistance to more
   than one person;

5. the suspect acting in his or her capacity as a health professional;

Against prosecution:

1. the suspect was wholly motivated by compassion;

2. the assistance or encouragement was only minor;

3. the suspect had sought to dissuade the would-be suicide, and participated only
   reluctantly;

4. the suspect reported the would-be suicide's death and co-operated fully with the
   police.

These factors span across excusatory, justificatory, and after-the-fact mitigating features of a case, but in a distinctive way. In D's favour, the factors are sensitive to excusatory features such as a compassionate motive or only reluctant participation, and to
'good citizenship' features such as reporting the death to, and co-operating with, the
authorities. On the other hand, against D, the factors are sensitive to whether someone
acts under a false cloak of justification (in his or her capacity as a professional, as a

---

[179] See, generally, C. Booth QC and D. Squires, *The Negligence Liability of Public Authorities* (2006).

commercial provider, or as a self-appointed actor 'in the public interest'). The logic of this approach is that it is precisely in those cases where someone sets themselves up as giving help or guidance in opposition to the law that a prosecution is desirable to underline the authority of the law itself.[180] By contrast, where someone acts from compassion, or only reluctantly (given the law's demands), whilst there is still a case for prosecution—after all, even reluctant murderers or thieves are still murderers or thieves—the public interest in the prosecution may be less compelling.

It is worth pursuing this point a little further, by making particular mention of factor 5 militating against prosecution, namely that the defendant was acting in their capacity as a health care professional. The Supreme Court has rejected the view that a medical professional's failure to assist in a suicide, requested by a patient unable to commit suicide without assistance, is a breach of that patient's Art. 8 right to respect for private life.[181] In that regard, in theoretical terms, the guidance is in line with this decision. The guidance places more emphasis on excusatory factors as militating in favour of non-prosecution (such as a relative's compassionate motive, in assisting), whereas action taken to assist suicide that carries with it an element of professionalism or the performance of public duty—a permissive or justificatory motive—will be scrutinized with a view to prosecution.

(f) 'MERCY' KILLING

This concept has no special legal significance in English criminal law, and there is no defence of mercy killing.[182] However, doctors may well avoid prosecution or conviction, if their actions evoke sympathy.[183] Where non-professionals are concerned, a not uncommon response is that 'legal and medical consciences are stretched to bring about a verdict of manslaughter by diminished responsibility'.[184] In Mackay's study of 157 cases in which diminished responsibility was raised, it seems that six were probably cases of mercy killing.[185] Practitioners commonly accept that worthy cases of mercy killing should be eased into diminished responsibility, but this informal approach provides the defendant with no legal basis for a defence. He or she is truly at the mercy of the psychiatrists, the prosecutor, and the judge.[186] The decision of the House of Lords

---

[180] See J. Horder, *Excusing Crime* (2004), 233.

[181] *R (On the application of Nicklinson) v Ministry of Justice* [2014] UKSC 38. See the discussion in Chapter 4.8(b).   [182] *Inglis* [2010] EWCA Crim 2637.

[183] For an (unsuccessful) prosecution of a family doctor for murder by administering high doses of morphine, see *Martin, The Guardian*, 15 December 2005, 8. The House of Lords Select Committee on Medical Ethics examined the issues and decided against recommending an offence of mercy killing, largely on the ground that existing provisions are sufficiently flexible to allow appropriate outcomes to be achieved, HL Select Committee on Medical Ethics, *Report* (Session 1993–94), i, paras. 259–60.

[184] CLRC 14th Report, para. 115; cf. *Cocker* [1989] Crim LR 740 with Lord Goff, 'A Matter of Life and Death' (1995) 3 Medical LR 1, at 11, and the findings of B. Mitchell, 'Public Perceptions of Homicide and Criminal Justice' (1998) 38 BJ Crim 453, at 460.

[185] Law Com No. 270, App B: 'The Diminished Responsibility Plea in Operation—an Empirical Study'. The estimate of six cases rests on inferences from Professor Mackay's descriptions of the relevant features of each case.

[186] On which see S. Ost, 'Euthanasia and the Defence of Necessity' [2005] Crim LR 355.

in the *Purdy* case (discussed in section (e)) to force the DPP to issue guidelines on prosecution policy in relation to the offence of assisting suicide is significant in relation to all these manoeuvres to escape the full force of the law of murder. It is an attempt to move to a more individual rights-governed approach, and away from the governance of the authoritarian principle in this field of law: where trust is placed in legal professionals and the jury to show mercy in the 'right' kinds of case.[187]

The Criminal Law Revision Committee (CLRC) regarded the bending of the law as unsatisfactory, and we have seen—in relation to diminished responsibility—that it may no longer be possible to engage in it in quite the same way under the post-2009 law.[188] The CLRC tentatively proposed a new offence of mercy killing where a person, out of compassion, unlawfully kills another who is, or is believed by him to be, permanently helpless or in great pain. The proposal attracted strong opposition, some arguing that it might withdraw legal protection from the weak and vulnerable, others arguing that the fundamental ethical problems could not be satisfactorily resolved by legal definition. In respect of doctors, some flexibility is achieved through such distinctions as that between bringing about a patient's death through omission (which may be lawful) and bringing it about by a positive act (which is not),[189] and between intending to cause death and intending to relieve pain while knowingly accelerating death.[190] A 'blind eye' may be turned to the practices of some doctors. But doctors cannot be assured that a 'blind eye' will be turned, and relatives and friends may be exposed to the strict law. In terms of protection for the vulnerable,[191] the chief difference between the present system and the CLRC's proposed offence is that the latter had a maximum penalty of two years' imprisonment, whereas life imprisonment is now available even where there is a conviction for manslaughter on grounds of diminished responsibility. The Law Commission concluded that a separate review and consultation on 'consensual' and 'mercy' killings would be necessary before well-founded proposals could be made.

(g) CONCLUSION: THE MURDER—MANSLAUGHTER BOUNDARY

In this section we have been examining the partial defences which mark out cases where, despite the presence of the mental element for murder, culpability is thought to be sufficiently reduced to warrant a reduction in the class of offence. Our discussion has taken a broad view of partial defences, commenting also on some possible defences which are not (yet) accepted in English law. Various reasons have been advanced for recognizing partial defences to murder. Some regard the mandatory penalty for

---

[187] For discussion of the authoritarian principle, see Chapter 4.5.

[188] Although, as we have seen, the re-definition of an abnormality of mental functioning as having to arise from a 'recognized medical condition' may assist some mercy killers suffering from the long-term stress of care without the need for any bending of the rules.

[189] The basis of the decision in *Airedale NHS Trust v Bland* [1993] AC 789, discussed in Chapter 5.4.

[190] The basis of the decision in *Adams* [1957] Crim LR 365, discussed in Chapter 5.6. See R. Tur, 'The Doctor's Defence and Professional Ethics' (2002) 13 KCLJ 75.

[191] Cf. M. Otlowski, *Voluntary Euthanasia and the Common Law* (1997), and J. Keown, *Euthanasia, Ethics and Public Policy* (2002).

murder as the chief, even the sole, reason for these doctrines. However, whilst highly significant, the mandatory penalty is not the only argument for partial defences. A key issue is the proper legal classification of an offence which contains strong exculpatory features: should killings influenced by diminished responsibility really be treated as cases of murder, whether or not the judge has flexibility on sentence? The Law Commission found strong support for the murder–manslaughter distinction, and for the view that partial defences should have the effect of reducing the crime from the most heinous to something lesser.[192] Worldwide, the label 'murder' (or its equivalent), and the stigma thought to accompany it, are very widely reserved for the most heinous group of killings,[193] with lesser forms of homicide classified differently where the culpability is significantly lower.[194]

The Law Commission recommended a three-tier structure for the law of homicide which includes two degrees of murder (first degree murder, second degree murder) and manslaughter.[195] Assuming—until we examine the matter in detail—that the scope of manslaughter corresponds roughly with the existing law of involuntary manslaughter, the Law Commission's recommendations would have three grades of conviction and therefore three thresholds to consider. To distinguish between first and second degree murder on the basis of the existence of an intent to kill or an intent to cause serious injury with an awareness of a serious risk of causing death may be acceptable, but it would focus much argument on the boundaries of 'serious injury' and of 'serious risk'. Similarly, the proposal that cases of intention to cause injury or fear or risk of injury with an awareness of a serious risk of causing death should qualify for conviction of second degree murder may be acceptable, but it will lead to much argument over the boundaries of 'injury' and of 'serious risk'.[196] Under the Law Commission's revised structure, the partial defences would reduce first degree murder to second degree murder, rather than from murder to manslaughter as under the current structure. The government chose not to explore further this three-tier structure for the law of homicide.

Arguments in favour of some of the partial defences have been set out above. Since it is possible that more than one defence might be raised in each murder case, sometimes in combination with a defence of lack of intent, or self-defence, a system of criminal law which offers a number of partial defences to murder risks undue complication and

---

[192] Law Commission, *Murder, Manslaughter and Infanticide* (2006).

[193] Some jurisdictions have terms for most serious forms of murder, such as the French concept of 'un assassinat': premeditated killing under Art. 221 of the Code Penale.

[194] See generally, J. Horder (ed.), *Homicide Law on Comparative Perspective* (2007); A. Reed and M. Bohlander (eds), *Loss of Self-control and Diminished Responsibility: Domestic, Comparative and International Perspectives* (2011).

[195] Law Com No. 304, 249. The term 'second degree' murder was employed by a Legislature as long ago as 1794, in Pennsylvania. A recommendation to divide the English law of murder into first and second degree murder can be dated back at least to the Royal Commission on Capital Punishment of 1866.

[196] See the valuable article by Richard Taylor, considering the implications for homicide trials of such these proposals for change: 'The Nature of Partial Excuses and the Coherence of Second Degree Murder' [2007] Crim LR, 345.

confusion in contested cases.[197] There is a risk—albeit small—that a jury may be divided over which partial defence applies, if any, on particular facts, leading to a situation in which no clear verdict can be reached. On the other hand, one merit of separate partial defences is that they focus the evidence and the legal argument, giving the jury (in contested cases) an opportunity to assess the particular arguments for partial exculpation. The challenges posed by having separate but closely allied defences, such as loss of control and diminished responsibility, could be overcome—as they are in some US states—by merging the two into a partial defence of 'extreme emotional disturbance', following the lead of the Model Penal Code.[198] This might encompass all those partial defences with an element of excuse in them. A provoked loss of self-control could fall within this new doctrine, as could diminished responsibility, although a general defence of mental disorder may be a better way of labelling and dealing with cases of clinical mental disorder. Cases now treated as infanticide often involve extreme emotional disturbance, as do mercy killings (although not those performed by professionals or commercial providers), suicide pacts, and cases of duress. One advantage of this amalgamation might be that there would be less potential for the jury to become confused, and yet the jury would still be empowered to reduce murder to manslaughter in appropriate cases. One disadvantage of the change might be that the more precise moral distinctions currently incorporated within the law would become submerged within the sentencing discretion, where the signposts are less clear and the arguments less structured.

A variant on this approach, a version of which is to be found under Art. 345 of the French Penal Code, is to give the jury in any murder case the right to find 'extenuating circumstances', which would mean—were it to be introduced in English law—that the judge would be free to pass an appropriate sentence rather than having to impose the mandatory life penalty. A sophisticated version of this was put forward as an amendment in the House of Lords during the debate that preceded the 2009 Act, but it was not adopted. It read:

56: Before Clause 46, insert the following new Clause—'Murder: extenuating circumstances

(1) In a trial for murder the trial judge may in the course of his summing up direct the jury that if they are satisfied that the defendant is guilty of murder, but are of the opinion that there were extenuating circumstances, they may on returning their verdict add a rider to that effect.

(2) The judge may not give such a direction unless there is evidence on which a reasonable jury might so find.

(3) Where the jury has so found, the judge shall not be obliged to pass a sentence of life imprisonment but may pass such other sentence as he considers appropriate having regard to any extenuating circumstances found by the jury.

---

[197] For criticism along these lines, see Horder, *Homicide and the Politics of Law Reform*, ch 8.

[198] Model Penal Code, s. 210.3.1(b). It must be said, however, that this partial defence is one of the least well received sections of the Code in the US, with only one or two adoptions: see J. Chalmers, 'Merging Provocation and Diminished Responsibility' [2004] Crim LR 198.

(4) If the judge passes a sentence other than a sentence of life imprisonment, he shall be obliged to state his reasons.

(5) If it appears to the Attorney General that the sentence so passed is unduly lenient he may refer it to the Court of Appeal under section 36 of the Criminal Justice Act 1988 (c. 33) (reviews of sentencing).[199]

This would be a highly sophisticated means of dealing with excusatory claims in homicide cases, although it is less clear that it would operate in a fair way when it is mental disorder that is the basis of the plea of extenuating circumstances. Juries are prone to find that horrific killings deserve to be treated as murder irrespective of the severity of any mental disorder that led the killer to do the acts in question. That is not fair to the killer whatever we may think of his or her acts, and does not ensure that he or she is treated more 'severely' in any event: prisoners with mental disorders may simply be transferred to hospitals for treatment.

It is arguable that both partial defences and 'extenuating circumstances' provisions only exist because legislatures in many countries have always wished to underpin the supposed uniqueness of murder, as a crime, with a unique (meaning uniquely severe) sentencing system to match, requiring a complex system for ensuring that at least some cases can fall down into a lesser (and less severely treated) category of homicide. Another alternative, then, would be to preserve the distinction between murder and manslaughter—but making it depend solely on the nature of the offender's fault element—and underpin this with separate but overlapping sentencing regimes for each offence. So, murder might involve a starting point of (say) fifteen years' imprisonment, going up to life imprisonment, whereas manslaughter might involve complete discretion over sentences up to a maximum of twenty years' imprisonment.[200]

8.5 'INVOLUNTARY MANSLAUGHTER'

The category of killings which has come to be known as involuntary manslaughter has nothing to do with involuntariness, properly so-called. These are not cases where the accused has caused death while in an involuntary state.[201] They are cases where death has been caused with insufficient fault to justify labelling it as murder, but with sufficient fault for a manslaughter verdict. The word 'involuntary' is therefore used merely to distinguish these killings from ones which have the necessary intent for murder but which are reduced to manslaughter by one of the doctrines just considered, such as loss of self-control or diminished responsibility. The legal debate in involuntary manslaughter is over the lower threshold of homicide liability—where to draw the line

---

[199] HL debates, 26 October 2009, col 1008–09, Lord Lloyd, adopting a proposal put forward by Professor John Spencer QC.

[200] The Sentencing Guidelines Council would, as now, have the function of designing guidelines for the kinds of cases, within manslaughter, that should attract lower or higher sentences.

[201] On which, see Chapter 4.2.

between manslaughter and cases of death by misfortune which are not serious enough to deserve a manslaughter conviction.

There are now three forms of involuntary manslaughter—two at common law (manslaughter by unlawful and dangerous act, manslaughter by gross negligence) and a statutory addition, corporate manslaughter. These three offences raise some deep issues of general principle. For example, manslaughter by unlawful and dangerous act is a species of constructive liability, which was briefly explained at the end of Chapter 4.7. In none of the cases of involuntary manslaughter is death or grievous bodily harm intended. Can constructive liability be justified by reference to the magnitude of the harm resulting, that is, death? Or would it be fairer to convict the wrongdoer of a lesser offence, thus ignoring the chance result of death occurring? Consider this example:

> D is arguing with V over whether V took D's place in the queue. V insults D, and D punches V in the stomach. V falls over, hits his head, and dies.

In law, so long as D is shown to have caused V's death, D commits manslaughter by unlawful and dangerous act in this example. The risk that V might die from D's punch is not relevant to the question of whether D is guilty of the crime. It is sufficient, as we shall see, that D commits the offence of assault (an act causing or posing a danger of 'some harm'), and that the assault causes death.[202]

The other two forms of involuntary manslaughter are based on liability for negligence, albeit gross negligence: as we saw in Chapter 6.4(a), this is regarded as insufficient for liability for most serious offences.[203] Is it right that liability for the second most heinous crime in English law, which carries a maximum penalty of life imprisonment, should be satisfied by this relatively low grade of fault?[204] These questions will be discussed in more detail once the elements of the offence have been outlined.

(a) MANSLAUGHTER BY UNLAWFUL AND DANGEROUS ACT

This species of involuntary manslaughter is based upon constructive liability. In broad terms, the law constructs liability out of the lesser crime which D was committing, and which happened to cause death. In fact, the courts have progressively narrowed this form of manslaughter over the last century or so:[205] there was a time when the mere commission of a tort or civil wrong sufficed as the 'unlawful act', and when there was no additional requirement of 'dangerousness' to be satisfied. What the prosecution must now prove is that D was committing a crime (not being a crime of negligence or a crime of omission), that in committing this crime he caused V's death, and that what

[202] Similarly, under the French Penal Code, an act of violence causing an unintended death is punishable by up to fifteen years' imprisonment: Art. 222–7. As we will see, English law goes much further, extending liability to unlawful and dangerous acts well beyond those that involve violence.

[203] Article 221–6. The offence is punishable with up to three years' imprisonment.

[204] It is, though, interesting to note that in French law causing death by negligence is the equivalent of manslaughter whether or not the negligence was 'gross', Art. 221–6. The offence is punishable with up to three years' imprisonment.

[205] R. J. Buxton, 'By Any Unlawful Act' (1966) 82 LQR 174.

he did when committing this crime was objectively dangerous. Let us examine each of these requirements in turn.

First, D must have been committing a crime. In many cases the crime which constitutes the 'unlawful act' will be a battery or an assault occasioning actual bodily harm, arising from a push, a punch, or a kick. The prosecution must establish that all the elements of the crime relied upon as the unlawful act were present: to this extent a mental element is required for this form of manslaughter, and so in assault or battery this would be the mental elements of intent or recklessness. This point had been overlooked by the trial judge in *Lamb*,[206] in assuming that an assault had taken place when two young men were joking with a revolver, without noting that fear was neither caused nor intended to be caused.[207] The point appears to have been overlooked by all the courts, including the House of Lords, in *Newbury and Jones*:[208] two boys caused the death of a railwayman by pushing a paving stone off a railway bridge on to a train below, but none of the judges identified the precise crime which constituted the 'unlawful act'. No doubt the boys' act was a crime (a form of criminal damage, or a specific railway offence), and so this case does not call into question the proposition that all the elements of the crime relied upon must be established. In *Dhaliwal*[209] D had subjected V to a long course of abuse, including physical assaults. One evening he abused her again, striking her once, and she subsequently committed suicide. The Court of Appeal quashed the manslaughter conviction, on the ground that V's severe emotional trauma caused by D's long course of abuse was not a recognized psychiatric condition and therefore not 'bodily harm'. Thus the abuse was not an unlawful act.

The 'unlawful act' requirement also means that D must not have any defence to the crime relied upon. Intoxication would supply a defence to a crime of specific intent in this context,[210] but in most cases the prosecution will rely on a crime of basic intent or recklessness and therefore intoxication would be no defence.[211] In a case where the prosecution relies on assault or battery as the 'unlawful act' and D claims that it was a justifiable use of force, the court must be satisfied beyond reasonable doubt that the force was not justified if it is to proceed to a manslaughter conviction.[212]

There appear to be two types of crime which will not suffice as the unlawful act—crimes of negligence and crimes of omission. The reasons for excluding crimes of negligence were stated in *Andrews* v *DPP*,[213] where a driver had killed a pedestrian whilst overtaking another car. There was little dispute that D had committed the offence of dangerous driving, but did that automatically make him guilty of manslaughter when death resulted? The House of Lords held that it did not: since the essence of dangerous driving was negligence, a driver should only be convicted of manslaughter if his

---

[206] [1967] 2 QB 981.   [207] For the law of assault, see Chapter 9.3(e).   [208] [1977] AC 500.
[209] [2006] 2 Cr App R 24, discussed by J. Horder and L. McGowan, 'Manslaughter by Causing Another's Suicide' [2006] Crim LR 1035, who conclude that on the facts, a prosecution for manslaughter by gross negligence would have been more likely to succeed.
[210] *O'Driscoll* (1977) 65 Cr App R 50.   [211] *Lipman* [1970] 1 QB 152, and generally Chapter 6.2.
[212] *Scarlett* (1994) 98 Cr App R 290.   [213] [1937] AC 576.

driving was so bad as to amount to the gross negligence required under the second head of involuntary manslaughter (see later). Whether or not the decision was motivated by tenderness towards motorists is hard to tell, but there is certainly some logic in keeping offences of negligence out of the 'unlawful act' doctrine when a separate head of manslaughter by gross negligence exists. The logic of the second exception is less evident, and cases of omission have not always been treated differently.[214] In *Senior*[215] a man who belonged to a religious sect called the Peculiar People refused to call a doctor to his child, who subsequently died; he was held guilty of manslaughter on the ground that he had committed an unlawful act (wilful neglect of the child) which caused death. However, this very reasoning was abjured in *Lowe*,[216] where D failed to ensure that medical help was summoned to his child, and it died. The Court of Appeal held that a manslaughter verdict would not necessarily follow from a conviction for wilful neglect:

> if I strike a child in a manner likely to cause harm it is right that if the child dies I may be charged with manslaughter. If, however, I omit to do something with the result that it suffers injury to health which results in death, we think that a charge of manslaughter should not be an inevitable consequence, even if the omission is deliberate.

This passage suggests that the law should, and does, draw a distinction between the blameworthiness of acts and omissions, even where the omission is deliberate. Yet the connection between withholding medical aid and subsequent death is surely closer than that between striking a child once and subsequent death. The father's duty in *Senior* and in *Lowe* is manifest and incontrovertible. If the 'unlawful act' doctrine is thought sound, these cases should fall squarely within it. If the doctrine is thought unsound, it should be abolished. This manifestation of the distinction between acts and omissions is morally untenable.[217]

Once it has been established that D was committing a criminal offence, the second step is to establish that this caused the death. In most cases of battery or actual bodily harm the causal connection will be plain, but cases involving drugs have presented difficulties. In *Kennedy (No. 2)*[218] D passed a syringe containing heroin to V, who injected himself and later died. The Court of Appeal upheld D's conviction for manslaughter, on the basis that the unlawful act was causing a noxious substance to be taken by V,[219] and that D was acting in concert with V and therefore bore joint responsibility for the offence. However, the House of Lords overruled this decision,[220] and re-affirmed

[214] For a fuller discussion, see A. Ashworth, 'Manslaughter by Omission and the Rule of Law' [2015] Crim LR 563.

[215] [1899] 1 QB 283.   [216] [1973] QB 702.

[217] In *Khan and Khan* [1998] Crim LR 830 the Court of Appeal suggested that omissions cases should be dealt with under gross negligence manslaughter.

[218] [2005] 2 Cr App R 23, criticized by D. Ormerod and R. Fortson, 'Drug Suppliers as Manslaughterers (Again)' [2005] Crim LR 819.

[219] Contrary to s. 23 of the Offences Against the Person Act 1861.

[220] [2008] 1 AC 269; for a review of the general topic, see W. Wilson, 'Dealing with Drug-Induced Homicide', in C. Clarkson and S. Cunningham, *Criminal Liability for Non-Aggressive Death* (2008).

the principle that a voluntary act (i.e. V's self-administration of the drugs) breaks the causal chain and prevents D from bearing responsibility for the death.

The third requirement is that the defendant's conduct in committing the crime must have been objectively dangerous. This was seen as a slight restriction of the doctrine when it was imposed in *Church*,[221] where the Court held that 'the unlawful act must be such as all sober and reasonable people would inevitably recognize must subject the other person to, at least, the risk of some harm resulting therefrom, albeit not serious harm'. The House of Lords has declined to narrow this test by requiring that D recognized the risk.[222] The test remains largely objective, but not entirely so. The dangers inherent in the situation should be judged on the basis of a reasonable person in that position, endowed with D's knowledge of the surrounding circumstances. Thus an ordinary person who burgled the house of an elderly resident would realize the possible dangers as soon as the age and frailty of the householder became apparent.[223] By contrast, the ordinary person would not know (if D did not know) that an apparently healthy girl of 15 had a weak heart;[224] but this decision must now be seen in the light of the decision of the Court of Appeal in *R v M*.[225] In this case, the victim was an apparently healthy 40-year-old doorman, who was in fact suffering from an asymptomatic renal artery aneurism. The defendants caused a violent disturbance outside the venue at which the victim was working, and the victim assisted in controlling the incident. The aneurism later ruptured causing fatal blood loss. The judge had ruled that the *Church* 'dangerousness' test could not be satisfied, but the Court of Appeal allowed an appeal by the prosecution.[226] The Court of Appeal held that the satisfaction of the *Church* test was predominantly one of fact, and on these facts, the criminal acts of the defendants might have been found by the jury to be such that any reasonable person would recognize that they posed a risk of some physical harm.

However, the reasonable person does not make unreasonable mistakes, and so the mistake of D who carelessly loaded a gun with a live cartridge thinking that it was blank was not taken into account.[227] One element of the *Church* test—'some harm . . . albeit not serious harm'—has been construed restrictively. In *Dawson*,[228] D, wearing a mask and carrying a pickaxe handle, approached a petrol-station attendant and demanded money; D fled when the attendant pressed the alarm bell, but the attendant then suffered a heart attack and died. The Court of Appeal held that the unlawful act would be regarded as 'dangerous' only if it was likely to cause physical harm, not if mere emotional shock (unaccompanied by physical harm) was foreseeable. The manslaughter conviction was quashed, partly because the trial judge had given the impression that conduct likely to produce emotional disturbance would be sufficient.

---

[221] [1966] 1 QB 59.

[222] *DPP v Newbury and Jones* [1977] AC 500.

[223] *Watson* [1989] 1 WLR 684.

[224] *Carey* [2006] Crim LR 842.

[225] [2012] EWCA Crim 2293.

[226] Under the Criminal Justice Act 2003, s. 58.

[227] *Ball* [1989] Crim LR 730.

[228] *Dawson* (1985) 81 Cr App R 150; cf. the strange interpretation of this decision in *Ball* [1989] Crim LR 730 and *Watson* [1989] 1 WLR 684.

Both the elements of 'unlawfulness' and 'dangerousness' in this form of manslaughter can be criticized.[229] One important criticism is that these elements together fail to identify sufficiently clearly conduct that is sufficiently blameworthy to justify conviction for manslaughter, but is not in essence conduct where negligence as to unforeseen consequences plays the crucial role in determining blameworthiness. For, as we saw just now in the discussion of *Andrews* v *DPP*, where negligence is playing that role it should ordinarily not be sufficient to justify liability for manslaughter unless it amounts to *gross* negligence in breach of a duty of care not to cause death (a basis for manslaughter is discussed in the next section). So, this form of manslaughter is open to serious criticism in terms of 'fair labelling', and by reference to the correspondence principle.[230] The correspondence principle is breached because the fault element does not have to relate to the death of the victim; indeed, the only fault element of substance relates to the unlawful (criminal) act, albeit that this act must be dangerous in the *Church* sense. The breach of the correspondence principle contributes to an absence of fair labelling in many such cases. In many instances where (say) a scuffle starts outside a public house, and no one is physically hurt, there may not even be police action or a prosecution; but if, as in *R* v *M*,[231] someone involved in the scuffle had a potentially lethal physical defect that was unfortunately triggered by the incident, leading to their death, then those unlawfully involved in the scuffle face conviction for 'manslaughter' and an almost inevitable prison sentence. The disparity between these possible outcomes, hinging simply on whether or not death is caused is what contributes to the sense of unfair labelling.

By contrast with English law, in French law, the focus in the equivalent offence is on neither the unlawfulness of conduct, as such, nor on the danger of minor harm that it poses. Instead, Art. 222-7 says simply that, 'acts of violence causing an unintended death' may be punished by up to fifteen years' imprisonment. Such a basis for a manslaughter conviction has been defended,[232] as a form of 'moderate constructivism'. It may be argued that an *intentional* attack on someone's physical integrity, in the form of wounding or actual bodily harm, rightly exposes someone to criminal liability for unintended consequences intrinsically linked to that attack, as well as for the attack's intended consequences. If I intentionally punch you with such force that I cause you injury, you fall to the ground, hit your head on the road, and die in consequence, there is an intrinsic link—physical harm done—between the injury intended and the death caused, that makes it morally permissible to hold me responsible as much in criminal as in civil law. Critics of such an approach insist that the problem of fair labelling in such cases is still unresolved: I am still being held liable for unintended and unforeseen consequences which may not even have been brought about through gross negligence. Further, it is argued, the fact that an attack is intentional makes the attack itself more

---

[229] See Horder, *Homicide and the Politics of Law Reform*, ch 5.

[230] On fair labelling and the correspondence principle, see Chapter 6.7(a).

[231] [2012] EWCA Crim 2293.

[232] For a defence of manslaughter on this basis, see Horder, *Homicide and the Politics of Law Reform*, ch 5.

serious, but leaves untouched the question whether it is right to find me criminally liable for the death caused.[233]

(b) MANSLAUGHTER BY GROSS NEGLIGENCE

This second variety of 'involuntary' manslaughter has suffered no fewer changes of direction than the first. Gross negligence became well established as a head of manslaughter in the nineteenth century, and then all but disappeared from the law in the 1980s. Thus in *Finney*,[234] where an attendant at a mental hospital caused the death of a patient by releasing a flow of boiling water into a bath, the test was whether he had been grossly negligent. In *Bateman*,[235] where a doctor had attended the confinement of a woman who died whilst giving birth, the Court of Criminal Appeal held that there must be negligence over and above that which is sufficient to establish civil liability, and which shows 'such disregard for the life and safety of others' as to deserve punishment. This test was approved by the House of Lords in *Andrews v DPP*.[236] In *Lamb*[237] two young men were joking with a gun; D pointed it at V and pulled the trigger, believing that it would not fire because neither bullet was opposite the barrel. The gun was a revolver, however, and it did fire, killing V. The Court of Appeal held that D might properly be convicted if his belief that there was no danger of the gun firing had been formed in a criminally negligent way.

The beginnings of a change of direction appeared in *Stone and Dobinson*,[238] where two people were convicted of manslaughter for allowing a sick relative, whom they had permitted to live in their house, to die without medical attention. The Court of Appeal's grounds for finding a duty of care in this case are scrutinized elsewhere.[239] The fault element required was expressed as recklessness, and defined thus: 'a reckless disregard of danger to the health and welfare of the infirm person. Mere inadvertence is not enough. The defendant must be proved to have been indifferent to an obvious risk of injury to health, or actually to have foreseen the risk but to have determined nevertheless to run it'. This passage contrasted 'mere inadvertence' with 'indifference to an obvious risk', perhaps foreshadowing the change that was about to take place. In the 1980s it was the concept of recklessness, in the *Caldwell* sense,[240] that came to dominate this variety of manslaughter. Both the House of Lords in *Seymour*[241] and the Privy Council in *Kong Cheuk Kwan*[242] propounded this as the proper test, and it was widely assumed that manslaughter by gross negligence had been absorbed into and replaced by reckless manslaughter.

In *Adomako*[243] the House of Lords re-established manslaughter by gross negligence, and jettisoned manslaughter by *Caldwell* recklessness. Lord Mackay held that

---

[233] A. Ashworth, 'A Change of Normative Position: Determining the Contours of Culpability in Criminal Law' (2008) 11 *New Criminal Law Review* 232.   [234] (1874) 12 Cox CC 625.

[235] (1925) 94 LJKB 791.   [236] [1937] AC 576.

[237] [1967] 2 QB 981.   [238] [1977] QB 354.

[239] A. Ashworth, 'The Scope of Criminal Liability for Omissions' (1989) 105 LQR 424, at 440–5.

[240] Discussed in Chapter 6.5(c).   [241] [1983] 1 AC 624.

[242] (1986) 82 Cr App R 18.   [243] [1995] 1 AC 171.

manslaughter by gross negligence requires the prosecution to prove (i) that D was in breach of a duty of care towards the victim, (ii) that the breach of duty caused the victim's death, and (iii) that the breach of duty amounted to gross negligence.

What determines the existence of a duty? Lord Mackay took the view that this was simply a matter of consulting the law of tort, and some decisions can be thus explained. Certain duty situations are well established, such as parent–child and doctor–patient. Others have been recognized in previous decisions: there are the omissions cases where D has a contractual duty to ensure safety,[244] and where D was initially responsible for creating a hazardous situation.[245] New duty-situations may be recognized, as in *R v West London Coroner, ex p Gray*,[246] where the Divisional Court recognized that police officers have a duty of care towards persons they arrest, particularly persons who are intoxicated. In *Prentice*[247] the Court of Appeal recognized the duty of an electrician to leave the house safe for the householder who employed him. A company has a duty to ensure the health and safety of its employees and of others affected by its activities,[248] for example. More recently, interest has focused on the criminal law's recognition of duties beyond those of the law of torts. This is not a new phenomenon, because the reasons adduced to support a duty to care for a sick relative in *Stone and Dobinson* (e.g. blood relationship, guest in house) remain controversial. In *Wacker*[249] D was involved in a plan to bring sixty illegal immigrants into the UK in a container on his lorry, and fifty-eight of them died from suffocation. The point was taken that, since the sixty would-be immigrants had concurred in the plan, D did not have an enforceable duty of care towards them because of their voluntary involvement in the illegality. The Court of Appeal responded that, while this may be the situation in the law of tort, the criminal law has the wider function of protecting the public and it is therefore not subject to the same restrictions as the law of tort. In *Willoughby*[250] D asked V to come to a disused public house that D owned and to help him set fire to it with petrol. The ensuing fire killed V and injured D. The Court of Appeal held that D was rightly convicted of the manslaughter of V, as well as the offence of arson endangering life, because D owed a duty to V. The Court held that the trial judge had been wrong to hold that the duty arose simply by virtue of D's ownership of the pub, but held that the duty stemmed from D's recruiting V to help and assigning him the dangerous task of spreading the petrol. As in *Wacker*, the effect is to go beyond duty-situations recognized by the law of negligence and to impose on D a duty towards people who are willing participants in the same enterprise. The decision in *Willoughby* recognizes that the existence of a duty is a question of law. But, in the absence of criteria for determining duty-situations,[251] this appears to be common law decision-making at its retrospective worst.

---

[244] *Pittwood* (1902) 19 TLR 37, the operator of a railway level crossing.

[245] *Miller* [1983] 2 AC 161, discussed in Chapter 4.4.   [246] [1988] QB 467.

[247] [1994] QB 302; this was the case that became *Adomako* in the House of Lords, the other three appellants in the consolidated appeal having had their convictions quashed by the Court of Appeal.

[248] *R v DPP, ex parte Jones* [2000] Crim LR 858.

[249] [2003] QB 1203.   [250] [2005] Crim LR 389.

[251] See the discussion by J. Herring and E. Palser, 'The Duty of Care in Gross Negligence Manslaughter' [2007] Crim LR 24.

It is in a way understandable that the courts should wish to avoid tying the concept of duty in the law of criminal negligence to the concept as it is currently understood in the law of tortious negligence. The duty concept has evolved in tort to reflect considerations concerned with monetary compensation of one private citizen for damage done by another (or by the State or one of its agents) that have no direct application in the substantive criminal law. So, for example, it can be a relevant consideration limiting the duty of care in tort that D might—if a duty were imposed—be exposed in a disproportionate way to an unlimited liability to compensate to an unlimited class of persons; but that concern is not relevant in the criminal law.[252] Moreover, in an ideal world, criminal trials would not be delayed (or followed) by lengthy secondary litigation over whether a duty of care arose in law, in the way that this heavily litigated question has pre-occupied civil courts for over a century. Accordingly, the criminal courts have settled for a simpler position, involving a two-step process: (a) the judge rules whether, as a matter of law, D's relationship with V was capable of giving rise to a duty, and if the ruling is that the relationship may involve in law a duty, then (b) it is for the jury to decide whether that duty arose on the facts of the case before them.

Much simpler though this approach may be, it sacrifices a great deal in point of certainty, in that it will be difficult for an ordinary person to know in advance when a duty of care will arise, and therefore whether they must do or not do certain things to avoid another's death if they are to escape criminal liability for manslaughter. A good example of the kind of retrospective lawmaking to which this approach can lead is to be found in *Evans*.[253] D had given her 16-year-old half-sister heroin at home, even though her sister was a recovering addict. V self-injected, and then began to show clear symptoms of having overdosed. D and her mother appreciated that there was a danger to V's health, but were afraid of getting into trouble if they called the emergency services. Consequently, they simply put V to bed and checked on her periodically, sleeping in the same room as her. By the morning, V had died from heroin poisoning. D was convicted of manslaughter and appealed, but the Court of Appeal upheld her conviction. It did so, however, not in virtue of D having supplied V with the heroin in the first place, but on the basis that, having *contributed* (by that act of supply) to the creation of a situation in which there was a risk of V's death, she had a duty to seek to rectify it by taking reasonable steps, and in the circumstances breached that duty in a grossly negligent way through failing to summon help before V died.

This finding involved an extension to the *Miller*[254] doctrine that the unjustified creation of a dangerous situation may lead to a duty to take reasonable steps to eliminate the danger (in that case, the danger posed by letting a cigarette fall and set fire to the room). The extension comes about because it was V who herself created the danger of death by self-injecting with heroin; D merely assisted in the creation of that danger by

---

[252] Although there is an analogous concern in the criminal law governing omissions not to impose duties to act in particular situations, breach of which would have the potential to be a criminal offence, on too wide a range of persons in that situation: see A. Ashworth, 'The Scope of Criminal Liability for Omissions' (1989) 105 LQR 424.

[253] [2009] EWCA Crim 650.   [254] [1983] 2 AC 161 HL.

V. Small extension to the *Miller* doctrine though it might seem, it does involve judicial extension of the ambit of criminal liability for manslaughter through case-by-case development. This is unsatisfactory, in that in the controversial area of dangerous drug-taking, the issues ought to be addressed through a proper consultative process that it is beyond the courts to undertake before they extend the law.[255] In French law, a combination of Art. 221-6 and Art. 121-3 provides for just the kind of situation encountered in *Evans*. By Art. 221-6, the causing of death by negligence is an offence punishable by up to three years' imprisonment, and by Art. 121-3, that offence can be committed in the following circumstances:

> natural persons who have not directly contributed to causing the damage, but who have created or contributed to create the situation which allowed the damage to happen who failed to take steps enabling it to be avoided, are criminally liable where it is shown that they have . . . committed a specified piece of misconduct which exposed another person to a particularly serious risk of which they must have been aware.

As a matter of doctrine, a less convoluted route to conviction in *Evans* might have been to say that D's supply of the heroin to V was a grossly negligent act that was itself still an operating cause of V's death. It was still an operating cause, in that—being only 16—V's decision to self-inject a controlled drug was not adequately free and informed, and hence did not break the chain of causation from D's supply; only self-injection by someone 18 years old or older (in full knowledge of the facts) would adequately meet the 'free, deliberate, and informed' criterion and hence break the chain of causation.[256] Even taking that course would, though, involve an extension of the scope of the law.

Once it is established that there was a duty, that it was breached,[257] and that this caused the death, there is the question of the terms in which the test of gross negligence is to be put to the jury. Lord Mackay LC in *Adomako* held that gross negligence depends:

> on the seriousness of the breach of duty committed by the defendant in all the circumstances in which he was placed when it occurred and whether, having regard to the risk of death involved, the conduct of the defendant was so bad in all the circumstances as to amount in the jury's judgment to a criminal act or omission.[258]

Lord Taylor CJ in the Court of Appeal had earlier stated that there were other types of case that might justify a finding of gross negligence, notably cases where there was

---

[255] See generally, G. Williams, 'Gross Negligence Manslaughter and Duty of Care in "Drugs" Cases: *R v Evans*' [2009] Crim LR 631; A. Ashworth, 'Manslaughter by Omission and the Rule of Law' [2015] *Criminal Law Review* 563.

[256] For the application of the 'free, deliberate, and informed' criterion, as an indication of when someone's intervention (including V's by, e.g., self-injecting) will break the chain of causation, see the decision of the House of Lords in *Kennedy (No. 2)* [2008] 1 AC 269.

[257] For a troubling decision concerned with the relationship between duty, and breach of duty, see *Phillips* [2013] EWCA Crim 358. This was another case where a conviction was upheld based on 'failure to assist' someone who had collapsed after an overdose; but in this case D had sought to assist by injecting the victim with adrenaline. The Court of Appeal did not appear to appreciate that the latter act might have regarded by the jury as discharging D's duty to assist, even though the assistance was unsuccessful.

[258] [1995] 1 AC at 187.

actual awareness of a risk combined with indifference to it or a grossly negligent attempt to avoid it.[259] It does not seem difficult to encompass these other cases within the *Adomako* test, so long as the focus remains on 'the risk of death'. If such a risk was reasonably foreseeable, then the jury must decide whether D's conduct fell so far below the expected standard as to justify conviction for manslaughter. It has often been observed that this test is circular: if members of the jury ask how negligent D must have been if they are to convict him of manslaughter, the answer is 'so negligent as to deserve conviction for manslaughter'. Significant as the circularity point may be, more powerful are the arguments that (a) it fails to meet the test of certainty properly required of a criminal law by Art. 7 of the Convention, and (b) its breadth leads to unfair inconsistencies in prosecution policy. The *Adomako* test was challenged on the former basis in *Misra* (2005),[260] and drew the unconvincing response that the question 'is not whether the defendant's negligence was gross and whether, additionally, it was a crime, but whether his behaviour was grossly negligent and consequently criminal'. This is a distinction without a difference and, despite the Court's discussion of some of the Strasbourg authorities, it should not be the last word on the subject. Indeed, Judge LJ went on to state that 'this is not a question of law, but one of fact'. Lord Mackay's words in *Adomako* make it clear that the jury is, in effect, deciding a question of law when it decides whether the conduct was bad enough to be classed as manslaughter. The second criticism of the *Adomako* test emerges from research by Oliver Quick into the decision-making of prosecutors in cases of fatal errors by medical staff,[261] finding a number of unexplained variations in prosecution decisions that the broad terminology of the offence permits.

Finally, we should note that, closely allied to manslaughter by gross negligence is the offence of manslaughter by (subjective) recklessness. There is some confusion over the relationship, in that in *Adomako* Lord Mackay indicated that it would not be wrong for a judge in directing the jury on the fault element in gross negligence manslaughter cases to use the term 'reckless' to describe D's conduct. However, it seems clear that causing death by recklessness is a form of manslaughter in its own right. In *Lidar*,[262] V died under the wheels of D's car when he lost his grip on the car as it was being driven at speed by D following a fight involving them both. D was convicted of manslaughter by recklessness. The Court of Appeal upheld Lidar's conviction on the basis that he had foreseen a risk that V might suffer death or serious injury if he (D) continued to drive at speed, and yet he continued to do so, and caused V's death thereby.

(c) CORPORATE MANSLAUGHTER

The Corporate Manslaughter and Corporate Homicide Act 2007 introduced a new form of manslaughter, corporate manslaughter, to English law. It was formerly possible

---

[259] *Prentice* [1994] QB 302, at 323.

[260] [2005] 1 Cr App R 21, on which see the comments of V. Tadros, *Criminal Responsibility* (2005), 85. Another (unsuccessful) ground of appeal was that the definition of the offence is so uncertain as to be incompatible with Art. 7 of the Convention.

[261] O. Quick, 'Prosecuting "Gross" Medical Negligence: Manslaughter, Discretion and the Crown Prosecution Service' (2006) 33 JLS 421.   [262] [2000] 4 *Archbold News* 3.

to convict a company of manslaughter by gross negligence at common law, but the 'identification doctrine' (discussed in Chapter 6.3) proved so restrictive in practice that only a few convictions of smaller companies were obtained.[263] Public concern at the considerable loss of lives resulting from companies' operations, and belief in the fairness of imposing the censure of homicide convictions (rather than merely of convictions under the Health and Safety at Work Act 1974) in bad cases, led to the lengthy and politically controversial process of bringing forward legislation.[264] The new offence can be committed only by an 'organization', and organizations can no longer be convicted of manslaughter by gross negligence (although individuals can). An individual cannot be held liable for the offence of corporate manslaughter, or for complicity in it.

The provisions of the Act are beset with considerable technicality,[265] but five key elements of the definition may be identified—(i) an 'organization' must (ii) owe a relevant duty of care and (iii) the way in which the activities were managed or organized must amount to a gross breach of that duty, (iv) a substantial element in that gross breach being the way that the organization's activities were organized by senior management, and (v) death must be caused by the way in which the activities were managed or organized. First, what qualifies as an 'organization' for the purpose of the Act? The definition goes well beyond companies and includes partnerships, some unincorporated associations, and most public bodies (such as hospital trusts, the police, and government departments).[266] The practical implications of these broad categories are considerably narrowed down by the second requirement, that the organization must owe a relevant duty of care to the deceased person. The concept of duty of care, elaborated in s. 2, is confined to duties recognized by the law of negligence.[267] Especially controversial in this respect was the prospect that liability could arise for deaths in custody, particularly where these occurred through a suicide that it is alleged could have been prevented. Initially, the government delayed making the 2007 Act applicable to such deaths, but since 2011 it has been applicable in that situation as specified in s. 2(2). There are also several exclusions in ss. 3 to 7 from duties that would otherwise apply—exclusions dealing with public bodies' decisions on resource allocation and public policy, military activities, the operations of emergency services, and duties under the Children Act 1989.[268] Whether there was a relevant duty of care is a question of law for the judge; the technicality of the tests and the exclusions may give rise to considerable legal argument.

[263] See generally C. Wells, *Corporations and Criminal Responsibility* (2nd edn., 2001); J. Gobert and M. Punch, *Rethinking Corporate Crime* (2003); and C. Wells, 'Corporate Manslaughter: Why Does Reform Matter?' (2006) 122 SALJ 646.

[264] C. Wells, 'Corporate Manslaughter: Why does Reform Matter?' (2006) 122 SALJ 646.

[265] For analysis, see D. Ormerod and R. Taylor, 'The Corporate Manslaughter and Corporate Homicide Act 2007' [2008] Crim LR 589; S. Field and L. Jones, 'Five Years On: The Impact of the Corporate Manslaughter and Corporate Homicide Act 2007: plus ça change?' (2013) 24 ICCLR 239.

[266] See s. 1(2) and Sch 1 to the Act.

[267] Compare the law of manslaughter by gross negligence (section 8.5(b)), where the courts have based liability on duties not recognized by the law of torts.

[268] For criticism of the 2007 Act's approach to the liability of public authorities, see Horder, *Homicide and the Politics of Law Reform*, ch 4.

Once the prosecution has satisfied the court that the defendant is an organization to which the Act applies, and that there was a relevant duty towards the deceased, the third element is that the way in which its activities were managed or organized amounted to a gross breach of the organization's duty. How can this be established? A breach is gross if the conduct allegedly amounting to the breach 'falls far below' what could reasonably be expected of the organization in the circumstances. This is a question of degree for the jury, similar to that which has to be decided when determining whether negligence is 'gross' for the purposes of manslaughter by gross negligence (section 8.5(b)). In this connection s. 8(2) requires the jury to consider whether there was a breach of health and safety legislation. If there was, then the jury should take account of how serious the breach was, how much of a risk of death it posed, and (by s. 8(3)) any evidence of what is often termed corporate culture, that is, evidence of 'attitudes, policies, systems or accepted practices within the organization that were likely to have encouraged' any breach of safety legislation. This broadens the time frame of the new offence, by reducing the possibility that the grossness of the breach is assessed simply on a 'snapshot' taken at the time of the fatal incident.

The fourth element in the definition is that the way in which the organization's activities 'are managed and organized by its senior management is a substantial element in the breach'. The term 'senior management' refers (s. 1(4)) to persons who play 'significant roles' in either decision-making about or actual managing of the whole or a substantial part of the organization's activities. This may prove to be a fairly restrictive definition, especially in relation to large organizations, since scrutiny falls only on those who play a significant role in relation to a substantial part of all the organization's activities. The test is probably a factual one (who played a significant role?), and courts are unlikely to be deflected by nomenclature. But then, once the persons who are senior managers are identified for the purposes of the Act, the jury must also be satisfied that those persons' role in the activities was a 'substantial element in the breach', a restrictive phrase that invites argument about the role of a particular employee's fault, and thereby revisits some of the problems of the 'identification doctrine' in corporate liability generally.[269]

The fifth requirement is that the way in which the organization's activities were managed caused the death. The issue of causation is not straightforward: presumably a 'more than minimal' cause is sufficient,[270] and, since there is no provision in the Act to prevent the application of normal principles, a voluntary intervening act (such as the conduct of an employee) would break the causal chain,[271] clearly not the intention behind the Act.

The new offence of corporate manslaughter is an important step towards recognition that corporate liability in this sphere is fair and that it has to be constructed

---

[269] J. Gobert, 'The Corporate Manslaughter and Corporate Homicide Act 2007: Thirteen Years in the Making but was it Worth the Wait?' (2008) 71 MLR 413, at 418.

[270] See the discussion of *Cato* [1976] 1 WLR 110 in Chapter 4.5.

[271] See the discussion of *Kennedy (No. 2)* [2008] 1 AC 269 in Chapter 4.5.

differently from individual liability. There are, however, various respects in which the Act could have been improved. The Act combines great technical complexity in some respects with considerable open texture in key terms, such as 'gross', 'significant', and 'substantial'. Moreover, it remains to be seen whether its application is easier and more extensive than the identification doctrine that applied previously: the notion of 'senior management' still requires the court to identify people within an organization who had a certain amount of influence and whose failure was a substantial element in the breach.[272] On the other hand, if the test proves to be applicable without difficulty to larger organizations, the kernel of this approach could and should be adapted to other forms of corporate liability. The requirement of the consent of the DPP for any prosecution is regrettable, since the possibility of private prosecution could have operated to prevent any official 'cover-ups'. The relationship between the new offence and offences under the Health and Safety at Work Act 1974 remains to be worked out:[273] a reconsideration of that legislation, with a view to reformulating its offences, would be a sensible next step. In the meantime, the Sentencing Guidelines Council has issued sentencing guidelines on both corporate manslaughter (for which only three forms of sentence—fines, remedial orders, and publicity orders—are possible) and offences under the Health and Safety at Work Act resulting in death.[274]

(d) THE CONTOURS OF INVOLUNTARY MANSLAUGHTER

The English law of manslaughter exhibits a tension between the significance of the harm caused and various principles of fairness such as the principles of correspondence and fair labelling. It is the resulting harm (death) which still dominates, and the enormous moral distance between D's conduct and the fatal result is evident from the fact that in many situations there may be nothing more than a conviction for common assault if death does not result (manslaughter by unlawful act if death results) or even no criminal offence at all (manslaughter by gross negligence if death results). Much is made of the unique significance of human life and the need to mark out, and to prevent, conduct which causes its loss. But does this really justify the present contours of the law of involuntary manslaughter?

It is important not to neglect the fact that manslaughter currently covers a wide range of culpability. The focus thus far has been on the lower borderline, but there are some forms of manslaughter that fall little short of murder, such as manslaughter by recklessness.[275] There is no doubting the substantial culpability of the person who embarks on a course of conduct knowing that there is a risk of death or serious

[272] See L. Price, 'Finding Fault in Organisations—Reconceptualising the Role of Senior Managers in Corporate Manslaughter' (2015) 35 *Legal Studies* 385.

[273] F. Wright, 'Criminal Liability of Directors and Senior Managers for Deaths at Work' [2007] Crim LR 949.

[274] See Sentencing Guidelines Council, 'Corporate Manslaughter and Health and Safety Offences causing Death' (2010); M. Woodley, 'Bargaining over Corporate Manslaughter—What Price a Life?' (2013) 77 Crim L 33.

[275] *Lidar* [2000] 4 *Archbold News* 3 confirms the existence of the crime of manslaughter by recklessness.

injury to another (e.g. the man who administered carbon tetrachloride to the woman in *Pike*,[276] knowing the danger of physical harm to her). We noted earlier that the Law Commission has recommended that some forms of reckless killing (where D intended to cause injury or fear or risk of injury, knowing that the conduct involved a serious risk of causing death) should be included in the new offence of murder in the second degree,[277] with lesser varieties falling within the offence of manslaughter.[278]

The main focus of our discussion above was on the lower threshold of manslaughter, where its minimum requirements form the boundary with accidental (non-criminal) homicide. It can be argued that to apply the label 'manslaughter' to the conduct of a person who envisaged no more than a battery, for example, by a single punch, is both disproportionate and unfair. On this view, it is only luck that makes the difference between the summary offence of common assault (maximum, six months' imprisonment) and the grave offence of manslaughter (maximum, life imprisonment). In such cases, so the argument goes, the manslaughter label exaggerates the amount of culpability, producing an extreme form of constructive liability.[279] The possibility of conviction for so serious an offence as manslaughter should not be such a lottery.[280] If D's conduct does not constitute reckless manslaughter, and does not amount to manslaughter by gross negligence, the proper course is simply to convict D of whatever other offence he has committed (unlawful wounding, or assault, say) and to pass sentence for that.[281] The Law Commission originally accepted this reasoning and recommended the abolition of unlawful act manslaughter,[282] but this has now been replaced—without detailed justification—by a recommendation that adopts the government's own formulation of a possible offence of manslaughter based on death caused by an act that D intended to cause injury or was aware carried a serious risk of injury.[283]

Where does this leave the crime of manslaughter by gross negligence? The Law Commission, after a review of the arguments, concluded that it is justifiable in homicide cases to criminalize gross negligence where D unreasonably takes a risk of causing death, where the failure to advert to the risk is culpable because the risk is obviously foreseeable and D has the capacity to advert to the risk.[284] The Commission recommends an offence of killing by gross negligence, with the following elements:

(1) a person by his or her conduct causes the death of another;

(2) a risk that his or her conduct will cause death would be obvious to a reasonable person in his or her position;

(3) he or she is capable of appreciating that risk at the material time; and

---

[276] [1961] Crim LR 547.   [277] Law Com No. 304, Part 2, discussed at section 8.3(b).

[278] Law Com No. 304, Part 2, paras. 3.52–56.   [279] See Chapter 6.7(a).

[280] CLRC 14th Report, para. 120.

[281] Although we should note once more the position in French law under which a violent act that causes an unintended death is an offence punishable by up to three years' imprisonment: see section (a) at n 238.

[282] Law Com No. 237, *Involuntary Manslaughter*, paras. 5.14–16.

[283] Law Com No. 304, paras. 3.46–49, adopting Home Office, *Reforming the Law on Involuntary Manslaughter: the Government's Proposals* (2000).

[284] Law Com No. 304, paras. 3.50–60, amending only slightly Law Com No. 237, Part 4.

(4) either

his or her conduct falls far below what can reasonably be expected of him or her in the circumstances; or

he or she intends by his or her conduct to cause some injury, or is aware of, or unreasonably takes, the risk that it may do so, and the conduct causing (or intended to cause) the injury constitutes an offence.[285]

This formulation has a number of good features. It incorporates a capacity requirement (3), and now insists that the objective risk must be one of death (2).[286] There is no special provision for omissions, but such cases should fall within (4) and the criteria for deciding whether or not there was a duty to act will continue to be left for development at common law. The formulation of condition (4)(a) does not go far in the direction of maximum certainty, but the Commission argues that at least the new test would not be circular (a criticism levelled at the *Adomako* test), and that the only alternative to leaving 'a large degree of judgment to the jury' would be 'to define the offence in such rigid and detailed terms that it would be unworkable'.[287] As for the second limb of (4), this is advanced as a test that may be simpler for juries to apply than the test in (4)(a), and one that is likely to be co-extensive in practice with (4)(a). It does not, of course, make any explicit reference to gross negligence, and its form is similar to the existing 'unlawful act' doctrine—a doctrine whose abolition the Law Commission originally recommended but whose retention, in modified form, the Commission now supports. The difference in this context is that condition (2) must be satisfied before condition (4)(b) would be applied. The Law Commission envisages that the maximum penalty for killing by gross negligence would be a determinate sentence, not life imprisonment, but no conclusions are reached on its precise grading. However, before we leave the question of how the law of involuntary manslaughter should be structured, it is important to assess various other homicide offences and to consider their proper place.

8.6 CAUSING OR ALLOWING THE DEATH OF A CHILD OR VULNERABLE ADULT

There has long been concern about the difficulty of achieving a homicide conviction when the death of a young child has been caused by one of the child's parents or carers but it cannot be proved which. Parliament has responded by introducing the offence of causing or allowing the death of a child or vulnerable adult, contrary to s. 5 of the Domestic Violence, Crime and Victims Act 2004. Whether the creation of a new offence

---

[285] Law Com No. 237, para. 5.34.

[286] This is the slight amendment made in Law Com No. 304, although it sits rather awkwardly with the Commission's view of unlawful act manslaughter. Cf. the Law Reform Commission of Ireland, *Homicide*, paras. 5.68–69, accepting a capacity requirement but not the objective risk of death.

[287] Law Com No. 237, para. 5.32.

was necessary, as distinct from special procedural means of bringing such cases within mainstream homicide offences, warrants further examination.[288]

8.7 CAUSING DEATH BY DRIVING

English law now contains some five offences of causing death by driving:

(1) causing death by dangerous driving, contrary to s. 1 of the 1988 Act;

(2) causing death by careless driving when under the influence of drink or drugs, contrary to s. 3A of the 1988 Act;

(3) causing death by careless driving, contrary to s. 2B of the 1988 Act;

(4) causing death by driving when unlicensed, disqualified, or uninsured, contrary to s. 3ZB of the 1988 Act;

(5) causing death by aggravated vehicle-taking, contrary to s. 1 of the Aggravated Vehicle-Taking Act 1992.

It is not possible to go into the detail of all these offences, but as they take the law of involuntary homicide well beyond the scope of gross negligence or unlawful and dangerous act manslaughter, it is worth considering the issues of principle that some of them raise.

The offence of *causing death by dangerous driving* replaced the former offence of causing death by reckless driving and, unlike that offence, is defined in the legislation. This is a considerable step towards greater certainty in the criminal law. In outline, s. 2A(1) provides that a person drives dangerously if '(a) the way he drives falls far below what would be expected of a competent and careful driver; and (b) it would be obvious to a competent and careful driver that driving in that way would be dangerous'. Section 2A(2) adds that a person also drives dangerously if it would be obvious to a competent and careful driver that driving the vehicle in its current state would be dangerous—for example, driving an obviously defective vehicle or driving with an unsteady load.[289] Section 2(3) defines 'dangerous' in terms of danger either of injury to any person or serious damage to property, and provides that any special knowledge possessed by the driver should be taken into account. This is an objective standard, but its extension to cases where only serious damage to property (and not death or injury) is foreseeable may be considered too wide. Since it applies to conduct on the road that falls 'far below what would be expected', the standard may therefore be higher than that of negligence in the law of tort, and is approaching (or equivalent to) a standard of gross negligence. The maximum for this offence is fourteen years, following the Criminal Justice Act 2003, compared with a maximum of five years for the offence of dangerous driving. It remains possible to convict drivers of murder where the required fault element can be

---

[288] Cf. Law Com No. 279, *Children: their Non-Accidental Death or Serious Injury* (2003).
[289] Cf. *Crossman* (1986) 82 Cr App R 333.

proved,[290] and likewise of manslaughter where the prosecution can establish, following *Adomako*,[291] that D was grossly negligent as to the risk of death, compared with
a high degree of negligence as to injury or damage, as required for causing death by
dangerous driving.

The Road Safety Act 2006 has introduced two further offences. The first is *causing death by careless driving*, with a maximum sentence of five years' imprisonment.
The Act states that careless or inconsiderate driving means driving that 'falls below
what would be expected of a competent and careful driver',[292] and this contrasts with
the dangerous driver whose driving must fall 'far below' that standard. However, the
offence of careless driving is chiefly intended to penalize small errors of judgment,
and it can hardly be said that the offence is intended to protect people's lives (unlike
dangerous driving). Thus it can be said that the moral distance between the underlying offence of careless driving—for which Parliament has provided only a fine as the
penalty—and causing death by careless driving, with its maximum of five years, is too
great, and that this is an improper use of a homicide offence. This is not to downplay
the concern and grief of the families of victims of these offences; but that must be responded to in a different way, rather than by excessive punishment of someone whose
error may have been both slight and momentary. The second new offence is *causing
death when driving while unlicensed, disqualified, or uninsured*. The essence of this offence is simply a minimal element of causation: if the driver causes death when he is
committing one of these three other offences (no valid licence, disqualified from driving, no insurance), he is guilty of this homicide offence without proof of any fault in the
driving.[293] Indeed, if there were fault in the driving, one would expect a prosecution
for one of the three offences with higher maxima. The reason for creating a homicide
offence for deaths caused in these circumstances is that the driver should not have been
on the road at all: his or her decision to drive when not permitted to do so was a *sine
qua non* of the incident that caused death. Parliament regarded this as the least serious
of the offences, assigning it a maximum penalty of two years' imprisonment. That may
be taken as an indication of the absence of a fault requirement for the actual driving.
However, research among members of the public shows unequivocally that this view
is widely rejected: where a disqualified driver takes to the road, and happens to cause
death through no fault in the manner of driving, most people regard this as more serious than causing death by careless driving[294]—whereas Parliament evidently viewed
it as less serious by a factor of 2 to 5. This research was commissioned in order to assist with the drafting of guidelines for sentencers, but in fact it made that task more
difficult, once it became apparent that there was widespread public rejection of the

---

[290] S. Cunningham, 'The Reality of Vehicular Homicides' [2001] Crim LR 679.

[291] [1995] 1 AC 171, discussed in section 8.5(b).

[292] Road Safety Act 2006, s. 30 (inserting a new s. 3ZA into the Road Traffic Act 1988).

[293] The controversial causal aspects of the offence were discussed in Chapter 5.3(a). See A. P. Simester and
G. R. Sullivan, 'Being There' [2012] 71 CLJ 29.

[294] B. Mitchell and J. V. Roberts, 'Public Attitudes to the Mandatory life Sentence for Murder: Putting
Received Wisdom to the Empirical Test' [2011] Crim LR 456.

hierarchy of maximum penalties that had been created. Most people, it seems, would wish to see a reversal of the maxima for causing death by careless driving and causing death when driving while unlicensed, disqualified, or uninsured; but the sentencing guidelines must reflect the law as it stands.[295]

Is there a need for these separate homicide offences? The first offence of causing death by dangerous driving was introduced in 1956, largely because juries were unwilling to convict culpable motorists of such a serious-sounding offence as manslaughter. Ever since its introduction there have been those who have pointed to its 'illogicality'.[296] The difference in practice between an offence of dangerous driving (maximum penalty of five years) and one of causing death by dangerous driving (maximum penalty of fourteen years) may simply be one of chance. Bad driving may or may not lead to an accident, depending on the chance conjunction of other factors and other people's behaviour. And an accident may lead to death (in which case the more serious offence is committed) or merely to serious injuries or to minor damage. The response to this 'illogicality'—which is, of course, the very problem with the law of involuntary manslaughter too—has varied. Both the James Committee in 1976[297] and the Criminal Law Revision Committee in 1980[298] recommended the abolition of the offence of causing death by dangerous driving, thereby accepting the 'illogicality' argument. This accords with the CLRC's proposal that 'unlawful act' manslaughter should be abolished.[299] However, the North Report on road traffic law reversed this trend. The report accepted the principle that, in general, persons should be judged according to the intrinsic quality of their driving rather than its consequences, but argued that the law should depart from this in cases where death is caused and the driver's culpability is already high.[300] There is a well-known risk in motoring that certain kinds of driving may cause accidents, and that accidents may cause death. The rules of the road are designed not only to produce the orderly and unhampered movement of traffic, but also to protect property, safety, and lives. One who deviates so manifestly from these rules as to drive dangerously ought to realize—because the driving test requires a driver to realize—that there is a considerable risk of an accident. If an accident happens as a result of driving which falls well below the proper standard, then that may well be a case of culpable negligence even if the driver had never thought of the risk in that particular case, because the driver is presumed to know the Highway Code.

Sound as this reasoning may be where it is dangerous driving that results in death, it is significantly less convincing in other cases.[301] Perhaps the next most serious cases would be those where D drives after taking considerable alcohol or drugs, and cases

---

[295] Sentencing Guidelines Council, *Causing Death by Driving Offences* (2008).

[296] Sir B. McKenna, 'Causing Death by Reckless or Dangerous Driving: a Suggestion' [1970] Crim LR 67.

[297] Report of the Interdepartmental Committee on the Distribution of Criminal Business between the Crown Court and the Magistrates' Courts (1975), App K.

[298] 14th Report (1980), paras. 140–8.   [299] 14th Report (1980), paras. 116–23.

[300] Road Traffic Law Review (1988), ch 6.

[301] See S. Cunningham, 'Punishing Drivers who Kill: Putting Road Safety First?' (2007) 27 LS 288.

where D drives after being disqualified from driving, and with both of these it is debatable whether the fault is sufficient to justify conviction and sentence for a homicide offence. One view is that it is sufficient—a decision to drive while intoxicated flies in the face of widely advertised safety campaigns, and a decision to drive while disqualified ignores the road safety reasons that led to the disqualification. Another view is that, in these cases and more generally, the current trend places far too much emphasis on the occurrence of death. These are not cases in which death is intended or knowingly risked: many of them are cases of negligence, to a greater (dangerous) or lesser (careless) degree, albeit that the risks to safety involved in motoring are well known. The great significance attributed to the accident of death is more appropriate to a compensation scheme than to a system of criminal law. Yet if the criminal law in motoring cases were to focus on 'intrinsic' fault rather than the consequences of the bad driving, it would come down much harder on many people who by good fortune did not cause any or much harm even though their driving fell appallingly below the required standard. Those who think it wrong that the courts should respond so readily to the 'accident of death' would equally have to harden themselves to reject the pleas of drivers who say 'at least I did no harm'. If the courts were to focus on the intrinsic fault in a defendant's driving, sentencing would become more difficult in itself and more controversial in the view of the mass media.

8.8 REVIEWING THE STRUCTURE OF THE LAW OF HOMICIDE

In this chapter we have discussed a wide array of different homicide offences. Towards the end of the chapter, questions about the proper contours and boundaries of the law of homicide have become more and more pressing. Although some suggestions and criticisms have been ventured at appropriate points, we may conclude the chapter with some broader reflections on the structure of the law of homicide.

Three main interlinked issues present themselves—questions about appropriate fault requirements, questions about appropriate labels, and questions about appropriate sentence levels.[302] Let us begin with fault: the principle should be that of equal treatment of offences of equal seriousness. There should therefore be an alignment of the minimum culpability requirements for homicide offences, unless there are strong reasons to the contrary. For example, manslaughter by gross negligence requires the risk of death to have been obvious, whereas causing death by dangerous driving may be committed if there was danger of injury or serious damage to property—requirements which are surely far too low for a homicide offence. The offence of corporate manslaughter is rather reticent on the whole issue, although s. 8 of the Corporate Manslaughter and Corporate Homicide Act 2007 does state that, where the death arose

---

[302] For fuller argument, see the chapters by Ashworth, Duff, and Tadros in C. Clarkson and S. Cunningham, *Criminal Liability for Non-Aggressive Death* (2008).

from a breach of health and safety regulations, the jury should consider how serious a risk of death existed.[303] However, we find major departures from this principle when it comes to the two new homicide offences of causing death by careless driving and causing death when driving while unlicensed, disqualified, or uninsured. Causing death by careless driving falls significantly below the threshold of fault required for manslaughter by gross negligence, and for causing death by dangerous driving. Moreover, the rationale for having an offence of careless driving is not so much to save lives (one purpose of the offence of dangerous driving) as to protect from injury and damage to property, so the claims for the new offence to be admitted as a form of criminal homicide are low. The arguments relating to causing death when driving while unlicensed, disqualified, or uninsured are different, because it is the initial criminal act of driving when not permitted to do so that colours the consequences. The parallel is therefore with manslaughter by unlawful act, and the question is whether the moral distance between the originating criminal act and the tragic (accidental) result is too great to justify its inclusion as a homicide offence. This does not mean that the defendant is not convicted, since the underlying criminal offence is still there, and the legislature could create another (non-homicide) offence if it were thought morally and socially appropriate. The chief argument in favour of including these as homicide offences is that the deliberate commission of a criminal offence changes D's normative position such that it is fair to hold him liable for the fatal (if unanticipated) consequences—a view which, as we have seen, begs enormous questions, such that the original progenitor of the 'change of normative position' reasoning no longer supports it.

This leads us into the second general issue, that of labelling. In principle the label applied to an offence should be a fair representation of the degree of culpable wrongdoing typically disclosed by the offence. It also seems fair that the labels used should be consistent. At present the term 'manslaughter' is used both for killings reduced from murder by a partial defence and for killings stemming from gross negligence or from an unlawful and dangerous act, as well as corporate manslaughter. The Law Commission has recommended that this common law confusion should be resolved by labelling the former as murder in the second degree while retaining the term manslaughter for the latter, and some counter-arguments were raised earlier.[304] Our present concern is at the lower boundary, where there is a contrast between manslaughter by gross negligence and causing death by dangerous driving (different labels, similar culpability), and where there are three other Road Traffic Act offences that use the formula, 'causing death by …'. In terms of nomenclature, it can be argued that the condemnatory term 'manslaughter' should be reserved for killings with more than the minimum culpability requirement—killings that currently amount to reckless manslaughter, not merely gross negligence, and certainly not unlawful and dangerous act cases.[305] This would

---

[303] It is not known how many cases will not involve a breach of health and safety regulations. If such cases exist, there appears to be no duty on the jury to consider the risk of death; if such cases do not exist, why beat about the bush?   [304] Section 8.4(i).

[305] Part of this argument would be that this group should includes killings reduced from murder by provocation or diminished responsibility: see Ashworth, n 57, 340.

mean that a fresh term should be sought for any group of killings that are considered sufficiently culpable to warrant a homicide conviction—perhaps a term such as 'culpable homicide', not hitherto used in English law.

This brings us to the third set of issues, relating to the sentencing of homicide offences. In principle there should not be a significant disparity between the condemnatory force of the offence label and the normal range of sentences. We should therefore reject the idea of a conviction for manslaughter by unlawful act, resulting from a single punch after an argument, that is followed by a community sentence or short custodial sentence. The sentence correctly indicates that the offence did not warrant that label in the first place.[306] On the other hand, as we have observed, sentence levels for causing death by dangerous driving are often higher than for gross negligence manslaughter. This difference calls for re-examination, as Michael Hirst argues,[307] but we may decide that it is right—in which case that would be a strong argument in favour of bringing the offence into an appropriate mainstream homicide offence. These are all questions that need to be examined on a wide canvas, and the starting point should be a general review of homicide offences—in other words, a wider review than the Law Commission has hitherto been able to carry out.

FURTHER READING

A. Ashworth, 'Principles, Pragmatism and the Law Commission's Recommendations on Homicide Law Reform' [2007] Crim LR 333.

A. Ashworth and B. Mitchell (Eds), *Rethinking English Homicide Law* (Oxford University Press, 2000).

C. M. G. Clarkson and S. Cunningham (eds), *Criminal Liability for Non-Aggressive Death* (Ashgate, 2008).

A. Cornford, 'The Architecture of Homicide' (2015) 34 OJLS 819.

J. Horder, *Homicide and the Politics of Law Reform* (Oxford University Press, 2012).

B. Mitchell and J. V. Roberts, 'Sentencing for Murder: Exploring Public Knowledge and Public Opinion in England and Wales' [2012] *British Journal of Criminology* 141.

A. Reed and M. Bohlander (Eds), *Loss of Self-control and Diminished Responsibility: Domestic, Comparative and International Perspectives* (Ashgate, 2011).

V. Tadros, 'The Homicide Ladder' (2006) 69 MLR 601.

R. Taylor, 'The Nature of "Partial Defences" and the Coherence of (Second Degree) Murder' [2007] Crim LR 345.

---

[306] See B. Mitchell, 'More Thoughts about Unlawful and Dangerous Act Manslaughter and the One-Punch Killer' [2009] Crim LR 502.

[307] M. Hirst, 'Causing Death by Driving and Other Offences: A Question of Balance' [2008] Crim LR 339.

9

NON-FATAL VIOLATIONS
OF THE PERSON

9.1 INTRODUCTION: VARIETIES OF PHYSICAL VIOLATION

In this chapter we shall be discussing two main forms of physical violation: the use of physical force, and unwanted sexual contact. As indicated in Chapter 3.2, physical and sexual integrity are intrinsically valuable personal goods by which people generally set great store: hence their importance in any scheme of criminal offences. Both kinds of good have, though, an interpersonal dimension that will raise questions for the criminal law. If I agree to fight you in the pub car park, can and should the criminal law be used against either of us respecting the blows struck? If X consents to sexual intercourse with Y, but then discovers that Y was aware that he was suffering from a serious sexually transmitted disease at the time, was X's consent a true consent? If so, the question whether Y raped X arises.

There may be considerable variations of degree: physical force can be anything from a mere push to a brutal beating which leaves the victim close to death, and unwanted sexual contact may be anything from a brief touching to a gross form of sexual violation. One problem for the criminal law, therefore, is how to grade the seriousness of the various forms of conduct: to have just a single offence of 'non-fatal harm' and a single offence of 'sexual violation' would come into tension with both the principle of fair labelling (see Chapter 6.7(a)) and the principle of maximum certainty (see Chapter 4.4(e)). Not only would it be contrary to principle, but it would also leave little to be decided at the trial and would transfer the effective decision to the sentencing stage.

The scheme of the chapter is to discuss non-fatal, non-sexual offences against the person first, including the contested question of the limits of consent, and possible reforms of the law. The second half of the chapter is devoted to the law of sexual offences under the Sexual Offences Act 2003, focusing on the main offences and the definition of consent, concluding with a review of the law's successes and failures.

9.2 REPORTED PHYSICAL VIOLATIONS

Crimes of violence constitute about 22 per cent of all crimes reported to, and recorded by, the police, with sexual offences constituting one per cent. Figures from the British Crime Survey 2012 show that, although the overall number of incidents of violent crimes doubled between 1981 and 1996, since then the number has declined. Slowly but steadily, the number of recorded crimes has come down by over 30 per cent to just below the number recording in 1981. Around 42 per cent of all incidents of violence involve no injury, and around 22 per cent involve an assault causing only minor injury.[1] Studies have begun to uncover the full extent of so-called 'domestic' violence as a proportion of violence in general,[2] but although police forces are moving towards more consistent policies of recording such incidents and dealing with them as true offences of violence,[3] different approaches are still found.[4] The British Crime Survey for 2012 puts the percentage of reported incidents of domestic violence at 14 per cent. Much of the violence that occurs takes place in the street, around transport facilities, or in pubs and clubs, the vast majority of both involving young men. In that regard, violent crime is committed in roughly equal proportions by strangers to, as by acquaintances of, the victim. It seems that the use of a weapon is important in determining the legal classification of offences (not surprisingly, since offences involving weapons may tend to have more serious consequences): some three-quarters of the serious woundings involved a weapon, whereas the proportion was only one-fifth for the less serious offences.[5]

Two particular points may be made about offences of physical violation. First, there is evidence of a strong correlation between drinking and violence. The 2007–8 British Crime Survey found that the victim said the offender was under the influence of drink in 45 per cent of cases and under the influence of drugs in a further 19 per cent of violent incidents, with higher averages in cases of stranger violence.[6] Even though most drinkers do not erupt into violence, the figures make it clear that the special rules relating to fault and intoxication, discussed in Chapter 6.2, come into play frequently. Thus

[1] <www.ons.gov.uk/ons/rel/crime-stats/crime-statistics/period-ending-march-2012/index.html>; C. Kershaw et al., *Crime in England and Wales 2007/08* (2008), 62–5.

[2] C. Mirrlees-Black, *Domestic Violence: Findings from a British Crime Survey Self-Completion Questionnaire* (Home Office Research Study No. 191, 1999).

[3] S. Grace, *Policing Domestic Violence in the 1990s* (Home Office Research Study No. 139, 1995); C. Hoyle, *Negotiating Domestic Violence* (1998); CPS Policy on Prosecuting Cases of Domestic Violence, at <www.cps.gov.uk>.   [4] L. Kelly et al., *Domestic Violence Matters* (Home Office Research Study No. 193, 1999).

[5] R. Walmsley, *Personal Violence* (Home Office Research Study No. 89, 1986), 8.

[6] Kershaw, *Crime in England and Wales 2007–08*, 76.

in Nigel Fielding's research into cases of violence that come to court, the defendant had been intoxicated at the time of the alleged offence in about a third of his sample of cases, and usually the degree of intoxication was considerable.[7] A second general point is that many offences of violence have consequences for the victim which extend well beyond any injury caused. There are psychological effects of fear and depression, which may significantly impair the victim's enjoyment of life long after the physical wounds have healed. Such effects are well-documented in the case of female victims of 'domestic' violence,[8] but many other victims of violence suffer lasting social and psychological effects stemming from the offence and from other circumstances (e.g. intimidation, long periods off work) that may follow it.[9]

The values which underlie the offences of physical violation are reflected in various Convention rights, such as Art. 3 (the right not to be subjected to 'torture or inhuman or degrading treatment'), Art. 5 (the right to liberty and security of person), and Art. 8 (the right to respect for one's private life). The principle of lifestyle autonomy makes its influence felt here, in the sense that one should have the liberty to decide for oneself the level of pain to which one subjects one's body (e.g. in sport, or for pure recreation). Central to this is the issue of the extent to which individuals may lawfully consent to the infliction of harm or injury on their bodies, which (as we shall see) raises questions about the justifications for State interference with the right to respect for private life in Art. 8.

9.3 OFFENCES OF NON-FATAL PHYSICAL VIOLATION

We have seen something of the various situations in which non-fatal physical harm might occur. How does the law classify its offences? How should it respond to these various invasions of physical integrity? One approach would be to create separate offences to cover different ways of causing injury and different situations in which violence occurs. This was the nineteenth-century English approach, and many such offences still survive in the Offences Against the Person Act 1861 (relating, for example, to injuries caused by gunpowder, throwing corrosive fluid, failing to provide food for apprentices, setting spring guns). A second approach would be to attempt to rank the offences by reference to the degree of harm caused and the degree of fault in the person causing it. The 1861 Act also contains some offences of this kind, but, as we shall see later, its ranking is impaired by obscure terms, uncertainties in the fault requirements, and some overlapping. Thorough reform of the law is long overdue, and will be discussed in subsection (k). A significant development in practice has been the promulgation, by the police and the Crown Prosecution Service, of charging standards

---

[7] N. Fielding, *Courting Violence: Offences Against the Person Cases in Court* (2006), 98–104.

[8] Hoyle, *Negotiating Domestic Violence*, ch 7; cf. Fielding, *Courting Violence*, 104–8, on victims, defendants, and courtroom tactics.

[9] J. Shapland, J. Willmore, and P. Duff, *Victims in the Criminal Justice System* (1985), ch 6, esp. at 99.

for the various offences against the person.[10] The expressed aim is to improve fairness to defendants, through greater uniformity of approach to charging, and to make the criminal justice system more efficient by ensuring that the appropriate charges are laid at the outset. The guidance will be referred to as each offence is discussed, although its impact in practice is difficult to assess.

(a) ATTEMPTED MURDER

If we were to construct a 'ladder' of non-fatal offences, starting with the most serious and moving down to the least serious, the offence of attempted murder should be placed at the top. There is an immediate paradox here: attempted murder may not involve the infliction of any harm at all, since a person who shoots at another and misses may still be held guilty of attempted murder. What distinguishes this offence is proof of an intent to kill, not the occurrence of any particular harm. The fault element for attempted murder is therefore high—higher than for murder, under English law, since murder may be committed by someone who merely intended to cause really serious injury and not death.[11] Nothing less than an intention to kill suffices to convict someone of attempted murder.[12] Beyond that, all that is necessary is proof that D did something which was 'more than merely preparatory' towards the murder.[13] Although a conviction is perfectly possible where no harm results—and such a case might still be regarded as a most serious non-fatal offence, since D tried to cause death—there are also cases—probably a majority—where D's attempt to kill results in serious injury to the victim. In such cases a prosecution might be brought for attempted murder—and will succeed if the intention to kill can be proved. However, the court might not be satisfied of that 'beyond reasonable doubt', and might find that D only intended to cause grievous bodily harm. In that event, the conviction will be for the offence of causing grievous bodily harm with intent, but both offences carry the same maximum punishment—life imprisonment.[14]

(b) WOUNDING OR CAUSING GRIEVOUS BODILY HARM WITH INTENT

Section 18 of the Offences Against the Person Act 1861 creates a serious offence which may be committed in a number of different ways. There are two alternative forms of conduct, and either of two forms of intent will suffice. The conduct may be either causing a wound or causing grievous bodily harm. A wound has been defined as an injury which breaks both the outer and inner skin. A bruise or a burst blood-vessel

---

[10] Now incorporated into the legal guidance set out at <www.cps.gov.uk/legal/l_to_o/offences_against_the_person/>.

[11] See the discussion in Chapter 7.3(c), where this is viewed as one argument against the 'GBH' rule for murder.   [12] Confirmed in *Fallon* [1994] Crim LR 519.

[13] This is the conduct requirement of all attempted crimes: see Chapter 11.3(b).

[14] The Sentencing Guidelines Council has conducted a consultation on whether sentences for attempted murder should be linked to those for murder (see Chapter 7.3(a)) or to those for other non-fatal offences: SGC, *Attempted Murder: Notes and Questions for Consultees* (2007).

in an eye does not amount to a wound,[15] whereas this requirement of the offence may be fulfilled by a rather minor cut. Grievous bodily harm is much more serious, although it has never been defined with any precision and the authoritative description is 'really serious harm'.[16] The harm does not have to be life-threatening or permanent, but it takes far less to cause serious harm to a young child or vulnerable person than to an adult in full health.[17] The harm may be a sexually transmitted disease with significant effects: the old case of *Clarence* (1888)[18] was against this, but *Dica* (2004)[19] establishes that infection with HIV can amount to grievous bodily harm.[20] The CPS guidance refers to injuries resulting in permanent disability or loss of sensory function, non-minor permanent visible disfigurement, broken or displaced limbs or bones, injuries which cause substantial loss of blood, and injuries resulting in lengthy treatment or incapacity.

Does the concept of 'bodily harm' extend to harm to the mind? This question has been raised in a number of cases of stalking and, although there is now specific legislation on stalking,[21] the substantive issue remains important under the 1861 Act. In *Ireland and Burstow* (1998)[22] the House of Lords heard appeals in two cases in which the defendants had repeatedly made silent telephone calls to their victims. Burstow had been convicted under s. 20 of the 1861 Act, of which grievous bodily harm is an element, and the House of Lords confirmed that 'bodily harm' includes any recognizable psychiatric injury. The House adopted the distinction, drawn by Hobhouse LJ in *Chan-Fook*,[23] between 'mere emotions such as distress or panic', which are not sufficient, and 'states of mind that are ... evidence of some identifiable clinical condition', which may be sufficient if supported by psychiatric evidence.[24] What must be proved, under either s. 18 or s. 20, is that the psychiatric injury was 'really serious'.

Turning to the fault requirements, the one most commonly relied on in prosecutions is 'with intent to cause grievous bodily harm'. The meaning of 'intention' here is the same as outlined earlier.[25] Where an attack involves the use of a weapon,[26] that may make it easier to establish the relevant intention. On the other hand, where psychiatric injury is alleged, it may be more difficult to prove that D intended to cause really serious harm of that kind. If the prosecution fails to establish intention, the offence will be reduced to the lower category, to be considered in section 9.3(c), so long as recklessness is proved. However, there is an alternative fault element for s. 18: 'with intent to prevent the lawful apprehension or detainer of any person'. Whilst the policy of this

[15] *C* v *Eisenhower* [1984] QB 331.

[16] *DPP* v *Smith* [1961] AC 290; cf. *Janjua* [1999] 1 Cr App R 91, where the CA held that 'serious harm', without the word 'really', was a sufficient direction in a case where a five-inch knife was used.

[17] *Bollom* [2004] 2 Cr App R 50.   [18] (1888) 22 QBD 23.

[19] [2004] QB 1257; see M. Weait (2005) 68 MLR 121; see also the discussion of *Konzani* (reference at n 99).

[20] See also *R* v *Golding* [2014] EWCA Crim 889, discussed later, in which it was held that, when genital herpes is passed on with the relevant fault element (and in the absence of V's consent to the risk of infection), this can amount to the malicious infliction of grievous bodily harm.

[21] Protection from Harassment Act 1997, discussed in section 9.3(g).   [22] [1998] AC 147.

[23] (1994) 99 Cr App R 147, at 152.

[24] This distinction was affirmed in *Dhaliwal* [2006] 2 Cr App R 348, rejecting any extension to psychological conditions.

[25] See Chapter 5.5(b).   [26] See n 4 and accompanying text.

requirement—classifying attacks on persons engaged in law enforcement as especially serious—is perfectly understandable, one result of the wording of s. 18 of the 1861 Act is that D can be convicted of this offence (with a maximum penalty of life imprisonment) if he intends to resist arrest and is merely reckless as to causing harm to the police officer.[27] It seems that consequences so serious as grievous bodily harm need not have been foreseen or foreseeable in this type of case,[28] which confirms this element of the crime as a stark example of constructive criminal liability.[29]

(c) INTENTIONALLY OR RECKLESSLY INFLICTING A WOUND OR GBH

Section 20 of the Offences Against the Person Act 1861 creates the offence of unlawfully and maliciously wounding or inflicting grievous bodily harm. The conduct element in this offence is similar to that for the more serious offence under s. 18, and the meanings of 'wound' and 'grievous bodily harm' are no different.[30] However, there has been an important recent extension of the offence to include recklessly passing on genital herpes.

In *Golding*,[31] D discovered that he had genital herpes, but did not tell a subsequent sexual partner after they began a sexual relationship, with the result that she too became infected. D was convicted of recklessly inflicting grievous bodily harm on her. The conviction and initial sentence of fourteen months' imprisonment were upheld by the Court of Appeal (although an adjustment was made to the sentence). Of course, what D did was very wrong; but the question is whether (a) there was fair warning that so serious an offence would be applied in such circumstances (see Chapter 4.4(e)), and (b) whether the incidence of genital herpes is so common that it is a risk everyone should realize that they are exposed to when having sexual intercourse (something like 1 in 20 men have genital herpes, compared with 1 in 360 people—predominantly men—who have HIV[32]). If the latter is true, then only a false assertion by D that he or she is free of the disease really ought to be caught by s. 20, if the disease is passed on. We will come back to this point later.

Considerable attention has been focused on the distinction between *causing* grievous bodily harm (s. 18) and *inflicting* grievous bodily harm (s. 20). Critics have long argued that it is illogical for the more serious offence to have the wider causal basis, but John Gardner has countered that it is perfectly rational to allow a wide causal basis (cause) when the fault element is narrow (intent) whilst restricting the causal basis (inflict) when the fault element is much wider (recklessness).[33] Even so, the exact

---

[27] *Morrison* (1989) 89 Cr App R 17; cf. *Fallon* [1994] Crim LR 519.

[28] The decision in *Morrison* did not clarify this; cf. *Mowatt*, n 41 and accompanying text.

[29] On which see Chapter 5.4(b).

[30] It will be recalled that *Burstow*, just discussed in relation to psychiatric injury as bodily harm, involved a conviction under s. 20.

[31] [2014] EWCA Crim 889. See the case comment by Karl Laird [2014] Crim LR 686.

[32] <www.nhs.uk/conditions/HIV/Pages/Introduction.aspx>.

[33] J. Gardner, 'Rationality and the Rule of Law in Offences against the Person' [1994] Camb LJ 502.

meaning of the more restrictive word 'inflict' in s. 20 is controversial. For many years it was believed to require proof of a sufficiently direct action by D to constitute an assault. This was decided in the old case of *Clarence* (1888),[34] where D had communicated venereal disease to his wife during intercourse that was held to be consensual. It was said that, as she consented, there was no assault, and so there could be no 'inflicting' within s. 20. A number of other decisions overlooked this requirement: convictions were returned in *Martin* (1881)[35] for harm caused by placing a bar across the exit to a theatre and shouting 'Fire!', and in *Cartledge* v *Allen* (1973)[36] for injury to a hand when a man threatened by D ran off and smashed into a glass door, although in neither case was there a clear assault. However, the House of Lords in *Wilson* (1984)[37] and subsequent cases[38] has decided that there can be an 'infliction' of grievous bodily harm without proof of an assault. The decisions are unsatisfactory in their reasoning, but may be explained as an attempt by the judiciary to improve the workability of an unsatisfactory mid-Victorian statute.[39]

The main difference between ss. 18 and 20 lies in the fault element, and it is a considerable difference. Section 18 requires proof of nothing less than an intention to do grievous bodily harm (apart from in cases of resisting arrest). Section 20 is satisfied by proof of intention but also by proof of recklessness, in the advertent sense of the conscious taking of an unjustified risk.[40] The fault element in s. 20 was broadened by the decision in *Mowatt* (1968).[41] The Court of Appeal held that there is no need to prove intention or recklessness as to wounding or grievous bodily harm themselves, so long as the court is satisfied that D was reckless as to *some* physical harm to some person, albeit of a minor character. This broad fault element—which goes against what might be an ordinary language reading of the wording of s. 20—has nonetheless been approved by the House of Lords.[42] Further, it must be kept in mind that the requirement for proof of recklessness is a requirement for proof only that there was foresight on D's part that his or her act *might* cause some harm.[43] The *Mowatt* extension is another example of constructive liability, and it complicates the process of developing out of the 1861 legislation a 'ladder' of offences graded in terms of relative seriousness. However, even without the *Mowatt* extension, one might ask whether the distinction between the intention only offence (s. 18) and the intention or recklessness offence (s. 20) in

---

[34] (1888) 22 QBD 23.   [35] (1881) 8 QBD 54.

[36] [1973] Crim LR 530. For further detail on the 1861 Act as a fledgling criminal code, see Chapter 2.4.

[37] *Wilson, Jenkins* [1984] AC 242.

[38] *Savage and Parmenter* [1992] 1 AC 699, *Mandair* [1995] 1 AC 208, *Ireland and Burstow* [1998] AC 147. See also the Australian decision of *Salisbury* [1976] VR 452, approved in *Wilson*, in which the term 'inflict' was interpreted to require some kind of violent conduct, even if not an assault as such.

[39] The decisions have important procedural as well as substantive implications: see G. Williams, 'Alternative Elements and Included Offences' [1984] CLJ 290.   [40] See Chapter 5.5(c).

[41] [1968] 1 QB 421.   [42] *Savage and Parmenter* [1992] AC 699.

[43] *Mowatt* [1968] 1 QB 421, confirmed in *Rushworth* (1992) 95 Cr App R 252. This accords with the normal definition of recklessness: see Chapter 5.5(c). Diplock LJ's judgment in *Mowatt* also includes the phrase 'should have foreseen', which wrongly suggests an objective criterion. The Court of Appeal has pointed this out, but judges occasionally fall into the error.

crimes of violence, which are often impulsive reactions to events, is so wide as to warrant the difference in maximum penalties between life imprisonment and five years' imprisonment.[44]

(d) AGGRAVATED ASSAULTS

Common assault is the lowest rung of the 'ladder' of non-fatal offences, with a maximum penalty of six months' imprisonment, and it is discussed in more detail in (e). Beyond common assault, certain assaults are singled out by the law as aggravated—assault with intent to rob, assault with intent to prevent arrest, assault occasioning actual bodily harm, racially or religiously aggravated assaults, and assault on a constable. Each of these will be discussed in turn.

Assault with intent to rob, like robbery, carries a maximum of life imprisonment;[45] it is, in effect, an offence of attempted robbery. *Assault with intent to resist arrest* or to prevent a lawful arrest, contrary to s. 38 of the 1861 Act, carries a maximum penalty of two years' imprisonment and may be charged where an assault on the police results in a minor injury. Another form of aggravated assault, which is usually regarded as representing the rung of the 'ladder' below recklessly inflicting a wound or grievous bodily harm (contrary to s. 20) but above common assault, is *assault occasioning actual bodily harm* (contrary to s. 47). The conduct element of 'actual bodily harm' has been given the wide definition of 'any hurt or injury calculated to interfere with the health or comfort of the victim' so long as it is not merely 'transient or trifling'.[46] However, in *Chan-Fook* (1994)[47] the Court of Appeal held that in most cases the words 'actual bodily harm' should be left undefined. Where there is no bodily contact it may be necessary to elaborate somewhat, but, as the House of Lords confirmed in *Ireland and Burstow*,[48] it should be made clear that any psychological effect on the victim must amount to psychiatric injury before it can fall within s. 47. Merely causing a hysterical or nervous condition is no longer sufficient.[49] This is a controversial restriction, even if it is arguably inherent in the word 'bodily', since research shows that immediate fright and lasting fear are produced by many attacks.[50] Harm of this magnitude ought to be given some recognition, but the courts have emphasized that only a clinical psychiatric condition, supported by expert evidence, falls within s. 47.[51] However, a kick that causes temporary unconsciousness has been held to be within s. 47, since it involves 'an

---

[44] The maximum sentence is seven years when the s. 20 offence is 'racially or religiously aggravated'. See n 56 and accompanying text.

[45] Theft Act 1968, s. 8(2); note that robbery itself (discussed in the context of property offences in Chapter 10.3) may also be classified as an offence of violence.

[46] *Donovan* [1934] 2 KB 498.   [47] [1994] Crim LR 432.

[48] [1998] AC 147, discussed in subsection (b).

[49] Dicta in *Miller* [1954] 2 QB 282 are no longer good law.

[50] Shapland, Willmore, and Duff, *Victims of the Criminal Justice System*, ch 6; M. Maguire and C. Corbett, *The Effects of Crime and the Work of Victim Support Schemes* (1987), ch 7.

[51] *Morris* [1998] 1 Cr App R 386 (evidence from general practitioner that V suffered sleeplessness, anxiety, tearfulness, fear, and physical tenseness not sufficient). To the same effect, *Dhaliwal* [2006] 2 Cr App R 348.

injurious impairment to the victim's sensory functions'.[52] The CPS guidance states that s. 47 should be charged where there is loss or breaking of a tooth, temporary loss of sensory function, extensive or multiple bruising, broken nose, minor fractures, minor cuts requiring stitches, and (reflecting *Chan-Fook*) psychiatric injury which is more than fear, distress, or panic.

The fault requirement for the offence of assault occasioning actual bodily harm reveals that it is an offence of constructive liability. All that needs to be established is the fault required for common assault, that is, intent or recklessness as to an imminent unlawful touching or use of force.[53] This clearly breaches the principle of correspondence (Chapter 6.4(a)). The Court of Appeal tried to remedy this deficiency, but the House of Lords overruled it.[54] Constructive liability therefore remains: a person who risks a minor assault may be held guilty of a more serious offence if 'actual bodily harm' happens to result. Moreover, the maximum penalty for the s. 47 offence is five years' imprisonment, with no apparent justification for the strange approach of making the penalty equivalent to the higher offence on the 'ladder' (the s. 20 offence), and the fault requirement equivalent to the lower offence on the 'ladder' (common assault, with a maximum of six months' imprisonment).[55]

A further form of aggravated assault is where an offence of assault occasioning actual bodily harm is *racially or religiously aggravated*. This is one of a group of aggravated offences created in order to signal the social seriousness of assaults that are either accompanied by, or motivated by, racial or religious hostility.[56] The essence of these offences 'is the denial of equal respect and dignity to people who are seen as "other"'.[57] The offence contrary to s. 28(1)(a) of the Crime and Disorder Act 1998 is committed when, at the time of the relevant offence (assault, and the offences contrary to s. 20 and s. 47 are included), the offender demonstrates racial or religious hostility towards V based on V's membership of a racial or religious group. The question of whether such hostility was demonstrated is an objective one for the jury. In *Rogers*, the House of Lords adopted a broad approach to the notion of race, holding that calling a group of women 'foreigners' when assaulting them demonstrated hostility based on a racial group. By contrast, the offence contrary to s. 28(1)(b) of the 1998 Act is subjective in nature. It is committed when the relevant offence is wholly or partly motivated by hostility towards members of a racial or religious group based on their membership of that group.[58] The effect of the aggravation is to raise the maximum penalty from five to seven years. It will be obvious

---

[52] *R (on the application of T) v DPP* [2003] Crim LR 622.

[53] Several s. 47 cases raise issues about whether there was an assault or battery, and these are discussed in subsection (e) on Common Assault.   [54] *Savage and Parmenter* [1992] 1 AC 699.

[55] Gardner, n 33, argues that this is not irrational: someone who has chosen to assault or risk assaulting another has crossed a moral threshold and is rightly held liable if more serious consequences result. See further Chapter 3.6(r).

[56] The definitions are to be found in the Crime and Disorder Act 1998 ss. 29 and 28, and the Anti-Terrorism, Crime and Security Act 2001 s. 39. For discussion of the former, see the sentencing guidelines decision in *Kelly and Donnelly* [2001] 1 Cr App R (S) 341.   [57] *Per* Baroness Hale in *Rogers* [2007] UKHL 8, at 12.

[58] For discussion of the distinction between the two offences, see *Jones v Bedford and Mid-Bedfordshire Magistrates' Court* [2010] EWHC 523.

that these offences do not cover all of the ground where 'hate crime' is concerned. For example, someone might be targeted because of hostility based on homophobia. The Law Commission has recommended that, alongside a full-scale review of existing offences, rather than extend existing offences to cover such examples, sentencing guidelines should be created specifically concerned with 'hostility-based offending' as an aggravating feature of an offence.[59] Were that done properly, the argument seems to be, then there would be no need for the current, cumbersome system of separate offences.

Brief mention should also be made of the offence, in s. 89 of the Police Act 1996, of *assaulting a police officer in the execution of his or her duty*. Procedurally speaking, this is not an aggravated assault, since it carries the same maximum penalty as common assault (six months' imprisonment) and is also triable summarily only. However, in practice the courts tend to impose higher sentences for assaults on the police, and it is therefore worth noting that this offence is committed even though D was unaware that he was striking a police officer. A decision by a single trial judge in 1865[60] is still regarded as authority for this proposition, but there is surely little justification for this today. The Draft Criminal Code is right to require actual or reckless knowledge that the person being assaulted is a constable,[61] leaving the possibility of conviction for common assault in other cases.

(e) COMMON ASSAULT

The lowest offence on the 'ladder' is what is known as common assault. Strictly speaking, the term 'assault' is used here in its generic sense, as including two separate crimes—assault and battery. In simple terms, battery is the touching or application of unlawful force to another person, whereas assault consists of causing another person to apprehend or expect a touching or application of unlawful force. Most batteries involve an assault, and in both popular and legal language the term 'assault' is often used generically to include battery. However, the Divisional Court in *DPP v Little* (1992)[62] held not only that the two offences are separate in law but also that they are statutory offences and not, as had been assumed, still offences at common law. Each offence is properly charged under s. 39 of the Criminal Justice Act 1988, which provides that they are triable summarily only with a maximum penalty of six months' imprisonment. We discuss battery first, and then assault.

The essence of a *battery* is any touching or application of unlawful force to another. Examples might include a push, a kiss, touching another's hair, touching another's clothing,[63] or throwing a projectile or water which lands on another person's body.

---

[59] Law Commission, *Hate-Crime: Should the Current Offences be Extended?* (Law Com No. 348, 2014), para. 1.44–1.62; C. Bakalis, 'Legislating Against Hatred: The Law Commission's Report on Hate Crime' [2015] Crim LR 192; A. Owusu-Bempah, 'Prosecuting Hate Crime: Procedural Issues and the Future of the Aggravated Offences' (2015) 35 *Legal Studies* 443. [60] *Forbes and Webb* (1865) 10 Cox CC 362.

[61] Law Com No. 177, cl. 76; awareness that the constable is or may be acting in the execution of duty is not required. [62] (1992) 95 Cr App R 28.

[63] *Thomas* (1985) 81 Cr App R 331 (touching the hem of a skirt and rubbing it), and *H* [2005] Crim LR 734, discussed in section 9.5(f).

Is it right that the criminal law should extend to mere touching, however trivial? The traditional justification is that there is no other sensible dividing line, and that this at least declares the law's regard for the physical integrity of citizens. As Blackstone put it: 'the law cannot draw the line between different degrees of violence, and therefore totally prohibits the first and lowest stage of it; every man's person being sacred, and no other having a right to meddle with it, in any the slightest manner'.[64] It is strange, then, that the draft Criminal Code originally defined assault in terms of applying force to, or causing an 'impact' on the body of, another (although that is not now the Law Commission's chosen path).[65] Would that include or exclude stroking another's hair or clothing? Individuals have a right not to be touched if they do not wish to be touched, since the body is private. Someone who knowingly touches V without V's consent violates this personal right as surely as if he had taken V's property, but does he use 'force'? The difficulty is most evident in cases of sexual assault, which may be committed by the least unwanted touching or stroking of one person's body by another. These are culpable acts, often regarded as being more serious than thefts of property. Should it be made clear that the offence really concerns the invasion of another's right not to be touched or violated in any way—a right not to suffer trespass to the person—and not necessarily an offence of 'violence'?[66] One consequence of defining the offence so widely is that reliance is placed on prosecutorial discretion to keep minor incidents out of court. The CPS guidance attempts to structure that discretion, but focuses more on the dividing line between s. 39 and s. 47. It states that 'although any injury can be classified as actual bodily harm, the appropriate charge will be contrary to s. 39 where injuries amount to no more than the following—grazes, scratches, abrasions, minor bruising, swellings, reddening of the skin, superficial cuts, a "black eye"'.

One disputed point about the ambit of the offence of battery is whether it can be committed by the indirect application of force, such as by digging a hole for someone to fall into. There are long-standing judicial dicta in favour of liability in these circumstances,[67] and the decision in *DPP* v *K* (1990)[68] now supports them. In this case a schoolboy, frightened that he might be found in possession of acid that he had taken out of a laboratory, concealed it in a hot air drier. Before he could remove it, another boy used the drier and suffered burns on his face. Parker LJ held that K had 'just as truly assault[ed] the next user of the machine as if he had himself switched the machine on'.[69] There are firm statements in two House of Lords decisions that are inconsistent with the possibility of an indirect battery,[70] but the Divisional Court continues

---

[64] W. Blackstone, *Commentaries on the Laws of England* (1768), iii, 120.

[65] Law Com No. 177, cl. 75; assault and battery are combined in a single offence under the code. For discussion of the Law Commission's most recent proposals for this offence, see text at n 181.

[66] See also Gardner, 'Rationality and the Rule of Law', and the discussion of sexual assaults, section 9.5(f).

[67] See *Clarence* (1888) 22 QBD 23, *per* Stephen and Wills JJ.

[68] (1990) 91 Cr App R 23 (reversed on other grounds by the House of Lords in *Savage and Parmenter* [1992] 1 AC 699).

[69] (1990) 91 Cr App R 23, 27; although it was not mentioned, the analysis might have been linked to the principle in *Miller* [1983] 2 AC 161, Chapter 4.4.

[70] See the argument of M. Hirst, 'Assault, Battery and Indirect Violence' [1999] Crim LR 557, relying on Lord Roskill in *Wilson* [1984] AC 242 and Lords Steyn and Hope in *Ireland and Burstow* [1998] AC 147.

to decide otherwise. Thus in *DPP* v *Santana-Bermudez* (2004)[71] a police officer asked D, before searching him, if he had any needles on him, and D falsely said that he had not. The officer put her hands into a pocket and her finger was pierced by a needle. The Court applied the principle in *Miller*[72] to hold that, since D had created the danger, his failure to avert the danger and its resultant materialization were capable of fulfilling the conduct requirement of battery.

Another problem is that, if the offence is defined so as to include all touching to which the victim does not consent, it seems difficult to exclude everyday physical contact with others. This could be resolved by assuming that all citizens impliedly consent to those touchings which are incidental to ordinary everyday life and travel; but the judicial preference seems to be to create an exception for 'all physical contact which is generally acceptable in the ordinary conduct of daily life'.[73] The cases decide that this exception extends to touching a person in order to attract attention, although there can be no exception when the person touched has made it clear that he or she does not wish to be touched again. The problem arose in *Collins* v *Wilcock* (1984),[74] where a police officer, not empowered to arrest D, touched D in order to attract her attention and then subsequently took hold of D's arm. D proceeded to scratch the police officer's arm, having previously made it clear—in colourful language—that she did not wish to talk to the police officer. The Divisional Court quashed D's conviction for assaulting a police officer in the execution of her duty, on the ground that the officer herself had assaulted D by taking hold of D's arm. The key issue here was D's obvious refusal of consent to any touching; in other cases there might be a question of whether the touching goes 'beyond generally acceptable standards of conduct'.[75] A number of decisions have suggested what appears to be an alternative approach: to ask whether D's touching was 'hostile'. This seems to be an inferior method of identifying the boundaries of permissible conduct. There has been disagreement whether this requirement forms part of the criminal law,[76] and the House of Lords applied it in *Brown*[77] whilst emptying it of almost all significance.

The essence of the crime of *assault*, as distinct from battery, is that it consists of causing apprehension of an immediate touching or application of unlawful force. It is therefore possible to have a battery without an assault (e.g. where D touches V from behind), as well as an assault without a battery (e.g. where D threatens to strike V but is prevented from doing so), but most cases involve both. Two disputed questions— whether words alone can constitute an assault, and how imminent the threatened force needs to be—have recently received considerable judicial and academic attention. The preponderance of authority until recently was that mere words, unaccompanied by any

---

[71] [2004] Crim LR 471.   [72] [1983] 2 AC 161, discussed in Chapter 4.4.

[73] *Per* Goff LJ, in *Collins* v *Willcock* (1984) 79 Cr App R 229, at 234.

[74] *Per* Goff LJ, in *Collins* v *Willcock* (1984) 79 Cr App R 229, at 234.

[75] *Per* Goff LJ, in *Collins* v *Willcock* (1984) 79 Cr App R 229, at 234; cf. *Donnelly* v *Jackman* (1969) 54 Cr App R 229.

[76] A requirement of hostility was re-asserted in *Brown* [1994] 1 AC 212, although Lord Goff in *Re F* [1990] 2 AC 1 held that it does not form part of the offence of assault.   [77] [1994] 1 AC 212, discussed in (f).

threatening conduct, could not amount to an assault,[78] but this was unsatisfactory if a primary purpose of the offence was to penalize the deliberate or reckless creation of fear of attack. As Lord Steyn put the point in *Ireland and Burstow*:[79]

> There is no reason why something said should be incapable of causing an apprehension of immediate personal violence, e.g. a man accosting a woman in a dark alley saying 'come with me or I will stab you.' I would, therefore, reject the proposition that an assault can never be committed by words.

In that case the argument was taken further, by recognizing that a person who makes silent telephone calls may also satisfy the conduct requirement for assault. The emphasis is now rightly placed on the intended or risked *effect* of what D did, rather than on the precise method chosen.[80]

That leaves the question of how immediate or imminent the threatened violence needs to be. In one case the Divisional Court held that assault was committed where a woman was frightened by the sight of a man looking in through the window of her house,[81] although there seems to have been little suggestion that the man was threatening to apply force either immediately or at all. The decision might be explained as a pragmatic attempt to remedy the absence of an offence which penalizes such 'peeping toms'.[82] Similarly in *Logdon v DPP* (1976)[83] D showed the victim a pistol in his desk drawer and said that it was loaded, and the Divisional Court held that this was an assault even though D had not handled the gun or pointed it. Presumably the threat was thought sufficiently immediate. Also in this case, D knew that the gun was a replica and was unloaded, but his actions and words caused the victim to believe otherwise. The fact that no harm was likely is immaterial, since the essence of the offence is the causing of apprehension in the victim.[84] The question of immediacy has been raised sharply by the cases of silent telephone calls, but not answered clearly. In *Ireland and Burstow*[85] Lord Steyn held that a caller who says 'I will be at your door in a minute or two' could satisfy the requirement of immediacy or imminence (Lord Steyn appeared to use the terms interchangeably), and that by the same token a silent caller who causes the victim to fear that he may arrive at her door soon could also satisfy the requirement. Lord Hope concluded that repeated silent telephone calls could satisfy the conduct requirement in assault if they created an apprehension of immediate violence.[86]

---

[78] Cf. *Meade and Belt* (1823) 1 Lew CC 184 with *Wilson* [1955] 1 WLR 493, and the discussion by G. Williams, 'Assaults and Words' [1957] Crim LR 216.

[79] [1998] AC 147, at 162; see also *Constanza* [1997] 2 Cr App R 492 for a case involving words, silence, and gestures.   [80] J. Horder, 'Reconsidering Psychic Assault' [1998] Crim LR 392.

[81] *Smith v Chief Superintendent of Woking Police Station* (1983) 76 Cr App R 234.

[82] This would only amount to the offence of voyeurism, contrary to s. 67(1) of the Sexual Offences Act 2003, if D, for the purpose of obtaining sexual gratification, observed V 'doing a private act'.

[83] [1976] Crim LR 121.

[84] Thus if the victim also believes that the gun is a toy or is unloaded, there can be no assault: see *Lamb* [1967] 2 QB 981.

[85] [1998] AC at 161; for reflections on the judicial function in thus developing the law see C. Wells, 'Stalking: the Criminal Law Response' [1997] Crim LR 463.   [86] [1998] AC 161, at 166.

The question was raised more directly in *Constanza* (1997),[87] particularly in respect of a letter put through V's door by D which caused V to fear that D had 'flipped' and might become violent at any time. D lived fairly close to V. The Court of Appeal contrasted a case where the feared violence would not occur before a time in the distant future, which would fall outside the definition of assault, and held that it would be sufficient 'if the Crown has proved a fear of violence at some time not excluding the immediate future'. In that case the appeal against conviction was dismissed. In *Ireland and Burstow* the House of Lords failed to discuss the *Constanza* test, but the two decisions taken together suggest a loosening of the 'imminence' requirement and perhaps the gentle drift of assault towards an offence of creating fear that does not require proof of a clinical psychiatric condition or proof of immediacy in a strict sense.

The fault element required for assault and battery is either intention or advertent recklessness as to the respective conduct elements.[88] The offence is summary only but, where the offence is racially or religiously aggravated,[89] it becomes triable in the Crown Court and has the higher maximum penalty of two years' imprisonment.

(f) QUESTIONS OF CONSENT

In order to explain why offences of violence are regarded so seriously, reference has been made to the principle of lifestyle autonomy. Lifestyle autonomy has both positive and negative aspects: on the one hand, it argues for liberty from attack or interference, whereas on the other hand it argues for the liberty to do with one's body as one wishes. In principle, just as the owner of property can consent to someone destroying or damaging that property,[90] so individuals may consent to the infliction of physical harm on themselves. We shall see below that consent may constitute the difference between the sexual expression of shared love between two people and serious offences such as rape or sexual penetration.[91] Should consent be given the same powerful role in relation to non-fatal injuries?[92] If a person wishes to give up her or his physical integrity in certain circumstances, or to risk it for the sake of sport or excitement, should the other person's infliction of harm on the willing recipient be criminalized?

A preliminary point in answering this question is whether the absence of consent is an element in the offence or the presence of consent is a defence. It seems more sensible to adopt the former alternative in relation to sexual offences. It would seem odd to suggest that every act of sexual intercourse constitutes the whole conduct element of rape, to which the consent of the 'victim' then provides a defence.[93] Similarly, touching

---

[87] [1997] 2 Cr App R 492.

[88] *Venna* [1976] QB 421, approved in *Savage and Parmenter* [1992] 1 AC 699.

[89] See n 53.   [90] Criminal Damage Act 1971, except in circumstances where life is endangered.

[91] See section 9.5(c).

[92] Cf. C. Elliott and C. de Than, 'The Case for a Rational Reconstruction of Consent in Criminal Law' (2007) 70 MLR 225.

[93] Likewise, it would seem strange to say that every appropriation of another's property amounts to theft unless there is the defence that the owner consents—although, as we shall see in Chapter 10.2 (a), the courts appear to have gone even further than that. For a contrary view, namely that even fully consensual sex can be a wrong calling for justification, see M. Madden Dempsey and J. Herring, 'Why Sexual Penetration Requires Justification' (2007) 27 OJLS 467.

between lovers, whether or not they might be labelled 'sexual', are surely not *prima facie* wrongs. So it is preferable to understand battery as an (unlawful) touching or application of force without the consent of the person touched. The defendant would normally raise the issue of consent, where relevant, but it should be for the prosecution to disprove it beyond reasonable doubt. The same burden of proof is borne where the defendant argues that the force was lawful, for example, in self-defence. It is sometimes considered that self-defence and consent involve, in law, 'justifications' for conduct: in particular, some judges have fallen into the error of believing that recognition of consent implies approval of the conduct involved.[94] In fact, this analysis mis-characterizes both defences, which have both been referred to in this work as involving 'permissions'. Something may be permissible, in law, even if in morality it is the wrong thing to do. In the case of consent, the law's respect for someone's lifestyle autonomy means that harmful but consensual conduct is permissible, so long as it is freely participated in by the parties (or willingly endured by one party),[95] even if that conduct provides no benefit to those involved or to others. What the law says is that respect for lifestyle autonomy is right, not that the conduct which then takes place is right.[96] The nature of consent, as a tolerance-based claim to acquittal, will be considered further below.

The ambit of effective consent in non-fatal offences remains a matter of common law, and it has been determined by the answer of the judges to three questions. First, what counts as consent to physical interference? Secondly, of what offences is the absence of consent an element? Thirdly, even when it is not an element in an offence, can consent be relevant in limited circumstances? The answer to the first question has been altered by recent decisions on the communication of HIV. The old case of *Clarence* (1888)[97] had held that, if V knew that she was consenting to sexual intercourse, her unawareness that D had a sexually transmitted disease did not negative that consent. This was so, even though the charge was inflicting grievous bodily harm, and she would clearly not have agreed if she had known the true facts. In *Dica* (2004)[98] the Court of Appeal held that consent to sex did not imply consent to bodily harm from a sexually transmitted disease, and that *Clarence* should not be followed. The crucial question of when consent is taken to be present was soon revisited in *Konzani* (2005),[99] where D (who knew he was HIV positive) had unprotected sex with three people without informing them of his condition. The Court of Appeal held that only fully informed consent will

---

[94] Compare the remark of Lord Lowry in *Brown* [1994] 1 AC 212, at 255, to the effect that allowing consent would give a 'judicial imprimatur' to what the defendants had done, with the more thoughtful approach of Lord Mustill.

[95] The effect of deception, threats, and other possible vitiating factors is considered in the context of sexual offences in section 9.5(d) and (e).

[96] The same is true of self-defence cases. Self-defensive conduct may be permissible in law, but morally questionable. An example might be where the only way in which I can stop a 9-year-old from picking up a real gun and shooting it at me is by shooting at the child myself, even though it was me who carelessly left the real gun within the child's reach.   [97] (1888) 22 QBD 23.

[98] [2004] QB 1257; see M. Weait, 'Criminal Law and the Sexual Transmission of HIV: *R v Dica*' (2005) 68 MLR 121.

[99] [2005] 2 Cr App R 13; see M. Weait, 'Knowledge, Autonomy and Consent: *R v Konzani*' [2005] Crim LR 673.

suffice, and that this means that if the other party is not aware of D's condition there can be no valid consent to the transmission of the disease.[100]

The Court claimed that it was upholding the principle of autonomy in its decision, but this is a contentious proposition. On the one hand, the decision is faithful to the view that (very broadly speaking) in supposedly consensual dealings between persons there is a duty to disclose facts known to be relevant to a person's willingness to enter into those dealings, if the person ignorant of those facts may otherwise suffer harm or loss.[101] On the other hand, the value in such an intensely personal and private matter as sexual intercourse has a fragile basis, one that is easily undermined by legal intrusiveness in a way that the value of the relationship between (say) buyers and sellers or trustees and beneficiaries is not. For that reason, one might take the more 'risk-positive' view that, if V has unprotected sex with D without asking D any questions about his sexual health, V is autonomously taking a well-known risk of a sexually transmitted disease. The Court's decision, though, is more risk-neutral: in effect, D must disclose his condition to V so that V can take an informed decision, and failure to do so means that no valid consent from V can be forthcoming. Thus the Court imposes the duty on D. It may be, though, that D must also be shown to have some understanding of the modes of transmission of HIV, before a duty to disclose can arise.[102] In line with the approach adopted here, in its Scoping Consultation Paper in 2014, the Law Commission took the provisional rule that the balance of considerations was against permitting criminal liability for an offence against the person to arise in cases of sexually transmitted infection, other than when the transmission was intentionally attempted.[103] 'Reckless' transmission would not be enough. There will be further discussion of the effect of fraud and threats on consent and autonomy, in the context of sexual offences.[104]

The answer to the second question has also become clearer in recent years, chiefly as a result of three decisions. In *Attorney General's Reference (No. 1 of 1980)*,[105] the reference concerned a fight in the street between two youths to settle an argument. The essence of the Court of Appeal's answer was that 'it is not in the public interest that people should try to cause or should cause each other actual bodily harm for no good reason'. In other words, the Court held that, if the fight merely involves assault or battery, consent can be effective as a defence. But if the results constitute actual bodily harm—which, as we saw in subsection (d), extends to 'any hurt or injury calculated to interfere with the health or comfort of the victim'[106]—consent cannot be a defence. In *Attorney General's Reference (No. 1 of 1980)* Lord Lane CJ suggested that it was sufficient if actual bodily harm was caused, even if D did not intend that consequence, but

---

[100] We saw at section 9.3(c) that the same approach was taken to the transmission of genital herpes in *Golding* [2014] EWCA Crim 889.

[101] *Hinks* [2000] 4 All ER 833 (HL); *Santana-Bermudez* [2004] Crim LR 471; *Richardson* [1998] 2 Cr App R 200; *Tabassum* [2000] 2 Cr App R 328; Fraud Act 2006, s. 3.

[102] Cf. S. Ryan, 'Reckless Transmission of HIV: Knowledge and Culpability' [2006] Crim LR 981 and R. Bennett, 'Should we Criminalize HIV Transmission?', in C. Erin and S. Ost (eds), *The Criminal Justice System and Health Care* (2007).

[103] Law Commission, *Reform of Offences Against the Person*, CP No 217 (2014), ch 6.

[104] See section 9.5(h) of this chapter.   [105] [1981] QB 715.   [106] *Donovan* [1934] 2 KB 498.

in Meachen[107] the Court of Appeal held that D must intend or be reckless as to actual bodily harm. Thus, where D had consensually penetrated V's anus with his finger for their sexual gratification, his conviction under s. 20 (she suffered serious anal injury) was quashed because he only foresaw a simple assault and her consent to that was valid. These decisions continue to place the dividing line between actual bodily harm (presence of consent generally irrelevant) and assault and battery (absence of consent an element). This dividing line was attacked by counsel for the appellants in Brown (1994),[108] but by a majority of three to two the House of Lords confirmed it. Whilst Lords Mustill and Slynn (dissenting) took the view that the absence of consent should be an element in any offence not involving grievous bodily harm, the majority rejected this change as unwise and unworkable.[109] The general rule is thus that consent may negative assault or battery, but not a more serious offence.

Thirdly, in what circumstances can consent be relevant, exceptionally, in relation to harms that might otherwise amount to assault occasioning actual bodily harm or even a more serious offence? The best-known modern statement of the position is that of Lord Lane CJ in Attorney-General's Reference (No. 6 of 1980):

> Nothing which we have said is intended to cast doubt on the accepted legality of properly conducted games and sports, lawful chastisement or correction, reasonable surgical interference, dangerous exhibitions, etc. These apparent exceptions can be justified as involving the exercise of a legal right, in the case of chastisement or correction, or as needed in the public interest, in the other cases.[110]

The closing words of this passage demonstrate the unsatisfactory basis of the prevailing judicial approach. How can it be said that dangerous exhibitions such as circus acts or trying to vault over twelve buses on a motorcycle are 'needed in the public interest'? The Supreme Court of Canada has attempted to answer this question by suggesting that stuntmen who agree to perform daredevil activities are engaged 'in the creation of a socially valuable cultural product', with benefits 'for the good of the people involved, and often for a wider group of people as well'.[111] This is not a convincing approach. It would be better to start with the high value placed on the principle of lifestyle autonomy (whatever the value of the activity engaged in, in the exercise of such freedom), and then examine reasons why particular consensual activities should be criminalized by way of exception to the general principle. This would require judges to look for distinct reasons for criminalizing particular consensual conduct, rather than holding it all to be criminal and then finding exceptions by dint of overblown claims about what is 'needed' in the public interest.

If we examine the exceptional categories in turn, cases of lawful chastisement do not belong here: they are hardly consensual, and in any event are subject to legal restrictions.[112] Cases of reasonable surgical interference encompass all the usual medical

---

[107] [2006] EWCA Crim 2414   [108] [1994] 1 AC 212.
[109] For discussion see D. Kell, 'Social Disutility and the Law of Consent' (1994) 14 OJLS 121; M. J. Allen, 'Consent and Assault' [1994] J Crim Law 183.   [110] [1981] QB 715, at 719.
[111] Jobidon [1991] 2 SCR 714.   [112] See Chapter 4.7.

operations,[113] but there are unanswered questions about non-essential interference such as plastic surgery (a proper manifestation of individual choice and autonomy?) and about the treatment of various disorders that can result in the voluntary amputations of limbs.[114] The exceptional category of sport has attracted many prosecutions in recent years arising from rugby and association football. In the leading case of *Barnes* (2005)[115] the Court of Appeal re-asserted the proposition that not every 'foul' committed in breach of the rules amounts to a crime. It is assumed that players do, and may lawfully, consent to physical force over and above the minimum permitted by the rules. This does not exclude the possibility of convictions for the use of physical force well beyond that which may reasonably be expected in a game: the borderline is vague, but courts should decide particular cases by reference to the degree of violence used, its relation to the play in the game, any evidence of intent, and so on. It is sometimes thought that an intent to cause injury carries a case across the threshold into criminality,[116] but there are examples (such as some short-pitched bowling in cricket) where that would lead to unexpected liability. Moreover, in boxing this is surely what each boxer is trying to do. However, it would be wrong to take the legality of boxing as a benchmark: as more is known about the incidence of brain damage among boxers, and as more deaths result from boxing, the question why boxing is still lawful needs to be approached with circumspection and without preconceptions.[117]

We now turn to two categories that were not mentioned in the passage from Lord Lane's judgment, 'horseplay' and sado-masochism. In *Jones* (1986)[118] the Court of Appeal held that schoolchildren could validly consent to 'rough and undisciplined play' so long as there was no intention to cause injury thereby. In that case boys were tossed in the air by others, and injuries were sustained when the others failed to catch them as they fell. This 'horseplay' exception was taken much further in *Aitken* (1992),[119] where officers in the RAF had been drinking and then began various mess games and pranks. At one stage they poured white spirit on the flying suits of some officers who were asleep and set fire to them, dousing the flames with no ill effects. They then seized V, who resisted only weakly, and poured white spirit on his flying suit. When they lit it, he was engulfed in flames and suffered 35 per cent burns. The Courts Martial Appeal Court quashed their convictions for inflicting grievous bodily harm, contrary to s. 20 of the 1861 Act. The reason for the decision was chiefly the judge advocate's failure to direct the jury clearly that a mistaken belief in consent would provide a defence. This implies that actual consent would have provided a defence to conduct that would otherwise amount to inflicting grievous bodily harm.

---

[113] For a dentistry case see *Richardson* [1998] 2 Cr App R 200, Chapter 9.5(h).

[114] See C. Erin, 'The Rightful Domain of the Criminal Law', in C. Erin and S. Ost (eds), *The Criminal Justice System and Health Care* (2007).   [115] [2005] 1 WLR 910.

[116] In *Barnes*, [2005] 1 WLR 910, Lord Woolf CJ remarked that every soccer player tackling another in order to win the ball has the recklessness needed to fulfil a s. 20 offence.

[117] M. J. Gunn and D. Ormerod, 'The Legality of Boxing' (1995) 15 *Legal Studies* 181.

[118] (1986) 83 Cr App R 375.

[119] (1992) 95 Cr App R 304; see also *Richardson and Irwin* [1999] 1 Cr App R 392.

Before commenting on the 'horseplay' exception recognized in *Jones* and *Aitken*, it
is appropriate to move on to the leading case on sado-masochism, *Brown* (1994).[120]
Here five men were convicted of assault occasioning actual bodily harm, and three of
them also of unlawful wounding.[121] They were found to have indulged in various homosexual sado-masochistic practices in private, involving the infliction of injuries on
one another but not requiring medical treatment. Having failed to persuade a majority
of the House of Lords to accept that the absence of consent should be an element in
the offences of actual bodily harm or unlawful wounding, the appellants' second argument was that consensual sado-masochism should be recognized as an exceptional
category. This was rejected by the Court of Appeal, according to which, 'the satisfying
of sado-masochistic libido does not come within the category of good reason'[122]—and
fared no better with a majority of the House of Lords. Lord Templeman condemned
the 'violence' and 'cruelty' of what the defendants had done;[123] Lord Lowry referred
to their desire to 'satisfy a perverted and depraved sexual desire';[124] Lord Jauncey was
particularly exercised by the possibility that others might follow the defendants' example if their convictions were not upheld. That is a controversial matter for a judge
to take into account, in this context, because in composing judgments judges are in a
good position neither reliably to assess the future impact of legal decision-making on
private or social activity, nor to weigh the competing considerations with the benefit of
empirical evidence and input from expert groups: these are all better seen as matters
for Parliament.[125]

What emerges from these three speeches is an overwhelming distaste for the defendants' activities, and a determination to describe it in language designed to produce
the conclusion that it should be criminalized. However, a court that looked for good
reason for regarding the conduct as lawful might well find the task more difficult than
one which looked for good reason to criminalize conduct that was private, consensual,
and imposed no burden on the health service. This point emerges with clarity from the
dissenting speech of Lord Mustill, who argued that the case was really about the criminalization of 'private sexual relations', and that the proper question was whether the
public interest required this. He, like his fellow dissentient Lord Slynn, found no compelling reasons for criminal liability. To characterize the conduct as 'violence' helped
the majority judges to their conclusion; if the infliction of pain had been recognized as
a desired part of a consensual sexual experience, the approach should have been different.[126] In Chapter 3.2, it was argued that people are entitled to set a low value on their
bodily integrity as an intrinsic good. That remains true, even when the thing preferred

---

[120] [1994] 1 AC 212.   [121] Discussed in the text at n 120.   [122] (1992) 94 Cr App R 302, at 309.
[123] [1994] 1 AC at 236.   [124] [1994] 1 AC at 255.
[125] See J. Horder, 'Judges' Use of Moral Arguments in Statutory Interpretation', in T. Endicott, J. Getzler,
and E. Peel, *Properties of Law: Essays in Honour of Jim Harris* (2006), ch 5.
[126] N. Bamforth, 'Sado-Masochism and Consent' [1994] Crim LR 661; but for a contrary view, see
D. Baker, 'Re-thinking Consensual Harm-doing' (2008) 12(1) *University of Western Sydney Law Review* 21.
For an alternative perspective, see J. Tolmie, 'Consent to Harmful Assaults: The Case for Moving Away from
Category Based Decision-Making' (2012) Crim LR 656.

in value is purely the pursuit of pleasure (which may have no intrinsic value) produced by the harmful-but-desired actions of another.

Beneath all these particular situations there are conflicting values which claim the law's attention. On the one hand, the liberty to submit to (the risk of) injury, however serious, ought to be respected, as an aspect of self-determination The point is conceded, so the argument might run, in the fact that suicide is no longer an offence, and it should therefore follow that consent to injury should negative any offence. On the other hand, that argument may not be regarded as decisive, because suicide assisted by another is a criminal offence,[127] as is euthanasia (treated as murder in English law), the explanation for that being that the involvement of others in the death changes and complicates the moral and legal issues.[128] One might have thought that many of the considerations at stake here, notably the fear of manipulation by the unscrupulous, would be less pressing and more manageable in respect of many kinds of non-fatal harm. However, the judiciary has maintained a restrictive approach, with a low threshold for consensual harm (only common assault), and two criteria ('good reason', 'needed in the public interest') for recognizing exceptions that allow consensual harms. Even if the low threshold is accepted, the approach to exceptions is manifestly unsatisfactory. The two criteria adopted by the judges fail to explain, let alone to justify, the categories of conduct included and excluded. There has been no attempt to explain why 'horseplay' should be recognized as an exception when sado-masochism is not. Possible explanations suggest themselves—the disgust of the judges for sado-masochism, the notion that the armed forces contain 'decent people' who sometimes act in 'high spirits'—but these are not principled explanations and are an unworthy basis on which to open a small window of liberty. Plainly the degree of injury caused is not conclusive: in both the 'horseplay' cases there were serious injuries requiring hospital treatment, as there may be in boxing, whereas in *Brown* no medical treatment was required. The fact that pain and injury are not self-inflicted certainly increases the likelihood that a public good may override what would otherwise be the rights of the participants in sado-masochistic activities; but (as argued later) no one has yet established a compelling, evidence-based case for such overriding.

A subsequent decision has muddied the waters still further. In *Wilson* (1996)[129] D had branded his initials on his wife's buttocks, at her suggestion, using a hot knife. The trial judge, following *Brown*, ruled that her consent could not be a defence to the charge of assault occasioning actual bodily harm. But the Court of Appeal quashed the conviction, saying that *Brown* does not establish that consent is never a defence to actual bodily harm. Exceptions are allowed, and the conduct in this case was equivalent to tattooing, which is an established exception. The Court added that there is surely no public interest in penalizing consensual activity between husband and wife in the privacy of their own home. However, it is difficult to see what reason there is for confining the privacy argument to husband and wife; and, of course, the approach of asking whether there are public interest reasons in favour of criminalization was the approach

---

[127] Under the Suicide Act 1961.   [128] See Chapter 8.4(h).   [129] [1996] 2 Cr App R 241.

of the minority, not the majority, in *Brown*. To add to the confusion, *Brown* was followed (and *Wilson* distinguished) in the case of *Emmett*.[130] In this case, D caused actual bodily harm to V when (with her consent) he set fire to lighter fuel on her breasts. The Court of Appeal said that D's conduct went 'beyond' what was involved in *Wilson*, and so upheld D's conviction.

The discussion so far has been conducted in the shadow of the European Convention on Human Rights. Article 8 of the Convention declares the right to respect for one's private life: should this not conclude the debate in favour of the minority in *Brown* and the Court of Appeal in *Wilson*? An answer to this question can be given, since the *Brown* case was taken to the European Court of Human Rights, where it became *Laskey* et al. v *UK*.[131] The Court held that the criminalization of consensual sado-masochism does violate the right to respect for one's private life in Art. 8.1, but it went on to conclude that the criminal law's interference with the right can be justified as 'necessary in a democratic society ... for the protection of health'. The Court regarded it as within each State's competence to regulate 'violence' of this kind, even though no hospital treatment was required by these defendants. The Court was urged to recognize that this case involved private sexual behaviour; it replied that, because of the 'significant degree of injury or wounding', the conduct might properly be regarded as violence.[132] The Court was urged to recognize that English law is biased against homosexuals, and it was referred to the *Wilson* case, in which violence in a heterosexual context was not criminalized. It replied that the facts of *Wilson* were not 'at all comparable in seriousness to those in the present case'.

The decision in *Laskey* v *UK* is a considerable disappointment to those who expected a rights-based approach, particularly one that respects privacy. However, it is evident that both the European and English courts will adopt a case-by-case analysis,[133] and the framework of Art. 8, supplemented by the Strasbourg jurisprudence, suggests that in future English courts will need to adopt rather more rigorous reasoning than that of the majority in *Brown*. In other respects, too, the approach of the English criminal courts to consent to injury requires re-appraisal. The Court of Appeal in *Wilson* was surely right to declare that the burden of finding strong arguments should lie on those who wish to criminalize consensual conduct, not on those who wish it to be lawful. This would mean that it is no longer necessary for judges to affirm that daredevil stunts are 'needed in the public interest' or that 'manly sports' help to keep people fit to fight for their country if necessary.[134] Instead, the question should be whether consensual boxing and 'horseplay', in so far as they are both expressions of lifestyle autonomy, do not go too far if there is a risk of serious injury resulting. This leads on to a further

---

[130] *The Times* 15 October 1999.   [131] (1997) 24 EHRR 39, on which see L. Moran (1998) 61 MLR 77.
[132] (1997) 24 EHRR 39 at para. 45, distinguishing the case from consensual non-violent homosexual behaviour in private, the criminalization of which has been held to breach Art. 8 in, e.g. *Dudgeon v United Kingdom* (1982) 4 EHRR 149.
[133] In *K.A. and A.D. v Belgium* (judgment of 17 February 2005, App No. 42758/98) the Strasbourg Court followed its *Laskey* judgment in holding that convictions based on consensual sado-masochism were a justifiable interference with the participants' Art. 8 rights.   [134] Sir Michael Foster, *Crown Law* (1762), 260.

criticism of the law—the absence of clear boundaries to the exceptions. Fair warning ought to be required, since this 'defence' establishes the boundaries of criminal conduct. The exceptional categories plainly apply to offences more serious than common assault, but no court has ever decided how far they go. If boxing is to remain lawful, then do all the exceptions apply, even to the level of causing grievous bodily harm with intent? The sanctity of life is a weighty value, and preservation from serious injury may not be far behind as a principle of protection. However, greater attention should be paid to the principle of lifestyle autonomy. Here, the 'respect' element is important, requiring the State to respect each individual's right to pursue his or her choices consensually with others (subject to such limitations as the absence of a mercy-killing defence, and the protection of the young). In relation to sport, there is in broad terms respect for autonomy, but in some other contexts paternalism, and even disgust, seem to take over as sources of guiding reasons to restrict liberty and choice.

Even so, Michelle Dempsey has sought to re-habilitate somewhat the views of the majority of the Law Lords in *Brown*. She provides a more sophisticated justification for the conviction than disgust or disapproval at the actions in question, with an initial focus on Lord Templeman's reliance on the 'cruelty' involved in the defendants' actions,[135] notwithstanding the victims' consent.[136] She argues that, in such cases, D is not justified in acting sadistically to cause V harm, even if V consents. Consent only gives permission to do the thing consented to (a point made earlier); it does not justify doing the thing itself. On Dempsey's argument, there must be further reasons, grounded in the consenting party's well-being, to make it right to go ahead as agreed. Here is an example of how the argument works. Suppose V, a stranger to D, comes up to D and asks D to slap him (V). When D asks, 'Why should I do that?', V says simply, 'Because I consent'. In this example, D has permission to slap V in virtue of V's consent. However, D has no positive V-focused reason to do as V asks, and so, in Dempsey's view, would not be justified in going ahead. Dempsey argues, similarly, that in *Brown*, although the victims may have consented to the harms inflicted, in itself that did not give the defendants a reason to go ahead, even if it involved a permission to do so. Satisfying their own sadistic desires, and even V's masochistic ones into the bargain, is (she argues) no such reason, as it fails to reflect the victim's well-being.

In moral terms, we should accept the view that consent is a permission that does not in itself justify performing the action consented to: positive reasons to go ahead are needed for such a justification. Even so, this insight does not advance the case for criminalization in *Brown* or similar cases. Where a mature V gives free and informed consent to an action by D, D may be perfectly justified in taking the view, as in the slap example just given, that it is *for V to decide* on his or her well-being with respect to the merits of the action when performed by D. It is, of course, a different matter if D has a special duty of care to look behind consent—and hence beyond the accompanying assumption that the person consenting knows their own mind, and has their own

---

[135] [1994] 1 AC at 236.
[136] M. Madden Dempsey, 'Victimless Conduct and the *Volenti* Maxim: How Consent Works' (2013) 7 *Criminal Law and Philosophy* 11.

reasons that can justify the action consented to—to deeper issues about V's well-being. Examples might be where D is V's parent or teacher. Outside of such special contexts, a liberal and democratic society gives people broad scope to form their own views on the merits of actions they allow to affect them: that is a feature of lifestyle autonomy. Those doing the 'affecting', like D in the slap example, are accordingly entitled to invoke that liberal and democratic permission when explaining their *ex hypothesi* consensual harm-causing conduct. The argument is a justificatory one. It is crafted in terms of an entitlement that the harm-causer has to act on the assumption that, in consenting to an act, the harm-sufferer has their own interest in self-determination at heart in so doing. That assumption is what provides D with a justification to go ahead, when V consents, rather than the consent itself. If Dempsey's argument rests on the view that we always have to be concerned for another's well-being in acting, because we should not assume and act on the view other people know their own best interests, then her theory is authoritarian-paternalistic, and hence inconsistent with liberal and democratic thinking.[137]

Suppose, though, that what has just been said about our entitlement to treat others as if they know their own minds is wrong. It is still possible to re-frame the argument in different terms. Unlike the civil law, the criminal law is much concerned with excuses. In excuse cases, there are reasons for the state to withhold liability, even though the reasons on which D acted were insufficient to justify the action. So, in the slap example, that V gave D consent to administer a slap can excuse D's action, even though it does not justify it. Consequently, D should be excused where he or she reasonably believed that V had reasons to agree to D's action, even if there were in fact no such reasons. More broadly, though, the defence in such cases is based on a toleration for consensual conduct: were there no consent, there would be scant reason for toleration. For example, some religious people believe in the importance of 'mortification' (punishment) of the flesh, by using a harm-causing instrument in many instances, as an aid in seeking to avoid sinful thoughts and actions.[138] Suppose V, who has a disability that prevents him or her from engaging in this practice unaided, asks D to perform the action in question, and D complies. By permitting consent as a defence, the law would appropriately show (appropriate) toleration of this practice, irrespective of whether it can be justified in terms of V's well-being. The same goes for sado-masochistic practices. From the perspective of the liberal and democratic thinking that informs this book,[139] to indulge the former whilst condemning the latter is the wrong path for the law (whatever people may think privately). To take an approach that involves picking over D's reasons for acting to see how they measure up at the bar of morality—did D

---

[137] See Chapter 2.5 for a discussion of liberal and democratic thinking.

[138] Pope Paul VI: 'True penitence, however, cannot ever prescind from physical ascetism as well ... The necessity of mortification of the flesh stands clearly revealed if we consider the fragility of our nature, in which, since Adam's sin, flesh and spirit have contrasting desires. This exercise of bodily mortification—far removed from any form of stoicism—does not imply a condemnation of the flesh which the Son of God deigned to assume. On the contrary, mortification aims at the "liberation" of man.' Apostolic Constitution *Paenitemini*, 17 February 1966.   [139] See Chapter 2.5.

act for an undefeated reason?—risks opening the door to intolerance and bigotry in determining the law's scope. V's consent is D's shield against criminal liability, even when D acts on that consent without sufficient (justificatory) reason.

That does not mean, 'anything goes' behind the shield of consent. There can still be reasons based on public goods[140] to deny that consent should be a defence in some cases, even on an excusatory basis. An example discussed earlier was the law's refusal to permit consent to be a defence for someone who performs female genital mutilation on a consenting adult woman.[141] In such cases, there are strong and compelling evidence-based 'public' reasons, reasons applicable to everyone living in a pluralistic society, to outlaw the practice (medical justifications apart). No such reasons exist, either in relation to consensual religious flagellation, or in relation to consensual sadomasochistic practices falling short of serious bodily harm. In seeking an outlet in the criminal law for their well-meaning authoritarianism, authoritarians should not seek to conjure such public reasons from mere aversion to what they (without evidence) regard as, 'corrupt[ion] by a culture of hedonistic permissiveness which aggravates tendencies to aggressive male behaviour'.[142]

The Law Commission produced a substantial Consultation Paper in 1995, ranging over many of the detailed topics on which consent to injury is an issue.[143] Although the paper contains much of value, the Commission adopts the rather impoverished starting point of trying to assess 'the prevailing Parliamentary culture' in respect of legislation on 'moral issues', allegedly finding 'a paternalism that is softened at the edges when Parliament is confident that there is an effective system of regulatory control'. Of course there are important issues of public pressure and political viability to be taken into account in making recommendations; but the Commission's primary task should surely be to separate the bad arguments from the good, and to avoid all vague references to 'the public interest'. Whether a quantitative criterion (i.e. the distinction between assault and assault occasioning actual bodily harm) should remain a central feature of the law of consent must also be doubted,[144] not least because of the uncertain dividing line between the two offences which the CPS guidance illustrates.

(g) PROTECTION FROM HARASSMENT ACT 1997

When discussing the range of offences against the person in subsections (b) to (e), it was noted that most of those offences have recently been applied by the courts so as to cover various manifestations of 'stalking' in so far as it causes psychiatric injury or, in respect of common assault, fear of violence.[145] More directly aimed at stalking are

---

[140] See Chapter 3.3.   [141] Chapter 4.2.

[142] Letter of Pope John Paul II to Women, <www.w2.vatican.va/content/john-paul-ii/en/letters/1995/documents/hf_jp-ii_let_29061995_women.html>.

[143] Law Commission Consultation Paper No. 139, *Consent in the Criminal Law* (1995), on which see S. Shute, 'The Second Law Commission Consultation Paper on Consent' [1996] Crim LR 684; P. Roberts, 'Consent in the Criminal Law' (1997) 17 OJLS 389; D. C. Ormerod and M. Gunn, 'Consent—a Second Bash' [1996] Crim LR 694.   [144] See Roberts (reference at n 143).

[145] See the study by E. Finch, *The Criminalisation of Stalking* (2001). See also <www.harassment-law.co.uk>.

the provisions of the Protection from Harassment Act 1997. The Act introduced civil remedies for harassment of another, and also created two new criminal offences. One is the summary offence in s. 2 of pursuing a course of conduct in breach of the prohibition of harassment in s. 1. Section 4 creates an offence, punishable with up to five years' imprisonment, of putting people in fear of violence: there must be 'a course of conduct [which] causes another to fear, on at least two occasions, that violence will be used against him',[146] and the fault element is either an intention to cause such fear or negligence, where 'a reasonable person in possession of the same information would think the course of conduct would cause the other so to fear'.[147] Although there is no doubt that these offences address a serious wrong that can cause considerable distress,[148] the combination of a negligence standard with a maximum penalty of five years is unfortunate. It may also be noted that the phrase 'fear of violence' contains neither an imminence requirement nor the need to show psychiatric injury. Statutory changes have now created an aggravated form of the offences under ss. 2 and 4 of the 1997 Act: where the s. 2 offence is racially or religiously aggravated, the maximum penalty rises from six months to two years; where the s. 4 offence is racially or religiously aggravated, the maximum penalty rises from five to seven years.[149]

(h) OFFENCES UNDER THE PUBLIC ORDER ACT 1986

Despite its title, the Public Order Act creates three serious offences which apply whether the conduct takes place in a public or a private place.[150] Of particular relevance here are those offences which involve violence or the threat of violence. The Act provides a 'ladder' of offences, of which the most serious is riot (s. 1). The essence of riot is the use of unlawful violence by one or more persons in a group of at least twelve persons who are using or threatening violence. The maximum penalty is ten years' imprisonment, compared with a maximum of five years for the lesser offence of violent disorder. The essence of violent disorder (s. 2) is the use or threat of unlawful violence in a group of at least three persons who are using or threatening violence.[151] Beneath violent disorder comes the crime of affray (s. 3), defined in terms of threatening or using unlawful violence towards another, and carrying a maximum of three years' imprisonment.[152] Affray may be committed by one individual acting alone. The term 'violence' includes conduct intended to cause physical harm and conduct which might cause harm (such as throwing a missile towards someone); and, for the two most serious offences of riot and violent disorder, 'violence' bears an extended meaning which includes violent conduct towards property.[153]

---

[146] See *DPP* v *Dunn* [2001] 1 Cr App R 352.

[147] This negligence standard has no exception for incapacity: *Colohan* [2001] Crim LR 845.

[148] As is evident from the facts of cases such as *Ireland and Burstow* [1998] AC 147, *Constanza* [1997] Crim LR 576, and *Morris* [1998] 1 Cr App R 386. See further Wells, 'Stalking: the Criminal Law Response'.

[149] Section 32 of the Crime and Disorder Act 1998, and s. 39 of the Anti-Terrorism, Crime and Security Act 2001; for sentencing guidelines see *Kelly and Donnelly* [2001] 2 Cr App R (S) 341.

[150] For general analysis see A. T. H. Smith, *Offences Against Public Order* (1987), and R. Card, *Public Order: The New Law* (1986).   [151] *NW* [2010] EWCA Crim 404.

[152] *Smith* [1997] 1 Cr App R 14;   [153] Public Order Act 1986, s. 8.

Three aspects of the breadth of these offences should be noted. First, not only are the definitions of 'violence' extended, but only one person need use this 'violence' whilst the remainder (eleven others for riot, two others for violent disorder) must be involved in threatening it.[154] There is no barrier to convicting only one person of riot or violent disorder, so long as there is evidence that others were also present and threatening 'violence'.[155] Secondly, despite the label 'public order offences', all the offences can be committed either in public or on private property.[156] And thirdly, although a key element in the offences is that the conduct be 'such as would cause a person of reasonable firmness present at the scene to fear for his personal safety', no such person need have been present. So in one sense these are offences of creating fear (and, in affray, one person causing fear in another)—supplementing common assault, and with much higher penalties—although in another sense they are not, since no person of reasonable firmness need actually be, or be likely to be, present. The odds, to put it bluntly, are stacked in favour of the prosecutor. Sentencing for these offences can result in several years' imprisonment where considerable violence is used and where D was the ringleader or prominently involved.[157]

The three serious offences are underpinned by three summary offences—causing fear or provocation of violence (s. 4), causing harassment, alarm, or distress with intent to cause it (s. 4A),[158] and causing harassment, alarm, or distress (s. 5). These summary offences do not involve actual violence, and the offence under s. 4 is inchoate in nature.[159] Where one of these offences is racially or religiously aggravated, it becomes triable on indictment, with a maximum penalty of two years' imprisonment.[160]

Is it necessary to have an extra ladder of offences so closely linked with the general ladder of offences against the person? One reason might be the unsatisfactory state of the law under the Offences Against the Person Act 1861; that Act fails to provide either a clear and defensible gradation of offences or any general offences of threatening violence against another.[161] A more frequent argument is that the provisions of the Public Order Act are needed to cope with 'group offending', which causes fear in ordinary citizens, and causes extra difficulties for the police and for prosecutors (in obtaining persuasive evidence). Offences committed by groups may well occasion greater fear than offences committed by individuals, and it may also be true that groups have a tendency to do things which individuals might not do: there may be a group bravado, fuelled by peer pressure, which may lead to excesses. On the other hand, the criminal law already makes some provision for such cases. The law of conspiracy is aimed at

---

[154] *Farmer* [2013] EWCA Crim 126.

[155] Cf. *Mahroof* [1989] Crim LR 72; see now *Mitsui Sumitomo Insurance (Europe) Ltd v The Mayor's Office for Policing and Crime* (2014) 1 All ER 422.

[156] See the interesting case of *Leeson v DPP* [2010] EWHC 994 (admin).

[157] *Keys and Sween* (1986) 8 Cr App R (S) 444, *Beasley* et al. (1987) 9 Cr App R (S) 504.

[158] Inserted by the Criminal Justice and Public Order Act 1994.

[159] On inchoate offences, see Chapter 12.   [160] See n 55.

[161] It does contain the offence of threatening to kill (s. 16), and we saw in subsection (e) that common assault may be committed by threatening unlawful force, but there are no general offences: see P. Alldridge, 'Threats Offences—A Case for Reform' [1994] Crim LR 176.

group offending, but that branch of the law is itself open to criticism.[162] The law of complicity and the new offence of encouraging or assisting crime enable the conviction of people who aid and abet others to commit offences, and spread a fairly wide net in doing so.[163] But the 1986 Public Order Act may be seen as a response to the call for a simplified and more 'practical' scheme of offences for dealing with group disorder. Central to this 'practicality' is the way in which the offence definitions go a long way in smoothing the path of the prosecutor, as we saw in relation to the provision that 'no person of reasonable firmness need actually be, or be likely to be, present at the scene'. This is 'practical' in the sense that the prosecution need not rely on members of the public to come forward and give evidence, which there is often a reluctance to do. But it is manifestly impractical from D's point of view, since it limits the opportunities for the defence to contest the issue.

The most prominent argument for having separate 'public order' offences is that group activities of this kind constitute a special threat to law enforcement and the political system. This argument comes close to a constitutional paradox—that people who are protesting against the fairness of the political system may find themselves convicted of serious offences if they adopt a vigorous mode of protest which may be the only effective one available to them because of their relative powerlessness. Article 11 of the European Convention declares a right of peaceful assembly, and where the *bona fide* exercise of this right happens to lead to some form of disorder it would be contrary to Art. 11 to hold the speakers or organizers liable if they did nothing to provoke violence.[164] To deal with such violence there is a whole range of general offences against the person, reviewed in the preceding paragraphs. But violence and threats in a context labelled 'public order' now attract higher sentences and lower evidential requirements under the Public Order Act, not to mention a concept of 'public order' that includes private premises and a definition of 'violence' broadened to include damage to property. Thus, 'public order' is a favoured concept among authoritarians and militant democrats,[165] used for political advantage and as a means of introducing wide discretionary powers and offences defined in ways that disadvantage the defence.[166] The more recent term 'public safety' may assume the same role, as a difficult-to-contest reason for introducing sweeping powers that ignore sound principle.

(i) ADMINISTERING NOXIOUS SUBSTANCES

The Offences Against the Person Act 1861 contains a number of crimes concerned with the administration of noxious or toxic substances. Section 22 penalizes the use of any overpowering drug or substance 'with intent to enable the commission of an arrestable offence' (maximum sentence of life imprisonment). Section 23 penalizes the

---

[162] See Chapter 12.4 and 12.5.
[163] See particularly *Jefferson* et al. (1994) 99 Cr App R 13; also Chapter 12.7 on encouraging and assisting crime.   [164] *Redmond-Bate* v *DPP* [1999] Crim LR 998.
[165] See Chapter 2.5. and Chapter 4.5
[166] See generally N. Lacey, C. Wells, and O. Quick, *Reconstructing Criminal Law* (4th edn., 2010), ch 2.

intentional or reckless administration of any poison or noxious thing which results in danger to the victim's life or grievous bodily harm (maximum sentence of ten years' imprisonment). A person who prepares a syringe and then hands it to another, who self-injects, does not administer, cause to be administered, or cause to be taken, within the meaning of the section.[167] Section 24 penalizes the administration of any poison or noxious thing, 'with intent to injure, aggrieve or annoy the victim' (maximum sentence of five years). This section has been applied so as to cover the administration of a drug which causes harm to the victim's metabolism by over-stimulation, if D's motive for this is malevolent rather than benevolent.[168] It has also been held that a substance may qualify as noxious when administered in a large quantity even if it would be harmless in a smaller dose.[169]

(j) TORTURE

In order to comply with its international obligations, the government introduced an offence of torture in 1988. Its essence is the intentional infliction of severe pain or suffering by an official or by someone else with the consent or acquiescence of an official, and the maximum penalty is life imprisonment.[170] The offence is committed whether the pain or suffering is physical or mental, and whether it was caused by an act or an omission. In almost all cases this would amount to the general offence of wounding or causing grievous bodily harm, but the reason for the separate offence is to mark the distinctive character of official violence, and also to give the offence a wider extra-territorial effect.

(k) THE STRUCTURE OF THE NON-FATAL OFFENCES

In this part of the chapter we have seen that, generally speaking, the existing range of offences seems to emphasize the result, the degree of foresight, the status of the victim, and any element of racial or religious aggravation as the critical issues in grading crimes of physical violation. The crimes in the 1861 Act form a somewhat shakily constructed ladder, with rather more overlapping of offences than is necessary and more elements of constructive liability than are justifiable.[171] Factors such as the existence of provocation, or the difference between premeditated and impulsive violence, are accorded no legal significance: however, they and other factors affect judgments of seriousness at the stages of prosecution and sentencing.[172]

There is an overwhelming case for reform of the 1861 Act. It is unprincipled, it is expressed in language whose sense is difficult to convey to juries,[173] and it may lead judges to perpetrate manifest distortions in order to secure convictions in cases where

---

[167] *Kennedy (No. 2)* [2007] UKHL 38, overruling previous authority.

[168] *Hill* (1986) 83 Cr App R 386.   [169] *Marcus* (1981) 73 Cr App R 49.

[170] Section 134 of the Criminal Justice Act 1988.   [171] For some doubts on the latter point see n 33.

[172] See E. Genders, 'Reform of the Offences Against the Person Act: Lessons from the Law in Action' [1999] Crim LR 689.   [173] N. Fielding, *Courting Violence (2006)*, 209–12.

there is 'obvious' guilt but where the Act falls down. How might the non-fatal offences be reformed? It is important to start by affirming the principle of maximum certainty, the principle of correspondence, and the principle of fair labelling, and in particular to ensure that the new scheme of offences is not so dominated by concerns about efficient administration (usually, prosecutorial convenience) as to produce wide, catch-all offences of the kind found in the public order legislation.[174] Proposals for reform were put forward by the Criminal Law Revision Committee (CLRC) in 1980, and revised by the Law Commission on various occasions culminating in a report and draft Bill in 1993.[175] The Labour government proclaimed its commitment to reforming this 'outmoded and unclear Victorian legislation', and a new draft Bill (based on the previous proposals) was circulated for comment in 1998.[176] The structure of the draft Bills places three major offences beneath attempted murder:

(i) causing serious injury with intent to cause serious injury;

(ii) causing serious injury recklessly;

(iii) causing injury either with intent or recklessly.

Offence (i) would be punishable by up to life imprisonment, offence (ii) by up to seven years' imprisonment, and offence (iii) by up to five years' imprisonment. Below these three offences would be common assault, punishable by up to six months' imprisonment at trial in the magistrates' court. Three forms of aggravated assault would be retained: assault on a police officer, causing serious injury with intent to resist arrest, and assault with intent to resist arrest.[177] The scheme depends chiefly on the seriousness of the harm caused and the degree of foresight, though in a much more structured fashion than the 1861 Act.[178]

There were some problems with the 1998 draft Bill. First, what is the meaning of 'injury'? Clause 15 follows the previous Bill in defining it as physical injury (including pain, unconsciousness, or any other impairment of a person's physical condition) and any impairment of a person's mental health. This seems to leave a wide and relatively indeterminate dividing line between causing injury and the lesser offence of assault (on which, see later). Minor cuts and bruises would be included, although the test of impairment of mental health is intended to exclude such conditions as alarm, distress, or anxiety and to be limited to clinical disorders.[179] This leaves various forms of mental distress uncovered, as we saw in the stalking cases discussed in subsections

---

[174] See Chapter 6.7(a) and Chapter 3.6 for discussion of the principles mentioned here.

[175] Criminal Law Revision Committee, *Offences against the Person*, 14th Report (1980); Law Com No. 218, *Legislating the Criminal Code: Offences against the Person and General Principles* (1993).

[176] Home Office, *Violence: Reforming the Offences Against the Person Act 1861* (1998).

[177] For criticism on this and other points see J. C. Smith, 'Offences against the Person: the Home Office Consultation Paper' [1998] Crim LR 317.

[178] In Ireland, the Non-Fatal Offences Against the Person Act 1997 follows the scheme of the English Bills to some extent, but includes specific offences of harassment, coercion, and attacking another with a syringe. It has now been in force for a decade.

[179] Cf. the existing test in *Ireland and Burstow*, n 85 and accompanying text.

(b), (c), and (d), and the definition of assault in the draft Bill makes no reference to fear: it is in the sanitized terminology of causing another 'to believe that such force or impact is imminent'.[180] The Law Commission revisited the issue in a Consultation Scoping Paper in 2014.[181] The Commission broadly endorsed the 1998 approach, with two changes. First, a new offence of 'intentionally or recklessly causing minor injury' was to be inserted into the offence ladder, between intentionally or recklessly causing injury, and assault. The crucial role of this offence is that it would be triable only in the magistrates' court (triable summarily). That ingenious suggestion is designed to avoid cases of relatively minor injury, where the degree of D's fault may not yet be known, being sent for an expensive trial in the Crown Court when they do not warrant such treatment. Secondly, in the light of developments (considered previously) that have meant that assault, as distinct from battery, is now an offence of much wider application, the Commission believed (probably rightly) that assault and battery should be treated as separate offences and not as two sides of one offence.

Great improvement though these reforms would be, there are still some question marks. It is not entirely clear that there is a compelling case for separating the offences of intentionally inflicting serious injury, and recklessly inflicting serious injury. A simpler solution would have been an offence of 'intentionally or recklessly inflicting serious injury', to match the offence beneath it of intentionally or recklessly inflicting injury. However, it must be admitted that to make the difference between the offences hinge only on the degree of injury suffered would invite plea-bargaining on an undesirable scale (see Chapter 1.3). Additionally, it is a loss not to have, as at present, an offence or offences of 'ulterior fault' in which D does X with intent to do Y, the current example being wounding with intent to do grievous bodily harm contrary to s. 18 of the OAPA 1861. On labelling grounds, there is a space unfilled in the reform proposals for offences such as, 'assault or battery with intent to do serious injury', notwithstanding the obvious point that in such circumstances an attempt to cause serious injury could be normally charged.

9.4 REPORTED SEXUAL ASSAULTS

A major change in the law brought about by the Sexual Offences Act 2003 will be discussed in the remainder of this chapter. However, an upward trend in reported sexual offences has been evident for several years. Among the most serious are rapes: recorded rapes of women and of men have increased considerably in recent decades.[182] In the last ten years, reported instances of rape of a woman increased from 6,281 in 1997 to 13,327 in 2005–06, dropping back to 11,648 in 2007–08, but then rising to 14,624 in

---

[180] Cf. the use of the notions of causing others to fear for their personal safety, and causing fear of violence, in the Public Order Act 1986 and the Protection from Harassment Act 1997.

[181] Law Commission, *Reform of Offences Against the Person*, CP No 217 (2014).

[182] There were 1,300 rapes reported in 1980, 2,900 in 1988, 4,600 in 1993: see further Kershaw et al., *Crime in England and Wales 2007–08*, Table 2.04.

2011 (a figure that may reflect changes in 2009–10 designed to improve the recording of rape complaints). Rape of a male has increased steadily from 347 in 1997 to 1,150 in 2006–07, and then to 1,310 in 2011.[183] However, it is difficult to tell to what extent this represents a real increase in the number of rapes or an increase in the reporting of them. The 2000 sweep of the British Crime Survey found that one in twenty women said that they had been raped since the age of 16, and one in ten had experienced some form of sexual assault (including rape).[184] It is not merely the numbers that have been increasing but also that the contours of rape have been confirmed to be different from the stereotype of attacks by strangers. Research has shown that some 45 per cent of rapes were said to have been committed by the victim's current partner, acquaintances accounted for 16 per cent, ex-partners 11 per cent, 'dates' 11 per cent, 'other intimates' 10 per cent, and strangers only 8 per cent.[185] Merely 20 per cent of the rapes and 18 per cent of all sexual victimization were reported to the police, and then only half of them by the victim.[186] Of rape victims who had contact with the police, 32 per cent were 'very satisfied' and 25 per cent 'fairly satisfied' with the police handling of the matter, compared with 16 per cent 'a bit dissatisfied' and 22 per cent 'very dissatisfied'.[187] Despite improvements made by the police over recent years, there is no doubt that reporting a rape may still be a strenuous and harrowing experience.[188] It is therefore likely to continue as an under-reported offence.

Even where a serious sexual offence is reported and recorded, however, there remain particular problems in securing a conviction. Significant numbers of rape complaints are discontinued or taken no further for lack of 'reliable' evidence, and rape convictions have declined as a proportion of reported rapes, as recorded rapes have increased—in 1979 some 32 per cent of reported rapes resulted in conviction for rape, compared with 6 per cent in a 2003–4 study for the Home Office.[189] In that study of some 700 reported rapes, some 13 per cent ended in conviction for an offence (6 per cent for rape, 7 per cent for lesser offences), but around 70 per cent of the original reported cases had already disappeared from the system, mostly on grounds of either withdrawal by the victim or insufficiency of evidence. Although there is now greater reporting of rapes between acquaintances, it cannot be inferred that the decline in conviction rates is because juries are more reluctant to convict in cases of acquaintance rape, and that stranger rapes are easier to prove. Indeed, in the Home Office study, stranger rapes had the same overall conviction rate (11 per cent) as acquaintance rapes, the only higher rate being for parents and other relatives (32 per cent).[190] Among other

---

[183] Kershaw et al., *Crime in England and Wales 2007–08*, 47; British Crime Survey 2011.

[184] A. Myhill and J. Allen, *Rape and Sexual Assault of Women: The Extent and Nature of the Problem*, Home Office Research Study 237 (2002), ch 3.

[185] Myhill and Allen, *Rape and Sexual Assault of Women*, 30.

[186] Myhill and Allen, *Rape and Sexual Assault of Women*, 49.

[187] Myhill and Allen, *Rape and Sexual Assault of Women*, 51.

[188] J. Temkin, *Rape and the Legal Process* (2nd edn., 2002), 3–8.

[189] A. Feist et al., *Investigating and Detecting Recorded Offences of Rape* (2007).

[190] See also J. Temkin and B. Krahé, *Sexual Assault and the Justice Gap* (2008), 19–22.

factors, evidence of injuries to the victim was strongly associated with conviction.[191] Longer sentences are now imposed on convicted rapists, so that whereas in the year before the guideline judgment in *Billam* (1986)[192] some 25 per cent of convicted rapists received sentences of five years or more, that percentage rose to 53 per cent in 1989 and to 74 per cent in 2000.[193] Sentencing guidelines may have increased that effect: they certainly increased the starting point for sentences for rape between (former) intimates to the same level as that for stranger rape.[194]

The sentencing guidelines take full account of the practical effects of sexual assault, which can be considerable. There are well-documented consequences of rape for many victims: some authors write of a 'rape trauma syndrome', signifying deep disruption of the victim's life-pattern and thought-processes not just in terms of the physical effects of rape (physical pain, inability to sleep, prolonged distress), but also in terms of the effects on well-being (newfound fears, mistrust of surroundings and other people, embarrassment, and so on). Young's New Zealand report concluded that 'rape is an experience which shakes the foundations of the lives of the victims. For many its effect is a long-term one, impairing their capacity for personal relationships, altering their behaviour and values and generating fear'.[195] The effects of sexual abuse of young children may be similar and long-lasting.[196] Indeed, there is no reason to suppose that such effects are confined to the victims of rape as traditionally defined: although sexual assaults vary in their degree, there may be many other forms of sexual assault which are serious enough to create such profound physical and psychological after-effects. Those effects may also tend to spread to the family and close friends of the victim, and then to reflect back on to the victim.[197]

9.5 NON-CONSENSUAL SEXUAL VIOLATION

The Sexual Offences Act 2003 was a major piece of law reform, and its provisions will be central to the discussion in the remainder of this chapter. The focus of this part of the chapter will be upon the offences of non-consensual sexual penetration. Before those offences are examined, however, we begin by exploring the rationale for taking sexual offences seriously, and then outline the structure and the aims of the 2003 Act.

(a) THE ESSENCE OF SEXUAL INVASION

What are the interests typically threatened or destroyed by sexual assaults? In section 9.4, the serious personal consequences of rape and other sexual assaults were described: in many cases rape causes a great deal of harm, and even lesser sexual assaults may have long-lasting psychological consequences that affect the quality of life. It is strongly

---

[191] Temkin and Krahé, *Sexual Assault and the Justice Gap*, 19–22, Table 4.6.
[192] (1986) 82 Cr App R 347.   [193] Temkin and Krahé, n 191, 37.
[194] *Milberry* [2003] 2 Cr App R (S) 142, superseded by Sentencing Guidelines Council, *Sexual Offences Act 2003* (2007).   [195] W. Young, *Rape Study: A Discussion of Law and Practice* (1983), 34.
[196] J. Morgan and L. Zedner, *Child Victims* (1992), ch 3.
[197] J. Shapland, J. Willmore, and P. Duff, *Victims in the Criminal Justice System* (1985), 107–8.

arguable, however, that it is not primarily the physical harmfulness of sexual invasions that makes them serious offences. Even where a sexual assault involves no significant physical force, it constitutes a wrong in the sense that it invades a deeply personal zone, gaining non-consensually that which should only be shared consensually.[198]

Highly significant, in understanding the seriousness of sexual offending, is the protection of the intrinsic value of personal and interpersonal goods connected to the lifestyle autonomy principle, discussed in Chapters 3.2 and 4.2. The development of a sexual identity that is freely endorsed is a personal good, with high intrinsic value for most people. No one should have to feel they have a significant stake in presenting themselves as, say, 'straight', when in fact they are gay or bisexual; still less should anyone be forced into such conduct. Similarly, sexual relations are an interpersonal good with high intrinsic value for most people,[199] so long as they exemplify lifestyle autonomy for those involved (they are not the product of coercion, and so on). However, our focus is what is important, in legal terms. The criminal law cannot rightly or sensibly be employed to protect you from yourself, by stopping you from 'living a lie' in pretending to be straight when you are gay or bisexual. Similarly, although perhaps more controversially, it cannot rightly protect you from bad sexual encounters with others that turn out to be value-less, simply on the grounds that these experiences were meaningless: occasions only for regret, shame or the feeling of having been 'used' by someone for their own ends. What is important, in legal terms, is not the value (or lack of it) in the activity, but whether it is engaged in through free choice, that is, autonomously.[200] So, for example, suppose that you engage in what turns out to be bad sex because your voluntary intoxication led you to be more susceptible to someone's advances, and you make a choice you know in retrospect that you should not have made. That will not be rape, if your choice was freely made, albeit influenced by intoxication.[201] Contrariwise, if a husband deliberately takes advantage of his wife's pathological intoxication[202] to have sexual intercourse with her, this will (other things being equal) be rape, if the prosecution can prove that she did not consent. In this example, as in other similar examples, in the words of John Gardner and Stephen Shute, rape is 'dehumanizing', because it is 'a denial of [the victim's] personhood'.[203] There is a denial

---

[198] See N. Lacey, *Unspeakable Subjects: Feminist Essays in Legal and Social Theory* (Hart, 1998), ch 4.

[199] Whether or not the value is instantiated is normally highly context-dependent. So, for example, for many people the value is sustained only where sexual relations take place within the bonds of marriage or in long-term relationships.

[200] The recent work of Michelle Madden Dempsey and Jonathan Herring may be considered as an attempt to cast doubt on this distinction. For example, in their view, even the penetration involved in fully consensual sexual intercourse can involve a *prima facie* wrong (something that is wrong unless a justification existed for engaging in the conduct), making it easier to accept that bad sex, as such, involves a transgression against the laws of rape or sexual assault. See M. Madden Dempsey and J. Herring, 'Why Sexual Penetration Requires Justification' (2007) 27 OJLS 467; See also J. Herring, 'Mistaken Sex' [2005] Crim LR 511.

[201] *Bree* [2007] EWCA Crim 804.

[202] Under the US Model Penal Code 2.08(5)(c), pathological voluntary intoxication, 'means intoxication grossly excessive in degree, given the amount of the intoxicant, to which the actor does not know he is susceptible.'

[203] J. Gardner and S. Shute, 'The Wrongness of Rape', in J. Horder (ed.), *Oxford Essays in Jurisprudence (4th Series)* (2000), 205.

of sexual autonomy and of bodily integrity here that applies in some measure to other sexual offences too. But the physical and psychological effects that typically flow from sexual offences (including humiliation and degradation) are also a large part of the justification for treating them so seriously.

So, the criminal law is not there to ensure you only ever make valuable, autonomy-enhancing choices in your sexual life. The criminal law is there to punish those who deprive you of a free choice over whether or not to have, or to continue with, the sexual experience in question at all (whether or not the experience turns out to be something of value to you).[204] In human rights terms, States have a positive obligation to have in place laws that protect citizens from unwanted sexual interference.[205] Thus the right to respect for one's private life in Art. 8 of the Convention recognizes that sexual choice is 'a most intimate aspect of affected individuals' lives'.[206] For this reason each citizen should have the right not to have others' sexual choices imposed on him or her. The State's laws should respect each individual's right to pursue his or her sexual choices consensually with others, subject to such limitations as public decency laws and to the protection of the vulnerable. This requires the State to ensure that its laws do not unjustifiably inhibit the expression of sexuality in consensual and non-offensive contexts.[207]

(b) THE STRUCTURE OF THE 2003 ACT

The Sexual Offences Act 2003 was the first fundamental reform of the relevant law for over a century, the Sexual Offences Act 1956 having been largely a consolidating measure.[208] Sections 1–4 of the Act create newly defined offences of rape and sexual assault, and new offences of assault by penetration, and causing sexual activity. All these offences turn on the absence of consent. Sections 5–8 create parallel offences in respect of child victims under the age of 13, and to these offences consent is irrelevant. Sections 9–15 then create a number of sexual offences against children under 16, with differing maximum penalties according to whether the offender is an adult or is under 18. Sections 16–24 contain various 'abuse of trust' offences, committed against persons under 18 by those in a position of trust. The new Act contains a number of reformulated familial sex offences, in ss. 25–9 and 64–5. Sections 30–44 create a range of offences, committed against persons with mental disorder by others (including care workers). Sections 45–51 amend the law to protect children against

---

[204] That is not to say that lack of free 'consent' should itself be the term employed by the law to mark the relevant distinctions. On this, see V. Tadros, 'Rape without Consent' (2006) 26 OJLS 515.

[205] *X and Y v Netherlands* (1986) 8 EHRR 235; *MC v Bulgaria* (2005) 40 EHRR 459.

[206] See, e.g., *Sutherland and Morris v UK* (1997) 24 EHRR CD22, para. 57.

[207] Hence the many judgments against States which have criminalized consensual homosexual acts, e.g. *Dudgeon v United Kingdom* (1982) 4 EHRR 149, and *ADT v United Kingdom* (2001) 31 EHRR 33.

[208] See, generally, P. Rook and R. Ward, *Sexual Offences: Law and Practice* (4th edn., 2010); J. Temkin and A. Ashworth, 'Rape, Sexual Assaults and the Problems of Consent' [2004] Crim LR 328 (on which much of the following analysis is based); J. R. Spencer, 'Child and Family Offences' [2004] Crim LR 347.

indecent photographs, pornography, and prostitution. Sections 52–60 alter the law relating to prostitution and trafficking for sexual exploitation. There are three preparatory offences in ss. 61–3, and then ss. 66–71 contain offences of exposure, voyeurism, sexual penetration of a corpse, and sexual activity in a public lavatory. Part 2 of the Act contains new notification requirements for sex offenders, and various new preventive orders for the courts to make.

(c) THE AIMS OF THE 2003 ACT

The 2003 Act was a far-reaching reform intended to mark a fresh start in the criminal law's response to sexual misconduct. The Sex Offences Review that preceded it was instituted in January 1999, consulted widely, and produced its report, *Setting the Boundaries*, in July 2000.[209] The government then announced its proposals[210] and brought forward a Bill in 2002, the details of which changed considerably as a result of parliamentary scrutiny.[211] The Sexual Offences Act 2003 has some 143 sections, of which the first seventy-one create offences. It had been a very long time since there had been a statute creating as many offences as this. At the risk of over-simplification, some seven purposes of the Act may be outlined.

First, the Act is intended to modernize the law of sexual offences and to bring it more closely into line with contemporary attitudes. Thus the Home Office criticized the former law as 'archaic, incoherent and discriminatory', and argued that it failed to reflect 'changes in society and social attitudes'.[212] This refers particularly to the attitudes of some men towards women, and one significant change had already been made a decade earlier when the marital rape exception was finally abolished.[213] But it is open to question whether high maximum penalties for consensual sexual conduct between children are closely in line with modern attitudes.

Secondly, and related to the first purpose, the Act mostly creates gender-neutral offences. Apart from the offence of rape, which can only be committed by a man as a principal offender, the offences can be committed by a male or female against a male or female. This ensures equality of protection and of criminalization, thereby avoiding discrimination that might violate a person's Convention rights.[214]

Thirdly, clarity was said to be an aim of the new law, so that people could know what behaviour was unacceptable. It may be an advantage that there are many separately labelled offences; but the Act adopts an unusually prolix style of drafting criminal

---

[209] *Setting the Boundaries: Reforming the Law on Sexual Offences* (Home Office, 2000). For critical comment, see N. Lacey, 'Beset by Boundaries: The Home Office Review of Sex Offences' [2001] Crim LR 3; P. Rumney, 'The Review of Sex Offences and Rape Law' (2001) 64 MLR 890; and Temkin, n 188.

[210] Home Office, *Protecting the Public* (2002).

[211] See, e.g., House of Commons Home Affairs Committee, *Sexual Offences Bill* (5th report, 2003), and the Joint Committee on Human Rights, *Scrutiny of Bills: Further Progress Report* (12th report, 2003).

[212] Home Office, n 210, para. 4.

[213] *R v R* [1992] 1 AC 599 and s. 142 of the Criminal Justice and Public Order Act 1994.

[214] E.g. *Sutherland and Morris* v *United Kingdom* (1997) 24 EHRR CD22 and *ADT* v *United Kingdom* (2000) 31 EHRR 33.

provisions, and there are many overlaps between offences. It is open to question whether this was the best means of trying to achieve the desirable objective of greater clarity.

Fourthly, the government was very keen to clarify the law relating to consent[215]—a vexed question for many years, and one where the nuances of sexual encounters and the power of ingrained attitudes interact to create considerable problems of applying any definition and standards.[216] However, as we shall see in paragraph (h), the new approach fails to fulfil the aspirations to certainty and clarity.[217]

Fifthly, the Act was intended to secure appropriate protection for the vulnerable, and to this end it includes (as we have already noted) several separate offences against children and also several separate offences against persons with mental disorder. One difficulty, to be discussed further in section 9.6, is that the Act's enthusiasm to criminalize sexual acts involving children succeeds in bringing many other children into the net of criminality, for what are perfectly normal and harmless teenage interactions. The government's reply is that prosecutors will use their discretion to ensure that youngsters are not prosecuted unless there is coercion or some other untoward element, but this is an unsatisfactory expedient, reliant on the authoritarian principle. Indeed, it may not constitute sufficient protection for young people's right to respect for private life under Art. 8. Kissing, fondling, and other consensual activities between 15-year-olds should surely not put the participants at risk of prosecution. One argument that young people of such an age in fact do have a right to engage in such activity is that—within limits—such conduct is a kind of 'horseplay' (discussed in section 9.3(f)) falling outside the scope of the relevant offence; but it should not be necessary to resort to such an argument: offences should be defined so as clearly to exclude minor 'sexual' acts to which consent has been given engaged in by young people.

Sixthly, one aim of the Act is to provide appropriate penalties to reflect the seriousness of the crimes committed.[218] Many of the maximum sentences are higher than before, and, even though the penalties for young offenders committing offences against children are lower than those for adults committing such offences, they are still very high bearing in mind the age of those involved.

Seventhly, the government hoped that the reformed law would play its part in reducing the attrition rate in rape cases and helping to convict the guilty. This was to be done by providing 'a clearer legal framework for juries as they decide on the facts of each case'.[219] With key terms such as 'consent' and 'sexual' under-defined, this aspiration always seemed more of a hope than an expectation, and the evidence suggests that it has not been realized.[220] Having said that, the Act expands the definition of rape, a change that, whether or not it ever turns out to be a way of increasing the number of convictions, is in many respects to be welcomed.

---

[215] Home Office, n 210, para. 30; Lord Falconer, HL Deb, vol. 644, col. 772 (13 February 2003).

[216] Cf. the discussions in Home Office, n 210, paras. 2.7 and 2.10.

[217] See, generally, C. Sjolin, 'Ten Years On: Consent under the Sexual Offences Act 2003' (2015) 79 J Crim L 20. [218] Home Office, n 210, para. 5.

[219] Home Office, n 210, para. 10; Lord Falconer, HL Deb, vol. 644, col. 771 (13 February 2003).

[220] D. Ormerod and K. Laird, *Smith and Hogan's Criminal Law* (14th edn., 2015), ch 18.2.

Reference will be made to these seven aims as various parts of the 2003 Act are examined. It is important to recall, however, that key concepts such as sexual autonomy and vulnerability cut both ways. As we saw in paragraph 9.5(a), a law of sexual offences that respects the principle of lifestyle autonomy and complies with Art. 8 of the Convention will attend to both the negative and positive aspects of the principle—that is, it will ensure that the law penalizes those whose conduct amounts to unwanted interference with a person's sexual autonomy, and it will ensure that the law does not penalize those who are engaging consensually in sexual activities (unless they are publicly offensive or involve vulnerable victims). The principle will also be referred to later, particularly in respect of sexual activity involving two children and familial sexual activity.

(d) RAPE

A reformed offence of rape was created by s. 1 of the 2003 Act, which provides:

(1) A person (A) commits an offence if—

(a) he intentionally penetrates the vagina, anus or mouth of another person (B) with the penis,

(b) B does not consent to the penetration, and

(c) A does not reasonably believe B consents.

One change was that rape now includes oral penetration with the penis. Under the old law, forced oral penetration could only be prosecuted as indecent assault, a label that manifestly failed to indicate the seriousness of the wrong. The opportunity to reform the law raised the question whether forced oral penetration should be classified as rape and thus aligned with vaginal and anal penetration, or whether it should be classified as assault by penetration, a new offence (see (e)) that also carries life imprisonment as its maximum sentence.[221] The Sex Offences Review concluded that penetration of the mouth is 'as horrible, as demeaning and as traumatizing as other forms of forced penile penetration'.[222] The Review decided that the fact that this was penetration by the penis justified placing it within the offence of rape, even though penetration by other objects (included within the offence of assault by penetration) was also an extremely serious violation.[223] Against the argument of principle, some raised the practical argument that bringing oral sex within rape might have the effect of devaluing rape, and that juries might be unwilling to return rape verdicts in such cases. The Home Affairs Committee concluded that this is unlikely to occur in practice,[224] and supported the principle behind the change.[225]

[221] In Irish law, assault by penetration is regarded as rape: Criminal Law (Rape) (Amendment) Act 1990. I am grateful to Ailbhe Oloughlin for this reference.   [222] Home Office, n 216, para. 2.8.5.

[223] The Court of Appeal has taken the view that, in sentencing for rape, judges should not adjust a sentence to reflect which orifice was penetrated: Ismail [2005] EWCA Crim 397.

[224] It seems that the Committee has been proved right, so far as juries' views on the scope of rape are concerned: n 220 earlier.   [225] Home Affairs Committee, Sexual Offences Bill, paras. 10–14.

The prosecution must prove that there was penetration by the penis,[226] and that it was intentional.[227] Since 'penetration is a continuing act from entry to withdrawal',[228] this means that the offence can be committed by intentionally failing to withdraw the penis as soon as non-consent is made clear. The prosecution must also establish the absence of consent (see (h)). The fault requirement in relation to consent has long been a matter of controversy. At common law a defendant could be convicted if he was reckless as to non-consent, in the sense that he 'could not care less' whether the victim was consenting.[229] However, at common law a defendant could be acquitted if he mistakenly believed that the victim was consenting, according to the *Morgan* decision.[230] There was much debate about whether there should be degrees of rape to reflect differing degrees of fault,[231] but in the end the government opted for the requirement that 'A does not reasonably believe that B consents'. The ramifications of this objective standard will be explored in paragraph (i), but it will be observed that the concept of recklessness plays no part in the reformed law.

(e) ASSAULT BY PENETRATION

This new offence carries a maximum sentence of life imprisonment, as does rape, but (like most other offences in the Act) it can be committed by a man or woman as a principal offender. Section 2 of the Act provides:

(1) A person (A) commits an offence if—

(a) he intentionally penetrates the vagina or anus of another person (B) with a part of his body or anything else,

(b) the penetration is sexual,

(c) B does not consent to the penetration, and

(d) A does not reasonably believe that B consents.

The conduct element of the offence includes penetration with any part of the body (such as a finger, but also including the penis, so that the offence overlaps with rape),[232] or penetration with an instrument, such as a bottle. The penetration must be sexual, a requirement discussed in paragraph (f), and it must be without consent. The sentencing guidelines are based on the view that penetration by a finger, or penetration with an instrument, can cause serious harm to young children and also significant psychological harm to adults, and the starting points are therefore substantial, depending on

---

[226] For this purpose, the vagina includes the vulva, and surgically reconstructed organs and orifices are included: s. 79(3).

[227] By contrast, under Scottish law, penetration may be committed recklessly as well as intentionally, a better legal position: Sexual Offences (Scotland) Act 2009, s. 1.

[228] Section 79(2).   [229] This test was supported in Home Office, n 216, paras. 2.12.5–6.

[230] Discussed in Chapter 6.5(d).

[231] See H. Power, 'Towards a Redefinition of the *Mens Rea* of Rape' (2003) 23 OJLS 379.

[232] Relevant in cases where the victim is unsure or incapable of telling what penetrated him or her: see *Minshull* [2004] EWCA 192 (where V was severely disabled).

the age of the victim.[233] The fault element for this offence is that the penetration must be intentional, and that the defendant must not reasonably believe that the victim consents (see paragraph (i)).

(f) SEXUAL ASSAULT

This offence is committed if A intentionally touches another person (B), the touching is sexual, B does not consent to it, and A does not reasonably believe that B consents. The questions of consent and reasonable belief will be discussed in paragraphs (h) and (i). The offence replaces indecent assault, and it will be noticed that both elements of the former crime are replaced. There must be a touching, not an assault; and it must be sexual, not indecent. But the offence of common assault remains, and the concept of assault is wider than touching, since it includes causing a person to apprehend bodily contact (see 8(3)(e)); the offence of assault can also be committed recklessly, whereas sexual assault requires an intentional touching.

What amounts to a touching? Section 79(8) states that it 'includes touching (a) with any part of the body, (b) with anything else, (c) through anything, and in particular includes touching amounting to penetration'. This is not an exhaustive definition, but it makes it clear that the touching does not have to be with the hands (and may be with an instrument), and that touching through clothes is sufficient. Thus in H[234] D made a sexual suggestion to V and took hold of her tracksuit bottoms, attempting to pull her towards him. She broke free and escaped. The Court of Appeal upheld the conviction for sexual assault, ruling that touching someone's clothing is sufficient to fulfil this requirement of the offence. Although s. 79(8) refers to touching through clothing, perhaps implying contact with V's body through clothing, the Court rightly held that this was not an exhaustive definition. Touching the clothes V is wearing is sufficient, Lord Woolf CJ held, so long as the other elements of the offence are fulfilled.

When is a touching 'sexual'? This question is important for the offences under ss. 2, 3, and 4 (among others). Section 78 provides that:

Penetration, touching or any other activity is sexual if a reasonable person would consider that—

(a) whatever its circumstances or any person's purpose in relation to it, it is because of its nature sexual, or

(b) because of its nature it may be sexual and because of its circumstances or the purpose of any person in relation to it (or both) it is sexual.

It will be evident that this section provides a framework for the decision but leaves much to the magistrates or jury to determine in each case. The framework involves a threefold division of cases,[235] and the standard is that of the reasonable person. Cases

---

[233] Sentencing Guidelines Council, *Sexual Offences Act 2003: Definitive Guideline* (2007). See *Corran* [2005] EWCA Crim 192.   [234] [2005] Crim LR 735.
[235] Largely following the previous leading case of *Court* [1989] AC 28.

falling within (a) are sexual by their very nature, and presumably include most touching of sexual organs and private zones of the body. On one view, even a proper medical examination of the vagina or penis is sexual (since the actor's purpose is irrelevant to this classification), although consent, or necessity, would justify it. However, such cases may be better regarded as falling within s. 78(b). This example shows that it may not be easy clearly to separate cases falling within (a) from those falling within (b).

Cases falling within (b) are ambiguous by their nature: reasonable people would disagree about whether or not they are inherently sexual. If the jury or magistrates decide that a touching might be sexual, the question whether this touching is sexual therefore depends on whether a reasonable person would consider that either the circumstances or the actor's motive or purpose was sexual. Thus in H^{236} the Court held that these questions had been properly put to the jury, resulting in the verdict that pulling at the woman's tracksuit bottoms might be sexual and, because of D's purpose, was sexual. In *Court* (1989)[237] a decision under the old law, D put a 12-year-old girl across his knee and spanked her on her shorts. He admitted that he had a buttock fetish. Under the 2003 Act, it is for the magistrates or jury to decide whether this falls within (b) in the sense that 'because of its nature it *may* be sexual'; if they so decide, then they could go on to hold that D's motive rendered it sexual.

The decision whether a case falls within (a) or (b) may be important from an evidentiary point of view. For example, in *Court*, when D was asked about his motivation for committing the offence, he admitted to having a 'buttock fetish'. Clearly, if that evidence was admitted at trial, it would virtually guarantee his conviction (as evidence lawyers say, the evidence was highly prejudicial). However, the way in which such evidence comes to be admitted may be affected by whether the case falls under (a) or (b). If the evidence was in law irrelevant to the prosecution's case, then it could not be led 'in chief', namely as part of the prosecution's direct case against D. How could such evidence possibly be irrelevant in that sense? Answer: if the case fell under (a) where D's purpose does not enter into the question of guilt, and so where evidence gratuitously given of it will create 'heat but no light'. So, ironically, it might seem as if a D who has made a pre-trial prejudicial admission about his sexual inclinations would be better off if his or her case fell under (a). However, there is still a trap for D in these circumstances. If he or she offers any purportedly innocent explanation of his or her behaviour—a justification, or a denial of the fault element, for example—the prosecution may then be able to introduce the prejudicial evidence. It may be able to do this not to show directly that D is guilty, but to show that his or her protestation of innocence should not be believed. If the jury hears the evidence tendered for this purpose by the prosecution, they are then likely to draw only one conclusion on the question of guilt.

Although s. 78 enumerates only two types of case, (a) and (b), there must logically be a third—cases where the touching is not such that a reasonable person would say that it might be sexual. Any touching of this kind cannot be 'sexual', whatever D's motives and whatever the circumstances. In *George* (1956)[238] D had attempted to remove a girl's

---

[236] [2005] Crim LR 735.   [237] [1989] AC 28.   [238] [1956] Crim LR 52.

shoe from her foot, admitting that this gave him sexual gratification. This was held not to amount to an indecent assault, but under the 2003 Act it could be a sexual assault. Everything turns on whether the jury or magistrates hold that a reasonable person would consider that 'because of its nature it may be sexual'.[239] Different tribunals may reach different conclusions: for example, attempting to remove a shoe might be held non-sexual whereas stroking a shoe might be held to be possibly sexual, within (b). One might ask to what extent interference with a shoe is perceived as an attack on someone's sexual autonomy, as distinct from their lifestyle autonomy as an owner of property (i.e. shoes). Fetishists may well do things that normally have no sexual connotation. Should the sexual motivation of the fetishist be sufficient to fulfil the offence, even in the third category? If we accept the 2003 Act's view that it should not, then are we sure that sexual motivation should be sufficient in ambiguous cases falling within (b)? Most of these cases amount to common assault, so it is not a question of conviction or not.[240] The present solution leads to uncertainty and probably inconsistency in practice, but it cannot be otherwise so long as we have category (b) and, by implication, a third category too.

(g) CAUSING SEXUAL ACTIVITY

Section 4 of the Act provides that a person commits an offence by intentionally causing another person to engage in an activity that is sexual. As with the offences in ss. 1–3, the victim must not consent and D must not reasonably believe that he or she consents. The essence of the conduct element is that D must cause the victim to engage in the sexual activity, and this presumably can be effected by explicit or implicit threats, or by use of a position of authority or dominance (simply by speaking words), rather than by actual physical coercion. Thus forcing V to masturbate in front of D,[241] or forcing two people to perform sexual acts for D's pleasure,[242] fall clearly within this new offence.[243] Similarly, P could be held to cause sexual activity by tricking D into believing that V wants sex when V does not, even if P cannot be convicted of complicity in rape.[244] It should probably be held that s. 4 creates two separate offences, since the causing of various penetrative sexual activities carries a maximum sentence of life imprisonment, whereas the causing of other non-penetrative activities has a maximum of ten years.

(h) ABSENCE OF CONSENT

Each of the offences in ss. 1–4 of the 2003 Act has two requirements that have not yet been examined—that B (the victim) did not consent, and that the defendant did not reasonably believe that B was consenting. Here we will discuss the absence of consent:

---

[239] The CA in H [2005] Crim LR 735 held that this would now be for the court to decide in each case.

[240] It is relevant to labelling, of course, and also to the imposition of notification requirements and other preventive measures under the 2003 Act, as well as to sentencing (on which see the Sentencing Guidelines Council, n 217).   [241] See Devonald [2008] EWCA Crim 527.

[242] Basherdost [2008] EWCA Crim 2883.   [243] This was the proposal in Home Office, n 216, para. 2.20.

[244] E.g. Cogan and Leak [1976] QB 217, discussed in Chapter 11.6; under the 2003 Act much would turn on whether D's mistake would prevent conviction.

the law on reasonable belief, which has a similar structure, will be examined in paragraph (i).

There are long-standing problems of defining what amounts to consent and to non-consent, and problems of proof. Indeed, the complexity of the 2003 Act's 'solutions' has led to a suggestion that the law should be re-structured so as to place minimal reliance on such a contested concept as consent.[245] However, the aim of *Setting the Boundaries*[246] and the 2003 Act was to set out a new approach to the difficult problems of consent. The Act puts forward a definition of consent in s. 74, and also further tackles the problems of definition and proof through lists of rebuttable and conclusive presumptions in ss. 75 and 76. The most straightforward course for the prosecution is to establish that B, the complainant, manifestly did not agree to the activity. Few cases are so straightforward and the Act therefore establishes three routes by which non-consent can be proved in cases of rape, assault by penetration, sexual assault, and causing sexual activity.[247] The first is to bring the circumstances within one of the conclusive presumptions in s. 76. The second is to make use of one of the rebuttable presumptions in s. 75. The third, residual approach is to rely on the general definition of consent in s. 74.

Conclusive Presumptions: Section 76(2) provides two sets of circumstances in which the absence of consent will be conclusively and irrebuttably presumed. If the prosecution can establish the relevant factual basis, the 'presumption' (in reality, a legal conclusion) arises and the defence has no answer. The first circumstance is that '(a) the defendant intentionally deceived the complainant as to the nature or purpose of the relevant act'. The common law also held that deception as to the nature of the act was fundamental, as where young girls had been invited to submit to acts in order to train their voice or to improve their breathing[248] and, unbeknown to them, the act which they were permitting was sexual intercourse.

Deception as to the purpose of an act is a significantly wider concept, which applies where D deceives V as to the ulterior reason for or objective of the act. The Court of Appeal held in *Jheeta*[249] that, since the presumption is a conclusive one, it ought to be construed narrowly. In that case B had submitted to intercourse because she had received text messages, allegedly from the police (but actually from D), ordering her to have sex with D; the Court held that this was not a deception as to the purpose of the act. The Court stated that the strongest case of deception as to purpose would be where D has deceived B as to the medical need for the particular procedure.[250] The Court held that there would be no deception as to purpose on the facts of *Linekar*,[251]

---

[245] V. Tadros, 'Rape without Consent' (2006) 26 OJLS 515.   [246] Home Office, n 211, part 2.10.

[247] However, it seems that the presumptions in ss. 75–6 do not apply to attempts and conspiracy to commit sex offences: Judge Rodwell, 'Problems with the Sexual Offences Act 2003' [2005] Crim LR 290.

[248] *Flattery* (1877) 2 QBD 410; *Williams* [1923] 1 KB 340.

[249] *Jheeta* [2007] EWCA Crim 1699.

[250] As in *Green* [2002] EWCA Crim 1501, where a qualified doctor induced young men to masturbate in front of him, allegedly to assess their potential for impotence but actually for his sexual gratification. A similar view might be taken of the facts of *Tabassum* [2000] 2 Cr App R 328, where women agreed to D examining their breasts for 'research work', when D represented that he was medically qualified and he was not.

[251] [1995] 2 Cr App R 49.

where D promised to pay a prostitute for intercourse but then reneged on the deal. Sir Igor Judge stated that 'she was undeceived about either the nature or the purpose of the act, that is, intercourse'.[252] Yet in the subsequent case of *Devonald*,[253] the Court held that where B was induced to masturbate in front of a webcam, believing that it was for the sexual pleasure of a woman whom he had 'met' on the internet when in fact D (a man) aimed to humiliate B, this was a deception as to purpose. Unusually, however, it was (in the context of the 2003 Act) a reverse deception—V thought that the purpose was sexual, whereas D intended the purpose to be humiliation.

A better decision is *Piper*,[254] where V agreed to be measured for a bikini by D on the (false) basis that it was necessary to determine her modelling potential, whereas in fact it was for D's sexual pleasure. D's conviction of sexual assault was upheld. This interpretation is more faithful to the concept of purpose. Following this more orthodox line is the decision of the Court of Appeal in *McNally*.[255] D deceived V as to her gender, pretending to be male. Thereby, D persuaded V to permit her (D) to penetrate V digitally. D was charged under s. 2 of the 2003 Act with assault by penetration. The Court of Appeal held that this was a case falling under s. 74, not s. 76, as there had been no deception as to the nature of purpose of the act.

In *B*,[256] the Court of Appeal confirmed that, in so far as the decisions in *Jheeta* and *Devonald* conflict, the decision in *Jheeta* is to be preferred to that of *Devonald*. In *B*, D had contacted V under a false name on a social networking site, and persuaded V to send D some photographs of V topless. D then threatened to publish the photographs, unless V engaged in sexual acts on a webcam, which V did. D was charged with causing a person to engage in sexual activity without consent.[257] The prosecution sought to rely on the conclusive presumption that V had not consented, because—they alleged—D had deceived V as to the purpose of the act. This is an odd case, in that, when D asked V to send him photographs of V topless, no non-sexual purpose in the request was specified by D, so V could have been in little doubt what the purpose was, namely sexual gratification. In relation to the performance of sexual acts on a webcam, whilst these were in a sense coerced and thus there may have no genuine consent, V could hardly have been in any doubt about the purpose involved here either. The Court of Appeal appears in essence to be suggesting that the prosecution should look to prove its case, on facts such as these, by relying on the general definition of consent in s. 74. If the prosecution pursues its case in that way, D will have the opportunity to argue that he did not have the fault element in that he reasonably believed that V was consenting, even if the conduct element was present in that V was not in fact consenting. With such a serious offence, the provision of such an opportunity is a requirement of fair labelling, other than in the most exceptional cases. For example, in 'dual purpose' cases, where D deceives V as to the purpose of the relevant act, but it is accepted that D's main motivation for engaging in the act may have been—as V was aware—something quite

---

[252] In *Jheeta* [2007] EWCA Crim 1699 at [27].   [253] [2008] EWCA Crim 527.
[254] [2007] EWCA Crim 2131.   [255] [2013] EWCA Crim 1051.
[256] [2013] EWCA Crim 823.   [257] Contrary to the Sexual Offences Act 2003, s. 4(1).

innocuous, then such a case should be pursued under s. 74 and D will be able to deny that he had the fault element.

This discussion raises a broader question concerning the kind of ulterior purposes that can fall within s. 76(2)(a). Examples include D deceiving V into having sex with D by falsely representing that D will (i) obtain a lucrative modelling contract for V,[258] or (ii) enter into a marriage or civil partnership with V.[259] In principle such cases are capable of falling within s. 76(2)(a), particularly if they are the only explanation for V's participation in sexual activity with D. Such cases raise fundamental questions about the nature of rape as a crime. In particular, there is a risk that the crime will become over-inclusive, and hence unable fairly to label some defendants who have used a deception concerning the purpose of the act, but where the deception was not the major causal influence on V's decision to engage in sexual intercourse with D. Under the old law, there was an offence less serious than rape called procuring a woman for intercourse by 'false pretences' that would have covered these kinds of case; but that offence was inexplicably abolished by the 2003 Act, rather than being modernized, leaving the cases involving sexual intercourse to be dealt with under s. 76 or s. 74 as 'rape or nothing'.

Section 76(92)(a) currently adds little of value to the law of sexual offences, beyond singling out for special treatment deceptions as to the 'nature of the act':[260] a special provision for the latter at least provides a small island of relative certainty on a key issue in this difficult moral terrain. Beyond well-established cases in which D falsely persuades V that V is engaging in a completely different act altogether,[261] policy considerations—rather than simple linguistic analysis—should come into the question of whether V has been deceived as to the 'nature of the act'. For example, the law does not currently regard deception as to whether a condom has been used as a deception concerning the 'nature of the act'; it is a matter to be dealt with under s. 74, not s. 76.[262] However, given the relative ease with which such a deception could be perpetrated, the seriousness of the possible consequences, and the especially intimate nature of the contact with V that D obtains through the deception, there is a strong case for ruling that such cases are covered by s. 76.

So far as reform relating to deceptions as to purpose is concerned, one possible reform would be to list in a legislative schedule particular kinds of deception as to purpose that fall within s. 76, leaving the rest to be dealt with under s. 74. Alongside

---

[258] For an example of this general type, see *Melliti* [2001] EWCA Crim 1563.

[259] For a helpful consideration of the broader issues, see K. Laird, 'Rapist or Rogue? Deception, Consent and the Sexual Offences Act 2003' [2014] Crim LR 491.

[260] The existence of a conclusive presumption of lack of consent, in cases covered by s. 76, might be thought—in labelling terms—to imply that the cases caught by the provision are the clearest examples of rape. Whilst that may be true of deception as to the nature of the act, what about the administration of drugs to stupefy V without consent? Or doing a sexual act while V is asleep or unconscious? Or, indeed, coercing V through immediate threats of violence? There is surely as good a case for including these within the conclusive presumptions as there is for the cases we have already encountered.

[261] See *Flattery* (1877) 2 QB 410.

[262] *Assange v Sweden* [2011] EWHC 2849 (admin); *R (On the application of F) v DPP* [2013] EWHC 945 (admin).

deceptions about condom use (in so far as they are not to be regarded as deceptions concerning the nature of the act), a plausible candidate for inclusion on the list might be deceptions based on supposed medical or other professional reasons for engaging in sexual intercourse. Alternatively, the 'deception as to purpose' element in s. 76 could simply be snipped off, leaving all cases of fraud—other than those concerning the nature of the act—to be dealt with under s. 74. Even so, a question arises over whether *every* case of sexual activity obtained by fraud should in principle be a sexual offence at all, in virtue of s. 74, even if one leaves aside the draconian impact of s. 76.[263] The same question would also be raised by the re-introduction of a reformed offence of (say) 'engaging in sexual activity or contact through deception'. There are no easy solutions, but—focusing on the fault element—we should note that, in the law of property crime, a fraud will not be criminal unless it is also a 'dishonest' fraud.[264] Analogously, whether for the purposes of s. 74 or for the purpose of any new, reformed lesser offence of engaging in sexual activity or contact through fraud, it should count as evidence that D did not have the fault element that he (or, in cases other than rape, she) reasonably believed that it was acceptable to keep the relevant information from V.[265] We will return to this issue later, in discussing Jonathan Herring's suggestion for an expanded law of rape. In essence, when crimes as stigmatic as sexual crimes are in issue, great sensitivity to the fault element is morally required alongside protection—in the definition of the conduct element—for the victim's right to lifestyle autonomy.

More controversially, are there some cases of sexual activity obtained by deception where we might argue that the prohibited conduct element was not present? Suppose that D (15 years old) falsely says to V (16 years old), 'I love you' to V, to induce V to kiss him which V does. Is this a sexual assault on V? Putting aside the question of whether or not D was, in the right way, at fault, there could be an argument that inducing consent to such an act by this kind of commonplace deception is, in these particular circumstances, permissible (tolerable if not admirable), and hence that the forbidden conduct element did not take place. However, such arguments almost certainly have no place in the modern law, even if they lead to the view that there is no public interest in prosecution. The fact a deception induced V to participate should be enough to establish that the forbidden conduct element took place.

The second circumstance in which the absence of consent is irrebuttably and conclusively presumed is where, '(b) the defendant intentionally induced the complainant to consent to the relevant act by impersonating a person known personally to the complainant'. The provision is really referring to the less well-known legal phenomenon of 'personation' (pretending to be a different person).[266] It cannot really mean to capture

---

[263] K. Laird, 'Rapist or Rogue? Deception, Consent and the Sexual Offences Act 2003' [2014] Crim LR 491.

[264] See Fraud Act 2006; Chapter 10.8.

[265] Were such a claim relevant to the fault element, whilst the decision in *Assange* might remain the same, the decision in *McNally* could have been different.

[266] Section 60 of the Representation of the People Act 1983 states that a person is guilty of 'personation' if he votes as someone else (whether that person is living, dead, or is a fictitious person), either by post or in person at a polling station as an elector or as a proxy.

the much broader concept of 'impersonation' (which extends to doing an impression of someone else). Otherwise, if V asks D to impersonate someone (X) that V finds sexually attractive, as by dressing and talking like X, and D's impersonation of X is so convincing that it induces V to consent to sexual intercourse with D, that would be rape. Even definitional maximalists about rape would probably draw the line there. In what follows, we should understand 'impersonation' to mean, 'personation'.

The previous law extended only to impersonating a spouse or partner,[267] whereas the 2003 Act extends to all impersonations other than those of a person who is not personally known to the complainant, such as a sports or television star. In one sense, this second conclusive presumption is less powerful than the first, since it requires the prosecution to establish that the impersonation induced V to consent: if the defence can create doubt about the causal link, this may be sufficient to prevent the presumption from arising. An important difficulty with the provision concerns the extent of the key notion that the impersonator (D) must be pretending to be someone 'known personally' to V. Is someone (X) that V has 'met' through contacting X on a social networking site someone 'known personally' to V? Suppose that V arranged to meet X, and an imposter (D)—knowing of the arrangement—took X's place and consequently engaged in sexual intercourse with V. Would D then be impersonating someone (X) personally known to V, such that the presumption would come into effect and D would be guilty of rape? Again, such a problematic case would be much more easily dealt with, had the 2003 Act retained and reformed the old offence of procuring a woman for intercourse through false pretences (deception). Compounding the uncertainty of this provision, is its arbitrariness. A deception in the form of a false claim to have professional qualifications, or to be a State official—false 'professional identity' claims— would, on policy grounds, appear to be more deserving of inclusion in s. 76; but they must now be dealt with under s. 74.[268]

For Jonathan Herring, the introduction of s. 76, and the abolition without replacement of the lesser offence of procuring a woman for the purposes of sexual intercourse by false pretences, provides an opportunity vastly to expand the law of rape into new and uncharted territory. On Herring's account of how the law should be understood,[269] rape ought to include all cases in which V went ahead with sexual intercourse (or any other form of sexual activity) with D on a mistaken basis, where (a) V would have changed his or her mind about going ahead if he or she had known the truth, and (b) D knew about or should have known about (a) at the time.[270] One can only marvel at the cases such an expansive reading of the 2003 Act would turn automatically into rape. Assume that V does not consent in the following examples. D continues to have sexual intercourse with his wife (V), whilst he is deriving sexual gratification from an image that has popped unbidden into his mind of his wife's attractive sister. As just indicated,

---

[267] See *Elbekkay* [1995] Crim LR 163.   [268] See the pre-2003 Act case of *Richardson* [1999] Crim LR 62.

[269] Described as 'frightening in its ramifications' by D. Ormerod and K. Laird (eds), *Smith and Hogan's Criminal Law* (14th edn., 2015), 843.

[270] Herring attributes no special significance, in this regard, to mistakes brought about by deception, or to the fact that the 2003 Act requires the deception to be as to the *purpose* of the act: Herring, n 200.

suppose—a hardly implausible supposition—that V would not have agreed to D's carrying on with sexual intercourse, had she known what D was thinking about when he continued, and that D was perfectly well aware of this (or, he should have been). The case then fits Herring's criteria for rape, notwithstanding the absence of a deception as to purpose. Herring would take the same uncompromising stance in a case where a man, engaged in a psychologically painful internal struggle over his true sexual identity, carries on having sexual intercourse with his wife even though he has fallen in love with a male colleague at work. If he was or should have been aware that his wife would be appalled by the idea that she is having intimate sexual contact with a man unsure of his sexuality, and would never have consented had she known of this lack of certainty, then on Herring's account he, too, is a rapist.

Added to this list of Herring's hitherto unaccounted for rapists will be every man who has sexual relations with V1, when he has separately been engaging in sexual relations with V2—or even just thinking about that possibility at the relevant time—without telling V1. Indeed, if he tells neither V1 nor V2 that he is in fact having sexual relations with both of them, then he is, on Herring's account, a multiple rapist, if neither would have gone ahead had they known the truth: opening up D's case to a fifteen years' imprisonment starting point for sentencing.[271] Every man who knowingly fails to disclose any of his religious or personal beliefs that he knows—or ought to know—would affect his partner's willingness to engage in sexual activity with him, will be guilty of rape, however important it is to him to keep his beliefs a private matter.

Liberal and democratic thinking rejects as inadequate the justification provided for such an approach, namely that its aim is to protect V's autonomy, because that claim does not show the same concern for the fault element as it does for the conduct element of sex crimes. Rape is a crime as much about D's fault as about V's lack of consent. Consider the point just made: Herring's theory dictates that, for fear of being exposed to a rape (or other sex crime) conviction, men cannot even keep their most profound religious beliefs private, when engaging in sexual relations with others who they appreciate would (might?) not go ahead if they knew about those beliefs. That being so, then—seen from the critical perspective of a liberal and democratic theory—every defendant is also a victim: a victim of state oppression.[272] Rights to privacy, to freedom of thought and religion, and to family life, may be impossible to sustain without an element of secrecy even if there is no right to secrecy as such.[273] Evidence shows that family members keep a great deal from one another, even whilst maintaining a stable and happy unit.[274] That is not to justify, morally, the failure to provide the information in any of the hypothetical examples given above. However, only a highly vindictive theory

[271] <www.cps.gov.uk/legal/p_to_r/rape_and_sexual_offences/sentencing/>.

[272] For a sophisticated account of how to deal with fraud cases in rape, see R. Williams, 'Deception, Mistake and Vitiation of the Victim's Consent' (2008) 124 LQR 132.

[273] See, on the inter-dependence of privacy and secrecy, S. Petronio (ed.), *Balancing the Secrets of Private Disclosures* (2014), xiii.

[274] L. Rosenfeld, 'Overview of the Ways Privacy, Secrecy, and Disclosure are Balanced in Today's Society' in Petronio (ed.), n 273, 34.

would (a) ignore the moral complexities involved in 'withheld information' cases, in order to concentrate only on V's perspective to the exclusion of D's legitimate concerns (perhaps including a concern for his family with V), and (b) apply one of the State's most condemnatory labels—a conviction for rape (or another sexual offence)—to mark D's moral failings. Suppose F has been raped in the past but, having found happiness with M, enters into a sexual relationship with M even though she (F) is aware that he (M) would never have agreed if he knew of her past (because M is very concerned about re-victimizing people in such situations). F is a sex criminal, on Herring's account, being guilty of intentionally causing M to engage in sexual activity, contrary to s. 4 of the 2003 Act. That is an outcome that is wrong legally, and distorted morally.

Fair labelling insists not only that there be a fault element, but that the fault element be appropriate for the nature of the crime in question. As suggested above, in 'withheld information' cases, defendants should be entitled to deny the fault element in sex crimes, on the grounds that they reasonably believed that the information could be withheld. This is an especially important basis for denying the fault element when fundamental rights and freedoms are engaged, such as the right to privacy, to family life and to freedom of thought and religion. Only those at ease with the application of the authoritarian principle[275] to sex crimes would suggest that a jury should not, even with the benefit of proper judicial directions, be trusted to judge a defendant's claim based on such a belief.

Rebuttable Presumptions: Section 75(2) enumerates six sets of circumstances giving rise to a rebuttable presumption of non-consent. Once the prosecution establishes the factual basis for one of the presumptions—that is, that the circumstance existed and that D knew it existed—that presumption operates against D until the defence adduce sufficient credible evidence 'to raise an issue as to whether he consented'. This does not place a burden of proof on D, but does require the defence to 'satisfy the judge that there is a real issue about consent that it is worth putting to the jury'.[276] Once this is done, the prosecution must prove absence of consent in the normal way, relying on s. 74. The six circumstances are:

(a) [where] any person was, at the time of the relevant act or immediately before it began, using violence against the complainant or causing the complainant to fear that immediate violence would be used against him;

(b) [where] any person was, at the time of the relevant act or immediately before it began, causing the complainant to fear that violence was being used, or that immediate violence would be used, against another person;

(c) the complainant was, and the defendant was not, unlawfully detained at the time of the act;

(d) the complainant was asleep or otherwise unconscious at the time of the relevant act;

---

[275] See Chapter 4.5.

[276] The words of Baroness Scotland, quoted by the Home Affairs Committee, *Sexual Offences Bill*, para. 29. For further discussion, see Temkin and Ashworth, 'Rape, Sexual Assaults and the Problems of Consent', 342–4.

(e) because of the complainant's physical disability, the complainant would not have been able at the time of the relevant act to communicate to the defendant whether the complainant consented;

(f) any person had administered to or caused to be taken by the complainant, without the complainant's consent, a substance which, having regard to when it was administered or taken, was capable of causing or enabling the complainant to be stupefied or overpowered at the time of the relevant act.

The prosecution has to prove that D knew that one of the circumstances existed, and does not have to show that it actually negatived consent, this being presumed. The practical operation of the provisions is complex,[277] and there appear to be few cases in which they have been relied on. Nonetheless, they do provide an incentive for D to give evidence in court, and in that—despite the law's professed neutrality on this issue more broadly—they embody a point of principle of special importance in this context, where trials may often come down to one person's word against another's.

The presumptions in (a) and (b) make an important statement about the effect of violence and threats of violence[278]—although conclusive presumptions would have made a stronger statement—but their ambit is limited to threats of immediate violence to V or to another person, such as a family member or friend.[279] Where the threat is no less realistic but is to use violence in the near future, the case falls outside these presumptions and must be dealt with under the general definition of consent. Similarly, other threats—relating, for example, to losing a job or being prosecuted for an offence—are also excluded from the presumptions. However, presumptions (a) and (b) are wider than the conclusive presumptions in one respect, since they contain no requirement that D be the author of the threats or violence. It is worth pointing out that many of these intricate legal niceties would have been unnecessary, had the 2003 Act not abolished the old offence of procuring sexual intercourse by threats.[280] Presumption (c) deals with cases of false imprisonment and kidnap. Presumption (d) applies to cases where V is either asleep or unconscious. The presumption applies not just to sleep, but to cases where V was unconscious through alcohol or otherwise. At common law, having sex with a person who was asleep would be rape, and thus there is an argument that this should be a conclusive presumption. However, what of the case where it is contended that V has signified to D that V enjoys being awoken from his or her slumbers by D doing something sexual to V? It must be borne in mind that these presumptions apply to all the offences in ss. 1–4, including the broad offence of sexual assault.[281] Presumption (e) refers to V's physical inability to communicate with D: there are already several offences in ss. 30–44 of the Act aimed at sexual acts with

---

[277] See the decision in *White* [2010] EWCA Crim 1929, where D's conviction was quashed because the judge had given what was found to be confusing and unnecessary direction to the just on s. 75.

[278] See *Dagnall* [2003] EWCA Crim 2441.

[279] The use of 'immediate' rather than 'imminent' restricts the range of this provision: cf. *Hasan* [2005] UKHL 22, discussed in Chapter 7.3(a).   [280] An offence under s. 2 of the Sexual Offences Act 1956.

[281] See further Temkin and Ashworth, 'Rape, Sexual Assaults and the Problems of Consent', 337–8.

those suffering some mental incapacity, but one purpose of this presumption may be to ensure that serious cases are treated as rape or assault by penetration.

Presumption (f) was added during the progress of the Bill,[282] and its drafting leaves open several questions. The first requirement is that someone (not necessarily D) administered to V or 'caused to be taken' a form of stupefying substance. Presumably, 'caused to be taken' includes cases where V is deceived into believing that what is being taken voluntarily is a substance with different properties, but it remains unclear whether this captures all forms of deception. Consent presumably bears the same broad and uncertain meaning as it has within the Act generally. As for the nature of the substance, the primary target is what are known as 'date rape drugs' such as rohypnol, but the presumption appears to extend to alcohol too. The substance must have been capable of stupefying or overpowering V, but it is not clear what degree of effect this will be held to require. Cases of unconsciousness fall within presumption (d), so a logical scheme would suggest that presumption (f) should apply where the effects of the substance on V's functioning are significant but not total. Once again, there is considerable room for interpretation in this provision, and this will determine the practical application of the law—and the 'messages' it sends out.[283] Finally, it should be reiterated that in order to rebut a presumption D needs only to adduce sufficient credible evidence to raise the issue. Thus even if the presumption is established—and that may depend on a jury question, such as whether V was asleep or unconscious or unlawfully detained—it will disappear if D satisfies the evidential burden and the case must then be fought on the general ground of non-consent.

Definition of Consent: Although the prosecution is likely to start by considering the application of the conclusive presumptions and the rebuttable presumptions to the case at hand, the general definition of consent will be relevant if the courts apply the narrow interpretation of the conclusive presumptions urged in *Jheeta* and where the defence satisfies the evidential burden in relation to a rebuttable presumption. Section 74 provides that 'a person consents if he agrees by choice, and has the freedom and capacity to make that choice'. This is intended to be a factual or 'attitudinal' definition, turning on what V felt rather than what V expressed.[284] Unfortunately, however, the section simply describes consent in terms of four other contested concepts—agreement, choice, capacity, and freedom. The concept of agreement may be construed either to mean simple assent to an act, or to entail a full consensus based on knowledge of the essential particulars. Similarly, the concept of choice may be construed to mean that the consent should be informed, so that where D has concealed from V a fact material to their sexual encounter this means that an informed choice was not made and that

---

[282] For detailed analysis, see E. Finch and V. Munro, 'Intoxicated Consent and Drug-assisted Rape Revisited' [2004] Crim LR 789.

[283] Many government statements at the time of the Bill emphasized that it was intended to send out 'clear messages' about what was acceptable and unacceptable: e.g. Home Office, n 210, para. 5, and Home Affairs Committee, *Sexual Offences Bill*, para. 30.

[284] Cf. P. Westen, 'Some Common Confusions about Consent in Rape Cases', (2004) 2 Ohio State JCL 333, and more fully, P Westen, *The Logic of Consent* (2005).

any consent was apparent and not real. However, the Court of Appeal has declined to accept this doctrine of informed consent in a case where D failed to disclose to V that he was HIV positive,[285] Latham LJ holding that V's consent to the sexual act was not vitiated but that D might be liable for an offence against the person by transmission of disease. The concept of capacity would seem to imply an adequate degree of under-standing of the acts and their significance, which is particularly relevant in cases of mental incapacity[286] and in cases where the complainant is intoxicated.

In *Bree*[287] both parties had been drinking alcohol for some time before they had sex. The Court of Appeal held that the proper approach in an intoxication case, where the complainant is not alleged to have been unconscious (and therefore within rebuttable presumption (d)), is whether she had sufficient capacity to choose whether to agree to sex and whether she did so: 'if through drink the complainant has temporarily lost her capacity to choose whether to have intercourse on the relevant occasion, she is not consenting'. The Court took a similar approach in *Hysa*,[288] holding that the case was wrongly withdrawn from the jury where V could not remember what she had said because she was so drunk. This decision is a very important one, in terms of the scope of protection for victims that the law provides. The Court cited with approval the law's pre-2003 Act view that

> [T]here is no requirement that the absence of consent has to be demonstrated or that it has to be communicated to the defendant for the actus reus of rape to exist ... It is not the law that the prosecution in order to obtain a conviction for rape have to show that the complainant was either incapable of saying no or putting up some physical resistance, or did say no or put up some physical resistance.

The central concept of freedom demonstrates how vague and contestable the statutory definition is: freedom of decision-making may be greater or less, depending on the impact of any deception, threats, or other perceived pressures, and the question is what degree of impairment should be taken to mean that any apparent consent was not free. Freedom cannot practically be defined in terms of a totally unconstrained choice, and we tend to use the term 'free' only 'to rule out the suggestion of some or all of its recognized antitheses'.[289] This indicates that the law might have been better drafted if it had focused on the effects of various forms of threat, deception, and other pressure in order to try to delimit the proper boundaries of consent. If it is argued that this was the aim of the presumptions in ss. 75 and 76, then the answer must be that they leave too many contested situations at large. No doubt the limits of consent will be elaborated in the case law, but the concepts of freedom, agreement, choice, and capacity do not provide sufficiently clear signposts to prevent inconsistent outcomes. Juries might be

---

[285] *E.B.* [2006] EWCA Crim 2945, following the decisions in *Dica* and *Konzani*, section 9.3(f), on this point.

[286] Section 30(2) of the Act refers to capacity in terms of whether D 'lacks sufficient understanding of the nature or reasonably foreseeable consequences of what is being done'.

[287] [2007] EWCA Crim 804. The conviction was quashed because of non-direction by the judge.

[288] [2007] EWCA Crim 2056.

[289] J. L. Austin, 'A Plea for Excuses', in H. Morris (ed.), *Freedom and Responsibility* (1961), 8.

told not to assume that V did agree freely just because V did not say or do anything, protest or resist, or was not physically injured;[290] that might have urged juries to challenge stereotypes, but no such model direction has emerged. However, the concept of agreement, in s. 74, should be interpreted as emphasizing that it is V's perception of choice and freedom that is crucial.[291]

What are likely to be the practical effects of the s. 74 'definition' on jury decision-making? Some clues are provided by research using mock juries.[292] They found that many jurors latched on to one or more of the four terms in s. 74 (agreement, choice, capacity, freedom) in order to justify quite different interpretations. As the authors comment, the fact that these four terms are 'within everyone's understanding does not mean that everyone understands them to mean the same thing, either in the abstract or in specific cases'.[293] Indeed, the terms did nothing to prevent some jurors from applying sexist stereotypes in their reasoning.[294] Thus where the woman complainant was intoxicated, some jurors readily assumed fault and therefore consent.

What are the contestable cases on consent? Numerous examples have already been mentioned. Taking deceptions first, if D deceives V into thinking that he intends to marry her and only for this reason does V agree to sex, does V agree by choice? Some jurors may conclude that this is nothing more than naivety, but if V regards it as crucial to her agreement, should a conviction for rape follow? Again, if D runs a modelling agency and promises V a glittering modelling career if he or she will have sex with him, does V agree by choice? Does it matter whether D is or is not likely to advance V's modelling career? What if D goes into a hospital dressed in a white coat and examines patients intimately at, say, a breast clinic or a clinic for testicular cancer?[295] And what of the case of *Linekar*,[296] where D deceived V into thinking that he will pay £25 for sex when he had no intention of doing so: does V agree by choice, in these circumstances? It is easy to say that V would not have agreed if all the circumstances had been known, but is it satisfactory that a requirement of a fully informed choice should lead to conviction of rape?[297] There is a strong argument that many of these cases should amount to a lesser offence, on the ground that the deception was not sufficiently fundamental, but the absence of a lesser offence in the 2003 Act, such as obtaining agreement to sexual activity by deception, may force courts to decide between rape and acquittal.

Turning to threats, we observed above that threats of non-immediate violence (e.g. 'I have some very nasty friends, and we know where you live') fall outside rebuttable presumptions (a) and (b), and so a jury or magistrate would have to decide whether such threats negative agreement by choice. If V, a sex worker who agrees to have sex with D for money, tells D that she has been forced to come to England and to work in this way,

---

[290] Home Office, n 210, para. 2.11.5; and see the passage cited from *Hysa* (reference at n 288).

[291] Cf. Lacey, *Unspeakable Subjects*, n 198, 114.

[292] E. Finch and V. Munro, 'Sexual Consent in the Jury Room' (2006) 26 LS 303.

[293] Finch and Munro, n 292, 315.

[294] For a summary and analysis of research, see Temkin and Krahé, n 190, ch 3.

[295] Cf. *Tabassum* [2000] 2 Cr App R 238 with *Richardson* [1998] 2 Cr App R 200, and section 9.3(f).

[296] [1995] QB 250.   [297] J. Herring, n 200, at 516; Laird, n 263; Williams, n 272.

D then knows that she cannot be said to be agreeing by choice, and he may be guilty of rape. In other cases, where D's conduct creates an atmosphere of fear, V may submit rather than risk a physical attack, even if there has been no actual violence or threats uttered. What if D tells V, an employee who has committed a disciplinary offence, that V will be dismissed unless willing to allow D to do a certain sexual act? Would the test of 'agreement by choice' be applied differently if V agreed to be fondled, or to be caned on a bare bottom, or to allow full sexual penetration?[298] Would the outcome be different if D were a police officer who stopped a motorist for a minor traffic offence, and said she would not report V if he engaged in a sexual activity with her?[299] One difficulty here is that, if the approach to deception is to require fully informed consent, the corresponding approach to threats cases may be that any credible and significant threat should be sufficient to negative choice or freedom.[300] If that were thought to carry criminal liability too far, then the concepts of 'choice' and 'freedom' would be at large again, without any indication of the degree of constraint needed to negative them.

(i) ABSENCE OF REASONABLE BELIEF IN CONSENT

For all the offences in ss. 1–4, it must not only be proved that V did not consent to what was done, but also that D did not reasonably believe that V was consenting. Subsection (2) of all those sections provides that 'whether a belief is reasonable is to be determined having regard to all the circumstances, including any steps A has taken to ascertain whether B consents'. This is clearly intended as a move away from the subjective test in *DPP* v *Morgan*,[301] which judged D on the facts as he or she believed them to be, however unreasonable that belief might be. Even if *Morgan* is defensible as a case on general principles, it is unacceptable as a rape decision. There are certain situations in which the risk of doing a serious wrong is so obvious that it is right for the law to impose a duty to take care to ascertain the facts before proceeding. Moreover, not only are serious sexual offences a denial of the victim's autonomy, but the ascertainment of one vital fact—consent—is a relatively easy matter. The subjective test of mistake has therefore been removed and replaced by a requirement of reasonable belief.

The same structure of conclusive and rebuttable presumptions applies as it does to consent itself. Thus, if any of the circumstances of deception in s. 76(2) is established, it is conclusively presumed that D did not believe that V was consenting. Similarly, if any of the six circumstances in s. 75(2) is established, D is to be taken not to have reasonably believed that V consented, unless sufficient evidence is adduced to raise an issue as to whether he reasonably believed it. The presumptions in ss. 75 and 76 were discussed in paragraph (h). The Sexual Offences Bill originally had a third conclusive presumption, for cases where V's willingness to engage in sexual activity with D was

---

[298] Cf. *McCoy* [1953] 2 SA 4.

[299] In Home Office, n 210, para. 2.10.9, it was suggested that threats such as 'losing a job or killing the family pet' should negative consent.

[300] Also relevant is the subtle difference between threats and inducements: see McGregor, *Is it Rape?* (2005), 169.   [301] [1976] 1 AC 182.

indicated only by a third party. If sexual autonomy is to be respected, is it not unreasonable that D should proceed on the basis of consent relayed by someone else, as in the notorious cases of *Morgan*[302] and *Cogan and Leak*?[303] In the end this provision was dropped for various reasons, including the possibility that it discriminated against some people with mental incapacity,[304] but such cases have caused controversy and the Act might have been expected to contain some reference to whether mistakes in such circumstances are reasonable.

The reference in subsection (2) to 'any steps A has taken to ascertain whether B consents' is important, in that it directs the court to consider whether D attempted to verify his assumption or belief about consent. But the more difficult question is whether the injunction to courts to have regard to 'all the circumstances' may undermine the objective test by letting in D's prejudices and belief system, or his beliefs about V's sexual history. Whilst recent decisions of high authority in other contexts suggest a general restrictiveness towards allowing the defendant's own characteristics to set the tone for what was 'reasonable' in the circumstances,[305] various government statements suggested that courts might properly take account of D's personal characteristics when deciding what was reasonable.[306] It is one thing to take account of a learning disability, but quite another thing to take account of stereotypical beliefs about, for example, women's behaviour. Thus account might properly be taken of the fact that D was suffering from Asperger's syndrome and hence prone to misunderstand V's intentions.[307] But there is a danger, borne out by Finch and Munro's research,[308] that the phrase 'all the circumstances' blunts the objectivity of the reasonableness requirement and allows juries to modify the standard to take account of a particular defendant's belief system. The Act does not indicate the levels or spheres of objectivity or subjectivity required by the test, allowing room for the operation of 'questionable socio-sexual myths'.[309] In *B*,[310] the Court of Appeal held that where D's belief in consent is attributable to psychotic illness or personality disorder, it could not be reasonable (D would have to plead insanity). However, Hughes LJ went on to add, evidence of more mild mental conditions that, for example, simply led D to misinterpret subtle social cues, could be admissible as showing that D's belief was reasonable. Possibly, evidence of mild Asperger's might satisfy that condition.

Another moot point is how the 'reasonable belief' test applies where D intentionally penetrates the vagina of someone he believes to be X (who has indicated that she would consent) but who turns out to be V (who does not consent). Although the drafting of the Act may be thought to indicate otherwise (in its references to A and B), such

---

[302] [1976] 1 AC 182; see Chapter 6.5(d).   [303] See Chapter 11.6.

[304] Further discussed by Temkin and Ashworth, n 276, 339.

[305] Notably the major decisions on duress in *Hasan* [2005] UKHL 22, discussed in Chapter 6.3.

[306] See Temkin and Ashworth, n 276, 341, for references.

[307] *T.S.* [2008] CLW 08/07/1. See, further, the thoughtful analysis by J. Stanton-Ife, 'Mental Disorder and Sexual Consent: Williams and After', in D. Baker and J. Horder (eds), *The Sanctity of Life and the Criminal Law: The Legacy of Glanville Williams* (Cambridge University Press, 2013), ch 9.

[308] See n 292.   [309] Finch and Munro, n 292, at 317.   [310] [2013] EWCA Crim 3.

a case of mistaken identity should be approached by treating the identity mistake as part-and-parcel of the consent mistake. In *Whitta*,[311] D and X agreed to have sex at a party they were attending. D, having become drunk, went upstairs and entering a bedroom, digitally penetrated V, who was not X but the sleeping mother of the party host. D claimed that, not having his glasses on, he had mistaken V for X, and indeed apologized and desisted when he realized that V was not X. The Court of Appeal took the view that:

> a possible alternative way of dealing with this very rare set of circumstances would be to hold that the offence is committed if a reasonable (and therefore sober) person would have realised that the person being penetrated or sexually touched was not the person whom the defendant thought he was consensually penetrating or touching.

The question is whether D's belief in consent is reasonable, which includes—although it is not decisive—the question of how reasonable the mistake as to identity was.

(j) THE EFFECT OF INTOXICATION: INTENTION CASES

We have already noted that the intoxicated state of the complainant may be relevant in various ways—unconsciousness (s. 75(2(d)), involuntary stupefaction (s. 75(2)(f)), or lack of capacity to consent (s. 74)—and also that D's intoxication may be relevant when deciding whether he held a reasonable belief in consent. But what is the relevance of D's intoxication to the other matters that must be proved for liability, notably in rape and sexual penetration (*intentional* penetration), in sexual assault (*intentional* touching), and in causing sexual activity (*intentionally* causing another to engage in sexual activity)?

The general effect of intoxication on criminal liability is not entirely clear, but one rule of thumb is that offences of basic intent (where intoxication is no defence) are those for which recklessness is sufficient, whereas offences of specific intent (where intoxication may be a defence) are those where intention alone is sufficient.[312] However, in *Heard*[313] D was convicted of sexual assault for exposing his penis and rubbing it against a police officer's thigh. D's defence was that he was drunk, but the judge ruled that this was inadmissible. The Court of Appeal upheld this ruling, concluding that the requirement of 'intentional touching' in sexual assault is one of basic intent. This looks like a pragmatic decision of the kind that abound in intoxication cases, and the attempts of Hughes LJ to align it with existing doctrine involved strain: his argument that 'a drunken accident is still an accident' may have the effect of blurring the boundaries of recklessness, and his narrowing of the concept of 'specific intent' to cases of purpose is a poor fit with the existing case law. The failure of the 2003 Act to deal with such an obvious issue as intoxication, while going into extraordinary complexity in other respects, is unfortunate. The key is whether, in deciding if D's belief in V's consent was reasonable in all the circumstances, the jury should have regard

---

[311] *Attorney General's Reference No. 79 of 2006 (Whitta)* [2007] 1 Cr App R (S) 752.
[312] See Chapter 7.2.   [313] [2007] EWCA Crim 125.

to D's drunken state. In principle, it seems wrong for a test of 'reasonable belief' to be adjusted to take account of drunken beliefs, and it now seems that—as under the old law—voluntary intoxication will not count as a relevant characteristic.[314]

9.6 OFFENCES AGAINST THE VULNERABLE

One of the central aims of the 2003 Act is to protect the vulnerable, and to this end Parliament enacted a wide range of overlapping offences against children.[315] We begin by discussing those offences against children under the age of 13 to which consent is irrelevant, and then consider each of the offences in ss. 9–15.

(a) OFFENCES AGAINST CHILDREN UNDER 13

Sections 5, 6, 7, 8 of the Act create offences parallel to those in ss. 1–4, save that they are only committed if the victim is under 13 and consent is not relevant. Section 5 creates the offence of rape of a child under 13, in the same terms as the offence in s. 1 but without any of the consent elements. Section 6 introduces an offence of assault of a child under 13 by sexual penetration, again without any consent requirements. The same approach is taken in respect of sexual assault of a child under 13 (s. 7) and causing a child under 13 to engage in sexual activity (s. 8). The other elements of these offences were discussed in section 9.5.

The main purpose of these offences is to provide for strong censure and punishment for adults who abuse young children. A major difficulty is that, in pursuit of the laudable aim of protecting young children and labelling those who abuse them sexually, these offences may result in the criminalization of other children. Sexual activity between children has long been widespread,[316] and some of it may involve boys and girls as young as 12. The serious offences in ss. 5–8 contain no exemptions for young persons, and so the conviction of two 12 year olds for kissing lustily in public is legally possible. The government sought to prevent this eventuality by assuring critics that there would be no such prosecutions, and the Crown Prosecution Service has published guidelines designed to ensure that the criminal law is not invoked inappropriately.[317] The CPS guidelines do mention that it is not in the public interest to prosecute children of a similar age (assuming that there was no coercion involved), and that would almost certainly dispose of the example of two 12 year olds kissing. But there may be circumstances when a young person is prosecuted, and is prosecuted for one of the four 'under 13' offences rather than for one of the lesser child sex offences mentioned in (b).

This is evident from G,[318] where G, aged 15, had sex with a girl of 12 whom he had met. G was charged with rape of a child under 13, contrary to s. 5. In the belief that the

---

[314] *Grenwal* [2010] EWCA Crim 2448.   [315] See the critique by Spencer, n 208.
[316] Spencer, n 208, at 354 and 360.   [317] See <www.cps.gov.uk>.   [318] [2008] UKHL 37.

offence imposes strict liability as to age, G was advised to plead guilty, but he did so on the basis that the girl consented in fact and told him that she was 15 too. Both the Court of Appeal and the House of Lords upheld his conviction for rape of a child under 13. Two principal arguments failed to persuade a majority of judges. First, there is the argument that imposing strict liability for such a serious offence is contrary to the presumption of innocence embodied in Art. 6.2 of the Convention. European authority for applying the presumption of innocence to the substantive criminal law, rather than to the burden of proof, is rather scanty, however.[319] This argument might have been better put on the basis of the 'constitutional principle' that 'unless Parliament has indicated otherwise, the appropriate mental element is an unexpressed ingredient of every offence'.[320] The reasons why this principle was asserted by the House of Lords were directly related to the injustices in cases of this kind; but whether such a judicially created presumption could properly be wielded against a recent legislative enactment which was clearly intended to introduce strict liability as to age in the 'under 13' offences is doubtful. More persuasive is the second argument, that convicting a boy of 15 of such a serious and stigmatic offence in these circumstances violates his rights under Art. 8. In many European countries there would have been no criminal law intervention in these circumstances. Here, once the basis of plea was established, the prosecution had the choice of (a) dropping the prosecution altogether or (b) dropping the s. 5 prosecution and charging G under s. 13 (and s. 9) with sexual activity with a child under 16, a lesser offence with a maximum sentence of five years for offenders under 18.[321] The majority in the House of Lords recognized that G's right to respect for his private life was engaged, but held that this was less important than the State's positive obligation to ensure that young people are protected from the sexual attentions of others. Baroness Hale emphasized the dangers of under-age sexual activity, referring to the long-term psychological effects to which it can give rise.[322] This is a powerful consideration, but it should not be regarded as the most powerful element in the case. The question for the courts was whether conviction of this very serious offence, carrying a maximum of life imprisonment, was a disproportionate interference with G's right to respect for his private life. The Court of Appeal had quashed the sentence of detention and substituted a conditional discharge; the gross disparity between conviction of a life-carrying offence and the ultimate sentence is a fair indication of the disproportionality involved. Yet the majority of the House of Lords allowed the conviction under s. 5 to stand.

The approach of the Sexual Offences Act 2003 to cases involving children or young people close in age is woefully inadequate and potentially unjust, as *G* demonstrates. Reliance on prosecutorial discretion is unsatisfactory in principle, and is unpersuasive in European human rights law.[323] Greater efforts should have been made to ensure

---

[319] See the commentary on the Court of Appeal decision at [2006] Crim LR 930.

[320] Per Lord Nicholls in *B* v *DPP* [2000] 2 AC 428, at 460; see also *K* [2002] 1 Cr App R 121.

[321] See Home Office, *Sexual Offences Act 2003: a Stock Take* (2006), para. 13, stating that in the first eight months of the Act coming into force, some 39 per cent of prosecutions for the s. 13 offence were for offences against children under 13 (as in the case of *G* [2008] UKHL 37).   [322] [2008] UKHL 37, at [45]–[51].

[323] The risk of prosecution is the key issue: e.g. *Sutherland and Monnell* v *UK* (1997) 24 EHRR CD22.

clarity in the law: if an age difference of up to two years is acceptable so long as no coercion (howsoever defined) is present, then that should be used as a model for legislation, as in other jurisdictions. Faced with the inadequacy of the legislation in this respect, the majority of the House of Lords in *G* should have followed human rights (and children's rights) reasoning more faithfully by focusing on the fairness of convicting this defendant on these assumed facts of this serious offence carrying life imprisonment.

(b) OFFENCES AGAINST CHILDREN UNDER 16

Sections 9–15 of the 2003 Act create a range of offences against children under age 16, which remains the age of consent in these matters. The original intention was that the first four of these offences, in ss. 9–12, would criminalize acts in respect of children aged 13–15 inclusive and would therefore complement the offences against children under 13 in ss. 5–8. When it became clear that this would create procedural difficulties where there was uncertainty about the victim's age, the remedy was to extend ss. 9–12 to cover offences against all children under 16.[324] This creates a manifest overlap between the two groups of offences when the victim is under 13, and raises serious questions about the need for such duplication.[325] We will return to this and other general issues after outlining this group of new offences.

Section 9 creates two offences of sexual activity with a child. The subsection (1) offence consists of sexual touching of a person under 16, an offence of enormous breadth that potentially criminalizes many normal touchings between young people. The subsection (2) offence consists of sexual activity involving penetration, with higher maxima. To these offences are added the offences in s. 10 of causing or inciting a child under 16 to engage in sexual activity (which run parallel to the offences in ss. 4 and 8). Further, s. 11 penalizes a person who engages in sexual activity in the presence of a child for the purpose of obtaining sexual gratification; and s. 12 creates an offence of causing a child to watch sexual activity, for the purpose of obtaining sexual gratification—such as watching a pornographic film, as in *Abdullahi*.[326] In that case the Court of Appeal confirmed that the sexual gratification need not be immediate, and that the requirement could be fulfilled if the purpose was to 'put the child in the mood' for a later gratification of D's desires.

The offences in ss. 9–12 have two common characteristics of note. One is that s. 13 states that, where any one of them is committed by a person under 18, the offence is triable summarily and, if tried on indictment, a lower maximum penalty of five years applies. This is a significant step in the direction of recognizing the need for a different approach to youngsters involved in sex cases, but it does not go far enough towards separating teenagers who sexually abuse other children (a significant social problem) from young people who consensually engage in sexual activities that are a fairly normal

---

[324] This explains why it would have been possible to charge G ([2008] UKHL 37) under ss. 13 and 9.

[325] Not least because a provision relating to the age of A (and of B) could easily have been inserted into ss. 1–4.   [326] [2007] 1 Cr App R 14.

part of growing up. Once again, supporters of the Act implicitly invoke the authoritarian principle by relying on prosecutorial discretion to mark this important difference and, for the reasons outlined earlier, this is unsatisfactory in general and not rendered more satisfactory by the actual guidelines issued by the CPS.[327]

The other common characteristic is that these offences are committed when 'either (i) B is under 16 and A does not reasonably believe that B is 16 or over, or (ii) B is under 13'. In terms of drafting, this is much clearer than ss. 5–8 in indicating strict liability where the child is 12 or under, compared with a reasonableness requirement where the child is aged 13–15 inclusive. But the question is whether it is fair: although there are some justifications for holding adults to strict liability where the child is aged 12 or less,[328] it is arguable that they should not hold sway in a stigmatic offence carrying life imprisonment; and for younger defendants this is unduly draconian, as the facts of G demonstrate.[329]

There are two further child sex offences in this part of the Act. Section 14 creates a wide-ranging offence of arranging or facilitating commission of a child sex offence (under ss. 9–13) in any part of the world. This covers much of the ground that the law of complicity would encompass (see Chapter 10), but goes beyond that by applying to offences that others may do. There is no lower penalty for offenders under 18, and yet this offence is committed by a teenager who arranges to meet his girlfriend (aged 15) for sex later in the day. Again, the drafting is so wide as to make no distinction between the abuser/exploiter and the consensual friend.

Section 15 introduces the much discussed offence of meeting a child following sexual grooming. This offence can only be committed by a person aged 18 or over. The conduct consists of either an intentional meeting, or where either party travels to a meeting, involving one person under 16, having met or communicated with that person on at least two previous occasions.[330] The required fault element is intending to do acts that constitute a relevant offence (mostly child sex offences under the Act), and not reasonably believing that the child is aged 16 or over. Proof of the intention to do 'relevant acts' is the principal narrowing feature of the offence: otherwise it is an offence in the inchoate mode, complete when D either intentionally meets a child or either party travels to such a meeting.

Efforts were made in Parliament to narrow the enormous reach of the offences in ss. 9–14 by ensuring that, at least, carers, teachers, and the medical profession are not drawn into the criminal law by virtue of conduct intended to protect or support children. Thus s. 14(3) lists a number of circumstances in which a person is taken to be acting 'for the protection of a child' and does not commit the offence—for once, Parliament did not rely on prosecutorial discretion. Reference may also be made here to s. 73, which creates exemptions from conviction for aiding, abetting, or counselling

---

[327] On the authoritarian principle, see Chapter 4.5.
[328] Cf. J. Horder, 'How Culpability Can, and Cannot, be Denied in Under-age Sex Crimes' [2001] Crim LR 15.
[329] [2008] UKHL 37; text at n 318.
[330] This reflects the broadened definition: see Criminal Justice and Immigration Act 2008, s. 73 and Sch 15.

several (but not all) offences in the Act for persons acting for the purpose of protecting the child rather than obtaining sexual gratification.

(c) ABUSE OF TRUST OFFENCES AGAINST PERSONS UNDER 18

The offence of abuse of a position of trust, introduced by the Sexual Offences (Amendment) Act 2000, was expanded into four new offences in the 2003 Act. Essentially, where a person over age 18 stands in a position of trust in relation to a person under 18, there is an offence if the person in trust has sexual activity with V (s. 16), causes or incites V to have sexual activity (s. 17), engages in sexual activity in the presence of V (s. 18), or causes V to watch sexual activity (s. 19). It will be seen that the substance of these offences parallels those in earlier sections—the drafting could have been much more concise—but the two key elements are the position of trust and the age of the younger person. Section 21 sets out definitions of 'positions of trust' that rely on the term 'looks after', whether in an educational institution, or in a hospital, or children's home, etc. The provision does not extend to others such as choirmasters, scoutmasters, or sports coaches, for whom the normal approach of aggravating the sentence is considered sufficient. Indeed, aggravation of sentence under ss. 9–12 would have dealt with all 'abuse of trust' offences in respect of children under 16, since the maximum sentences for those offences are already high. The significance of ss. 16–19 is that they apply where the young person is 16 or 17, over the age of consent but still (it is thought) vulnerable to abuse by those trusted to care for them. The question is whether the law should have gone further to attempt to separate abusive relationships from loving ones, or whether it is sufficient to state that there shall be no lawful sexual relationships of any kind between persons of 16 or 17 and those trusted to care for them. English law does not say this, since marriage between such persons is lawful. Other legal systems attempt to penalize those elements of pressure that indicate abusive relationships,[331] whereas English law criminalizes all such relationships and then attempts the necessary differentiation at the sentencing stage.[332]

(d) FAMILIAL SEX OFFENCES

The 2003 Act contains two sets of offences aimed at familial sexual activity. We deal first with ss. 25–9 on 'familial child sex offences', which apply where one of the family members is under age 18. Child sexual abuse is not merely a sexual offence, but one of the deepest breaches of trust which can take place in a family based society. The home ought to be a safe haven, the place where young people can go to get away from fear and violence, and this fundamental feeling of safety can be destroyed by sexual abuse. Incest was introduced into English law as a distinct offence by the Punishment

---

[331] Spencer, n 208, referring to French law.
[332] Sentencing Guidelines Council, *Sexual Offences* (2007), 60–1, refers to such factors as the degree of vulnerability of the young person, the age gap between the parties, and the presence of coercion.

of Incest Act 1908.[333] Although the eugenic risk (that the child of an incestuous relationship between father and daughter or brother and sister will have congenital defects) was known at the time and was probably a factor, most of the arguments of the
reformers were based on the protection of children from sexual exploitation. Those arguments have great force today, as increasing evidence of child abuse within the family
comes to light and as this hitherto 'private' realm is opened up.[334] Fathers may use their
considerable power within the home to lead a daughter into sexual activity from a relatively early age. All kinds of pressure may be exerted on the child to keep quiet about
the behaviour, with sometimes disastrous effects on his or her emotional development.

The essence of the two main offences is that s. 25 penalizes sexual touching of a family
member under 18, with higher penalties where penetration is involved and lower penalties where the offence is committed by a family member also under 18; and that s. 26
penalizes the incitement of a family member to engage in sexual touching. As observed
in relation to the 'position of trust' offences, the objective of labelling these offences
separately could have been achieved much more simply by applying ss. 9 and 10 in the
relevant sets of circumstances. That would still necessitate a definition of a 'family relationship', and s. 26 now expands this beyond close blood relations to cover a range of
step-relations and foster parents living in the same household and regularly involved in
caring for the young family member. Sexual abuse by such persons remains an important
matter, of course, but it is already punishable whenever the child is under 16. So, again, it
is a question of criminalizing those who commit offences against family members aged
16 and 17, whom (as a matter of law) they may be free to marry. Section 28 creates an
exception for parties who are lawfully married, but that is not a convincing resolution
of the issue of consensual sexual relations between adult members of the household
and young family members aged 16 and 17. No attempt has been made to identify what
is abusive about some of those relationships, and the same applies to sexual relations
between young siblings in the same family—some of which are abusive, others not sufficiently wrong or harmful to warrant criminal liability. Again, the discretion to prosecute and the sentencing discretion are regarded as the proper methods of making the
necessary distinctions, even though prosecution and conviction are momentous events.

Later in the Act appear two offences of sex with adult relatives. Section 64 creates
the offence of sexually penetrating a relative aged 18 or over, and s. 65 creates an offence of consenting to being sexually penetrated by a relative aged 18 or over. Both
offences have a maximum sentence of two years' imprisonment, and both now apply
to adoptive relations.[335] This extends the previous law of incest to cover oral, anal, and
vaginal sex and to include penetrative acts between consenting males. However, the
rationale of punishing exploitation of the young is no longer applicable here, since the

---

[333] See V. Bailey and S. Blackburn, 'The Punishment of Incest Act 1908: A Case Study in Law Creation'
[1979] *Crim LR* 708, and S. Wolfram, 'Eugenics and the Punishment of Incest Act 1908' [1983] Crim LR 308.
[334] See L. Zedner, 'Regulating Sexual Offences within the Home', in I. Loveland (ed.), *The Frontiers of
Criminality* (1995), on the interaction of the State and the family, privacy, and regulation.
[335] Criminal Justice and Immigration Act 2008, s. 73 and Sch 15.

parties are adults. The offences appear to go against the Art. 8 principle of respecting the right of adults to engage in consensual sex in private, but the Sexual Offences Review concluded that 'the dynamics and balance of power within a family require special recognition, and we were concerned to ensure that patterns of abuse established in childhood were not allowed to continue into adulthood'.[336] Thus the relevant sentencing guidelines identify exploitation or long-term grooming as factors that render the offence serious enough for a custodial sentence.[337]

(e) OFFENCES AGAINST PERSONS WITH MENTAL DISORDER

For the protection of these vulnerable people the Act introduces three sets of offences, each set being broadly parallel to the scheme for child sex offences in ss. 9–12 (i.e. sexual touching, causing or inciting sexual activity, engaging in sexual activity in the presence of such a person, and causing such a person to watch sexual activity). Thus ss. 30–3 contain offences against persons with a mental disorder impeding choice. Section 30(2) defines such persons in terms of being either unable to communicate their choice or lacking the capacity to choose whether to agree. In C[338] the Court of Appeal held that the mental disorder would usually have to be severe if it were to negative the capacity to choose, and that V's irrational fear of the defendant could not be equated with lack of the capacity to choose. The second set of offences, in, ss. 34–7, create offences of using inducement, threat, or deception in respect of a person with mental disorder. Sections 38, 39, 40, 41, 42, 43, 44 penalize care workers for persons with mental disorder who commit these offences.

It is important to ensure that the mentally disordered are properly protected from sexual abuse, but once again the Act contains prolix drafting and overlapping offences. On the one hand prosecutors are left to decide which of various applicable offences to select; on the other hand prosecutorial discretion is the only means of ensuring that sexual conduct between persons with a learning disability is not prosecuted unless there is strong evidence of coercion or other exploitative elements. As with the child sex offences, the Act fails to deal adequately with 'consensual' conduct between two people who both fall into the 'vulnerable' category. It is not possible to rely on the same principle of sexual autonomy here as with 'normal' adults, but the question remains whether relationships that are non-exploitative should be criminalized.

9.7 OTHER SEXUAL OFFENCES

Attention should be drawn briefly to some of the other crimes in the Sexual Offences Act 2003. Reference has already been made to the offences relating to photographs of children and child pornography in ss. 45–51,[339] and to various offences relating to

---

[336] Home Office, n 210, para. 5.8.3.   [337] Sentencing Guidelines Council, *Sexual Offences* (2007), 92–3.
[338] *The Times*, 9 June 2008.
[339] See A. Gillespie, 'The Sexual Offences Act 2003: Tinkering with Child Pornography' [2004] Crim LR 361.

prostitution and trafficking in ss. 52–60. The Act introduced three new preparatory sexual offences: s. 61 penalizes the intentional administration of a substance with intent to stupefy or overpower,[340] s. 62 creates the very broad crime of committing any offence with intent to commit a sexual offence,[341] and s. 63 criminalizes trespass with intent to commit a sexual offence.[342] The new offence of exposure of genitals (s. 66) is limited by the requirement that D intends that someone will thereby be caused alarm or distress. Section 67 creates the offence of voyeurism for the purpose of obtaining sexual gratification. Section 69 creates offences of sexual intercourse with an animal (maximum sentence, two years). Sexual penetration of a corpse is criminalized by s. 70. And s. 71 creates an offence of engaging in sexual activity in a public lavatory.[343]

9.8 RE-ASSESSING SEXUAL OFFENCES LAW

The Sexual Offences Act 2003 marked an important advance in many ways. Reform of the essentially Victorian law was long overdue, and the need to reflect modern attitudes manifest. As we noted in section 9.5(c), there were some seven aims of the 2003 Act, many of them laudable. The law of sexual offences is now almost as gender-neutral as it could be. In some respects it goes further towards respecting human rights. And it makes considerable and well-signalled strides towards protecting the vulnerable from sexual exploitation.

There are, however, various respects in which the Act falls short of its promoters' ideals. Both the Sexual Offences Review and the 2003 Act set out to create a law that respects sexual autonomy and protects the vulnerable, but are these goals attained? Respect for sexual autonomy has both its positive and negative sides, as argued earlier, and two significant manifestations of paternalism—the criminalization of consensual sex between adult relatives (see 9.6(d)), and the failure to recognize consent to sado-masochistic practices as part of sexual offences law[344]—amount to considerable restrictions. Respect for sexual autonomy also requires a clear and sensitive attempt to define 'consent', but it was argued earlier that the Act's scheme in ss. 75 and 76, and particularly the broad 'definition' in s. 74, fall well short of the ideal. Too many issues are left to interpretation, risking not only inconsistent decisions, but also the infiltration of old stereotypes which are at odds with the Act's aims. Thus the Act fails to give any signposts in relation to three obvious types of case—those involving intoxication, or non-fundamental deceptions, or non-violent threats. Moreover, the repeal of the former offences of obtaining sex by deception or by threats places even more strain on

---

[340] Cf. the terms of the presumption in s. 75(2), discussed in section 9.5(h).

[341] This was applied to kidnapping with intent to commit a sex offence in *Royle* [2005] 2 Cr App R (S) 480.

[342] Previously s. 9 of the Theft Act 1968 covered entry as a trespasser with intent to commit rape, whereas the new crime applies to any sexual offence.

[343] For detailed treatment of these and other offences in the Act, see Rook and Ward, n 208.

[344] Discussed in relation to the *Brown/Laskey* decision in section 9.3(f).

the general definition of consent and its four opaque elements (freedom, choice, agreement, and capacity).[345]

As for the protection of the vulnerable, in section 9.6 we noted the many offences protecting children, young people aged 16 and 17 (often referred to in the Act as children), and the mentally disordered. Unfortunately, as also observed earlier, the Act goes too far in the direction of criminalizing members of these very groups, especially children. Almost all the child offences, and particularly the most serious ones in ss. 5–8, apply to young defendants as much as to adults. The injustice to which this can lead is demonstrated by the events and the outcome in G,[346] which fails to give adequate protection to D's human rights. This underlines the inadequacy of the government's assurances that no children will be prosecuted unless there is coercion or some other untoward feature of the case. Reliance on prosecutorial discretion is insufficient protection of accused children's Art. 8 rights under the Convention—making teenagers liable to conviction for normal consensual activities also abridges their sexual autonomy—and the actual guidelines of the Crown Prosecution Service are relatively flexible too. Much more effort should be made, as in other jurisdictions, to give statutory protection to young defendants by means of higher minimum ages or age gaps. For example, in Scotland, s. 37 of the Sexual Offences Act 2009 marks out for separate treatment some kinds of sexual activity when engaged in by older children, and distinguishes between cases where that activity is sexual and when it is not. Further, under s. 39 of the 2009 Act, it is a defence in Scotland if minor sexual acts were engaged in by older children (13–16 years old) when the age gap between them was no more than two years.

Related to English law's reliance on prosecutorial discretion is the reluctance of policymakers and Parliamentary Counsel to try to capture the core of the wrongs, resulting in offence definitions that are overly broad. CPS guidance states that sexual activity between teenagers will not be prosecuted unless there is coercion, deception, or other untoward circumstances: why cannot something along those lines be put into the statute? The answer may be that it is difficult to prove. And yet in other sections, such as 11, 12, 18, and 19, a person may not be convicted unless the prosecution proves that the acts were done 'for the purpose of sexual gratification'—a requirement that goes to the core of the wrong, and may well be difficult to prove, but which is (rightly) included in the Act.[347]

A further point about autonomy concerns the use of objective standards and strict liability in the Act. It was argued in Chapter 5.4 and 5.5 that respect for individual autonomy militates in favour of subjective tests for criminal liability (intention,

---

[345] The government appears content with the statutory definition as construed by the courts in decisions such as *Bree*: see Office for Criminal Justice Reform, *Convicting Rapists and Protecting Victims: Justice for Victims of Rape* (2006) and *Convicting Rapists and Protecting Victims: Response to Consultation* (2007).

[346] [2008] UKHL 37; text at n 318.

[347] The same point may be made about the laudable effort, in ss. 14 and 73, to define the circumstances in which people who are acting in order to protect a child are exempted from liability—rather than leaving it to prosecutorial discretion.

knowledge), and against strict liability, save perhaps in respect of minor offences with low penalties. The Sexual Offences Act 2003 is probably the first major statute to introduce widespread negligence liability for serious offences carrying life imprisonment, or fourteen or ten years' imprisonment, in the requirement that 'A does not reasonably believe that B consents'. Is this a justifiable derogation from the subjective principle? It has been argued here and in previous editions that this is justifiable, because of the physical proximity of the parties in these offences and the important values (notably the sexual autonomy of both parties) that ought to be known to be at stake. Does that also justify strict liability as to age when the child is under 13, as ss. 5–12 provide? This is much more difficult to justify, particularly for young defendants. Perhaps it was thought too favourable to defendants to adopt a 'reasonable belief' requirement here too, since it is much easier to feign ignorance or mistake in these cases. But that is an assertion that is little tested. The House of Lords' declamations about the 'constitutional principle' of requiring subjective belief[348] may have been unconvincing in their precise application to sexual cases, but the case for requiring reasonable belief on the question of age, as with consent, is much stronger.

Both the Sex Offences Review and the government made much of the Act's aim of introducing greater clarity into sexual offences law, particularly (as noted in section 9.5(c)) in respect of consent to sexual activity. Maximum certainty is one aspect of the principle of legality, as we saw in Chapter 3.4(i), and serves to protect rule-of-law values for defendants, victims, and courts. Unfortunately there are serious doubts about whether the Act goes as far towards achievement of this aim as it should.[349] It is not merely a question of prolix drafting, overlapping offences, and reliance on prosecutorial discretion. Key terms such as 'consent' and 'sexual' are not satisfactorily defined, leaving the possibility (which the research of Finch and Munro tends to strengthen)[350] that different juries and magistrates may interpret them differently and that old stereotypes will continue to exert an influence. In a statute with high maximum penalties which undoubtedly takes sexual offending seriously, this is one of several unfortunate shortcomings. The Home Office's 'stocktake' of the Act came before some of the problems indicated were properly manifest, and even then it was commented that many of the changes in the law could not produce increased conviction rates unless 'stereotypes and myths surrounding rape' are addressed and changed.[351] Thus, even if the definitions and drafting cannot be improved[352]—and that is highly doubtful—steps should be taken to incorporate into model directions some warnings against the use of sexual stereotypes in decisions about consent and reasonable belief.[353] Yet to make significant

---

[348] In *B v DPP* discussed in Chapter 6.5(a)(iii).
[349] See C. Elliott and C. de Than, 'The Case for a Rational Reconstruction of Consent in Criminal Law' (2007) 70 MLR 225.   [350] See n 292 and text.
[351] Home Office, *Sexual Offences Act 2003: a stocktake of the effectiveness of the Act since its implementation* (2006), paras. 45–6; see also Criminal Justice System, *Convicting Rapists and Protecting Victims—Justice for Victims of Rape* (2007).
[352] For a proposal for radical re-structuring, see V. Tadros, 'Rape without Consent' (2006) 26 OJLS 515.
[353] See further Temkin and Krahé, n 190, chs 2, 8, and 9.

inroads into the disparities between the attrition rate in rape cases and other crimes, not only is procedural reform likely to be as effective as reforming the substantive law, but changing public attitudes seems to be necessary in order to make any progress at all. Education in its widest sense seems necessary in order to reduce the effect of sexual stereotypes.[354]

FURTHER READING

NON-FATAL OFFENCES

C. ERIN, 'The Rightful Domain of the Criminal Law', in C. Erin and S. Ost (eds), *The Criminal Justice System and Health Care* (Oxford University Press, 2007), ch 14.

J. GARDNER, 'Rationality and the Rule of Law in Offences against the Person', in J. Gardner, *Offences and Defences* (Oxford University Press, 2007), ch 2.

HOME OFFICE, *Violence: Reforming the Offences against the Person Act 1861* (1998).

J. HORDER, 'Reconsidering Psychic Assault' [1998] Crim LR 392.

LAW COMMISSION, *Reform of Offences Against the Person: A Scoping Consultation Paper* CP 217 (2014).

M. MADDEN DEMPSEY, 'Victimless Conduct and the *Volenti* Maxim: How Consent Works' (2013) 7 *Criminal law and Philosophy* 11

P. ROBERTS, 'Consent in the Criminal Law' (1997) 17 OJLS 389.

SEXUAL OFFENCES

E. FINCH and V. MUNRO, 'Breaking Boundaries? Sexual Consent in the Jury Room' (2006) 26 LS 303.

J. GARDNER and S. SHUTE, 'The Wrongness of Rape', in J. Gardner, *Offences and Defences* (Oxford University Press, 2007), ch 1.

J. HERRING, 'Mistaken Sex' [2005] Crim LR 519.

N. LACEY, *Unspeakable Subjects: Feminist Essays in Legal and Social Theory* (Hart Publishing, 1997), ch 4.

C. SJOLIN, 'Ten Years On: Consent under the Sexual Offences Act 2003' (2015) 79 J Crim L 20.

J. R. SPENCER, 'Child and Family Offences' [2004] Crim LR 347.

V. TADROS, 'Rape without Consent' (2006) 26 OJLS 515.

J. TEMKIN and A. ASHWORTH, 'Rape, Sexual Assaults and the Problems of Consent' [2004] Crim LR 328.

P. WESTEN, 'Some Common Confusions about Consent in Rape Cases' (2004) 2 Ohio St. LJ 333.

---

[354] Temkin and Krahé, n 190, ch 10.

10

OFFENCES OF DISHONESTY

10.1 INTRODUCTION

The principal statutes in this part of the criminal law are the Theft Act 1968 and the Fraud Act 2006. The principal offence in the former statute is referred to as theft or stealing. These terms seem to convey the idea of permanently taking another's property, but in fact the definitions in the Theft Act extend the notion of stealing to a wide variety of dishonest violations of another's property rights. The Theft Act shifted the emphasis of the offence from protecting possession to protecting ownership, and also encompassed a much wider range of property rights than the old law of larceny.[1] Now it is more a question of infringing another's property rights than of 'taking' property. There is no requirement that D should have permanently deprived V of the property, although it must be proved that D *intended* to do so. D's conduct does not have to amount to a potential destruction of V's ability to use the property or act as owner: on the contrary, the courts have held that the merest interference with any right of an owner may suffice, so long as it is accompanied by dishonesty and an intention permanently to deprive. One might therefore say that, in broad terms, these are crimes where what matters most in law is that D's conduct manifests a dishonest 'proprietorial' *intention*. In this way, the law runs contrary to what common sense might suggest, which is that the law is and should be concerned with conduct that involves a dishonest acquisition of *property as such*; but that does not necessarily mean that the law's focus is wrong.

---

[1] For discussion see A. T. H. Smith, *Property Offences* (1994), 1–17; for criticism of the consequent breadth of the offence, see S. P. Green, *Thirteen Ways to Steal a Bicycle: Theft Law in the Information Age* (2012), ch 1.

Even if the vast majority of thefts and frauds do involve dishonestly depriving others of their property, the law may be justified in spreading the net further. It may do this in order to catch conduct that (a) undermines the security of property interests without necessarily involving a taking of property—as when someone's computer is hacked and malware placed on the hard drive, or a secret photograph is taken of their PIN number—or conduct that (b) involves the manipulation of information crucial to someone's prospects for financial gain or loss—as when someone advises a client to invest in a company without disclosing that she (the adviser) has a financial stake in the company, or that she does not have a licence to give financial advice. Unsurprisingly, thus, the Fraud Act 2006 is even more wide-ranging than the law of theft: the broad concept of dishonesty is at its core, and its principal offence consists of making a false representation, intending thereby to make a gain or cause a loss. This and the other main offences are even more overtly inchoate in nature than theft, penalizing the dishonest making of the false representation rather than any obtaining of property. The 2006 Act can be considered to be the most advanced expression of the idea, just mentioned, that what matters in law is conduct that embodies a dishonest proprietorial intention, rather than dishonest conduct that leads to the deprivation of another's property. Indeed, the 2006 Act extends wrongdoing beyond a strictly 'proprietary' approach, to focus on dishonest 'financial intentions' in a contractual context more broadly, intentions that cover not only gains but also losses and the mere risk of losses to others. For example, it seems reasonably clear that fraud under the 2006 Act now effectively makes all but redundant the offence of false accounting contrary to s. 17 of the 1968 Act. Whilst a notion of individual property rights still shapes the law of theft and fraud, the law also treats the integrity and stability of financial transactions, alongside property interests more generally, as a public good (as explained in Chapter 3[2]) worthy of protection.

The great variety of offences of dishonesty, and the breadth of their definitions, raises problems of proportionality and the proper limits of the criminal sanction. The proportionality issues revolve partly round the problem of deciding what concept of property rights should be employed (discussed in the next paragraph) and partly round the prevalence of 'white-collar crime'.[3] For many years there has been criminological interest in the notion of 'white-collar crime', particularly deprivations of property perpetrated in commercial settings, but this has not really been reflected by changes in the law or in enforcement practice. The police have traditionally concerned themselves more with stealing from shops and burglary than with embezzlement and the various forms of frauds upon and by companies. This is an ironic development, in some ways, since the government has been busy downgrading shoplifting: it is triable only summarily for those under 18 when the value is less than £200,[4] and can now be met with a fixed penalty rather than a prosecution in some instances.[5]

---

[2] See Chapter 3.3 and 3.4.

[3] See D. Nelken, 'White-Collar Crime', in M. Maguire, R. Morgan, and R. Reiner (eds), *The Oxford Handbook of Criminology* (5th edn., 2012); S. P. Green, *Lying, Cheating and Stealing: a Moral Theory of White-Collar Crime* (2006).   [4] Anti-Social Behaviour, Crime and Policing Act 2014, s. 176.

[5] Penalties for Disorderly Behaviour (Amount of Penalty) Order 2002, SI 2002/1837.

The modernization of property offences achieved by the Theft Act 1968 did have the effect of freeing the law from such constricting notions as thieves having to 'take and carry away' property in order to be convicted. However, the 1968 Act provides little indication of a determination to treat white-collar offences as equivalent to other forms of theft: only ss. 17 and 19, on false accounting and on false statements by company directors, point in this direction. Perhaps in consequence, the 1980s saw the creation of several new quasi-regulatory offences in the spheres of white-collar crime and 'city fraud' outside the Theft Acts and the proposed Criminal Code.[6] This development has made it difficult to claim that such offences are integrated into a new scheme of property offences which achieves a realistic proportionality among the degrees of offending. A good example is provided by Parliament's response to the 2009 MPs' expenses scandal.[7] In order to avoid the harsh treatment that might be meted out to them under the Fraud Act 2006 (maximum sentence, ten years' imprisonment), Parliamentarians decided to create a new 'white collar' offence applicable only to MPs, in s. 10 of the Parliamentary Standards Act 2009. The offence is committed when an MP provides information for the purposes of an expense claim that the member knows to be false or misleading in a material respect. Laughably (given the high trust position occupied by MPs), but predictably, the maximum sentence MPs thought they could possibly bear following conviction for such an egregious abuse was—as compared with that available for fraud—literally decimated, at one year's imprisonment.

The enactment of the Fraud Act 2006 is significant in that it does extend further into the realm of 'white-collar crime'. However, the Companies Acts, Financial Services and Markets Act 2000, and other legislation are still regarded as 'regulatory' in nature, despite the indictable offences they contain, and despite some maximum penalties (e.g. seven years for misleading statements or practices contrary to s. 397 of the 2000 Act, and for fraudulent inducement to make a deposit contrary to s. 35 of the Banking Act 1987) which are the same as for theft[8] and only slightly less than the maximum for fraud (ten years' imprisonment). This chapter's discussion of the 'traditional' property offences will attempt to keep the 'new' offences of dishonesty well in sight.

Historically, one explanation for the difference in treatment between theft or fraud in the streets, and theft or fraud in the 'suites', is that the police have lacked the expertise and resources to investigate and prosecute complex white-collar crimes, not least when they involve transactions overseas. It is generally always going to be much simpler and cheaper to investigate a burglary at someone's home (whether or not the offender is caught), than it is to investigate, say, a complex fraud or bribery, the perpetrators of which are companies registered in England and Wales seemingly controlled by a network of companies outside the jurisdiction. With financial crime estimated at £38 billion per year in England and Wales (£30 billion of this being attributable to fraud), it is not surprising that governments have invested in specialist agencies to tackle the

---

[6] See Law Com No. 177, cll. 139–77, which cover only the offences under the Theft Act and forgery.
[7] R. Winnett and G. Rayner, *No Expenses Spared* (2009).
[8] Section 26(1) of the Criminal Justice Act 1991 reduced the maximum for theft from ten to seven years.

problem, the Serious Fraud Office (SFO) being the most important example.[9] The City of London police have also set up specialist units to tackle the problem, examples being the Overseas Anti-corruption Unit, and the Insurance Fraud Enforcement Department, together with the government-funded National Fraud Intelligence Bureau.[10] The work of the SFO is also now supported by the work of the National Crime Agency (taking in the work of the now defunct Serious Organised Crime Agency and the National Fraud Authority). So, whatever else may be missing from the effort to tackle financial crime, it is not a lack of bureaucratic agencies devoted to the task. We have also seen that new measures such as Deferred Prosecution Agreements have been brought in, to secure corporate compliance in fraud and bribery cases amongst others, avoiding the need for a costly and uncertain trial process.[11]

The broad and uncertain idea of 'dishonesty', explored in the context of the crime of theft in section 10.2(e), is one concept which binds these offences together; but as indicated above, they are not bound together by a focus on the protection of property as such. Whilst the protection of property rights is an important public good, so is the integrity of financial investments and transactions.[12] Taken as a whole, the offences of theft, fraud, and market-based offences seek to protect both of these public goods, whereas the older law was focused more—if not solely—on property rights alone. We return, in sections 10.2(a) and 10.2(e), to the question whether the offences under discussion in this chapter are essentially property offences, or broader dishonesty offences protecting the integrity of transactions. Simester and Sullivan, who strongly believe that they should be cast as property offences, argue that by penalizing theft, 'the criminal law both protects individuals from any particular loss they may suffer and safeguards the regime of property law more generally'.[13] This may be true, but there is more at stake here than the law's regime for protecting property rights.

How serious, relatively speaking, are theft and kindred offences? There has long been an allegation that English criminal law is too concerned with property offences—at the expense of offences against the person and against the environment. This cannot be more than a general allegation, since it is easy to construct a comparison between theft of some vital and valuable item of property and a minor assault. In broad terms, however, two points should be made about the proposition that property offences are treated too seriously. First, the allegation may concern enforcement as much as the written laws. The police investigate and prosecute relatively fewer crimes within business and commercial circles. This may, in turn, be because offences are dealt with informally in other ways, by dismissing an employee who has been caught committing an offence, for example.[14] In the 1980s the Serious

---

[9] <www.sfo.gov.uk>.

[10] <www.cityoflondon.police.uk/advice-and-support/fraud-and-economic-crime/nfib/Pages/default.aspx>.

[11] Chapter 1.3.   [12] See Chapter 3.4.

[13] A. P. Simester and G. R. Sullivan, 'The Nature and Rationale of Property Offences', in R. A. Duff and S. P. Green (eds), *Defining Crimes* (2005), 172.

[14] See M. Levi, 'Suite Revenge? The Shaping of Folk Devils and Moral Panics about White-Collar Crimes' (2009) 49 B J Crim 1.

Fraud Office (SFO) was created as part of a stated determination to pursue commercial frauds more vigorously. The SFO's criteria for accepting a case for investigation are that it involves £1 million or more, that it has significant international dimensions, that widespread public concern is likely, that investigation requires highly specialized knowledge, or that the SFO's special powers are likely to be necessary.[15] The Crown Prosecution Service handles many other fraud cases. The Department for Business, Innovation & Skills (BIS) also investigates and prosecutes some offences relating to the financial markets, including the crime of 'insider dealing' in shares.

Significant as these developments may be, they are on such a comparatively small scale that they do little to redress the imbalance in law enforcement between 'crime in the streets' and 'crime in the suites'. Secondly, there is the question whether the threshold of the criminal law is lower in property offences than elsewhere. Civil law has a far greater involvement in offences of dishonesty than in violent or sexual offences; the very questions of property ownership and property rights are the subject of a complicated mass of rules relating to contracts, trusts, intellectual property, restitution, and so forth. Many property losses could be tackled through the civil courts, by suing under one of these heads of civil law. It may be true that the amounts concerned are often too small to justify the time and expense of civil proceedings, but should that not make us pause to consider whether the criminal sanction is being properly deployed here, and whether adequate weight is being given to the policy of minimum criminalization? If the criminal law is to be reserved for significant challenges to the legal order, should there not be vigilance about the extension of the criminal sanction into spheres in which civil remedies exist, or where some non-criminal procedures might be more proportionate? Is it not true that many dishonest dealings which amount to criminal offences are in practice the subject of nothing more than regulatory action or civil penalties, from commercial frauds to income tax frauds? How, then, can one justify prosecuting ordinary people for the relatively petty thefts that are the everyday business of the criminal courts? These are questions to which we will return at the end of this chapter.

Attention should also be drawn at this introductory stage to the respective roles of the legislature and the courts in property crimes. Parliament has, through the Theft Act 1968 and the Fraud Act 2006, provided some fairly broad offences. The appellate courts have, in dealing with appeals, developed the law in ways which often extend the ambit of already wide offences in order to criminalize persons whose conduct seems wrongful. Although the decisions have not been all one way, there is much evidence here of the influence of the authoritarian principle, and hence of the relative impotence of the principle of maximum certainty in relation to legislators, and of the principle of strict construction in relation to judges.[16]

---

[15] See <www.sfo.gov.uk>.
[16] See the discussion in Chapter 4.4(e), 4.4(f), and 4.5.

10.2 THE OFFENCE OF THEFT

Theft is not the most serious of the English offences against property,[17] but it must be discussed first, because it is an ingredient of some more serious offences, notably robbery and burglary. The offence of theft, contrary to s. 1 of the Theft Act 1968, may be divided into five elements. The three conduct elements are that there must be: (i) an appropriation; of (ii) property; which (iii) belongs to another. The fault elements are that this must be done: (iv) with an intention of permanent deprivation; and (v) dishonestly. The essence of stealing is the violation of another's property rights; unlike fraud, it does not require a particular wrongful method of achieving this.[18] Discussion of each of the five elements in turn will demonstrate just how extensive the English law of theft is in some directions, and how restrictive in other directions.

(a) APPROPRIATION

Before the Theft Act 1968, English law used to require proof that D had taken and carried away the property, a requirement far too stringent for some types of property (e.g. bank balances), and yet a requirement which at least ensured that certain overt physical acts had to be established before conviction. The Theft Act broadened the law's basis by requiring merely an appropriation. In most cases this will involve taking possession of someone else's property without consent. Section 3(1) of the Act begins by defining an appropriation as 'any assumption by a person of the rights of an owner', and then extends the concept to cover a case where D has come by the property without stealing it and where D subsequently assumes 'a right to it by keeping or dealing with it as owner'. This includes cases where D finds property which he does not initially intend to keep (perhaps intending to report the finding), but later decides to do so. Thus the wording of s. 3(1) implies that a simple change of mind, unaccompanied by any overt act, constitutes appropriation. Put another way, the mere omission to return the goods or to report the finding constitutes (together with the change of mind) the keeping which amounts to an appropriation. This is a dramatic demonstration of how far the law has retreated from the requirement of 'taking and carrying away' which characterized the previous law, and of how little is required in order to constitute the conduct element of theft. It also raises questions about the justification for this omissions liability, and whether citizens have fair warning of it.

Let us explore the ambit of appropriation by returning to the main defining words, 'any assumption of the rights of an owner'. Does this mean that one can appropriate property even if one obtains it with the consent of the owner? On the face of it, this might seem absurd: surely there cannot be any stealing of property if the owner consents to part with it. But the House of Lords has pointed out that the definition of theft does not include the phrase 'without the consent of the owner', as did the previous

---

[17] The classic study is that of Smith, n 1; substantially more up to date is *Smith's Law of Theft* (9th edn., 2007), by D. Ormerod and D. H. Williams, and Green, n 1.   [18] See Green, n 3, ch 6.

offence; and in *Lawrence*[19] it held that a taking can amount to theft, even though the owner consents. The facts in that case were that V, an Italian who spoke little English, arrived in England and wished to hire a taxi to take him to an address in London. He offered D, the taxi-driver, enough money to cover the lawful fare, but D asked for more and, as V held his wallet open, D took more notes from it. The defence argued strenuously that this could not be theft because V consented to D taking the extra money, but the House of Lords held this irrelevant. The definition of theft does not expressly *require* the taking to be without the owner's consent, and the House of Lords held that the term 'appropriates' does not imply an absence of consent. Thus D had appropriated V's property dishonestly and with the intention of depriving V permanently of it. This decision has given rise to much controversy and to diverse interpretations.[20] One technical question is whether the money still belonged to V when D took it from V's wallet: if it was V's intention that ownership should pass to D, maybe the second element in theft was missing. But perhaps the most regrettable fact is that D was prosecuted for theft at all, since the case seems to be an obvious example of fraud (formerly, obtaining by deception). An English appeal court cannot alter the charge, or order a retrial on the different charge, and so the choice lay between quashing the conviction of a manifestly dishonest person and doing 'rough justice' at the risk of destabilizing the law of theft. The courts preferred the latter course to the former.

Apparently inconsistent with *Lawrence* was the later decision in *Morris*.[21] The essence of the two cases consolidated in the appeal was that D took goods from a supermarket shelf, replaced their existing price-labels with labels showing lower prices, and then took them to the checkout, intending to buy them at the lower price. As in *Lawrence*, the cases proceeded on theft charges rather than on obtaining or attempting to obtain by deception. The House of Lords upheld the convictions, but propounded a more restrictive idea of appropriation. Lord Roskill stated that the concept of appropriation involves 'an act by way of adverse interference with or usurpation of' the owner's rights, and that this will generally require D to have committed some unauthorized act. This was clearly fulfilled in *Morris*, since the attaching of price-labels by customers is unauthorized. However, if the case had proceeded on the *Lawrence* basis that consent is irrelevant, the customers would have been held to have appropriated the goods as soon as they took hold of them, and before tampering with the price-labels.

The conflict between these two decisions was resolved by the House of Lords in *Gomez*.[22] D, an employee at an electrical store, persuaded his manager to sell goods to a friend in exchange for cheques which he knew to be worthless. As in the two previous cases (and several others over the years), facts which obviously supported a charge of obtaining property by deception (now, fraud) resulted in a prosecution for theft. The House of Lords, by a majority, preferred *Lawrence* to *Morris* on the ground

---

[19] [1972] AC 626.   [20] See especially G. Williams, 'Theft, Consent and Illegality' [1977] Crim LR 127.

[21] [1984] AC 320.

[22] [1993] AC 442; for analysis of this and other decisions, see A. Halpin, *Definition in the Criminal Law* (2004), 166–86.

that the remarks on appropriation in the latter were *obiter dicta* whereas in the former they were part of the *ratio decidendi*. Not only did the House of Lords therefore hold that whether the act was done with the owner's consent or authority is immaterial, but they also stated this as a general proposition on 'appropriation', not confined to cases in which there is an element of deception.

The result of *Gomez* is that the offence of theft is now astoundingly wide. Any act in relation to property belonging to another constitutes an appropriation of that property, and liability for theft then turns on the presence of dishonesty and of an intention permanently to deprive the owner. The breadth of this test is emphasized by one dictum from *Morris* that was incorporated into the *Gomez* formulation: that 'the assumption of *any* of the rights of an owner in property amounts to an appropriation of the property'.[23] Thus all that D needs to do is to assume any one right of an owner, and the conduct element in theft is complete. A customer who touches a tin of beans in a supermarket has appropriated them, even though the owners of the supermarket are quite content for customers to take goods from the shelves and even to replace them later, provided that when they reach the checkout they pay for the goods that are to be taken away.[24]

The breadth of the *Gomez* test has been confirmed (and, some argue, further extended) in a series of decisions on the receipt of 'gifts'. In *Mazo*[25] D had received substantial gifts from her employer, an elderly woman whose mental state was apparently deteriorating: the Court of Appeal quashed the conviction and stated that a person cannot be guilty of theft of property received as a valid gift. In *Kendrick and Hopkins*[26] that proposition was doubted, and the convictions were upheld where defendants who organized the affairs of a confused woman secured several payments to themselves, ostensibly for their services to her. In *Hinks*[27] D received substantial gifts from a man of limited intelligence whom she had befriended. The House of Lords held, by a majority of three to two, that the conviction of theft should be upheld. It does not matter that there was a valid gift of the property according to the civil law: if D had appropriated the property dishonestly, a conviction for theft may follow.[28] One advantage of the *Hinks* decision is the practical benefit of simplicity, since there is no need to instruct juries on the intricacies of the civil law. However, many critics of the decision are concerned that it appears to bring the criminal law and civil law into conflict: it is said to be absurd that a person can be convicted of a criminal offence on the basis of what was, according to the law of personal property, the receipt of a perfectly valid gift.[29] In fact, the absurdity reduces to vanishing point if three further points are taken into account. First, the civil law and criminal law may be pursuing different purposes: no contradiction exists, Simon Gardner argues, because, 'the civil law is rightly concerned to respect established property rights, even if unsatisfactorily acquired, whilst the criminal law rightly

[23] [1984] AC 320, *per* Lord Roskill at 332.

[24] The Court of Appeal in *Gallasso* (1994) 98 Cr App R 284 held that there is only an appropriation if there is a 'taking', but this goes against the preponderance of authority: see *Smith's Law of Theft*, n 17, 26–7.

[25] [1997] 2 Cr App R 518.   [26] [1997] 2 Cr App R 524.   [27] [2001] 2 AC 241.

[28] *Hinks* was followed by the Privy Council in *Wheatley* v *Commissioner of Police of the British Virgin Islands* [2006] 1 WLR 1683.

[29] E.g., J. C. Smith in [2001] Crim LR 162; J. Beatson and A. P. Simester in (1999) 115 LQR 372.

concentrates on penalizing the unsatisfactory manner of acquisition'.[30] Secondly, it could be argued that *Hinks* supports the institution of property by criminalizing those who indirectly threaten the system of property rights by committing a wrong against another,[31] the wrong residing in the dishonest behaviour and the potential harm being further instances of similar conduct. Thirdly, to what extent was the transfer in *Hinks* truly consensual? It can be argued that the criminal law is protecting the vulnerable against exploitation by penalizing dishonest transactions of this kind, and that it is a separate concern that the civil law fails to accomplish this properly.[32] Notably, under the French Penal Code, conduct such as that engaged in by the defendants is dealt with (in more serious cases) by a specific offence under Art. 223-15-2:

> fraudulently abusing the ignorance or state of weakness of a minor, or of a person whose particular vulnerability due to age, sickness [or] infirmity . . . is apparent or known to the offender ... in order to induce the minor or other person to act or abstain from acting in any way seriously harmful to him ...

A number of other questions arise about the ambit of appropriation, some affected by *Gomez*, others not. First, is appropriation an instantaneous or a continuing act? There is no definite answer, but if the question itself is analysed, a plausible answer may be found. The question is not whether the appropriation continues throughout the time when the thief is in possession of the property, and whenever he uses it. That is implausible. The question ought to be whether appropriation is complete as soon as D does an act in relation to the property and, if so, whether it can also be said that the appropriation continues throughout the period when D is engaged in that act. It follows from *Gomez* that D could be convicted of theft on the basis of his first act (e.g. seizing a victim's jewellery, getting into a car hired to him). Is it then inconsistent to hold that the appropriation continues whilst D is engaged in that particular piece of conduct (e.g. whilst D is in the victim's house after seizing the jewellery, whilst D is driving the car hired to him)? There is authority to support the view that appropriation does continue throughout the act or 'transaction',[33] not being exhausted by the first act in relation to the property, and this corresponds with the law relating to the conduct element in rape.[34]

Connected with this is a second point about the time factor in appropriation. The result of *Gomez* and *Hinks* is that a person appropriates property even if the owner's consent is given, yet it remains necessary to establish that the appropriation was of 'property belonging to another' (see the further discussion in (c)). It seems that the *Gomez–Hinks* position is that at the moment when D appropriates it, or immediately before, the money still belongs to the donor.[35] What of the case where D goes to a

---

[30] S. Gardner, 'Property and Theft' [1998] Crim LR 35, at 42.

[31] S. Shute, 'Appropriation and the Law of Theft' [2002] Crim LR 445.

[32] See the carefully argued article by A. Bogg and J. Stanton-Ife, 'Protecting the Vulnerable: Legality, Harm and Theft' (2003) 23 *Legal Studies* 402.

[33] *Hale* (1979) 68 Cr App R 415 (section 10.3); *Atakpu and Abrahams* (1994) 98 Cr App R 254; *Smith's Law of Theft*, n 17, 51–2.

[34] Section 79(2) of the Sexual Offences Act 2003, discussed in Chapter 8.5(a).

[35] R. Heaton, 'Deceiving without Thieving?' [2001] Crim LR 712; cf. now the Fraud Act 2006, section 10.8.

restaurant, orders food, and eats it before payment? What if D goes to a petrol station and fills up with petrol? In both cases the owner intends ownership of the food or petrol to pass to D. However, ownership has passed by the time D finishes eating or filling the tank with petrol, and the relevant act of appropriation has taken place. If, therefore, having eaten the food or filled the tank, D *then* decides to leave without paying for the food or petrol, there can be no conviction of theft because the appropriation ended and ownership in the property passed before the dishonest intention was conceived.[36] A court might hold that the act or 'transaction' should be construed so as to include paying for the property, so that the dishonest intent would be contemporaneous with the appropriation, but since D did not pay either the restaurant or the petrol station this argument would be based on hypothetical rather than real facts.

A third, related point is that the act which constitutes the appropriation does not need to be the act which is intended to deprive the owner permanently. The act of appropriation need only be an act done in relation to the property: so long as it was done with the dishonest intent required, theft has been committed at that point. It does not matter that D's act of swapping the price-labels on two items was part of a plan to offer the higher-priced goods to the cashier with the lower price-label on them, and that that plan had not been executed. *Morris*[37] holds that D does not have to intend permanent deprivation by the act of appropriation; he may intend to deprive by some act in the future. This confirms that the offence of theft in English law criminalizes people at a much earlier point than they would generally suppose. A stark example is provided by *Chan Man-Sin* v *Attorney-General for Hong Kong*,[38] where D wrote unauthorized cheques on his employers' accounts. It was argued that this was not an appropriation since, when the bank discovered that the cheques were forged, it would have to make good the companies' accounts. The Privy Council upheld the theft conviction, stating that D had assumed a right of the owner and that it is not necessary to show that the appropriation would be 'legally efficacious'. The decision penalizes dishonesty, but reduces appropriation to a will-o'-the-wisp.[39]

In exploring the concept of appropriation, the phrase 'act in relation to the property' has been used. We have already noted that an omission (or, at least, a private decision) can suffice, as in the case of a person who finds property and subsequently decides to keep it: s. 3(1). What is the minimum conduct that might suffice? In *Pitham and Hehl*[40] it was held that a person who went to the house of a man who was in prison and offered to sell that man's furniture to the two defendants had thereby appropriated the furniture: he 'showed them the property and invited them to buy what they wanted'. The Court of Appeal held that it was clear that this amounted to 'assuming the rights of the owner', untroubled by the fact that no hands may have been laid on the furniture. Although there were undoubtedly better ways of framing the charge in this case, it may be said after *Gomez* that the person who offered to sell the furniture was assuming

---

[36] *Edwards* v *Ddin* (1976) 63 Cr App R 218, *Corcoran* v *Whent* [1977] Crim LR 52.
[37] [1984] AC 320.   [38] (1988) 86 Cr App R 303.   [39] See the criticism by Smith, n 1, 162.
[40] (1977) 65 Cr App R 45.

a right of the owner. However, in *Briggs*[41] the Court of Appeal held that there was no sufficient act of appropriation where D ensured that conveyancers transferred to her the proceeds of the sale of a house belonging to two elderly relatives. The case was properly one of fraud, since D had obtained the relatives' consent by deception, but one of the charges was theft and the Court held that appropriation requires a physical act rather than merely ordering another to transfer a credit balance in her favour. The decision in *Gomez*, which would support the opposite conclusion, was not discussed.

Before re-assessing the concept of appropriation, mention should be made of the exception in s. 3(2) of the Theft Act. If a person acquires property for value in good faith, no later assumption of the rights D believed he had acquired can amount to an appropriation, even if D then knows that he has not acquired good title. This applies when D keeps the goods or gives them away, but if D sells them and represents expressly or impliedly that he has the title to do so, he will commit the offence of fraud.[42]

Leaving aside this exception, what is the ambit of appropriation? As a result of *Gomez*,[43] any act in relation to property that can be said to assume a right of the owner of the property constitutes appropriation, and the consent of the owner is irrelevant. Courts view this as an 'objective' factual question, but it is arguable that the notion of appropriation (as developed) includes an element of 'proprietary subjectivity', that is, that a mental act of proprietorship helps to mark the distinction between appropriations and non-appropriations.[44] Nonetheless, the notion of appropriation is now considerably more expansive than its framers could have anticipated, and it can be criticized in four ways. First, the definition is not faithful to the intentions of the Criminal Law Revision Committee (CLRC) or of Parliament. That the CLRC intended the concept of appropriation to cover only unauthorized acts is set out plainly in the dissenting speech of Lord Lowry in *Gomez*. A person can now be guilty of theft even though the transaction was effective in passing ownership to D.[45] As a matter of statutory interpretation the decision of the majority of the House of Lords in *Gomez* is untenable; but it is the law, and the House of Lords in *Hinks* applied it not only to cases where the transfer of property was voidable, but also to cases of valid gift.

A second and related criticism is that the new definition violates the principle of fair labelling by lumping together thieves and swindlers. One effect of *Gomez* is that many cases of fraud (formerly, obtaining property by deception) are also cases of theft, except those relating to land.[46] Once again this contradicts the intentions of the CLRC and Parliament: 'obtaining by false pretences is ordinarily thought of as different from theft … To create a new offence of theft to include conduct which ordinary people would find difficult to regard as theft would be a mistake.'[47] The distinction between the two kinds of conduct is morally relevant: there are situations in which one would think differently

[41] [2004] 1 Cr App R 34.   [42] See section 10.8.   [43] [1993] AC 442.
[44] See E. Melissaris, 'The Concept of Appropriation and the Offence of Theft' (2007) 70 MLR 581, although somewhat reliant on *Gallasso* (reference at n 24).
[45] Cf. *Kaur v Chief Constable of Hampshire* [1981] 1 WLR 578.
[46] Cf. Heaton, n 35, for a few contrary possibilities.   [47] CLRC, *Theft (General)* (1965), para. 38.

of a thief and of a swindler.[48] It can therefore be argued that the law ought to attach different labels to people who violate property rights in such different ways. This is particularly so in view of the difference in maximum penalties between fraud (ten years) and theft (now seven years). Having said that, we should point out that some legislatures roll up theft and fraud (and other offences) into a single offence without much difficulty, an example being this offence under s. 484-502-9 of the Californian Penal Code:

> 484. (a) Every person who shall feloniously steal, take, carry, lead, or drive away the personal property of another, or who shall fraudulently appropriate property which has been entrusted to him or her, or who shall knowingly and designedly, by any false or fraudulent representation or pretense, defraud any other person of money, labor or real or personal property, or who causes or procures others to report falsely of his or her wealth or mercantile character and by thus imposing upon any person, obtains credit and thereby fraudulently gets or obtains possession of money, or property or obtains the labor or service of another, is guilty of theft.

Thirdly, the *Gomez* definition is so broad that it exhibits no respect for the principle of maximum certainty and, by making conduct criminal when it would not even amount to a civil wrong, fails to give fair warning to citizens about the boundaries of the law of theft. For example, there is no civil wrong involved in eating a restaurant meal or filling a car's tank with petrol before paying, but both acts amount to appropriation and, if accompanied by a dishonest intent at the time, may result in a conviction for theft.[49] Persuading someone to make a substantial gift in one's favour may lead to a valid gift at civil law, and yet receipt of the gift may constitute appropriation. The point about fair warning might be thought to be overdone: after all, a person who acts dishonestly takes the risk that the conduct will be held to be criminal. But that is an unsatisfactory basis for the criminal law. In everyday life, in business, and in financial dealings, there is often a fine line between unlawful dishonesty and merely exploiting gaps in the law—in taxation matters, this is expressed as the distinction between evasion and avoidance.[50] Whilst it is often impossible to frame a criminal provision precisely, without excluding a number of cases that ought to be included and without rendering the law unintelligible, the result of *Gomez* is that the law of theft incorporates no attempt at precision at all. The appropriation need not be a civil wrong, or involve an unauthorized act, or be an overt act, etc.: in effect, any dishonest acquisition can amount to theft. Appropriation is effectively removed from the equation in most cases: the whole weight falls on the concept of dishonesty,[51] discussed and criticized in subsection (e).

A fourth and related criticism is that the judicial approach severely reduces the amount of manifest criminality in the offence of theft.[52] In other words, liability is imposed for conduct that is not manifestly theftuous: s. 3 of the Theft Act 1968 contains

---

[48] S. Shute and J. Horder, 'Thieving and Deceiving: What is the Difference?' (1993) 56 MLR 548; C. M. V. Clarkson, 'Theft and Fair Labelling' (1993) 56 MLR 554.

[49] Cf. the lesser offence of making off without payment, mentioned in section 10.8(f).

[50] See Green, n 3, 243–5.   [51] Shute, n 31, 452–3.

[52] M. Giles and S. Uglow, 'Appropriation and Manifest Criminality in Theft' (1992) 56 J Crim Law 179, adapting G. Fletcher, *Rethinking Criminal Law* (1978).

elements of this, in its reference to a later assumption of rights by a finder of property, but the three House of Lords decisions (*Lawrence, Morris, Gomez*) take it much further by labelling as a thief any person who assumes a right of the owner in respect of another's property, with or without that other's consent, provided that the two fault elements (dishonesty, intention to deprive permanently) can be proved. Some would say that this proviso is sufficient to rebut the criticism, since the dishonest intent should be the key factor. But this raises questions about the ambit of the criminal law: quite apart from the fact that it may exceed the ambit of the civil law here, the offence of theft now has the breadth and the characteristics of an inchoate offence, and yet it is extended further by the crime of attempted theft. The result is an extremely wide conduct element, not distinguished from ordinary honest transactions save by the intent.

This fourth criticism is an argument against the judicial expansion of the conduct element in theft, rather than against the assimilation of deception to theft achieved in *Gomez* itself. The two points are treated differently by Peter Glazebrook, who applauds *Gomez* on the grounds that:

> Holding swindlers to be thieves does no injustice, will save much inconvenience in cases where it transpires only late in the day that a crook has resorted to deception, and avoids the extreme absurdity of denying the name of thief to those who misappropriate property received as a result of a mistake that they have induced while according it to those who had done nothing to bring about the mistaken transfer: Theft Act 1968, section 5(4).[53]

The point about s. 5(4), which is discussed in subsection (c), is that no absolutely satisfactory line can be drawn between theft and fraud in all instances. Moreover, as we saw earlier, the relevant offence under the Californian Penal Code is drafted so as to avoid unnecessarily fine distinctions between offences in this area of the law. Having said that, there is a substantial case for making the effort to draw the theft–fraud distinction in many clear cases. It may be argued that holding swindlers to be thieves obscures a clear category difference in many cases. What has exercised the judges, particularly in appellate courts, has been the prospect of quashing a theft conviction simply because the police and the Crown Prosecution Service have alleged the wrong offence. This is largely a procedural error: it ought to be remediable by procedural means either at the trial or on appeal, rather than being allowed to distort the development of the law.

Whilst procedural change is needed to avoid the acquittal of swindlers simply because they have been wrongly charged as thieves, the substantive definition of theft ought to be reconsidered too. Glazebrook, following Glanville Williams, argues that since theft is an offence of dishonesty, 'legal logic requires that the conduct constituting its external elements be unlawful—either tortious, or a breach of trust, or, if the property belongs to a company, a fraud on its creditors or shareholders'.[54] One desirable effect of this definition would be to state clearly that there can be no theft if the owner consented to D dealing with the property as D has done.[55] On the other hand, the

---

[53] P. R. Glazebrook, 'Revising the Theft Acts' [1993] Camb LJ 191.   [54] Glazebrook, n 53, 192.

[55] For Glazebrook, however, it would be subject to the rider 'unless that consent is obtained by duress or by deceit, that is, tortiously'. This would perpetuate the overlap between theft and fraud, argued against in the text.

arguments in favour of *Hinks* suggest that any reconsideration of the relationship between civil and criminal liability should not assume that the civil law's approach is correct, or that a divergence between the approaches is indefensible.[56] The links with the concept of dishonesty are also close, and we will return to this issue in subsection (e).

(b) PROPERTY

In order to be stolen, the object concerned must be 'property' within the meaning of the Theft Act 1968. Section 4(1) appears to be couched in very broad terms: 'property includes money and all other property, real or personal, including things in action and other intangible property'.[57] Thus in certain circumstances, as we shall see in subsection (c), D can steal P's bank balance.[58] But there are limits. There is no property capable of being stolen in a dead body or its parts.[59] Nor does electricity fall within the definition of 'property', although s. 13 of the Theft Act 1968 provides an offence of dishonestly abstracting electricity. More importantly, there is no property in confidential information, such as business secrets and examination papers. Thus, if D purloins a confidential document of this kind, photocopies it, and replaces it, he cannot be charged with theft: not only is it difficult to argue that D has an intention to deprive the owner permanently of the information, but what has been taken does not constitute property.[60] Injunctions may be obtained in the civil courts to prevent interference with, or the abuse of, such secrets, but the criminal offence of theft does not extend so far. The problem has become more pertinent with the increasing use of computers as means of storing information: if D 'hacks into' V's computer system, retrieving from it some confidential information which is then noted down, it appears that no 'property' has been stolen. The House of Lords was invited to extend the law of forgery to cover cases of 'hacking' in *Gold and Schifreen*,[61] and its refusal to extend the law in this direction helped to precipitate specific legislation on the subject. The Computer Misuse Act 1990 created three offences of unlawfully entering another's computer system, with dishonest intent.[62] It is right that this form of property violation should be the subject of special provisions: an artificial extension of the present structure of the law of theft to cover such cases, which lie far from the ordinary stealing of tangible property, would probably be less successful and might have unexpected side-effects. It is also right that the law should criminalize this kind of property violation, which might be much more serious financially than many of the takings which fulfil the basic definition of theft. This is one instance in which there was judicial self-restraint and strict construction, in *Gold and Schifreen*, and it was followed by remedial legislative action.[63]

---

[56] See the arguments of Gardner and of Shute, discussed earlier at n 30 and 31.

[57] See S. Green, 'Theft and Conversion: Tangibly Different?' (2012) 128 LQR 564.

[58] *Kohn* [1997] 2 Cr App R 445.   [59] See the discussion by A. T. H. Smith, *Property Offences*, 46–9.

[60] *Oxford* v *Moss* (1979) 68 Cr App R 183, and generally R. G. Hammond, 'Theft of Information' (1984) 100 LQR 252.

[61] [1988] AC 1063.   [62] M. Wasik, *Crime and the Computer* (1991); Smith, n 1, ch 11.

[63] See Chapter 4.4(f).

There are further limitations in s. 4. In the first place, the general proposition is that land cannot be stolen. There are some exceptions to this, and of course it is quite possible to convict someone of theft of title deeds or of fraud in relation to them, but the land itself, being of a certain permanence, remains. Section 4(3) effectively excludes from the law of theft the picking of mushrooms or of flowers, fruit, or foliage from plants growing wild, unless the picking is 'for reward or for sale or other commercial purpose'. It should be noted that this exception is confined to wild mushrooms, flowers, etc., and that the term 'picking' would seem to exclude a person who digs up a wild plant or cuts down a tree. Section 4(4) provides that a wild creature cannot be stolen, unless it is ordinarily kept in captivity (e.g. at a zoo) or has already been reduced into possession (e.g. game birds already shot and retrieved by a landowner). Much of the conduct thus excluded from the law of theft falls within long-standing offences of poaching.

(c) 'BELONGING TO ANOTHER'

The old law of larceny was concerned mainly to penalize those who took possession of property from those in possession, whereas there are many other ways of depriving a legal owner of property. How far should the law go in criminalizing appropriations of property from persons other than the legal owner? Section 5 of the Theft Act 1968 succeeds in spreading the net wide: property is regarded as belonging 'to any person having possession or control of it, or having in it any proprietary right or interest (not being an equitable interest arising only from an agreement to transfer or grant an interest)'. The first phrase, 'possession or control', may be wide enough to enable D to be convicted of theft of, say, suits from a dry-cleaning shop even though the suits had only been placed there temporarily by their owners. There is no need to establish the precise legal relationship between the possessor and the supposed owner of the goods; for Theft Act purposes, the goods are treated as belonging to the temporary possessor, too. So, D can be convicted of theft if he or she steals the drugs that V illegally has in his or her possession.[64] However, if it appears that property has been abandoned by its previous owner or that the previous owner intended to part with her or his entire interest in it, there can be no theft because the property no longer belongs to another.[65] The same should not be true of the proceeds of unknown crimes.[66]

The second phrase of the definition encompasses various situations in which D might regard himself as owner or part-owner of the property. Only three years after the enactment of the Theft Act, s. 5(1) led the Court of Appeal in *Turner (No. 2)*[67] to affirm the conviction of a man who had seized his own car back from a garage that had just

---

[64] *Smith* [2011] EWCA Crim 66.

[65] *Dyke and Munro* [2002] 1 Cr App R 30 (members of the public intended to part with their entire interest when putting money in a charity collecting box); see also *Wood* [2002] EWCA Crim 832 (D who takes property believing that it has been abandoned does not commit theft).

[66] Cf. *Sullivan and Ballion* [2002] Crim LR 758, where the commentary by J. C. Smith is more notable than the first instance decision reported.   [67] (1971) 55 Cr App R 336.

repaired it. D certainly intended to avoid paying for the repairs, but the question was whether he had appropriated 'property belonging to another'. The Court held that the garage was clearly in 'possession or control' of the car. It was parked outside the garage, and they had a set of keys for it. However, D would only have appropriated property belonging to another if the garage had what civil lawyers call a 'lien' over the car, and the Court of Appeal held, unsatisfactorily, that the issue of a lien should be disregarded.

Section 5(1) certainly provides that one part-owner of property can be convicted of theft from the other part-owner. For example, a business partner who appropriates partnership property in order to deprive the other partner of it may be liable for theft so long as the other elements (notably dishonesty: there must be no claim of right) are present.[68] A controversial question is whether company controllers may be convicted of stealing the property of the company—meaning by 'company controllers' one or more persons who, between them, own the entire shareholding in a company. If D and E (being the sole shareholders) transfer money from the company's account to their personal accounts, it might seem strained to say that the company's property 'belongs to another' when the sole shareholders are the very persons who are doing the appropriating. However, it has been held[69] that such cases may in principle amount to theft because the company is a separate legal entity from its controllers, and this view has been reinforced by the decision in *Gomez*[70] to the effect that the owner's consent does not prevent an appropriation in law. Thus in this sphere, too, theft liability turns largely on proof of dishonesty. Whether the same applies to transfers of company property by the controllers in order to put it out of the reach of creditors, in circumstances of actual or pending insolvency, remains doubtful.[71]

In view of the gain and of the dishonesty, company cases are surely as proper a concern of the criminal law as shoplifting. Whether they should be classified as theft or fraud, or dealt with under the Companies Act offence of fraudulent trading,[72] bears on such matters as the stigma of conviction (theft may be more stigmatic than a 'breach' of the Companies Act) and the mode of enforcement. Thus there are arguments in favour of criminalization—and against the marginalization of such offences—by placing them within the Theft Act or Fraud Act. Whether the troubled concept of appropriation and the existing definitions within s. 5 are adequate to the purpose is doubtful, and legislative amendment seems desirable.

There is also the question whether there is an appropriation of property belonging to another when D acquires part or the whole of P's bank balance. D does not acquire cash from P, but is the recipient of either a credit transfer or a cheque. In *Hilton*[73] D, an officer of a charity who was a signatory of the charity's bank account, instructed the bank to transfer some of the charity's money to other accounts in order to pay

---

[68] *Bonner* (1970) 54 Cr App R 257.

[69] *Attorney-General's Reference (No. 2 of 1982)* [1984] QB 624, and *Philippou* (1989) 89 Cr App R 290.

[70] [1993] AC 442, particularly the speech of Lord Browne-Wilkinson.

[71] Cf. G. R. Sullivan, [1991] Crim LR 929, replying to D. W. Elliott, 'Directors' Thefts and Dishonesty' [1991] Crim LR 732.   [72] Companies Act 1989, s. 41.   [73] [1997] 2 Cr App R 445.

his debts. The Court of Appeal upheld his conviction for theft, on the basis that he appropriated the charity's chose in action (i.e. its right to sue the bank for the relevant money). He did not *obtain* property belonging to another, because what P had before the transaction was the right to sue P's bank for the relevant amount, and P's right is either diminished or extinguished, but it is not P's right that is obtained by D but a new and separate right. However, it was accepted that, as a result of *Gomez*, D appropriated (destroyed) the charity's chose in action in respect of that money. It might alternatively be claimed that he appropriated the money itself, because he did an act in relation to that amount which assumes a right of the owner. This would be so if D instructed a particular person at P's bank to make the transfer, or if the transfer were accomplished automatically by the CHAPS process used in modern banking, so long as D initiated the process. The courts have yet to adopt this reasoning.[74] A similar argument can be constructed where D has obtained a cheque from P which D subsequently pays into his account. On the basis of the wide definition in *Gomez*, it can be argued that D appropriates P's bank balance by his act in relation to it, that is, presenting the cheque drawn on P's account. This analysis assumes that P's account is in credit, but it is no different if P is overdrawn and has an agreement with the bank for an overdraft, since that too is a contractual right against the bank. The conclusion, then, is that D *appropriates* property belonging to another by dealing with it in any of these ways.

The question has arisen also in the context of train tickets. In *Marshall*,[75] D and others collected from travellers on the London Underground tickets that had been used but were still valid, and re-sold them to other travellers. The Court of Appeal, in upholding the convictions, did not address the question whether the tickets were 'property belonging to another', in particular, whether the ticket belonged (in any sense) to London Underground. Instead it decided the case on the ground that there was an intention permanently to deprive London Underground of the tickets, because when they were finally handed in the virtue would have gone out of them. However, as Sir John Smith argued, the prior question is whether the conduct element in theft was made out. To whom did the tickets belong at the relevant time? Much depends on the conditions of issue, and whether they were brought to the travellers' attention, matters not discussed in *Marshall*.

Turning to the other parts of s. 5 of the Theft Act, they elucidate, and perhaps extend, the definition of 'belonging to another' in certain ways. Section 5(2) states that when property belongs to a trust, those entitled to enforce the trust should be treated as owners of the property.[76] Section 5(3) expressly includes property received 'from or on account of another' where the person receiving it is under an obligation to the other 'to retain and deal with that property or its proceeds in a particular way'. This

---

[74] For further discussion, see *Smith's Law of Theft*, n 17, 72.

[75] [1998] 2 Cr App R 282, discussed by J. C. Smith, 'Stealing Tickets' [1998] Crim LR 723.

[76] A provision that appears to have been overlooked when quashing the conviction in *Dyke and Munro* [2002] Crim LR 153 (n 60); as Sir John Smith pointed out in the commentary, the Attorney General has the right to enforce charitable trusts.

applies to the treasurer of a sports club or a holiday fund who holds money on behalf of others. However, it is to be noted that s. 5(3) states that the obligation must be 'to the other,' and in *Floyd* v *DPP*[77] the Divisional Court upheld D's conviction for theft from a Christmas hamper company, in circumstances where money had been collected from work colleagues over several months and where the obligation to deal with the money was evidently owed to the colleagues, not to the company. Section 5(3) does not extend, in the ordinary way, to the travel agent or other trader who receives a deposit for a purchase and then fails to fulfil the contract.[78] It provides only for those cases where D is responsible for holding a particular sum of money or its proceeds on another's behalf:[79] this case involves an obligation to deal with the money received in a particular way, as part of a distinct fund, whereas payments to a business are usually payments into the general funds of that business. It has also been held that the manager of a public house who made secret profits by selling beers not brewed by his employers fell outside s. 5(3), since he was merely accountable for the profits of the public house and was under no obligation to 'retain and deal with' them.[80] Some might argue that this is an arbitrary way to draw the line between criminal liability and mere civil liability, but it tends to be justified on the basis that a remedy for breach of contract is usually sufficient for the latter type of case. However, the civil law has been altered by the Privy Council:[81] a secret profit is now deemed to be held on constructive trust for the principal, and so it seems that the manager of the public house would be convicted of theft since s. 5(3) would apply.

Section 5(4) extends the definition of 'belonging to another' to cases where D 'gets property by another's mistake and is under an obligation to make restoration (in whole or in part)'. The obvious example of this is the mistaken overpayment: if money is credited to D's bank account in error, and D resolves to keep it, this amounts to theft of the overpaid sum.[82] If the overpayment is by a bookmaker, there is no legal obligation involved and so s. 5(4) cannot be invoked to support a theft conviction.[83]

Finally, on 'belonging to another', it is worth looking at two interesting cases. In *Sullivan and Ballion*,[84] the defendants took £50,000, the proceeds of drug dealing, from the body of a friend who had died of natural causes. They were charged with theft of the money. The judge dismissed the charges on the grounds that the money was ownerless at the time of the appropriation. That cannot be right. The money must have belonged to someone, such as those entitled to inherit under his will. However, even

[77] [2000] Crim LR 411.
[78] *Hall* [1973] QB 126; *aliter* if the contract provides that the money must be held specifically for this purpose. Cf. *Breaks and Huggan* [1998] Crim LR 349.
[79] In most such cases a trust would be created, and s. 5(1) itself could be applied: cf. *Arnold* [1997] Crim LR 833. Cf. also the use of s. 5(3) in *Klineberg and Marsden* [1999] 1 Cr App R 427 to avoid problems arising from *Preddy* [1996] AC 815.
[80] *Attorney-General's Reference (No. 1 of 1985)* (1986) 83 Cr App R 70.
[81] *Attorney-General for Hong Kong* v *Reid* [1994] 1 AC 324, noted by Sir John Smith at (1994) 110 LQR 180.
[82] *Attorney-General's Reference (No. 1 of 1983)* [1985] QB 182; it is arguable whether s. 5(4) is needed to achieve this result after the civil case of *Chase Manhattan Bank NA* v *Israel-British Bank* [1981] ch 105.
[83] *Gilks* (1972) 56 Cr App R 734.   [84] [2002] Crim LR 758.

had the judge so ruled, there would have been the question of the fault element. If the defendants believed that the property was ownerless, that would be a basis on which to deny that the appropriation was dishonest. Secondly, in *Toleikis*,[85] D took clothes that had been left by the owners in marked bags outside their homes to be collected by a charity. Again, the question was whether the clothes 'belonged to another' (had they been left on the owners' property, rather than outside, they would certainly have been regarded as still belonging to the owners[86]). The Court held that the clothes belonged to, and thus were stolen from, the charity. That seems doubtful, because a gift requires not only an intention to give but (in some form) delivery of the gift. Nonetheless, the Court in *Toleikis* found 'delivery' in the form of leaving the clothes out for collection. More plausibly, the good should have been regarded as still in the ownership of the original donors, because the clothes had not been abandoned, only left out for collection by a specific organization.

(d) 'THE INTENTION PERMANENTLY TO DEPRIVE'

It must be proved that D intended that the person from whom he appropriated the property should be deprived of it permanently. We have already seen that permanent deprivation itself is not necessary for theft: a temporary appropriation will suffice. But the ambit of the offence is restricted by the need for an *intention* permanently to deprive. Thus, the essential minimum of the offence is temporary appropriation with the intention of permanent deprivation.

The Theft Act does not define 'intention permanently to deprive'. Intention presumably bears the same meaning as elsewhere in the criminal law,[87] and therefore covers cases where D knows that a virtually certain result of the appropriation will be that the other is deprived of the property permanently. Most cases will fall into place fairly easily, but the requirement of intention 'means that it is still not theft to take a thing realizing that the owner may not, or probably will not, get it back'.[88] Thus there will be no theft where D takes property and then abandons it where it might be found, and the description 'stolen car' is inaccurate if it refers to a car taken from its owner and abandoned some distance away, since it is well known that cars are normally returned to their owners by the police.[89] Section 12 of the Theft Act 1968 provides a special offence of taking a car without the owner's consent, which does not require proof of an intention permanently to deprive (discussed in section 10.3). A car *would* be stolen, however, if it were taken with a view to changing its identity marks and then re-selling it.

Is there an 'intention permanently to deprive' if D takes someone else's money, intending to repay it before the owner notices its absence? At first sight it would appear

---

[85] [2013] EWCA Crim 600.

[86] For analogous reasons, it is theft to help oneself to golf balls someone else has lost on a golf course, because they belong to the club that owns the course even if they have been abandoned by the hapless original owner–user of the ball: *Hibbert v McKiernan* [1948] 1 All ER 860.

[87] See Chapter 6.5(b).   [88] Smith, *Property Offences*, 187.   [89] E.g. *Mitchell* [2008] EWCA Crim 850 (no theft committed).

not: an intention to repay surely negatives an intention to deprive permanently. Yet if the property taken is money, it is highly unlikely that D intends to replace exactly the same notes (or coins) that were taken. It would therefore be correct to hold that D did intend to deprive the owner permanently of the notes and coins that were taken, and the Court of Appeal confirmed that this is the law in *Velumyl* (1989).[90] A manager had taken money from his company's safe, intending to repay it the following day when a debt was repaid to him. The Court held that an intention to return objects of equal value is relevant on the issue of dishonesty, but does not negative the intention to deprive the owner permanently of the original notes and coins. The Court added that taking someone else's property in these circumstances amounts to forcing on the owner a substitution to which he or she does not consent.[91] Some would argue that this is both pedantic and unrealistic, since money is fungible and one £10 note is for all purposes the same as another. On the other hand, there may be situations in which the owner wants a particular denomination (e.g. £1 coins for a slot machine, whereas D takes ten and leaves a £10 note) or needs to use the money earlier than expected. One merit of the strict rule here is that, by foreclosing what might otherwise be a defence of lack of intent to deprive permanently, it ensures that the wider rights and wrongs are assessed in the context of the dishonesty requirement.

Does it matter if the intention is conditional? One answer to this is that most intentions in theft are conditional in some respect, and so it should not matter greatly. Particular difficulty has been caused in cases of attempted theft, where D has not yet appropriated any property but is searching a container (a pocket, handbag, suitcase, car boot) in order to find something worth stealing. In these circumstances it would be unsatisfactory to convict D of attempting to steal a purse, for example, if D had already examined the purse and decided not to take it. This may explain the rather sweeping statement of the Court of Appeal in *Easom*[92] that 'a conditional appropriation will not do'. Subsequently the Court of Appeal held that the correct form of indictment in these 'container' cases would be to charge D with attempting to steal 'all or any of the contents' of the bag, vehicle, or other container.[93] However, it has been pointed out that this is hardly more satisfactory in a case like *Easom*, where D had examined all the contents of the handbag and had found nothing worth taking. It is an offence to attempt something that turns out to be impossible,[94] and so the better wording is to charge D with simply attempting to steal from the container.[95]

Neither of the two problems just discussed is mentioned in the Theft Act itself. The Act does not define 'an intention permanently to deprive', but it does provide, in s. 6, an extension of the concept. It states, in a poorly drafted compromise provision,[96]

[90] [1989] Crim LR 299.   [91] Adopting the words of Winn LJ in *Cockburn* (1968) 52 Cr App R 134.

[92] [1971] 2 QB 315; for analysis see K. Campbell, 'Conditional Intention' (1982) 2 *Legal Studies* 77.

[93] *Attorney-General's References (Nos. 1 and 2 of 1979)* [1980] QB 180, *Smith and Smith* [1986] Crim LR 166.

[94] See Chapter 11.3(c).   [95] *Smith's Law of Theft*, n 17, 120.

[96] See J. R. Spencer, 'The Metamorphosis of Section 6 of the Theft Act' [1977] Crim LR 653.

that where D's intention is, 'to treat the thing as his own to dispose of regardless of the other's rights', this is equivalent to an intention permanently to deprive. The Court of Appeal in *Fernandes*[97] held that this key phrase applies to 'a person in possession or control of another's property who, dishonestly and for his own purpose, deals with that property in such a manner that he knows he is risking its loss'.[98] Another example is the ransom principle, where D takes V's property, telling V that he will return it only if V pays the asking price. D is clearly treating the property as 'his own to dispose of regardless of the other's rights', in that he is bargaining with the owner (in effect) to sell it back. Thus in *Raphael*,[99] where D drove off in V's car and then offered to return it for a cash payment, the Court of Appeal held that this was a clear case of D treating the car as his own to dispose of regardless of V's rights. It is right to bring such cases within theft, inasmuch as they are takings where, as s. 6 puts it, D does not mean 'the other permanently to lose the thing itself', and yet where the substance of D's intended taking and V's intended loss is little different from permanent deprivation. However, the Divisional Court effectively broadened s. 6(1) in *DPP v Lavender*,[100] where D had taken two doors from a council house undergoing repair and had fitted them to another council house to replace damaged doors. The Court did not refer to the dictionary definition of 'dispose of', but appeared to hold that 'dealing with' the doors could amount to 'disposing of' them. The Court therefore held that D should be convicted of stealing the doors, even though they had simply been transferred from one council property to another. This is unsatisfactory.

Section 6 goes on to deal with two specific types of case. One, set out in s. 6(2), is where D parts with V's property under a condition as to its return which D may be unable to fulfil; the obvious example of this is pawning another's property, hoping to be able to redeem it at some time in the future. The other example, in s. 6(1), is where D borrows or lends V's property: this may amount to D treating it as his own to dispose of 'if, but only if, the borrowing or lending is for a period and in circumstances equivalent to an outright taking or disposal'. Although this is an extension of the idea of intending permanent deprivation, the final few words may prove fairly restrictive. Their scope was considered by the Court of Appeal in *Lloyd*,[101] where a cinema employee removed films from the cinema for a few hours, thereby enabling others to copy the films with a view to selling 'pirate' copies. The employee always intended to return the films, and always did. Clearly, his conduct in allowing others to make copies did significantly reduce the value of the films, but it is not possible to say, as s. 6(1) requires, that his borrowing was equivalent to an outright taking. He did not render the films valueless, even though he did reduce their commercial value by enabling the production of copies. Fewer people might pay to watch the films at the cinema. Lord Lane CJ stated the effect of s. 6(1) in these terms: '[a] mere borrowing is never enough to constitute the

---

[97] [1996] 1 Cr App R 175, at 188.
[98] Cf. *Mitchell* [2008] EWCA Crim 850 (no theft because D always intended to, and did, abandon the car).
[99] [2008] Crim LR 995.   [100] [1994] Crim LR 297.   [101] [1985] QB 928.

necessary guilty mind unless the intention is to return the "thing" in such a changed state that it can truly be said that all its goodness or virtue has gone'.[102]

The application of this test may be illustrated by D, who takes V's railway season-ticket, which expires on 31 January, and maintains that it was always his intention to return it on 1 February. His intention clearly is to return the ticket, which may be physically unchanged, but, since it will no longer be valid, it is fair to describe it as being in a 'changed state'. 'All its goodness' will have gone by 1 February and so D is liable to conviction. But if D maintains that it was always his intention to return the ticket on 30 January, it will still be valid for one more day and, on the *Lloyd* test, D would have to be acquitted (if the court believed the story). Thus, by using the word 'all', Lord Lane made it clear that few borrowings will amount to theft. Some might argue that the wording of s. 6 is slightly more flexible—'in circumstances making it *equivalent* to an outright taking'—but the only way of introducing greater flexibility would be to hold that an intention substantially to reduce the value of the property would suffice, and such a broad reading would go against the principle of maximum certainty (see Chapter 3.5(i)). The real problem here is that, without a general offence of temporary deprivation, judicial attempts to stretch an offence based on an intention permanently to deprive are likely to produce difficulties.

Is there a strong case for dispensing with the requirement of an intention permanently to deprive? At present there are only two offences of temporary deprivation in the Theft Act—s. 12, penalizing the taking of cars, bicycles, etc. without the owner's consent; and s. 11, penalizing the removal of an article on display in places open to the public, such as museums and galleries. Among the arguments for penalizing temporary deprivation generally,[103] probably the strongest are that the chief value of many items lies in their use and that many modern objects are intended for fashion or for a relatively short active life. If someone deliberately takes an item for a period and deprives the other of its use for the same period, that is wrong, and there may be far more gain and loss involved than in many cases of theft in which there is an intention permanently to deprive. In many similar cases where deception is used, there will be an offence of fraud;[104] but if the advantage is gained boldly, without deception, it rarely amounts to an offence at present. The usual counter-argument is that the criminal law would be extended to many trivial 'borrowings' without consent, and that the police and courts would be flooded by such cases. However, this does not appear to have occurred in those European and Commonwealth jurisdictions which have extended their law of theft in this way. For example, in France the basic offence of theft is very simply defined under Art. 311-1 without reference to a need for an intention permanently to deprive the victim: 'Theft is the fraudulent appropriation of a thing belonging to

---

[102] [1985] QB 836; in *Bagshaw* [1988] Crim LR 321, the Court of Appeal commented that this restrictive reading of s. 6(1) was *obiter*. The convictions in *Marshall* (n 70 and accompanying text) for re-selling London Underground tickets were upheld by the Court of Appeal purportedly by applying s. 6(1).

[103] See G. Williams, 'Temporary Appropriation Should Be Theft' [1981] Crim LR 129; Smith, n 1, 191; Law Com No. 228, *Conspiracy to Defraud* (1994), 32–4.

[104] See section 10.7(a).

another person'. Moreover, there could be exceptions to cater for many non-serious cases. The real question is whether a sufficiently strong case for extending the ambit of the criminal law has been made: police and prosecutorial discretion might serve to eliminate minor cases, but are there major cases that justify criminalization? Could any major types of case, such as unauthorized copying of materials and other commercial malpractices, be covered adequately by specific offences? Would this approach not have the further advantage of removing the need for the over-complicated provisions in s. 6? These are questions for a broad review of dishonesty offences.

(e) THE ELEMENT OF DISHONESTY

Perhaps the core concept in the Theft Act is dishonesty. The breadth of the definition of appropriation means that the finding of dishonesty may often make the difference between conviction and acquittal. From the fact that there is also the requirement of an intention permanently to deprive, it is evident that 'dishonesty' performs a separate function. The fault necessary for theft is not expressed simply in terms of intent, reck-lessness, or other *mens rea* terms. The dishonesty requirement imports considerations of motivation and excuse directly into the offence conditions. Let us consider the details.

The 1968 Act does not provide a definition of dishonesty, but it does stipulate in s. 2 that, in each of three instances, an appropriation may *not* be considered dishonest for the purposes of the crime of theft.[105] The first instance, in s. 2(1)(a), is where D believes that he has the legal right to deprive V of it. An example of this is where D seizes money from V, believing that V owes him the money.[106] In many cases under this provision there will be a mistake of law (usually, of civil law), and the main question will be whether the court is satisfied that D actually had the mistaken belief claimed—or, to reflect the burden of proof, whether the prosecution has established beyond reasonable doubt that this was not D's actual belief. The second instance, in s. 2(1)(b), is where D believes that V would have consented if V had known of the circumstances. The third, in s. 2(1)(c), is where D believes that the owner of the property cannot be discovered by taking reasonable steps. This applies chiefly to people who find property and conclude that it would be too difficult to trace the owner.

The main feature of s. 2, then, is that it removes three types of case from the possible ambit of 'dishonesty', making it clear that it is the personal beliefs of defendants which are crucial here. These are, effectively, excuses—which could have been drafted so as to include objective elements, but were not.[107] The only other legislative clue to the meaning of 'dishonesty' is the declaration in s. 2(2) that an appropriation may be dishonest even though D is willing to pay for the property. Apart from that, the definition of dishonesty is at large ('morally open-textured'),[108] and the courts have been

---

[105] Section 2 does not apply to the term 'dishonesty' as used in other offences under the Theft Act such as false accounting and handling, nor to conspiracy to defraud.   [106] *Robinson* [1977] Crim LR 173.

[107] J. Horder, *Excusing Crime* (2004), 49; cf. the discussion of mistaken beliefs in Chapter 6.4 and 6.5.

[108] Horder, n 107, 49.

left to develop an approach. Whilst insisting that the meaning of dishonesty is a matter for the jury or magistrates and not a matter of law, the judges have laid down the proper approach to the question. It seems that there are three stages. First, the court must ascertain D's beliefs in relation to the appropriation—the reasons, motivations, explanations. Secondly, the jury or magistrates must decide whether a person acting with those beliefs would be regarded as dishonest according to the current standards of ordinary decent people. Thirdly, if there is evidence that D thought that the conduct was not dishonest according to those general standards, D should be acquitted if the court is left in reasonable doubt on the matter.

The first and second stages in the test were laid down in *Feely*,[109] where D had 'borrowed' money from his employer's safe despite a warning that employees must not do so. D's explanation was that he intended to repay the sum out of money which his employer owed him (which amply covered the deficiency). The Court of Appeal held that the key question for the court should have been whether a person who takes money in those circumstances and with that intention is dishonest according to the current standards of ordinary decent people. The third stage was added by *Ghosh* (1982),[110] where the Court of Appeal tried to reconcile two lines of earlier cases. The example given by the court was of a foreigner failing to pay when travelling on English public transport in the belief that it is free. However, as has been pointed out,[111] this is a poor example, which would render the third stage superfluous. D's own beliefs are already considered at the first stage, so that, in the example given, the court would then consider at the second stage whether a foreigner with that belief would be dishonest according to the ordinary standards of reasonable and honest people. The answer would surely be no. Moreover, even though the third stage does not provide a defence where D acts on strong moral or social beliefs which he knows are not shared by 'reasonable and honest people', it may provide a defence for the person who thinks that those people would not regard his conduct as dishonest. Whether people who are so out of tune with current standards should be acquitted is a difficult issue. But the overall complexity makes it hardly surprising that the Court of Appeal has declared that the third stage should not be mentioned to a jury unless the facts specifically raise it—which is highly unlikely in a case where the dishonesty was obvious.[112]

The three-stage test of dishonesty evolved by the courts is complex and controversial. Moreover, its sphere of operation is enormous: around one-half of all indictable charges tried by the courts include a requirement of dishonesty. The few specific instances covered by s. 2 are relevant only to a small minority of theft charges: most theft cases and all other dishonesty offences under the Theft Act are decided on the three-stage judicial test. Yet that test is open to serious objections.[113] The root of the

---

[109] [1973] QB 530.   [110] [1982] QB 1053.

[111] See K. Campbell, 'The Test of Dishonesty in *R v Ghosh*' [1984] CLJ 349.

[112] *Roberts* (1987) 84 Cr App R 117 and *Price* (1990) 90 Cr App R 409, criticized by A. Halpin, 'The Test for Dishonesty' [1996] Crim LR 283, at 289, 291–2.

[113] E. Griew, 'Dishonesty: The Objections to *Feely* and *Ghosh*' [1985] Crim LR 341; Halpin, n 22, 149–66.

problem has been the assumption, first stated by the CLRC[114] and then espoused by the courts in the 1970s,[115] that dishonesty is easily recognized and that the concept should therefore be treated as an ordinary word. Neither part of this assumption is well founded. Dishonesty may be easily recognized in some situations, but it is far more difficult in situations with which a jury or magistrates are unfamiliar—such as alleged business fraud or financial misdealing.[116] For example, some competition law experts supported the government's removal of the dishonesty requirement in cartel offences for just this reason:

> [A]s a number of practitioners and academics have pointed out, dishonesty works well in the law of *theft* because juries are very rarely directed to consider it in a given case. The dishonesty inherent in the alleged theft is considered so obvious that the judge usually takes it as given. Even in *fraud* cases, dishonesty can generally be inferred from a false representation. Price fixing is inherently objectionable, but dishonesty is not immediately obvious because the act is more subtle than theft or fraud. Price fixing does not require a positive misrepresentation; all that is required is secrecy and a desire to act like a monopolist.[117]

It may be countered that there would be no objection to expert evidence being given to support the evidence for and against regarding a given cartelization as dishonest, and further, that without the dishonesty requirement the competition offence seems morally to be less serious than it is meant to be. However, the point being made is an important one, and s. 47 of the Enterprise and Regulatory Reform Act 2013 removed the element of 'dishonesty', replacing it (in broad terms) with a defence to a cartel offence that an agreement was reached openly.[118]

Moreover, much depends on who is responsible for characterizing conduct as dishonest. In a multicultural society with widely differing degrees of wealth, it may often happen that someone who is poor or is a member of a minority community may have his or her conduct characterized as honest or dishonest by people who are relatively wealthy and are members of the majority community. There may also be an element of hypocrisy in this, since it is well known that practices which are strictly dishonest abound in the business or private lives of people at all levels.[119] Many, or most, forms of employment have their 'perks' according to which some practices of employees taking or using company property have become so traditional as to be thought of almost as an entitlement, and employers are content to 'turn a blind eye' to this. The same might with justification have been said in the past of MPs in relation to some of their 'expense'

---

[114] Criminal Law Revision Committee, 8th Report, *Theft and Related Offences*, Cmnd 2977 (1966), para. 39.

[115] But strongly criticized in Australia: see, e.g., *Salvo* [1980] VR 401.

[116] LCCP 155, *Fraud and Deception*, 7.49–53

[117] <www.competitionpolicy.wordpress.com/2012/03/19/the-uk-cartel-offence-laying-the-dishonesty-requirement-to-rest/ (Andreas Stephan), discussing the BIS 2012 Paper: <www.gov.uk/government/uploads/system/uploads/attachment_data/file/31879/12-512-growth-and-competition-regime-government-response.pdf>.

[118] But see now, P. Whelan, 'Section 47 of the Enterprise and Regulatory Reform Act 2013: A Flawed Reform of the UK Cartel Offence' (2015) 78 *Modern Law Review* 493.

[119] J. Braithwaite, *Inequality, Crime and Public Policy* (1979).

claims.[120] This all tends to suggest that there are situations in which dishonesty cannot be regarded as an ordinary word with a clear, shared meaning. Yet, because it is not easy to devise a law that includes the culpable and excludes the non-culpable, it has been argued that such an issue is better resolved by a jury or lay magistrates assessing the facts of the case, rather than by inevitably crude legal rules.[121]

This, however, brings us to some strong objections to using the 'ordinary standards of reasonable and honest people' as a test for establishing dishonesty. It derogates from the rule of law in various ways. Its uncertainty may mean that, for some defendants, the judgment of dishonesty comes as an *ex post facto* assessment of their conduct, not knowable at the time of acting. Its uncertainty also brings it into conflict with the principle of maximum certainty in the criminal law.[122] Under the European Convention on Human Rights, an offence definition does not pass the 'quality of law' test unless it is sufficiently certain, which means that it must 'describe behaviour by reference to its effects' rather than relying solely on a morally evaluative term.[123] That cannot be said of 'dishonesty', and it appears that theft, deception, and other dishonesty offences only satisfy the Convention because 'dishonesty' is merely one of several elements in the definition of the offence[124]—a proposition that overlooks the considerable dependence of theft on 'dishonesty' after *Gomez* and *Hinks*. A further rule-of-law criticism is that the breadth of the concept increases the risk of different courts reaching different verdicts on essentially similar sets of facts, and leaves room for the infiltration of irrelevant factors. The *Feely* problem of borrowing money without permission is not unusual, but differently constituted juries might take a different view of its dishonesty. On the other hand, it is true to say that this alleged inconsistency of practice is not supported by any evidence, and that the impact of the alleged uncertainties of definition should not be exaggerated.[125]

It is far easier to criticize the test, however, than to propose a replacement which overcomes all the objections. Some years ago D. W. Elliott proposed that the requirement of dishonesty should be jettisoned; that the three types of case now covered by s. 2(1) should be declared not to be theft; and that the statutory definition of appropriation should exclude all appropriations 'not detrimental to the interests of the owner in a significant practical way'.[126] This would have the advantages of greater simplicity than *Ghosh* and of confining the decisions of juries and magistrates to whether the taking was too trivial to justify conviction, but it would fall well below the principle of maximum certainty until the courts had developed some specific criteria. Somewhat

---

[120] See section 10.1 earlier.

[121] R. Tur, 'Dishonesty and Jury Questions', in A. Phillips Griffiths (ed.), *Philosophy and Practice* (1985); J. Horder, 'Excusing Information-Provision Crimes in the Bureaucratic State' (2015) 68 CLP 197, esp. at 204–9.

[122] See Chapter 4.4(e); Shute, n 31, at 452–3.

[123] *Hashman and Harrup* v *United Kingdom* (2000) 30 EHRR 241.

[124] *Hashman and Harrup* v *United Kingdom* (2000) 30 EHRR 241, para. 39.

[125] See further Bogg and Stanton-Ife, n 32, 407–14.

[126] D. W. Elliott, 'Dishonesty in Theft: A Dispensable Concept' [1982] Crim LR 395, adapting the words of McGarvie J in the Australian case of *Bonollo* [1981] VR 633, at 656.

similar are the proposals of Peter Glazebrook, which stem from the proposition that no conduct that is not legally wrongful should be sufficient for theft.[127] From this starting point, Glazebrook assumes the presence of dishonesty unless the case can be brought within one of a number of listed exceptions. The first three exceptions correspond to those in the existing s. 2(1), and two others correspond to s. 3(2) (purchasers in good faith) and s. 4(3) (pickers of wild produce not for a commercial purpose). Whilst Glazebrook does not list a *de minimis* exception of the kind proposed by Elliott, he deals explicitly with one group of cases that Elliott assumed would be excluded by his *de minimis* exception. Thus one of Glazebrook's exceptions is that a person who appropriates property is not to be regarded as dishonest if:

> the property is money, some other fungible, a thing in action or intangible property, and is appropriated with the intention of replacing it, and in the belief that it will be possible for him to do so without loss to the person to whom it belongs.

What convinces both Elliott and Glazebrook that these 'borrowing' cases should not be theft? Elliott does not deny that they involve civil wrongs, but would exclude them because and in so far as they are not serious enough to justify criminalization. Presumably D's belief in the ability to make repayment is one central factor in this judgment, along with surrounding circumstances about the significance of the event for the owner which may suggest that it is sufficient to treat it as a civil matter. This may, however, mean that the differential treatment of employee 'pilfering' and ordinary small-value shoplifting is perpetuated, though this time under the guise of judgments about relative significance. In theory Elliott's test could become the gateway to the decriminalization of much shoplifting, on the basis that a small-value taking is hardly likely to be detrimental in a significant practical way to the interests of Tesco, Sainsbury, or other major retailers, but courts are unlikely to adopt this reading. Glazebrook's formula is concerned more directly with the 'borrower' of money, and would lead to an acquittal in cases such as *Feely*.[128] Here again, the 'borrower' clearly commits a civil wrong, violating the owner's right to decide how and by whom the property may be used,[129] and so presumably the argument for putting them beyond the criminal sanction is that they are insufficiently serious. The provision is narrower in scope, and would be easier to administer since it requires no normative judgment from the court. But it remains a considerable distance from the existing law. At present we have an extremely wide definition of appropriation which leaves most criminalization decisions to the court's judgment of dishonesty—a judgment with few parameters and much scope for differences of perspective. The Glazebrook approach would confine the definition of appropriation, notably by requiring proof of a civil wrong, with the consequence that a far less flexible and extensive definition of dishonesty would be required. Legal certainty would be enhanced, and legalism would triumph over the variable populism of the *Ghosh* test.

---

[127] Glazebrook, 'Revising the Theft Acts' [1993] Camb LJ 191.
[128] See n 109 and accompanying text.   [129] Halpin, n 112, 294.

10.3 TAKING A CONVEYANCE WITHOUT CONSENT

Although an appropriation of another's property without an intention to deprive the other of it permanently does not normally amount to an offence under English law, there are a few exceptions. The best known and most frequently invoked is the offence of taking a conveyance without the owner's consent, contrary to s. 12 of the Theft Act 1968. In the early 1990s there was growing public concern over 'joy-riding' by young drivers who took cars in order to race them and to give 'displays', and this concern was heightened when some of the offences ended in the deaths of pedestrians or other road users. In 1992 Parliament passed the Aggravated Vehicle-Taking Act, empowering courts to impose harsher sentences in many such cases. The Act was mentioned in Chapter 7.6 during the discussion of serious motoring offences, and reference will be made to it later since it is an aggravated form of the basic offence under s. 12 of the Theft Act.

10.4 ROBBERY

Robbery can be one of the most serious offences in the criminal calendar, and average sentences are higher than for any other crime apart from rape and murder. The definition of the offence is within the Theft Act 1968, but the crime involves the use or threat of violence and is triable only in the Crown Court. The number of recorded robberies was around 63,000 in 1997, doubling to 121,000 in 2001, dropping back to 85,000 in 2007–08, and then down again to 75,000 in 2009–10.[130] Some of these offences are planned attacks on persons in charge of money or other valuables at banks, building societies, or in security companies. However, as we shall see in the paragraphs that follow, many fairly minor forms of snatching a bag or mobile phone can be charged as robbery. This creates a problem of fair labelling: a sudden, impulsive bag-snatching falls into the same legal category as a major armed robbery. The offence is extremely wide, and its drafting owes more to efficiency of administration than to fairness of labelling. Sentences for robbery of a bank or security vehicle in which firearms were carried and no serious injury done can now range as high as twenty-five years' imprisonment,[131] with smaller-scale robberies of building society branches often sentenced in the range from four to seven years, and street robberies in which a weapon is produced having a starting point of four (adults) or three (young offenders) years.[132] Against that sentencing background, it is worth noting that some 28 per cent of robberies involve the theft of nothing more than a mobile telephone.[133] It is, then, the use or threat of force in committing the theft that must bear the weight of justification for

---

[130] C. Kershaw et al., *Crime in England and Wales 2007/08*, 49; J. Flatley et al., *Crime in England and Wales, 2009–10, Findings from the British Crime Survey and Police Recorded Crime* (2010), 32.

[131] *Thomas* et al. [2012] 1 Cr App R (S) 252.

[132] See Sentencing Guidelines Council, *Robbery: Definitive Guideline* (2006).

[133] Home Office Press Release 25 June 2007.

the high starting points in sentencing robbers; but as we will see, the courts have construed 'force' widely, for the purposes of s. 8. The detection rate for robbery is also very
low, with no more than one-fifth of robberies 'cleared up'.[134]

The legal elements of robbery contrary to s. 8 of the Theft Act 1968 are theft accompanied by the use or threat of force. It follows from this that if D has a defence to theft,
there can be no conviction for robbery. Thus where D took V's car by threat of force,
intending to abandon it later (and doing so), this was not robbery because it was not
theft, the intention permanently to deprive being absent.[135] Again, where D brandished
a knife at V in order to get V to hand over money which D believed he was owed, it was
held that this could be neither theft nor robbery if the jury found that D did believe
that he had a legal right to the money (and so was not dishonest: s. 2(i)(a)).[136] Conviction for another offence, such as possessing an offensive weapon or blackmail, might be
possible on these facts. But if there is no theft, there can be no robbery.

Turning to the amount of force needed to convert a theft into a robbery, s. 8 of the Act
requires it to be proved that, immediately before or at the time of stealing, and in order to
steal, D 'used force on a person or put or sought to put any person in fear of being then
and there subjected to force'. Several points of interpretation arise here. The force, threat,
or attempted threat of force must take place immediately before or at the time of the theft:
this seems to exclude the use of force immediately after the offence, but the Court of Appeal has circumvented this limitation by holding that the appropriation element in theft
continues while the thieves are tying up their victims so as to make good their escape.[137]
This strained view of 'appropriation' does linguistic violence to the notion of a 'continuing act', although it does illustrate that there is perhaps a gap in the law. There is possibly
a case for an offence of using or threatening violence to prevent any attempt to re-take
property stolen by the person making the threat, although that would not cover the facts
of *Hale*,[138] where the defendants were really guilty of theft, followed by assault and false
imprisonment in tying up the victims. Finally, the force must be used in order to steal,
not merely on the same occasion as the stealing. Where there is a threat of force, the
threat must be to subject a person (not necessarily the victim of the theft) to immediate
violence—a threat to injure at some time in the future would be insufficient for robbery.

One question which has engaged the attention of the courts is, at first sight, a perfectly simple one: what does the phrase 'uses force on a person' mean? *Dawson and
James*[139] seems to hold that bumping into someone so as to knock him off balance
may be sufficient force. The result of *Clouden*[140] seems to be that pulling V's handbag

---

[134] For further analysis see A. Ashworth, 'Robbery Reassessed' [2002] Crim LR 851. Kershaw et al., *Crime
in England and Wales 2007/08* report a detection rate of 20 per cent for robbery in 2007–08.

[135] *Mitchell* [2008] EWCA Crim 850; see section 10.2(d).

[136] *Robinson* [1977] Crim LR 173; cf. *Forrester* [1992] Crim LR 792.

[137] *Hale* (1979) 68 Cr App R 415, n 33 and accompanying text.

[138] (1979) 68 Cr App R 415.   [139] (1976) 64 Cr App R 150.

[140] [1987] Crim LR 56; the decision also goes directly against the Criminal Law Revision Committee's view
(8th Report (1966), para. 65), that 'we should not regard mere snatching of property, such as a handbag, from
an unresisting owner as using force for the purpose of the definition, though it might be so if the owner resisted'.

in a way which causes her hand to be pulled downwards amounts to using force on a person. None of the defendants in these cases could claim any social or moral merit in their activities, but should they be classified as robbers rather than mere thieves? Of course it is difficult to draw the line between sufficient and insufficient force, but if robbery is to continue to be regarded as a serious offence, triable only on indictment and punishable with life imprisonment, surely something more than a bump, a push, or a pull should be required. It may be true that the significant feature of robbery 'is not merely that D usurps V's property rights, but how she does so',[141] but that does not support the existence or structure of the current offence, which was pushed well beyond its old boundaries in *Clouden*. At common law, the (threat of) 'force' in robbery had to be used to facilitate the stealing, as by overcoming V's resistance; it was not enough that force was involved in the taking of the property,[142] but in *Clouden* the Court refused to carry over this older view into its interpretation of s. 8. However, a case taking a more restrictive view of robbery is *P v DPP*.[143] D had snatched V's cigarette from V's hand, and was convicted of robbery. The Divisional Court quashed the conviction, as there had been no contact between D and V. It was held that the appropriate charge should have been theft, even though it was accepted that, for the purposes of s. 8 'force' could applied by D to V indirectly.

A radical solution would be to abolish the offence of robbery, leaving prosecutors to charge theft together with an offence of violence at the appropriate level—although, interestingly, there are no general offences of threatening or attempting to threaten the use of force, other than common assault (maximum penalty six months) and threatening to kill or inflict serious harm. Another solution would be to divide the offence of robbery, so that the use or threat of lesser degrees of force in order to steal is differentiated from major robberies involving considerable violence or firearms. The principle of fair labelling (Chapter 6.7(a)) is readily adopted for offences against the person, and no one would argue in favour of a single offence of using or threatening force (of any degree) against another. The present definition of robbery plainly breaches that principle.[144]

10.5 BLACKMAIL

The crime of blackmail has attracted a good deal of attention from scholars in recent years, not least because the combination of the internet, and of computer and telephone 'hacking', open up many new ways to gain information for the purposes of blackmail that did not exist before.[145] It was noted earlier that the criminal law does

---

[141] Simester and Sullivan, n 13, 194; Green, n 3, ch 17.
[142] *Gnosil* (1824) 1 C & P 304; *Harman's Case* (1620) 2 Roll Rep 154, discussed by Ormerod and Laird, *Smith and Hogan's Criminal Law* (14th edn., 2015), 962.
[143] [2012] EWHC 1657 (admin).   [144] Ashworth, n 134, 855–7.
[145] See the symposium of articles on blackmail in (1993) 141 U Pa L R 1565.

not penalize all threats of violence,[146] although we have just seen that robbery is committed if a person uses a threat of immediate violence in order to steal property. The essence of blackmail contrary to s. 21 of the Theft Act 1968 is the making of a demand, reinforced by menaces, with a view to making a gain or inflicting a loss. Blackmail is therefore wider than the other offences committed by threats, since it is not confined to threats of violence.[147] The word 'menaces' has been held to extend to threats of 'any action detrimental to or unpleasant to the person addressed',[148] and may involve a threat to disclose some compromising information. On the other hand, blackmail is narrower than some other 'threat' offences, in that the offence is committed only where D makes the demand 'with a view to gain for himself or another or with intent to cause loss to another'. The definitions of 'gain' and 'loss'[149] are supposed to establish blackmail as a property offence (although the notion of 'gain' has been applied to the obtaining of a pain-killing injection from a doctor),[150] whereas it is surely the use of coercive threats (especially where they involve violence) that constitutes the gravamen of the offence.[151]

In 2009–10 there were 1,400 recorded instances of blackmail.[152] Modern technology has created greater opportunities for blackmail in a number of ways. An unusual example is one in which D posted cute pictures of a pet rabbit online, and then threatened to kill and eat it unless those who had viewed the pictures paid him.[153] It may now be possible, whether or not legally, remotely to access sensitive information about someone that only personal knowledge of the individual would have revealed in the past. Perhaps particularly where sexual indiscretions are concerned, the threats in question may be ones respecting which the victim may be especially keen to avoid publicity. It may also be possible simply to gain access to someone's computer system and threaten to wreck it unless some demand is met, as in instances of 'ransomware' in which blackmailers threaten to deny a user access to his or her account on a game website unless money—perhaps in the form of bitcoins—is paid.[154]

It has been said that the criminalization of blackmail creates a paradox: it may be legal to reveal another's secret, and it may be legal to ask another person for money, but when D asks V for money as the price of not disclosing a secret, a serious offence, triable only in the Crown Court, is committed. A more plausible analysis would emphasize the element of coercion involved in obtaining something that ought only to be

---

[146] See section 10.3(e).

[147] See the symposium of articles on blackmail in (1993) 141 U Pa L R 1565–989.

[148] *Thorne* v *Motor Trade Association* [1937] AC 797. See also *Ceesay* [2013] 1 Cr App R(S) 529 (involving a faked kidnap). [149] In s. 34(2) of the Theft Act 1968.

[150] *Bevans* (1988) 87 Cr App R 64. [151] Simester and Sullivan, n 13, 188.

[152] J. Flatley et al., *Crime in England and Wales, 2009–10, Findings from the British Crime Survey and Police Recorded Crime* (2010), Table 2.04.

[153] Ormerod and Laird, n 142, 1071n45, discussing S. E. Sachs, 'Saving Toby: Extortion, Blackmail and the Right to Destroy' (2006) 24 Yale Law and Policy Rev 251.

[154] <www.uk.businessinsider.com/hackers-found-a-way-to-blackmail-gamers-2015-3?r=US&IR=T> ; see Ormerod and Laird, n 142, 942, citing M. Griffiths, 'Internet Corporate Blackmail: A Growing Problem' (2004) 168 JP 632.

yielded by consent.[155] In practice many prosecutions concern the betrayal or threatened revelation of sexual secrets, so the rationale of the offence may also include the protection of certain forms of privacy.[156]

10.6 BURGLARY

One of the aims of the Theft Act 1968 was to reduce the earlier mass of prolix offences to a reasonable minimum. The law thus abandoned a definition which distinguished between burglaries of dwellings and other premises. However, by virtue of a change in sentencing law there are now separate offences of burglary in a dwelling and other burglaries again, although they share the same definition. The Criminal Justice Act 1991 reduced the maximum penalty for non-residential burglary to ten years, retaining the fourteen-year maximum for burglary in a dwelling. This separation of maximum penalties has the procedural effect of creating separate offences,[157] and the prosecution must specify which form of burglary is being charged. However, the legal definition continues unchanged, with no reference to the psychological harm which constitutes the *gravamen* of burglary in a dwelling. These psychological effects are well documented: Maguire and Bennett found that about a quarter of victims 'are, temporarily at least, badly shaken by the experience', and that a small minority of victims suffer longer-lasting effects.[158]

The offence of burglary contrary to s. 9 of the Theft Act 1968 has a wide ambit, but its essence may be summarized thus: it may be committed either by entering a building as a trespasser with intent to steal, or by stealing after entering a building as a trespasser. 'Entry' does not require entry of the whole body: it is sufficient if, say, an arm is put through a broken window to take goods from within.[159] What if D inserts a pole through V's letter box to obtain the house key so that he or she can gain access to the property, but is arrested before getting a chance to use the keys?[160] At common law, the issue was whether the instrument employed was to be used to commit the offence (which would be burglary), or whether it was to be used merely to gain entry (which would not be burglary). On that view, the pole-user would not be guilty of burglary, because he or she was using the pole merely as a means to access an easy means of gaining entry; but it is unlikely that such a narrow view would be taken of the offence under s. 9. In this example, D 'enters' (through the medium of the pole) as a trespasser on V's property, and does so with the ulterior intention of committing (we may assume) an offence mentioned in s. 9.

What must be entered is a building or part of a building: this is drafted so as to cover the person who enters the building itself lawfully, but then trespasses by going into a

---

[155] For deeper discussion see G. Lamond, 'Coercion, Threats and the Puzzle of Blackmail', in A. P. Simester and A. T. H. Smith (eds), *Harm and Culpability* (1996).

[156] P. Alldridge, '"Attempted Murder of the Soul": Blackmail, Privacy and Secrets' (1993) 13 OJLS 368; see the case of *Davies* [2004] 1 Cr App R (S) 209.

[157] *Courtie* [1984] AC 463.   [158] M. Maguire and T. Bennett, *Burglary in a Dwelling* (1982), 164.

[159] *Brown* [1985] Crim LR 611.   [160] *Horncastle* [2006] EWCA Crim 1736.

forbidden part of the building. The forbidden part does not have to be a separate room: it has been held that a customer in a shop who goes into the area behind a service counter enters part of a building as a trespasser.[161] The requirement of trespass places a civil law concept at the centre of the offence. There is no general offence of trespass in English law—it is regarded as merely a civil matter between the parties—but a stealing or intent to steal converts trespass into the serious offence of burglary. In broad terms, someone who trespasses in another person's building is one who enters it without permission. Usually the permission will take the form of a direct invitation, but there may be cases of implied permission which raise difficulties of interpretation.

Two Court of Appeal decisions have been responsible for developing the requirement of entry as a trespasser in different, and possibly inconsistent, ways. In *Collins*[162] it was held that it is not enough that D would be classified as a trespasser in civil law: the criminal offence of burglary requires that D knew that, or was reckless as to whether, he was a trespasser. This protects from conviction the person who enters at the invitation of the householder's daughter, without realizing that she is unauthorized to give such permission. This decision kept the offence fairly narrow, by insisting on a fault element on this point, but the decision in *Smith and Jones*[163] broadened it by suggesting that the fault element is sufficient in itself. The defendants here had entered the house of Smith's father and stolen two television sets. The father maintained that his son would never be a trespasser in his house, but this did not prevent the Court of Appeal from upholding the convictions. The Court reasoned that Smith had entered 'in excess of the permission' given by his father, since the father's general permission surely did not extend to occasions when his son intended to commit a crime on the premises. The result of this decision seems to be that anyone who enters another person's building with intent to steal is a trespasser by virtue of that intention. This approach has what some would see as the great merit of removing questions of civil law from the centre of the offence and replacing them with a straightforward test more appropriate to criminal trials: did D enter the building with the intention of stealing? More turns on D's intent than on the technicalities of trespass.

Simplicity is a virtue in the criminal law, and yet *Smith and Jones* introduces difficulties. In the first place, it seems inconsistent with *Collins*, where D had a (conditional) intent to rape the woman who invited him in, but this was not held to invalidate her permission.[164] More importantly, the boundaries of burglary are being pushed wider than is necessary or appropriate. Surely the proper label for what was done in *Smith and Jones* is theft, and the availability of the charges of theft and attempted theft makes it unnecessary to strain the boundaries of trespass by inserting unstated reservations into general permissions given by householders. There is no element of suspicion, fear, or threat when the person who enters is someone who is generally permitted to do so. Of course, part of the problem here is that the present definition of burglary includes

---

[161] *Walkington* (1979) 68 Cr App R 427.   [162] [1973] QB 100.   [163] (1976) 63 Cr App R 47.

[164] Entering as a trespasser with intent to rape has now been absorbed into the broader offence of trespass with intent to commit a sexual offence under Sexual Offences Act 2003, s. 63.

no reference to the factors which make it such a serious crime in some cases. Convictions for the offence might be rare if the prosecution had to prove that D intended to cause, or was reckless as to causing, fear, alarm, or distress—a burglar might try to avoid such effects by entering a house when the occupier is out and taking property without damaging or ransacking the premises—but even then the crime can cause considerable distress and fear (feelings that one's property has been sullied by another, for example, or that one's home is no longer a safe place).[165] The difficulty is that the real *gravamen* of many burglaries lies in an unintended, unforeseen, or even unwanted effect upon the victim. It is fair to fix the general level of sentences by reference to that element,[166] since the psychological effects ought to be widely recognized, but it is more problematic to make it a requirement in the definition of the offence.

Section 9 creates two forms of burglary. The first, contrary to s. 9(1)(a), is a truly inchoate offence: entering a building as a trespasser with intent to steal, etc. The offence is complete as soon as D has entered with the requisite intent. What ordinary people might regard as an 'attempted burglary', since D has not yet stolen anything, is in fact the full offence. The section refers to entry with intent to steal 'anything therein', and in most cases it will not matter that D's intent was a conditional one, to steal only if something worth stealing were found.[167] The second form is, having entered as a trespasser, stealing or attempting to steal, etc. (s. 9(1)(b)). Either form of the offence becomes the more serious crime of aggravated burglary (s. 10, punishable with life imprisonment) if D is carrying any firearm or imitation firearm, any weapon of offence, or any explosive. In most of these instances there could, in any event, be a conviction for an additional offence in respect of the weapon. Section 10 incorporates the aggravating element into the label, but in one decision the Court of Appeal took this too far when extending the offence to D who, having used a screwdriver to effect entry, then prodded the householder in the stomach with it.[168]

Burglary also has another unexpected element. Not only does it have the inchoate form of entering a building with intent, but it also covers three different intents. The discussion thus far has concentrated on the intent to steal, since that is what one would expect. But, in fact, burglary is also committed by entering a building as a trespasser with intent to inflict grievous bodily harm or to commit criminal damage. This means that s. 9(1)(a) burglary functions as an inchoate violent offence, so that a person who enters a house carrying a weapon has committed the offence at that point. This illustrates the considerable reach of s. 9(1)(a) burglary, going beyond that of an attempt to commit the substantive crime (e.g. grievous bodily harm or criminal damage). If it can be justified, it is on the ground that entering a building as a trespasser is a non-innocent act which should be sufficient (when combined with evidence of

---

[165] See Maguire and Bennett, *Burglary in a Dwelling*, ch 5.

[166] See the sentencing guidelines in Sentencing Council, *Burglary Offences* (2012).

[167] See *Smith's Law of Theft*, n 17, 263, arguing that D might fall outside the section if his intention was only to steal a specific item if, on examination, it had certain characteristics.

[168] *Kelly* (1992) 97 Cr App R 245.

a proscribed intent, often inferred from surrounding circumstances or from the absence of any other plausible explanation) to warrant criminal liability. D has crossed the threshold between conceiving an intent and taking steps to translate the intent into action. It should also be noted that, where the charge is burglary contrary to s. 9(1)(b), only two types of further offence convert the crime into burglary: D must have entered as a trespasser and then have either stolen or inflicted grievous bodily harm, or attempted either offence. Criminal damage is not relevant to this form of burglary.[169]

We have seen that what makes most residential burglaries more serious than most thefts is the element of invasion, with all the possible psychological effects which make it a more personal offence. It should therefore be mentioned that there are other offences which 'protect' the home: the Protection from Eviction Act 1977 (as amended) criminalizes the unlawful eviction or harassment of a residential occupier, and there are various offences in Part II of the Criminal Law Act 1977, which penalize the adverse occupation of residential premises. These offences are restated in the Draft Criminal Code.[170] More recently, in response to media-highlighted concerns about 'squatting' (occupying premises as a trespasser), Parliament has passed s. 144 of the Legal aid Sentencing and Punishment of Offenders Act 2012, creating an offence in the following terms:

(1)   A person commits an offence if—

   (a)   the person is in a residential building as a trespasser having entered it as a trespasser,

   (b)   the person knows or ought to know that he or she is a trespasser, and

   (c)   the person is living in the building or intends to live there for any period.

(2)   . . .

(3)   For the purposes of this section—

. . . (b) a building is 'residential' if it is designed or adapted, before the time of entry, for use as a place to live . . .

(5)   A person convicted of an offence under this section is liable on summary conviction to imprisonment for a term not exceeding 51 weeks or a fine not exceeding level 5 on the standard scale (or both).

In itself, trespass has to this point been in law purely a civil wrong, and the new offence is meant to reflect the frustrations of owner–occupiers with the delays that can be encountered in the civil law to securing the removal of trespassers from residential

---

[169] There were formerly four offences specified by s. 9(1)(a), the intent to rape being the fourth. This has now been repealed and replaced by s. 63 of the Sexual Offences Act 2003, which penalizes trespass with intent to commit a sexual offence, with a maximum sentence of ten years.

[170] Law Com No. 177, cll. 187–96.

property. The question is whether it is a proportionate response to this problem to make it an imprisonable offence that extends to cases where someone trespasses without even necessarily realizing that they are trespassing, since the offence extends to cases in which this is something they 'ought to know'. There is already a power under s. 7 of the Criminal Law Act 1977 to enter premises and arrest a trespasser who has refused to leave. It might also be argued that the offence is unnecessary because trespassers living on residential premises will almost inevitably commit one or more offences in order to maintain their existence there: such as the abstraction of electricity (contrary to s. 13 of the Theft Act 1968), theft (of food, etc.) or criminal damage (to locks or doors, etc.). An illegal trespass continuing for more than a few hours ought to give rise to a reasonable suspicion that one of these offences is being committed, giving the police the right to enter the property and arrest suspected offenders (although in some instances a warrant would be needed for this purpose).

10.7 HANDLING STOLEN GOODS AND MONEY-LAUNDERING

In this section we deal first with the offence of handling, and then with the money-laundering offences that are also concerned with subsequent dealings with stolen property or its proceeds. It has often been said that if there were fewer receivers of stolen goods, there would be fewer thieves. This may well be true—there are professional 'fences' who act as outlets for stolen goods, and goods are sometimes stolen 'to order'[171]—although it is doubtful whether this is a sufficient justification for keeping the maximum penalty for handling stolen goods at fourteen years, double the maximum for theft. Stuart Green has argued that the offence has both a backward-looking and a forward-looking justification.[172] The backward-looking justification concerns the wrongful interference with the owner's goods, and the forward-looking justification concerns the encouragement that handling provides to would-be thieves.

Even so, s. 22 of the Theft Act 1968 considerably extended the liability of persons concerned in dealing with stolen goods, creating a broad offence which covers many minor acts of assistance which might more naturally fall within inchoate offences or complicity.

The essence of the offence of 'handling' is dealing with stolen goods. The concept of stolen goods includes goods obtained by means of theft (including robbery and burglary), fraud, or blackmail, and it also covers the proceeds of such goods. Goods may, however, lose their legal classification as stolen if returned to their owner or to police custody, even temporarily.[173] The fault elements required for handling are dishonesty, and that D must 'know or believe' that the property is stolen, terms which

---

[171] See C. B. Klockars, *The Professional Fence* (1975), and Maguire and Bennett, *Burglary in a Dwelling*, 70–5. For sentencing guidelines on handling, see *Webbe* [2002] 1 Cr App R (S) 82.

[172] Green, n 1, 180–94.   [173] For an example see *Attorney-General's Reference (No. 1 of 1974)* [1974] QB 744.

include 'wilful blindness'[174] but not suspicion, even strong suspicion.[175] The prohibited conduct may take one of four forms, but merely touching stolen property does
not amount to the offence. 'Handling' is simply the compendious name for the four
types of conduct. Type (i) is 'receiving' stolen property, which means taking control
or possession of it. This is the most usual form of the offence, and applies to the 'fence'
who takes the property from the thief for resale, and to the person who buys stolen
goods from another. Type (ii) is 'arranging to receive' stolen goods, and here we meet
the broadening of the offence. If D agrees to buy stolen goods from the thief, who is
to deliver them later, D has 'arranged to receive' even before the thief has taken any
action to bring the goods to him. Type (iii) is 'undertaking or assisting in their retention, removal, disposal or realization by or for the benefit of another person'. This is an
extremely wide provision designed to criminalize those who help a thief or a receiver.
It is rendered even wider by type (iv), which penalizes arrangements to do an act or
omission within (iii). Thus, a person who does, assists in, or arranges to do or assist
in any of the acts or omissions within type (iii) is criminally liable—on one condition.
The condition is that it must be 'by or for the benefit of another person'. In the leading
case of *Bloxham*[176] D bought a car, subsequently realizing that it was stolen. He then
sold the car to someone else and was charged with type (iii) handling. The House of
Lords quashed his conviction, on the ground that he sold the car for his own benefit,
not for the benefit of another. He did not sell the car for the benefit of the original thief
or handler, of whom he knew nothing; and it would be ridiculous to suggest that he
sold it for the buyer's benefit. Moreover, D was originally a purchaser in good faith,
and the policy of the Theft Act is not to criminalize such purchasers, even if they later
discover the unwelcome truth about their purchases.[177]

The purpose of broadening the definition of handling was 'to combat theft by making it more difficult and less profitable to dispose of stolen property'.[178] This purpose
has now been taken further by the enactment of legislation on money-laundering and
the disposal of the proceeds of crime. There is now a complex body of law that extends the reach of the criminal law considerably beyond the confines of handling stolen goods. No attempt can be made here to examine the details of this legislation, but
it is important to outline the three principal offences of money-laundering under the
Proceeds of Crime Act 2002.[179] Section 327 of the Act creates the offence of concealing,
disguising, converting, transferring, or removing from the jurisdiction any 'criminal

---

[174] Discussed in Chapter 6.5(d).
[175] Cf. *Grainge* [1974] 1 WLR 619 with *Brook* [1993] Crim LR 455. See further S. Shute, 'Knowledge and
Belief in the Criminal Law', in S. Shute and A. P. Simester (eds), *Criminal Law Theory: Doctrines of the General Part* (2002), at 172–6.
[176] [1983] 1 AC 109, responding to the promptings of J. R. Spencer, 'The Mishandling of Handling' [1981]
Crim LR 682.
[177] Section 3(1) and (2) of the Theft Act; see further *Smith's Law of Theft*, n 17, 373–4.
[178] CLRC, 8th Report (1966), para. 127.
[179] For full analysis, see *Mitchell, Taylor and Talbot on Confiscation and the Proceeds of Crime* (3rd edn.,
2002) for a critical appraisal of the policy, see P. Alldridge, *Money Laundering Law* (2003), esp. chs 3 and 9.

property'. Section 328 creates an offence of becoming concerned in an arrangement to facilitate the acquisition, retention, use, or control of criminal property by another person. Section 329 creates offences of acquisition, use, or possession of criminal property. All the offences are punishable with up to fourteen years' imprisonment, the same maximum as handling. There are two key elements in the offences. The first is that they all relate to 'criminal property', defined as 'a person's benefit from criminal conduct' or 'property that directly or indirectly represents such a benefit'. It will be noticed that this goes beyond stolen goods to encompass the proceeds of all crimes, notably drug offences. The second key element also forms part of the definition of 'criminal property'—that D must 'know or suspect that it constitutes such a benefit'. In other words, it only qualifies as 'criminal property' if the launderer has this state of mind. This is the only fault element in the offences under ss. 327 and 329; the offence under s. 328 additionally requires that D knows or suspects that the arrangement will facilitate the acquisition, retention, use, or control of the property. These fault elements are entirely subjective, with the minimum requirement being that D suspects that the property may be 'criminal'—a form of recklessness, requiring D to believe that there is a risk of the property being the proceeds of crime. This use of 'suspects' takes these offences considerably beyond the 'belief' requirement for handling stolen goods; and whereas type (iii) handling is only criminal if done for the benefit of another, a similar requirement applies only to the s. 328 offence and not to the other offences.

Offences of money-laundering are required by international conventions, but the extent to which such broad offences are justifiable has been questioned. The confiscation provisions in the Proceeds of Crime Act 2002 are so draconian, and not dependent on a conviction, that it may be thought unnecessary to add further offences to the existing crimes of handling and of encouraging or assisting crime.[100] The ostensible purpose is to catch the 'godfathers' who live off organized crime. But the breadth of the offences is such that it may encourage prosecutors to charge money-laundering when a person appears to have no lawful means of support but plenty of money, even though it cannot be proved what particular offences D has committed or acquired proceeds of.[181]

10.8 OFFENCES UNDER THE FRAUD ACT 2006

The Theft Act 1968 introduced the offences of obtaining property by deception (s. 15) and obtaining a pecuniary advantage by deception (s. 16). Those offences, and further offences in ss. 1 and 2 of the Theft Act 1978 that were designed to plug gaps in the law, were repealed and replaced by offences under the Fraud Act 2006. The new offences overlap with a considerable number of other offences of fraud scattered through the statute-book and at common law. Among the statutory offences are two under the

---

[180] Alldridge, n 179, 64–9.
[181] Cf. the conflicting CA decisions in *Craig* [2007] EWCA Crim 2913 and *NW* et al [2008] 3 All ER 533.

Theft Act 1968, false accounting (s. 17) and false statements by company directors (s. 19), several under the Forgery and Counterfeiting Act 1981, the offence of fraudulent trading (Companies Act 1985, s. 458), and various offences of false and misleading statements under such statutes as the Banking Act 1987, the Financial Services and Markets Act 2000, and the Enterprise Act 2002. Among the common law offences are cheating the public revenue (which is based on fraud, and does not require deception[182]) and conspiracy to defraud, which will be examined in section 10.9. Notice that an important contrast between the latter offences, and the offences under s. 15 and s. 16 of the 1968 Act, is that the former required proof of a consequence element: the obtaining of property, or of a pecuniary advantage (brought about by a deception). The removal of that consequence element in the offences under the 1968 Act, and hence the transformation of those offences into 'inchoate' offences, have been key elements of the 2006 reform.

The most prominent characteristic of the Fraud Act offences is that they are drafted in the inchoate mode: they set out to penalize fraudulent conduct, whether or not it succeeds in deceiving anyone and whether or not it leads to the obtaining of any property. In this way, two of the main difficulties of the previous law—proving that someone was deceived, and proving that the deception caused the obtaining[183]—are removed, although (as we shall see) there are some problems with the new law. The focus below will be on the four main offences introduced by the Fraud Act: fraud by false representation, fraud by failing to disclose information, fraud by abuse of position, and obtaining services dishonestly. Most of the general concepts will be dealt with in relation to the first offence, which is likely to be the most widely prosecuted.[184] The maximum sentence upon conviction under the 2006 Act is ten years' imprisonment.[185]

(a) FRAUD BY FALSE REPRESENTATION

This offence, like those in (b) and (c), is created by s. 1 of the Act and then defined by a subsequent section, in this case s. 2. Thus, fraud by false representation is, technically, simply one way of committing the offence of fraud. Section 2(1) provides that this form of fraud is committed if D 'dishonestly makes a false representation, and intends, by making the representation, to make a gain for himself or another, or to cause loss to another or to expose another to the risk of loss'. It will be observed that it is the dishonest making of a false representation with the required intention that constitutes the offence: as stated earlier, there is no requirement that anyone is deceived or that anything is actually obtained, let alone that it must be property rather than

---

[182] See *Mavji* (1987) 84 Cr App R 34, *Redford* (1989) 89 Cr App R 1, and the thorough study by D. Ormerod, 'Cheating the Public Revenue' [1998] Crim LR 627, who argues that the offence should be abolished.

[183] See the 5th edn. of this work, at 397–401.

[184] For fuller analysis, see D. Ormerod, 'The Fraud Act 2006—Criminalising Lying?' [2007] Crim LR 193, and *Smith's Law of Theft*, n 17, ch 3.

[185] See now Sentencing Council, Fraud, *Bribery and Money Laundering Offences Definitive Guideline* (2014).

services.[186] The conduct element or *actus reus* has two components, a representation that is also false; the fault element or *mens rea* has three elements—knowledge, dishonesty, and the intent to cause loss or make a gain.

(i) *Conduct Elements:* The first point is that the representation made by D must be false. This means, according to s. 2(2), that it must be either untrue or misleading. A representation can be untrue if in any particular it is inaccurate; in other words, it is not necessary that the whole representation is untrue, so long as one element of it is untrue. Any argument to the effect that the untruth was so minor as to be immaterial goes to the dishonesty requirement: an example of how much of the work done to distinguish criminal from non-criminal acts in borderline cases under the 2006 Act is done by that requirement. The term 'misleading' is different, since it posits a particular effect of what was said or done by D. Presumably the term usually bears an objective meaning, that is, what is likely to mislead the ordinary person. But if D has any special knowledge of the person to whom the representation is addressed—for example, that that person is particularly gullible, or on the other hand that he is so knowledgeable that he will not be misled—this could be relevant in determining whether the representation is misleading.

The requirement that D makes a representation does not suggest that it must be received by another, let alone acted upon. If the representation is not communicated to its intended recipient (perhaps because that person is deaf, or because a written representation is intercepted before arrival), that does not negative the *actus reus* of the offence. Section 2(3) provides that representations as to fact or law are included, as is a representation 'as to the state of mind of the person making the representation or any other person'.[187] This will be particularly relevant in cases where D promises to make payment next week if goods are delivered today, assuming that it can be proved (usually by inference) that at the time he made the promise D did not intend to pay the following week. Section 2(4) provides that 'a representation may be express or implied'. This applies equally to representations by words and by conduct.[188] Many everyday transactions are conducted on certain assumptions which it would be tedious to spell out to or check on every occasion. We assume that the woman wearing a police uniform is a policewoman, or that the man wearing a Royal Mail uniform is a postman. We also assume that when a person pays by cheque there will be the funds to meet the cheque. The representations implied by giving a cheque in payment have now been formalized in a number of decisions: it is implied (i) that the drawer has an account at the bank; and (ii) that the cheque will be met when presented, which may mean in practice that there are sufficient funds in the account, or that sufficient funds will be paid in

---

[186] In *Idress* [2011] EWHC 624 (Admin), D persuaded X to sit his (D's) driving test by representing that he (X) was D. D's conviction under s. 2 was upheld. The case illustrates that 'gain' and 'loss' need not involve financial gain (s. 5(2)(a)), but extend to other property, presumably here including a driving licence.

[187] For an example, see *Shabbir* [2012] EWCA Crim 1482.

[188] A case illustrating the importance of determining when there is, and is not, an implied representation—in this case, concerning possible future changes in financial circumstances—is *UAE v Allen* [2012] EWHC 1712 (admin).

before the cheque is presented, or that there is an arrangement with the bank for a sufficient overdraft facility.[189] Finally, s. 2(5) is a complicated provision intended to bring representations to machines within the offence: 'a representation may be regarded as made if it is submitted in any form to any system or device designed to receive, convey or respond to communications (with or without human intervention)'.

(ii) *Fault Elements:* The first of the three fault elements is to be found, strangely, in the definition of 'false'. A representation is only false, according to s. 2(2)(b), if 'the person making it knows that it is, or might be, untrue or misleading'. This is a requirement of knowledge, which seems (by the words 'or might be') to extend to a form of reckless knowledge.[190] As noted in Chapter 5.5(d), some cases of 'wilful blindness' may be held to fall within the requirement of knowledge. The second of the fault elements is dishonesty, and it is clear that this was intended to bear the meaning placed on that concept in *Ghosh*.[191] However, in the law of theft the concept of dishonesty is narrowed by s. 2 of the Theft Act, which excludes three kinds of case from its ambit. There is no equivalent of s. 2 in the Fraud Act, and so cases of belief in legal right will fall to be dealt with according to the *Ghosh* test of the ordinary standards of reasonable and honest people. As indicated earlier, in view of the inchoate nature of the offence, and the breadth of the requirement of knowledge that the representation 'might be' misleading, many cases are likely to turn on the magistrates' or jury's view of D's honesty or dishonesty. For example, exaggerated claims by sellers might be commonplace in particular markets: D must know that they might be misleading, but in the circumstances is it dishonest to indulge in such over-statements? Or, to put the matter differently, would it be considered sufficiently dishonest to constitute fraud?[192]

To give a more concrete example, companies are often under regulatory obligations to provide complex terms and conditions data, along with their own advertising and other transactional material designed to encourage customers to invest in products. If the companies appreciate that such data may confuse customers, given that the data is part of an overall package of material intended to make a gain for the company, is an offence committed? It would create great uncertainty if each case depended on how integral the former (the data) was to the latter (the promotional material). The company may have to rely on an absence of dishonesty, although the law of fraud is often of marginal relevance in such cases because they are already governed by context-specific regulatory offences.

The third fault element for this offence is that D 'intends, by making the representation', to cause a gain or a loss. It should be noted that this incorporates a requirement of causation—that the intention must be to cause the gain or loss 'by making the representation'—so that if D argues that he did not intend the false representation to be

---

[189] *Gilmartin* (1983) 76 Cr App R 238.

[190] Confirming the need for subjective fault is *Augunas* [2013] EWCA Crim 2046.

[191] See the discussion of theft in section 10.2(e).

[192] This is admittedly a re-formulation of the dishonesty requirement, but it points to the element of uncertainty in the definition and to how it might be resolved. Cf. the discussion of whether the 'definition' of dishonesty complies with the 'quality of law' test in the Convention, section 10.10.

a causal factor (merely an embellishment), he may create a doubt that this element of the offence is satisfied.[193] In most cases, however, proof of an intent to make a gain or to cause a loss will not cause difficulty. The definition of gain and loss in s. 5 is similar to that for the offence of blackmail (see section 10.5), extending to temporary or permanent losses of money or property, and also covering cases where D intends only to expose the other to the risk of a loss.

(b) FRAUD BY FAILING TO DISCLOSE INFORMATION

This offence is created by s. 1(2)(b) of the Fraud Act and defined in s. 3. Its essence is dishonestly failing to disclose information that D has a duty to disclose. It is therefore an offence of omission: it is designed to deal with some cases that presented a difficulty for the previous offence of obtaining by deception, but in doing so it overlaps considerably with the offence in s. 2, as we shall see. The fault elements for the s. 3 offence are dishonesty and an intention, by the failure to disclose the information, to make a gain or to cause a loss. These run parallel to the corresponding requirements for the offence of fraud by false representation, and will not be discussed further. More significant are the two elements of the *actus reus*, the failure to disclose and the information that D has a duty to disclose.[194] It might be thought that 'failing to disclose' is clear enough, but there may be questions over partial or insufficiently full disclosure in some cases. Essentially, if D does not disclose everything that must be disclosed, the defence may have to rest its case on the absence of dishonesty. Turning to the duty to disclose, this was intended to reflect the duties that exist under statute and at common law. It is as plain as can be that the intention of the legislature was that there must be an existing legal duty,[195] and that there is no scope for creating special duties under criminal law (as, for example, in relation to gross negligence manslaughter).[196] In *White*,[197] for example, the Court of Appeal found that there was no duty, when applying for a mortgage, to inform the company that the applicant is unemployed. It therefore behoves the prosecutor to spell out the duty and its source,[198] and whether the duty did indeed exist is a question of law. By contrast, whether D fulfilled the duty, or failed to disclose that which was required, is a question for the jury. Some of these cases might be prosecuted under s. 2, by arguing that D made an implied representation by conduct or by omission, but in principle it will usually be easier for the prosecution to proceed under s. 3.

---

[193] For the importance of this, see now *Gilbert* [2012] EWCA Crim 2392, where the Court of Appeal found that the trial had failed to direct the jury to acquit, if false statements made to a bank, in order to secure the opening of an account, were not made in order to make a gain or cause a (risk of) loss to another at a later point.

[194] An example would be a failure to disclose previous convictions when applying for a job. See *Daley* [2010] EWCA Crim 2193; *Razoq* [2012] EWCA Crim 674. For a more complex case, see *Forrest* [2014] EWCA Crim 308. [195] Law Com No. 276, *Fraud* (2002), paras. 7.28–9.

[196] Chapter 8.5(b). [197] [2014] EWCA Crim 714.

[198] This was the issue in *Forrest* [2014] EWCA Crim 308.

(c) FRAUD BY ABUSE OF POSITION

This offence, created by s. 1(2)(c) of the Act and defined in s. 4, is the most controversial of the trio. This is because its key terms threaten to crumble away into vagueness when scrutinized. Indeed, it looks distinctly less like a fraud offence than either of the other two. Its central element, dishonest abuse of position, appears not to require any fraud or falsity at all—a brazen taking would seem to suffice. Although dishonesty and a corrupt intent are not to be equated, in some respects, the s. 4 definition has more in common with the offence of bribery than with fraud.

What are the conduct elements of this offence? Three main requirements may be identified—the occupation of a position, the expectation that financial interests will be safeguarded, and the perpetration of abuse. First, what kind of position must D occupy? It seems plain that the intention of the legislature was that the concept of 'position' should not be restricted to recognized fiduciary positions. Indeed, examples given by the government include cases where V has allowed D access to his or her financial records, or business records, as well as cases where an employee of a care home deals with a resident's financial affairs.[199] Thus employees or others who stand in a particular relationship to another may be brought within the concept of 'position',[200] a penumbra of uncertainty that fails to give fair warning of the law's impact. Secondly, the position must be one 'in which [D] is expected to safeguard, or not to act against, the financial interests of another person'.[201] Many employees who are not expected to safeguard their organization's financial interests may nevertheless be expected not to act against them. Beyond that, this requirement has all the rigidity of a hot marshmallow. The statute does not say 'may reasonably be expected' but 'is expected', so the obvious question is: whose expectation is relevant? The meaning would vary too much if it depended on the victim's expectation, and it could hardly turn on D's own expectation, so it seems that the courts may well develop a notion of 'reasonable expectation'. Once again, there is no fair warning of the law's impact. Thirdly, there is the requirement that D 'dishonestly abuses that position'. This is the only active element in the *actus reus* of this offence, and it may be fulfilled by an act or an omission: s. 4(2). An employee who awards contracts to friends or who fails to bid for a particular contract in order to allow a friend to obtain it seems likely to fulfil this requirement: here is the analogy with bribery, mentioned above, in that such an action by D would undoubtedly be corrupt even if it did not involve bribery as such. It is not clear whether 'abuse' implies the actual making of a gain or loss, but it may be interpreted more broadly as acting

---

[199] See on this point, *Marshall* [2009] EWCA Crim 2076. See further, *Smith's Law of Theft*, n 17, 170–3. Cases like *Hinks* [2001] 2 AC 241 (discussed in section 10.2(a)) would fall clearly within the new offence. Cf. the extensive definition of 'positions of trust' in the Sexual Offences Act 2003, ss. 21–2.

[200] How would this apply to the facts of *Silverman* (1988) 86 Cr App R 213, where D had done building work for V and her family for many years and D, on request, gave V a quotation for building work that was excessively high? V undoubtedly trusted D. Did D 'occupy a position' in which he was expected not to act against her financial interests? Does actual or reasonable reliance create such a position or expectation?

[201] For a recent application of this principle, see *Waqanika* [2014] EWCA Crim 902.

(or failing to act) improperly or against the financial interests of V, irrespective of the outcome. The Court of Appeal has said that the term 'abuse' can be explained as, 'uses incorrectly', or 'puts to improper use'.[202]

The fault elements for this offence are twofold—dishonesty, and the intention, by the abuse of position, to cause gain or loss. It is evident that the dishonesty requirement will be particularly important in this offence, in view of the uncertain boundaries of the key *actus reus* elements. However, if there has been an apparent abuse of position (in whatever wide sense that is understood), there is likely to be a whiff of dishonesty in most cases. The employee who deviated from appropriate procedures in order to ensure that a friend obtained a contract—whether a local government official, a chief constable, or a car salesperson—may be confronted with the prospect of conviction for a serious offence carrying a maximum of ten years' imprisonment. It is not clear how widely known this change in the law is, but the fact that s. 1(2)(c) applies in this situation helps, as indicated above, to buttress the law of bribery and corruption. The Bribery Act 2010 punishes corruption in cases like this only where, amongst other things, a person conferring an advantage (the contract) does so knowing or believing that its acceptance by another person would constitute the improper performance of a relevant function or activity.[203] So, suppose D offered the contract to a lover or close friend who, in accepting it, would not themselves become involved in the improper performance of an existing function or activity with which they have been entrusted. It is, in such a case, the abuse of position offence that must be employed to criminalize D's conduct, rather than the 2010 Act offence;[204] but the similarity between the offences is nonetheless striking.

(d) OBTAINING SERVICES DISHONESTLY

This offence, created by s. 11 of the Fraud Act, replaces the offence of obtaining services by deception contrary to s. 1 of the Theft Act 1978. It will be noted immediately that the element of deception required by the previous law has gone, and that the concept of dishonesty is once again the centrepiece of the new offence. There is also a major difference between this offence and the three Fraud Act offences just considered: whereas those offences are drafted in an inchoate mode, this offence requires an actual obtaining.

There are three elements in the *actus reus* of this offence. First, D must obtain services for himself or another by an act. The reference to an act has been taken to imply that an omission will not suffice for this offence.[205] There is no definition of 'services', and it may be construed widely so as to include, for example, the unlawful downloading of music.

---

[202] *Pennock* [2014] EWCA Crim 598. In this case, the defendants had withdrawn a large sum from a joint account; but as they were both signatories to the account, this could not be an 'abuse' of their position.

[203] Bribery Act 2010, s. 1(2).

[204] See further, Law Commission, *Reforming Bribery* (Report No 313, 2008), paras. 3.126–32. In this kind of example, depending on how much they know, the lover or friend could be complicit in the fraud offence committed by D, or found guilty of the inchoate offence of assisting or encouraging the commission of the fraud when they accept the offer.   [205] *Smith's Law of Theft*, n 17, 178.

The ambit of 'services' is restricted by the second requirement, that the services 'are made available on the basis that payment has been, is being or will be made for or in respect of them'. This rules out services provided on a complimentary basis, but will cover most cases. However, the High Court has held that it does not extend to 'credit'. So, where D tops up his mobile phone by charging the cost to other mobile users, D is obtaining credit, not services.[206] Thirdly, D must 'obtain [the services] without any payment having been made for or in respect of them or without payment having been made in full'. This seems to exclude cases where D pays for services by using a credit or debit card that he is not authorized to use—since the issuing company will make the payment if the card transaction is completed.[207] However, it clearly includes cases where D obtains a reduced rate of payment to which he is not entitled (whether or not any fraud or deception is involved).

There are three fault elements for the offence. First, D's act must be dishonest. This is a reference to the *Ghosh* test and is likely, once again, to be a crucial issue for the magistrates or jury in determining whether or not D has committed the offence. Secondly, D must know, when he obtains the services, that either they are being made on a payment basis or 'that they might be'. This introduces a requirement of reckless knowledge, to cover cases where D realizes there is a risk that payment might be required but does not enquire further. And thirdly, D must intend that 'payment will not be made, or will not be made in full'. This requirement of an intent to avoid payment means that this offence does not apply to cases where D's dishonest obtaining of services amounts to getting something to which D is not entitled but intends to pay for fully—as where parents lie about their religion in order to get their child into a faith school, intending to pay the full fees for the child's education. This would not be an offence under s. 2 either.

10.9 CONSPIRACY TO DEFRAUD

The elements of the common law crime of conspiracy to defraud were restated in *Scott v Metropolitan Police Commissioner*.[208] The offence may take one of two forms. If it is directed at a private person, what is proscribed is an agreement between two or more persons 'by dishonesty to deprive' that person of something to which he or she is or may be entitled, or to injure some proprietary right of that person, with intent to cause economic loss.[209] It seems that an intention to do acts which will defraud is sufficient, and a 'good motive' cannot negative that.[210] If the offence is directed at a public official, what is proscribed is an agreement between two or more persons 'by dishonesty'

---

[206] *Mikolajczak v Poland* [2013] EWHC 432 (admin).

[207] Most such cases will amount to an offence under s. 2, since there will be an implied false representation and an intent to cause loss or the risk of loss.   [208] [1975] AC 819.

[209] An attempt has been made to narrow the scope of the crime to cover only actual or potential 'injury' to a proprietary right or interest of the victim: *Evans* [2014] 1 WLR 2817; but that might be too narrow bearing in mind the breadth of the definition of the offence in *Scott*. See P. Jarvis, 'Conspiracy to Defraud: A Siren to Lure Unwary Prosecutors' [2014] Crim LR 738.   [210] *Wai Yu-tsang* [1992] 1 AC 269.

to cause the official to act contrary to his or her public duty. There seem to be few prosecutions for conspiracy to defraud directed at public officials.[211] The controversies mainly concern the first form of the offence.

It is, in the first place, a crime of conspiracy. Conspiracy is one of the three inchoate offences in English criminal law, to be discussed in Chapter 11, but conspiracy may also be charged when the acts agreed upon have actually been committed. The definition of conspiracy to defraud is so wide that it criminalizes agreements to do things which, if done by an individual, would not amount to an offence. In its 1994 report the Law Commission accepted that in principle this is objectionable, but maintained that there are 'compelling' practical reasons for retaining the offence, at least until a general review of dishonesty offences is completed.[212] In its final 2002 report, the Law Commission criticized the offence for being 'so wide that it offers little guidance on the difference between fraudulent and lawful conduct', and recommended its abolition as part of the reforms that became the Fraud Act 2006.[213] However, the government declined to put forward a provision abolishing conspiracy to defraud, taking the view that prosecutors needed to have time to determine whether the Fraud Act offences would cover all the types of case or whether some lacunae would exist.[214] The matter is therefore to be reviewed in a few years, and in the meantime prosecutors will continue to enjoy the advantages of rolling together a number of instances into a single charge of conspiracy to defraud, within the guidance laid down by the Attorney General.[215] In the extradition case of *Norris v United States of America*[216] the House of Lords emphasized the importance of the certainty requirement under human rights law and held that there was no authority for regarding price-fixing as constituting conspiracy to defraud. There remains a strong argument that the offence is too uncertain to satisfy the requirements of the Convention, an argument accepted by both the Law Commission[217] and the Joint Committee on Human Rights.[218] The government disagrees, and a challenge has yet to be made (necessarily, in a case where the conduct alleged would not amount to conspiracy to commit an existing offence).

10.10 DISHONESTY, DISCRETION, AND 'DESERT'

There is a wide range of issues of principle raised by the approach of the legislature and the courts to offences of dishonesty. The most obvious of these is the government's refusal to accept that the offence of conspiracy to defraud fails to measure up to the principle of legal certainty, and the strong suspicion that the ubiquitous requirement of 'dishonesty'

---

[211] Cf. *Moses* [1991] Crim LR 617.   [212] Law Com No. 228, *Conspiracy to Defraud*, summarized at [1995] Crim LR 97 and discussed by Sir John Smith at [1995] Crim LR 209.

[213] Law Com No. 276, *Fraud* (2002), para. 1.6.

[214] See *Smith's Law of Theft*, n 17, 219–25, for an examination of the arguments.

[215] Attorney General, *Guidance on the Use of the Common Law Offence of Conspiracy to Defraud* (2007).

[216] [2008] UKHL 16.   [217] Law Com No. 276, para. 5.28.

[218] Joint Committee on Human Rights, *Legislative Scrutiny: Fourteenth Progress Report* (2006).

is also lacking in certainty. Apart from the three exceptions in s. 2 of the 1968 Act, which apply only to offences of theft, the meaning of 'dishonesty' is left at large, with only the 'ordinary standards of reasonable and honest people' to steer the jury or magistrates towards a conclusion. This ample discretion—which is what it amounts to, since there is no touchstone of social honesty—opens the way to retrospective standard-setting (which derogates from the rule of law because D did not have an opportunity to adjust his conduct to the standard), to inconsistent decisions (which amount to arbitrariness that detracts from the rule of law), and to discriminatory decisions (which detract from equality before the law). No doubt, prosecutors and some judges regard flexibility as a great virtue in the law, but it runs counter to any principles which regard Art. 7 and the principle of legality and respect for individual autonomy as central values.[219] As the Law Commission now accepts, following the Human Rights Act, efforts must be made to redefine at least some of the property offences in a way which cuts down or structures this wide discretion. It is a great irony that the CLRC, in the report that preceded and proposed the Theft Act 1968, purported to recognize, 'the principle of English law to give reasonable guidance as to what kinds of conduct are criminal'.[220]

The definitions of some of the offences under the Theft Act are notable for their breadth. Theft and robbery cover wide areas of minor and major wrongdoing, without differentiation in the label. Some offences spill over into areas normally occupied by inchoate offences or by law of complicity. The inchoate mode of definition is used with regard to burglary contrary to s. 9(1)(a), 'entering as a trespasser with intent to steal', and—more significantly—it is adopted for the crime of theft itself: the main conduct element is an 'appropriation', which may be fulfilled by any assumption of the right of an owner, even if it is with the owner's consent.[221] One consequence is to push back the crime of attempted theft even further, so that in *Morris*[222] theft was constituted by swapping labels on goods in the supermarket, and attempted theft would presumably be committed by such acts as trying to peel off the labels prior to swapping them. This presses criminal liability too far. The Fraud Act 2006 accentuates this tendency, since its main offences are phrased in an inchoate mode. Another example is provided by the offence of handling, for which the legislature has cast the net so wide (assisting in, or arranging to assist in, the retention, removal, disposal, or realization of stolen goods) as to cover conduct which would normally be charged as aiding and abetting, etc.[223] Again, one consequence of this is that the law of complicity applies so as to extend the boundaries of the wide offence of handling still further. Just as attempted theft might be termed a doubly inchoate offence, so aiding and abetting an offence of handling stolen goods might be called a doubly secondary offence.

Thus the flexibility of the 'broad band' approach to definitions in the Theft Act 1968, together with the anomalous contours of criminalization, has meant that the outer boundaries of the law (and particularly the lower boundaries) are uncertain and shifting.

---

[219] See the fairness principles discussed in Chapter 4.   [220] CLRC, 8th Report (1966), para. 99(i).
[221] See section 10.1(a), discussing *Gomez*.   [222] [1984] AC 320.
[223] See section 10.9.

One consequence of *Gomez*[224] combined with *Hinks*[225] is that the focus of the law of theft has been moved from the misappropriation of others' property towards the punishment of dishonesty. This has caused a great deal of fuss from those who hold that the criminal law should not punish unless there is also a civil wrong, a point that might also be argued against the present definition of blackmail, whereas the stronger objections to the effects of *Hinks* on the law of theft are the deficit in fair warning that comes from reliance on the term 'dishonesty', a contestable concept that invites variable social and moral judgments and is insufficient to guide citizens in the regulation of their conduct.[226]

The legislative and judicial development of dishonesty offences charted in this chapter shows little attachment to a policy of minimum criminalization, and indicates ready resort to the criminal sanction as 'social defence' against relatively minor forms of dishonesty. The Fraud Act may be a much-needed modernization of the law, but it is also a significant extension of the ambit of the criminal law. No efforts have been made to remove many of the lesser appropriations, frauds, and handlings from the criminal law. The problem appears to be that it is hard to find a workable distinction between these minor forms of dishonesty and dishonest appropriations of property which are quite serious. English law has no provision equivalent to the *de minimis* section of the Model Penal Code, allowing a defence where the conduct was not serious enough to warrant conviction.[227] There is a provision in the *Code for Crown Prosecutors in England* which states that it is not in the public interest to bring a prosecution where only a nominal penalty would be likely.[228] However, when such guidance has to be relied on frequently, it takes on the character of authoritarianism criticized in Chapter 4.5, because the matter becomes one largely of discretion controlled by officials, leaving the boundaries of the criminal law in a distinctly uncertain state. The point is strengthened by the presence of civil remedies for many acts of dishonesty concerning property. One approach is to regard the value of the appropriated goods or services as the crucial element, and to place all cases below a certain sum into a separate category—cancellation of the offence if the taker repays what was taken within seven days, for example, as in the French bad-cheque law.[229] English law has now quietly taken a momentous step in this direction, mentioned earlier,[230] of empowering the police to issue a Penalty Notice for Disorder (NPD) in respect of any retail theft under £200, although the expectation is that thefts of £100 or over will only exceptionally be dealt with by a PND. This echoes a radical proposal made twenty years ago,[231] and may be seen as a small step towards recognizing the minor nature of many shop thefts.[232]

---

[224] [1993] AC 442.   [225] [2001] 2 AC 241.

[226] See section 10.2(e), and cf. the further discussion by Bogg and Stanton-Ife, n 32, with Ormerod, n 184, 635–41, on the problems of 'dishonesty' in fraud offences.

[227] Model Penal Code, s. 212.   [228] *Code for Crown Prosecutors* (5th edn., 2004), para. 5.10(a).

[229] For an outline see C. Anyangwe, 'Dealing with the Problem of Bad Cheques in France' [1978] Crim LR 31.

[230] Section 10.1.

[231] See A. Ashworth, 'Prosecution, Police and the Public: A Guide to Good Gate Keeping' (1984) 23 Howard JCJ 621.

[232] There may be disadvantages of such measures, in terms of police power and the treatment of very poor offenders: see A. Ashworth and M. Redmayne, *The Criminal Process* (4th edn., 2010), ch 6.

Of course, there are possible objections against each of these alternatives, not least the claim that offences of dishonesty have a significance in one's judgment of people which transcends the sum involved. But this is where we meet serious problems of proportionality and of social ambiguity or hypocrisy.[233] Many forms of conduct amounting to dishonesty offences are routinely dealt with in some non-criminal manner—large companies required to repay money on government contracts, for example, executives dismissed from employment, tax fraudsters required to pay double the underpaid tax rather than being prosecuted, and so forth. A Law Commission Working Paper argued that there is no need to criminalize those who deliberately use another person's profit-earning property in order to make secret profits, since it is generally adequate to leave the owner to sue the malefactor; yet restaurant bilkers who make off without paying a few pounds are routinely subjected to the criminal sanction.[234] Moreover, as argued above, there are few social standards of dishonesty which do not vary according to the background and circumstances of the group of citizens who are making the judgment. The argument is clearly one meant to counter the predominance of authoritarianism. The present legal definitions are so broad that they give no clear steer on how the law should be enforced, leaving a large discretion that the police and prosecutors tend to exercise on 'conventional' assumptions. As a result, enforcement practices fail to ensure equality before the law, by subjecting many minor offenders to conviction whilst adopting a different approach to some who dishonestly cause large losses to others.

There are, then, at least five conflicting principles in dishonesty offences. The principle of proportionality militates in favour of a more clearly structured restatement of these offences so as to integrate crimes from the Companies Acts and elsewhere into the general framework and emphasize their seriousness. The principle of maximum certainty urges that such a restatement should be less reliant on such broad terms as 'dishonesty', which affords insufficient guidance to citizens. The principle of fair labelling would suggest that the offence of robbery is far too wide and should be subdivided, and indeed that the offence of theft (subdivided in several other European countries) should also reflect the difference between a small taking and a substantial theft. The principle of minimum criminalization argues in favour of a reconstruction of these offences (including the new fraud offences) so as to exclude some minor forms of dishonesty and to include some major ones. On the other hand, the same principle would support the exploration of non-criminal means of dealing with some forms of dishonesty: this has been the pattern for many years, but it has generally meant that companies and well-connected persons have succeeded in avoiding the criminal sanction, when others of lowlier status have been convicted. This goes against the principle of equality before the law, since it discriminates on grounds of wealth and social position. Some propose to resolve this conflict by maintaining non-criminal means of dealing

---

[233] See the sources drawn together by N. Lacey, C. Wells, and O. Quick, *Reconstructing Criminal Law* (4th edn., 2010), 328–45.

[234] Pointed out by A. T. H. Smith, 'Conspiracy to Defraud' [1988] Crim LR 508, at 513, commenting on the Law Com. Working Paper No. 104.

with commercial fraud, since these can be more effective,[235] whilst redoubling efforts to narrow down the ambit of the criminal sanction for minor forms of dishonesty. Unfortunately, the present tendency is towards the former but not the latter.[236]

FURTHER READING

S. P. Green, *Lying, Cheating and Stealing: a Moral Theory of White-Collar Crime* (Oxford University Press, 2006).

S. P. Green, *Thirteen Ways to Steal a Bicycle: Theft Law in the Information Age* (Harvard University Press, 2012).

D. Ormerod, 'The Fraud Act 2006—Criminalising Lying?' [2007] *Criminal Law Review* 193–219.

D. Ormerod and D. H. Williams, *Smith's Law of Theft* (9th edn., Oxford University Press, 2007).

A. T. H. Smith, *Property Offences* (Sweet & Maxwell, 1994).

---

[235] Cf. J. Braithwaite and B. Fisse, 'The Allocation of Responsibility for Corporate Crime' (1988) 11 Sydney LR 468, with Levi, *Regulating Fraud*.

[236] Royal Commission on Criminal Justice, *Report*, Cm 2263 (1993), para. 7.63; Serious Fraud Office, *Annual Report 1993–94* (1994).

11

COMPLICITY

11.1 INTRODUCTION

The question of complicity may arise when two or more people play some part in the commission of an offence.[1] It has already been noted, in discussing the various public order offences,[2] and will be emphasized later, when discussing conspiracy,[3] that the criminal law regards offences involving more than one person as thereby enhanced in seriousness. Joint criminal activity often involves planning and a mutually reinforcing determination to offend. The fact that any activity is known by the participants to be group activity will—even when it is spontaneously undertaken—usually make it difficult for an individual to withdraw for fear of letting the others down and losing face. When, more specifically, people act as a group in committing crime, their offending may escalate in nature or broaden in scope as a feature of group dynamics.[4]

Having said that, there are, of course, different degrees of involvement in a criminal enterprise. For example, someone (X) may not as such be part of a joint criminal enterprise involving A, B, and C, but may agree in exchange for payment to provide A, B, and C with some goods or services known by X to be a part of A, B, and C's plans for the commission of the crime. In this case, X is not part of the group committed to the joint criminal venture him or herself, but may still be treated in law as an accessory to

---

[1] See the monograph by K. J. M. Smith, *A Modern Treatise on the Law of Criminal Complicity* (1991); Law Commission, *Participating in Crime* (Law Com No. 305, 2007), Part 2 and App B.

[2] See Chapter 9.3(g).   [3] See Chapter 12.4.

[4] N. Kumar Katyal, 'Conspiracy Theory' (2003) 112 Yale LJ 1307. See now *R v Jogee* [2016] UKSC 8, para 11.

the crime if it is committed by A, B, and C.[5] More remotely, Y—a bystander—may see the crime in progress as it is committed by A, B, and C, but do nothing to assist the police when they try to arrest A, B, and C, perhaps jeering instead at the officers' efforts. Is Y's reprehensible conduct enough to make him or her complicit in the offence? One of the main issues in the law of complicity is the proper scope of criminal liability: how much involvement should be necessary, as a minimum, if someone is to be regarded as complicit in a crime committed by another person?

Let us take a hypothetical example of a burglary, in which A plans the theft of certain valuable articles from a country house. He talks to B and C, who agree to carry out the burglary for him by breaking into the house and stealing the articles. They approach D, who has worked at the house, for information which will help them to gain entry. They arrange for E to drive them to the house in a large van and to transport the stolen goods after the burglary; and they agree with F that he should come and position himself near the main gates of the house in order to warn them if anyone approaches. If A, B, C, D, E, and F all do as planned, what should be the extent of their criminal liability? As we will see, the law treats them all as guilty of burglary, irrespective of the differences between their contributions to the offence.

It is apparent that B and C are the only ones to have fulfilled the definition of the crime of burglary, by entering the house as trespassers and stealing property from it.[6] They are guilty as what the law calls 'principal' offenders. It should then be asked whether there is sufficient justification for bringing A, D, E, and F within the ambit of the criminal law at all. Would the law not be more effective if it concentrated on the principal offenders? The main difficulty in answering this question is that, in some crimes, the conduct of the accomplices may be no less serious or significant than that of the principals. Here, A is the 'mastermind' behind the offence and, although B and C freely accept his invitation to become involved, A's planning is a decisive factor. In effect, the joint criminal enterprise involves A, B, and C together. At a different level, D, E, and even F are knowingly involved in advancing the criminal endeavour agreed on by A, B, and C. They have voluntarily lent their support to the offence: the culpability resides in the decision to support the commission of the crime agreed on by A, B, and C, and the role they accept in the crime is a practical manifestation of that support.

Further, with joint criminal activity, such as that engaged in by A, B, and C, (assisted by D, E, and F) in the example just given, the culpability question is not just about measuring each participant's personal contribution to the enterprise on its own; that would be too individualistic. There is a sense in which the wrongdoing as a whole is greater than the sum of the parts, morally and hence legally. An extra element of culpability

---

[5] It has been suggested that those who merely assist or encourage a joint enterprise (or who assist or encourage an individual intending to commit or committing the crime) should be guilty only of the inchoate offence of assisting or encouraging crime: see the Law Commission, Consultation Paper No 131, *Assisting and Encouraging Crime*, 1993. However, the New South Wales Law Commission recommended retention of the English common law approach, in this respect, under which assisting or encouraging the commission of an offence makes one an accessory to, and open to conviction of, the offence itself: Report 129 (2010), *Complicity*.   [6] Theft Act 1968, s. 9; see Chapter 10.5.

comes from the fact that, however small an individual's own practical contribution may have been (it may have been no more than an agreement and intention to take part, with no action to follow this up), he or she knew as a matter of common sense that, by joining in and hence assisting or encouraging a larger scheme of activity, that contribution played a part in constituting or sustaining the larger scheme itself. For example:

> P asks D to provide him with a copy of a stolen key that P says is the key to a family home. D—who knows P well—agrees in exchange for payment, realizing that P must be intending to enter the house as a trespasser with intent either to rape or to steal. P subsequently uses the copied key to enter to house and commit rape.

In this example, D may be convicted of rape, along with P. Most importantly, it will not be legally relevant that D says, 'although I must take some blame for helping P to commit an offence, I am not tainted by the fact that the offence was a sexual offence because I would have helped P whether the offence was rape or theft; I was personally indifferent to which it would be'. In the eye of the law, this claim cannot prevent D being rightly labelled a sex offender. From the moment that D realizes that a rape is one of the two offences that P may commit in the house, yet nonetheless intentionally assists P to complete the one of P's plans that involves rape, D's conduct in providing the copy of the key is regarded as so tainted by the sexual nature of the offending it assisted, that D is regarded as justifiably convicted of rape itself, and not just of an inchoate offence such as assisting rape.[7]

There are, broadly speaking, three forms of participating in crime:

> *First*, as a principal;

> *Secondly*, as an accomplice who (in the language of the Accessories and Abettors Act 1861) 'aids, abets, counsels or procures' the offence, or who is liable as a participant in a joint venture with the principal(s); and

> *Thirdly*, as someone who becomes involved in assisting the offenders only after the crime has been committed (without having agreed to this beforehand), as by helping to conceal its commission.

We will be concerned only with the first two of these modes of complicity, because they involve participation in the offence committed by the principal or principals (including the case where someone agrees *beforehand* to assist after the commission of the crime, as by concealing weapons used). We will not be concerned with those who, without any prior involvement, assist only *after* the crime has occurred, an example being where P, having committed a crime, then confesses it to his unsuspecting parents who then decide to help him to try to conceal his involvement.[8]

---

[7] See *R v Jogee* [2016] UKSC 8, para 1.

[8] This kind of assistance is dealt with by other criminal offences concerned with assisting offenders and attempting to pervert the course of justice.

It also needs to be kept in mind that the rules and principles of complicity are supported by a set of inchoate offences created by the Serious Crimes Act 2007: in particular, offences of assisting or encouraging the commission of an offence, contrary to one of the offences created by ss. 44–46 of the 2007 Act. Discussion of the offences under the 2007 Act is postponed to Chapter 12.7, since they are essentially inchoate offences. In other words, D can be found guilty of assisting or encouraging an offender under the 2007 Act even though the offence itself never takes place. An example would be where D provides P with a weapon to commit a murder, but P changes her mind or dies before committing the offence. In this example, there is no substantive offence committed by P in which D can be complicit, but D may be guilty of the inchoate offence of 'assisting murder' under the 2007 Act. However, it will be apparent that those offences overlap considerably with the forms of complicity,[9] and reference to the interaction of the two sources of liability will be made throughout this chapter.

11.2 DISTINGUISHING PRINCIPALS FROM ACCESSORIES

The simplest way of drawing this distinction is to say that a principal is a person whose acts fall within the legal definition of the crime, whereas an accomplice (sometimes called an 'accessory' or 'secondary party') is anyone who aids, abets, counsels, or procures a principal.[10] It does not follow from this that where two or more persons are involved in an offence, one must be the principal and the others accomplices. As indicated in the last section, two or more persons can be co-principals, so long as together they satisfy the definition of the substantive offence and each of them engaged in some part of the external element of the offence with the required fault. Indeed, English law goes further, holding that two or more persons can be co-principals, if each of them by his own act contributes to the commission of the external element of the offence: if all their acts together fulfil all the conduct elements, and if each of them has the required mental element:[11]

> D1 and D2 have planned to rob V. D1 holds V's arms, forcing V to drop her purse, and D2 picks up the purse before they both make their escape.

In this example, D1 and D2 are in fact co-principals even though it might superficially seem as if D1 simply helps D2 to commit the robbery. The conduct element of robbery is theft involving the use or threat of force before or at the time of the theft. That being so, D1 (with the fault element for robbery) engages in one part of the conduct element of robbery by using force against V, and D2 (also with the fault element for robbery)

---

[9] A complexity in the working of the overlap is that the 2007 Act uses the modern terminology of 'assist' and 'encourage' whereas the Accessories and Abettors Act 1861 uses the language of 'aid, abet, counsel and procure'. Whilst aiding, abetting, and counselling are broadly the same as assisting and encouraging, 'procuring' an offence is arguably something different, but we will come to that point later.

[10] *Gnango* [2011] UKSC 59, para 129 (Lord Kerr).   [11] K. J. M. Smith, n 1, 27–30.

engages in a different part of the conduct element of robbery, namely the theft. So, they are co-principals. Had a third party to the robbery plan (D3) been involved solely as a look-out, then D3 would have been an accomplice, rather than a principal. D3 may have had the fault element for robbery, but by keeping look-out D3 would not thereby have engaged in a part of the external or conduct element of robbery. Being an accomplice in a robbery, albeit not perpetrating it as a principal, will nonetheless mean that D3 will also stand to be convicted of robbery along with D1 and D2.

Some criminal offences are so defined that they can only be committed by two or more co-principals. The public order offences of riot and violent disorder are clear examples of this.[12] There can also be accomplices to such offences, casting the net of criminal liability even wider so as to encompass those who encourage and intend to encourage the principals.[13]

Although English law maintains the distinction between principals and accessories, in practice the substantive criminal law almost always treats them in a similar way where completed offences are concerned. The leading statute is the Accessories and Abettors Act 1861, which provides that anyone who 'shall aid, abet, counsel or procure the commission of any indictable offence … shall be liable to be tried, indicted and punished as a principal offender'. It is hard to over-estimate the significance of this provision, and it has been the source of a great deal of controversy (although common law jurisdictions have sometimes found it hard to manage without taking this approach[14]). For example, during the Apartheid era in South Africa, a provision that drew inspiration from the 1861 Act—s. 18 of the Riotous Assemblies Act 1956—was very broadly construed to impose criminal liability on leaders of dissident or protest organizations who had arranged political meetings at which offending was engaged in by one or more of those at the meetings.[15] As the wording of the 1861 Act indicates, accessories (those who aid, abet, counsel, or procure) are liable to be tried as punished *as principal offenders*. So, if D (the accessory) assists or encourages P (the principal) to commit murder, however minor D's assistance or encouragement, D is liable to be convicted of murder itself, along with P, and will accordingly also receive the mandatory life sentence (albeit, perhaps, with a slightly shorter initial period in prison than P). In cases other than murder, D will be convicted of the same crime and P and may receive up to and including the maximum penalty for the substantive offence. As we pointed out earlier, though, an accessory could be as much or more to blame than a principal offender. An example might be where D is P's tyrannical father, and threatens P with a beating unless P commits a crime, which P consequently does.

Of equal importance are the procedural consequences of the rule laid down in the 1861 Act. It means that the prosecution can obtain a conviction without specifying in advance whether the allegation is that D is a principal or an accomplice, or what form

---

[12] See Chapter 9.3(g).   [13] *Jefferson* et al. (1994) 99 Cr App R 13.
[14] See New South Wales Law Commission, n 5.
[15] The real controversy in such cases stemmed from the fact that—in breach of the participants' human rights—the political meetings themselves were illegal, thus paving the way for the application of a 1861 Act-style form of liability on the organizers in relation to criminal activity arising from the meetings.

the alleged complicity took.[16] This is because, whoever was in fact the accessory and who in fact the principal does not matter in terms of the offence for which they are tried: the 1861 Act says they can all be tried, convicted, and punished as principal offenders. This is undoubtedly a great convenience for the prosecution in certain types of case. Thus in *Giannetto*,[17] the prosecution case, based on circumstantial evidence, was that G certainly either killed his wife or was an accomplice by virtue of hiring someone else to kill her; but there was insufficient evidence to show clearly which kind of involvement characterized G's role. The Court of Appeal upheld the conviction, holding that the jury 'were entitled to convict [of murder] if they were all satisfied that if he was not the killer he at least encouraged the killing'. The Court added that 'the defendant knows perfectly well what case he has to meet',[18] that is, both those allegations.

Does this amount to adequate notice of the charge(s) to be met? While appellate courts have repeatedly encouraged prosecutors to frame indictments in as much detail as possible,[19] it is also clear that 'if the Crown nail their colours to a particular mast, their case will, generally, have to be established in the terms in which it is put'[20]— which creates a disincentive to framing the indictment in detail. Challenges to these rules of criminal law and procedure under the Human Rights Act, on the basis that the charge fails to satisfy the Art. 6(3)(a) requirement to inform a defendant 'in detail of the nature and cause of the allegation against him', have not met with success,[21] but there remains the point of principle whether defendants in such cases always receive fair warning.

The 1861 English statute is sometimes compared unfavourably with such systems as that in Germany, which restricts the maximum penalty for an accomplice to three-quarters that of the principal;[22] but the comparison is not a straightforward one. It is true that accomplices are normally less blameworthy than principals and therefore deserve less severe sentences. It is also true that a law which produces a conviction of murder and a sentence of life imprisonment for giving relatively minor assistance to a murderer is unjust (though the injustice stems as much from the mandatory penalty for murder as from the law of complicity). But systems like the German system seem not to provide for those cases in which the accomplice is no less culpable or even more culpable, than the principal, as indicated. One way of providing for all degrees of complicity would be to retain the legal power to impose any lawful sentence on the principal, but to respect the accomplice's right not to be punished more severely than is proportionate to the gravity of his contribution by declaring a general guideline that

---

[16] See *Montague* [2013] EWCA Crim 1781.   [17] [1997] 1 Cr App R 1.

[18] *Per* Kennedy LJ at 8–9, following (*inter alia*) the Supreme Court of Canada in *Thatcher* v *R* (1987) 39 DLR (3d) 275, where Dickson CJC asked (at 306): 'why should the juror be compelled to make a choice on a subject which is a matter of legal indifference?'.

[19] *Maxwell* v *DPP for Northern Ireland* [1979] 1 WLR 1350 (HL); *Taylor, Harrison and Taylor* [1998] Crim LR 582 (CA); cf. P. R. Glazebrook, 'Structuring the Criminal Code', in A. P. Simester and A. T. H. Smith (eds), *Harm and Culpability* (1996), at 198–201.   [20] *Giannetto* [1997] 1 Cr App R 1, at 9.

[21] *Mercer* [2001] All ER (D) 187 confronted the point directly; *Concannon* [2002] Crim LR 215 dismissed a different and less persuasive argument.   [22] See G. Fletcher, *Rethinking Criminal Law* (1978) 634ff.

the starting point in sentencing accomplices should be that they receive no more than half the sentence of the principal. This more regulated approach to sentencing would be a significant step, at least for so long as English law fails to reflect the different degrees of involvement in crime by assigning different legal labels.

Finally, how does the law of complicity cope with cases where it can be proved that each of two defendants was at least an accomplice but cannot be proved which one was the principal?[23] Where, in a case of a child's death caused by drugs, it can be shown that one or other parent administered methadone to their young child whilst one or the other stood by, it matters not that the prosecution cannot establish which parent administered it because the other parent must at least be an accomplice, having failed to intervene to save the child.[24] Having said that, if in such a situation it cannot be established that both parents were present throughout, then it follows that it cannot be proved that both of them were at least accomplices, and the prosecution must fail.[25] To deal with this situation, as we saw earlier,[26] the Domestic Violence, Crime and Victims Act 2004 contains a new offence: causing or allowing the death or serious physical harm to a child or vulnerable adult, reinforced by inferences from silence, in an attempt to fill this gap.

11.3 THE CONDUCT ELEMENT IN COMPLICITY

We have seen that the 1861 Act refers to those who 'aid, abet, counsel, or procure' a crime. As a matter of history, it seems that this Act was intended only to declare the procedure whereby accomplices could be convicted and sentenced as principals, and not to provide a definition of complicity. Earlier statutes had used a wide range of terms—contriving, helping, maintaining, directing—and the wording of the 1861 Act was probably intended merely as a general reference to the existing common law on accomplices. However, the words have taken on an authority of their own. In 1976 the Court of Appeal declared that each of the four verbs should be given its ordinary meaning,[27] but, as we shall see, there are several decisions on the scope of the four terms. One factor that formerly had considerable importance was presence during the commission of the crime. So long as the other conditions for liability were fulfilled, presence turned the accomplice into an aider or abettor, absence into a counsellor or procurer.[28] However, it appears that the distinction no longer has any practical consequences in English law.[29] Whether an accomplice is described as an aider, abettor, counsellor, or procurer seems to depend partly on ordinary language and partly on

---

[23] *Gianetto* [1997] 1 Cr App R 1; *Montague* [2013] EWCA Crim 1781.

[24] *Russell and Russell* (1987) 85 Cr App R 388; *Emery* (1993) 14 Cr App R (S) 394.

[25] *Lane and Lane* (1986) 82 Cr App R 5. See, most recently, *Banfield* [2013] EWCA Crim 1394.

[26] Chapter 8.6.   [27] *Attorney-General's Reference (No. 1 of 1975)* [1975] QB 773.

[28] See, e.g., Lord Goddard CJ in *Ferguson v Weaving* [1951] 1 KB 814, and generally J. C. Smith, 'Aid, Abet, Counsel or Procure', in P. R. Glazebrook (ed.), *Reshaping the Criminal Law* (1978).

[29] *Howe* [1987] AC 417, overruling *Richards* [1974] QB 776.

specific judicial decisions. In relation to the use of these terms, we should note that the modern judicial preference is to use 'encourage' in place of 'counsel', and 'assist' in place of 'aid' and 'abet'. In the recent case of *R v Jogee*,[30] the Supreme Court used the terms 'encourage' and 'assist' almost exclusively, when setting out the modern law.[31] However, tempting though it may be to do so, one cannot simply replace the older terms with the more modern ones. For example, as we shall see, 'counselling' is broader than 'encouraging' because it includes the mere provision of advice or information.

(a) AIDING AND ABETTING

It has been traditional to consider the modes of complicity in terms of the two time-honoured pairings: 'aid or abet', and 'counsel or procure'. In fact, the concept of abetment seems to play no independent role now. Abetting involves some encouragement of the principal to commit the offence and this usually accompanies, or is implicit in, an act of aiding. Aid may be given by supplying an instrument to the principal, keeping a look-out, doing preparatory acts, and many other forms of assistance given before or at the time of the offence. As long as it has been shown that the accomplice's conduct helped or might have helped the principal in some way, it does not have to be established that the accomplice caused the principal's offence. Causation requirements often function so as to fix the threshold of legal liability. However, one cannot, in general, trace causal responsibility through the voluntary and intentional act of another person[32]—so it will not usually be possible to hold that an accomplice *caused* the principal to act, save in a rather diluted form of 'causing'.[33] Sanford Kadish has argued that the law does require a form of causation: the courts must be satisfied that the accomplice's help *might* have made a difference to whether the principal's offence was actually committed, in the sense that one could not be sure that it would have been committed but for the accomplice's assistance.[34] However, it is not easy to reconcile all decisions with this approach.

Thus in *Wilcox v Jeffery* a jazz enthusiast attended a concert, applauding the decision of an American jazz musician to give an illegal performance. No point was taken in court about whether the musician was actually encouraged by the defendant's acts.[35] Indeed, in cases where several people applaud or encourage some kind of unlawful spectacle, it would be difficult to maintain that the performer(s) drew actual encouragement from the acts of any one of the spectators. In *Giannetto*[36] the Court of Appeal stated that 'any involvement from mere encouragement upwards would suffice', and did not dissent from the trial judge's suggestion that, if another man had said to D that he was about to kill D's wife, as little as patting him on the back, nodding and saying 'Oh goody' would be sufficient to turn D into an aider and abettor. This suggests that even

---

[30] *R v Jogee* [2016] UKSC 8.
[31] Although, in *Jogee*, at para 12 of the judgment, counselling is equated with encouraging.
[32] See Chapter 5.6(a) and (b).
[33] Cf. H. L. A. Hart and T. Honoré, *Causation in the Law* (2nd edn., 1985), 388.
[34] S. Kadish, *Blame and Punishment* (1987), 162.   [35] [1951] 1 All ER 464.
[36] [1997] 1 Cr App R 1, at 13.

at this late stage a small amount of encouragement, giving moral support to or showing solidarity with the principal, is thought to be sufficient for liability.

What if the principal is unaware of the help given by the secondary party? In the famous American case of *State* v *Tally*,[37] Judge Tally, knowing that his brothers-in-law had set out to kill the deceased, and knowing that someone else had sent a telegram to warn the victim, sent a telegram to the telegraph operator telling him not to deliver the warning telegram. The telegraph operator complied, and the brothers-in-law committed the offence. The judge was convicted of aiding and abetting murder, even though the brothers-in-law were unaware of the judge's assistance when they killed the victim. There was a causal connection in this case, but no meeting of minds between D and P. The absence of the latter might raise a question over whether the judge's act should be sufficient for complicity, although, as we will see below, it amounts to the inchoate offence of encouraging or assisting an offence contrary to s. 44 of the Serious Crime Act 2007. However, as D1 can become complicit in D2's offence by simply agreeing that the offence will be committed (or where D1 and D2 share a common intention to commit the offence),[38] or by giving encouragement as part of a crowd, even though neither act assists or encourages D2 as such, it would be anomalous if D1's crucial act of knowing assistance was insufficient to make D1 complicit in D2's crime.

(b) ACCOMPLICE LIABILITY AND SOCIAL DUTIES

The key question here, in accessorial liability, is simple to state: can a person be convicted as an accomplice merely for standing by and doing nothing while an offence is being committed? If mere presence at the scene during the principal's offence were sufficient for accomplice liability, this would amount to recognizing a citizen's duty either to leave straight away or to take reasonable steps to prevent or frustrate any offence which is witnessed.

The courts have held that non-accidental presence, such as attending a fight or an unlawful theatrical performance, is not conclusive evidence of aiding and abetting.[39] At a minimum there must be an act of encouragement (accompanied by an intention to encourage, discussed in section 11.4), although in unusual instances—where D1's 'forbidding presence' is itself meant to and does encourage D2 to commit a crime, mere presence could be enough.[40] Some judgments suggest that it must be shown that encouragement was not just given but also had some effect on the principal,[41] but this has not usually been required. The factual questions are for the jury or magistrates. The requirement of an act of encouragement is not satisfied merely by going to the place where the performance is taking place, but payment and applause may suffice;[42] however, in one case it was held that remaining in a vehicle that was being used to obstruct

---

[37] *State* v *Tally* (1894) 15 So 722.   [38] *Rook* [1993] 2 All ER 955.   [39] *Coney* (1882) 8 QBD 534.
[40] *Robinson* [2011] UKPC 3, para 14 (Sir Anthony Hughes). See *R* v *Jogee* [2016] UKSC 8, para 12.
[41] Hawkins J in *Coney* (1882) 8 QBD 534, and *Clarkson* [1971] 1 WLR 1402.
[42] *Wilcox* v *Jeffery* [1951] 1 All ER 464.

the police, in circumstances showing that D supported the actions of the driver, might amount to aiding.[43] The position of spectators who happen upon an illegal fight or event and stay to watch it is similar: simply sitting or standing nearby is unlikely to be sufficient for liability, but any cheering or applause would probably tip the balance in favour of conviction. The problems are particularly acute in cases of public disorder. To impose duties on bystanders, even the duty to move away, might be regarded as an incursion on a citizen's right to freedom of assembly (declared in Art. 11 of the European Convention). What must be proved, to amount to aiding and abetting one of the offences in the Public Order Act, is that D was present, was giving encouragement, and was intending to encourage others to commit the specified offence.[44] Mere presence should not be sufficient, particularly in view of Art. 11.[45]

Are there arguments in favour of the law going further and imposing a duty to take steps to prevent crime? The public disorder example may be complicated by the impotence of individuals to do anything to stop the disturbance and, indeed, the imprudence of their trying to do so. But is it not arguable that there should be at least a duty to alert the police? If so, should failure to do so constitute a distinct offence (as in French law[46]) or complicity in the public disorder? Another example, which does not involve public disorder, occurs where a woman is living with a man who she discovers is dealing in drugs. If the police raid the dwelling and find drugs on the premises, should the law treat her as an accomplice even if there is no evidence of active assistance or encouragement of the drug dealing? In the case of *Bland* (1988)[47] the Court of Appeal quashed the woman's conviction as an accomplice in such circumstances. Cases such as this demonstrate a vivid conflict between individuals' rights of privacy in their personal relationships and the social interest in suppressing serious crime. Would it be right for the law to co-opt husbands against wives, parents against children, house-sharing friends against friends in order to increase public protection?[48]

Probably the only way to answer this question is to balance the relative centrality of the right against the seriousness of the offence involved—not a simple exercise, but an inevitable one if the true nature of the problem is to be confronted. The same applies to the situation in *Clarkson*.[49] Two soldiers happened to enter a room where other

[43] *Smith* v *Reynolds* et al. [1986] Crim LR 559; for another decision based on voluntary presence, see *O'Flaherty* [2004] Crim LR 751.

[44] *Jefferson* et al. (1994) 99 Cr App R 13, at 22; for a summary of the main public order offences, see Chapter 9.3(h).

[45] More generally it should be noted, though, that D1's presence at the scene of the crime has never been necessary to make D1 an accessory. The relevant assistance or encouragement could have been given long before the crime is committed by D2, at a time when D1 is far away: *Stringer* [2011] EWCA Crim 1396.

[46] Article 223(1) of the French Penal Code, discussed by A. Ashworth and E. Steiner, 'Criminal Omissions and Public Duties: The French Experience' (1990) 10 *Legal Studies* 153.

[47] [1988] Crim LR 41; cf. also *Bradbury* [1996] Crim LR 808.

[48] Cf. s. 80 of the Police and Criminal Evidence Act 1984, which makes a husband or wife (but not a non-spouse) compellable as a witness on a charge of violence towards a child under 16 in the household; and the offence under s. 5 of the Domestic Violence, Crime and Victims Act 2004, which criminalizes any 'member of the same household' (including lodgers and frequent visitors) who fails to take steps to protect a child from the risk of serious harm.   [49] [1971] 1 WLR 1402.

soldiers were raping a woman. It was not found that they did not do anything other than watch, but they certainly did nothing to discourage continuance of the offence. The Courts Martial Appeal Court quashed their convictions for aiding and abetting, because the judge had not made it clear that there should be proof of both an intent to encourage and actual encouragement. Nothing was said about a duty to alert the authorities immediately in the hope of preventing the crime's continuance. What if three persons came upon one man raping a woman? If it was within their power to put a stop to the offence and to apprehend the offender, should they have a duty to do so—or at least a duty to inform the police?[50] The practical possibilities will vary from case to case, but the real issue is whether there is to be a principle that citizens ought to take reasonable steps to inform the police when they witness an offence. The decision in Allan[51] is against this, emphasizing the requirement of encouragement and adding that, even if D would have joined in if necessary, it would be unacceptable 'to convict a man on his thoughts, unaccompanied by any physical act other than the facts of mere presence'. However, variations in the facts of cases could be accommodated by requiring the citizen only to take 'reasonable steps',[52] and no law should require a person to place his or her own safety in jeopardy. Even if this were accepted, there would remain the question whether it is fairer to convict the defaulting citizen of a new offence of failing to inform the police rather than making the citizen into an accomplice to the principal crime. The former is surely more appropriate in terms of fair labelling.

Can a person be said to aid an offence by an omission?[53] There would surely be no awkwardness in describing the cleaner of a bank who, in pursuance of an agreed plan, purposely omits to lock the doors when leaving as 'aiding' a burglary of the bank. In such a case, there is a clear duty and a failure to perform it, and the causation question is answered (in so far as it is relevant to aiding) in the same way as for omissions generally.[54] Another example would be the driving instructor who is supervising a learner driver and who realizes that the learner is about to undertake a manoeuvre which is dangerous to other road users. If, as in *Rubie v Faulkner*,[55] the instructor fails to intervene, either by telling the learner not to do it or by physically acting to prevent it, then this failure in the duty of supervision is rightly held to be sufficient to support liability for aiding and abetting the learner driver's offence.

From these cases of duty we turn to cases of legal power, and the so-called 'control principle'. The owner of a car who is a passenger when the car is being driven by another has the legal power to direct this other person not to drive in certain ways;[56] the licensee of a public house has the legal power to require customers to leave at closing-time;[57] the owners of a house have the legal power to direct the behaviour of

---

[50] Cf. the proviso to the new offences in the Serious Crime Act 2007, to be discussed in Chapter 12.7.

[51] [1965] 1 QB 130; see further G. Williams, 'Criminal Omissions—the Conventional View' (1990) 107 LQR 86.   [52] See n 44.

[53] Smith, n 1, 39–47.   [54] See Chapter 4.5(c).

[55] [1940] 1 KB 571, discussed by M. Wasik, 'A Learner's Careless Driving' [1982] Crim LR 411, and D. J. Lanham, 'Drivers, Control and Accomplices' [1982] Crim LR 419.

[56] *Du Cros v Lambourne* [1907] 1 KB 40.   [57] *Tuck v Robson* [1970] 1 WLR 741.

their children and of visitors to their premises. In the first two cases the courts have held the car owner and the licensee liable as accomplices to the crime of the offender who drives carelessly or remains drinking after hours. What is unusual about these cases is that they rest on the legal *power* of control of, respectively, the car owner and the licensee and not, like *Rubie* v *Faulkner*, on the existence of a legal *duty* to ensure compliance with the law. A similar analysis is found in *JF Alford Transport Ltd*,[58] where the company's convictions for aiding and abetting drivers to falsify their tachograph records were quashed. If the prosecution had proved the power of control, knowledge, and encouragement by non-intervention, that would have been sufficient. The court re-asserted the control principle, although this case, unlike the previous two, did not involve D's presence during the commission of the offences; and knowledge, or wilful blindness, was held not to have been established. The control principle departs from the usual approach of not imposing liability for an omission unless a clear duty exists. What the courts have done, in effect, is to assimilate these cases of 'power of control' to cases of duty, thereby creating a new class of public duty. Even though English law does not impose liability for failing to take reasonable steps to prevent an offence which occurs in the street, these cases hold that a property owner will be liable for failing to take reasonable steps to prevent an offence which occurs on or with that property (and with the owner's knowledge). The law has, in effect, co-opted property owners as law enforcement agents in respect of their own property, and *JF Alford Transport* provides for employers to be co-opted in respect of their employees' conduct at work. The Law Commission rightly recommends the abolition of the control principle, narrowing liability to cases of failure to discharge a legal duty.

Does it amount to aiding if a shopkeeper sells an item to P knowing that P intends to use it in a crime, or if a borrower returns an article to its owner knowing that the owner intends to use it in crime? These could be said to be acts of assistance, in the sense that the physical conduct of selling or returning goods helps an offender. Should such acts, if accompanied by the required mental element, amount to aiding the principal? The problem is that the shopkeeper is simply selling goods in the normal course of business, and the borrower is merely fulfilling a duty to restore the goods to their owner (respectively, an exercise of a power and the performance of a duty). If the law were to regard either of these acts as 'aiding', it would lead to considerable confusion over when a criminal law duty is to take precedence over a civil law power or duty.

In *National Coal Board v Gamble*, Devlin J said: 'if one man deliberately sells to another a gun to be used for murdering a third, he may be indifferent whether the third man lives or dies and interested only in the cash profit to be made out of the sale, but he can still be an aider and abettor'.[59] Applied in every case, this view would make shopkeepers accomplices whenever they continued with a sale in spite of their knowledge of D's criminal intent. The same analysis would apply in cases where D1 returned something owned by D2, knowing of D's intent to use the thing to commit a crime.

---

[58] [1997] 2 Cr App R 326.   [59] *NCB* v *Gamble* [1959] 1 QB 11.

However, Devlin J's view must now be read in the light of the decision of the Supreme Court in *R v Jogee*.[60] Devlin J's indifferent gun seller cannot now be found liable for a crime committed by the gun purchaser, unless the seller intended to assist or encourage the purchaser to carry out his or her intent. Mere indifference to the carrying out of the intent is not enough.

(c) COUNSELLING AND PROCURING

The characteristic contribution of the counsellor or procurer is to incite, instigate, or advise on the commission of the substantive offence by the principal. One way of expressing this is to describe the role as 'encouraging' the perpetrator. Some European legal systems provide a higher maximum penalty for an accomplice who incites or instigates than for a mere helper, and a general justification for this can readily be found. No offence might have taken place at all but for the instigation, and this is surely more reprehensible than assisting someone who has already decided to commit a crime. In practice, however, there are many shades of culpability between helpers and instigators, a point which strikes the English lawyer more forcefully because of the uncertain limits of the terms 'counselling' and 'procuring'. The ordinary meaning of 'counselling' may fall well short of inciting or instigating an offence, and covers such conduct as advising on an offence and giving information required for an offence; whereas the ordinary meaning of 'procuring' is said to be 'to produce by endeavour',[61] which goes beyond mere instigation.

The forms of counselling and procuring recognized by English law probably stretch from the giving of advice or information through encouraging or trying to persuade another person to commit the crime to such conduct as threatening or commanding that the offence be committed. Generally speaking, the accomplice's culpability increases as one proceeds towards the extreme of a command backed by threats. In that extreme situation the principal may have the defence of duress,[62] and may be regarded as an innocent agent of the threatener, who then becomes the principal.[63] There are also cases in which the principal does not realize that someone is trying to bring about an offence: for example, if D surreptitiously laces P's non-alcoholic drink with some form of alcohol and P subsequently drives a car, unaware of the consumption of alcohol, P will be liable to conviction for drunken driving and D could be convicted of procuring the offence, so long as it was shown that D knew P was intending to drive. Such conduct fulfils the ordinary definition of procuring: 'you procure a thing by setting out to see that it happens and taking appropriate steps to produce that happening'.[64] Such a case is, though, really one in which D should be regarded as committing the offence,

---

[60] *R v Jogee* [2016] UKSC 8, para 10.   [61] *Attorney-General's Reference (No. 1 of 1975)* [1975] QB 773.
[62] See Chapter 7.3.   [63] See *Bourne* (1952) 36 Cr App R 125, discussed in section 11.6.
[64] See *Attorney-General's Reference (No. 1 of 1975)* [1975] QB 773. Cf. P. Alldridge, 'The Doctrine of Innocent Agency' (1990) 2 *Criminal Law Forum* 45.

by causing an unwitting P to engage in the relevant conduct (which is criminal only in virtue of the fact that offence in question is one of strict liability), but where D cannot be found guilty of the offence as a principal because D did not drive: P did. The Law Commission has proposed that such odd cases be dealt with through a new offence of 'causing another to commit a no fault offence'.[65]

The ordinary meaning of procuring, 'to produce by endeavour', is not restricted to cases where the principal is unaware of the accomplice's design. One can take the appropriate steps to bring about a crime by persuading another to do the required acts—for example, by shaming someone into committing an offence by taunts of cowardice—but conduct such as hiring 'hit-men' to carry out an offence is probably better described as counselling.[66] It can be said that in cases of procuring there is a causal relationship between the accomplice's procuring and the principal's act, and it is proper to say that the principal acts *in consequence of* the accomplice's conduct.[67] These cases, then, represent the high-watermark of causal connection among the various types of accessorial conduct, headed by the case of procuring an unwitting principal (where D laces P's drink), in which there is no meeting of minds between principal and accomplice. Such a strong causal connection is not found in counselling, which may merely involve the supply of information, advice, or encouragement. This led Professor Sir John Smith to conclude that: 'procuring requires causation but not consensus; encouraging requires consensus but not causation; assisting requires actual help but neither consensus nor causation'.[68] If cases of hiring hit-men are classified as counselling or encouraging, then all that is required is that the accomplice and principal reached some kind of agreement on what was to be done, with the accomplice encouraging the principal (usually by offering money) to carry out the crime.[69]

(d) THE PROBLEMS OF THE CONDUCT ELEMENT

We should note at this point some of the difficulties of the conduct element. It is not just that the four key terms are opaque and that basic questions of principle and policy (concerning, for example, omissions liability and social duties) are resolved on a case-by-case basis. There are two more fundamental difficulties, stemming largely from the breadth of the concept of 'aiding'. The first is that any contribution by the accomplice seems to suffice for liability, no matter how small. This brings both uncertainty and the potential for injustice. The second and related difficulty is that the element of causation stemming from the accomplice's assistance may be slight. Should cases where D's contribution has no causal impact on P's commission of the offence lead to D's liability for the substantive offence, let alone the sentence for it, particularly if that sentence is

---

[65] Law Com No. 305, Part 4.
[66] As on the facts of *Richards* [1974] QB 776, and of *Calhaem* [1985] QB 808.
[67] Hart and Honoré, n 31, 51–9, and Chapter 4.5(d).
[68] Smith, n 28, 134; perhaps the words 'actual or potential help' might be preferable.
[69] *Calhaem* [1985] QB 808.

mandatory (as in murder)? In *R v Jogee*, the Supreme Court had this to say about the supposed causal element:

> Once encouragement or assistance is proved to have been given, the prosecution does not have to go so far as to prove that it had a positive effect on D1's conduct or on the outcome: *R v Calhaem* [1985] QB 808. In many cases that would be impossible to prove.[70]

However, one might ask rhetorically, 'how can someone be complicit in a crime when it cannot be proved that they have contributed anything?' Is not such a person guilty only of an inchoate offence of assisting or encouraging, contrary to part 2 the Serious Crime Act 2007, even if the principal offender happens to carry out the crime in question? A partial answer to these questions may be that, at least in some cases, one must distinguish between D1's individual contribution to D2's offence, by way of encouraging or assist-ing, and D1's contribution to that offence by way of his or her role in a collective act of encouraging or assisting. For example, as the Supreme Court goes on to point out in the passage immediately following the quotation above, when the question is whether D1 encouraged D2 by shouting, when D1's shouts were only a small contribution to a wall of sound created by thousands of people, D1's causal contribution to encouraging D2 must be understood in terms of the contribution made collectively by D1 and thousands of others. The same might be true in a case of assisting, where D1 plays a role along with dozens of others, in forming a circle of people preventing participants in an illegal fight from escaping the fight. In such an example, even if D1 never him or herself has to pre-vent a contestant escaping, his or her contribution to the formation of the circle should be enough to convict him of offences committed by the contestants themselves.

Where the contribution is small and non-essential—such as driving P to a place close to where the offence is to be committed[71]—the sufficiency of the influence of the causal contribution may also be questioned.[72] Under the Serious Crime Act 2007, it would now be a separate offence of encouraging or assisting crime, but the penalty structure is the same.

11.4 THE BASIC FAULT ELEMENTS IN COMPLICITY

The fault required for conviction as an accomplice differs from that required for all other forms of criminal liability. This is because it concerns not merely the defendant's awareness of the nature and effect of his own acts, but also his awareness of the inten-tions of the principal. It is a form of two-dimensional fault, which brings with it various complexities: the would-be accomplice's knowledge of the principal's intentions may be more or less detailed, and in any event the principal might not do exactly as planned.

There are two basic fault elements that must be proved in all cases. First, the ac-complice must intend to do whatever acts of assistance or encouragement are done,

---

[70] *R v Jogee* [2016] UKSC 8, para 12.   [71] As in *Bryce* [2004] 2 Cr App R 35.
[72] See the strong arguments by G. R. Sullivan, 'First Degree Murder and Complicity' (2007) 1 Crim Law & Phil 271; cf. J. Gardner, 'Complicity and Causality' (2007) 1 Crim Law & Phil 127, at 137.

and must be aware of their ability to assist or encourage the principal.[73] Secondly, the accomplice must know the 'essential matters which constitute the offence'.[74] The scope of this oft-quoted phrase is unclear. It seems that it includes the facts, circumstances, and other matters that go to make up the conduct element of the principal offence; but, there is uncertainty about the extent to which the accomplice must know the details of the offence. Some issues can be resolved by basic propositions. If the aider knows the nature of the offence which the principal intends to commit but does not know when it is to occur, that should be immaterial: time is rarely specified as an element in the definition of a crime. The same applies to the location of the offence: so long as the aider knows that the principal plans to burgle a bank, ignorance as to the particular bank is immaterial to accomplice liability.[75] The real difficulties begin when the aider or counsellor does not know precisely what offence the principal intends to commit, and has only a general idea. Should this be sufficient?

Let us suppose that D lends P some mechanical cutting equipment, knowing full well that P intends to use it in connection with a forthcoming crime but having no precise idea of the crime intended: D does not ask, and P does not tell. In fact, P uses the equipment in a burglary. On facts similar to these, the decision in *Bainbridge*[76] held that neither mere suspicion nor broad knowledge of some criminal intention is sufficient: the minimum condition for accomplice liability is knowledge that the principal intends to commit a crime of the *type* actually committed. This decision clearly goes against, or beyond, the basic requirement that the accomplice should know the essential matters that constitute the principal's crime.[77] Should this extension of liability be opposed, since knowledge of the particular crime committed ought to be required, because the theory is that the accomplice's liability derives from the principal's offence? Or, should it be accepted as a pragmatic solution which avoids the acquittals of those who assist willingly without knowing the precise form of offence envisaged? This might depend on the breadth of the term 'type', and some light is thrown on this by the decision of the House of Lords in *Maxwell v DPP for Northern Ireland*.[78] Maxwell was persuaded to drive a car for a group of terrorists, knowing broadly what offences they *might* commit, but not knowing which one or ones they *would* commit. It was held that he was liable as an accomplice to the offence of doing an act with intent to cause an explosion, so long as he contemplated that offence as one of the possible offences and intentionally lent his assistance. As Lord Scarman put it: 'an accessory who leaves it to his principal to choose is liable, provided always the choice is made from the range of offences from which the accessory contemplates the choice will be made'.[79] So, as far as inchoate liability is concerned—where the principal does not go on to commit the crime assisted or encouraged, i.e. the matter is now dealt with by the offence in s. 46 of

---

[73] Smith, n 1, 141.   [74] *Johnson* v *Youden* [1950] 1 KB 544.   [75] *Bainbridge* [1960] 1 QB 219.

[76] *Bainbridge* [1960] 1 QB 219.

[77] See *Johnson* v *Youden* [1950] 1 KB 544. The Law Commission was prepared to describe the *Bainbridge* judgment as an 'evasion' of this basic requirement: LCCP, *Assisting and Encouraging Crime*, para. 3.22.

[78] [1978] 3 All ER 1140.   [79] *Maxwell* was approved in *R v Jogee*: [2016] UKSC 8, para 15–16.

the Serious Crime Act 2007, of encouraging or assisting offences believing that one or more will be committed. As its name suggests, this offence aims to deal with the very situation that arose in *Maxwell*, and it does so by the creation of this new offence in the inchoate mode—an offence committed whether or not the principal goes ahead.[80]

11.5 COMPLICITY AND FAULT-BASED OFFENCES

(a) ASSISTING OR ENCOURAGING AN OFFENCE WITH A FAULT ELEMENT

In the preceding section, we saw that the basic elements of complicity that must be proved against someone alleged to be an accomplice are (a) an intention to assist or encourage the offence, and (b) knowledge of the circumstances of the offence.[81] These basic elements must be proved against an alleged accomplice even when the offence committed by the principal is a strict liability offence. There is no inconsistency in strict liability cases, in insisting that the accomplice must be shown to have satisfied the basic elements, including knowledge of the circumstances, whilst no fault need be proved against the principal. On the one hand, someone (the principal offender) can engage in forbidden conduct without knowing or having reason to know that they have done so, and hence be found strictly criminally liable. On the other hand, someone cannot sensibly be said to have been an 'accomplice' to the commission of the offence, or 'complicit' in it, without some fault element being proved against them.[82]

By contrast, an issue we have not yet addressed directly is the effect on what must be proved against the accomplice when the principal's offence involves proof of fault on the principal's part. Must an alleged accomplice be shown to have intentionally assisted or encouraged the principal to act with the fault element of an offence, as well as intentionally assisting or encouraging the principal to engage in the conduct element, in the relevant circumstances and with the relevant consequence elements (if any)? In short, following the Supreme Court's decision in *R v Jogee*,[83] the answer is 'yes', it must be proved against the alleged accomplice that he or she intended to encourage or assist the principal to act with the fault element:

> **Example1:** D2 (the alleged accomplice) is said to have assisted or encouraged D1 (the principal) to commit burglary. The evidence is that D2 rang D1 to tell D1 that a property would be empty on a particular day, and so it would be possible to gain access to that property without being noticed (so, what D2 says probably constitutes both a bit of encouragement and assistance). Acting on this information, D1 gains access to the property on the day in question, and steals some valuable paintings.

---

[80] The offence is discussed in Chapter 12.7(c).

[81] *Johnson v Youden* [1950] 1 KB 544; *R v Jogee* [2016] UKSC 8, para 9. In *Jogee*, the terminology of 'existing facts' is used instead of 'circumstances of the offence', but the latter is preferable for reasons discussed below in section 11.5(d) .

[82] *Johnson v Youden* [1950] 1 KB 544; *Callow v Tidstone* (1900) 83 LT 411 (DC).

[83] *R v Jogee* [2016] UKSC 8.

Other things being equal, D1 is clearly guilty of burglary as a principal offender. Will D2 also be guilty of burglary, as D1's accomplice? What the law now requires is that the prosecution show that D2 intentionally assisted or encouraged D1 not only to enter the property as a trespasser—the conduct and circumstance elements of the offence—but also to do this with the relevant fault elements.[84] In burglary, the fault elements D1 must possess, and hence with which D2 must intentionally encourage or assist D1 to act, are, first, awareness that he or she (D1) was or might be a trespasser when entering, and secondly, an intent to steal (amongst other possibilities) when entering.[85] As the Supreme Court has put it succinctly, 'If the crime requires a particular intent, D2 must intend to assist or encourage D1 to act with such intent…[*i.e.* with] whatever mental element is required of D1'.[86]

The facts of *Jogee* illustrate this principle. Jogee and the principal offender, Hirsi, were arguing with a man (V) and a woman at her home. Not long previously, Jogee had been in the house and angrily waved a knife around saying that he and Hirsi should 'shank' V. Jogee and Hirsi left the house, but then returned. Hirsi was standing in the entrance hallway where V also was, armed with a knife he had just taken from the kitchen, whilst Jogee was outside with a bottle shouting encouragement to Hirsi to attack V. Jogee then went up to the doorway and leant past Hirsi, saying that he (Jogee) wanted to smash the bottle over V's head. Hirsi then stabbed V to death. Respecting the liability of Jogee, the trial judge had directed the jury that Jogee could be found guilty of murder if they were sure that Jogee had encouraged an attack on V, realising or foreseeing that Hirsi might use the knife on V with intent to kill or cause serious harm. The jury found Jogee guilty of murder. The Supreme Court quashed Jogee's conviction for murder, on the basis that the jury should have been directed to consider whether they were sure that Jogee's intention, in encouraging Hirsi to attack V, was that Hirsi should act with the fault element for murder. It was not enough that Jogee encouraged Hirsi to attack V, merely foreseeing that Hirsi *might* act with the intent for murder.

(b) THE SIMPLIFYING EFFECT OF *R V JOGEE*

The adoption by the Supreme Court of a simple, intent-based foundation for law governing accomplice liability does away with a considerable amount of case law that had left much doubt hanging over the question of what fault element was required of the accomplice, in relation to the fault element of the principal.[87] Some authorities required

---

[84] See *Clark* (1985) 80 Cr App R 344, where the assistance by D2 in a burglary was provided by someone who in fact intended the burglars to be captured in the act by the police. The Court of Appeal held that, in spite of his good motive (motive being irrelevant to fault elements in the criminal law, generally), D2 fulfilled the requirements of accomplice liability, in that he knew that the principal offender would act with the fault elements for burglary. However, D2 might nonetheless rely on a 'law enforcement' defence.

[85] S. 9 of Theft Act 1968.

[86] *R v Jogee* [2016] UKSC 8, para 10. Although the Supreme Court confines its analysis to assisting and encouraging, the analysis will also apply to counselling, under the Accessories and Abettors Act 1861.

[87] For a detailed discussion, see the 7th edition of this book.

D2 to intend that D1 act with the fault element for the offence,[88] where 'intent' is understood in its ordinary legal sense to include foresight of a virtual certainty, alongside direct intention. Such cases remain good law. Other cases appeared to suggest that it is sufficient if D2 is proved to have been reckless whether D1 might act with the fault element, when D2 is alleged to have encouraged or assisted D1 to engage in the conduct element (in the relevant circumstances, with the relevant consequences, if any). For example, in *Webster*,[89] D2 had permitted D1 to drive even though D2 knew D1 was drunk. D1 drove dangerously, and a passenger was killed in an ensuing accident. The Court of Appeal held that what must be shown, in relation to D2, was merely that, knowing that D1 was drunk whilst driving, D2 foresaw (a kind of recklessness) that D1 was likely to drive dangerously. This case is no longer good law. Following *Jogee*, the relevant test would now be whether, knowing that D1 was driving whilst drunk, D2 intended (including an inference of intent from foreseeing it as certain) that D1 drive dangerously.

More significantly, the simple, intent-based test[90] for complicity in crimes involving a fault element has swept away a much larger body of case law dealing with the liability of accomplices in so-called 'joint enterprise' cases. At the beginning of section 11.1, an example was given in which A planned the theft of valuables from a country house, and persuaded B and C to carry out the burglary for him. They then approached D, who had worked at the house, for information that would help them to gain entry. It was pointed out that, in this example, only B and C are principal offenders, the ones who fulfil both the conduct and fault elements. However, we also said that A is part of what has been called the 'joint criminal enterprise' of burglary, along with B and C. This is because A, B, and C have a plan in common to commit burglary, whereas D is not part of this plan. D merely assists those (A, B and C) who are party to the plan, to the joint criminal enterprise. After *Jogee*, the test now applicable to determine D's liability for the burglary was set out above: did D intentionally assist A, B and C to carry out their plan? Proving this involves proving, first, that D intended to provide assistance with respect to the conduct and circumstance elements of burglary to be committed by one or more of A, B and C. It also involves, secondly, proof that D intended one or more of A, B and C to act on his assistance with the fault element for the crime in issue (burglary). However, before *Jogee*, a different approach was taken to those involved in the joint criminal enterprise itself (in our example, A, B and C), depending on the circumstances.

To illustrate the circumstances that previously gave rise to much difficulty, let us take our example a bit further. Suppose that B and C enter the house as trespassers with intent to steal, as agreed with A. However, they unexpectedly come across the householder who tries to push them out of the house. Angered by this, B and C take turns repeatedly to punch and kick the householder in the head. As a result, the householder is killed. Assuming that B and C acted with at least an intention to cause serious harm

---

[88] *NCB v Gamble* [1959] 1 QB 11 (DC); *Bryce* [2004] EWCA Crim 1231.
[89] [2006] EWCA Crim 415.
[90] Intentionally assisting or encouraging an offence, intending that the principal act with the fault element.

to the householder, then they stand to be convicted of his or her murder; but what about A? Under the pre-*Jogee* law, as a party to the joint criminal enterprise of burglary, A would clearly not be found guilty of murder if he never anticipated that B and C might go beyond burglary to commit murder. However, if it had crossed A's mind at a relevant point that, should B and C encounter a householder, they might well form and act on the intention to kill or cause serious injury to the householder, then A would also be guilty of murder along with B and C if the householder was killed with the intent for murder. In other words, for participants in a joint criminal enterprise, if one of them went beyond the agreed scope of enterprise and committed some other crime, the others could also be found guilty of that other crime in the following circumstances: if they went ahead with the joint enterprise, despite realising or foreseeing that the other crime might be committed by one of their number during the course of the enterprise.[91] There were some exceptions to this rule,[92] but in effect, the rule meant that a participant in a joint enterprise (D2) could be found guilty, as a complicit or secondary party, of a crime he or she merely foresaw might be committed during the enterprise by another party to the joint enterprise (D1), even though D2 had no intention that this other crime be committed, and no intention to assist or encourage its commission by another party to the enterprise.

Pre-*Jogee* there were, then, two separate tests for secondary liability or complicity. There was an intention-based test for those assisting or encouraging a crime to the commission of which they were not a party (like D, in our example above), and an awareness of risk or foresight-based test for those who were parties to a joint enterprise (like A, in our example above). In itself, the existence of two different tests—one for assisting or encouraging, and one for joint enterprise—is not necessarily a flaw. US Federal Law has lived with such a distinction for many years.[93] Having said that, the latter test—the foresight of risk test—has widely been considered too broad.[94] The argument runs as follows. If D2 is engaged in a joint criminal enterprise with D1 to steal apples, but also foresees that D1 may attack the apple trees' owner if the latter confronts them, why should that mere foresight of a possibility be sufficient to fix D2 with liability for D1's attack, if D2 neither intended such an attack, nor intended to assist or encourage D1 in such an attack, nor even thought such an attack likely to occur?[95] The simple fact that the foreseen attack took place during the course of a criminal joint enterprise to commit theft might seem too insubstantial a moral and legal basis for justifying D2's liability for D1's attack. The 'foresight' test is re-evaluated below.

---

[91] *R v Powell; R v English* [1999] 1 AC 1; *Chan Wing-Siu v The Queen* [1985] AC 168.

[92] In particular, where there was a 'fundamental difference' between what D realized that another participant in the joint enterprise might do, and what that other participant actually did: see *R v Rahman* [2008] UKHL 45, and the more detailed analysis in section 11.5(d) below.

[93] See US Model Penal Code s. 2.06 (assisting and encouraging, although that is not the language used), and *Pinkerton v US* (1946) 328 U.S. 640, 66 S.Ct. 1180, 90 L.Ed. 1489 (joint enterprise, although the case is actually concerned only with joint enterprises arising from a conspiracy).

[94] See, for example, Beatrice Krebbs, 'Joint Criminal Enterprise' (2010) 73 MLR 578.

[95] *R v Collinson* (1831) 4 Car and P 565.

Following *Jogee*, there appears to be only one test for accomplice liability in all contexts, which will thus be applied in an example such as the apple-theft example:

> [T]he mental element in assisting or encouraging is an intention to assist or encourage the commission of a crime, and this requires knowledge of any existing facts necessary for it to be criminal. If the crime requires a particular intent, D2 [the alleged accomplice] must intent to assist or encourage D1 to act with such intent.[96]

On this view, what would have to be shown in the apple-theft example is that D2 intended to assist or encourage D1 (with the relevant intent) to attack the apple trees' owner, should they encounter the owner in the course of stealing the apples. During a discussion of liability in joint enterprise cases, the Supreme Court suggests this, when holding that:

> There can be no doubt that if D2 continues to participate in crime A with foresight that D1 may commit crime B, that is evidence, and sometimes powerful evidence, *of an intent to assist D1 in crime B*. But it is evidence of such an intent (or, if one likes, of "authorisation"), not conclusive of it.[97] (our emphasis)

In this passage from the Supreme Court's judgement, it is an intention on D2's part to assist or to encourage D1 to commit crime B, with the fault element for that crime (should the need to commit it arise during the course of an agreed plan or joint enterprise to commit crime A) that plays a pivotal role in determining whether or not D2 is liable for crime B as well as for crime A. That view is bolstered by passages in the judgment where the Supreme Court places emphasis on the claim that an 'association' (understanding; agreement) between D1 and D2 —like D2's presence in attendance at the scene of D1's crime— is only possible, 'evidence on the question whether assistance or encouragement was provided'.[98]

However, more detailed analysis is required to understand the foundations of the new law. Consider this example.

Example 2: D1 and D2 agree to commit crime A, and each understands that in the course of committing crime A, it may be also be necessary for one or other of them to commit crime B. During the course of committing crime A, D1 finds it necessary to commit crime B.

What is the basis for convicting D2 of crime B as well as of crime A? On the facts, it may be that D2 provided no specific encouragement or assistance at all to D1 to

---

[96] *R v Jogee* [2016] UKSC 8, paras 9 & 10. This formula bears some resemblance the test for complicity set out in section 2.06(3) of the US Model Penal Code, 'A person is an accomplice of another person in the commission of an offense if: (a) with the purpose of promoting or facilitating the commission of the offense, he (i) solicits such other person to commit it, or (ii) aids or agrees or attempts to aid such other person in planning or committing it, or (iii) having a legal duty to prevent the commission of the offense, fails to make proper effort so to do ...'. The difference is that *Jogee* applies such a formula to joint enterprises, as well as to non-joint enterprises, whereas US Federal law takes a different approach to crimes committed in furtherance of a conspiracy or joint enterprise: see the end of 11.5(c) below.

[97] *R v Jogee* [2016] UKSC 8, para 66.

[98] Ibid., para 11. See, in defence of this kind of approach, W. Wilson and D. Ormerod, 'Simply Harsh to Fairly Simple: Joint Enterprise Reform' [2015] Crim LR 53, an article which must surely have influenced the Supreme court in *Jogee*, even if it was not mentioned in the single judgment.

commit crime B, and may even have been unaware that D1 was committing crime B (perhaps it was committed by D1 in another room of a house D1 and D2 were burgling, whilst D2 was elsewhere). So, what links D2 to D1's commission of crime B is *not* necessarily particular acts of assistance or encouragement provided by D2 to D1 to commit crime B, but the fact that the commission of crime B was, for both D1 and D2, an anticipated—albeit quite possibly unwanted—element in the agreement between them to commit crime A. In *Jogee*, the Supreme Court addresses such cases and says that, on such facts, D2 can be convicted of crime B, along with D1:

> If the jury is satisfied that there was an agreed common purpose to commit crime A, and if it is satisfied also that D2 must have foreseen that, in the course of committing crime A, D1 might well commit crime B, it may in appropriate cases be justified in drawing the conclusion that D2 had the necessary conditional intent that crime B should be committed, if the occasion arose; or in other words, that it was within the scope of the plan to which D2 gave his assent and intentional support. But that will be a question of fact for the jury in all the circumstances.[99]

Central to this analysis is the concept of 'conditional' intention to do something ('We will do X, if circumstances Y arise'). Not all cases of assisting or encouraging will involve 'conditional' intentions. *Jogee*, for example, did not involve such an intention. In law, what mattered was quite simply whether or not Jogee, through his encouragement, intended Hirsi to act with the intent for murder.

However, a joint enterprise may involve contingency plans applicable if things turn out in a certain way, and thus involve 'conditional' intention. Suppose that D2 has agreed with D1 on a plan to commit crime A, where the plan also includes the possible commission of crime B by one or other of them. Then, D2's agreement to commit crime A carries with it explicit or implicit support (encouragement) for the commission of crime B, should the circumstances arise in which it is anticipated that crime B will be committed. So, in joint enterprise cases —common purpose cases—D2's liability for crime B committed by D1 is based on intentional encouragement after all. The encouragement comes in the form of an agreement with D1 that crime B should be committed, if the agreed circumstances arise for its commission during the course of committing crime A. Whereas the old law, applicable only in joint enterprise cases, made D2 liable for crime B if D2 had merely foreseen that crime B might well be committed, the new law makes D2 liable for crime B only if D2 *conditionally intended* that crime B should be committed, if the agreed circumstances arise for its commission in the course of crime A. These circumstances are often thought of as negative ones to be avoided if possible: 'Will we need to hit someone during the course of our burglary?' However, we should note that they may also be 'positive' circumstances, to be sought after: 'When we are damaging V's house, if anyone sees something worth stealing, they should steal it!'

Similarly, in non-joint enterprise cases (where D2 encourages or assists D1, but is not part of any shared plan to commit the offence in question), conditional intention may play an important role. Suppose D1 goes to a house shared by D2 and D3, and asks them

---

[99] Ibid., para 94.

to provide D1 with a murder weapon. D2 provides a knife, and D3 provides a gun. D1 says to both D2 and D3 that he will use the weapon that seems most appropriate when he encounters V. In the event, D1 uses the gun to kill V. In such a case, assuming both D2 and D3 intend D1 to act with the intent for murder, both could conceivably be convicted of murder. First, D3 can be convicted on the basis of intentionally assisting murder (D3 provided the murder weapon). D2 can be convicted on the basis of intentionally encouraging (the provision of the knife, although not used in the murder itself, may be a form of encouragement to commit the murder, in the circumstances). Secondly, both D2 and D3 intend to assist or encourage D1 to commit murder, because both 'conditionally' intend D1 to use the weapon they have provided: if the circumstances call for the use of that weapon by D1.

The same analysis, in terms of conditional intention, is applicable if, say, D2 sells D1 what is in fact a highly unreliable gun, for D1's planned murder. In such a case, D2 still intends D1 to act with the intent for murder, if certain conditions obtain, namely that the gun does in fact fire as D1 intends when D1 fires at V. Indeed, it seems likely that, in this kind of case, even if D2 sells D1 a highly unreliable weapon *in order to* make it less likely that D1 will succeed (perhaps D2 would not want to see D1 jailed for life), D2 can still be convicted of murder if D1 is in fact successful in shooting V with the gun. In such an example, it will still be true to say that that D2 assisted D1 knowing that D1 would be successful in carrying out his or her murderous intent (D2's oblique intent), if—here is the contingency or conditio—the gun fired as D1 intended it to and as D2 knew it could. This is the kind of example where, in the words of the Supreme Court, D2 can be convicted because:

> D2 gives intentional assistance or encouragement to D1 to commit an offence and to act with the mental element required of him, but without D2 having *a positive intent* that the particular offence will be committed.[100]

More generally, comparing the old law and the new law on the secondary party's fault element in joint enterprise cases, there are without question important differences between (conditional) intention and foresight, as states of mind. Intention normally involves a kind of provisional (revisable) *decision* to act in a certain way. By contrast, foresight is a purely a cognitive state of mind over which people do not necessarily exercise the same degree of control as they do over their intentions. Foresight of a possible consequence may simply 'come to me' unbidden, through the unconscious working of my mind (so to speak, popping into my head) whether I welcome it or not. It is, then, generally speaking, more blameworthy to form a conditional intention to do something wrong than it is simply to foresee that one might do something wrong. However, the main advantage of the new law's approach is not, in fact, that it greatly narrows the scope for finding D2 liable for crime B, by making such liability turn on whether D2 'conditionally intended' crime B to be committed, rather than merely foreseeing that crime B might well be committed. Few indeed are likely to be the cases where D's liability turns on this precise question, although no doubt there will be plenty of scope to 'coach' alleged accessories into presenting an account of their role events in terms of possible foresight, but not ('Never, honestly!') in terms of conditional intention. More significant is the fact that there is no longer any need

---

[100] *R v Jogee* [2016] UKSC 8, para 10.

to have a set of rules governing joint enterprise cases that is separate and different from the rules governing non-joint enterprise cases. *Jogee* is a case that exemplifies the importance of a single set of rules, because on the facts it was unclear which of the two sets of old rules would have applied. Did Jogee and Hirsi form a joint plan to attack V before they returned to the house, in which case the old joint enterprise rules would have applied? Or, was the attack on V only started once the two had returned to the house, when Jogee encouraged Hirsi to attack V, but without himself having planned this beforehand with Hirsi, in which case the non-joint enterprise rules would have applied? These questions are no longer a significant issue, because the test is the same: did Jogee intentionally encourage Hirsi to attack V, and to attack V with the intent for murder?

(c) DOES *JOGEE* NARROW THE LAW, OR SIMPLY BROADEN IT IN DIFFERENT WAYS?

Having said all this in favour of *Jogee*, the focus in point of controversy in some instances will simply switch. It will switch from whether crime B was foreseen as a possible incident of committing the agreed crime A, to whether—even if there was no express agreement—there was 'tacit' or 'implicit' agreement that crime B might be committed if certain circumstances arose. This is because it is made clear in *Jogee* that D1's commission of crime B will fall within the scope of a joint enterprise agreed with others if it is, 'expressly *or tacitly* agreed' (our emphasis) that crime B may be committed during the course of the enterprise.[101]

In discussing this issue, one point of law needs to be made clear. If D1's conduct in committing crime B fell outside of any explicit or tacit understanding between the parties to the joint enterprise, then the other parties cannot be found complicit in crime B. In such a case D1 will, as Sir Michael Foster put it as long ago as the middle of the 18th century, 'stand single in that offence, and the person soliciting will not be involved in his guilt'.[102] This principle probably also applies when D1 acts for reasons to which the other parties to the joint enterprise did not agree could form a basis for committing crime B, even if crime B itself was a crime that the members of the joint enterprise agreed might be committed, during the course of crime A:

> **Example 3:** D1 and D2 agree to burgle a house and to kill anyone who resists, if need be. During the burglary, D2 goes into an upstairs room and unexpectedly encounters her boyfriend (V) in bed with the householder. V gets out of bed to push D2 out of the room, and an enraged D2 attacks and intentionally kills V.

In this example, D2 has—as D1 and D2 agreed might happen—intentionally killed someone resisting the burglary. However, it is clearly arguable that D2 has stepped outside the agreed (contingency) plan by doing this, if the reason for killing V was D2's violent and jealous rage, and not the need to prevent resistance to the burglary.[103]

---

[101] Ibid., at para 93.
[102] Sir M. Foster, *Crown Law*, 3rd ed. (1809), affirmed in *R v Jogee* [2016] UKSC 8, at para 19.
[103] See further *R v Calhaem* [1985] QB 808.

In that regard, there was a contentious result that could arise under the pre-*Jogee* law that has also now been avoided. Pre-*Jogee*, even in a case involving an agreed (non-lethal) attack on V by D1 and D2 in which D1 intentionally killed V, if D2 was found not to have foreseen that D1 might act with the intent for murder, then D2 could be found guilty of neither murder *nor* manslaughter.[104] The logic of this argument was that if, in killing V with the intent for murder, D1 stepped outside the scope of the agreed plan (a non-lethal attack on V), then the killing of V was outside the scope of the plan, period. The fact that D2 possessed the fault element for unlawful and dangerous act manslaughter,[105] and that V was killed in the course of the agreed unlawful attack, was not sufficient to justify convicting D2 of manslaughter. This was thought to be because unlawful and dangerous act manslaughter involves causing an unexpected death through the unlawful act; and in the circumstances just outlined, V's death was not 'unexpected' but the produce of a murderous act by D1 that D2 had not foreseen. It is hard to resist the logic of that argument, but prior to the decisions in *Chan Wing-Siu*[106] and *Powell; English*,[107] the law did in fact convict D1 of murder and D2 of manslaughter in most such situations.[108] *Jogee* has now restored this older approach—D1 guilty of murder; D2 of manslaughter—to the law.[109] However, there may still be some examples, perhaps variations on Example 3 above – in which, even when there has been an agreed (non-lethal) attack on V by D1 and D2, D1's murderous act in killing should still be regarded as an act too far from the original plan to justify convicting D2 of manslaughter. *Jogee* confirms that this is the case.[110]

Important though it is, putting this point on one side, how far do the supposedly narrower and more humane *Jogee* rules of complicity truly extend? Quite far, if parties to a joint enterprise to commit crime A can be found liable for the commission of crime B by one of their number, when they are found to have 'tacitly' agreed to the commission of crime B (if the circumstances for its commission by one of their number arise). Here is a simple example to illustrate the problem:

> **Example 4:** D1 and D2 plan a house burglary, giving no express thought to whether they would encounter a householder in the course of the burglary, and hence giving no thought to what they would do in such circumstances. During the burglary, D1 unexpectedly encounters the householder, and knocks him out, so that he can complete the burglary with D2. That evening, D2 is overheard in a public house telling D1, 'You did exactly what I would have done in the circumstances; well done, mate!'

Is D2 complicit in D1's assault on the householder? We can certainly say that D2 did not actually foresee that D1 might commit an assault in the course of the burglary. So, perhaps ironically, D2 would clearly be acquitted of assault under the old—and supposedly harsher—rules governing joint enterprise, because foresight is always, as it were, 'explicit' and not 'tacit'. Foresight is in one's conscious mind, if it is there at all. Obviously, if what D2 says in the pub is simply praise of D1 after the fact to bolster

---

[104] *R v Powell; R v Daniels* [1999] 1 AC 1.   [105] See chapter 8.5.   [106] [1985] AC 168.
[107] [1999] 1 AC 1.   [108] *R v Smith (Wesley)* [1963] 1 WLR 1200; *R v Betty* (1964) 48 Cr App R 6.
[109] *R v Jogee* [2016] UKSC 8, paras 27-35.   [110] Ibid., para 33.

D1's confidence, then clearly that *ex post facto* encouragement cannot provide a basis for finding D2 liable for D1's crime. Other things being equal, D2 must possess the relevant fault element at the time he does the acts that assist or encourage the offence. However, there is a different way of looking at the facts in this example.

In Example 4, D2's words could be said to show that there was in fact a tacit or implicit element to his agreement to commit burglary with D1, which is that either one of them would, if need be, do something to fend off or incapacitate a householder during the course of the burglary. On that view, D2's words have the potential to inculpate him in D1's offence as a secondary party, in a way that the foresight test would not. Some might argue that there is nothing wrong with that. A great deal of conversation and joint activity involve taken-for-granted assumptions lying behind what is explicitly discussed or done together, assumptions that neither party can simply disavow when it suits them. These assumptions reduce the incidence of interpretive error in interaction.[111] For example, putting aside unusual situations, if I say, as your boss, 'Take a taxi to the theatre, if your car has broken down', it should simply never occur to you that my instruction encompasses stealing a taxi to get to the theatre. Consequently, if you did steal a taxi to get to the theatre, and were blamed for the theft,[112] your blame could not be reduced in any way morally by you saying, 'But I was ordered to take a taxi to the theatre!' Having said that, applying such a 'language game' analysis as a mean of inculpating D2 in the outcome of a joint criminal enterprise is a contentious step,[113] not least because joint enterprises may take the form of nothing more sophisticated than the spontaneous coming together of a group of people bent on committing one or more offences.[114]

A potential problem with *Jogee*, then, is that it shifts the focus away from actual foresight of what might happen in the course of crime A, to what was agreed— most importantly, including what was tacitly (impliedly) agreed—by the parties to the joint enterprise, as part of their contingency planning for the commission of crime A. Consequently, *Jogee* makes the application of the law governing the liability of secondary parties vulnerable to what juries choose to regard as 'tacitly' agreed. Example 4 is an illustration of this, and there might be many such examples, including cases decided under the old rules, such as *R v Powell; R v English*,[115] or *Chan Wing-Siu v The Queen*.[116] That may actually make it more likely, rather than less likely, than it would have been under the old law, that a secondary party in a plan to commit crime A will be found to have (tacitly) agreed that, if the relevant circumstances arise, crime B may be committed. The old law at least required actual foresight that crime B might be committed in the course of crime A, and nothing less.

The law must be considered settled by *Jogee* now, unless Parliament intervenes. Should Parliament intervene, is there an alternative approach that avoids the Trojan

---

[111] For a discussion in the context of implied terms in contracts, see C. J Goetz and R. E. Scott, 'The Limits of Expanded Choice: An Analysis of the Interactions between Express and Implied Contract Terms' [1985] 73 California Law Review 261.

[112] We are not talking here about legal blame under s. 1 of the Theft Act 1968, but blame in a more general non-legal sense.

[113] We mean 'language game' in Wittgenstein's sense: L. Wittgenstein, *Philosophical Investigations* (1999).

[114] *R v Jogee* [2016] UKSC 8, para 95.   [115] [1999] 1 AC 1.   [116] [1985] AC 168.

horse constituted by the rule that secondary parties will be taken to have agreed what the jury regards as 'tacitly' agreed, as well as what was expressly agreed? One possible approach would be to say that secondary parties to a joint enterprise to commit crime A are liable for crime B, when committed by one of their number, if they foresaw not simply that crime B might be committed in the course of crime A, but that it might be committed in order to *further* the joint enterprise to commit crime A. That would prevent secondary parties becoming liable for any crime (B) that it happens to be within their contemplation that the principal may commit during the course of crime A. The test would restrict their liability to a crime B that is intrinsically linked to the commission of crime A, namely a crime committed to further or advance crime A. On this view, then, an alleged secondary party (D2) would be guilty of a full offence if:

(i)   (Crime A) D2 intentionally assisted or encouraged D1 to commit a crime. Where the crime is fault-based, D's intention must extend to D1 committing the crime with the fault element;[117] or

(ii) (Crime A and crime B) D2 satisfies the conditions in (i) above in relation to crime A, and also, D2 intends or foresees a realistic possibility that D1 might commit crime B in the course of and in order to further (including the avoidance of detection, *etc.* of) the successful commission of crime A.

It should be noted that, in employing a test based on foresight, this test is considerably more generous to the accused than analogous rules applicable in most US jurisdictions. In those jurisdictions, a doctrine of 'natural and probable consequences' applies to implicate D2 in crime B, even if crime B was not foreseen by D2 as a way that D1 might seek to further the joint enterprise. So, suppose that D2 agrees to act as a lookout for D1 during a robbery, but during the robbery D1 intentionally shoots dead a police officer who resists. In most US jurisdictions, both D1 and D2 will be guilty not only of robbery but also of murder in such a case, because the murder will be regarded as a reasonably foreseeable consequence of the bank robbery.[118] The US Supreme Court has taken a similar approach to D2's liability for crime B when it is committed in furtherance of a conspiracy (a key form of joint enterprise).[119] In *Pinkerton v US*,[120] the US Supreme Court found that a crime (crime B) could be attributed to all conspirators if it furthered the conspiracy, or if it could reasonably have been foreseen as a necessary or natural consequence of carrying out that unlawful agreement.

(d) PROBLEMS THAT REMAIN, POST-*JOGEE*

We have seen that a great advantage of the decision in *Jogee* is that it applies a single test for the major forms of accomplice liability. This is the test of whether D2 intentionally assisted or encouraged the commission of the crime by D1, knowing the facts

---

[117] This is the position under *Jogee*.

[118] This example is discussed in these terms by J. Dressler, *Understanding Criminal Law*, 3rd ed. (2001), at 478.

[119] *Pinkerton v US* 328 U.S. 640, 66 S.Ct. 1180, 90 L.Ed. 1489 (1946). Joint enterprises are wider than conspiracies because they include cases in which D2 simply joins in with crime being committed by D1, and they then act in common without having any express or implied agreement: see *R v Jogee* [2016] UKSC 8, para 95.

[120] Pinkerton v US 328 U.S. 640, 66 S.Ct. 1180, 90 L.Ed. 1489 (1946).

necessary for its commission and (where relevant) intending to assist or encourage D1 to act with the relevant fault element.[121] It was suggested in 11.5(c) that this great advantage was to some extent counter-balanced by the introduction of an uncertainty, in cases involving a joint enterprise or common intent. This uncertainty involves the extent to which it will prove to be fair or just to hold secondary parties liable for what the prosecution claims was 'tacitly' (impliedly) agreed might happen – the commission of crime B – in certain circumstances. What else are we to make of the decision in *R v Jogee*?

To begin with, we must try to make sense of what the Supreme Court says about the alleged accomplice's fault element, in relation to D1's commission of a crime with a fault element:

> [T]here can be cases where D2 gives intentional assistance or encouragement to D1 to commit an offence and to act with the mental element required of him, but without D2 having a positive intent that the particular offence will be committed. That may be so, for example, where at the time that encouragement is given it remains uncertain what D1 might do; and arms supplier might be such a case.[122]

On the face of it, a requirement that D2 intentionally assist or encourage D1 not merely to do the act, but to do it with the fault element, seems bizarre. Suppose that D1 goes to a gun seller (D2) and says to D2, 'I can't make up my mind whether or not to kill a business rival, so I thought I would buy a gun in case I decide to do so'. D2 sells a gun to D1, who subsequently goes on to murder the business rival. In order to convict D2 of the murder, along with D1, the prosecution has to show that D2 gave intentional assistance to D1 to act with the fault element for murder. Does that really mean the prosecution would have to show that, when confronted with D1's explanation for buying the gun, D2 did not merely sell it to him but, for example, positively encouraged D1 to make up his mind to kill and stick to that intention? It seems unlikely that the Supreme Court meant to narrow the scope of secondary liability that far.

It is clear from the passage just cited that the accomplice need not share the principal's intent. So, the gun seller can be found liable for the murder even if he has no view on whether or not D1 should carry out the killing. So, what does it mean to say that D2 need not share the principal's intent, but must be shown to have intentionally assisted or encouraged the principal to act with the relevant fault element? It may mean that the prosecution must show that D2 intentionally assisted or encouraged D1 to commit the crime, knowing that if D1 committed it, D1 would do so with the relevant fault element.[123] In the arms seller example just given, this requirement can be satisfied. D2 knows that, if D1 goes on to use the gun he has sold him, D1 will act with the intent for murder. Yet if that is the test, the law would barely have changed, post-*Jogee*, because it would be essentially foresight-based in relation to D1's intent. Alternatively, as argued above, the Supreme Court may mean that D2 must intend (which may include foreseeing as virtually certain) D1 to commit the crime in question, even if D2 does not desire it as such. If that is right, the most of those who sell weapons illegally will not be complicit in the acts of those who commit crime with the weapons the sellers have provided (the sellers will still be guilty of serious offences relating to the sales).

[121] *R v Jogee* [2016] UKSC 8, paras 9–10.   [122] Ibid., para 10.
[123] See *R v Bryce* [2004] EWCA Crim 1231.   [124] *R v Jogee* [2016] UKSC 8, para 9

A second point involves a puzzle arises over the Supreme Court's claim that the basic elements of accomplice liability involve proof that D2 had knowledge, at the time of the act of assistance or encouragement, of 'existing facts' necessary to make D1's act criminal.[124] Suppose that D2 offers D1 a place to store the goods that D1 intends to steal the following day. At the point that this offer of assistance is made (an offer that in itself assists D1 by giving him or her more options), there are no stolen goods, and thus there are no 'existing facts' necessary to make D1's act criminal: D1 is yet to engage in such an act. The Supreme Court must surely mean here that what matters is whether D2 knows that, when D1 acts on D2's assistance or encouragement, the facts making D's act criminal will exist at that (later) time.[125] Indeed, later in the judgment, the Supreme Court reverts to the traditional formula, stating that what matters is that, 'an intention to assist or encourage the commission of an offence requires knowledge by D2 of any facts necessary to give the principal's conduct *or intended conduct* its criminal character'.[126]

Thirdly, and finally the Supreme Court appears to have abolished the so-called 'fundamental difference' rule,[127] as it applies to murder cases, but without quite saying so, in so many words, leaving its status unclear. It was in murder cases that the need for the fundamental difference rule seemed most pressing, given the mandatory life sentence that follows upon conviction. The need for the rule arose because the fault element in murder can take two forms: an intention to kill, or an intention to do serious harm.[128] Consider a joint enterprise case in which D1 and D2 agree on a plan to give V, 'the beating of his life'. D1 takes this to mean that V is to be intentionally killed through beating, but D2 assumes this means the two of them will inflict only serious harm on V, leaving V alive. When they encounter V, D1 stabs V through the heart. In spite of the (morally) highly significant difference between what each intends to do, D1 and D2 nonetheless in law agreed on a plan, a plan to launch a murderous assault on V: an assault that will involve acting on either an intention to kill or an intention to inflict serious harm. Consequently, both stands to be convicted of murder.

Even so, under the pre-*Jogee* law, in this kind of example, D2 was entitled to argue that, although acting with a murderous intent was anticipated by both parties as part of the plan, there was a 'fundamental difference' between what D2 thought the plan involved, and what D1 actually did, that could justify D2's acquittal of murder.[129] The 'fundamental difference' could be expressed in different ways. There may have been (i) a different and more dangerous 'act' on D1's part (stabbing not beating) with a weapon D2 did not realise that D1 had or would use. There may have been (ii) a graver intention on D1's part (intent to kill), using the same weapon. Finally, there might (iii) have been both factors (i) and (ii) present (more dangerous weapon used (that D2 did not know D1 had or would use), and a graver intent held by D1. Depending on which older case or judgment you read, the result should be an acquittal on the murder charge, at least in cases (i) and (iii), but possibly also in (ii). In short, the law was a mess. What does *Jogee* say about the 'fundamental difference' rules?

---

[125] See the discussion of this issue, in relation to conspiracy, in Chapter 12.5(c).
[126] *R v Jogee* [2016] UKSC 8, para 16 (our emphasis).   [127] See section 11.5(b), n 12.
[128] See Chapter 8.
[129] *R v English* [1999] 1 AC 1. In such circumstances, D2 would now stand to be convicted of manslaughter: see section 11.5(c).

The problem never directly confronted in *Jogee* about such cases is that it cannot in any straightforward way be said that, by intentionally killing V, D1 clearly departed from the plan and was thus acting on a frolic of his own in intentionally killing, in which case D2 would be acquitted of homicide completely, or perhaps convicted only of manslaughter.[130] This cannot be said because, as already indicated, D1 and D2 shared a plan to launch what was, in law, a murderous assault on V. The Supreme Court in *Jogee* said about the fundamental rule that:

> [T]here will *normally* be no occasion to consider the concept of 'fundamental departure' as derived from *English* … If [the] crime is murder, then the question is whether he [D2] intended to assist the intentional infliction of grievous bodily harm at least … [D2] may think that D1 has an iron bar whereas he turns out to have a knife, but the difference may not at all affect his intention to assist, if necessary, in the causing of grievous bodily harm at least. Knowledge or ignorance that weapons generally, or a particular weapon, is carried by D1 will be evidence going to what the intention of D2 was, and may be irresistible evidence one way or the other, but it is evidence and no more.[131]

Here, the Supreme Court appears to rule out (i) above, as a basis for acquittal of murder on the basis of fundamental difference, namely where D1 simply acts with a more dangerous weapon than anticipated. However, the Supreme Court does not address either situation (ii), or in particular situation (iii) where D2 neither agrees to nor anticipates that D1 will act both with a graver intent and with a more dangerous weapon. We are left to ponder what is meant by the statement at the beginning of the passage just cited that, 'normally', the fundamental difference rule can henceforth be ignored.

The simplest solution would be to regard the fundamental difference rule as abolished by *Jogee*. The rule arose because of the width of the fault element in murder, and because of the application of the mandatory life sentence in murder cases to accessories as well as to principals, under the Accessories and Abettors Act 1861. One, or other—and in particular the former—problem with the law of murder needs to be resolved by Parliament, with beneficial consequences for the rules of complicity. It is no longer appropriate for the courts to seek to make the tail wag the dog, by continuing to apply the fundamental difference rule to murder cases where D1 intended to kill, D2 intended only serious harm, but both shared a plan to act with murderous intent. Whether or not that is right, it seems likely that we have not heard the last of 'joint enterprise' in the higher courts.

(e) SAME OFFENCE, DIFFERENT RESULT

What is the position where P commits the same type of offence as D had envisaged but by some unexpected method, or against an unintended victim? In a case where, in the course of a joint enterprise, P aims to kill V1 but misses and hits V2, the law employs the transferred malice principle[132] in taking the same approach towards accomplices as it does to offences by individuals. In such a case, D—if he or she had the relevant awareness of what P might so—would still be guilty of murder. A modern example is *Gnango*.[133] In

---

[130] See the analysis towards the start of 11.5(c) for discussion of this issue, and at n 22.
[131] *R v Jogee* [2016] UKSC 8, para 98 (our emphasis).
[132] See Chapter 6.7(d).   [133] [2011] UKSC 59.

this case, D1 met D2 and the two men exchanged fire, each intending to kill the other, but a bullet fired by one of them struck a by-stander and killed her. It is not entirely clear, in this case, that the judge correctly directed the jury on the nature of crime A, the agreed offence, which might have been affray, or something of that nature. However, assuming some such crime was the agreed offence, both D1 and D2 foresaw that, in the course of it, one or other of them might be killed (the relevant fault element at that time). That being so, in law, the fact that V by accident turned out to be someone else is not relevant. Both men were guilty of murder.

Similarly, where the intended result occurs by an unexpected mode (e.g. death caused by a stab through the eye rather than in the chest), this does not affect the accomplice's liability. In so far as the policies of transferred liability and the other analogous rules are sound for individuals, they should apply to principals and accomplices. The same should presumably be said of constructive liability: thus, if D helps P in an assault on V, as a result of which V unexpectedly dies, a law which renders P liable for manslaughter should also apply so as to render D an accomplice to manslaughter.[134] These propositions all apply the logic of English law's 'derivative' theory of complicity, whereby the accomplice's liability derives from that of the principal.

The common factor in the above group of cases is that the result was unexpected by both P and D. The problem of D's liability is different in cases where P deviates intentionally from the agreed course of conduct. In the famous old case of *Saunders and Archer*,[135] D (P's lover) had advised P to kill his wife by means of a poisoned apple.[136] P placed the apple before his wife, but the wife passed the apple to their small child, who ate it and died. P is reported as having said to his wife, just before she gave the apple to the child, 'Apples are not good for little children'. D was held not to have been an accomplice in the child's murder, on the basis that (although these are not the court's words) P's non-intervention amounted to a free, deliberate, and informed intervention breaking the chain of causation. Although P did not actually give the apple to the child, he sat by and allowed the child to eat the apple when it was his parental duty to intervene. This failure to prevent the miscarriage of the plan was treated as equivalent to approval by P, and thus as a voluntary intervening act (omission) it was enough to negative D's complicity in the actual result.

(f) DIFFERENT, LESS SERIOUS OFFENCE

The House of Lords decision in *Howe* (1987)[137] holds that, where D aids or counsels P to commit a certain offence, and P deviates by committing a less serious offence, D may be convicted as an 'accomplice' to the intended (more serious) offence. Suppose D encourages P to murder V, but that when P sees V P simply fires into the air to frighten V.

---

[134] *Baldessare* (1930) 22 Cr App R 70; cf. *Mahmood* [1994] Crim LR 368.   [135] (1573) 2 Plowd 473.

[136] A woman's role in using an apple to poison someone conjures, of course, a biblically inspired image of her role in man's fall, but also thereby an image of her power as the originator of (in the original sense) 'awful' events. See further, in relation to *Saunders and Archer*, P. Crofts, 'The Poisoned Apple of Malice' [2013] *Griffith Law Review* 150.   [137] [1987] AC 417.

However, the bullet deflects down from a high brick wall and hits V causing V's death. In this case, P might only be guilty of manslaughter by unlawful and dangerous act. However, D can be still be guilty of murder. That might seem in one way sensible and just, but it is hard to square with the idea that D is an 'accomplice,' because P commits a crime different—less serious—from that which D encouraged.

The House of Lords in *Howe* disapproved of an earlier decision in *Richards*.[138] In *Richards*, the court had followed the 'not an accomplice' logic, and laid down a different rule. In that case a woman paid two men to beat up her husband so as to put him in hospital for a few days. Her hope was that this experience would lead her husband to turn to her for comfort, thus repairing their relationship. She was charged with wounding with intent to do grievous bodily harm. The hired men inflicted less serious injuries than she had asked them to, and were convicted of the lesser offence of malicious wounding. It was held that she could not be convicted, as an 'accomplice' to the higher offence of wounding with intent, unless she was present at the scene (an ancient rule now of no relevance). The effect of *Howe* was to sweep away such restrictions, but therefore also to move away from the derivative theory of liability, the theory that D's crime is dependent on and derived from P's. The accomplice is liable although the (intended) higher offence was never committed, and so the accomplice's liability cannot derive from any such offence. The theory underlying the *Howe* ruling is that the culpability of the accomplice should be viewed as a separate issue from that of the principal (contrast the *English–Rahman* approach), and based upon what the accomplice intended to happen or believed would happen. This result could now be achieved on the facts of *Richards* by charging the wife with the inchoate offence assisting or encouraging wounding with intent to do grievous bodily harm (see Chapter 12.7).

11.6 DERIVATIVE LIABILITY AND THE MISSING LINK

We now come to another set of cases in which the English courts have departed from, or at least modified, the derivative theory of accessorial liability. If the would-be principal is not guilty of the substantive offence, because of the absence of a mental element or the presence of a defence, does this mean that the accomplice must also be acquitted? A straightforward application of the derivative theory would lead to the acquittal of the accomplice. One cannot be said to have aided and abetted an offence, if the offence did not take place; for then, there is nothing from which the accomplice's liability can derive. Yet, the would-be accomplice has done all that he or she intended to do in order to further the principal's crime, and, considered in isolation, the accomplice is surely no less culpable than if the principal had been found guilty. It is therefore not surprising that English courts have responded by stretching the doctrine of complicity.

---

[138] [1974] QB 776, discussed by Kadish, *Blame and Punishment*, 184–6.

In *Bourne*[139] D threatened and forced his wife to commit bestiality with a dog, and his conviction for aiding and abetting bestiality was upheld despite the fact that his wife would have had a defence of duress if charged as the principal. In *Cogan and Leak*[140] Cogan had intercourse with Leak's wife, believing, on the basis of what Leak had told him, that Mrs Leak was consenting. Leak knew that his wife was not consenting. Cogan's conviction for rape was quashed because his defence of mistaken belief in the woman's consent had not been properly put to the jury, but Leak's conviction for aiding and abetting rape was upheld. There is a difference between the cases. In *Bourne*, P committed the *actus reus* with the *mens rea*, albeit under duress. So, present in that case were the all the required elements of a crime in which D could be complicit. Crucially, one might argue, the defence available to P did not depend on a denial of those elements. By contrast, under the law of rape as it then stood, although P engaged in the *actus reus* of rape, he did not have the *mens rea*. So, it might be argued, there was no crime in which D could be complicit, and the court should have taken the view that D was guilty only of the incitement of P to rape, and not of rape itself.

However, the courts have not drawn any such distinction. In *DPP v K and B*[141] two girls aged 14 and 11 threatened and bullied another girl, aged 14, to remove her clothes and submit to penetration by a boy. The boy was never identified, nor was his age known, and the defence argued that if he was under 14 (as suggested) he may not have been liable to conviction as a principal in rape (because of the presumption of *doli incapax*, which then applied to children aged between 10 and 14[142]). If the boy could not have been convicted as principal, could the two girls be convicted of procuring rape? The Divisional Court held that they could. The case can be understood as analogous to *Bourne*, in that—one might say—the old presumption of incapacity to commit rape under the age of 14 is akin to a defence, like duress, that leaves both the fault element and the conduct element intact for D to be complicit in. On the other hand, it might be said that, by way of contrast with the position in *Cogan and Leak*, in *K and B* unless the prosecution could satisfy the jury that the boy was 14 or over, there was not even an *actus reus*, let alone *mens rea*, precisely because the boy was—at that time—presumed to be *incapable* of committing the offence as a principal.

The judgments in these cases contain little elaboration of the theoretical basis for conviction. They extend the derivative theory of liability by making it possible to convict D as an accomplice, when the 'principal' has committed only the *actus reus* or 'wrongful act,' in the absence of a mental element (or the presence of a defence available to P). This approach has significant theoretical and practical limitations. One requirement of accomplice liability is that the accomplice must know the essential elements of the offence (including the principal's mental element); but in these cases the accomplice usually knows that the would-be principal lacks an element necessary for conviction. Bourne knew that his wife was acting because of his threats; Leak knew that Cogan was

---

[139] (1952) 36 Cr App R 125.   [140] [1976] 1 QB 217.   [141] [1997] 1 Cr App R 36.
[142] For discussion see Chapter 5.2(a).

acting because of his lies.[143] The same difficulty arises in respect of *Millward*,[144] where D was convicted of procuring the offence of causing death by reckless driving by sending an employee out in a tractor with a defective trailer which led to the death of another motorist. The employee was acquitted of the principal offence, but the Court of Appeal upheld the employer's conviction for, essentially, procuring the *actus reus*. This was the explicit ground for finding liability in *DPP v K and B*: 'there is no doubt whatever that W was the victim of unlawful sexual intercourse ... The *actus reus* was proved. The respondents procured the situation which included the sexual intercourse.'[145]

This extension of the derivative theory does not, however, give the courts grounds for overturning the decision in *Thornton v Mitchell* (1940).[146] A bus conductor was directing the driver in reversing a bus when an accident was caused. The driver was acquitted of careless driving, because he was relying (reasonably) on the conductor's guidance, and it was held that the conductor must therefore be acquitted of aiding and abetting. Since the *actus reus* of careless driving was not committed, the suggested extension of the derivative theory would yield the same result.

What is the most suitable legal technique for dealing with these cases? The new inchoate offences relate to encouraging or assisting a crime or an offence whether or not it takes place. So, one might rest content with convicting D of encouraging or assisting the crimes in question. A different approach might involve invoking the doctrine of innocent agency. A clear example of this would be where an adult urges or orders a child under the age of criminal responsibility to commit crimes, such as stealing from a shop. The young child is deemed 'innocent' in law, and so it is said that the adult commits the crime through the innocent agency of the child. No such notion is possible where two adults are involved, since it is presumed that adults are autonomous beings acting voluntarily, save in exceptional circumstances. How much further can the doctrine of innocent agency be taken? If D gives a bottle to the carer attending a child, V, telling her that it contains a prescribed medicine when in fact it contains poison, D should surely be liable as the principal when the carer administers the contents of the bottle to V, who dies. The carer would be regarded as an innocent agent because he or she was acting under a mistake which would prevent criminal liability for the acts.[147] If this is accepted, it would seem to follow that where (as in *Cogan and Leak*) D persuades P to have sexual intercourse with D's wife by inducing P to believe that she consents to this, P's mistake would mean that he drops out of the picture as an innocent agent and that D should be liable as a principal for rape.[148]

Various objections might be raised against this conclusion. The major counter-argument is that the doctrine of innocent agency should not be used where it is

---

[143] The same cannot be said of *DPP v K and B*, where, even if the girls had known the boy's age, they would not have known its legal significance. [144] [1994] Crim LR 527.

[145] *Per* Russell LJ [1997] 1 Cr App R at 45.

[146] [1940] 1 All ER 339; cf. R. Taylor, 'Complicity and the Excuses' [1983] Crim LR 656.

[147] *Michael* (1840) 9 C and P 356, Chapter 4.5(b)(i).

[148] See generally the discussion by Kadish, *Blame and Punishment*, Essay 8. Under the modern law of rape contained in the Sexual Offences Act 2003, P's belief, induced by D, would have to be based on reasonable grounds.

linguistically inappropriate. It is appropriate to describe D as killing (or, at least, caus-ing the death of) V in the case involving the carer, but it is manifestly inappropriate to describe a person as driving with excess alcohol in his blood if what he has done is to lace the drink of someone else who is about to drive a car,[149] or to describe D as having raped a woman if D tricked another man into having sexual intercourse with that woman,[150] or to describe D as having committed bigamy if she induced someone else to believe (er-roneously) that the other person's marriage had been legally terminated and to remarry on the strength of this belief.[151] The conflict here is plain. The law has to be expressed in words, and some verbal formulas are hedged about with linguistic conventions which do not necessarily correspond to moral or social distinctions in responsibility. It seems right that D who gives poison to the carer to administer unwittingly should be convicted as the principal in murder, because D was the cause of the death. That element of causation remains prominent in the other examples of the 'lacer' of drinks, the encourager of non-consensual intercourse, and the orchestrators of bigamy, and the moral/social argument for criminal liability seems no less strong; but the conventions of language erect a barrier. Some offences are phrased in terms which imply personal agency (rape is said to be one) or which apply only to the holder of a certain office or licence. However, there is no reason why the law should be constrained by a barrier that is linguistic rather than substantive.

The Law Commission has recommended a set of new clauses designed to overcome these and other problems.[152] There would be a new innocent agency provision, render-ing D liable as a principal for causing P (an innocent agent) to commit the conduct ele-ment of an offence when not liable because of infancy, insanity, or lack of the required fault element. There would also be a new offence of causing another to commit a no-fault offence, designed to cater for cases such as *Attorney-General's Reference (No. 1 of 1975)*.[153] Additionally, a special provision is recommended to make it clear that D may be guilty of assisting or encouraging an offence even if the offence is one that may be committed only by someone of a particular description and D does not meet that de-scription. It is arguable that these recommendations are somewhat over-elaborate,[154] but legislation is certainly needed and the Law Commission's scheme (perhaps with some streamlining) would be a significant advance.

11.7 SPECIAL DEFENCES TO COMPLICITY

(a) WITHDRAWAL

Complicity is often focused on the words or deeds of an accomplice prior to the principal's crime. If the accomplice has a change of heart before the principal commits the offence, can the accomplice's liability be removed? It can be argued that withdrawal should be

---

[149] *Attorney-General's Reference (No. 1 of 1975)* [1975] QB 773.

[150] *Cogan and Leak* [1976] 1 QB 217; at this time a husband could not be convicted of the rape of his wife, but that rule has now been abrogated: see Chapter 8.5(d).

[151] *Kemp and Else* [1964] 2 QB 341.   [152] Law Com No. 305.   [153] See n 68 and accompanying text.

[154] R. D. Taylor, 'Procuring, Causation, Innocent Agency and the Law Commission' [2008] Crim LR 32.

rewarded in so far as it may negative culpability in relation to P's offence, and that the availability of the defence gives the accomplice an incentive to take action to prevent the substantive offence from happening.[155] In some cases a withdrawal may indeed amount to a denial of the conduct element of complicity, as where the supplier of an instrument takes it back from the principal or where the giver of encouragement supplants this with discouragement.[156] In most cases, however, the contribution of the accomplice may have some enduring influence over the principal by way of either encouragement or assistance, and one might expect the law to require not merely a change of mind communicated to the principal, but some endeavour to 'undo' the effect of the contribution already made. The older decisions tend to speak in terms of the principal acting with the authority of the accomplice, and withdrawal as a countermanding of that authority.[157] Modern decisions have emphasized the significance of the stage which the principal's actions have reached. Thus, where D's contribution consists of giving information to the principal about property to be burgled, and then, a week or so before the planned burglary, D tells the principal that he does not wish to be involved and does not want the burglary to take place, this may be an effective withdrawal.[158] This rule may be thought unduly favourable to D, since the advice or help may well have assisted or even encouraged P.[159]

In *Becarra and Cooper* (1975),[160] however, the situation was rather different. B had given C a knife to use if anyone disturbed them during the burglary they were carrying out. When B heard someone coming, he told C of this, said 'Come on, let's go', jumped out of a window, and ran off. C did not follow: he stabbed the inquisitive neighbour fatally with the knife. B was convicted as an accomplice to murder, and this was upheld in the Court of Appeal. When events have proceeded so far, an effective withdrawal was held to require far more than a few words such as 'let's go'. The Court held that 'where practicable and reasonable there must be a timely communication of the intention to abandon the common purpose', in such a form that serves 'unequivocal notice' of the withdrawal.[161] In *Becerra* the imminence of danger was taken to require something 'vastly more effective' than the few words spoken: it seems clear that if C had already been using or preparing to use the knife against the inquisitive neighbour, an effective withdrawal might have required B to go so far as to try to restrain C physically. Thus the essence of withdrawal in complicity is that the accomplice must not only make a clear statement of withdrawal and communicate this to the principal, but must also (if the crime is imminent) take some steps to prevent its commission.

The application of these kinds of rules can be difficult, in cases where a joint enterprise arises spontaneously, and (say) suddenly erupts into violence. In *Rajakumar*,[162]

---

[155] A. Reed, 'Repentance and Forgiveness: Withdrawal from Participation and the Proportionality Test', in A. Reed and M. Bohlander (eds), *Participation in Crime: Domestic and Comparative Perspectives* (2013); Cf. the unavailability of withdrawal as a defence to criminal attempts, Chapter 12.3(a).

[156] K. J. M. Smith, 'Withdrawal in Complicity: A Restatement of Principles' [2001] Crim LR 769. See also *R v Jogee* [2016] UKSC 8, para 12.   [157] E.g. *Saunders and Archer* (1573) 2 Plowd 473, at 476.

[158] *Whitefield* (1984) 79 Cr App R 36.   [159] Cf. K. J. M. Smith, n 165, 779–82.

[160] (1975) 62 Cr App R 212; see also *Baker* [1994] Crim LR 444.

[161] *Otway* [2011] EWCA Crim 3.   [162] [2013] EWCA Crim 1512.

the Court of Appeal suggested that, 'what may suffice to constitute withdrawal in spontaneous and unplanned violence may not necessarily so suffice in pre-planned group violence'. This can hardly be a rule of law, as the distinction between spontaneous and pre-planned violence is one of degree. In *Robinson*,[163] the Court of Appeal has said:

> [I]n those rare circumstances [where D purports to withdraw from a crime he or she initiated] communication of withdrawal must be given in order to give the principal offenders the opportunity to desist rather than complete the crime. This must be so even in situations of spontaneous violence unless it is not practicable or reasonable so to communicate ...[164]

The closer the principal's offence is to commission, the more active the intervention required of the accomplice for effective withdrawal. In a sense, the argument is similar to but stronger than the *Miller* principle—that one has a duty to prevent harm resulting from a train of events which one has started[165]—since the accomplice is knowingly involved in initiating the train of events, whereas Miller did so unknowingly, and it may be possible to say that D has some causal responsibility for P's subsequent act(s).[166] The Law Commission recommends that any possible defence of withdrawal should be narrowed, so that the accomplice would have a defence only if, 'he or she had negated the effect of his or her acts of assistance, encouragement or agreement before the principal offence was committed'.[167] In Canada, the rule is not quite so strict. D must, bearing in mind the nature and degree of his or her participation, have taken reasonable steps to negate that contribution.[168] This is analogous to a 'due diligence' defence, in relation to crimes of otherwise strict liability.[169]

(b) THE *TYRELL* PRINCIPLE

In *Tyrell* (1894)[170] it was held that a girl under 16 could not be convicted as a secondary party to an offence of unlawful sexual intercourse committed with her. Lord Coleridge CJ stated that Parliament could not have intended 'that the girls for whose protection [the Act] was passed should be punishable under it for the offences committed upon themselves'. Although the Court's reasoning was based on statutory interpretation, the decision has subsequently been treated as authority for a general principle that victims, particularly victims of sexual offences, cannot be convicted of complicity if the offence was created for their protection.[171] The Law Commission has recommended a restatement of this 'protective principle',[172] but whether this will deal satisfactorily with the uncertainties left by the Sexual Offences Act 2003 is doubtful.[173]

---

[163] (2000) 5 Arch News 2.   [164] Ibid.   [165] [1983] 2 AC 161.

[166] See the argument in J. Gardner, 'Complicity and Causality' (2007) 1 *Criminal Law and Philosophy* 127.

[167] Law Com No. 305, para. 3.67.   [168] *Gauthier* [2013] SCC 32.   [169] Chapter 6.4(a).

[170] [1894] 1 QB 710.   [171] E.g. *Whitehouse* [1977] QB 868.

[172] Law Com No. 305, 114–19 and draft Bill, cl. 6.

[173] M. Bohlander, 'The Sexual Offences Act 2003 and the *Tyrell* Principle—Criminalising the Victims?' [2005] Crim LR 701.

(c) CRIME PREVENTION

There is authority that a form of 'choice of evils' defence may be available to someone who would otherwise be an accomplice.[174] In *Clarke* (1984)[175] D's defence was that he joined other burglars once the offence had been planned, and did so in order to assist the police. The Court of Appeal held that this could form the basis for a defence if the jury were satisfied that D's conduct was 'overall calculated and intended not to further but to frustrate the ultimate result of the crime'. However, the law is in confusion, since there are other decisions on analogous points which have effectively denied the defence recognized in *Clarke*.[176] The Law Commission recommends a circumscribed defence of acting to prevent the commission of an offence or to limit the occurrence of harm,[177] although Parliament has enacted a somewhat broader defence that only applies to the new offence of encouraging or assisting crime.[178]

11.8 CONCLUSIONS

The decision of the Supreme Court in *R v Jogee* has done much to clarify and simplify the nature of the fault element, in particular, required to be proved against the accessory to the principal's crime. However, significant ambiguities remain. For example, firstly, the basic proposition that the liability of the accomplice is 'derivative'—derived from the liability of the principal—has been qualified in a number of respects that threaten the intellectual coherence of the basic proposition.

Secondly, the early part of this chapter was concerned with the ambit of complicity liability: what forms of conduct should suffice? The old terms 'aid, abet, counsel, and procure' continue to be relied upon,[179] and it is hardly true to say that each term bears its ordinary meaning. The variations in the level of accomplices' contributions is great. Someone who procures another to commit an offence by threats or by implanting a false belief may have substantial causal influence. This suggests that a rule restricting the penalty for the accomplice to half or three-quarters of the maximum for the principal would be too crude. In contrast, acts of aiding or encouraging may be minor and hardly significant, if any encouragement such as saying 'Oh goody' really is sufficient.[180] It would be difficult to attempt a legislative listing of all the types of conduct

---

[174] For discussion of such defences see Chapter 5.9.   [175] (1984) 80 Cr App R 344.

[176] Compare *Smith* [1960] 2 QB 423, and *Yip Chiu-Cheung* [1995] 1 AC 111, discussed in Chapter 12.5(c), both denying the defence. For further discussion see A. Ashworth, 'Testing Fidelity to Legal Values' (2000) 63 MLR 633, at 653–8.

[177] Law Com No. 305, 110–14 and draft Bill, cl. 7.

[178] Serious Crime Act 2007, s. 50, discussed in section 11.7.

[179] E.g. in s. 50 of the Anti-Terrorism, Crime and Security Act 2001, which penalizes anyone who 'aids, abets, counsels, or procures, or incites' an offence relating to biological, chemical, or nuclear weapons outside the United Kingdom. By contrast these old terms have been replaced, in relation to the offence of assisting suicide contrary to the Suicide Act 1961, by the modern language of 'doing an act capable of encouraging or assisting suicide': Coroners and Justice Act 2009, s. 59.

[180] *Giannetto* [1997] 1 Cr App R 1, section 11.3(a).

which might amount to complicity, although some progress can be made in that direction.[181] Yet the obvious expedient of allowing prosecutorial discretion to determine (in practice) the lower threshold of criminal complicity leaves scope for prosecutors to exert pressure on fringe participants in offences to choose between facing prosecution and testifying in offences against the others.

The law of complicity has also become the focal point for a number of arguments about the duties of citizens. The normally restrictive approach of English law towards liability for omissions has already been discussed,[182] but complicity is one sphere in which the courts have abandoned their general reluctance. In a sense, this may be compatible with the idea that the accomplice may be held in some way responsible for the conduct of the principal, a notion implicit in the terminology of 'authority' which is sometimes used, and also in the requirements for withdrawal from complicity. But the idea of legal responsibility as an accomplice for the acts of those whose conduct one has the power to control—rendering the publican, the car owner, and the house owner liable for the conduct of their guests, and employers liable for those of their employees[183]—is a bold step towards omissions liability under the camouflage of the law of complicity.[184] Moreover, as we saw at the beginning of section 11.5, welcome though it has been, the Supreme Court's decision in *R v Jogee*[185] has not resolved all the problems of complicity. For example, the case did not deal with the relationship— if any—between counselling and encouraging. The case did not explain the nature and relevance of 'conditional' intentions to assist or encourage. The case seemed equivocal at best on the question of whether an accomplice's knowledge of the 'essential matters' of the principal's offence extends to matters not yet in existence but which the accomplice believes will or may be in existence at the time the offence is committed (such as whether stolen goods to be handled by the principal and the accomplice will have been stolen at time when they are intended to be handled).

FURTHER READING

B. KREBS, 'Joint Criminal Enterprise' (2010) 73 MLR 578.

LAW COMMISSION, *Participating in Crime*, Law Com. No. 304 (2007).

NEW SOUTH WALES LAW COMMISSION, *Complicity* (Report No. 129, 2010).

A. P. SIMESTER, 'The Mental Element in Complicity' (2006) 122 *LQR* 578.

J. C. SMITH, 'Criminal Liability of Accessories: Law and Law Reform' (1997) 113 *LQR* 453.

K. J. M. SMITH, *A Modern Treatise on the Law of Criminal Complicity* (Oxford University Press, 1991).

W. WILSON and D. ORMEROD, 'Simply Harsh to Fairly Simple: Joint Enterprise Reform' [2015] Crim LR 53.

---

[181] See the draft produced by P. Glazebrook, 'Structuring the Criminal Code', in A. P. Simester and A. T. H. Smith (eds), *Harm and Culpability* (2005), 212.

[182] See Chapter 5.4(b) and (c).   [183] On the last point, recall *JF Alford Transport*, section 11.3(b).

[184] See A. Ashworth, 'The Scope of Criminal Liability for Omissions' (1989) 105 LQR at 445–7; Law Com No. 177, cl. 24(3).   [185] *R v Jogee* [2016] UKSC 8.

12

INCHOATE OFFENCES

12.1 THE CONCEPT OF AN INCHOATE OFFENCE

The word 'inchoate', not much used in ordinary discourse, means 'just begun', 'undeveloped'. The common law gave birth to three general offences which are usually termed 'inchoate' or 'preliminary' crimes—attempt, conspiracy, and incitement. A principal feature of these crimes is that they are committed even though the substantive offence (i.e. the offence it was intended to bring about) is not completed and no harm results. An attempt fails, a conspiracy comes to nothing, words of incitement are ignored—in all these instances, there may be liability for the inchoate crime. However, the legal landscape has changed in several ways.

In the first place, the Law Commission recommended and Parliament decided that the inchoate offence of incitement should be abolished and replaced by a more extensive set of offences of assisting or encouraging crime, and these are examined in section 12.7. Secondly, those offences take their place alongside others that criminalize conduct at an early stage, well before the stage of a criminal attempt. Examples are 'grooming' children for sexual purposes,[1] making or supplying articles for use in frauds,[2] and the offence of engaging in 'any conduct in preparation for giving effect to' an intention to commit acts of terrorism in s. 5 of the Terrorism Act 2006.[3] Thirdly, in

---

[1] Sexual Offences Act 2003, s. 15.   [2] Fraud Act 2006, s. 7.
[3] See V. Tadros, 'Justice and Terrorism' (2007) 11 New Crim LR 658.

many instances, the law of inchoate offences also applies to these offences defined in an inchoate mode, driving criminal liability even further back: so, it would be possible to charge someone with conspiracy or attempt to 'groom' a child, or to make or supply articles for use in fraud. Fourthly, crimes of possession are also essentially inchoate: it is not the mere possession, so much as what the possessor might do with the article or substance, which is the reason for criminalization. These developments in the criminal law will be assessed after a discussion of the two remaining common law inchoate offences—attempt and conspiracy—and the new statutory inchoate offences of encouraging or assisting crime.

12.2 THE JUSTIFICATIONS FOR PENALIZING ATTEMPTS AT CRIMES

(a) INTRODUCTION

It might be thought that if there is a justification for making the doing of 'X' criminal, then there must automatically be a justification for criminalizing an attempt to do 'X'; but matters are not so straightforward.[4] Let us begin with three examples: (i) X goes to the house of his rival, V, with a can of petrol, some paper, and a box of matches; he soaks the paper in petrol and is about to push it through the letter box when he is arrested before he can do anything more; (ii) Y drives a car straight at V, but V jumps out of the way at the last moment and is uninjured; (iii) Z is offered money to carry a package of cannabis into Britain; she accepts, brings the package in, but on her arrest it is found that the package contains dried lettuce leaves. These are all cases in which there may be a conviction for attempt.[5] The first feature to be noticed is that no harm actually occurred in any of them—no damage was done, no injury caused, no drugs smuggled. Normally, criminal liability requires both culpability and harm: X, Y, and Z may appear culpable, but they have caused no harm. Why, then, should the criminal law become involved? One answer is that harm does indeed have a central place in criminal liability, but that the concern is not merely with the occurrence of harm but also with its prevention. According to this view, the first decision for legislators is exactly which harms and wrongs should properly be objects of the criminal law (see Chapter 3). Once this has been decided, and taking the aims of the criminal law into account, the law should not only provide for the punishment of those who have culpably caused such harms, but also penalize those who are trying to cause the harms. A person who tries to cause a prohibited harm and fails is, in terms of moral culpability, not materially different from the person who tries and succeeds: the difference in outcome is determined by chance rather than by choice, and a censuring institution such as the criminal law should not subordinate itself to the vagaries of fortune by focusing on results rather than on culpability. There is

---

[4] R. A. Duff, *Criminal Attempts* (1996), ch 5 and *passim*.

[5] Depending on the accused's intention and beliefs at the time: see section 12.3(a).

also a consequentialist justification for the law of attempts, inasmuch as it reduces harm by authorizing law enforcement officers and the courts to step in *before* any harm has been done, so long as the danger of the harm being caused is clear.

(b) TWO KINDS OF ATTEMPT

The rationale for criminalizing attempts can best be appreciated by drawing a theoretical distinction (which the law itself does not draw) between two kinds of attempt. First, there are incomplete attempts, which are cases in which the defendant has set out to commit an offence but has not yet done all the acts necessary to bring it about. Our first example, of X about to put petrol-soaked paper through the door of V's house, is such a case: he has still to light the paper or push it through the door. Contrast this with the second kind of attempt, which will be called a complete attempt. Here the defendant has done all that he intended, but the desired result has not followed—Y has driven the car at V, intending to injure V, but he failed; and Z has smuggled the package into the country, believing it to be cannabis when in fact it is a harmless and worthless substance.

It is easier to justify the criminalization of complete attempts than incomplete attempts, and the two sets of justifications have somewhat different emphases. The justification for punishing complete attempts is that the defendant has done all the acts intended, with the beliefs required for the offence, and is therefore no less blameworthy than a person who is successful in committing the substantive offence. The complete 'attempter' is thwarted by some unexpected turn of events which, to him, is a matter of pure chance—the intended victim jumped out of the way or the substance was not what it appeared to be. These are applications of what were called the 'subjective' principles earlier, the essence of which is that people's criminal liability should be assessed on what they were trying to do, intended to do, and believed they were doing, rather than on the actual consequences of their conduct.[6] Rejection of this approach would lead to criminal liability always being judged according to the actual outcome, which would allow luck to play too great a part in the criminal law. Of course, luck and chance play a considerable role in human affairs, and we have already seen how important the chance result of death is in the law of involuntary manslaughter.[7] However, there is no reason why a system for judging and formally censuring the behaviour of others should be a slave to the vagaries of chance. The 'subjective principle' would also be accepted by the consequentialist as a justification for criminalizing complete attempts: the defendant was trying to break the law, and therefore constituted a source of social danger no less (or little less) than that presented by 'successful' harm-doers.

What about incomplete attempts? The subjective principle does have some application here, inasmuch as the defendant has given some evidence of a determination to commit the substantive offence—though the evidence is likely to be less conclusive than in cases of complete attempts. There is one distinct factor present in incomplete

---

[6] Chapter 8.5(a).   [7] See Chapter 6.4(a).

attempts, which is the social importance of authorizing official intervention before harm is done. Since the prevention of harm has a central place in the justifications for criminal law, there is a strong case for stopping attempts before they result in the causing of harm. Detailed arguments about the point at which the law should intervene are discussed in section 12.3(b). Once this point has been reached, then the agents of law enforcement may intervene to stop attempts before they go further. The culpability of the incomplete attempter may be less than that of the complete attempter because there remains the possibility that there would have been voluntary repentance at some late stage: after all, it may take greater nerve to do the final act which triggers the actual harm than to do the preliminary acts. But so long as it is accepted that the incomplete attempter has evinced a clear intention to commit the substantive offence by doing some further acts, there is sufficient ground for criminalization. Federico Picinali has argued that the final acts in an attempt may indeed provide a basis for inferring a clearer intention to commit the offence than might have been the case at an earlier stage.[8] He says this is because such final acts will be accompanied by a belief—not present at the earlier stage—that the time to commit the act is now. In many cases, that test may be helpful, but it will perhaps provide less guidance when it is a series of acts that must be done to complete the crime rather than a final act.

Although there are sufficient grounds for criminalizing both complete and incomplete attempts, it may be right to reflect some differences between them at the sentencing stage. It may be argued that incomplete attempts should be punished less severely than the full offence—because of the possibility of voluntary abandonment of the attempt, because it takes greater nerve to consummate an offence, and because it may be prudent to leave some incentive (i.e. reduced punishment) to the incomplete attempter to give up rather than to carry out the full offence. For complete attempts the case for reduced punishment is less strong, although there may be an argument for some reduction of punishment in order to give the complete attempter an incentive not to try again—otherwise D might reason that there is nothing to lose by this.[9] However, on the 'objectivist' approach to attempts advocated by Antony Duff, lesser punishment for completed attempts would be important to mark the fact that D failed to produce the intended effect in the real world.[10] It will be noticed that these arguments for reduced punishments are consequentialist in nature. Following the principle of 'desert', there is little reason for reducing the punishment of the complete attempter, although there is some reason for recognizing the possibility that the incomplete attempter might yet desist.

---

[8] F. Picinali, 'A Retributive Justification for not Punishing Bare Intentions or: On the Moral Relevance of the "Now Belief"' (2012) 31 *Law and Philosophy* 23.

[9] The longest determinate sentence in English law, forty-five years' imprisonment, was given for the offence of attempting to place on an aircraft a device likely to destroy the aircraft: see *Hindawi* (2008) 1 Cr App R(S) 156.   [10] Duff, n 4, ch 4 and 351–4.

12.3 THE ELEMENTS OF CRIMINAL ATTEMPT

The relevant English law is now to be found in the Criminal Attempts Act 1981, which followed a Law Commission report on the subject.[11] It will be discussed by considering three separate aspects of the offence in turn—the fault element, the conduct element, and the problem of impossibility.

(a) THE FAULT ELEMENT

It has been said that, where a person is charged with an attempt, 'the intent becomes the principal ingredient of the crime'.[12] English law on this point appears clear, in that s. 1(1) of the Criminal Attempts Act 1981 begins by stating that D must be shown to have acted, 'with intent to commit an offence to which this section applies'.[13] There have been appeals in cases where D has been charged with attempting to cause grievous bodily harm by driving a car at another person, and the defence has been that D did not intend to injure the other. These appeals have led the courts to establish that purpose is not required for the crime of attempt: what is needed, according to James LJ in *Mohan* (1976),[14] is proof of 'a decision to bring about ... [the offence], no matter whether the accused desired that consequence of his act or not'. This is supposed to align the meaning of intent here with its meaning in the general law, so as to include foresight of virtual certainty.[15] Some writers have misgivings about this 'extension':[16] can I really be said to be attempting to do X when I was not trying to bring X about but only foresaw X's occurrence as a virtually certain consequence of doing something else that I did set out to achieve? To include cases involving foresight of virtually certain consequences within attempts, is really to include some kinds of intentional 'endangerment' within attempts. That may not be wrong, on policy grounds, but it takes us away from a plain and simple focus on attempts (as we will see shortly).

Accepting that an attempt must involve intention, whether direct or inferred from a foresight of virtual certainty, a further question then arises: which of the elements of the offence—any? all? some?—must be intended? Section 1(1) of the 1981 Act speaks of an, 'intent to commit an offence', but that wording is ambiguous on this crucial point. Consider an example in which D is caught as he is about to throw a stone in the direction of a window, and D is charged with attempted criminal damage. Criminal damage contrary to the Criminal Damage Act 1971 is committed if, without lawful

---

[11] Law Com No. 102, *Attempt, and Impossibility in Relation to Attempt, Conspiracy and Incitement* (1980). See further I. Dennis, 'The Criminal Attempts Act 1981' [1982] Crim LR 5 and A. Ashworth, 'Criminal Attempts and the Role of Resulting Harm under the Code, and in the Common Law' (1988) 19 *Rutgers* LJ 725.

[12] *Per* Lord Goddard CJ in *Whybrow* (1951) 35 Cr App R 141, at 147. For further general discussion, see Duff, n 4, ch 1.

[13] The 1981 Act applies to offences triable on indictment, but not to summary offences.

[14] [1976] 1 QB 1, applied to the 1981 Act in *Pearman* (1985) 80 Cr App R 259.

[15] See now *Woollin* [1999] AC 92, discussed in Chapter 5.5(b); the Law Commission proposes no change: Law Com Consultation Paper No. 183, *Conspiracy and Attempts* (2007), 14.32.

[16] Cf. Duff, n 4, 17–21.

excuse, D intentionally or recklessly damages or destroys property belonging to an-other. Suppose D says that his intention was to throw the stone in the general direc-tion of the window, but not directly at the window: in other words, he admits only recklessness—not intention—with regard to damaging the window, if he performs the action of throwing the stone that way. For the purposes of convicting D of an attempt to commit this offence, it is clear that the prosecution will have to establish that, in throwing the stone, D actually intended to damage the window (the conduct/consequence element of the offence). That is for the following reason. There is no general crime of 'reckless endangerment' of persons or property in English law. A requirement, in the law of attempts, for mere recklessness as to the conduct/consequence element of causing damage to the window would turn the offence of attempting criminal damage into one of recklessly endangering property: something the 1981 Act did not envisage or authorize.[17] So, although recklessness with regard to damaging the window would suffice as the fault element for criminal damage itself, had the window actually been damaged by the stone when thrown, it is an insufficient fault element for the crime of attempting to commit criminal damage. Nothing short of an intention to cause damage—the conduct/consequence element—will suffice.

It is, though, also an element of the basic offence of criminal damage that the win-dow belongs to another person. Does it follow that, in order to fulfil the requirements of s. 1 of the 1981 Act, D must also be proved to have intended to damage *another per-son's* window, or is it sufficient that D was reckless as to whether the window belonged to another person? The fact that the property damaged belongs to another person is a 'circumstance' element of the crime, and not a conduct or consequence element (un-like damaging the window: the conduct/consequence element). Arguably, the require-ment of intention in criminal attempts relates only to the 'agent-causal' elements of the crime, the conduct and consequence elements, rather than to 'non-causal' elements of the crime. The latter are the circumstance elements that go towards describing or explaining why what D does will be an offence, but with D's *causal* role in events re-moved from the picture. The fact that property 'belongs to another' is clearly an es-sential element of the offence of criminal damage. However, it not an agent-causal element: something that D 'does', as a matter of basic action—'damaging'—and its con-sequences, if any. Instead, the fact that property belongs to another is a non-causal element, an essential feature of the crime that can be described without reference to D's conduct and its consequences. Where non-causal ('circumstantial') elements of the crime are concerned, it is open to the law to hold that, if recklessness suffices for this element when the completed crime is in issue, it also suffices when an attempt to com-mit the crime is in issue. In that regard, a point of importance for the later discussion is that, confusing though this may be, non-causal (circumstance) elements of an offence can be fault elements. In rape cases, the requirement that D has no reasonable belief

---

[17] Until now, English law has filled this gap pragmatically, by creating a few specific offences of endanger-ment to deal with reckless behaviour on the roads and in other situations where there is a risk, but no actual occurrence, of serious consequences.

in V's consent, when intentionally engaging in sexual intercourse with V, may be so described. The absence of reasonable belief in V's consent is a non-causal state of mind that must, together with its mirroring circumstance element—that V did not in fact consent—accompany the agent-causal element of intentional intercourse.

However, the law has never been entirely clear on this crucial point. There were some indications that the courts—although reserving the right to interpret the elements of each offence in such a way as seems appropriate in context—were moving towards a general distinction between conduct or consequence (agent-causal) elements, which must be intended, and circumstance (non-causal) elements, where the fault element will be the same as for the completed offence.[18] The well-respected case of *Khan*[19] is authority for the view that, in cases of attempted rape, whilst sexual intercourse (the conduct element) must be intended, it is sufficient to show that D had the fault element for the full offence of rape with respect to V's lack of consent (circumstance element).[20] However, in *Pace and Rogers*,[21] without any broad review of the authorities, a much stricter approach was taken, and doubt cast on *Khan* as an authority for the fault element in attempts generally. The Court of Appeal held that the prosecution had to prove not only that the conduct and consequence elements were intended, but also that the circumstance elements were intended.

Following a surveillance operation, the defendants in *Pace and Rogers* had been charged with and initially convicted of attempting to commit an offence contrary to s. 327 of the Proceeds of Crime Act 2002: concealing, disguising, or converting criminal property, knowing or suspecting that the property was the proceeds of crime.[22] Undercover officers had gone to the defendants' scrap metal yard, and offered them metal that the officers indicated had been stolen (it was not in fact stolen, but belonged to the police). The defendants agreed to buy the metal. That being so, had the metal in fact been stolen, they would have committed the completed offence just described, if they were proved to have known or suspected that the property was the proceeds of crime. However, given that the metal they agreed to buy was not in fact stolen metal, the defendants could only be charged with an attempt to conceal, disguise, or convert the metal (the criminal property): what is known as a case of 'factually impossible' attempt.[23] So, far as the fault element is concerned, had the Court of Appeal followed the well-established approach in *Khan*,[24] that would have meant the prosecution had to prove that, intending to convert the property (the agent-causal, conduct element), the defendants 'knew *or suspected*' that the property was stolen (non-causal, circumstance

---

[18] *Whybrow* (1951) 35 Cr App R 141 is authority for the view that consequence elements must be intended. In that case, it was admitted that the judge has mis-directed the jury when telling them that the fault element for attempted murder could include an intention to cause grievous bodily harm, even though proof of that would suffice for the full offence. For attempted murder, proof of an intention to cause death (the consequence element) must be demonstrated.

[19] (1990) 91 Cr App R 29.

[20] At that time, the circumstance-fault element was recklessness as to a lack of consent, but is now an absence of reasonable belief in consent.

[21] [2014] EWCA Crim 186.   [22] The completed offence is in s. 327 of the Proceeds of Crime Act 2002.

[23] See the discussion in section 12.3(c).   [24] (1990) 91 Cr App R 29.

element), this being the fault element for the completed offence. However, the Court of Appeal instead held that there could be no conviction in such a case—a case of attempt—unless the defendants actually *knew* that the metal was stolen. Proof of suspicion that the property was stolen property was not enough for the inchoate offence of attempt, even if it was enough for the completed offence.

The logic of *Khan* is that where circumstance (non-causal) elements are concerned, a charge of attempt involves proof of the same fault element as required for the completed offence. Disagreeing with that approach, the Court of Appeal in *Pace and Rogers* confined the authority of *Khan* to rape cases.[25] There was also some suggestion that the circumstance-fault element of crimes should be stricter in cases of impossible attempt, such as *Pace and Rogers*. In *Khan*, the attempt was not factually impossible, in that, had D gone on to have non-consensual intercourse with V, rape would have been committed. However, the drawing of such a distinction—between possible and impossible attempts— would be wholly contrary to the policy of the 1981 Act,[26] and cannot be accepted.[27]

Having said that, in favour of the decision in *Pace and Rogers*, the Court of Appeal was right to point out that its approach, requiring circumstance or non-causal elements to be known about, was consistent with the law's approach to the same issue in conspiracy cases. If D1 and D2 agree to handle 'stolen' goods for D3, there will be no conspiracy unless it is shown that D1 and D2 knew that the goods would be stolen at the time of the handling; suspicion that the goods might be stolen would not be enough on a conspiracy charge.[28] Moreover, a number of academic commentators[29] also favour a narrower approach to the fault element in inchoate crime that requires the prosecution to prove, in attempts cases, that (as was put in *Pace and Rogers*[30]):

> Turning, then, to s 1(1) [of the Criminal Attempts Act 1981] we consider that, as a matter of ordinary language and in accordance with principle, an 'intent to commit an offence' connotes an intent to commit all the elements of the offence. We can see no sufficient basis, whether linguistic or purposive, for construing it otherwise.

Regrettably, the Court of Appeal did not allude to the recent Report of the Law Commission on attempts and conspiracy, in which it had recommended that, whilst attempts and conspiracy should certainly be treated in essentially the same way so far as the circumstance-fault element is concerned, the way to treat them the same is by (broadly speaking) following the *Khan* approach to the circumstance-fault element in *both* crimes.[31]

---

[25] Where, in any event, its authority will have to be re-considered, in the light of the change in the circumstance fault element of rape to an absence of reasonable belief in consent, rather than recklessness: Chapter 9.5(i).

[26] See the Criminal Attempts Act 1981, s. 1(3)(b).

[27] See the criticism of F. Stark, 'The *Mens Rea* of a Criminal Attempt' (2014) 3 Arch Rev 7; G. Virgo, 'Criminal Attempts—The Law of Unintended Consequences' (2014) 73 CLJ 244.

[28] *Saik* [2006] UKHL18.

[29] J. Child and A. Hunt, 'Pace and Rogers and the Mens Rea of Criminal Attempt: Khan on the Scrapheap?' (2014) 78 J Crim Law 220; P. Mirfield, 'Intention and Criminal Attempts' [2015] Crim LR 140.

[30] [2014] EWCA Crim 186.

[31] Law Commission, *Conspiracy and Attempts* (Law Com No. 318, 2009).

One possible, if unlikely, path the law may now take involves the courts seeking to circumvent any intent-as-to-circumstance-element requirement, by arguing that, in cases requiring proof of lack of consent, the typical defendant 'conditionally' intends to have non-consensual sexual intercourse.[32] That is to say, D intends to have sexual intercourse if V consents, but D also intends to have sexual intercourse if D does not consent. Given the high scholarly authority for that approach, namely the late Professor Glanville Williams, at some future point the Supreme Court may consider it.[33]

One difficulty facing the courts, whether or not the law is reformed along such lines, is to distinguish between the 'agent-causal' elements of the offence (the conduct and consequence elements), and the 'non-causal' (circumstance) elements, where a particular offence makes the distinction a hard one to draw. An example is the aggravated offence, contrary to s. 1(2) of the Criminal Damage Act 1971, of damaging or destroying property, being reckless as to whether life is endangered thereby.[34] Suppose D tries to drop a piece of concrete from a bridge over a motorway, but he is unable to heave it off the ledge as it is too heavy. When arrested, D says that his intention was solely to damage a car, although he realized that danger might be posed to the driver. For the purposes of securing a conviction for attempt to commit the offence contrary to s. 1(2), will it be necessary for the prosecution to show not merely that D intended to damage the car (the conduct element), but also that D intended to endanger someone's life thereby? Or, will it be enough that D was reckless as to this element of the 'aggravated' offence under s. 1(2)?

On analogous facts, in *Attorney-General's Reference (No. 3 of 1992)*,[35] the Court of Appeal held that a person can be convicted of attempted aggravated arson if he intends to cause damage to property by fire while reckless as to whether the life of another would thereby be endangered. The case has been criticized for its failure to require intention as to both elements of the offence, on the basis that they are either conduct or consequence elements, but are not circumstance elements.[36] If the decision is eclipsed by *Pace and Rogers*, then, of course, intention is required as to all elements of the offence irrespective of whether they are agent-causal (conduct/consequence) or non-causal (circumstance) elements. Putting that possibility on one side, caution is needed here before endorsing the criticism of the court's decision. First, an element of an offence may be a conduct, circumstance, or a consequence element, depending either on how the offence as a whole is defined or on the way in which the prosecution makes its case. For example, the dangerousness of 'dangerous driving' is a conduct element if

---

[32] Conditional intention was ruled out, as a basis for understanding the fault element in attempts by *Husseyn* (1978) 67 Cr App R 131, but the decision has been heavily criticized.

[33] See G. Williams, 'Intents in the Alternative' (1991) 50 CLJ 120.

[34] See J. Child, 'The Structure, Coherence and Limits of Inchoate Liability: The New Ulterior Element' (2014) 34 *Legal Studies* 537–59.

[35] *Attorney General's Reference (No. 3 of 1992)* (1994) 98 Cr App R 383.

[36] See D. W. Elliott, 'Endangering Life by Damaging or Destroying Property' [1997] Crim LR 382. See also See J. Child, 'The Structure, Coherence and Limits of Inchoate Liability: The New Ulterior Element' (2014) 34 *Legal Studies* 537–59.

the focus is on the manner in which D drove, but it can be a circumstance element if the danger came not from the manner of D's driving, as such, but from the fact that, say, D had crammed twelve people into a small car designed to carry only four people. Secondly, a complicating factor is that a fault element can be a circumstance element. For example, as indicated earlier, in rape cases, the requirement that D have no reasonable belief in V's consent, when intentionally engaging in sexual intercourse with V, may be so described.

In the case of s. 1(2) of the 1971 Act, in proving the completed offence, D must be shown to have been reckless whether life was endangered by the damage D caused. Crucially, it is not necessary to show that life was in fact endangered by D's action. That indicates that this element of the offence is best described as a non-causal, circumstance-fault element, and not as an agent-causal, consequence element. It follows that, as it is a circumstance element, the prosecution must prove only the same thing on an attempt charge that it is obliged to prove when charging the completed offence: namely, that D was reckless whether life was endangered by the damage he or she caused. There is no need to prove that D intended life to be endangered thereby, because no such consequence need ensue for the completed offence to be committed. In other words, that feature of the offence does not feature agent-causally.

This analysis is undoubtedly complex, and many will understandably believe that the way to banish complexity is to follow the *Pace and Rogers* approach, requiring intention as to all elements. Unfortunately, thing are not so simple. Even if one is broadly disposed to follow the *Pace and Rogers* approach, it only makes sense to require *intention* as to the 'doing' part of the attempt, the agent-causal element(s). For the other, non-causal, elements (if any)—the circumstance elements—requiring the prosecution to prove *knowledge*, not intention, is the right requirement. On a restrictive, *Pace and Rogers* approach, it is, for example, more sensible to say that I must 'know' that goods will be stolen when I handle them, not that I must be shown to have 'intended' them to be stolen. Yet, in order to adopt this common-sense approach, a distinction between agent-causal (conduct/consequence) and non-causal (circumstantial) elements of the offence must still be drawn, as under the *Khan* approach. Even so, it must be admitted that a lack of clarity over the meaning of 'knowledge', in law, is likely to prove problematic in this context. Just because someone tells me that goods are stolen, does that mean that I hence 'know' that they are? If a known drug dealer asks me to post a sealed package through someone's letter box, do I 'know' that the package contains drugs? The answer is 'no', in the ordinary sense of 'knowledge', in both cases, although the law is clearly free to adopt a wide definition of 'knowledge' to catch such cases if policy considerations so dictate. Such definitional contortion could, though, be avoided by the simple expedient of following the *Khan* approach. Barring special kinds of exception, there should be a general rule requiring in attempts the same kind of fault to be found in the completed offence in issue; and in the absence of any fault requirement in the completed offence, imposing a requirement to prove intention as to conduct or consequence elements and recklessness in relation to circumstance elements, when an attempt is charged.

(b) THE CONDUCT ELEMENT

Since the effect of the law of attempts is to extend the criminal sanction further back than the definition of substantive offences, the question of the minimum conduct necessary to constitute an attempt has great importance.[37] The issue concerns incomplete attempts: when has a person gone far enough to justify criminal liability? Two schools of thought may be outlined here. First, there is the fault-centred approach, arguing that the essence of an attempt is trying to commit a crime, and that all the law should require is proof of the intention plus any act designed to implement that intention. The reasoning is that any person who has gone so far as to translate a criminal intention into action has crossed the threshold of criminal liability, and deserves punishment (though, for the reasons given earlier—the possibility of abandonment, for example— the punishment would be less than for a complete attempt). Secondly, there is the act-centred approach, of which two types may be distinguished. One type bases itself on the argument that one cannot be sure that the deterrent effect of the criminal law has failed until D has done all the acts necessary, since one could regard the law as successful if D did stop before the last act out of fear of detection and punishment. This suggests that only acts close to the substantive crime should be criminalized. The other type of act-centred approach is adopted by those who see great dangers of oppressive official action—to the detriment of individual liberties—if the ambit of the law of attempts is not restricted tightly. If *any* overt act were to suffice as the conduct element in attempts, wrongful arrests might be more numerous; convictions would turn largely on evidence of D's intention, so the police might be tempted to exert pressure in order to obtain a confession; and miscarriages of justice might increase, especially when inferences from silence are permissible (see subsection (c)). To safeguard the liberty of citizens and to assure people that justice is being fairly administered, the law should require proof of an unambiguous act close to the commission of the crime before conviction of an attempt.[38] Otherwise, we would be risking a world of thought crimes and thought police.

The choices for the conduct element in attempts might therefore be ranged along a continuum. The least requirement would be any 'overt act' (manifesting the relevant fault element), but that would be objectionable as risking oppressive police practices and as leaving little opportunity for an attempter to withdraw voluntarily. The most demanding requirement would be the 'last act' or 'final stage', but that goes too far in the other direction, leaving little time for the police to intervene to prevent the occurrence of harm and allowing the defence to gain an acquittal by raising a doubt whether D had actually done the very last act. In the US the Model Penal Code requires D to have taken a 'substantial step' towards the commission of the full offence.[39] This might appear to breach the principle of maximum certainty (Chapter 4.4(e)), but the Model

---

[37] Duff, n 4, ch 2; Ashworth, n 11.

[38] This was the clear inference from the empirical research on public opinion by P. Robinson and J. Darley, *Justice, Liability and Blame* (1995), 20–8.

[39] Model Penal Code, s. 2.5.01, discussed by Ashworth, n 11, 751–3.

Penal Code seeks to avoid this by listing a number of authoritative examples of a 'substantial step'. Thus, the approach recognizes the inevitable flexibility in questions of degree such as this but seeks to give some firm guidance. The Criminal Attempts Act 1981 requires D to have done 'an act which is more than merely preparatory to the commission of the offence'. Opinions differ on whether this is closer to the fault-centred approach than is the 'substantial step' test, but it is certainly more vague (since there are no authoritative examples), and the Act leaves the application of the test entirely to the jury, once the judge has found that there is sufficient evidence of an attempt.[40] At the earlier stage of arrest, it leaves much to the judgment of the police officer.[41]

On a plain reading of the Act the proper test is whether D was still engaged in merely preparatory acts, in which case he is not guilty of attempt, or whether his conduct was *more* than merely preparatory. This is inevitably a question of degree, and the Court of Appeal has not been wholly consistent in its classification of different cases. Thus, in *Jones* (1990)[42] D bought a gun, shortened its barrel, put on a disguise, and then jumped into the back seat of his rival's car. D pointed the loaded gun at his rival and said 'You are not going to like this', but his rival then grabbed the gun. The defence argument was that this could not amount to attempted murder: what D had done was not more than merely preparatory, because he still had to release the safety catch, put his finger on the trigger, and pull it. The Court of Appeal dismissed this argument, which was more appropriate to the 'last act' test, and held that once D had climbed into the car and pointed the gun there was ample evidence for a jury to hold that attempted murder had been committed. A more difficult case is *Campbell* (1991)[43] where the police had received information about a planned post office robbery. They watched D in the street outside the post office. They arrested him as he approached the door of the post office, and found him to be carrying an imitation firearm and a threatening note, and carrying (but not wearing) sunglasses. The Court of Appeal quashed D's conviction for attempted robbery, holding that it is extremely unlikely that a person could be convicted of an attempt when he 'has not even gained the place where he could be in a position to carry out the offence'.[44] He had not entered the post office, and was no longer wearing the sunglasses.[45] This decision was followed in *Geddes* (1996),[46] where the Court of Appeal quashed a conviction for attempted false imprisonment. D had been seen loitering around the lavatory block

[40] Criminal Attempts Act 1981, ss. 1(1) and 4(3).

[41] Under ss. 24(3)(b) and 24(4)(b) of the Police and Criminal Evidence Act 1984 it is lawful to arrest without warrant a person reasonably suspected of committing an attempted crime; and under s. 24(7)(b) a constable may arrest without a warrant anyone reasonably suspected to be *about to commit* an arrestable offence.

[42] (1990) 91 Cr App R 351; cf. the earlier decision in *Gullefer* [1987] Crim LR 195.

[43] (1991) 93 Cr App R 350.

[44] D's conduct went beyond 'reconnoitering the place intended for the commission of the offence', which is sufficient for an attempt under the Model Penal Code but was intended to lie outside the English test: Law Com No. 102, para. 2.33.

[45] These decisions were considered in *Attorney-General's Reference (No. 1 of 1992)* (1993) 96 Cr App R 298, where the Court of Appeal held that a conviction for attempted rape could be proper even if the man had not yet attempted penetration.

[46] [1996] Crim LR 894; cf. *Nash* [1999] Crim LR 308, where the Court of Appeal upheld convictions on two counts on facts that were a considerable distance short of the commission of the substantive offence.

of a boys' school, and the prosecution case rested on a can of cider found in a lavatory cubicle, D's rucksack (containing a large kitchen knife, rope, and masking tape) found in nearby bushes, and evidence from a third party that D was sexually fascinated by young boys. The Court harboured no doubt that D's intentions were as the prosecution alleged, but held ('with the gravest unease') that, since D had not spoken to or confronted any pupil at the school, his conduct had been merely preparatory and no more. On the other side of the line fell *Tosti* (1997),[47] where convictions for attempted burglary were upheld. D and another man were seen crouching by the door of a barn, examining the padlock. When disturbed they tried to run away, and D was caught. His car was found nearby, and there was oxy-acetylene cutting equipment concealed in a hedge. The Court of Appeal took the view that D had done an act showing that he had tried to commit the offence, rather than merely putting himself in a position to do so.

The Court of Appeal's various endeavours to reformulate the statutory test so that it can be applied meaningfully to the facts of differing cases have not been conspicuously successful. It is hardly helpful to refer to the steering of a 'mid-way course' between the 'last act' test and the penalization of merely preparatory acts.[48] The Court in *Tosti* rightly emphasized the distinction between preparatory acts, which may constitute an attempt, and *merely* preparatory acts, which may not; but that distinction is difficult to apply to *Campbell*, where one might suggest that D had gone beyond mere preparation, whereas *Geddes* is closer to the dividing line. Sheer physical proximity to the intended victim or targeted property may be the only sensible distinction between the convictions upheld in *Jones* and in *Tosti* and the other decisions, but of course, in the age of instant electronic communication, physical proximity to a victim may be a guide to whether or not the test has been satisfied in only a limited range of situations. In *R*,[49] D was charged with and convicted of attempting to arrange a sexual offence with a child (itself a partially inchoate offence), contrary to s. 14 of the Sexual Offences Act 2003. D had texted a prostitute to ask if she knew of any 12-year-olds available for sex. R's conviction was upheld, although—appalling though D's action was—it might easily be argued that the text message was purely preparatory to any attempt to make a genuine 'arrangement' to commit a child sex offence.

The Law Commission proposes that the law should penalize 'criminal preparation' by those who are 'in the process of executing a plan to commit an intended offence'; that the test should be 'defined with a degree of imprecision' so as to enable courts to deal fairly with a variety of circumstances; and that there should be a list of statutory examples to guide the courts in applying the new test.[50] The Commission denies that

---

[47] [1997] Crim LR 746.

[48] The words of Lord Lane in *Gullefer*, considered by K. J. M. Smith, 'Proximity in Attempt: Lord Lane's Midway Course' [1991] Crim LR 576. For more recent cases, see, e.g., *Moore v DPP* [2010] EWHC 1822 (admin), driving on private land can be more than merely preparatory to driving on public land; *Mason v DPP* [2009] EWHC 2189 (Admin), opening the car door not more than merely preparatory to drink-driving; *Ferriter* [2012] EWCA Crim 2211, struggling with V and putting one hand in her trousers can be more than merely preparatory to a sexual offence.

[49] [2009] 1 WLR 713.   [50] LCCP 183, *Conspiracy and Attempts*, 16.8 to 16.17.

the new test would enlarge the current law of attempts and, since no case for extending the law has been made out, the new offence must be carefully drafted so as to ensure this. The use of examples, pioneered in the USA,[51] may well be a fruitful device for achieving consistency in judicial rulings.

(c) THE PROBLEM OF IMPOSSIBILITY

Just as the conduct element in attempts relates chiefly to incomplete attempts, so the problem of impossibility usually arises in connection with complete attempts.[52] Once again, there are fault-centred and act-centred perspectives to be considered, according to whether one takes the view that D's beliefs or the reality of D's conduct should be the primary determinant of liability.

The fault-centred approach to impossible attempts is a straightforward application of the subjective principle (see Chapter 6.4(a)): a person should be judged on the facts or circumstances as he or she believed them to be at the time. So, where D *believes* that he is doing acts which amount to an offence, it is justifiable to convict of an attempt to commit that offence. D's state of mind is just as blameworthy as it would be if the facts *were* as they are believed to be. Thus, we are justified in convicting the person who smuggles dried lettuce leaves in the belief that they are cannabis, and the person who puts sugar in someone's drink in the belief that it is cyanide, and the person who handles goods in the belief that they are stolen. In all these cases there is no relevant moral difference between their culpability and the culpability in cases where the substances *really* are cannabis, cyanide, and stolen goods.

The act-centred approach points to the absence of actual danger in these cases. Thus it is argued that there is a risk of oppression if the law criminalizes people in objectively innocent situations.[53] Part of the concern here is that convictions might be based on confessions which are the result of fear, confusion, or even police fabrication.[54] Without the need to establish any objectively incriminating facts, the police might construct a case simply on the basis of remarks attributed to the accused person. Anyone carrying a bag might be liable to be arrested and to have attributed to him or her the remark: 'I thought it contained drugs'. These arguments based on the threat to individual rights are too important to be dismissed peremptorily, particularly since the Criminal Justice and Public Order Act 1994 provides that adverse inferences may be drawn from a suspect's silence in the face of key questions, without also providing that statements attributed by the police to the suspect, which are

---

[51] See n 25, and I. Dennis, 'The Law Commission Report on Attempt: The Elements of Attempt' [1980] Crim LR 758.   [52] Duff, n 4, ch 3.

[53] Three expressions of the act-centred view are J. F. Stephen, *History of the Criminal Law* (1883), ii, 225; J. Temkin, 'Impossible Attempts: Another View' (1976) 39 MLR 55; and Lords Bridge and Roskill in *Anderton v Ryan* [1985] AC 560.

[54] This is one of the concerns expressed in the lengthy discussion of attempts by G. Fletcher, *Rethinking Criminal Law* (1978), 137ff.

unrecorded and which the suspect denies, should be inadmissible in evidence.[55] There has been no shortage of research findings to the effect that new controls on the police tend to be manipulated in practice so that the intended goals may not be achieved.[56] It may therefore be unsafe to expect the laws of criminal procedure to prevent any dangers to individual rights: if a fault-centred law leads to police malpractice which cannot otherwise be prevented, it ought to be narrowed. This leaves untouched the fault-centred argument that there really is no difference in terms of moral culpability or dangerousness between persons who actually do make an impossible attempt and many ordinary attempters.[57] However, there are also principled arguments in favour of at least a partly objectivist law of attempts, either allowing impossibility as a defence in those relatively unusual circumstances where D's endeavour fails to connect with the real world, or more broadly developing the view that actual consequences make a significant moral difference.[58]

There would be little difference between the two approaches over the case of D, who fired a shot at V and missed because his aim was not good enough. That is a classic criminal attempt. But what is the difference between that and a case in which E puts sugar in X's drink in the belief that it is cyanide? On the act-centred approach there is no social danger in the latter case, because sugar is innocuous; yet it is equally true that there is no danger in the first case, because shooting and missing is innocuous. Some might say that D might try again and the shot might not miss; yet it is equally possible that E might try again and might choose an ingredient which actually is poisonous. It seems, then, that the act-centred approach incorporates one limb of the subjective principle—that people should be judged on the consequences they intend to happen—but not the other (belief) limb—that people should be judged on the facts as they believe them to be. There is no principled explanation for accepting one and not the other, apart from the argument about police powers and individual liberty, which ought (if possible) to be tackled directly, and not through a distortion of the law of attempts.

The recent history of English law contains evidence of both approaches. The House of Lords in *Haughton* v *Smith*[59] adopted an act-centred stance, but the Law Commission accepted the arguments above and recommended a fault-centred approach, in which impossibility would be no defence to liability. Debate continued during the passage of the new law, and one result of further changes of mind by the government was two strangely worded provisions in s. 1(2) and (3) of the Criminal Attempts Act 1981. The Act purported to follow the Law Commission and to criminalize impossible

[55] For a review of the case law see I. Dennis, 'Silence in the Police Station: The Marginalisation of Section 34' [2002] Crim LR 25.

[56] See, e.g., I. McKenzie, R. Morgan, and R. Reiner, 'Helping the Police with their Inquiries' [1990] Crim LR 22; T. Bucke and D. Brown, *In Police Custody: Police Powers and Suspects' Rights under the Revised PACE Codes of Practice* (1997).   [57] A view meticulously criticized by Duff, n 4, chs 9–12.

[58] There is not space here to do justice to the careful arguments of Duff, n 4, especially at 206–36 and 378–84.

[59] [1975] AC 476.

attempts, but the House of Lords interpreted the provisions so as not to achieve this result, and it was only in *Shivpuri* (1986)[60] that it was settled that, in the English law of attempts, D is judged on the facts as he or she believed them to be. Thus, if a person buys electronic equipment believing that it is stolen (when it is not), that constitutes an attempt to handle stolen goods.

The fault-centred approach here has been limited to beliefs about facts. If D is mistaken about the law, believing that certain conduct is an offence when it is not, there is no liability for an attempt. Thus, where D believed that he was smuggling currency into the country but there is no offence of importing currency, there could be no conviction.[61] This is easily explained: there is no crime to be attempted, only an imaginary crime. But it can also be seen as a corollary of the maxim that ignorance of the law is no excuse: a mistake about the criminal law neither exculpates nor inculpates. By contrast, a mistake as to the facts may exculpate (subject to other policies relevant to mistakes)[62] or inculpate (as an impossible attempt), since the general principle is that D is judged on the facts as he or she believed them to be.[63]

(d) REFORM

The Law Commission has consulted on a set of proposals for reforming the law of attempts, as noted at various points earlier. The major argument is that completed attempts should be distinguished from incomplete attempts (as this work has always maintained), and that two separate offences should be devised to cater for this—the offence of attempt, for those who are engaged in the last acts towards committing the substantive offence, and 'criminal preparation', for those caught at an earlier stage. The Commission is right to emphasize that the 'ordinary language' approach to criminal attempts is ill-suited to deal with incomplete attempts, but whether the solution of two separate offences is either necessary or practical seems doubtful.[64] On the other hand, the Commission's other proposals—on the fault element, on the use of examples to bring consistency to decisions on the conduct element, and on including attempts by omission—are to be welcomed. However, the Commission acknowledges that the proliferation of statutory offences of preparation has become opportunistic rather than principled, and the question of the overall reach of the criminal law needs to be re-assessed.[65]

---

[60] [1987] AC 1, overruling the House's own decision of the previous year in *Anderton v Ryan* [1985] AC 560. A considerable influence in bringing about this judicial *volte-face* was the article by G. Williams, 'The Lords and Impossible Attempts' [1986] Camb LJ 33.

[61] *Taaffe* [1984] AC 539.

[62] See Chapter 6.5(d), and Chapter 7.5.

[63] See Chapter 6.4(a).

[64] Cf. J. Rogers, 'The Codification of Attempts and the Case for "Preparation"' [2008] Crim LR 937.

[65] LCCP 183, *Conspiracy and Attempts*, 16.66.

12.4 THE JUSTIFICATIONS FOR AN OFFENCE OF CONSPIRACY

The essence of conspiracy is an agreement between two or more persons to commit a criminal offence. The reason for criminalization is largely preventive, as in the law of attempts, since it enables the police and the courts to intervene before any harm has actually been inflicted. Whereas in attempts the doing of a 'more than merely preparatory' act is required as evidence of the firmness of the intent, in conspiracy it is the fact of agreement with others which is regarded as sufficiently firm evidence that the parties are committed to carrying out the crime. Another part of the justification for an offence of conspiracy is that persons who go so far as to reach an agreement to commit a crime, and are caught before the agreement is carried out, may not be significantly less blameworthy or less dangerous than persons who conspire and succeed in bringing about the substantive offence.

However, this fairly traditional analysis of conspiracy as an inchoate offence neglects the other social functions which conspiracy law has been called upon to perform. In the nineteenth century, it was accepted that a conviction for criminal conspiracy could be based on an agreement to do any unlawful act, even though that act was not criminal but only a civil wrong, such as a tort or breach of contract. This gave the criminal law a long reach, particularly with regard to the activities of the early trade unions, and the courts upheld conspiracy convictions for what were, in effect, no more than agreements to go on strike, until the law was changed by the Conspiracy and Protection of Property Act 1875 and the Trade Disputes Act 1906.[66] In social terms, the criminal law lent its authority to those who wished to suppress organized industrial action. In legal terms, the reasoning seemed to be that acts which were insufficiently anti-social to justify criminal liability when done by one person could become sufficiently anti-social to justify criminal liability when done by two or more people acting in agreement. Such a combination of malefactors might increase the probability of harm resulting, might in some cases increase public alarm, and might in other cases facilitate the perpetration and concealment of the wrong.[67] Prosecutions were often brought in cases where the agreement had been carried out and the unlawful acts done, since there was no substantive criminal offence to be prosecuted (in that the conspiracy was to do an unlawful but non-criminal act). Thus the legal definition turned on an 'agreement', but the social reality centred upon the actual commission of the tort or breach of contract, from which a prior agreement was inferred. In these contexts, conspiracy functioned more as an additional substantive offence than as an inchoate crime.

---

[66] For a general account of the social history of conspiracy see R. Spicer, *Conspiracy Law, Class and Society* (1981); see also G. Robertson, *Whose Conspiracy?* (1974).

[67] For further discussion see P. E. Johnson, 'The Unnecessary Crime of Conspiracy' (1973) 61 Cal LR 1137, and I. Dennis, 'The Rationale of Criminal Conspiracy' (1977) 93 LQR 39.

In the 1960s and 1970s the House of Lords, pursuing a broad policy of social defence, expanded the law of conspiracy considerably by criminalizing various agreements to do non-criminal acts;[68] but in *DPP* v *Withers* (1975)[69] their Lordships called a halt, holding that there was no such offence as conspiracy to cause a public mischief. This presaged the Law Commission's report on conspiracy in 1976, which recommended that the offence of conspiracy should be coextensive with the substantive law.[70] Conspiracies should be criminal only if the conduct agreed upon constitutes a crime when done by one person. The principles of non-retroactivity and maximum certainty were accepted, even to the point of asserting that if some new form of wickedness were to arise which did not fall within existing offences, the proper approach would be to await a response from the legislature rather than for the judges to exploit the elasticity of the law of conspiracy.[71] Parliament adopted the substance of the Law Commission's report, and enacted the Criminal Law Act 1977. Part I of the Act created the offence of statutory conspiracy, limited to agreements to commit one or more criminal offences; Part II provided a handful of offences of trespass on residential premises.[72] An agreement to commit one of these distinct trespass offences is a statutory conspiracy, and the common law offence of conspiracy to trespass, upheld in *Kamara*,[73] was abolished.

The 1977 Act did not, however, accomplish a clean sweep of common law conspiracy. The Law Commission had been unable to complete its examination of conspiracy to defraud and any new offences which might be needed to replace it (see Chapter 10.8); and another committee was engaged in a review of the laws on obscenity, which led the government to exclude from the 1977 Act conspiracies to corrupt public morals and to outrage public decency.[74] Thus the controversial decision in *Shaw*[75] remains authoritative on conspiracy to corrupt public morals, as does the decision in *Knuller*[76] on conspiracy to outrage public decency, and also *Scott* v *Metropolitan Police Commissioner*[77] on conspiracy to defraud, whose precepts owe more to the 'thin ice' doctrine associated with the authoritarian principle (Chapter 4.5) than to any notion of maximum certainty in criminal law (Chapter 4.4(e)). The only small retrenchment is that conspiracy to outrage public decency is now a form of statutory conspiracy, as a result of the decision in *Gibson* to the effect that the offence of outraging public decency is a substantive offence that one individual can commit.[78]

---

[68] The high watermarks were *Shaw* v *DPP* [1962] AC 220 (conspiracy to corrupt public morals), *Knuller* v *DPP* [1973] AC 435 (conspiracy to outrage public decency), and *Kamara* v *DPP* [1973] 2 All ER 1242 (conspiracy to trespass).   [69] [1975] AC 842.

[70] Law Com No. 76, *Conspiracy and Criminal Law Reform* (1976).   [71] Law Com No. 76, paras. 1.8–9.

[72] The Criminal Justice and Public Order Act 1994 has now added the offences of aggravated trespass (s. 68), trespassory assembly (s. 70), and unauthorized camping (s. 77). In that regard, see now the new 'squatting' offence in the Legal Aid Sentencing and Punishment of Offenders Act 2012.

[73] [1973] 2 All ER 1242.

[74] The Williams Committee, which subsequently reported on *Obscenity and Film Censorship*, Cmnd 7772 (1979), but whose recommendations were not adopted in legislation.

[75] [1962] AC 220.   [76] [1973] AC 435.   [77] [1975] AC 819.

[78] *Gibson* [1990] 2 QB 619: the combined effect of this decision and s. 5 of the Criminal Law Act 1977 is that conspiracy to outrage public decency becomes a statutory conspiracy. It is undecided whether the same applies to corrupting public morals.

Leaving aside the common law conspiracies to defraud, to corrupt public morals, and to outrage public decency, is it true to say that statutory conspiracy functions primarily as an inchoate offence? Few conspiracies can be prosecuted at the stage of agreement, because meetings of conspirators usually take place in private and it is rare for sufficient evidence to become available until some acts in furtherance of the agreement have been done and observed. So the rationale of early prevention, even before an attempt has been committed, is often far from the social facts. However, another function of inchoate offences is to criminalize those who try and fail, as well as those who are caught before they have the chance to succeed or fail. Conspiracy does fulfil this function, being used against those who join together to commit a crime in circumstances in which it is impossible to do so.[79] Yet there remains a way in which even statutory conspiracy also functions as an extra criminal offence.

The rules of evidence in conspiracy cases are somewhat wider than those in other trials: for example, the statements of one co-conspirator are admissible in evidence against another if they relate to an act done in furtherance of the conspiracy, by way of exception to the general rule that the admissions of one co-defendant cannot be adduced in evidence against the other.[80] Moreover, all that has to be proved for conspiracy is the agreement, and that may be inferred from behaviour. Prosecutors who wish to take advantage of these rules may prefer to charge conspiracy instead of the substantive crime even in a case where the substantive offence has been committed: it is bad practice for them to charge both conspiracy and the substantive crime,[81] but it is no answer to a conspiracy charge alone that the substantive offence was in fact committed. In the terminology of English criminal procedure, a conspiracy does not 'merge' with the substantive offence. Thus the prosecution may defend its use of a conspiracy charge as giving a more rounded impression of the nature of the criminal enterprise, in terms of planning and the different roles of the various participants.[82]

Despite this use of the crime of conspiracy as an extra substantive offence, its primary justifications remain those of an inchoate offence. An individual who declares an intent to steal certain property has committed no offence; two or more individuals who agree to do the same thing may be convicted of conspiracy to steal. How strong are the justifications? Three arguments may be considered. First, criminal groups generate a 'special social identity' that leads to loyalty, commitment, and indeed a certain loss of control by individuals as a group dynamic takes over, with individuals being afraid to withdraw and participants spurring each other on. Some psychological research

---

[79] The 1977 Act contained no provision on impossibility, but s. 5 of the Criminal Attempts Act 1981 makes it clear that impossibility is no more a defence to conspiracy than it is to attempt.

[80] See *Liggins* et al. [1995] Crim LR 45 and commentary. The same rule applies to principals and accomplices.

[81] See the case of the Shrewsbury pickets, *Jones* et al. (1974) 59 Cr App R 120, and the Practice Direction [1977] 2 All ER 540.

[82] This 'rounded impression' argument is much emphasized by prosecutors, but the Law Commission seems unpersuaded that a similar effect could not be achieved by using the existing law of complicity: Law Commission Consultation Paper 155, *Fraud and Deception* (1999), paras. 4.36–4.38. See further Chapter 10.9.

suggests that even hastily formed groups may quickly generate this kind of identity and loyalty.[83] The implication is that such joint criminal ventures may acquire a momentum of their own and may render the commission of further offences more likely, and that this justifies singling them out.[84] Secondly, where several people are involved, this may enable individual members to distance themselves from the actual harm to be caused by looking little further than their own acts of assistance. This 'technique of neutralization' may make crime easier to carry out.[85] Thirdly, the involvement of several people in an offence may create greater fear in victims and greater public alarm. One could imagine an individual more terrifying than two bungling offenders, but this casts little doubt on the qualitative difference between most criminal gangs and the activities of most lone offenders. In many cases group crimes are more terrifying, and sentencers may well be justified in treating this as an aggravating factor, as is the case under French law when an offence is committed by 'several people acting as an organized gang'.[86]

Whether considerations such as these justify the creation of special public order offences aimed at group behaviour, with separate rules of proof favouring prosecutors, was questioned earlier.[87] Do they justify the law of conspiracy, especially now that Part 2 of the Serious Crime Act 2007 has introduced wider-ranging inchoate offences of encouraging and assisting crime?[88] What if the doctrine of merger were extended, so that conspiracy ceased to be chargeable if the substantive offence had been committed? No special characteristic of group criminality would be lost, because there remains the doctrine of complicity. The law of principals and accomplices may lack some of the evidentiary advantages to the prosecution which conspiracy has, but it does favour the prosecution procedurally by not requiring it to charge defendants separately as accomplices or principals.[89] And, other than in murder cases, there is the same discretion at the sentencing stage to reflect the element of aggravation in planned group offending.

A similar question about the dispensability of the offence of conspiracy may be asked in relation to its inchoate function. Many conspiracies will already have been carried far enough to fulfil the test for criminal attempt, under the existing or the proposed law, or the new offences of encouraging or assisting crime. Much of the ground might therefore be covered by the law of attempts and by prosecutions for complicity in attempts. This leaves only the few cases where clear evidence is obtained of an agreement to commit a crime, without any action having yet been taken to implement the agreement. The Law Commission argues that the offence remains vital to deal with these cases, particularly where the police or security services possess intelligence about a planned terrorist incident that enables them to prove an agreement and thus to

---

[83]   N. K. Katyal, 'Conspiracy Theory' (2003) 112 Yale LJ 1307, cited in LCCP 183, *Conspiracy and Attempts*, Part 2.

[84]   See the discussion of joint enterprise in complicity in Chapter 11.5.   [85]   Katyal, n 84, 1323.

[86]   See French Penal Code, Art. 221–4–8, and more generally A. Ashworth, *Sentencing and Criminal Justice* (4th edn., 2005), ch 5.2.2.   [87]   See text at n 81.   [88]   See section 12.7.

[89]   See further Chapter 10.2, and *DPP for Northern Ireland* v *Maxwell* [1978] 3 All ER 1140.

intervene early.[90] Even if this is conceded, it seems likely that the offence of conspiracy will continue to be used much more broadly, in cases where the doctrine of complicity also applies, because prosecutors like having the powers that it gives them.[91] These powers raise a range of other questions. Agreements usually involve words, and so, issues of privacy, freedom of speech, and freedom of association may arise here,[92] in the sense that the existence of this offence might encourage the police to use intrusive tactics (such as bugging premises). To advocate freedom to commit crimes would be unsupportable, but one must avoid the risk of inhibiting the development of controversial ideas. Furthermore, there is the danger of conviction based on inference and mere association, which leave opportunities for prosecutions to be brought without much hard evidence. The offence of conspiracy may be defended as a vital tool against organized crime, but the difficulty is that it may bear oppressively on some of the individuals who are caught within its ample net.

12.5 THE ELEMENTS OF CRIMINAL CONSPIRACY

(a) AN AGREEMENT BETWEEN TWO OR MORE PERSONS

Agreement is the basic element in conspiracy. The idea of an agreement involves a meeting of minds, but that 'meeting' must be something more than several people independently forming the intention to commit an offence. In *Mehta*,[93] Toulson LJ put the point in this way:

> [A]lthough each conspirator need not necessarily know of the identity or even the existence of all the other conspirators, there must be a shared criminal purpose or design in which all have joined, rather than merely similar or parallel ones.[94]

It follows that there is no need for a physical meeting of the persons involved so long as they reach a mutual understanding of what is to be done.[95]

Whether the understanding amounts to an agreement may be a matter of degree: if the parties are still at the stage of negotiation, without having decided what to do, no criminal conspiracy has yet come into being. But what if the parties have reached agreement in principle, leaving matters of detail to be resolved afterwards? In *Broad* (1997)[96] there was evidence that the defendants had agreed to manufacture certain substances that would undoubtedly be Class A drugs, even though it was not yet clear or decided which drug would be manufactured by the processes they had commenced. The Court of Appeal held that it was sufficient for conspiracy liability that

---

[90] LCCP 183, *Conspiracy and Attempts*, para. 2.9.

[91] A consideration surprisingly treated by the Law Commission as a justification for retaining the offence: see LCCP 183, *Conspiracy and Attempts*, para. 2.34.

[92] Articles 8, 10, and 11 of the European Convention on Human Rights.   [93] [2012] EWCA Crim 2824.

[94] [2012] EWCA Crim 2824, para 20. See further, *Shillam* [2013] EWCA Crim 160; P. Jarvis and M. Bisgrove, 'The Use and Abuse of Conspiracy' [2014] Crim LR 261.

[95] G. Orchard, '"Agreement" in Criminal Conspiracy' [1974] Crim LR 297.   [96] [1997] Crim LR 666.

each defendant had participated in the processes knowing that one of these substances would be produced.[97] What if arrangements have been made, but may be unscrambled later? The judicial tendency is to regard these as conspiratorial agreements, and this is consistent with the rule that there is no defence of withdrawal for a person who has become a party to a conspiracy.[98] Moreover, since all human arrangements are vulnerable to changes in circumstances, the possibility that a planned robbery might be cancelled if there are police in the vicinity at the time does not negate the existence of a conspiracy. Further problems over 'conditional' agreements are discussed in section 12.5(b).

Certain agreements are excluded from the law of conspiracy. First, by s. 2(2)(a) of the Criminal Law Act 1977, agreements between husband and wife only (without a third person) cannot amount to criminal conspiracies. This rule places the value of marital confidence above the public interest in having conspirators brought to justice, a priority which has been partly abandoned in other areas of the law (e.g. by compelling one spouse to give evidence against the other in certain proceedings).[99] If a husband and wife go so far as to commit an attempt or a substantive offence, they can be convicted jointly of that. Secondly, by s. 2(2)(b), agreements in which the only other person is under the age of criminal responsibility cannot result in D's conviction for conspiracy—an application of the rule of criminal capacity. Thirdly, by s. 2(2)(c) of the Act, agreements in which the only other person is an intended victim cannot result in D's conviction for conspiracy. This parallels the rule that a person who falls within the class protected by the offence (e.g. persons under a given age) cannot be convicted as a party to that crime.[100] Fourthly, s. 4(1) provides that a prosecution for conspiracy to commit one or more summary offences requires the consent of the Director of Public Prosecutions. Although this appears to restrict the practical use of conspiracy charges, it should be noted that the crime of attempt does not apply to summary offences at all. Once again, the 'double life' of conspiracy as an inchoate and a quasi-substantive offence is evident. One argument is that the deliberate planning of numerous offences, even if summary only, may justify prosecution as a conspiracy. Presumably, also, the number of persons involved in an agreement to commit summary offences might persuade the Crown Prosecution Service that it is in the public interest to prosecute for a single conspiracy rather than bringing various separate small charges.

Agreement is the basic element in criminal conspiracy, but the evidence offered to a court may often amount to inferences from behaviour rather than direct testimony or recording of a meeting of conspirators. Thus the typical process is to infer a prior agreement from behaviour which appears to be concerted. However, courts sometimes

---

[97] The Court dismissed the relevance of any defendant's ignorance that the substances were, in law, Class A drugs.

[98] Compare *Mulcahy* (1868) LR 3 HL 306, and *Thomson* (1965) 50 Cr App R 1, with the arguments in section 12.8.

[99] Police and Criminal Evidence Act 1984, s. 80. The Law Commission rightly propose the abolition of this exemption: LCCP 183, *Conspiracy and Attempts*, Part 9.

[100] *Tyrell* [1894] 1 QB 710, discussed in Chapter 10.7(b).

overlook the fact that, if the charge is conspiracy, it is the conduct agreed upon and not the conduct actually carried out that is the basis of the offence.[101]

(b) THE CRIMINAL CONDUCT AGREED UPON

We move now to the subject-matter of the agreement. The Criminal Law Act 1977, s. 1(1), provides that a conspiracy is criminal if it is agreed that 'a course of conduct will be pursued which, if the agreement is carried out in accordance with their intentions ... will necessarily amount to or involve the commission of any offence or offences by one or more parties to the agreement'. The essence, therefore, is that two or more persons should agree on the commission of a crime. It is well established that they need not know that the agreed course of conduct does amount to a crime—ignorance of the criminal law does not excuse here.[102] The 'course of conduct' includes not only the acts agreed upon but also the intended consequences: conspiracy to murder requires not only an agreement to shoot at a person but also the intention that the shots should cause death.[103]

In interpreting the section, one's eyes are drawn to the word 'necessarily': can it ever be said that, if an agreement is carried out in accordance with the parties' intentions, it will *necessarily* involve the commission of an offence? This unduly concrete term seems to run counter to the proposition that all agreements are conditional in some way or another, and thus to ignore the possibility of an unexpected failure (the bomb which fails to detonate, the shot which misses, etc.). Does it therefore leave all fallible agreements outside the law of conspiracy? Is it enough for the defence to raise a reasonable doubt that the plan might have miscarried for some reason? Such an argument would put the principles of statutory interpretation to a stern test: should the court apply the plain meaning of 'necessarily' on the principle of strict construction—and acquit—or should it apply the purposive approach and the policy of social defence—and convict?

One challenge to the wording was heard in *Jackson* (1985).[104] Four men arranged for one of their number to be shot in the leg; the aim was to provide mitigation in the event of his being convicted at his trial for burglary. He was shot in the leg before the end of the trial. On a charge of conspiracy to pervert the course of justice, it was argued that there was no certainty that he would be convicted and therefore the agreement would not necessarily lead to a perversion of the course of justice. The Court of Appeal rejected the argument, drawing a distinction between the inevitability of the substantive offence being committed (which s. 1(1) does not require) and the inevitability that it would be committed if the agreement was carried out in accordance with their intentions. The Court approved the example of two people agreeing to drive from London to Edinburgh within a time that could only be achieved without breaking the speed

---

[101] For an unsatisfactory decision see *El-Kurd* [2001] Crim LR 234. See also P. Jarvis and M. Bisgrove, 'The Use and Abuse of Conspiracy' [2014] Crim LR 261.

[102] *Churchill* v *Walton* [1967] 2 AC 224.

[103] As for attempted murder, an intention to cause grievous bodily harm is not sufficient: see O'Connor LJ in *Siracusa* (1990) 90 Cr App R 340, at 350.   [104] [1985] Crim LR 442.

laws if traffic conditions were particularly favourable, and agreeing to break the speed limits if necessary.[105] This would not be a conspiracy to exceed the speed limit because it would be possible to do everything agreed upon without breaking the law. However, it can be argued that this is too favourable to the parties, who have plainly agreed to commit one or more offences if certain contingencies arise.[106] In principle, these cases should be dealt with through the rules on conditional intention, bearing in mind that most intentions are conditional to some extent.[107]

Section 1(1) of the 1977 Act was amended by s. 5 of the Criminal Attempts Act 1981 to make it clear that impossibility is no more a defence to conspiracy than to a charge of attempt. It is sufficient to establish that the agreement *would* have involved the commission of an offence but for the existence of facts which rendered it impossible. The justifications for this follow those outlined in section 12.3(c).

(c) THE FAULT REQUIREMENTS

The basic fault requirements for conspiracy would appear to be twofold: first, that each defendant should have knowledge of any facts or circumstances specified in the substantive offence, either knowing that present facts exist or (as the case may be) intending that certain facts or circumstances will exist at the time of the substantive offence; and, secondly, that each defendant should intend the conspiracy to be carried out and the substantive offence to be committed, although we will see below that this requirement is in doubt.

Section 1(2) makes it clear that these requirements of full intention and knowledge as to facts and circumstances apply no matter what offence is agreed upon. Thus full knowledge and intent are required, even for conspiracies to commit offences of strict liability, negligence, or recklessness. Why is the fault element for conspiracy kept so narrow? If the substantive offence is satisfied, say, by recklessness as to some elements, why should the crime of conspiracy not likewise be satisfied? The answer seems to lie with the remoteness principle encountered elsewhere: that inchoate crimes are an extension of the criminal sanction, and the more remote an offence becomes from the actual infliction of harm, the higher the degree of fault necessary to justify criminalization. Thus, in *Saik*[108] D changed large amounts of money at his currency exchange on behalf of others. He pleaded guilty to conspiracy to convert the proceeds of drug trafficking, contrary to s. 93(2) of the Criminal Justice Act 1988 (now superseded by the Proceeds of Crime Act 2002), but the basis of his plea was that he merely suspected that the money was the proceeds of crime. The House of Lords held that his conviction should be quashed: although the substantive offence would be committed if D had 'reasonable grounds to suspect' that the money was the proceeds of crime, a charge of

---

[105]*Reed* [1982] Crim LR 819.

[106] See the discussion in the decision of the House of Lords in *Saik* [2007] 1 AC 18; G. Virgo, 'Laundering Conspiracy' (1996) 65 Cambridge LJ 482.   [107] See further LCCP 183, *Conspiracy and Attempts*, Part 5.

[108] [2007] 1 AC 18.

conspiracy could only be sustained, on the proper interpretation of s. 1(2), by proof of full knowledge. This demonstrates one drawback for prosecutors of using a conspiracy charge when there is evidence on which the substantive offence could have been charged instead: proof of full knowledge and intention is required on a conspiracy charge, when it may not be for the full offence.

Should such a narrow approach to the fault element in conspiracy be retained? If X and Y agree to go to a woman's room and to have intercourse with her, hoping that she will consent but not caring whether she does or not, are they guilty of conspiracy to rape? The wording of s. 1(2) of the 1977 Act suggests not. Yet it was argued earlier[109] that there should be a conviction for attempted rape in parallel circumstances, and that argument might apply no less strongly to conspiracy. The Law Commission takes this view, arguing that X and Y are sufficiently culpable because their agreement shows that they are 'prepared to go ahead with the plan even if it turns out that V does not consent'.[110] On this view, as with the Commission's recommendations for attempt, the fault element should be intention for the conduct and (if any) consequence elements, but recklessness as to circumstance elements where no fault or only negligence-based fault is required.[111]

In applying the 1977 Act, the concern of the courts has not in fact been with these arguments but with other questions about the meaning of s. 1(1). In *Anderson*,[112] the House of Lords chose to reinterpret the words of the section in order to uphold a conviction. D was convicted of conspiring to effect a break-out from prison. D had agreed that his part would involve suppling diamond wire to cut prison bars. His defence was that he never intended the break-out to succeed, and was only interested in obtaining payment for playing his part. Determined to uphold Anderson's conviction in the face of this somewhat flimsy excuse, the House of Lords held, first, that a person may be convicted of conspiracy even without intending the agreement to be carried out; and, secondly, that a person is guilty of conspiracy if, and only if, it is established that he or she intended to play some part in the agreed course of conduct. Both these propositions are open to doubt. It seems extraordinary that a person can be held liable for conspiring to commit an offence when he does not intend it to be committed, particularly since that might mean that none of the conspirators needs to intend the substantive offence to be committed. The Privy Council has now held, in *Yip Chiu-cheung*,[113] that the prosecution must establish that each alleged conspirator intended the agreement to be carried out. This is the better view, although *Anderson* remains high authority to the contrary. The second proposition appears to run counter to one of the rationales of

---

[109] See section 12.3(a), discussing *Khan* (1990) 91 Cr App R 29 and *Attorney-General's Reference (No. 1 of 1992)* (1994) 98 Cr App R 383.

[110] LCCP 183, *Conspiracy and Attempts*, para. 4.109.

[111] Unless the full offence requires a subjective state of mind, such as suspicion, belief, or knowledge that the circumstance will exist at the time of the offence, in which case it is these forms of fault that the prosecution must prove: Law Com No. 318, paras. 1.48 and 1.50.

[112] [1986] AC 27.

[113] [1995] 1 AC 111. This was not a statutory conspiracy contrary to the 1977 Act, but the common law is surely no different on this point.

conspiracy, which is to bring those who plan offences but do not take part in them (the 'godfathers') within the ambit of the criminal sanction. The second *Anderson* proposition was later reinterpreted by the Court of Appeal in *Siracusa*[114] so as to mean the opposite of what the House of Lords said. According to *Siracusa*, a passive conspirator who concurs in the activities of the person(s) carrying out the crime without becoming involved himself is guilty of criminal conspiracy. Had the inchoate offence of assisting crime existed at that time, Anderson would almost certainly have been guilty of that offence, but it did not, and so the law of conspiracy was stretched beyond its intended boundaries to catch such activity. The precedents are therefore in a mess, and the Law Commission rightly proposes clarification that each conspirator should intend that the agent-causal conduct and any consequence element will occur.[115]

12.6 INCITEMENT

The third of the trio of inchoate offences in English criminal law was incitement. The courts had developed it along rather different lines from those of attempt and conspiracy, both of which have been put into statutory form in recent years. The Law Commission gave several reasons for regarding the offence of incitement in its present form as unsatisfactory and, rather than proposing a revised statutory version of the offence, recommended its abolition and replacement with new and broader offences of assisting and encouraging crime.[116] These new offences, created by Part 2 of the Serious Crime Act 2007, came into force on 1 October 2008 and are examined below. However, it must be noted that there remains a whole range of statutory offences of incitement which are unaffected by the abolition of the common law offence—from long-standing offences such as incitement to disaffection from the armed forces, to the offence under s. 1 of the Terrorism Act 2006 of publishing a statement likely to be understood 'as a direct or indirect encouragement' of acts of terrorism.[117]

12.7 ENCOURAGING OR ASSISTING CRIME

The statutory context of the new offences is instructive: they are set out in Part 2 of the Serious Crime Act 2007, between Part 1 (which introduces Serious Crime Prevention Orders) and Part 3 (entitled 'Other Measures to Prevent or Disrupt Serious or Other Crime'). In other words, the new offences are conceived as part of a raft of measures against serious and organized crime.[118] However, nothing in the statute limits them to

---

[114] (1990) 90 Cr App R 340.

[115] LCCP 183, *Conspiracy and Attempts*, para. 4.22 *et seq*; Law Com No. 318, at paras. 1.20 and 1.22. See also the new offences of encouraging and assisting crime, discussed in section 12.7.

[116] Law Com No. 300, *Inchoate Liability for Assisting and Encouraging Crime* (2006), ch 3.

[117] For analysis, see A. Hunt, 'Criminal Prohibitions on Direct and Indirect Encouragement of Terrorism' [2007] Crim LR 441.   [118] Home Office, *New Powers against Organized and Financial Crime* (2006).

such types of crime, and so they take their place as general inchoate offences. Part 2 of the 2007 Act creates three new offences of encouraging or assisting crime, and they will now be considered in turn. The three offences are supported by some twenty sections of further detail, rendering this one of the more complex legislative innovations in the criminal law. The aim here will be to identify and to appraise critically the principles of the new offences, without the distraction of too much detail.[119]

(a) INTENTIONALLY ENCOURAGING OR ASSISTING AN OFFENCE

The first of the three new inchoate offences is that provided by s. 44 of the Serious Crime Act 2007, which is committed if (a) D does an act capable of encouraging or assisting the commission of an offence and (b) D intends to assist or encourage its commission. Many of the features of this offence also apply to the other two offences, and so they will be discussed here. It is immediately obvious that this offence applies independently of whether the principal offence is committed or not: so if D uses encouraging language to P with respect to the commission of an offence, or if D assists P by lending him equipment, D commits this offence irrespective of whether P is in fact encouraged by D's words, or whether P actually uses D's equipment, to commit the principal offence. This must be right in principle, as argued in section 12.2: D has crossed the threshold of culpability, whether P responds to his promptings or not. But that principled argument does not necessarily justify the extent of the liability for this offence, which we must now examine.

The conduct element of the s. 44 offence is doing 'an act capable of encouraging or assisting the commission of an offence'. Thus it seems that any act will satisfy the section, howsoever small or insignificant, so long as it is *capable of* amounting to encouragement or assistance. We have already noted that there is no requirement that D's act in fact encourages or assists, which means that there is no requirement that P even knew of D's act, since the focus of this offence is on D. What is capable of amounting to encouragement or assistance depends on the meaning of each of those terms, but the Act, replete as it is with all manner of other qualifications and extensions, contains no definition of either of these key words.[120] Thus s. 65(1) states that encouragement includes 'threatening another person or otherwise putting pressure on' him or her, but in other respects the concept is left for the courts to develop. Under the 2007 Act, any act, however small, suffices for this offence so long as it is capable of encouraging or assisting the commission of the anticipated offence.[121] Admittedly, though, the difficulty

---

[119] See J. Child and A. Hunt, 'Mens Rea and the General Inchoate Offences: Another New Culpability Framework' (2012) 63 NLQ 247; J. Child, 'The Structure, Coherence and Limits of Inchoate Liability: The New Ulterior Intent' (2014) 34 LS 537.

[120] Although, in fairness to the Law Commission whose Report provided the basis for Part 2 of the 2007 Act, the Commission indicated that 'encouraging' should bear broadly the same meaning that 'incitement' had at common law: Law Com No. 300, para. 5.37.

[121] Further, the maximum penalty for the anticipated offence applies even though the conviction is under s. 44 and not for the anticipated offence.

for the legislature here is in devising a test that will determine what is to count in law as only a 'small' influence on P by way of encouragement or assistance. So, it is easy to understand the temptation to leave this as a matter (a) for prosecutors in deciding whether it is in the public interest to prosecute someone whose contribution was minimal, and (b) for judges when considering the issue of sentence, rather than seeking to decide that question as a matter of law. Further, as the Law Commission pointed out when discussing this issue,[122] given that the offences in the 2007 Act are inchoate, if the jury had to decide whether or not someone's assistance or encouragement was only 'small', or 'trivial' when the offence itself had not taken place, how could they go about their task? They would be answering a very speculative and hypothetical question.

Section 65(2) states that 'an act capable of encouraging or assisting' includes taking steps to reduce the possibility of criminal proceedings being brought in respect of that offence (as by helping P to flee the country after his crime) and includes failing to take steps to discharge a duty (as by leaving a window open to help burglars to gain access to premises); s. 65(3) excludes a failure to respond to a constable's request to assistance, but that exclusion suggests that in other respects the question whether there was a duty is for the court, applying general principles.

The main fault element required for conviction of the s. 44 offence appears to be purpose: subsection (1)(b) states that D must intend by his act to encourage or assist the commission of the anticipated offence, and subsection (2) states that it is not enough that encouragement or assistance was 'a foreseeable consequence of his act'. The implication is therefore that foresight of virtual certainty (oblique intention) will never suffice for liability here: presumably this is intended as a counterweight to the potentially wide reach of the conduct element of this offence. However, since the essence of s. 44 is 'encouraging or assisting *an offence*', D must also have fault in relation to the full offence he is encouraging or assisting—an offence means conduct plus fault on the part of P, the perpetrator whose offence it is D's purpose to encourage or assist. The Act's provisions on this are complex.

Where P's offence is one that requires fault, it must be proved that D believed that P would do it with the required fault or that D was reckless as to whether or not P would have the required fault, or that D's state of mind was such as that if he (D) had done the conduct that he anticipated P would do, he (D) would have had the required fault.[123] That last provision caters for cases where D seeks to trick P into doing something (such as sexually penetrating V) which is not an offence for P (because P has been tricked and therefore lacks fault): since D has the fault, D is liable for the s. 44 offence nonetheless. And that is not all. If the anticipated offence is one requiring proof of particular circumstances or consequences or both, it must be proved that D believed or was reckless as to whether P's conduct would be done in those circumstances or with those consequences.[124] This would have obvious implications for charges of encouraging or assisting offences under the Sexual Offences Act 2003, where many of the offences

---

[122] Law Com No. 300, at para. 5.51.   [123] Serious Crime Act 2007, s. 47(5)(a).
[124] Serious Crime Act 2007, s. 47(5)(b).

specify circumstances such as the age (under 13, 13 to 15) or the mental capacity of the complainant. For example, if D is to be convicted of encouraging P to engage in a sexual act (conduct) with someone under the age of 16 (circumstance), D must know or be reckless as to whether, were P to go ahead with the act, P would do so with a person under the age of 16. Both these kinds of provisions make perfect sense; indeed the scheme would be unduly punitive, and lack any element of fair labelling, without them. However, the extent to which the provisions complicate the statutory scheme perhaps indicates that it might have been better, with the benefit of a steer from the Law Commission, to leave the courts to fill in such details.

(b) ENCOURAGING OR ASSISTING AN OFFENCE BELIEVING IT WILL BE COMMITTED

Whereas the essence of the s. 44 offence is D's purpose to assist or encourage, the s. 45 offence is committed if D believes, when he does an act capable of encouraging or assisting the anticipated offence, that it will be committed. Thus if D, the manager of a garden centre, sells weed killer to two customers whom he overheard talking about using it to poison someone, he will be guilty of the s. 45 offence if he believes they intend to carry out the poisoning, but not if he thinks they were speaking hypothetically or were joking. For s. 45, the focus is not D's purpose or desire that P will commit the offence, but D's *belief* that P *will* commit it. Thus the conduct element for the s. 45 offence is the same as that under s. 44—an act capable of encouraging or assisting—and all the extensions and exclusions mentioned in (a) earlier apply equally here. As with s. 44, the s. 45 offence is committed irrespective of whether P actually commits the anticipated offence or even realizes that D is trying to encourage or assist him to do so.

There are two main fault elements for this offence. First, D must believe that the offence he is encouraging or assisting 'will be committed'. What kind of mental state is believing that something will happen? To act with a belief is to act without any significant doubt on the matter: here, a belief that P is virtually certain to commit the offence should be sufficient. When the term 'belief' is combined with the term 'will', this indicates a high degree of confidence in D's mind that P is going to commit the anticipated offence.[125] Also, as under s. 44, D must believe that P will commit the full offence (with its conduct and fault elements), or be reckless as to that; and, as with s. 44, if D has the fault element for that offence and knows that P does not, D may be convicted under s. 45.[126] Similarly, D must believe that any circumstances or consequences specified in the anticipated offence will be fulfilled.[127] Turning to the second fault element for the s. 45 offence, D must believe that his act will encourage or assist P. It is doubtful whether this requirement adds a great deal to the offence, since it will

---

[125] Cf. the test in joint venture cases in complicity, where it is sufficient that D realizes there is a risk that a greater offence than D has agreed to will be committed: Chapter 11.5. Note also that s. 49(7) of the 2007 Act provides that a conditional belief (that the offence will be committed if certain conditions are met) is enough.

[126] See s. 47(5)(a) and the discussion at n 103.   [127] See s. 47(5)(b) and the discussion at n 104.

usually be satisfied if the other conditions are fulfilled. Finally, Sch 3 to the 2007 Act lists a number of offences to which s. 45 cannot apply: these include conspiracies and attempts, and several statutory incitement offences. Whereas there can be convictions under s. 44 where it is D's purpose to encourage or assist such offences, liability in cases where D merely believes that P will commit one of those offences is thought to go too far.

(c) ENCOURAGING OR ASSISTING OFFENCES BELIEVING ONE OR MORE WILL BE COMMITTED

Section 46 of the 2007 Act creates an offence aimed at resolving a difficulty in the law of complicity, where D assists or encourages P in a criminal enterprise without knowing which of a number of possible offences P might commit.[128] Thus the essence of the s. 46 offence is that D does an act capable of encouraging or assisting one of a number of offences, believing that one or more of those offences will be committed. D may be convicted even if he does not know which of the offences will be committed, and irrespective of whether any of them are committed. The conduct element for this offence follows the pattern of ss. 44 and 45, requiring an act capable of encouraging or assisting. All the extensions and exclusions mentioned in (a) apply. The only difference here is that the act must be capable of encouraging or assisting 'the commission of one or more of a number of offences', that number being two or more. The prosecution must specify the offences on which it wishes to rely, but not all the possible offences that D's act might have encouraged or assisted. The Court of Appeal has rejected an appeal based on the submission that the s. 46 offence was so vague in nature that it should be declared incompatible with the requirement for certainty under Art. 7 of the European Convention.[129]

The fault element for the s. 46 offence is complex. As under s. 45, D must believe that his act will encourage or assist the commission of one or more of the offences. D must believe that one or more of the offences 'will be committed', which suggests no substantial doubt on the matter.[130] According to s. 47(4), it is sufficient if D believes that one of the group of crimes will be committed, without any belief as to which one. Also, as with ss. 44 and 45, D must believe that P will commit the crime with the relevant fault element, or be reckless as to that; and D must believe that any circumstances or consequences specified in the anticipated offence(s) will be present, or be reckless as to that.[131] The s. 46 offence is meant to deal with this kind of case:

> P asks D to provide him with a sawn-off shotgun. D provides P with the gun, feeling sure that P will use it to commit either robbery, murder, or the infliction of grievous bodily harm. P is subsequently arrested when he threatens a police officer with the gun, and so does not go on to commit robbery, murder or grievous bodily harm.

---

[128] Discussed in Chapter 11.5.   [129] *R v S&H* [2011] EWCA Crim 2872.
[130] See text at n 122, which applies here.   [131] See discussion at n 123 and n 124.

In this example, D may be prosecuted for either assisting murder, or assisting robbery, or assisting the infliction of grievous bodily harm, even though none of these offences actually took place (the s. 46 offence is an inchoate one, like the offences under ss. 44 and 45).[132] However, D may not be prosecuted for assisting P to resist arrest, to be in possession of an illegal weapon in a public place, or for any threats offence. This is because these crimes were not ones on a list of offences, one of which D was sure P was going to commit at the time he provided P with the gun.[133]

(d) SPECIAL DEFENCES

Part 2 of the 2007 Act provides two special defences to the three new crimes, as well as spelling out (in s. 47(b)(c) and (d)) that ignorance of the law is no defence, so that if D encourages or assists P in doing certain conduct, without being aware that that constitutes a criminal offence, D will still be liable. The two special defences are a reasonableness defence and an exemption for persons in protected categories.

The presence of the reasonableness defence is unusual in applying to crimes of general application, such as those created by Part 2 of the 2007 Act. The Law Commission had recommended that it should not apply to the offence now created by s. 44 of the 2007 Act, namely doing an act capable of encouraging or assisting crime, believing that the offence will be committed.[134] The Commission's argument was that if D directly intends to assist or encourage an offence by his or her act, then the law's policy should be to prevent D being able to raise a defence that his or her act was simply a 'reasonable' thing to do (other than when that issue arises under an existing defence such as, for example, the defence of duress). If D could raise such an open-ended defence, even though he or she intended to assist or encourage the commission of a crime, it might seem to call into question the solidity of the basis for making conduct of the kind in which D engaged in an inchoate criminal offence in the first place. However, so far as the offence now created by s. 45 is concerned, the Law Commission took the view that a reasonableness defence to this offence was desirable in the interests of preventing inchoate liability stretching too far into ordinary conduct. The Commission gave the following example:

> D is driving at the maximum speed limit in the outside lane of a motorway. D sees P coming rapidly up behind her, and so moves into the middle lane to allow P to pass in the outside lane, even though D is aware that P must be speeding in excess of the maximum limit.[135]

In this example, D assists P to continue committing a speeding offence, by moving out of P's way. However, many people would be surprised to discover that such conduct was a criminal offence to which there was no defence. Accordingly, the Law Commission recommended that a 'reasonableness' defence (with the burden of proof lying on D) should be applicable in such a case. The government of the day agreed with this

---

[132] It would appear that it is not necessary that all the possible offences in contemplation appear on the indictment, because this would create complete overlap between s. 46 and s. 45: *Sadique* [2013] EWCA Crim 1150; G. Virgo (2013) 7 Arch Rev 4.

[133] For sentencing under this provision, see *McCaffery* [2014] EWCA Crim 2550.

[134] Law Com No. 300, para. 6.24.   [135] Law Com No. 300, para. 6.18.

approach, but decided to extend the defence to cases covered by s. 44 as well, namely where D directly intended to assist P. Primarily, this was to ensure that, for example, undercover officers who intentionally assisted or encouraged offenders only to maintain their 'cover', could avail themselves of the defence (although the Law Commission had proposed a separate 'prevention of crime' defence to deal with such cases). However, the reasonableness defence is not restricted to such cases. In theory, it would, for example, be open to D to raise a defence of 'reasonableness' to a charge of assisting rape where D had encouraged P to commit the rape of a girl because, in D's home country, this would be a reasonable course of action if the girl had refused to accept a marriage proposal agreed by the families. No doubt, a jury would reject the defence, but should it even be open to D to plead it in such cases?

The ambit of the reasonableness defence is uncertain, since so much will depend on the view taken by the jury or magistrates. The burden of proof is on the defendant, contrary to the presumption of innocence,[136] and what D must prove is that he knew or reasonably believed that certain circumstances existed, and that in those circumstances it was reasonable for him to act as he did. Section 50(3) provides that, in determining whether D's conduct was reasonable, the court must consider among other factors the seriousness of the anticipated offence, and any purpose or any authority claimed by D for his conduct. Cases of authority or purpose might include someone acting in order to expose another's wrongdoing, or another's susceptibility to temptation.

Section 51 provides that an offence under ss. 44, 45, or 46 cannot be committed if the anticipated offence is a 'protective offence' and D falls within the particular category of persons whom the offence was designed to protect. Thus if D (aged 12) encourages P to touch him sexually, D does not commit an offence under the 2007 Act because the anticipated offence under s. 9 of the Sexual Offences Act 2003 is designed to protect children under 16. However, it is unclear what happens in the situation that arose in *G* (2008),[137] where both D and P are under 16 and therefore within the protected category; if the act was consensual, is it right that only one of them should have a defence under s. 51?

(e) CONCLUSIONS: THE NEW INCHOATE OFFENCES

There are several points in favour of this new group of inchoate offences. They ensure that liability depends on D's culpability, irrespective of whether P goes on to commit the anticipated offence. To make D's liability turn on whether or not P went on to commit the substantive offence is to allow chance to play too significant a role. Seen as replacements for the common law offence of incitement, the new offences avoid some of the stranger twists and turns of the former case law, and that is beneficial. The offences also remedy some gaps in the law of complicity, a branch of the criminal law that awaits reform.

---

[136] See Chapter 4.5.   [137] [2008] UKHL 37, discussed in Chapter 8.6.

However, the enactment of Part 2 of the Serious Crime Act 2007 also brings several undesirable features.[138] Creating a statutory offence of incitement, and adding an offence of facilitation of crime, could have been a simpler and no less effective model. Simplicity and clarity were not high on the draftsman's agenda; taken together with the complexities of the Corporate Manslaughter and Corporate Homicide Act, it may be concluded that 2007 was not a good year in this respect.[139] Substantively, there are concerns about the breadth or indeed the virtual absence of the conduct requirement for assisting—any act that is capable of providing assistance is sufficient. The s. 46 offence also spreads its net wide, much wider than the *Maxwell* doctrine.[140] The absence of definition of the two key terms, encouragement and assistance, is an ironic feature of this technically complex edifice.[141] Whether the new extensions to criminal liability have an impact on organized or serious crime remains to be seen, but it seems most likely that they will merely become everyday additions to the prosecutor's armoury.

12.8 VOLUNTARY RENUNCIATION OF CRIMINAL PURPOSE

In view of the inchoate nature of attempt, many conspiracies, and the new offences of encouraging and assisting crime, the question arises of the legal effect of a change of mind before the substantive offence is committed. What if D abandons the attempt or withdraws from the conspiracy? English law has generally taken the view that this cannot alter the legal significance of what has already occurred: there is no defence of voluntary renunciation of criminal purpose, and it is a matter for mitigation of sentence only.[142] On the other hand, many other European systems allow such a defence,[143] the American Model Penal Code also makes provision for it,[144] and of course there is a limited doctrine of withdrawal in complicity.[145] What are the main arguments on either side?

The main argument against allowing such a defence is that it contradicts the temporal logic of the law. The definitions of attempt and conspiracy, and of the new offences of encouraging or assisting crime, are fulfilled once D, with the appropriate culpability,

---

[138] See HC Justice Committee, 'Post-Legislative Scrutiny of Part 2 (Encouraging or Assisting Crime) of the Serious Crime Act 2007', HC 639 (2013). The scrutiny makes many criticisms of the 2007 Act, but such criticisms are not legitimate '*post*-legislative' scrutiny unless they identify problems that have been encountered in practice. The Justice Committee could identify no such problems. Indeed, use of the 2007 Act has steadily increased without significant problems being encountered: <www.publications.parliament.uk/pa/cm201314/cmselect/cmjust/918/918.pdf>.

[139] Without entering into a detailed critique, several of the subsections could have been run together (e.g., subsections (2), (3), and (4) of s. 47) and others could have been avoided (e.g., s. 47(7)(b)).

[140] See Chapter 11.4.

[141] See further, D. Ormerod and R. Fortson, 'Serious Crime Act 2007: The Part 2 Offences' [2009] Crim LR 389.

[142] *Lankford* [1959] Crim LR 209, and Law Com No. 102 (1980), para. 2.133; cf. M. Wasik, 'Abandoning Criminal Intent' [1980] Crim LR 785.

[143] Fletcher, *Rethinking Criminal Law*, 184–97.   [144] Model Penal Code, s. 5.01(4).

[145] Discussed in Chapter 11.7(a).

does the 'more than merely preparatory' act, or reaches the agreement, or does an act capable of encouraging or assisting a crime. Anything that happens subsequently cannot undo the offence: it has already been committed. The situation is no different from that of the thief who decides to return the stolen property: theft has been committed and the offence cannot be undone, even though voluntary repentance may well justify substantial mitigation of sentence. A subsidiary argument is that it would in any event be difficult for a court to satisfy itself of the voluntariness of the renunciation of criminal purpose, and that such occasions might well involve a mixture of motives on D's part. This makes the matter much more suitable for the sentencing stage than the trial itself.

Against this, and in favour of a defence of voluntary renunciation, may be ranged various moral and prudential arguments. The principal argument is that it is the intent or criminal purpose which is the essence of inchoate offences, and that voluntary renunciation shows that the original criminal purpose was not sufficiently firm. This coincides with the view that it often takes more 'nerve' to go through with a crime than merely to plan or encourage it. Thus, D can be said to 'undo' the offence by a change of mind, because the criminal purpose is a continuing one—not a once-and-for-all mental state—and its effect can be neutralized by subsequent decision or action on D's part. The situation is different from that of the thief who voluntarily decides to return the property to its owner, for theft is a substantive offence and is not criminalized simply because it is one stage on the way to another crime. The argument for allowing a defence of voluntary renunciation becomes stronger as the conduct element in the inchoate offences is taken further back from the occurrence of the harm, as in the new offences of encouraging or assisting crime. A further argument is that if D renounces before the harm is caused, this may show that the threat of the criminal sanction has had a deterrent effect. To punish D nonetheless would be needless, and the case should be regarded as a success for the law rather than a failure.

Those systems which have a defence of voluntary renunciation do not appear to find it problematic,[146] members of the public seem to regard it as fair,[147] and it has not caused great problems in English complicity law.[148] The defence is rarely raised, and the issue usually turns on the voluntariness of the change of mind, which may then be explored in a trial setting rather than at the sentencing stage. At a theoretical level, there is a strong argument for reduced culpability, but this does not conclude the case for a complete defence. The allocation of excuses as between the liability and the sentencing stages turns on questions of degree (see Chapter 6.8), and one might well take the view that voluntary renunciation is not sufficiently fundamental to warrant a complete defence to criminal liability.

---

[146] See the discussion by Fletcher, *Rethinking Criminal Law*, 184–97.
[147] Robinson and Darley, *Justice, Liability and Blame*, 23–8.   [148] See Chapter 11.7(a).

12.9 THE RELATIONSHIP BETWEEN SUBSTANTIVE AND INCHOATE CRIMES

We have seen that the general function of inchoate crimes is to penalize preparation, planning, or encouragement towards the commission of a substantive offence. It has also been noted that the crime of conspiracy is sometimes invoked where the substantive offence has occurred, and that 'complete' attempts are cases in which D has done everything intended for the commission of a crime: in both those instances, the inchoate offences come very close to substantive crimes. The same phenomenon also appears the other way round: modern legal systems often define what are essentially inchoate offences in the terms of substantive crimes.

Some five variations of these crimes defined in an inchoate mode, or crimes of ulterior intent, have been distinguished:[149]

(1) committing a lesser crime, intending to commit a greater one;

(2) committing a crime, intending to do some non-criminal wrong;

(3) committing a civil wrong, intending to commit a crime;

(4) doing something overtly innocent intending to commit a crime;

(5) crimes where the intent is by its nature ulterior.

The principal offences introduced by the Fraud Act 2006, and the offence of preparing for terrorism under the Terrorism Act 2006, are examples of the increased use of type (4) offences in recent years. Three related points may be made—the effect of doubly inchoate offences, the case for a general threats offence, and the spread of offences of possession.

(a) DOUBLY INCHOATE OFFENCES

Where the offence is in the third category, such as burglary (entering as a trespasser with intent),[150] or in the fourth category, such as doing an act with intent to impede the apprehension of an offender,[151] the prosecution's task is made easier: they do not have to establish that D caused a certain result if they can persuade the court that he did an act with intent to produce that result. Moreover, since these are substantive offences, liability can be incurred additionally through the inchoate offences. Thus there can be an attempted burglary or an attempted bomb hoax, which criminalizes D's conduct at an even earlier point than the doing of an act with intent to cause harm. There is little evidence that these extensions of the criminal law are carefully monitored, or that the implications of applying the inchoate offences to crimes defined in the inchoate mode have

---

[149] J. Horder, 'Crimes of Ulterior Intent', in A. P. Simester and A. T. H. Smith (eds), *Harm and Culpability* (1996), 156–7; for other discussions see A. Ashworth, 'Defining Criminal Offences without Harm', in P. F. Smith (ed.), *Criminal Law: Essays in Honour of J. C. Smith* (1987), and Duff, n 4, 354–8.

[150] See Chapter 10.6.   [151] Criminal Law Act 1967, s. 4.

ever been systematically considered. It appears that there may be liability under s. 44 of the Serious Crime Act 2007 for encouraging or assisting an attempt or a conspiracy, and perhaps liability for attempting or conspiring to encourage or assist a crime. The reach of criminal liability is pushed further and further, without evidence of an overall scheme.

(b) THREATS OFFENCES

English law already contains a miscellany of threats offences:[152] for example, it has long been an offence to threaten to kill,[153] and common assault is committed by causing another to apprehend the use of force, but there is no comprehensive structure of threats offences.[154] Sections 4 and 5 of the Public Order Act 1986 criminalize some threats of harm in some circumstances, but the general issue remains. Peter Alldridge points out that the values of consistency and clarity in the law do not favour the creation of a general inchoate offence of threatening to commit a crime, in place of the present array of ad hoc accretions, since one might achieve consistency and clarity by abolishing most threats offences and retaining only a few well-known ones.[155] He identifies two key elements in the making of threats. First, uttering a threat is evidence that D has thought about committing the threatened crime and may be willing to do so. It may therefore appear similar in quality to an attempt, although some threats are conditional. Secondly, a primary characteristic of threats is the creation of fear. Since this should be the main target of threats offences, it is therefore inappropriate simply to regard threats as a fourth form of inchoate liability: consideration must be given to the kinds of fear and of circumstances for which criminalization is necessary.[156] There is already the offence of blackmail, which penalizes the making of unwarranted demands with menaces,[157] and this should be the starting point. In the meantime, threatening another to persuade him or her to commit a crime may amount to encouraging crime for the purpose of the offences under the Serious Crime Act 2007.[158]

(c) POSSESSION OFFENCES

Another prominent example of offences defined in the inchoate mode is possession—possessing offensive weapons, possessing instruments for use in forgery, and possessing drugs. A major difference here is that many of these articles are non-innocent, in the sense that their possession calls for an explanation at least.[159] That certainly cannot

---

[152] P. Alldridge, 'Threats Offences—A Case for Reform' [1994] Crim LR 176.

[153] Put into statutory form in s. 16, Offences Against the Person Act 1861.

[154] Contrast the position under the French Penal Code, where there is an offence of threatening to commit any felony or misdemeanour (Art. 222–17), with increased penalties for repetition or in the case of a threat to kill.

[155] P. Alldridge, 'Threats Offences—A Case for Reform' [1994] Crim LR 176, at 180.

[156] Cf. J. Horder, 'Reconsidering Psychic Assault' [1998] Crim LR 392, discussed in Chapter 9.3(e).

[157] Chapter 10.5.   [158] See section 12.7, and Serious Crime Act 2007, s. 65.

[159] Cf. the critical questions raised by D. Husak, 'Reasonable Risk Creation and Overinclusive Legislation' (1998) 1 Buffalo Crim LR 599, at 618.

be said of offences defined so as to penalize 'any act done with intent', although it can perhaps be said of an offence of burglary, which penalizes the entering of a building as a trespasser (a civil wrong) with intent to steal. Much depends on the way in which a legal system uses and defines its offences of possession, but there is at least one major objection to them, namely, that they presume a further criminal intent from the very fact of possession. In effect, they are abstract endangerment offences, presuming danger (without specifying it) from a given fact.[160] We have seen that the concept of possession itself is artificially wide;[161] some possession offences leave no opportunity for D to argue that the possession was for a non-criminal reason, and so are the ideal offences for police and prosecutors.[162] Others, like the offensive weapons law, impose on the defendant the burden of proving 'lawful excuse' or 'reasonable excuse' for the possession.[163] Now it is true, and worth bringing into the calculation, that possession offences often have the merit of certainty; there is nothing vague about the warning they spell out to citizens.[164] Yet it must be questioned whether this is enough to outweigh the remoteness from harm and the absence of a need for the prosecution to prove criminal intent which characterize most crimes of possession.[165] One might have thought that, as with the fault element for attempt and conspiracy, the more remote offences should be confined to cases of proven intention that the substantive crime be committed. Many offences of possession have no such requirement at all.

12.10 THE PLACE OF INCHOATE LIABILITY

There appear to be sound reasons for including inchoate offences within the criminal law, both on the consequentialist ground of the prevention of harm and on the 'desert' ground that the defendant has not merely formed a culpable mental attitude directed towards wrongdoing and harm, but has also manifested it. Indeed, our argument has gone further in suggesting that some inchoate offences are no different, in terms of culpability, from substantive offences. This is true of so-called complete attempts, where D has done everything intended, but some unexpected—or at least, undesired—circumstance has prevented the occurrence of the harm. The same may apply to some impossible conspiracies, and to some of the new offences of encouraging or assisting crime. The subjective principles (see Chapter 6.4(a)) are fulfilled no less in these cases than in substantive crimes. Various challenges to this approach have been noted, and

---

[160] See now, A. Ashworth, 'The Unfairness of Risk-Based Possession Offences' (2011) 5 *Criminal Law and Philosophy* 237; M. Dubber, 'The Possession Paradigm', in R. A. Duff and S. P. Green (eds), *Defining Crimes* (2005), 101.   [161] Chapter 5.3.

[162] Dubber, 'The Possession Paradigm', 96. Cf. s. 5(4)(b) of the Misuse of Drugs Act 1971, providing a defence for those who take possession of drugs for the purpose of handing them to the police or other authorities.

[163] Prevention of Crime Act 1953, s. 1; see Chapters 4.5 and 5.3. Despite Art. 6.2 of the Convention, it seems that the burden of proof will remain on defendants for this type of offence: *Lynch v DPP* [2002] Crim LR 320.

[164] On the principle of maximum certainty see Chapter 4.4(e).   [165] Husak, n 159, 616–26.

there are prominent desert theorists who oppose it. Thus Nils Jareborg is sceptical of the prominence given to culpability in this approach, arguing that the criminal law is primarily designed for preventing certain types of harm, that a focus on mental states is inappropriate for the large anonymous communities of modern States, and that the proper role of culpability should therefore be to exculpate and not to inculpate.[166] Antony Duff has argued for an objectivist approach that gives fuller recognition to the significance of actual harm.[167] However, shifting the focus to the occurrence or non-occurrence of harm attributes too much significance to matters of chance. This may be appropriate in a system of compensation, but not in a system of public censure such as the criminal law. There is a respectable conception of fairness, connected to principles of individual autonomy, that favours penalizing people who tried and failed—even if, because of some fact unknown to them, their attempt, encouragement, or assistance was bound to fail. On the view advanced here, the moral difference between those who fail and those who succeed in causing the harm is too slender to justify exempting the former from criminal liability.

While there is a good in-principle justification for liability, there are five contrary arguments that have greater or lesser strength in particular contexts. First, as recognized in section 12.3(c), conditions in a particular jurisdiction may be such that a properly developed law of inchoate offences places too much power in the hands of the police and puts innocent citizens at risk. Unless procedural or other means of rectifying this problem can be found, this is a strong argument against these extensions of criminal liability. Secondly, this argument applies with particular vigour to possession offences. Since they typically require no proof of any further intent, they place considerable power in the hands of the police, and effectively leave D to come up with some mitigating circumstances at sentence, since conviction normally follows on from detection. Thirdly, and connected to this, is the uncertainty of key definitional terms: the conduct element in attempts has been drawn so vaguely in English law that it sacrifices values of legality (see 12.3(a) and 4.4(e)), and there are also uncertainties over the conduct element in conspiracy (12.5(b)) and in the new offences of encouraging or assisting crime (12.7) which, if they cannot be reduced, tell against these extensions of the law. The proposal of statutory examples to promote consistency in dealing with attempts cases is important here, but the Serious Crime Act 2007 contains scant guidance on what should and should not amount to assistance or encouragement.

Fourthly, there seems to be absolutely no principled supervision of the reach of the criminal law. It has been noted that the offences under the Fraud Act 2006 are in the inchoate mode, so that an offence of 'making a false representation' is then extended by the law of attempts to penalize more than merely preparatory steps towards making such a representation. Similarly in R[168] the question was whether R had attempted

---

[166] N. Jareborg, 'Criminal Attempts and Moral Luck' (1993) 27 Israel LR 213.
[167] Duff, n 4, particularly ch 12 (criticizing the subjectivist use of 'moral luck' arguments) and ch 13 (constructing an objectivist law of attempts).   [168] [2008] EWCA Crim 619.

the offence under s. 14 of the Sexual Offences Act 2003, which penalizes a person who 'arranges or facilitates' something that he intends another to do in contravention of ss. 9–13 of the Act. R had twice approached an adult prostitute asking her to find him a girl prostitute of 12 or 13. The Court of Appeal held that asking the adult prostitute was capable of amounting to an attempt to arrange an act of sexual activity with a child. Thus a statutory provision worded so as to catch preparatory acts is extended still further by the operation of the law of attempts. This is not to say that the extension is unjustifiable, only that the effects of the law of attempts on new offences seem to receive little principled appraisal.

Fifthly, there now seems to be acceptance by the Law Commission of the remoteness principle—that the inchoate offences should be subjected to more restrictive fault requirements than other crimes, so that intention and knowledge alone are generally required for the inchoate offences, and recklessness is insufficient.[169] To what extent this should apply in cases of intention as to consequences coupled with recklessness as to circumstances has been discussed earlier.[170] Section 44 of the Serious Crime Act 2007 requires purpose for its basic offence of encouraging or assisting crime; but on the other hand, lesser forms of fault are sufficient under ss. 45 and 46. However, no trace of this principle is to be found in the possession offences. A further principle urged earlier is that the reach of the inchoate offences should increase with the seriousness of the harm—meaning, for example, that the law should stretch further against crimes of violence than against mere property offences. English law has no such scheme:[171] the title of the Serious Crime Act 2007 has it right, but not the contents of Part 2. The only trace is that the crime of attempt does not apply to summary offences (nor does conspiracy, unless the Crown Prosecution Service decides otherwise); the offence under s. 46 of the 2007 Act is triable only on indictment, but no such restriction applies to the offences under ss. 44 and 45.

It has long been realized that the way forward is to reconsider the law of inchoate offences together with the law of complicity in order to create a coherent and principled scheme for liability. The Law Commission is making efforts in that direction,[172] but it cannot succeed unless the myriad offences of possession and distinct preparatory offences are brought into the scheme. Appendix C to the Law Commission's Consultation Paper catalogues a multitude of offences of possession and preparation under different statutes.[173] Moreover, as indicated earlier, there is an increasing trend to define new criminal offences in the inchoate mode—when the general inchoate offences extend them further. Much of this legislation originates from different government departments. The result is an unprincipled whole.

---

[169] LCCP 183, *Conspiracy and Attempts*, paras. 1.6 and 4.49; cf. para. 4.62.

[170] Cf. the treatment of recklessness as to circumstances, in sections 12.3(a) (attempt) and 12.5(c) (conspiracy).												[171] See Ashworth, n 11, 764–6.

[172] See the assessment by W. Wilson, 'A Rational Scheme of Liability for Participating in Crime' [2008] Crim LR 3.												[173] LCCP 183, *Conspiracy and Attempts*, 257–63.

FURTHER READING

A. ASHWORTH, 'The Unfairness of Risk-Based Possession Offences' (2011) 5 *Criminal Law and Philosophy* 237.

J. CHILD and A. HUNT, 'Mens Rea and the General Inchoate Offences: Another New Culpability Framework' (2012) 63 NILQ 247.

M. D. DUBBER, 'The Possession Paradigm' in R. A. Duff and S. P. Green (eds), *Defining Crime* (Oxford University Press, 2005).

R. A. DUFF, *Criminal Attempts* (Oxford University Press, 1996).

R. FORTSON, *Blackstone's Guide to the Serious Crime Act 2007* (Oxford University Press, 2008).

P. JARVIS and M. BISGROVE, 'The Use and Abuse of Conspiracy' [2014] Crim LR 261.

N. K. KATYAL, 'Conspiracy Theory' (2003) 112 *Yale LJ* 1307.

LAW COMMISSION, *Inchoate Liability for Assisting and Encouraging Crime* (Law Com No. 300, 2006).

LAW COMMISSION, *Conspiracy and Attempts* (Law Com No. 318, 2009).

D. ORMEROD and R. FORTSON, 'Serious Crime Act 2007: The Part 2 Offences' [2009] Crim LR 389.

BIBLIOGRAPHY

A comprehensive bibliography is now available free of charge online. Readers can quickly and easily locate specific references by using the online, alphabetized bibliography, or alternatively can download and print the entire listing.

In addition to this, all references are available in full in the footnotes throughout the text.

Go to www.oxfordtextbooks.co.uk/orc/ashworth8e/

Ashworth's Principles of Criminal Law - 8th edition

Bibliography

Abbott WM, "Anticlericalism and Episcopacy" in Buchanan S and Fissel MC (eds), *Law and Authority in Early Modern England* (University of Delaware Press 2007).

Alexander L, "Criminal Liability for Omissions: An Inventory of Issues" in Shute S and Simester AP (eds), *Criminal Law Theory: Doctrines of hte General Part* (Oxford: Oxford University Press 2002).

Alge D, "Negotiated Plea Agreements in Cases of Serious and Complex Fraud in England and Wales: A New Conceptualisation of Plea Bargaining?" (2013) 19(1) Web Journal of Current Legal Issues.

Alldridge P, "The Coherence of Defences" [1983] Criminal Law Review 665.

— "Developing the Defence of Duress" [1986] Criminal Law Review 433.

— "The Doctrine of Innocent Agency" (1990) 2 Criminal Law Forum 45.

— "What's Wrong with the Traditional Criminal Law Course?" (1990) 10 Legal Studies 38.

— "'Attempted Murder of the Soul': Blackmail, Privacy and Secrets" (1993) 13(3) Oxford Journal of Legal Studies 368.

— "Threats Offences - A Case for Reform" [1994] Criminal Law Review 176.

— "Dealing with Drug Dealing", in P SA and Smith ATH (eds), *Harm and Culpability* (Oxford: Oxford University Press 1996).

— "The Sexual Offences (Conspiracy and Incitement) Act 1996" [1997] Criminal Law Review 30.

— *Relocating Criminal Law* (Ashgate Publishing 2000).

— *Money Laundering Law* (London: Butterworths 2003).

Allen MJ, "Consent and Assault" (1994) 58 Journal of Criminal Law 183.

Alridge A, "The Trial of Dr. Moor" [2002] Criminal Law Review 31.

American Law Institute, *Model Penal Code* (revised edn with commentaries 1980).

Andanaes J, "Error Juris in Scandinavian Law" in Mueller G (ed), *Essays in Criminal Science* (London: Sweet & Maxwell 1961).

Andrews JA, "Wilfulness: a Lesson in Ambiguity" (1981) 1 Legal Studies 303.

Anyangwe C, "Dealing with the Problem of Bad Cheques in France" [1978] Criminal Law Review 31.

INDEX